Callie Marie Rennison and Mary Dodge highlight the interactions of victims, criminal justice professionals, and offenders and bring out the controversial issues within the criminal justice process.

A Focus on Offenders in Prison and the Community

Joshua Benjamin sustained a traumatic brain injury as a young child. His injury and a charge of sexual assault against a child have left devastating consequences that will remain with Joshua for life. You will see how a person charged with a crime is processed in the criminal justice system.
While incarcerated, Joshua experienced sexual assault and underwent psychiatric therapy. You will also see what life is like for a former convict and how, even though released from prison, his conviction has had a lasting effect.

"I enjoyed reading this text. It was well organized and well written. The updated trend information has been needed in an introduction to criminal justice text for some time."

—Jennifer Riggs
Eastern New Mexico University, Ruidoso

A Focus on Restorative Justice

Chris Farias was arrested multiple times for driving under the influence. Through Chris's story, you will see the consequences of Chris's decisions to drive intoxicated. Although Chris did enter a restorative justice program, his arrest and conviction had far-reaching effects on his personal life, finances, and business.

"I really liked the way the book began, with the case studies and real-life examples. I also liked the ethical issues and decision-making scenarios within each chapter. It is very engaging for the student."

—James Stewart
Calhoun Community College

Cultivate Critical Thinking

🔧 CONTEMPLATING CAREERS

CONTEMPLATING CAREERS boxes introduce students to the skills, responsibilities, salary, work environment, and even the personality characteristics that make up an ideal candidate. Video interviews of people who work in these fields are available through the Interactive eBook.

📋 POLICY ISSUES

"I loved the Policy Issues boxes and would use them often in class discussion. They provide a great way for students to connect the materials to some current event and to see how what we discuss in class relates to policy issues."

—Jacqueline M. Mullany,
Triton College

POLICY ISSUES boxes provide a foundation for understanding how policy decisions are made. Students are also asked to consider the complexities of policy making and to think critically about the policies currently in place.

❓ COMMON MISCONCEPTIONS

"One of the things I try to do in my intro course is dispel myths, and I think these [Common Misconceptions boxes] do a great job of pointing out common myths my students presume."

—Jamie Ann Snyder,
University of West Florida

COMMON MISCONCEPTIONS boxes emphasize and explain the important distinctions between systems and policies that students often struggle to fully comprehend.

⚖️ ETHICAL ISSUES

"The Ethical Issues boxes are very beneficial. This is because the human element of the system is the hardest aspect to explain and/or predict. Having good examples of how system actors find the sweet spot on the continuum between the best practice and the street is very helpful."

—Charles E. Hogan,
Georgia State University

ETHICAL ISSUES boxes in each chapter present hypothetical situations wherein the chapter's topic results in a real-world ethical dilemma.

DIVERSITY IN THE JUDICIARY

Women in the Judiciary

An emphasis on **DIVERSITY** provides students with insight into this undeniably powerful force in our criminal justice system.

Ties to Technology

SAGE COURSEPACKS: OUR CONTENT TAILORED TO YOUR LEARNING MANAGEMENT SYSTEM

SAGE Coursepacks makes it easy to

- Import our quality instructor and student resource content into your school's learning management system (LMS)

- Customize course content to meet your students' needs

- Intuitive and simple-to-use, SAGE Coursepacks do not require special access codes

Sharpen Your Skills with SAGE edge!

SAGE edge offers a robust online environment featuring an impressive array of tools and resources for review, study, and further exploration, keeping both instructors and students on the cutting edge of teaching and learning. SAGE edge content is open access and available on demand.

ENHANCED INTERACTIVE EBOOK

- The easy-to-follow Interactive eBook gives you access to the same content and page layout of the traditional printed book, but in a flexible digital format.

- Hear firsthand from the victims and criminals in the running cases in video clips accessed through the Interactive eBook.

- **Available for FREE when bundled with the printed text,** or available for purchase.

SAGE was founded in 1965 by Sara Miller McCune to support the dissemination of usable knowledge by publishing innovative and high-quality research and teaching content. Today, we publish over 900 journals, including those of more than 400 learned societies, more than 800 new books per year, and a growing range of library products including archives, data, case studies, reports, and video. SAGE remains majority-owned by our founder, and after Sara's lifetime will become owned by a charitable trust that secures our continued independence.

Los Angeles | London | New Delhi | Singapore | Washington DC | Melbourne

Dear Student,

We want to take a moment to introduce you to our new edition of *Introduction to Criminal Justice: Systems, Diversity, and Change.*

But before we do, we simply want to say that we hope this course will infuse in you the same excitement and passion we have for the criminal justice system. In our book, we present contemporary and, at times, controversial coverage of the criminal justice system. We anticipate that this course and our textbook will ignite your interest in criminal justice and the various topics it encompasses.

If you are like us, you respond to real stories. They are memorable. They have a narrative drive. And they show the interconnected nature of criminal justice. In this book, we use real-world examples to illustrate the theoretical concepts necessary to understand the criminal justice system. The examples portray the relations among the police, the courts, and the corrections system by highlighting interactions of victims, criminal justice professionals, and offenders, which illuminate controversial issues in the criminal justice process.

During your journey through the criminal justice system you will meet Jennifer Schuett, an 8-year-old girl who was abducted from her bedroom, brutally raped, nearly decapitated, and left for dead by a police impersonator. Her case will teach you about investigative difficulties and victim engagement. Next, you meet Chris Farias, a man who had multiple DUIs before he was jailed and entered a restorative justice program, which helped change his life—for the better. We follow with the introduction of Joshua Paul Benjamin, a young man who was convicted of sex offenses against children. We will chronicle his journey through the criminal justice system and discuss his adult life as a law-abiding citizen. Last, you will encounter Danny Madrid, who as an adolescent became involved with a group of delinquent peers. Together, they spray-painted graffiti around their Southern California neighborhood. This behavior escalated to minor street crimes, and eventually gun violence. After a shooting left a rival gang member paralyzed, Danny served time in prison. By weaving these actual case studies throughout the chapters, we offer a fresh, exciting, and real-world glimpse of the connectedness of the criminal justice system.

You will also be exposed to topics often underrepresented in criminal justice textbooks. We introduce you to criminal justice policy and how policymakers' decisions affect our lives; victimology, or the study of victims; and diversity, an undeniably powerful force in our criminal justice system.

We hope that you find your introductory course engaging and that you will develop a passion to learn more about the dynamic field of criminal justice.

All the best,

Callie Marie Rennison

Mary Dodge

INTRODUCTION TO
CRIMINAL JUSTICE

Second Edition

From Callie:

This work is dedicated to two professors who changed the trajectory of my professional life: Jon Lorence, PhD, and Robert Erikson, PhD

From Mary:

For Lucie, Michael, and Phillip and in memory of Gilbert Geis

INTRODUCTION TO
CRIMINAL JUSTICE

SYSTEMS, DIVERSITY, AND CHANGE

2 EDITION

CALLIE MARIE RENNISON
UNIVERSITY OF COLORADO DENVER

MARY DODGE
UNIVERSITY OF COLORADO DENVER

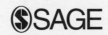

Los Angeles | London | New Delhi
Singapore | Washington DC | Melbourne

FOR INFORMATION:

SAGE Publications, Inc.
2455 Teller Road
Thousand Oaks, California 91320
E-mail: order@sagepub.com

SAGE Publications Ltd.
1 Oliver's Yard
55 City Road
London EC1Y 1SP
United Kingdom

SAGE Publications India Pvt. Ltd.
B 1/I 1 Mohan Cooperative Industrial Area
Mathura Road, New Delhi 110 044
India

SAGE Publications Asia-Pacific Pte. Ltd.
3 Church Street
#10-04 Samsung Hub
Singapore 049483

Printed in Scotland by Bell and Bain Ltd, Glasgow.

Names: Rennison, Callie Marie, author. | Dodge, Mary, 1960- author.

Title: Introduction to criminal justice : systems, diversity, and change / Callie Marie Rennison, University of Colorado Denver, Mary Dodge, University of Colorado Denver.

Description: Second edition. | Thousand Oaks, CA : SAGE, [2017] | Includes bibliographical references and index.

Identifiers: LCCN 2016036798 | ISBN 9781506347721 (pbk. : alk. paper)

Subjects: LCSH: Criminal justice, Administration of—United States. | Crime—United States.

Classification: LCC KF9223 .R46 2017 | DDC 364.973—dc23
LC record available at https://lccn.loc.gov/2016036798

This book is printed on acid-free paper.

Acquisitions Editor: Jessica Miller
Editorial Assistant: Jennifer Rubio
Production Editor: Veronica Stapleton Hooper
Copy Editor: Jim Kelly
Typesetter: C&M Digitals (P) Ltd.
Proofreader: Dennis W. Webb
Indexer: Jeanne Busemeyer
Cover and Interior Designer: Scott Van Atta
Marketing Manager: Amy Lammers
eLearning Editor: Laura Kirkhuff

MIX
Paper from responsible sources
FSC® C007785

18 19 20 10 9 8 7 6 5 4

BRIEF CONTENTS

DETAILED CONTENTS

iStockphoto.com/sangakur

PART II: LAW ENFORCEMENT 97

Chapter 4. The History of Policing 98

Chapter 5. On the Streets: Organization, Responsibilities, and Challenges 124

Reuters/Jim Young

© DarrenMower

Chapter 12. Prison Life and Life After Prison .. 314

PART V. BEYOND THE BASICS 339

Chapter 13. The Juvenile Justice System..........340

Chapter 14. Exploring Specialized and Topical Issues 364

AP Photo/Jay Pickthorn

DISTINCTIVE CHARACTERISTICS OF THIS TEXT

Format: The eBook

A distinctive characteristic of the text is its format, which is available in traditional format as well as in a dynamic eBook. Universities are incorporating an increasing number of online and hybrid classes, and this trend toward high-tech learning will continue to increase exponentially for future generations of students. With a text + eBook format, students can easily access learning materials on devices such as computers, netbooks, iPads, Kindles, and smartphones regardless of their physical location, which encourages reading.

The text + eBook approach also includes relevant links in the margins, allowing easy access to NPR, YouTube video links, author and expert videos, Instructor and Student Study websites, journal articles, government websites, and other important information. This approach provides up-to-date, interactive criminal justice material with traditional classroom pedagogy to create an enhanced learning environment in and out of the classroom. We believe that if students can access materials online using an eBook and other sources, they will be more likely to actually use and learn from them. Furthermore, these nimble formats make interacting with this important material easier using a variety of devices while traveling, commuting, or sitting in public or places other than behind a desk.

Special Topic Boxes

Special topic boxes focusing on *policy issues*, *ethical issues*, *common misconceptions*, and *contemplating careers* associated with the criminal justice system are included in each chapter.

Get FREE access to the interactive eBook with the purchase of a new printed text.

Learn more at edge.sagepub.com/rennison2e/access

 VIDEOS **Videos:** Links are provided to videos that correlate to the chapter content and increase student understanding.

CASE STUDY VIDEOS **Case study videos:** Available only in the Interactive eBook, these clips include interviews with victims and former offenders in the running case studies and cement the concepts and cases for the students.

AUTHOR VIDEOS **Author videos:** Available only in the Interactive eBook, original videos showcase authors Callie Marie Rennison and Mary Dodge, introducing each chapter and giving students insights into tough concepts.

CAREER VIDEOS **Career videos:** Available only in the Interactive eBook, interviews with criminal justice professionals discussing their day-to-day work and current issues related to technology, diversity, and cutting-edge developments in their field are available.

JOURNAL ARTICLES **Journal articles:** Articles from highly ranked SAGE journals such as *Crime and Delinquency*, *Theoretical Criminology*, *Criminal Justice Review*, and more can be accessed.

AUDIO LINKS **Audio Links:** Links are provided to audio clips that enhance student comprehension of chapter content.

WEB LINKS **Web Links:** Links are provided to relevant websites that further explore chapter-related topics.

The purpose of these boxes is to engage and enhance students' critical thinking skills by considering difficult topics or concepts associated with the system. Policy issues are largely absent from existing books, whereas they are highlighted in our chapters. The policy issues we consider, for example, include difficulties in counting crime, the appropriate role of law enforcement officers, and policing domestic violence. Ethical Issues boxes are integrated into each chapter to reinforce and emphasize text narrative. Ethics in the criminal justice system is a subject often treated in an isolated manner, summarily covered in five or so pages. We believe that ethical behavior and decision making apply to all aspects of the system and provide the opportunity to approach each topic in a more thoughtful and continuous manner. Ethical topics covered include, but are not limited to, self-defense and the castle doctrine, the use of marijuana by those in the criminal justice system, and off-duty officer behavior. Many concepts and terms related to the criminal justice system are widely misunderstood by students. Using Common Misconceptions text boxes, we offer clarity about terms such as *prison, jail, parole, probation, robbery, burglary, discretion,* and *discrimination.* Finally, each chapter presents information related to criminal justice careers that students might wish to explore further. Information provided includes characteristics and skills needed by individuals in these roles, responsibilities associated with the careers highlighted, and additional information such as work environment and salary. This career-specific information is designed to engage student interest in a variety of fields in criminal justice.

End-of-Chapter Features

Aside from the features described above, the text offers several end-of-chapter features designed to further enhance students' learning experiences:

- *Key points.* Students are provided with summary statements that emphasize major concepts that are important to grasp after reading the chapter.
- *Key terms.* Basic and, perhaps, unfamiliar words and concepts introduced in the chapter are defined to help improve study skills.
- *Review questions.* These questions are designed to help students review for exams and determine whether they fully understand key topics covered in the chapter.
- *Critical thinking matters.* These questions are offered to spur independent thought about topics or to be used by the professor or instructor to promote class discussion. These questions show that many issues are not black and white but rather far more complex in nature and outcome.

FOR WHOM IS THIS BOOK SUITED?

In writing this text, our primary audience of interest was undergraduates in criminology, criminal justice, sociology, public policy, and political science. While the book would be useful in a variety of classes devoted to these topics, we see the adoption of this text primarily in undergraduate introduction courses. We also believe that this text can be widely adopted in undergraduate study abroad programs. Our comprehensive and engaging presentation of the criminal justice system will help those around the world better understand the reality—that is, the good, the bad, and the ugly—of the criminal justice system in the United States.

WHAT'S NEW IN THIS EDITION

This edition builds on the solid foundation of the first edition. A major change is the inclusion of a new case study focused on gang violence. In this second edition, students are introduced to Danny Madrid, who as a gang member was charged with attempted murder and spent time in prison as a result. We learn about his entrance into gang life, his crimes, his incarceration, and the difficult transition during reentry. Students will learn about his successes and his setbacks and how his interaction in the criminal justice system continues to influence him today.

A second improvement is the expanded coverage of diversity. Where possible, we included additional information on groups such as Asians, American Indians, and members of the LGBTQ community. Over time, with more and more research focused on these groups, we will continue to increase our coverage.

Third, this edition includes updated statistics and estimates on crime, victimization, and elements of the criminal justice system.

Fourth, we reorganized the material in Chapters 8 and 9 at the request of our reviewers and to facilitate student learning. All chapters are similar in length, which facilitates teaching this material over the course of a 15-week semester or 10-week quarter. Additionally, current challenges, new approaches, and changes in technology for policing, courts, and corrections were added to provide up-to-date perspectives on policing, courts, and corrections.

Finally, with the assistance of experienced and helpful reviewers, several spelling and grammar mistakes were corrected and unclear concepts more fully explained. This second edition offers a more powerful and comprehensive introduction to the criminal justice system that will enhance teaching and learning.

The white-collar crime case study following Doctors Asch, Stone, and Balmaceda that appeared in the first edition can be found online: edge.sagepub.com/rennison2e.

$SAGE edge™

Sharpen your skills with SAGE edge at edge.sagepub.com/rennison2e. SAGE edge for Students provides a personalized approach to help you accomplish your coursework goals in an easy-to-use learning environment. You'll find action plans, mobile-friendly eFlashcards, and quizzes as well as video and web resources to support and expand on the concepts presented in this chapter.

THANK YOU

This book benefited from the contributions of many. I hope to sufficiently thank them all, though it seems impossible. Still, I will do my best. First, I extend a heartfelt thanks to Jennifer Schuett, Joshua Paul Benjamin, Chris Farias, and Danny Madrid. These individuals graciously shared their stories as our four case studies in the book, and as a result, this text offers readers a deeper understanding of the complexities of the criminal justice system and how it touches *all* people. Your experiences highlight the consequences of crime on victims, offenders, criminal justice workers, family members, friends, and citizens. Without your generous sharing, these important dimensions of the criminal justice system could not have been portrayed in this text.

Because of the multitude of people who spend their lives thinking about and researching topics related to victims, statistics, police, courts, white-collar crime, terrorism, technology, advocates, corrections, and other relevant criminal justice topics, this book was possible. These dedicated researchers include my coauthor, Mary Dodge. When Mary and I first met, we talked about our areas of interest, learning that substantively we worked in very different areas. We also discovered that in important ways we were quite similar: We are both dedicated to teaching about the criminal justice system in a passionate, dynamic, and realistic way that engages students. I think our collaborative effort in this text reflects this approach.

A hefty thank-you is extended to the University of Colorado Denver's School of Public Affairs. The School of Public Affairs offers a supportive and engaging atmosphere, with fascinating colleagues, eager students, and a gorgeous physical setting. I feel so fortunate to be able to conduct my work in such an environment. Extra thanks go to Dean Paul Teske for his continued support for this work and all of the research I do.

This book would simply not exist without the support and guidance of Jerry Westby and his team at SAGE. Some team members came and went throughout this process, but each is deserving of my gratitude. Aside from Jerry, the team members included Jessica Miller, Nicole Mangona, Laura Kirkhuff, Jim Kelly, and Veronica Stapleton Hooper.

A part of SAGE's work was to line up numerous reviewers as the book progressed. This panel of reviewers clearly spent their valuable time providing thoughtful feedback and criticisms that improved our work. A special thanks to the following:

REVIEWERS OF FIRST EDITION

Dr. George Ackerman, Palm Beach Community College

Brandon L. Bang, Washington State University

Lauren M. Barrow, PhD, Chestnut Hill College

Ellen G. Cohn, PhD, Florida International University

Daniel Dexheimer, Santa Clara University

Colin Glennon, Fort Lewis College

Kelly L. Gould, Sacramento City College

Elizabeth Gurian, PhD, Norwich University

Alan Harland, Temple University

Ann C. Hathaway, Indiana University–Purdue University at Fort Wayne

Charles E. Hogan, Georgia State University

Z. Dennis Kalam, Miami Dade College

Deniese Kennedy-Kollar, PhD, Molloy College

David J. MacDonald, Eastfield College

Shana L. Maier, Widener University

Danielle McDonald, Northern Kentucky University

James R. McDonald, Valencia College

William (Bill) Mixon, Columbus State University

Jacqueline M. Mullany, PhD, Triton College

James Newman, Rio Hondo College

Paul Nunis, Arkansas State University

Pat Patterson, Eastfield College

James Kane Record, JD, LLM, California University of Pennsylvania

Jennifer Riggs, Eastern New Mexico University–Ruidoso

Donna Lee Ross, JD, Mount Ida College

Jamie Ann Snyder, University of West Florida

Katie L. Swope, PhD, Stevenson University

Angela Taylor, Fayetteville State University

Arnold R. Waggoner, Rose State College

Tracey Woodard, University of North Florida

Kevin Wright, Arizona State University

REVIEWERS OF SECOND EDITION

Dr. Kimberly Casey, Northwest Missouri State University

Mark C. Fields, Administration of Justice

Doris Hall, California State University, Bakersfield

Marilyn Horace-Moore, Eastern Michigan University

Iryna Malendevych, University of Central Florida

Eric Metchik, PhD, Salem State University

Scott Moller, Monterey Peninsula College

Selena M. Respass, Miami Dade College

Jennifer Sumner, California State University, Dominguez Hills

Carol L. S. Trent, PhD, University of Pittsburgh

And last, but by no means least, I deeply thank my husband and best friend, Dave Vaughan. He has quietly lived with me as I toiled away on chapters in the throes of workaholism and absenteeism. During this process, he has spent a lot of time outside climbing, riding, and hiking without me. He's never complained and always encouraged. There aren't really the words needed to express how much your support means to me. Thank you.

—*Callie Marie Rennison*

Like Callie, I share deep gratitude for all the people willing to invest their time and energy in this book, including the SAGE team, reviewers, and my colleagues at the School of Public Affairs. Thanks go to all my students, many of whom are now colleagues, who have inspired and challenged me over the years. Special thanks to Joe Airey, Steve Addison, Carolyn Berry, Alison Burke, Dan Burke, Megan Burns-Pratt, Fran Gomez, Victoria Josupait, Tracie Keesee, Kaitlin Levy-Liotard, Fireman Ross, Carol Peeples, Skylar Steele, Jace Valcore, Vicki VanAntwerp, David Walcher, Nicole Weiffenbach, Jerry Williams, Daneilla Johner, Kate Jimmerson, Nancy Contreras, Jessica Rosenthal, Patricia Woodin, Katie Didier, Annie Miller, Katyie Wells, and all the students in my Introduction to Criminal Justice courses. My deepest appreciation goes to my family and friends Lucie Sarkisian, Mike and Phillip Dodge, Kelly Keating, Tammy and David Fenimore, Valerie and Craig MacDonald, and Jere, Mary, and Fred Stahl for their unconditional love and acceptance. Also, I wish to acknowledge the incredible scholars and colleagues who have inspired my work and who will be deeply missed: Gilbert Geis, Bill Chambliss, Joan McCord, Rita J. Simon, John Irwin, and Dale Sechrest.

—Mary Dodge

ABOUT THE AUTHORS

Callie Marie Rennison is the associate dean of faculty affairs and a full professor in the School of Public Affairs, University of Colorado Denver. She earned a PhD in 1997 in political science from the University of Houston, University Park. Her areas of research interest include investigating the nature, extent, and consequences of violent victimization, with an emphasis on research methodology, quantitative analysis, and measurement. Much of this research focuses on violence against women, violence against minority groups such as African Americans and Hispanics, crime data, and victim interaction with the criminal justice system. Callie recently served on a National Academies committee examining domestic sex trafficking of minors in the United States. Her research has appeared in numerous journals, including the *Journal of Quantitative Criminology, Justice Quarterly, Violence and Victims,* and *Violence Against Women.* Callie teaches a variety of graduate and undergraduate courses, including statistics, research methods, murder in America, crime and the media, and introduction to criminal justice.

Callie was awarded the School of Public Affairs Research and Creative Activities Award in 2013, the Teaching Award in 2011, and the Service Award in 2015. In 2016, she was awarded the American Society of Criminology's Bonnie S. Fisher Victimology Career Award to recognize significant contributions in the area of Victimology over her lifetime.

Mary Dodge earned her PhD in 1997 in criminology, law, and society from the School of Social Ecology at the University of California, Irvine. She received her BA and MA in psychology from the University of Colorado at Colorado Springs. She is a full professor at the University of Colorado Denver in the School of Public Affairs. Her research articles have appeared in the *American Journal of Criminal Justice, Women & Criminal Justice, Contemporary Issues in Criminology,* the *International Journal of the Sociology of Law, The Prison Journal, Police Quarterly,* the *Journal of Contemporary Criminal Justice,* and the *Encyclopedia of White-Collar and Corporate Crime.* Her most recent articles explore public opinion and white-collar crime and misconduct by policewomen. She and Gilbert Geis coedited the book *Lessons of Criminology* and share authorship on the book *Stealing Dreams: A Fertility Clinic Scandal.* She is also the author of *Women and White-Collar Crime.* Her research and writing interests include women in the criminal justice system, white-collar crime, policing, prostitution, and courts.

Mary was the 2007 recipient of the campuswide University of Colorado Denver Excellence in Teaching Award. She received the School of Public Affairs Teaching Award in 2001, 2005, and 2006 and the Research and Creative Activities Award in 2002 and 2004. In 2011, she received the School of Public Affairs and University of Colorado's awards for excellence in service. Her research often involves collaboration with local and national police departments and law enforcement agencies.

PART I

FOUNDATIONS

© SpeedliteModifier

1

AN INTRODUCTION TO CRIME AND THE CRIMINAL JUSTICE SYSTEM

> "Justice is open to everyone in the same way as the Ritz Hotel."
>
> —Judge Sturgess (1928)

> "The more laws the more offenders."
>
> —Thomas Fuller, *Gnomologia* (1732)

LEARNING OBJECTIVES

After finishing this chapter, you should be able to:

1.1 Identify the paths on which a crime may be handled in the criminal justice system.

1.2 Summarize why consensus for an exact definition of crime is difficult and why crime definitions may change over time.

1.3 Review the five perspectives of the criminal justice system.

1.4 Critique how the consensus and conflict models help and hinder public policy.

1.5 Identify key elements in the relationship between crime and the media.

1.6 Distinguish how the fear of crime and actual risk of being victimized are often misinterpreted by the public.

1.7 Differentiate between criminal justice and criminology.

INTRODUCTION: MAKING OUR WAY THROUGH THE CRIMINAL JUSTICE SYSTEM

The **criminal justice system** comprises institutions, policies, and practices with the goal of maintaining social control and deterring crime through sanctions and rehabilitation. The criminal justice system is explored in a great number of books. Many of these books present the cold hard facts in chapters that make it difficult for students to *really* understand the system and its ties to ethics, policy, and our everyday lives. Many students have firsthand experience with the criminal justice system. At a minimum, most have been exposed to elements of the criminal justice system (not all accurate) through the media. Perhaps you were convicted of driving while intoxicated or received a speeding ticket. Or perhaps a family member was incarcerated or served a community corrections sentence. Maybe you have had experience as a victim. Maybe your credit card numbers were stolen and used to make purchases online. Or your bank account was hacked and your life's savings taken. Perhaps your car was stolen or your home was burglarized. Many people grieve over the homicide of a family member or friend. As unpleasant as any of these scenarios are, they all provide a glimpse into the complexities of the huge industrial nature of the criminal justice system.

Students in criminology, criminal justice, and sociology courses often comment that textbooks appear unconnected to the real world. In general, those who become involved in the criminal justice system through peripheral or direct contact will assure others that the processes and procedures are different from the material and stories frequently portrayed in books and the media.

Crime and the criminal justice system commonly are sensationalized in the books we read, the television shows we watch, and the gruesome headline news stories we see daily. The real stories in the criminal justice system can be complex, and each case touches individuals in far-reaching ways. The goal of this book is to demonstrate how the system works in reality and familiarize you with the complicated path from first contact with it—whether as victims or offenders—to exiting the system (for those who do exit). To demonstrate how this happens, we introduce four real people and describe their actual experiences with the criminal justice system throughout the book. None wanted to be involved with the system, but for years, and even decades, their lives have been intertwined and entangled with law enforcement, courts, and corrections. For some, if not each one, involvement with the system will continue until their deaths. The true stories related to their cases and experiences are used to enhance and inform the contextual material presented in each chapter. This chapter introduces Jennifer Schuett, Chris Farias, Joshua Paul Benjamin, and Danny Madrid.

criminal justice:
The system of institutions, policies, and practices with the goal of maintaining social control and deterring crime through sanctions and rehabilitation.

CASE STUDY

Jennifer Schuett: A Case of Attempted Murder and Rape

Jennifer Schuett

Eight-year-old Jennifer Schuett. What type of person would harm a little girl? How should the criminal justice system handle such an offender?

On August 10, 1990, 8-year-old Jennifer was abducted from her bedroom at 2:30 a.m. The offender, a complete stranger, covered her mouth, assuring her that she was safe because he was a police officer. He told her this while running down the sidewalk with her in his arms. He placed Jennifer in his car and sped away from the apartment complex where she lived with her mother. The man later stopped the car and brutally raped Jennifer. In an effort to remove the only witness to his heinous crime, he slashed her throat from ear to ear and left her in a vacant lot, thinking she was dead.[1]

The Jennifer Schuett case reminds us that crime generally involves victims. Too often, accounts of crime fail to acknowledge the individuals harmed in incidents. Historically, work in criminology and criminal justice overlooked victims, rendering them little more than witnesses at a trial (if a trial occurred). In some cases, when a victim was acknowledged, he or she was blamed for part of or the entire incident.[2] The past several decades have witnessed an emphasis on the role of the victim in the criminal justice system. Victims now have increased resources and assistance to help in recovery, and policy and research efforts provide greater understanding of victimization. We follow Jennifer and her forced introduction to the criminal justice system throughout this text.

Chris Farias: A Case of Driving Under the Influence

Chris Farias grew up in an Italian family on the East Coast in which large gatherings of relatives were frequent.[3] The adults in Chris's family celebrated get-togethers and holidays with copious amounts of wine. The children in the family grew accustomed to celebrating with alcohol. While his parents taught the children to respect alcohol, their actual perceptions and experiences were quite different. As Chris and his siblings matured, they recognized that their father's alcohol consumption was a lifestyle rather than a celebratory event. Chris's dad was an alcoholic. Concerned about his drinking problem, the family attended Al-Anon meetings and engaged in various interventions to convince their father to quit drinking. Sadly, none of these attempts were successful. Chris's father was forced into a treatment program after seven DUIs. His rehabilitation was somewhat successful, and he had no further tangles with the law, although he started drinking again during the last 10 years of his life.

Chris spent the first half of his life trying desperately not to be like his father. He went to college and obtained a degree in teaching, and he spent almost a decade in the classroom. Chris, like his dad, had an innate desire to build and repair things. Eventually, he quit teaching and opened a construction company. Chris also consumed alcohol and drank to the point of impairment. In time, Chris recognized that along with alcohol abuse, his personality was like his father's: defiant, addictive, and careless. Over the years, Chris was arrested multiple times for driving under the influence. In the following chapters, we follow the consequences of Chris's decisions, his entanglement with the criminal justice system, and how it has affected his personal life, finances, and business.

Chris Farias. How did a DUI affect the life of this hard-working businessman? Did the criminal justice system go too far with his case?

Joshua Paul Benjamin: A Case of Sexual Assault

Joshua Paul Benjamin was a happy boy living with his parents and sister in a Midwestern city.[4] He liked building intricate towers of blocks and speeding around the house on his plastic push motorcycle. Like many little boys, he was bright, curious, and active. Though Joshua was high energy, he was also caring and patient, and loved to cuddle with his mother.

Tragedy struck when Joshua was only 3 years old and the front door to his home was left unlocked. Joshua discovered this unlocked door and rushed outside, eager to visit a friend who lived across the street. He never arrived. As Joshua darted out from between two parked vehicles on the street, an oncoming car hit him. The accident happened so quickly that the driver never had time to hit the brakes.

Joshua was rushed to the hospital in critical condition, where doctors informed his parents that he would either die or have brain damage as a result of his injuries. After about 10 days, Joshua emerged from a coma unable to communicate, with a paralyzed left side. At home following discharge, Joshua dragged himself through the house on the floor. His life changed dramatically after charges of sexual assault against a child emerged, and the ensuing events, as described in later chapters, resulted in his lifetime involvement in the criminal justice system.

Tragedy struck Joshua when he was a toddler. He was hit by a car while crossing the street. Could anyone have known that the resulting injury would ultimately lead to his entanglement in the criminal justice system?

Danny Madrid: A Case of a Gang Member and Attempted Murder

As a young boy growing up in a predominantly Latino and Black neighborhood in South Los Angeles, Danny Madrid dreamed of one day becoming an astronaut. Danny's dreams as a small child faded when he became involved with a gang at the age of 13. He was asked to join the gang by the older boys in the neighborhood, and because he had known their younger siblings since early childhood, life on the streets with these boys seemed natural. With his new peer group, Danny engaged in graffiti, drug crimes, and other street-level crimes in the Los Angeles area. Not surprisingly given these offenses, Danny's clashes with law enforcement increased substantially. In addition, violent conflicts with rival gangs were common. Although he already affiliated with his gang, Danny was assaulted or "packed" by a group of rival gang members. In retaliation, he and a friend got in a car with a gun to seek revenge against the rivals. That day in 1990, Danny's life took a turn for the worse.

Danny Madrid found himself a member of a gang at a young age. Not surprisingly, this led to several interactions with law enforcement. How did such a young person become involved in this life?

Case Study Video 1.1:
Interviews with case study participants

Audio:
Rising Incarceration Rate Isn't Reducing Crime

law enforcement:
One of the three main components of the criminal justice system. Law enforcement agencies are charged with investigating crimes and arresting individuals alleged to have committed crimes.

courts: One of the three main components of the criminal justice system. The courts are responsible for interpreting and applying the law.

corrections: Functions to protect society from criminals through housing, monitoring, and other community-based programs.

WHAT IS THE CRIMINAL JUSTICE SYSTEM?

Laws that define crime represent a small portion of the legal field and create a large web of entanglements. Society needs a way to deal with individuals who violate these laws and those who are victims of crime, hence the development of the criminal justice system. The criminal justice system comprises three primary components: law enforcement, courts, and corrections.[5] **Law enforcement** is charged with investigating crime and apprehending individuals alleged to have committed crimes. **Courts** are responsible for interpreting and applying the law in these cases. The correctional component protects society from criminals through housing, monitoring, and other community-based programs. In some instances, **corrections** involves incarceration in jails or prisons, while in other cases it consists of supervision in the community, parole, or probation. In the most extreme cases, it means putting an offender to death. The death penalty is a controversial issue and is addressed more fully when we discuss courts and sentencing later in the text. Part of the debate over capital cases focuses on issues of retribution and the chance of executing an innocent person. Another important aspect of the criminal justice system—one that has received improved and much deserved attention in recent years—is the victim. Increased emphasis on incorporating victims into the system and paying attention to their needs and wishes is more apparent in law enforcement, courts, and corrections today.

Size of the System

The criminal justice system is enormous and costly even in light of reductions in violent and property crimes since the early 1990s. Through 2007, annual growth in the system was dramatic (it has declined slightly since). Why is the criminal justice system in the United States so large and costly? The system is large because an enormous proportion of the juvenile and adult population is under the control of the criminal justice system. By the end of 2014 in the United States more than 6.8 million individuals (6,851,000) were being supervised in the adult correctional system, which includes incarceration in local jails, prisons, or on parole or probation. This corresponds to 1 in every 36 adults, or 2.8% of all adults, being under some form of criminal justice supervision at the end of 2014. The majority of these adults were being supervised in the community (3,864,100 on probation, and 856,900 on parole). An additional 2.2 million adults were incarcerated at the end of 2014 (i.e., 2,224,400 in total, with 744,600 in local jails and 1,561,500 in prisons).[6] The prison and jail populations are so enormous that some describe the United States as "addicted to incarceration."[7]

COMMON MISCONCEPTIONS

The Differences Between Prison, Jail, Parole, and Probation

Students, citizens, and the media often confuse the terms *prison*, *jail*, *parole*, and *probation*. As will be presented in greater detail in subsequent chapters, these terms designate different institutions and conditions.

Jails are local facilities managed by cities and counties that perform a somewhat overlapping but distinct purpose from prisons and penitentiaries. While prisons hold individuals convicted of crimes, jails hold both those convicted of crimes and individuals who have not been convicted. Jails, for example, detain people who have not been offered bail and those who cannot make bail prior to a trial. Prisons hold persons convicted of more serious offenses serving longer sentences; jails typically detain individuals who have been convicted of misdemeanors serving sentences of less than 1 year (in some jurisdictions jails may hold inmates for longer periods of time). Another exception is the case of prison overcrowding—jails may then incarcerate state and federal felony prisoners serving longer sentences (for a fee).

Probation and parole are types of sentences. Probation is a sentence that suspends or delays a term of full-time incarceration in prison or jail. In return for the suspended or delayed sentence, the judge orders the offender returned to the community, where he or she must abide by certain rules and conditions. Since its inception, the use of probation (and other intermediate sanctions) has become the most common form of sanction administered in the United States. Typically, a person given probation has not served time in a jail or prison for that particular offense. A person just released from prison may be placed on parole as part of his or her sentence. Parole operates like probation in that the offender is released from prison back into the community, where he or she must abide by certain rules and conditions. Failure to comply with those rules often means returning to prison.

Think About It

1. Do jails hold only those convicted of minor crimes for which a sentence of less than 1 year is given? Explain.

2. If someone is on parole, does this mean he or she has never served time in prison? Why or why not?

3. Do local jails hold federal prisoners? Explain.

Gender, Race, and Hispanic Origin in the System

The adult imprisonment rate differs greatly by the offender's gender, race, and Hispanic origin. At the end of 2014, men were imprisoned at a rate of 890 per 100,000, which is almost 14 times greater than the 65 per 100,000 rate characterizing women (see Figure 1.1).[8] Black non-Hispanic men were imprisoned at a rate of 2,724 per 100,000, which is almost 6 times the rate of 465 per 100,000 that characterizes white non-Hispanic men.[9] At the close of 2014, differences in the imprisonment rate were apparent for women by race and Hispanic origin as well. Black non-Hispanic women were imprisoned at a rate of 109 per 100,000, while their white non-Hispanic and Hispanic counterparts were imprisoned at about half that rate: 53 per 100,000 and 64 per 100,000, respectively.[10]

Not all of the differences in imprisonment rates are based solely on variation in criminal behavior. Research indicates that some personal characteristics are associated with a greater likelihood of harsher punishment.[11] In other words, a white woman and a black man committing the same criminal act may be treated differently in the system. The white woman may never be arrested, while the black man may find himself incarcerated. This lack of equity in justice is reflected in the quotation by Judge Sturgess found at the beginning of this chapter: "Justice is open to everyone in the same way as the Ritz Hotel." In other words, powerful citizens who are wealthy and in the majority may receive lenient treatment, while the poor and minorities are

Web:
Bureau of Justice Statistics

Figure 1.1 ■ Year-End 2014 Imprisonment Rates by Race, Hispanic Origin, and Gender of Offender

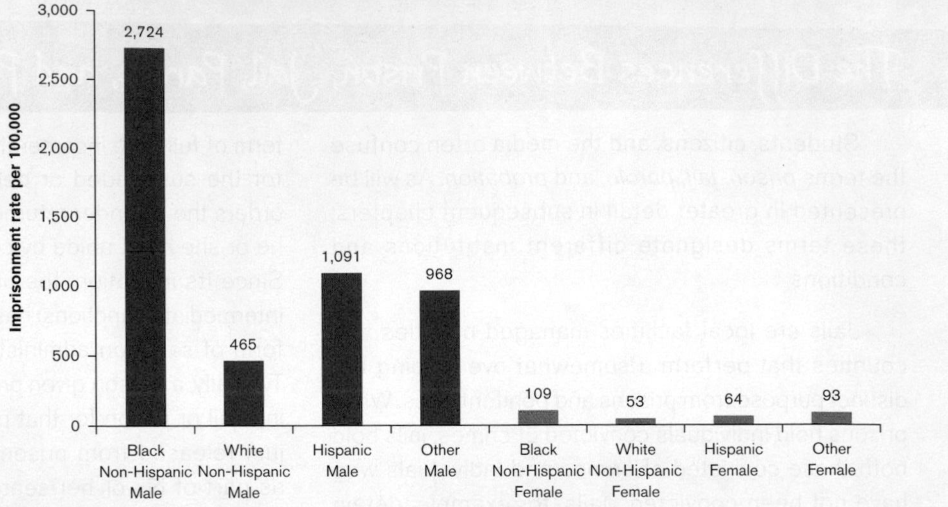

Imprisonment rate per 100,000

Black Non-Hispanic Male	2,724
White Non-Hispanic Male	465
Hispanic Male	1,091
Other Male	968
Black Non-Hispanic Female	109
White Non-Hispanic Female	53
Hispanic Female	64
Other Female	93

How does incarcerating such a large number of our citizens benefit our society? How does it harm it? "Other" includes American Indians and Alaska Natives; Asians, Native Hawaiians, and other Pacific Islanders; and persons of two or more races.

Source: Carson, E. A. (2015). *Prisoners in 2014*, September, 2015. Washington, DC: U.S. Department of Justice, Bureau of Justice Statistics.

treated harshly. Given the serious consequences of being incarcerated, this inequity is important to recognize.

Differences in the likelihood of being sanctioned in the community or incarcerated also are associated with characteristics of the victim. One example is capital punishment. In theory, we reserve capital punishment for our most extreme criminals. Is this the reality? A look at statistics demonstrates that fewer than 2% of murderers were given death sentences. What accounts for why such a small percentage of offenders were sentenced to death when 98% of murderers were not? Some research points to specific factors associated with a greater likelihood of getting the death penalty. These aspects include murders committed with torture, grave risk of death to others, being a black offender, and committing a murder with another felony. Furthermore, research shows that a black defendant who kills a nonblack victim has the highest likelihood of being sentenced to death compared with black-on-black, nonblack-on-nonblack, and nonblack-on-black homicide. These findings hold true even when other characteristics, such as torture, risk to others, and additional felonies, are taken into account.

The Cost of the Criminal Justice System

Video 1.1:
The true cost of incarceration in Baltimore's poorest neighborhoods

The enormous size of the criminal justice system, particularly in corrections, stems partly from the public's desire for longer and harsher sentences. Policymakers who wanted to be "tough on crime" and gain favor with voters implemented legislation such as three-strikes, habitual offending, and mandatory sentencing laws. The result was a massive expansion of the criminal justice population, a large number of people working in the system, and an equally dramatic increase in the cost of the system. In 2013, Ted Gest noted that the U.S. criminal justice employed 2.4 million people at an annual cost of $212 billion. To put this in perspective, each person in the United States, regardless of age, paid $670 in 2013 to support the criminal justice system.[12] Costs differ by location. The cost of state incarceration (a part of the overall criminal justice system), for example, varies greatly. Henrichson and Delaney estimated that the 2010 total taxpayer cost of state prisons in Arizona was $1,002,553,000, while in Colorado it was $606,208,000.[13] In contrast, California taxpayers paid $7,932,388,000 in 2010, while those in Texas footed a bill of $3,306,358,000. Even when considering only state incarceration, the criminal justice system is expensive for taxpayers.

In some locales, scarce economic resources as well as massive overcrowding have highlighted the need to consider options other than incarceration. Since 2009, California had been under a federal court order to reduce overcrowding in the system. The 2009 court order was finally met in early 2015 after the implementation of Proposition 47, which lowered the penalties for many crimes such as forging checks, stealing vehicles, and possessing small amounts of illegal drugs. Overall, the California prison population has decreased by 45% since 2006.

This change reflects a backing away from previously enacted "get-tough" on crime policies. Politicians throughout the nation are increasingly fans of releasing nonviolent prisoners or using punishment that incorporates more parole and probation versus incarceration in order to save money. Yet public safety continues to be an important concern, and policymakers are vying for public approval. Consequently, legislation in the United States continues to lean toward harsh punishment, despite the financial costs.

For most people, a courthouse or jail symbolizes the criminal justice system. In reality, it is a large system that includes law enforcement, courts, and corrections. What does it mean to you?

HOW DOES THE CRIMINAL JUSTICE SYSTEM WORK?

The criminal justice system is large, varied, and complex, encompassing many systems and services found among governments at the local, state, and federal levels. For this reason, no single description or illustration can accurately describe *the* criminal justice system, as no single component acts in isolation. The entire system requires that particular steps be taken to offer citizens due process and minimize undue governmental intervention. Figure 1.2, developed by the Department of Justice's Bureau of Justice Statistics, illustrates the most common steps found in the criminal justice system. While this depiction offers the most common pathways, in reality each section of the criminal justice system overlaps and functions with feedback from others. Conventional wisdom suggests that police officers, for example, arrest a suspect following an investigation. Then they present the suspect and information from the investigation to the prosecutor for consideration of charges. In reality, law enforcement officers may or may not arrest a suspect based on input from a district attorney during the investigation. Some research indicates, for example, that arrest for rape and sexual assault is more likely if the prosecutor feels that the case can be won at trial, based on whether there is evidence that the offender committed the crime. This results in instances in which weak evidence that a rape occurred can be associated with an alleged offender's evading arrest and remaining free to reoffend.

A Road Map

The criminal justice system process begins when a crime becomes known to law enforcement. In many instances, crimes fail to come to the attention of law enforcement. In 2014, for example, only about 46% of violent crimes and 37% of property crimes were reported to the police. In other words, more than half of all violent and property crimes are never reported to law enforcement. Furthermore, there is great variation in the degree of reporting by type of crime. About 61% of robbery is reported, while only about 29% of property theft becomes known to law enforcement. Motor vehicle theft is the most likely of street crimes to be reported; about 83% of these crimes are brought to the attention of law enforcement.[14]

Once alerted, law enforcement agents investigate whether a crime has occurred. If a determination is made that a crime occurred, attempts to identify and apprehend the offender(s) are

Figure 1.2 ■ A Road Map of the Criminal Justice System

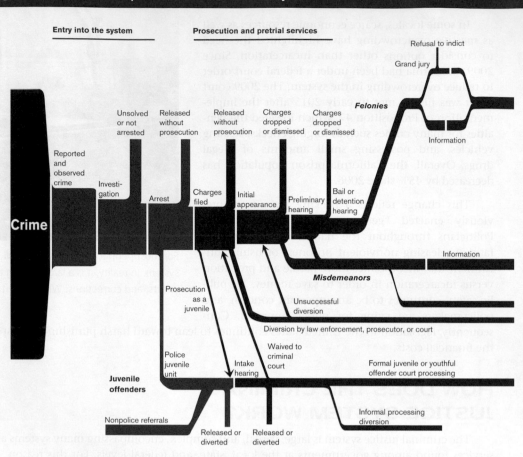

The criminal justice system is complex. Does it need to be? How would you design a system that is fair and takes into account the victim, offender, and community?

Source: Bureau of Justice Statistics. (2014). Criminal Justice System Flowchart. Retrieved from http://www.bjs.gov/content/largechart.cfm.

nolle prosequi: Latin for "be unwilling to pursue," this is commonly used by a prosecutor to willingly terminate legal proceedings before trial or before a verdict. The statement is often construed as an admission that the charges cannot be proven.

No bill: A decision made by a grand jury that indicates that insufficient evidence is present to proceed with the case.

nolo contendere: A plea made by a defendant in which he or she neither admits nor disputes guilt. It is commonly referred to as a "no-contest" plea.

made. Evidence gathered from the investigation is presented to a prosecutor, who, using his or her discretion, determines whether formal charges will be filed. If no charges are filed, the accused is released from his or her involvement in the system. If charges are filed, the prosecutor may proceed toward plea bargaining or trial, or may decide to drop charges in an act known as **nolle prosequi**.

Once charged, the accused appears before a judge or magistrate in person or via video and is informed of the charges against him or her. Several other things may happen at this point depending on the jurisdiction and elements of the crime. First, the determination of guilt and punishment may be dispensed. Or the defendant may be assigned a public defender if the charges are serious enough and the accused lacks sufficient resources to retain an attorney independently. Also, the judge or magistrate may determine if bail is warranted.

In some jurisdictions a grand jury may be convened to investigate and issue an indictment or no bill. **No bill** indicates that insufficient evidence is present to proceed with the case, and the accused is released if he or she is in jail.

The next step is generally an arraignment. At the arraignment the charges are read, the defendant is informed of his or her rights, and the defendant enters a plea—whether it be guilty, not guilty, or **nolo contendere** (i.e., accepting penalty without admitting guilt). The judge may or may not accept the plea, and the defendant may or may not be sentenced immediately. Some defendants opt for trial by jury, while others request trial by judge.

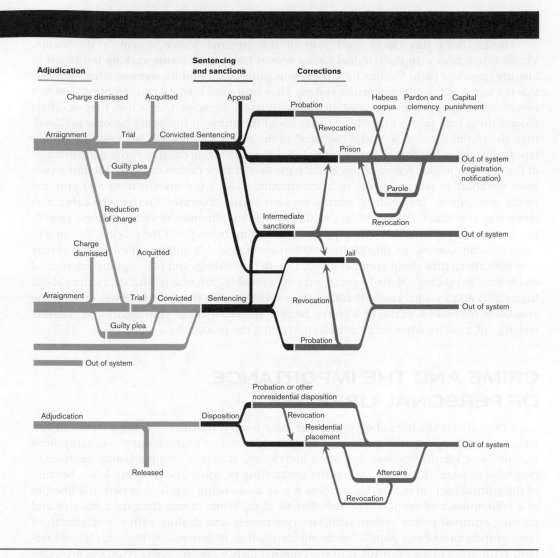

At trial, the prosecution and defense present evidence and question witnesses, while the judge rules on legal issues. At the conclusion of the trial, a conviction or acquittal on the charges is levied. Following this verdict, the sentence is imposed either immediately or in a second hearing by the judge or, in capital cases, the jury. Some defendants may appeal the case on the basis of procedural or constitutional errors—not on the basis of an alleged "wrong" outcome.

Punishment differs greatly. Those sentenced to a year or less incarceration generally spend that time in a jail. Those sentenced to longer stays are usually sent to a prison. The length of the punishment is more often indeterminate (i.e., not based on a fixed number of years) than determinate (i.e., based on a fixed number of years). That is, in most cases, the judge sentences the offender to an **indeterminate sentence** in the form of a range of years to be served (e.g., 3 to 15 years). Often, parole boards determine when the convicted individual is released following any mandatory time in prison. Parole boards also set conditions of the release. Violation of parole conditions may mean that the offender is returned to prison to complete his or her sentence.

In some cases, those accused avoid jail and/or prison. These individuals may be sentenced to house arrest, boot camps, intensive supervision, drug treatment, and/or electronic monitoring. Especially in cases like these, the development and use of continually improving technology play a greater role.

indeterminate sentence:
Sentence given to a defendant in the form of a range of years to be served (e.g., 3 to 15 years).

The Victim

Missing from this classic road map of the criminal justice system is the victim. Victim interaction with the criminal justice system takes many forms, making it difficult to identify one clear path. Victims have numerous things to attend to, some of which are outside the scope of the criminal justice system. They may need medical care, emotional and/or psychological support, and/or assistance with insurance agencies. One action they or others around them may take is to alert the police about the crime. If the police become involved, then the victim becomes a crucial "witness" to the crime. Victims will be questioned, often repeatedly, about the crime. They may feel that they are losing control as the machinations of the criminal justice system churn ahead regardless of their desires or input. Victims report great variation in playing a role or being informed about the investigation and criminal justice proceedings. Increasingly, victims are paired with advocates. **Victim advocates**, also referred to as victim service providers, victim/witness coordinators, or victim/witness specialists, are trained professionals who support crime victims throughout the process. Working to support victims, advocates provide information about available options. These resources may help educate victims about criminal justice system proceedings and offer options for needed emotional, psychological, or financial support available. Advocates educate victims about their rights and in some cases attend court proceedings with the victims. If you or someone you know becomes a victim of a crime, become informed about your rights and consider seeking out a victim advocate to assist in navigating the process.[15]

CRIME AND THE IMPORTANCE OF PERSONAL LIBERTIES

Crime affects the lives of everyone. For some people, this means being a victim of violence, having property stolen, having a home burglarized, or losing money to unscrupulous businesses or identity thieves. For other individuals, it means losing a family member to homicide or watching a loved one suffer devastating personal and property losses because of the criminal acts of others. Or for some it may mean being deprived of personal liberties as a consequence of criminal conduct. For all of us, crime means funding a massive and growing criminal justice system with taxpayer money and dealing with the aftermath of large proportions of our population being confined or monitored by the correctional system. With more money flowing into the criminal justice system, fewer resources are available for other social institutions, such as community centers, prevention programs, and education. These consequences are felt by students who are forced to pay higher tuition or forgo an education altogether.

victim advocates:
Trained professionals who support crime victims as their cases move through the criminal justice system.

inalienable rights:
Rights that are universal and not contingent on laws or beliefs specific to a particular government or culture.

The consequences of crime also affect us all in terms of personal liberties. A strong relationship exists between increased criminalization of behavior and greater loss of personal freedoms. On one hand, in order to ensure the greatest good for the greatest number (also referred to as utilitarianism), legislation is required to prohibit certain behaviors. Constitutional freedoms, on the other hand, ensure certain **inalienable rights**. Legal controversies over the rights afforded by the U.S. Constitution are common and often depend on whether a strict interpretation of the language is applied. In contrast, some legal experts believe that changes in contemporary society require a broader interpretation.

President Obama signs an executive order. Should he have extended the PATRIOT Act? Should the government be able to conduct wiretaps on citizens?

Chip Somodevilla/Getty Images

Judicial activism is said to occur when decisions are influenced by personal or political underpinnings. Balancing personal freedoms and public safety concerns can present difficult policy challenges.

Some commentators and scholars argue the 2001 **USA PATRIOT Act** (Uniting and Strengthening America by Providing Appropriate Tools Required to Intercept and Obstruct Terrorism), signed into law by President George W. Bush, is one example of how citizens are losing personal freedoms.[16] The September 11, 2001, terrorist attacks in New York, Virginia, and Pennsylvania, arguably the greatest contemporary tragedy to occur on U.S. soil, changed domestic and foreign policies and law enforcement in ways that have affected the entire populace. The USA PATRIOT Act, among other things, reduced restrictions on intelligence collection and broadened discretion in detaining and deporting immigrants suspected of terrorist activities. In May 2011, President Barack Obama signed a 4-year extension of the provisions for roving wiretaps, searches of business records, and surveillance of individuals with no connection to a particular terrorist group. Opponents of the act argue that the provisions overextend the powers of the Federal Bureau of Investigation (FBI) and allow monitoring of telephone calls, emails, and financial records without the added safeguard of a search warrant.[17] Contemporary evidence and the information revealed by Edward Snowden, a former Central Intelligence Agency and National Security Agency (NSA) employee, supports the notion that records of individual U.S. citizens are being collected. Many portions of the PATRIOT Act that lacked congressional approval expired in 2015. During the same year, the **USA Freedom Act** was passed, which halted the NSA from gathering a massive amount of phone data. Instead, the USA Freedom Act allows phone companies to retain phone data that can be accessed by the NSA once federal court permission is obtained.

WHAT IS CRIME?

Sometimes the most difficult questions to answer are the simplest ones. For example: What is **crime**? The most commonly accepted answer is that crime is the breaking of a law for which the criminal justice or some other governing authority prescribes punishment. Crimes are defined differently across geographic regions such as localities, states, and nations. Additionally, what constitutes a crime may be contingent on the characteristics of the person committing the act or the person being victimized. For instance, some acts by minors are illegal (i.e., status offenses), whereas the same actions by adults are legal. Definitions of crime are not static; they change over time. Certain actions once illegal are now legal, and new restrictions on behavior may have been unthinkable years ago.

Street Crimes

When asked to identify a crime, most people will respond by listing offenses regularly portrayed in the media: murder, rape, or robbery. But these responses represent an incomplete set of crimes. These acts are commonly referred to as street crimes. **Street crimes** are considered those that are relatively common and serious, involving a victim and an offender who come together in space and time. This includes crimes such as homicide, rape, sexual assault, robbery, and physical assault. Some people view street or violent crimes as those involving a stranger who commits a crime. Although this happens, a large proportion of violent crime occurs between people known to each other. In 2010, for example, 40% of male victims and 64% of female victims of nonfatal violence reported that they knew the offenders.[18] People generally perceive violent or street crimes as involving deadly weapons such as firearms, knives, or clubs. In reality, most street crime does not involve weapons (see Figure 1.3). The public frequently views street crimes with great fear, believing that offenses will inevitably lead to injury or even death. In reality, street crime is relatively unlikely to lead to injury or death, though it can and does happen.

Property Crimes

The public also is familiar with **property crime**, which includes motor vehicle theft, burglary, and property theft. Regardless of the year considered, property crimes are far more

judicial activism: This refers to deviation from the literal meaning of the Constitution, to take into account the present situation including complex societal advances.

USA PATRIOT Act: The 2001 Uniting and Strengthening America by Providing Appropriate Tools Required to Intercept and Obstruct Terrorism Act was signed into law by President George W. Bush to strengthen security measures designed to protect the United States from attack.

USA Freedom Act: A 2015 law that came into effect the day after the USA PATRIOT Act expired. This act restored many provision of the PATRIOT Act but limited the collection of telecommunication metadata of citizens by the National Security Agency.

crime: The breaking of a law for which the criminal justice system or some other governing authority prescribes punishment.

street crimes: These crimes are relatively common and serious, involving a victim and offender who come together in space and time.

property crime: Crime against property. The most common forms of property crime include burglary, property theft (aka larceny), and motor vehicle theft.

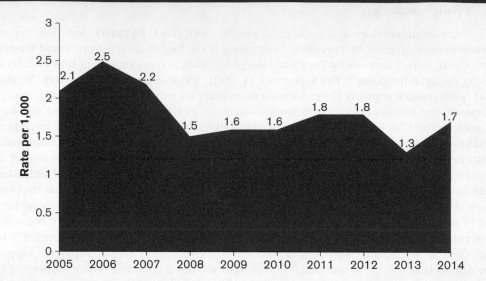

Figure 1.3 ■ Rate of Nonfatal Firearm Victimizations, 2014

Estimates of nonfatal firearm victimization rates per 1,000 people are relatively stable year to year. What may account for the general stability in rates?

Source: Adapted from Table 2 in *Criminal Victimization 2014*. Jennifer L. Truman & Lynn Langton. September 2015. U.S. Department of Justice, Office of Justice Programs, Bureau of Justice Statistics.

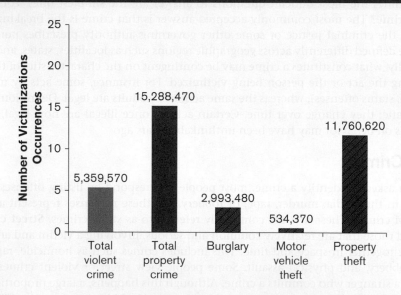

Figure 1.4 ■ Count of Violent and Property Crimes in the United States, 2014

Do you find it surprising that there are far fewer violent crimes than property crimes in the United States? What may influence people to believe that violent crime is so much more common?

Source: Adapted from Tables 1 and 3 in *Criminal Victimization 2014*. Jennifer L. Truman and Lynn Langton. September 2014. U.S. Department of Justice, Office of Justice Programs, Bureau of Justice Statistics.

common than violent street crimes, much to the surprise of those who are influenced by media accounts of unlawful incidents (see Figure 1.4). A consistent finding is that motor vehicle theft is the least common form of property crime and property theft is the most common form of property crime in the United States. Additional information on property crime is presented in Chapter 2.

POLICY ISSUES

Protecting U.S. Citizens

As a result of the 9/11 terrorist attacks, airport security measures now include full-body scans and pat-downs. Additionally, the federal government's Terrorist Screening Center established the No-Fly List during the George W. Bush administration (not to be confused with the Terrorism Watch List, which is substantially longer). Those on the No-Fly List are prohibited from boarding commercial aircraft, or from traveling to or from the United States. The number of names on this list changes as threats and intelligence change, but overall, it has grown over time. In 2011, 10,000 names were on this list (not all citizens of the United States). In 2012, that number increased to 21,000, and by 2013, there were 47,000 names on the No-Fly List. At the time of this writing, in mid-2016, the website no-fly-list.com indicated that 100,208 names were on the No-Fly List. Opponents argue that the No-Fly List violates civil liberties and due process. One appellate court noted, "Tens of thousands of travelers have been misidentified because of misspellings and transcription errors."

The increase in suspect names likely is attributable to the actions of Umar Farouk Abdulmutallab, the underwear bomber. On Christmas Day in 2009, the Nigerian man boarded a plane to Detroit and, in a failed attempt, tried to ignite a bomb hidden in his underwear. In 2012, he was sentenced to life in prison. At the sentencing hearing he showed no remorse and said he was "proud to kill in the name of God." This incident shows the importance of tracking individuals suspected of terrorism.

In contrast to the Abdulmutallab case is the story of Rahinah Ibrahim, who was detained, handcuffed, and questioned for 2 hours at San Francisco International Airport after being identified as being on the No-Fly List. The woman, a mother of four, was a doctoral student at Stanford University flying to Malaysia to present a research paper. The next day she was allowed on a plane, but she was refused entry back into the United States, and her visa was revoked. Ibrahim eventually was paid $225,000 in a settlement claiming wrongful detention by the local police department and a Transportation Security Administration contractor. This incident shows the importance of accuracy to the No-Fly List and the consequences of being mistakenly placed on it.

Think About It

1. Should we be willing to detain individuals with little or no probable cause?

2. Has the government overstepped its legal authority and trampled on constitutional rights?

3. Are we willing to surrender some due process to ensure our safety against terrorism? Why or why not?

Victimless Crimes

Some crimes historically referred to as **victimless crimes** involve illegal behavior that does not (in theory) directly affect another individual.[19] Commonly cited examples of victimless crimes include prostitution, drug use, and gambling. While some people indicate that there are no victims of these crimes, others disagree. For example, drug use may increase rates of burglary as users attempt to gain more resources to continue their habit. Prostitution may increase violence because these women and men are frequently assaulted as a result of their status. Prostitution also may be directly responsible for the trafficking of minors, as meeting the demand of clients (criminal offenders) requires the control of younger and younger people forced into the sex trade. Gambling may lead to financial ruin, requiring families to be supported through governmental programs. Are these really victimless crimes?

White-Collar Crimes

As noted, when people think about criminals and the criminal justice system, they tend to focus on street or property crimes and how law enforcement, courts, and corrections

victimless crimes:
These criminal offenses are thought not to involve victims because they do not directly harm individuals other than the offenders.

handle them. Rarely do people envision white-collar crimes, which affect far more people than street or property crime. Edwin Sutherland, in his presidential address to the American Sociological Society, first recognized white-collar crime as a serious problem in 1939.[20] (The name of this organization was later changed to the American Sociological Association to avoid the embarrassing acronym.) Sutherland described white-collar crime as a "crime committed by a person of respectability and high social status in the course of his occupation."[21] White-collar crime is ill defined, but generally conceived of as lying, cheating, and stealing by occupational, corporate, and government professionals using a wide range of frauds. While there is no consensus, the following are often considered white-collar crimes:

- bribery
- securities fraud
- Ponzi schemes
- mortgage fraud
- misuse of pension funds
- bank fraud
- unsafe products

- violations of public trust
- medical fraud
- insider trading
- price fixing
- toxic dumping
- fiduciary fraud
- religious fraud

White-collar crimes are *not* victimless crimes. A single fraud or scam can destroy a corporation, bankrupt families through lost savings and pensions, lead to home foreclosures, introduce toxic elements in the environment, and ultimately cost investors and taxpayers billions of dollars. Though rarely thought of, and often given brief mention in criminal justice texts, white-collar crime affects more people than street and property crime combined. David Friedrichs, a distinguished scholar, noted that losses from white-collar crime might be as high as $250 billion annually, compared with the estimated $4 billion annually attributed to losses involving robbery and burglary.[22] Major corporate scandals like the collapse of Enron have focused more attention on white-collar criminals. Enron CEO Kenneth Lay was indicted on 11 counts of securities fraud and other charges and later found guilty of 10 of those. Lay was sentenced to just over 24 years in prison (but died before he began serving his sentence). Xuyen Thi-Kim Nguyen, another white-collar criminal, was convicted of one count of conspiracy, two counts of mail fraud, and seven counts of wire fraud in conjunction with mortgage fraud. She disappeared in 2005 before sentencing. She is currently a fugitive and is wanted by the FBI.[23]

Much of the debate over the definition of white-collar crime exemplifies the slippery slope of distinguishing what should be regarded as criminal. An academic argument between Sutherland and Paul Tappan developed into an important basis for thinking about the crime label.[24] Sutherland questioned the legal definition of criminal behavior. He believed that the conviction of a criminal act was an unnecessary condition for determining whether a person committed an offense.[25] Tappan argued, however, that sociological constructs such as antisocial behavior, conduct norms, and deviance fail to differentiate criminal versus noncriminal. In other words, in a much more legalistic approach, Tappan believed that only people convicted of crimes with specific penalties could be considered criminals. While their argument may appear to be a matter of semantics, what constitutes white-collar crime continues to vary, and unethical behavior today may later be labeled as criminal.[26]

Bernie Madoff was responsible for one of the largest financial frauds in history and stole over $17 billion from investors. He was sentenced to 150 years in prison. At the time Madoff was in his 70s and was likely to die in prison. How might longer sentences for white-collar crime deter other financial fraudsters?

Cybercrime

A relatively new and rapidly growing type of crime is **cybercrime**. Broadly, cybercrime is illegal activity committed using a computer or computer networks as the primary method of commission. Examples of cybercrime include the following:

- network intrusions
- dissemination of computer viruses, malicious code, botnets, and various email scams such as phishing
- denial-of-service attacks
- identity theft
- stalking

- bullying
- fraud
- theft of service
- online gambling
- trade secret theft
- securities fraud
- child pornography

This list of cybercrimes reveals a controversy as to whether the offenses represent unique and different types of crime. Consider that decades ago, several of these crimes (e.g., network intrusions, dissemination of malicious code, viruses, botnets, phishing, denial-of-service attacks) were nonexistent, given lesser technology that was available. Overall, these crimes fail to neatly fit in a typology of violent and property crime. Yet it appears that some cybercrime refers to a different method used to commit violent crimes (e.g., bullying, stalking), property crimes (e.g., identity theft), and white-collar crimes (e.g., securities fraud). Clearly, there is some overlap, as even the FBI releases statistics on what it refers to as "white-collar cybercrime."[27] Additional overlap is found between cybercrime and terrorism because some incidents of the latter are being committed using computers. In time, greater clarity defining the boundaries of cybercrime will emerge.

Xuyen Thi-Kim Nguyen, fugitive. Like violent crime, white-collar crime is committed more by men than women. Why is that? Are women just less likely to commit criminal acts? Or do they generally have less access to ways of committing white-collar crimes? What do you think?

Terrorism

Terrorism is a crime that receives a great deal of attention in the public and in academic studies.[28] Though a variety of definitions of terrorism are used by different agencies and groups, in recent years, it generally includes these characteristics:

- It is committed by subnational or extremist clandestine groups that may or may not include groups in the United States.
- It is premeditated.
- Targets are noncombatants.
- Acts have the purpose of influencing an audience.
- Acts tend to be cross-national (international vs. domestic terrorism).
- Acts generally seek political, social, or economic change.

Though public awareness has increased since the 9/11 attacks, terrorism has a long history in the United States. A relatively recent act of domestic terrorism was the 1995 bombing of the Alfred P. Murrah Federal Building in Oklahoma City. Several domestic terrorists were responsible for this deadly bombing. The two most widely known were Timothy McVeigh and Terry Nichols. Lesser known were accomplices Michael and Lori Fortier. Michael Fortier was McVeigh's army roommate. All of these individuals were sympathizers of the American Militia Movement and self-proclaimed survivalists. They were especially incensed because they believed that the government was infringing on their right to bear arms. In addition, these individuals were enraged about past government actions at Ruby Ridge and Waco.

McVeigh was responsible for actually detonating the ammonium nitrate fertilizer–based bomb at the Murrah Federal Building. He parked a van, which hid the 4,800-pound bomb, in a loading zone and detonated it using a 5-minute and a 2-minute fuse. Nichols built the bomb. The Fortiers were considered accomplices given their knowledge of the attack as well as their assistance in the planning. As a result of these actions culminating in the blast on April 19, 1995, 680 people were injured and 168 people lost their lives. Nineteen of those killed were under age 6, as a day care center operated in the building.

McVeigh was tried and found guilty on 11 counts of murder and conspiracy. He was sentenced to death and executed on June 11, 2001. Nichols also was found guilty and ultimately sentenced to 161 consecutive life terms without the possibility of parole. Michael Fortier was

Video 1.2:
Everyday cybercrime

cybercrime: A form of illegal activity using a computer or computer networks as the primary method of commission. Examples of cybercrime include network intrusions, dissemination of computer viruses, and phishing.

terrorism: The completed or threatened use of coercion and/or violence against a population of people with the goal of changing political, religious, or ideological positions.

The Alfred P. Murrah Federal Building, Oklahoma City, shortly after a domestic terrorist bombing in 1995. How did this act of terrorism differ from 9/11? What explanations account for the government's failure to respond to this act of terror in the same way it did following 9/11? What would you have done after the Oklahoma City bombing to minimize the possibility of future terrorist acts?

tried and sentenced to 12 years in prison and a $75,000 fine. In 2008, after serving 10 years, Fortier was released and entered the Witness Protection Program, in which he was given a new identity. Lori Fortier was given immunity, and as a result she was never tried or convicted.

International terrorism continues to receive increased attention as the number of terrorist organizations and attacks increase. Terrorism goes beyond all geographic boundaries and ethnicities. The most prominent group is the Islamic State of Iraq and the Levant (also known as ISIS or ISIL), which is responsible for many recent bombings and murders worldwide. In June 2016, for example, nearly 40,000 Fallujah citizens were trapped when ISIS militants surrounded the Iraqi city with snipers and cut off food supplies. Additionally, four people were arrested in Germany after one member of a sleeper cell revealed their plot to bomb German metro stations. And three Minnesota men were found guilty of plotting to join ISIS. These three incidents are only a small fraction of the threats and actions of ISIS in just one month.

CRIME DEFINITIONS CHANGE OVER TIME

Crime is not new. Where there have been people, there has been crime. What *has* remained constant is the notion that crimes can be either *mala in se* or *mala prohibita*.

Mala in se refers to behavior that is immoral and inherently wrong by nature. *Mala prohibita* describes behavior that is prohibited by law. Until recently, marijuana use was considered illegal as a result of *mala prohibita*. What constitutes *mala prohibita* has changed over time. In some cases, previously illegal behavior has become decriminalized, while in other instances, what had been ordinary behavior is now illegal. As of mid-2016, four states (Washington, Colorado, Oregon, and Alaska) and the District of Columbia had legalized the possession of small amounts of marijuana for personal consumption, though the drug remains illegal under federal law. By mid-2016, 24 states had legalized medical marijuana. As the quotation at the beginning of the chapter indicates, with more laws, we have more criminals. Through **decriminalization**—the reduction or abolition of penalties associated with behaviors—we have fewer offenders. Decriminalization examples include justifiable homicide and adultery.

Justifiable Homicide

While **justifiable homicide**—the lawful and intentional taking of another's life—has always been legal, what constitutes justifiable homicide has changed over time. For an act to be defined as justifiable homicide, there must be evidence that the suspected offender (e.g., a burglar) presented an imminent threat to the life or well-being of another. This threat includes murder, manslaughter, armed robbery, and rape. Law enforcement officers or citizens killing in self-defense or to defend others, state-sanctioned executions, and killing during times of war are all considered justifiable homicides.

Recent changes in some state laws have expanded situations in which justifiable homicide is possible. Historically if a burglar were to enter one's home or business, it was expected that the resident or business owner obey a *duty to retreat*. That is, the resident had to first try to avoid conflict and take steps to retreat in order to avoid a confrontation with the offender. Only after attempts at de-escalation could the homeowner or business owner use force. Currently, many states, including (but not limited to) Florida, Texas, Pennsylvania, and Tennessee, have adopted laws referred to as the "Castle Doctrine."

Broadly, the **Castle Doctrine** and Make My Day Laws state that residents are no longer required to retreat if threatened by intruders. Instead, they may justifiably use force,

mala in se: One of two types of illegal behavior. *Mala in se* refers to behavior that is sinful and inherently wrong by nature.

mala prohibita: One of two types of illegal behavior. *Mala prohibita* describes behavior that is prohibited by law. What constitutes *mala prohibita* is dynamic and has changed over time.

decriminalization: The act of ending or reducing criminal penalties associated with some behaviors.

justifiable homicide: The lawful killing of another person such as when a law enforcement officer or a citizen kills in self-defense or to defend another.

Castle Doctrine: A legal doctrine that states that homeowners are no longer required to retreat if threatened by intruders. In some states it extends beyond homes.

including deadly force, against intruders, if they or other individuals are threatened. There is some variation in how expansively the Castle Doctrine applies. In some states, such as Texas and Florida, it applies to one's home or business, one's motor vehicle, public places, and any other location a person has a right to be. In Colorado, an offender must enter a "dwelling" in order for a claim of justifiable homicide to be made.

Adultery

Another example of decriminalization of behavior is **adultery**. Historically, adultery was criminal behavior defined as sex between a *married woman* and a person other than her spouse. The basis for this distinction focused on paternity. That is, this law sought to prevent a husband from supporting or leaving an inheritance to another man's child or children because of his wife's adulterous behavior.

A crash resulting from drunk driving. Given the aftermath of some drunk driving accidents, do you feel the offense should be dealt with more harshly or less harshly than it currently is? What do you think is the appropriate BAC threshold making DUI a crime?

Over time most states have decriminalized adultery; however, definitions of adultery and the associated punishment vary by state. Currently, in New York, adultery occurs when two people engage in sexual activities and at least one of the members of the pair has a living spouse. In Minnesota, adultery occurs when a married woman has sex with a man who is not her husband. In this scenario both the man, whether married or not, and the woman have committed adultery. In Michigan, adultery is a felony punishable with jail or some other intermediate sanction. In contrast, adultery results in a $10 fine in Maryland. In the U.S. military, adultery is an offense for which one can be court-martialed. The prosecution of adultery, while uncommon, still occurs in the military.

Driving Under the Influence

While marijuana and adultery are examples of decriminalization, in other instances behavior has become increasingly criminalized. By expanding what is considered criminal behavior, we have increased the number of offenders and the number of persons under control of the criminal justice system. One example of increased criminalization applies to driving under the influence. Consider, for example, people who drink alcohol or take drugs and then get behind the wheel of a vehicle or on a motorcycle, and drive. At times, this behavior results in terrible and deadly accidents. While it has been prohibited to drive drunk in some places for more than a century, convictions were rare. New York was the first state to implement a drunken driving law, in 1910; however, there was no specific definition of what constituted driving while intoxicated. In general, the accepted limit was 0.15% blood alcohol content (BAC). This means that a person with a BAC of 0.15% has 15 grams of alcohol in 10 liters of blood. Drunk drivers rarely received jail or prison time, and victims received no restitution or justice. The offenders would merely go home and try to deal with their "problem" in a private and personal way. This approach to drunk driving changed in the late 1970s and is now associated with serious penalties.

Leading this change was Candace Lightner, the founding president of Mothers Against Drunk Driving (MADD).[29] In 1980, Lightner's 13-year-old daughter Cari was hit from behind by a drunk driver as she walked to a church carnival in her neighborhood. The driver, who had momentarily blacked out because of too much alcohol, regained consciousness after killing Cari and drove off, leaving her badly mutilated body in the street. The man was a repeat offender who was out on bail following a separate hit-and-run drunk driving incident only 2 days before he killed Cari. Cari's death represented his fifth offense in 4 years. Four days after Cari's death, Lightner started MADD when she discovered that the offender who had been apprehended would not receive any jail or prison time for killing Cari.

Since then, there has been a flurry of changes to the laws related to drunk driving and punishment. Currently, all states have clearly defined BAC levels that result in criminal charges and penalties, though the laws and punishment vary by state. In most states, the legal BAC limit is 0.08%. In some states a separate offense (driving while ability impaired, 0.05% BAC) may also be charged.

Journal:
Mandatory minimum sentences for DUIs

adultery: In general, sex by a married person with someone other than his or her spouse; specific laws differ by state, as does the level of criminality associated with it.

rape: A type of violent crime considered *mala in se* that includes "penetration, no matter how slight, of the vagina or anus with a body part or object, or oral penetration by a sex organ of another person, without the consent of the victim."

The first time Chris Farias was pulled over driving while intoxicated, he took a plea bargain that lowered his drunk driving charge to public intoxication. A few years later, he was pulled over again for DUI. This arrest resulted in a substantial monetary fine and some time in jail. Unfortunately, Chris's defiant personality interfered with any change in his behavior. He continued drinking and driving. Two years after his second DUI incident, Chris attended a tailgating party in preparation for the fun of drinking during a college football game. After the game he was unable to get a cab because of the crowds (and the large number of intoxicated people using cabs), and he made the poor decision to ride his motorcycle home, thinking that if he took the back roads he could avoid the police. To this day, he is angry at his decision because his home was mere blocks away—he could have easily walked. An officer noticed a man riding a motorcycle extraordinarily slowly on a cold night and pulled Chris over. Once again, he was arrested. What Chris failed to realize was that the change in drunk driving laws where he lived meant that even his first offense was to be treated as a DUI. With this third DUI, he confronted much more severe consequences with harsher punishment. Chris faced the risk of losing everything—his construction business, girlfriend, friends, home, and driver's license—because of the zero-tolerance policy now connected with DUI laws.

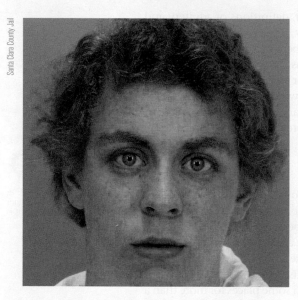

Santa Clara County Jail

California changes Sexual Assault Definition. Brock Turner was a college student who sexually victimized an unconscious female college student by a trash container at a fraternity party. Turner was convicted of three felony charges, including two for sexual assault based on penetrative actions. According to the FBI definition, the penetrative actions constituted rape. According to the law in California at the time of his conviction, his actions constituted sexual assault, and Turner was released from jail after serving only three months of a six month sentence. Citing Turner's sentence, California Assemblywoman Cristina Garcia introduced a bill to revise California's Penal Code so that "all forms of nonconsensual sexual assault may be considered rape for purposes of the gravity of the offense and the support of survivors." The bill was passed by the Assembly and signed into law, becoming effective January 1, 2017. Some are shocked at how short Turner's sentence was. Others who are more familiar with the way sexual violence is handled in the criminal justice system are shocked that he was found guilty and served any time at all. What would you call the crimes committed by Turner? Rape? Sexual Assault? Why? Do you think Turner served enough time? Not enough? Why?

Rape and Sexual Assault

Rape is another example of a crime that has seen an expansion in its definition over time. While rape has always been a crime and considered *mala in se*, how it has been legally defined has changed. For example, originally, the FBI defined rape as the "carnal knowledge of a female forcibly and against her will."[30] In 2011, the FBI definition was changed to broaden the behaviors that are considered rape: "penetration, no matter how slight, of the vagina or anus with a body part or object, or oral penetration by a sex organ of another person, without the consent of the victim." This change included boys and men as victims as well as behavior beyond the penetration of a vagina by a penis. In 2013, the FBI removed the word *forcibly* from this definition to further reflect contemporary understanding of this violence. Rape does not necessarily involve force, but it does involve a lack of consent, such as when a person is unconscious. A recent highly publicized example is that of Brock Turner. According to the police report, Turner, a student at Stanford University, was caught in the act, and ultimately convicted of three felony charges: assault with intent to rape an intoxicated woman, sexually penetrating an intoxicated person with a foreign object, and sexually penetrating an unconscious person with a foreign object. Turner's victim was unconscious during the attack, as it happened by a trash container outside of the Kappa Alpha fraternity house on campus. According to the FBI definition, the penetrative actions constituted rape. According to the law in California at the time of his conviction, Turner's actions constituted sexual assault (the California law was changed shortly thereafter to reflect nonconsensual penetrative actions as rape). As of October 2017, Turner is currently appealing his convictions.

Additional changes in laws included those that recognize that rape can occur between married partners. Prior to 1975, rape by definition could not occur between marital partners.[31] Currently, all states have marital rape laws, although it took almost 20 years to recognize the seriousness of rape between a

ETHICAL ISSUES

Shoot or Don't Shoot?

In many states, homeowners have the right to confront and use deadly force when unwanted intruders enter their homes. In some jurisdictions, laws specifically state that people who are defending their property may shoot a burglar or another criminal only in a "dwelling." In one case, a man who freed himself after being tied up during a home invasion grabbed his gun and ran outside and began shooting at the burglar, who had stolen his car. He killed the driver, who then crashed the vehicle into a neighbor's home. In another case in the same state, a man shot and killed a person who was stealing from his storage shed. In the first case, prosecutors decided not to file charges against the homeowner.

In the second example, the man was charged with voluntary manslaughter. Other difficult cases have arisen when inebriated people have entered the wrong house and were shot by property owners.

Think About It

1. If a burglar leaves your house with your money, television, and stereo, would you give chase and shoot?

2. If a person is breaking into an unattached garage, do you think this qualifies as a dwelling?

3. Is the taking of another person's life an ethical or moral issue? Explain.

rape shield laws were enacted to protect the privacy of victims. Rape shield laws restrict a defendant's ability to cross-examine a rape victim about past sexual behavior and prohibit the revealing of the identity of a rape victim.[32] In some states, protections are even broader.

Before these statutes were enacted, rape victims' prior behaviors were used as evidence to mitigate the crime, which had a chilling effect on the willingness of victims to go forward. In the case of Jennifer Schuett, one would think that she would not have had to worry about being accused of luring her attacker given her age and the rape shield laws. It seems unthinkable that anyone would accuse a child of such a thing. Yet it happens. Consider the case of an 11-year-old Cleveland, Texas, girl who was gang-raped by 18 men in 2010.[33] The defendant's attorney publicly portrayed the young victim as a "seductive man-luring spider." Changes in these laws are one step in the right direction to convey that rape is a crime of violence and that victims are not responsible for their victimization. Like the perpetrator in the Schuett case, evidence points toward rape being an act of power and control by the perpetrator.[34]

THE CRIMINAL JUSTICE SYSTEM: PURPOSE AND PERSPECTIVES

People often are surprised by the lack of agreement related to the *purpose* of the criminal justice system. Some individuals believe its purpose is to control and punish offenders and to protect society. Others view rehabilitation as the purpose of the system. And yet others believe the purpose of this massive system is to ensure that all accused are treated fairly and/or to restore justice. This section identifies the major perspectives on the purpose of the criminal justice system. While each is presented as a distinct *perspective*, they are not necessarily mutually exclusive.

Crime Control

A popular view is that the role of the criminal justice system is to prevent crime by shrewdly and harshly punishing offenders. This viewpoint, referred to as the **crime control perspective**, finds that when punishment is weak or avoided, offenders do not fear apprehension and continue to commit crimes. As a result, the public is left unprotected and crime increases. This model holds that all offenders—violent or not—are greedy, impulsive, and/or thrill-seeking

crime control perspective: A popular view of the role of the criminal justice system. This perspective states that the goal of the system is to prevent crime by shrewdly and harshly punishing offenders.

Is it possible to both rehabilitate and punish offenders for unlawful behavior? Or are these two goals diametrically opposed? What policies would you implement to both punish and rehabilitate offenders?

individuals. Offenders choose to commit the crime and must be punished. In order for a system operating under this perspective to function properly, effective law enforcement, long sentences, and strict mandatory punishment (especially the use of prison time) are required. This expensive and punitive perspective of the criminal justice system is currently in vogue and has resulted in part in the enormous growth of individuals under the supervision of the criminal justice system. This growth occurred until recently despite documented declines in violent and property offending that started in the early to mid-1990s.

Research indicates that, while popular, in practice the crime control model is not effective, efficient, or economically sound. About two thirds of all offenders commit additional crimes even after being punished. Recidivism rates this high indicate a level of ineffectiveness in terms of deterring future criminal behavior. Furthermore, the implementation of longer and tougher sentences coupled with high rates of recidivism often results in families being torn apart. Children are raised in an environment of less (or no) supervision, and spouses left behind must frequently turn to public assistance (i.e., your tax dollars) to survive. This approach has fueled an increase in prison construction at great financial and social expense. Also, more law enforcement officers and criminal justice workers are being hired, resulting in further increased costs.

Rehabilitation

Another perspective holds that the purpose of the criminal justice system is to rehabilitate offenders. This **rehabilitative perspective** asserts that the role of the criminal justice system is to care for and treat people who cannot take care of themselves. The rehabilitative perspective is based on the notion that offending is the result of blocked opportunities such as employment (and no money), inadequate education, lack of transportation, and poor adult role models. In essence, those who commit crime are victims of social inequality. Many people believe that when individuals are provided with the opportunity to achieve and support themselves through legitimate means, they will do so and avoid the consequences of committing crime. This perspective is based on the underlying belief that people commit crime because it is their only option.

Based on this concept, the role of the criminal justice system is to provide individuals with the means to improve their lives through education, training, and social skills. With these necessary tools, individuals can support themselves in legitimate ways once released. The rehabilitative perspective also comes with a large price tag. Offender education and rehabilitation are costly. Some experts, however, argue that the price in terms of money and damage by offending is even greater if we allow those least able to survive to continue their deviant and offending ways. Society can pay now in terms of offering skills, or pay later in terms of incarceration.

Due Process

The **due process perspective** focuses on the criminal justice system's purpose of ensuring that all people accused of crimes are treated fairly and equally. The basis of the due process perspective is found in the U.S. Constitution. Specifically, the Fifth and Fourteenth Amendments speak to each citizen's right to due process in the administration of justice. The due process clauses exist to protect citizens accused of crimes from capricious detainment and denial of freedom, inequitable use of capital punishment, and/or the taking of property by the government as a result of a criminal or civil proceeding. Everyone accused of a crime should be treated equitably by law enforcement, the courts, and corrections. This perspective means that

rehabilitative perspective: A view that the purpose of the criminal justice system is to rehabilitate offenders.

due process perspective: A perspective that views the role of the criminal justice system to be to ensure that all people accused of crimes are treated fairly and equally in the system.

Figure 1.5 ■ Restorative Justice Approaches

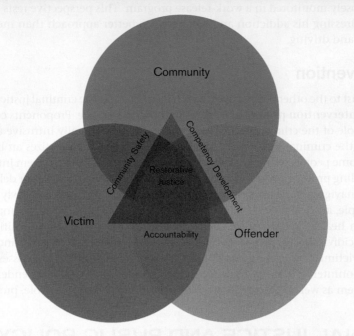

Restorative justice approaches actively engage the victim in the process. Other approaches are not as victim-centric. Should dealing with the offender involve the victim? Why or why not?

Source: Center for Restorative Youth Justice.

detainment should be fairly distributed, every person should receive fair hearings and trials, engaged and competent attorneys should represent the accused, and sentencing (if appropriate) should be evenhanded. The due process perspective holds that the criminal justice system should not allow inequitable treatment based on any characteristics, including the accused person's race, ethnicity, age, income, or religious preference.

A system that operates contrary to the principles of due process is the antithesis of the U.S. Constitution and what our criminal justice system stands for. Unfortunately, as discussed throughout this text, there are myriad examples in which the criminal justice system has failed to uphold its due process purpose. Arrest, incarceration, and the death penalty are not equitably distributed. Documented cases indicate that competent legal representation and judicial behavior are not evenhandedly dispersed throughout the system.

Restorative Justice

The **restorative justice perspective** finds that the appropriate role of the criminal justice system is to repair the harm caused by criminal behavior. This perspective holds that the criminal justice system should not operate through punishment, but rather though cooperation among victims, offenders, and members of the community. Together, some or all of these actors share with one another how the crime affected them and reach consensus on a satisfactory method of resolution (Figure 1.5). Whereas other perspectives tend to focus on punishing the offender and satisfying legal principles, this approach focuses on the victims of crime. Victims are able to share in detail with offenders (if appropriate) how their crimes harmed them. The community is involved because local citizens (versus the state) are considered victims as well. Offenders are expected to take responsibility for their actions and to "pay" for them through agreed-upon means. The outcome may include paying restitution, repairing damaged property, and/or serving the community. Though not widely implemented in the United States, research finds that restorative justice results in the highest rate of victim satisfaction and offender accountability.

Web:
Restorative justice

restorative justice perspective: This perspective indicates that the appropriate role of the criminal justice system is to restore justice as best as possible through repairing the harm caused by criminal behavior.

Chris Farias's most recent DUI was dealt with through a restorative justice approach. He was allowed to undergo special treatment, provided with counseling (at personal financial cost), and closely monitored in a work-release program. This perspective rests on the assumption that addressing his addiction and behavior is a better approach than merely punishing his drinking and driving.

Nonintervention

In contrast to the other perspectives, which identify what the criminal justice system should do, the **nonintervention perspective** argues for noninterference. Proponents contend that the appropriate role of the criminal justice system is to be as minimally intrusive as possible. Any intrusion by the criminal justice system is harmful because it stigmatizes an individual as an "offender." Some people believe that the stigma from criminal justice system interaction results in a self-fulfilling prophecy whereby offenders view themselves as failures or delinquent and, as a result, find navigating the noncriminal world more and more difficult. Newly minted offenders, for example, are less able to find work given their records and often are unable to establish and maintain healthy relationships. Taken together, these increased difficulties enhance the chances of recidivism. This perspective advocates for the decriminalization and legalization of nonserious, victimless crimes such as public drunkenness, vagrancy, and possession and use of marijuana. Noninterventionists argue for the release of all nonviolent offenders from the correctional system as well as the release from oversight of others (e.g., parole, probation).

CRIMINAL JUSTICE AND PUBLIC POLICY

The beginning of the chapter noted how everyone is affected by the criminal justice system through public policy. The criminal justice system is our method of social control and reflects both a **consensus model** and a **conflict model**. Social control represents the methods used to ensure conformity and compliance among its members. The government and laws typically accomplish formal social control. Informal social control may be instilled, for example, through peer pressure to act a certain way. A closely related concept is the idea of a social contract. This perspective developed from the work of early philosophers who believed that organized societies are created by an agreement that is mutually beneficial to the whole. The social contract gives power to the government or state to provide protection and ensure well-being among citizens.

Consensus Model

A consensus model, which supports the idea of a social contract, originated from the work of John Locke and is based on the view that everyone in the criminal justice system works in unison to achieve justice. The consensus model operates on the notion that there is general agreement about what behaviors are harmful to the majority of the public and that these behaviors are deemed criminal. This model recognizes that criminal law then serves a social control function designed to protect citizens and maximize peace.

Conflict Model

A conflict model is based on the notions of division and disparity among members of society and the struggles for power that this causes. The conflict model has roots in the ideology espoused by Karl Marx and focuses on the power struggle between the haves and have-nots—or, stated differently, those with and without power. According to the conflict model, those with power define what is criminal and, in doing so, exert control over the powerless. By exerting this power, those in powerful positions are able to maintain their dominance and privilege over the less fortunate. Given the relationship between race, ethnicity, and gender and power in the United States, it is not surprising that evidence exists pointing to the use of the criminal justice system to control persons of color and women. In this chapter, and those that follow, you will encounter evidence of both the consensus and conflict models at all levels of the system.

The importance of crime and public policy is essential to our understanding of all components of the criminal justice system. Public concerns about gun violence, gangs, human

nonintervention perspective: A view that the appropriate role of the criminal justice system is to be as minimal and nonintrusive as possible.

consensus model: A theoretical view of the criminal justice system that highlights the collaborative nature of the system. The components of the criminal justice system work in unison to achieve justice.

conflict model: A theoretical view of the criminal justice system that highlights the adversarial nature of the system. Components of the criminal justice system work in competition to produce a fair outcome or justice.

trafficking, and other high-profile crimes increase pressure on lawmakers to respond. Legislative efforts seeking harsher punishments are common and create political common ground. No political party or potential candidate can be against tougher laws for reducing crime and violence. Social scientists and empirical research provide the evidence for many of the decisions driving our lawmakers. Joan Petersilia and James Q. Wilson, pioneers in crime and public policy, warn of avoiding two mistakes in approaching policy. First, we still are identifying the problems and searching for solutions. This lack of knowledge creates a need for *action*. Second, researchers can inform policy, and abdicating responsibility to law enforcement, judges, and politicians is a mistake. Their position emphasizes collaboration.[35] The interaction among criminologists, practitioners, and lawmakers to solve crime problems is discussed throughout the following chapters.

CRIME AND THE MEDIA

The criminal justice system and media such as newspapers, blogs, the Internet, television shows, movies, and books are engaged in a troubled relationship that almost everyone is exposed to. Separating the two is impossible.[36] The media are dominated by stories of crime and victimization, and while there is nothing inherently wrong with the media being preoccupied with these things, much of what is conveyed to the public projects inaccuracies about crime, victimization, and the criminal justice system. This situation is troubling because most people gain their understanding about crime, victimization, and the criminal justice system from the media. From these stories the public identifies what it feels are important criminal justice–related issues. These issues come to the attention of policymakers, who in turn enact legislation that influences our lives. Unfortunately, this process means that some critical (but unsexy) criminal justice issues are ignored while other rare or unimportant issues gain a great deal of resources and attention. The implementation of memorial criminal justice policies often reflects this process. These policies are named for persons who were victims of crime. This book covers many of these memorial policies, including Megan's Law and Amber Alerts. Other policies well known to the public are those in memory of Adam Walsh and Polly Klaas. While no one can argue that the crimes against these individuals were not tragic, whether these memorial policies improve the criminal justice system is debatable.

Framing

Crime is portrayed in the media through **framing**. Framing means that criminal justice and crime stories are packaged into tidy presentations that make sharing the information easy. Frames simplify criminal events and make processing, labeling, and understanding crimes easier for the audience. Unfortunately, frames fail to allow the expression of important variation and nuances in the crimes. It is vital to recognize that frames are tied to the criminal justice policies (also oversimplified) designed to address the problem. Sasson offers five common crime-and-justice frames found widely in the media in the United States[37]:

- faulty criminal justice system
- blocked opportunities
- social breakdown
- racist system
- violent media

The faulty criminal justice system frame indicates that crime occurs because of a dearth of law and order in the country. Presentations using this frame indicate that crimes are committed because criminals feel they can get away with them. This frame contends that criminal sanctions are a joke and that criminals are rarely held accountable. This frame depicts prisons as having

"TV violence made him do it. Says he'll name shows if we drop the charges."

Research indicates that stories portrayed in the media are associated with heightened fear. Should the media be required to present a more accurate view of crime? Or is it okay that the media tend to highlight only the most heinous of all crimes?

Audio:
Despite grim media reports, crime rates are actually down in the U.S.

Author Video:
Crime and the media

framing: The packaging of criminal events in the media into tidy presentations that make sharing the information easy.

faulty criminal justice system frame: Suggests that crime occurs because of a dearth of law and order in the country and that criminals offend because they feel they can get away with it.

Blocked opportunities frame. As a policymaker, what would you do to reduce crime? Would you act to reduce poverty, unemployment, and discrimination? How might those actions influence crime?

blocked opportunities frame: This frame indicates that crime results from a lack of legal options. Offenders live in poverty, are uneducated, unemployed, and discriminated against, and because of that commit crime.

social breakdown frame: Indicates that crime is the result of a breakdown in family and community.

racist system frame: Indicates that the problem is not crime, but rather that law enforcement, courts, and corrections are racist agents of oppression.

violent media frame: This frame finds that crime is depicted as a direct result of the violent media present in television, movies, video games, and music.

infotainment: The marketing of a highly edited and distorted combination of entertainment and information purported to be truthful and comprehensive.

revolving doors and blames bleeding-heart liberals for the chaos in which we all live. Because the problem is clearly framed as a lack of adequate sanctions, the policies required to address crime are clear: Enact sanctions that are swift, certain, and severe. Offenders must be punished brutally, and the crime problem will be solved.

A second common crime frame found in the media is the **blocked opportunities frame**. This perspective suggests that crime results from a lack of legal opportunities among offenders. Offenders live in poverty and are uneducated, unemployed, and discriminated against. Therefore, those living in these conditions are left with no other option but to commit crimes. Given this tidy explanation for the presence of crime, the solution is simple and clear: Enact policies that lift people out of poverty, educate them, offer them skills to enhance employability, and end discrimination. Given the right opportunities, offenders will not commit crime.

The **social breakdown frame** presents crime as the obvious result of a breakdown in family and community. Alleged evidence of this collapse includes high divorce rates, cohabitation of unmarried people, out-of-wedlock births, same-sex marriage, and other nonconventional family units. This frame also contends that the availability of welfare has further enabled families and the community to disintegrate. This clear framing of the issue identifies the policies needed to correct crime: Enact policies that promote family and community values, and end handouts.

The fourth common crime frame found in the media is the **racist system frame**. This perspective holds that the problem is not crime, but rather the criminal justice system. In this frame, law enforcement, courts, and corrections are depicted as racist agents of oppression. The criminal justice system, then, is used as a means to oppress people of color. Given this simple problem, the solution is clear: Enact policies that ameliorate racial injustices, and include the banding together of people of color to gain the justice that they deserve.

And finally, the **violent media frame** depicts crime as a direct result of the violent media that bombard us in television, movies, video games, and music. This frame holds that this constant display of violence leads to a lack of respect for human life and increased violence in the nation. To remedy this situation, the required policy is clear: Enact policies that would regulate widespread violent imagery available to the masses.

Infotainment

An unfortunate offspring of the relationship between media and crime is infotainment. **Infotainment** is the marketing of a highly edited and distorted combination of entertainment and information purported to be truthful and comprehensive. Infotainment leads the viewing public to feel that they are being educated with facts and information about crime and the criminal justice system in the United States. In reality, the public is receiving a highly edited and narrow view of the topic. There are endless examples of false beliefs held by the public that is commonly portrayed in the media:

- Women are more likely to be victims of violence than men.
- Murder is one of the most frequent types of violence committed.
- Children are at higher risk of being violently victimized at school than away from school.

- Most crime committed in the United States is violent in nature.
- Offenders are crazed monsters.
- Most violence is committed by armed offenders.
- Strangers commit most crimes.
- Only guilty people confess to crimes.
- Most violent crimes result in injuries to the victims.
- Blacks are more likely to violently victimize whites than other blacks.
- Most individuals accused of crimes go to trial.

Do you believe supporters of the Black Lives Matter movement see the criminal justice system through the racist system frame? What other frames might explain their position?

All of these statements are false. Yet most believe them to be accurate, and as a result many people live in unwarranted fear of becoming victims of crime. This misinformation also misleads the public into believing they know what an offender really looks or acts like. This misinformation can be dangerous or deadly if it leads some to fail to understand who may actually be a threat to them. Sadly, these commonly held misunderstandings can lead people who were violently victimized to question whether they were in fact victimized: The offender was a friend, there was no weapon, I was not seriously injured . . . was it really a crime? Misunderstandings about the reality of crime and victimization in the United States distort policies, waste time and resources, create unnecessary fear, and may endanger individuals.

Narrow-Casting

Further exacerbating the distorted presentation of crime in the media is the contemporary practice of **narrow-casting**. Once upon a time, there were few media outlets, which meant that each needed to offer a wide range of perspectives on crime. Broad coverage was required to appeal to their viewership. Today, there are countless media channels, and most offer narrow and often distorted views of reality. Viewing audiences are smaller and more homogeneous, and the infotainment presented to them, described as factual and comprehensive, is not. Failure to tune in to a multitude of media and nonmedia sources and an inability to critically consume information lead to uninformed and misinformed citizens.

Viewers must understand that the media constitute a for-profit business. The primary goal of the media—including so-called news programs—is not to inform and educate members of the public. The ultimate goal of these for-profit businesses is to deliver viewers to advertisers. This agenda is seldom accomplished by offering truthful and comprehensive accounts of crime. Rarely is it accomplished by offering the nuances of crime, mundane criminal events, and difficult policy discussions. Rather, delivery of viewers to advertisers is best achieved by emphasizing the most heinous of crimes, the most vulnerable of victims, and titillating topics, packaged in easy-to-digest frames. This approach leaves an audience that feels crime is perpetually out of control.

CRIMINAL JUSTICE VERSUS CRIMINOLOGY

What is the difference between criminal justice and criminology? Many use the terms interchangeably, and while there is some overlap, they refer to two disciplines. Adding to the confusion is the lack of agreement over the degree of overlap or differences between criminology and *criminal justice*. Criminal justice refers to the system—that is, the system of law enforcement, courts, and corrections. This approach involves investigating

narrow-casting:
The presentation of a narrow view of information in the media to small homogeneous audiences.

CONTEMPLATING CAREERS

Contemplating a Career in Criminal Justice

The information in this chapter is indicative of a large and far-reaching criminal justice system. The size and breadth of the criminal justice system have implications in terms of the many career and job opportunities available. Positions include victim advocates; researchers; probation and parole officers; federal, state, and local law enforcement agents; prosecutors; defense attorneys; judges; prison psychologists; reentry specialists; law clerks; and corrections officers. Each of these positions (and others not noted here) benefit from individuals wishing to help others and improve society.

Additional personal characteristics, such as being a leader, inquisitive, detail oriented, and organized, may point to specific careers for you. In the remainder of the text, many of these important careers and specific personality characteristics associated with them are highlighted.

Career Video:
A federal agent discusses his experience and current issues in the field.

the practices of these three institutions, including laws relating to crime and offenders, approaches to deterring future crime, sanctioning and/or rehabilitating offenders, and recidivism. In contrast, *criminology* refers to the study of the nature, extent, and causes of criminal offending and criminal victimization. Some scholars suggest that criminal justice refers more to the policy aspects of crime, whereas criminology applies more to the behavioral aspects of offending and victimization. While these perspectives offer tidy descriptions, separating the two in practice is messy. For instance, some scholars conduct research on the behavior of police officers. Others conduct research on the interaction of victims with policing agencies. Others examine jurors' responses to victims of violence and their likelihood to render a guilty verdict based on the characteristics of the offender.

The fields of criminal justice and criminology are extensive, and opportunities for careers as academics, practitioners, and advocates are widely available. Overall, the two disciplines are intertwined in ways that are often indistinguishable. Many criminal justice programs offer courses in criminology, and many criminology departments offer courses in criminal justice. Content and research cannot easily be pigeonholed into one or the other category. The material presented in this text reflects that overlap. You will be exposed to criminal justice as well as criminology material. Together, this information offers a comprehensive overview.

CHAPTER WRAP-UP

Author Video:
Skills students need to excel in criminal justice

This chapter explored the nature of crime and the controversies surrounding definitions, types of crimes, different perspectives, and legal changes over time. The material and examples demonstrated that the criminal justice system fluctuates over time, changes given advances in technology, and is believed by many to act differently dependent on the characteristics of the victim, the offender, and the crime committed. The problematic relationship between crime and the media also was addressed in this chapter. Understanding crime and the media is vitally important for all students of criminal justice. We hope that this inclusion offers the basics and raises questions that lead to greater exploration of the topic. We introduced four individuals personally entangled with the criminal justice system as victims or offenders and their stories. The remainder of this text continues their stories as they wend their way through the system. Keeping in mind the road map as well as the role of the victim in the system, you will follow each of our case studies as it takes its unique path through the system.

criminology:
An academic discipline that investigates the nature, extent, and causes of criminal offending and criminal victimization.

KEY POINTS

- Crime affects everybody either directly or indirectly.

- Crime is not uniformly defined, encompasses a variety of acts, differs across jurisdictions, evolves over time given available technology, and changes to reflect cultural norms and mores.

- The popular view of crime tends to be narrow and to focus on street crimes such as robbery, rape, murder, and burglary. In fact, crime is far more expansive and includes white-collar crimes, cybercrimes, so-called victimless crimes, and terrorism.

- The criminal justice system is a large array of institutions with three main components: law enforcement, courts, and corrections. Traditionally overlooked, the victim is an integral part of the criminal justice system.

- The criminal justice system has expanded dramatically in the past several decades. Only recently has the growth in some areas slowed and in some cases even reversed course. Some commentators and scholars argue that the criminal justice system affects particular subpopulations (e.g., the disadvantaged) more than others.

- There is no single criminal justice system; rather, it is composed of many local, state, and federal systems that operate differently across jurisdictions. In addition, some people argue that the criminal justice system experience differs based on characteristics of the offender, the victim, and the event.

- Not everyone agrees on the purpose of the criminal justice system. Some view it as a mechanism to punish offenders to deter them from future offending. Some view it as a way to rehabilitate offenders to be productive citizens. Others view it as a system that deals with the offender, victim, and community to make whole the damage from a crime. And finally, many feel that the system's role should be greatly reduced as it does more harm than good.

- Public policies established in response to crime and the criminal justice system influence every person's life. Evidence exists that policies may disproportionately affect the disadvantaged to a greater degree than others.

- Though criminal justice and criminology are distinct disciplines, there is overlap between the two. Basically, *criminal justice* refers to the system of law enforcement, courts, and corrections. Investigating the practices of these three institutions includes how laws relate to crime and offenders, approaches to deterring future crime, sanctioning and/or rehabilitating offenders, and recidivism. *Criminology* refers to the study of the nature, extent, and causes of criminal offending and criminal victimization.

- One can neither study criminal justice without considering the role of the victim and victimization nor study it without giving attention to the role of diversity among victims and offenders.

- The purpose of the media is to deliver viewers to advertisers, not necessarily to educate the public about crime and the criminal justice system. Media depictions of crime are more likely to come in the form of infotainment, be narrow-casted, and offer the viewer a false sense of full and accurate information.

KEY TERMS

Adultery 19

Blocked Opportunities
   Frame 26

Castle Doctrine 18

Conflict Model 24

Consensus Model 24

Corrections 6

Courts 6

Crime 13

Crime Control
   Perspective 21

Criminal Justice 4

Criminology 28

Cybercrime 17

Decriminalization 18

Due Process
   Perspective 22

Faulty Criminal Justice
   System Frame 25

Framing 25

Inalienable Rights 12

Indeterminate Sentence 11

Infotainment 26

Judicial Activism 13

Justifiable Homicide 18

Law Enforcement 6

Mala in Se 18

Mala Prohibita 18

Narrow-Casting 27

Nolle Prosequi 10

No Bill 10

Nolo Contendere 10

Nonintervention
   Perspective 24

Property Crime 13

Racist System
   Frame 26

REVIEW QUESTIONS

1. How are policies related to crime and our personal liberties associated?

2. Why is crime difficult to define? What are some issues that make it difficult?

3. What type of behaviors does crime encompass?

4. How does increased criminalization and decriminalization of behaviors influence your life?

5. What is the difference between *mala prohibita and mala in se*?

6. What causes crime to change over time?

7. What is the criminal justice system? What are its primary components?

8. What factors account for high incarceration rates?

9. What personal characteristics are related to one's likelihood of being incarcerated?

10. What are the major perspectives regarding the purpose of the criminal justice system?

11. Why is narrow-casting a departure from past portrayals of crime in the media?

CRITICAL THINKING MATTERS

1. **Achieving Justice and Fairness.** In what ways can the criminal justice system ensure equal and fair treatment for all? Are there methods that could be used to streamline the system and still respect due process rights? How can the criminal justice system operate in a more cost-effective manner and still protect the public from offenders? How can the system better care for victims? How could the system have helped in the case of Jennifer Schuett? Is expecting the system to assist victims going beyond the boundaries of what a criminal justice system should focus on?

2. **How Do You Distinguish Terrorism?** What makes a domestic terrorist attack different from traditional violent crime? How is it that what Timothy McVeigh and Terry Nichols did in Oklahoma City is terrorism, when the Columbine massacre is a school shooting? Are we drawing a false distinction in violent acts? Why should it matter whether a terrorist act was one of domestic or international origin? What difference does it make to the victims, the offenders, or the citizens of the nation?

3. **Policy and Drunk Driving Laws.** Research shows that drivers with BAC levels higher than 0.10% are responsible for more than 80% of drunk driving deaths. Yet in most states, the legal BAC limit is 0.08%, and MADD is continuing to work toward lowering this threshold. What is the right thing to do? Should we use resources to lower the legal BAC if these drivers are not likely to be involved in fatal accidents? Should the legal limit go to 0.10% to focus on the worst offenders? Should persons under age 18 be held to tougher BAC thresholds? Have drunk driving laws created an industry allowing attorneys to get rich while costing citizens their reputations, opportunities at employment, and high fines? Has Chris Farias been caught up in a system that continues to criminalize benign behavior and "create" more offenders? Or have the tough drunk driving laws made our society safer? Was Chris Farias a criminal who needed to be taken off the street at the expense of the taxpayer?

4. **Crime and the Media.** Many people have distorted views of the criminal justice system given that their knowledge is based on media portrayals only. Does having a distorted view of criminal justice matter? Is there any harm in remaining uninformed? Should the government step in and regulate portrayals of crime in the media to ensure that the public is better educated? What are the advantages and disadvantages of such a policy? Or should the education system do a better job at teaching individuals the truth about the criminal justice system? What can be done to make a more educated populace, and does it really matter?

5. **Male Rape and Marital Rape.** Many people find it difficult to understand how a man can be raped. Gabe Wright was raped at gunpoint after being beaten while on a fishing trip. Was this rape? Do we need specific laws to address rape when the victim is male? Why or why not? Similarly, many struggle to understand how rape can occur between married people. Consider the stories of Karen Carroll (http://thevoicesandfacesproject.org/V&F/index.html#!folio/carroll.html) and Victoria Sherden (http://thevoicesandfacesproject.org/V&F/index.html#!folio/sheridan.html), who were each raped by their husbands. After reading their stories, do you view these to be incidents of rape? Prior to changes in law, these husbands could not have been charged with rape. Are these changes in statutes a positive or negative thing? Why?

6. **Frameworks and Gang Violence.** Danny Madrid was raised by his mother and grandmother in an impoverished Latino and black neighborhood in Los Angeles. In this environment he became a gang member, committing minor and serious crimes. Given the little you know about Danny, what framework do you believe explains his descent into offending? Were his criminal acts a result of a faulty criminal justice system—a system that is easy on crime and one in which criminals know they can get away with their deeds? Or is it the lack of opportunities made available to Danny to become an astronaut that steered him to a life of violence? Perhaps you find that the breakdown of his family was the culprit? Danny's father was a "rolling stone" who was primarily absent from his life, and when he was around, he could be violent. Danny's last interaction with his father was when he was 14, when an argument resulted in Danny's being beaten by his father with a broomstick. Does this sort of breakdown have something to do with Danny's story? What role does the fact that Danny is Latino in what some consider a racist country play? Which of these do you believe account for his eventual gang membership and criminal behavior and why? Given the framework that you have selected, what solutions are indicated? As a policymaker, what would you do to maximize the chances of other little boys growing up in the same situation to become law-abiding citizens?

7. **Violence and Crime.** Although a great deal of violence is portrayed in the media, does it influence behavior? Or are aggressive people drawn to aggression depicted in the media? Does watching a movie or playing a violent video game make one commit an act of violence? Does watching a violent movie make you feel like acting out in a violent fashion? If the media are so influential, why is most crime that is committed property crime? If people become more violent by watching violence in the media, why do most violent crimes committed result in uninjured victims? Should it be the government's role to step in and regulate what we see in the media? Or does such a proposal trample our freedoms? How do you moderate viewing of violence for yourself and your family? Or do you? Does it matter?

DIGITAL RESOURCES

⑤SAGE edge™

Sharpen your skills with SAGE edge at edge.sagepub.com/rennison2e. SAGE edge for Students provides a personalized approach to help you accomplish your coursework goals in an easy-to-use learning environment. You'll find action plans, mobile-friendly eFlashcards, and quizzes as well as video and web resources and links to SAGE journal articles to support and expand on the concepts presented in this chapter.

2 THE NATURE AND EXTENT OF CRIME

LEARNING OBJECTIVES

After finishing this chapter, you should be able to:

2.1 Identify how crime is measured in the United States.

2.2 Summarize the many issues that make counting crime difficult.

2.3 Identify and criticize the major sources of national crime data in the United States.

2.4 Review the advantages and disadvantages of each source of national crime data used to measure crime in the United States.

2.5 Summarize the nature and extent of violent, property, and white-collar crime in the United States.

2.6 Identify the difficulties inherent in recognizing and measuring cybercrime, terrorism, and white-collar crime.

2.7 Demonstrate an understanding of criminological theories used to explain crime and criminality.

INTRODUCTION: WHY AND HOW IS CRIME MEASURED?

Why measure crime? Because doing so provides essential information. First, measuring crime reveals the extent and nature of crime, which serve as one measure of the well-being of the nation. High crime is indicative of serious societal problems, especially for vulnerable populations. Continued measurement may indicate that crime has declined, which offers information on improvements in society that affect everyone. Second, measuring crime can be used to evaluate the benefits of policy. A policy may be implemented to improve some aspect of the criminal justice system or to reduce the risk of crime. Only through measurement can we identify if the policy was successful or unsuccessful. As noted in the quotation that opens this chapter, better measurement can lead to programs that are more effective at reducing crime. Third, measuring crime helps identify groups in society that are suffering disproportionate amounts of victimization and allows efficient and targeted assistance in addition to addressing the needs of all victims. Fourth, measuring crime allows researchers to discover the root causes of crime, offending, and victimization. Better understanding of causes allows federal, state, and local policymakers to combat crime, reduce victimization, and ensure that encounters with the criminal justice system are efficient and evenhanded.

Researchers collect data to measure crime using a variety of methods. They can ask people if they or

The J. Edgar Hoover Building in Washington, DC, is the FBI headquarters. A little-known but vitally important role of the FBI is to collect crime data. What type of crime data do you think the FBI should be gathering?

their homes have been crime victims. They can ask individuals if they have committed crimes. They can observe people in a natural setting to witness crimes being committed. Researchers can enter prisons and jails and ask inmates about the crimes they committed. Or they can gather official reports from police or other authorities to make a determination about the extent and nature of crime. When it comes to measuring the extent and nature of crime for the nation, two of these methods are used: gathering data from official law enforcement records and asking people if they have been victims of crimes.

These methods represent the efforts of the two bureaus in the Department of Justice (DOJ) charged with (among other things) gathering crime data. One DOJ bureau that collects a wide variety of crime data is the Federal Bureau of Investigation (FBI).[1] Estimates of crime in the United States reported by the FBI are found in the **Uniform Crime Reports (UCR)**,[2] the **Supplementary Homicide Reports (SHR)**,[3] and the **National Incident-Based Reporting System (NIBRS)**.[4] Crime data gathered by the FBI are gathered directly from law enforcement agencies, which submit it voluntarily.

The Bureau of Justice Statistics (BJS)[5] is another DOJ bureau that gathers a wide variety of national crime data. Most notably for efforts related to estimating the nature and extent of violent and property victimization in the United States, BJS sponsors the **National Crime Victimization Survey (NCVS)**.[6] This work has enhanced our knowledge about who victims of crime are, the characteristics of crime, and the characteristics of offenders according to victims.

Journal:
Utilizing mail and telephone surveys

Uniform Crime Reports (UCR): This program, started by the International Association of Chiefs of Police and then moved under the umbrella of the FBI in 1929, is a compilation of crime data.

Supplementary Homicide Reports (SHR): Supplemental reports to the FBI's Uniform Crime Reporting System that gather details about homicides in the United States, including information about offenders, victims, and incidents.

National Incident-Based Reporting System (NIBRS): A large and complex national data collection system designed to gather incident-based crime information from law enforcement.

National Crime Victimization Survey (NCVS): A nationally representative survey of victims of property and personal violence in the United States.

MEASURING VIOLENT AND PROPERTY CRIME

FBI Measurement of Crime

Ask a member of the public about the role of the FBI, and the response will likely focus on the bureau's crime-fighting responsibilities. Others may comment on the FBI's relatively new terrorist-fighting duties. A lesser known but valuable responsibility of the FBI is as the collector, analyzer, and archiver of crime data through the Uniform Crime Reporting (UCR) Program. The UCR Program represents the nation's oldest unified national crime data collection effort.[7] Prior to this program, there was a long history of crime data collection in numerous jurisdictions using an assortment of definitions for a variety of crimes (see Figure 2.1). Gathering data in this fashion was problematic because no two jurisdictions or states defined crimes or collected information in a standardized way. As a result, one could neither aggregate the existing crime data in any meaningful way nor make comparisons across jurisdictions or over time within one jurisdiction. What was needed was a uniform system to gather crime data using the same (i.e., uniform) definitions for a standardized set of crimes. This uniformity was necessary, as jurisdictions then and now differ in terms of statutory definitions and elements of crime.

In 1790 when the DOJ was established, Congress mandated that it report on crime statistics. The actual act of uniformly reporting crime information took much longer and occurred outside the purview of the DOJ. In the mid-1800s, some of the first documented appeals for unified national crime data gathering were made. Widely cited are calls for this activity at the convention of the National Police Association (later known as the International Association of Chiefs of Police [IACP])[8] during a meeting in St. Louis. Approximately 50 years later, in 1927, after many years of discussion about this need, the IACP established the Committee on the Uniform Crime Records to develop a program and procedures for uniformly collecting information about crime across jurisdictions in the United States.

Uniform Crime Reports

The product of the work of the committee was the UCR Program. Launched in 1929–1930, the UCR Program was designed to provide unified, reliable, and systematic information on a set of frequently committed serious crimes reported to law enforcement agencies across the country. Using these data, police chiefs could accurately compare crime across jurisdictions and over time. Furthermore, data about these crimes could be aggregated in a meaningful fashion. The IACP managed the UCR Program for several years until the FBI was charged with oversight of the program (some sources place the FBI takeover of the UCR Program in 1935).

Crime analysts investigate the nature and extent of crime in the United States. Without the work of analysts and the statistics they produce, how different might our criminal justice system look? How much crime would you think there is?

Since that time, the FBI has managed the UCR Program as it compiles crime reports submitted voluntarily by law enforcement agencies. (Some states mandate reporting to the FBI.) The crime reports are submitted either directly from local, state, federal, and tribal law enforcement agencies or through centralized state agencies from across the nation. When launched, the UCR Program was based on reports from 400 law enforcement agencies in 43 states, describing crimes occurring in about 20% of the population. Currently, the program gathers crime reports from approximately 17,000 (of the more than 18,000) law enforcement agencies from

Author Video:
The importance of measuring crime

Web:
FBI Uniform Crime Reporting

Table 2.1 ■ FBI UCR Part I and Part II Crimes as of 2015

Part I Crimes	Part II Crimes	
• murder and nonnegligent manslaughter • rape (the term *forcible* was removed in 2013 following definitional improvements) • robbery • aggravated assault • burglary • larceny/theft • motor vehicle theft • arson (added in 1979) • human trafficking—commercial sex acts (added in 2013) • human trafficking—involuntary servitude (added in 2013)	• other assaults (simple) • forgery and counterfeiting • fraud • embezzlement • buying, receiving, and possessing stolen property • vandalism • possession and carrying of a weapon • prostitution and commercialized vice • sex offenses (except rape and prostitution and commercialized vice) • drug abuse violations • gambling • offenses against family and children	• driving under the influence • liquor law violations • drunkenness • disorderly conduct • vagrancy • all other violations of state or local laws not specified (except traffic violations) • suspicion (arrested and released without formal charges) • curfew and loitering violations (persons under age 18) • assisting and promoting prostitution • purchasing prostitution

Why is it necessary to separate crimes into Part I and Part II types? What advantages come from this distinction? What disadvantages?

Source: U.S. Department of Justice, Federal Bureau of Investigation. (2013, June 20). *Criminal Justice Information Services (CJIS) Division, Uniform Crime Reporting (UCR) Program: Summary Reporting System (SRS) user manual.* Retrieved from https://ucr.fbi.gov/nibrs/summary-reporting-system-srs-user-manual.

Figure 2.1 ■ Timeline of Crime Reporting, 1790 to Present

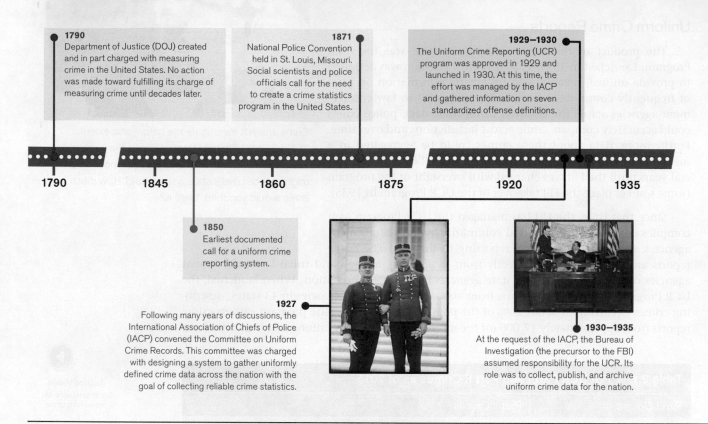

1790
Department of Justice (DOJ) created and in part charged with measuring crime in the United States. No action was made toward fulfilling its charge of measuring crime until decades later.

1871
National Police Convention held in St. Louis, Missouri. Social scientists and police officials call for the need to create a crime statistics program in the United States.

1929–1930
The Uniform Crime Reporting (UCR) program was approved in 1929 and launched in 1930. At this time, the effort was managed by the IACP and gathered information on seven standardized offense definitions.

1790   1845   1860   1875   1920   1935

1850
Earliest documented call for a uniform crime reporting system.

1927
Following many years of discussions, the International Association of Chiefs of Police (IACP) convened the Committee on Uniform Crime Records. This committee was charged with designing a system to gather uniformly defined crime data across the nation with the goal of collecting reliable crime statistics.

1930–1935
At the request of the IACP, the Bureau of Investigation (the precursor to the FBI) assumed responsibility for the UCR. Its role was to collect, publish, and archive uniform crime data for the nation.

Photo credits: 1927: Library of Congress; 1930–1935: © Corbis; 1961: © iStockphoto.com/wragg; 1976: © iStockphoto.com/belterz; 1992: © iStockphoto.com/shironosov

all states, the District of Columbia, and some U.S. territories. Furthermore, the UCR Program describes crime occurring in almost the entire nation. The purpose of the UCR Program has always been to serve the needs of law enforcement agencies.

The UCR Program gathers information on a broad range of personal and property criminal offenses. These crimes may occur to a person of any age as well as to businesses (e.g., burglary of a business). UCR crimes are partitioned into **Part I and Part II crimes**. Part I crimes include the most serious and regularly occurring crimes. Part II crimes include less serious and less regularly occurring crimes (Table 2.1).

The traditional UCR Program (in more recent years referred to as the **Summary Reporting System [SRS]**) primarily offers *counts* of each type of crime (see Form 2.1). In general, the UCR was not designed to gather information on characteristics of crime victims or offenders, though some exceptions existed. SRS data, for example, include whether a rape was completed or attempted, whether a burglary involved forcible entry, the type of motor vehicle stolen, and whether a robbery involved a weapon. While this information is valuable, the lack of additional detail for all SRS crimes limited understanding about crime. For example, one could not determine the victim-offender relationship in an assault, whether a weapon had been used during a rape, or myriad other characteristics of events, victims, and offenders. Understanding the time in which the SRS was developed is important to recognize, given the unavailability of computing power and computer technology. Gathering aggregate counts of crime from a large geographic area was an impressive task in the beginning. Nonetheless, it was recognized that without a greater understanding of specific characteristics of crime, efforts to reduce it were greatly hindered.

Part I and Part II crimes: Designation of crime types under the UCR's Summary Reporting System. Part I includes common and serious crimes, while Part II crimes are less common and less serious.

Summary Reporting System (SRS): The original aggregated crime data collected under the FBI's Uniform Crime Reporting Program.

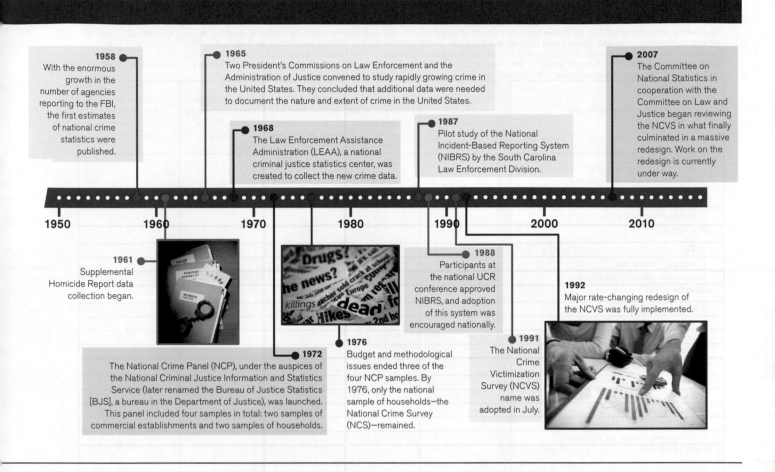

1958
With the enormous growth in the number of agencies reporting to the FBI, the first estimates of national crime statistics were published.

1965
Two President's Commissions on Law Enforcement and the Administration of Justice convened to study rapidly growing crime in the United States. They concluded that additional data were needed to document the nature and extent of crime in the United States.

1968
The Law Enforcement Assistance Administration (LEAA), a national criminal justice statistics center, was created to collect the new crime data.

1987
Pilot study of the National Incident-Based Reporting System (NIBRS) by the South Carolina Law Enforcement Division.

2007
The Committee on National Statistics in cooperation with the Committee on Law and Justice began reviewing the NCVS in what finally culminated in a massive redesign. Work on the redesign is currently under way.

1950   1960   1970   1980   1990   2000   2010

1961
Supplemental Homicide Report data collection began.

1972
The National Crime Panel (NCP), under the auspices of the National Criminal Justice Information and Statistics Service (later renamed the Bureau of Justice Statistics [BJS], a bureau in the Department of Justice), was launched. This panel included four samples in total: two samples of commercial establishments and two samples of households.

1976
Budget and methodological issues ended three of the four NCP samples. By 1976, only the national sample of households—the National Crime Survey (NCS)—remained.

1988
Participants at the national UCR conference approved NIBRS, and adoption of this system was encouraged nationally.

1991
The National Crime Victimization Survey (NCVS) name was adopted in July.

1992
Major rate-changing redesign of the NCVS was fully implemented.

While imperfect, the traditional UCR SRS offers many benefits in our efforts to measure and better understand crime. First, it has been ongoing for almost a century, with remarkably stable methodology. This stability enables meaningful trend analysis. Second, UCR SRS data allow analyses at many levels of geography, including cities, regions, and the nation. Third, this system offers crime information on a broad range of offenses. Thus, rather than focusing only on street crimes (i.e., homicide, robbery, and assault), the UCR SRS offers information on crimes such as embezzlement, drunkenness, and vagrancy. Fourth, the UCR SRS gathers information from a broad range of law enforcement agencies covering all 50 states, the District of Columbia, and some U.S. territories. Fifth, the UCR SRS collects crime information regardless of the age of the victim or offender. And sixth, the SRS gathers information on crimes against people as well as those against businesses. If a vehicle was stolen from a business, for example, it would be recorded in the SRS if reported to the police.

Supplementary Homicide Reports

The 1960s marked the beginning of collecting crime details with the initiation of the SHR. Data from this program have been archived since 1976. Using the SHR forms (Form 2.2), the FBI began gathering detailed information on homicides, including the victim's age, sex, and race; the offender's age, sex, and race; weapon type (if any); victim-offender relationship; and the circumstances that led to the homicide.[9] The patterns uncovered by this information have been used in the development of policy recommendations focused on homicide.

Form 2.1 ■ SRS Reporting Form

RETURN A - MONTHLY RETURN OF OFFENSES KNOWN TO THE POLICE

This report is authorized by law Title 28, Section 534, U.S. Code. Your cooperation in completing this form will assist the FBI, in compiling timely, comprehensive, and accurate data. Please submit this form monthly, by the seventh day after the close of the month, and any questions to the FBI, Criminal Justice Information Services Division, Attention: Uniform Crime Reports/Module E-3, 1000 Custer Hollow Road, Clarksburg, West Virginia 26306; telephone 304-625-4830, facsimile 304-625-3566. Under the Paperwork Reduction Act, you are not required to complete this form unless it contains a valid OMB control number. The form takes approximately 10 minutes to complete. Instructions for preparing the form appear on the reverse side.

1-720 (Rev. 02-22-13)
OMB No. 1110-0001
Expires 07-31-16

CLASSIFICATION OF OFFENSES	DATA ENTRY	2 OFFENSES REPORTED OR KNOWN TO POLICE (INCLUDE "UNFOUNDED" AND ATTEMPTS)	3 UNFOUNDED, I.E., FALSE OR BASELESS COMPLAINTS	4 NUMBER OF ACTUAL OFFENSES (COLUMN 2 MINUS COLUMN 3) (INCLUDE ATTEMPTS)	5 TOTAL OFFENSES CLEARED BY ARREST OR EXCEPTIONAL MEANS (INCLUDES COL. 6)	6 NUMBER OF CLEARANCES INVOLVING ONLY PERSONS UNDER 18 YEARS OF AGE
1. CRIMINAL HOMICIDE						
a. MURDER AND NONNEGLIGENT HOMICIDE (Score attempts as aggravated assault) If homicide reported, submit Supplementary Homicide Report	11					
b. MANSLAUGHTER BY NEGLIGENCE	12					
2. RAPE TOTAL	20					
a. Rape	21					
b. Attempts to Commit Rape	22					
Historical Rape (See Instruction #15 below)						
3. ROBBERY TOTAL	30					
a. Firearm	31					
b. Knife or Cutting Instrument	32					
c. Other Dangerous Weapon	33					
d. Strong-Arm (Hands, Fists, Feet, Etc.)	34					
4. ASSAULT TOTAL	40					
a. Firearm	41					
b. Knife or Cutting Instrument	42					
c. Other Dangerous Weapon	43					
d. Hands, Fists, Feet, Etc. - Aggravated injury	44					
e. Other Assaults - Simple, Not Aggravated	45					
5. BURGLARY TOTAL	50					
a. Forcible Entry	51					
b. Unlawful Entry - No Force	52					
c. Attempted Forcible Entry	53					
6. LARCENY - THEFT TOTAL (Except Motor Vehicle Theft)	60					
7. MOTOR VEHICLE THEFT TOTAL	70					
a. Autos	71					
b. Trucks and Buses	72					
c. Other Vehicles	73					
GRAND TOTAL	77					

CHECKING ANY OF THE APPROPRIATE BLOCKS BELOW WILL ELIMINATE YOUR NEED TO SUBMIT REPORTS WHEN THE VALUES ARE ZERO. THIS WILL ALSO AID THE NATIONAL PROGRAM IN ITS QUALITY CONTROL EFFORTS.

☐ NO SUPPLEMENTARY HOMICIDE REPORT SUBMITTED SINCE NO MURDERS, JUSTIFIABLE HOMICIDES, OR MANSLAUGHTERS BY NEGLIGENCE OCCURRED IN THIS JURISDICTION DURING THE MONTH.

☐ NO SUPPLEMENT TO RETURN A REPORT SINCE NO CRIME OFFENSES OR RECOVERY OF PROPERTY REPORTED DURING THE MONTH.

☐ NO LAW ENFORCEMENT OFFICERS KILLED OR ASSAULTED REPORT SINCE NONE OF THE OFFICERS WERE ASSAULTED OR KILLED DURING THE MONTH.

☐ NO AGE, SEX, AND RACE OF PERSONS ARRESTED UNDER 18 YEARS OF AGE REPORT SINCE NO ARRESTS OF PERSONS WITHIN THIS AGE GROUP.

☐ NO AGE, SEX, AND RACE OF PERSONS ARRESTED 18 YEARS OF AGE AND OVER REPORT SINCE NO ARREST OF PERSONS WITHIN THIS AGE GROUP.

☐ NO MONTHLY RETURN OF ARSON OFFENSES KNOWN TO LAW ENFORCEMENT REPORT SINCE NO ARSONS OCCURRED.

DO NOT USE THIS SPACE	
	INITIALS
RECORDED	
EDITED	
ENTERED	
ADJUSTED	
CORRES	

Imagine the time and effort needed collectively across the nation to voluntarily provide the FBI with SRS data.

Source: Federal Bureau of Investigation.

COMMON MISCONCEPTIONS

Burglary Versus Robbery

Burglary refers to a property crime in which someone enters a dwelling without permission. Homes, trailers, sheds, apartments, hotel rooms, and offices are examples of dwellings that can be burglarized. *Robbery* refers to a personal violent crime. Robbery involves an incident in which someone takes or attempts to take something of value directly from another person.

Remember, a house is never robbed; a house is burglarized—it is a person who is robbed.

Think About It

1. Why does it matter if one uses burglary and robbery interchangeably?

2. Are there other types of crime for which people frequently use the wrong term to describe an act?

3. Does it make sense to you that crimes against a person and crimes against property are described differently? Why or why not?

National Incident-Based Reporting System

The important information gained by gathering details of homicide made clear the benefits of doing the same for nonfatal crimes. Following expert evaluations and recommendations made in the late 1970s and early 1980s, the *Blueprint for the Future of the Uniform Crime Reporting Program* (1985)[10] outlined a set of new procedures that formed the basis for the NIBRS. In addition, the increased availability of technology and computing power made NIBRS feasible. Introduced in the mid-1980s, NIBRS augments the SRS by gathering detailed incident information about crimes, including the nature and types of crimes committed during each incident, victim and offender characteristics, type and value of stolen and recovered property, and characteristics of arrested individuals. Furthermore, NIBRS included new crimes and adopted some contemporary definitions that were not used by the SRS. Initially in the traditional SRS, for example, forcible rape was by definition a crime experienced only by a girl or a woman. In contrast, NIBRS defined forcible rape as "the carnal knowledge of a *person*,"[11] counting boys and men as victims of these offenses when appropriate. (In 2013, both systems dropped *forcible* and now refer to this type of crime as "rape"). With the implementation of NIBRS, data on a new offense category of crime are included: "crimes against society." Crimes against society consist of drug and narcotic offenses, trafficking in pornography or obscene material, prostitution, and gambling offenses. The modernization, enhancements, and improvements reflected in NIBRS over the SRS have resulted in data that better serve the needs of the system's primary constituency—law enforcement. Furthermore, NIBRS offers greater information to policymakers and the public about victimization risk.

Like the traditional UCR SRS, reporting to NIBRS is voluntary. And like the traditional SRS, NIBRS data reflect only crimes known to the police. Though similar, NIBRS differs from the traditional SRS in several important ways. One difference is that the SRS nomenclature of Part I and Part II offenses was replaced in NIBRS with **Group A and Group B** classes of offenses.[12]

Multiple criteria were used to determine which crimes should be Group A and Group B offenses. For example, those placed in Group A are more serious and frequently occurring offenses, those most likely to come to the attention of law enforcement, with the greatest

Group A and Group B crimes: Two major clusters of crimes gathered by the FBI in NIBRS. Group A includes 22 crimes covering 46 offenses including homicide and robbery. Group B includes 11 offenses such as loitering and drunkenness.

Form 2.2 ■ Actual Document Used to Record Homicides

1-704 (Rev. 1-12-11)
OMB No. 1110-0002
Expires 8-31-17

SUPPLEMENTARY HOMICIDE REPORT

This report is authorized by law Title 28, Section 534, U.S. Code. While you are not required to respond, your cooperation in using this form to list data pertaining to all homicides reported on your Return A will assist the FBI in compiling comprehensive, accurate data regarding this important classification on a timely basis. Any questions regarding this report may be addressed to the FBI, Criminal Justice Information Services Division, Attention: Uniform Crime Reports/Module E-3, 1000 Custer Hollow Road, Clarksburg, West Virginia 26306; telephone 304-625-4830, facsimile 304-625-3566. Under the Paperwork Reduction Act, you are not required to complete this form unless it contains a valid OMB control number. The form takes approximately 9 minutes to complete.

1a. Murder and Nonnegligent Manslaughter

List below for each category specific information for each murder and nonnegligent homicide and/or justifiable homicide shown in item 1a of the monthly Return A. In addition, for justifiable homicide list all justifiable killings of felons by a citizen or by a peace officer in the line of duty. A brief explanation in the circumstances column regarding unfounded homicide offenses will aid the national Uniform Crime Reporting Program in editing the reports.

Incident	Situation*	Victim** Age	Sex	Race	Ethnicity	Data Code — Do Not Write In These Spaces Offender** Age	Sex	Race	Ethnicity	Weapon Used (Handgun, Rifle, Shotgun, Club, Poison, etc.)	Relationship of Victim to Offender (Husband, Wife, Son, Father, Acquaintance, Neighbor, Stranger, etc.)	Circumstances (Victim shot by robber, robbery victim shot robber, killed by patron during barroom brawl, etc.)

* - Situations

A - Single Victim/Single Offender
B - Single Victim/Unknown Offender or Offenders
C - Single Victim/Multiple Offenders
D - Multiple Victims/Single Offender
E - Multiple Victims/Multiple Offenders
F - Multiple Victims/Unknown Offender or Offenders

Use only one victim/offender situation code per set of information. The utilization of a new code will signify the beginning of a new murder situation.

** - Age - 01 to 99. If 100 or older use 99. New born up to one week old use NB. If over one week, but less than one year old use BB. Use two characters only in age column.

Sex - M for Male and F for Female. Use one character only.

Race - White - W, Black or African American - B, American Indian or Alaska Native - I, Asian - A, Native Hawaiian or Other Pacific Islander - P, Unknown - U. Use only these as race designations.

Ethnicity - Hispanic or Latino - H, Not Hispanic or Latino - N, Unknown - U.

Source: Federal Bureau of Investigation.

likelihood that law enforcement is the best channel for gathering data on the offenses. Group A consists of the following 23 crimes covering 52 offenses:

- homicide offenses (murder and nonnegligent manslaughter, negligent manslaughter, justifiable homicide [justifiable homicide, while collected here, is not included in the criminal offense statistics])
- sex offenses (rape, sodomy, sexual assault with an object, fondling, incest, and statutory rape) (in 2013, the term *forcible* was removed from these offenses)
- robbery
- assault offenses (aggravated, simple, intimidation)
- burglary/breaking and entering
- larceny/theft offenses (pocket-picking, purse-snatching, shoplifting, theft from building and theft from coin-operated machine or device, theft from motor vehicle, theft of motor vehicle parts)
- motor vehicle theft
- arson
- bribery
- counterfeiting/forgery
- destruction/damage/vandalism of property
- drug/narcotic offenses
- pornography/obscene material
- prostitution offenses (prostitution, assisting or promoting prostitution, and purchasing prostitution)
- embezzlement
- extortion/blackmail
- fraud offenses (e.g., ATM fraud, impersonation, wire fraud, identify theft[a], hacking/computer invasion[a])
- gambling offenses (e.g., betting/wagering, promoting/assisting/operating gambling, sports tampering)
- kidnapping/abduction
- human trafficking (both commercial sex acts and involuntary servitude)
- stolen property offenses
- weapon law violations

Group B offenses consist of 10 offenses (only arrest data are collected):

- bad checks
- curfew/loitering/vagrancy violations
- disorderly conduct
- driving under the influence
- drunkenness
- family offenses/nonviolent
- liquor law violations
- peeping tom
- trespass of real property
- all other offenses

Note: Runaway was previously a Group B offense in NIBRS. The FBI discontinued the collection and publication of arrest data for runaways in January 2011.

[a]These cyber offenses took effect in 2016.

A second important difference in NIBRS compared with the SRS concerns the **hierarchy rule**.[13] In the SRS, only the most serious crime committed during a criminal event is reported to the FBI. That is, if an incident included a rape and a homicide, only the homicide information was forwarded to the FBI in the SRS because it is the more serious crime. Some people erroneously report that the hierarchy rule has been completely suspended in NIBRS, but this is incorrect, as three exceptions remain: motor vehicle theft, arson, and justifiable homicide. First, if a motor vehicle is stolen (motor vehicle theft) and there were items in the car stolen (property theft), only the motor vehicle theft is reported in NIBRS. Second, when an arson is part of a multiple-offense incident, two Part I offenses are reported: the arson and the additional Part I offenses committed with the arson. And finally, in the event of a justifiable homicide, two offenses are reported: the felonious act by the offender that led to the justifiable homicide and the actual justifiable homicide.[14] Still, the near total abandonment of the hierarchy rule in NIBRS means that the FBI gathers far more crime information than under the traditional SRS.

An important difference between NIBRS and the SRS is that the former distinguishes between an attempted and a completed crime for most incidents, and the SRS does not. And unlike the SRS, NIBRS allows one to link victim, offender, and crime attributes to a particular offense. Previously, using the traditional SRS, with the exception of homicide, links among offender, victim, and incident information with a particular crime event were unavailable. NIBRS also allows linked data on victims, offenders, offenses, and arrestees.[15] This change dramatically enhances the value of NIBRS data over SRS aggregate data.

Given that NIBRS is an augmentation of the traditional SRS data collection effort, it is no surprise that it is characterized by several of the same advantages as the SRS. But NIBRS offers advantages not found in the SRS. An important benefit of NIBRS is that it offers incident-level details for every crime reported. NIBRS also provides information on all reported crimes occurring within an incident and not just the most serious crime committed during the incident. An additional advantage of NIBRS is the ability to disaggregate data by multiple victim, offender, and incident characteristics and to link these components of a criminal incident.[16] These advantages also hint at the enormous size of NIBRS data.

Like all data, the traditional SRS and NIBRS are imperfect. Easily forgotten is that both reflect only those crimes reported to the police. If the police fail to learn about a crime, it will not be measured in SRS or NIBRS. Research is clear that many crimes are not reported to the police. In fact, only about half of all violent crime comes to the attention of the police. A second potential issue with SRS and NIBRS data is that they can be manipulated for political and other purposes given that the data originate from law enforcement agencies. While data manipulation by law enforcement officials is uncommon, it can happen and has happened. Third, because the SRS and NIBRS are voluntary, they are subject to a lack of reporting, or incomplete reporting, by participating law enforcement agencies. When crime data are not submitted, or the submitted data fail to meet the FBI's guidelines for completeness and accuracy, the FBI imputes the missing crime data. Research suggests that the degree to which UCR data are imputed at the national level is sizable, varies by jurisdiction, and fluctuates year to year.[17]

An additional disadvantage of NIBRS, not shared by the SRS, is its limited coverage.[18] That is, while the SRS collects crime data from nearly all states, the District of Columbia, and U.S. territories, NIBRS coverage is narrower (Figure 2.2). As of 2013, data from 43% of law enforcement agencies in 33 states, describing about 29% of the U.S. population, were represented in NIBRS. As recently as 2005, no agency covering a population of more than 1 million provided data to the NIBRS, an issue referred to as "small agency bias." In sum, NIBRS crime data fail to constitute a representative sample of the population, law enforcement agencies, or states.

The coverage of NIBRS continues to grow as the FBI shifts its focus to NIBRS, rather than dividing attention and resources between NIBRS and the SRS. In fact, the UCR Program will officially sunset the SRS on January 1, 2021. As a result, all states are currently transitioning to NIBRS. In addition, a new data collection system is under way: the

hierarchy rule: Used to facilitate counting crime, this rule ranks crimes from least to most serious. In a criminal incident, only the most serious crime committed during the incident is counted.

ETHICAL ISSUES

Misreporting in the UCR

In 2009, the *Dallas Morning News* revealed that the Dallas Police Department had been purposefully recording attempted burglaries as acts of simple vandalism. The same news agency discovered that police also misreported violent crimes. In several instances, the police department recorded violent attacks as less serious crimes. Specifically, the police department reported 75 of 500 assaults as aggravated, while listing the remainder as simple assaults. Simple assaults—because they are not Part I crimes—are not used in the calculation of the official crime rate. An investigation indicated that 40 of the crimes reported as simple assaults should have been recorded as aggravated assaults because the incidents involved victims' being attacked with various weapons, including bottles, pipes, bats, rocks, bricks, chairs, and bar stools. Others involved attempted strangling, serious injuries, and the brandishing of a knife as well as a rifle. The extent of this misreporting was large enough to make it appear that Dallas's violent crime rate was decreasing. FBI experts and the Texas Department of Public Safety, which manages the UCR data collection effort, confirmed the findings of the news. With appropriate reporting, the violent crime rate may still have shown a decline, but not as dramatic.

Detroit has also been plagued with problematic reporting. The Detroit Police Department admitted in 2001 that it had misreported rape and murder numbers throughout the 1990s. With the erroneous reporting, the department appeared to have one of the highest arrest rates, though the data were so flawed that it is unclear how many suspects were actually arrested. The errors were so large that Detroit's homicide arrest figures skewed the FBI's homicide arrest statistics for the entire nation. Detroit reported that it had been arresting murder suspects at three times the national rate and rape suspects at twice the national rate. The department maintains that the misreporting was not an effort to deceive, but rather honest errors.

Though not widespread, these examples highlight one potential problem with using data from the UCR or other official police records: deliberate misreporting.

Think About It

Pretend that you are the mayor of a city and discover that your police department has been misrepresenting crime data for your jurisdiction.

1. **How would you ethically handle this in terms of informing the public and holding responsible parties accountable?**

2. **What if you are an analyst working in the city and your boss asks you to alter the data to make the city look safer? How would you ethically handle this?**

National Crime Statistics Exchange (NCS-X). This collaborative effort between BJS and the FBI (and other organizations) will produce nationally representative incident-based statistics on crimes using both data reported to law enforcement agencies and a sample (see Figure 2.2). As noted by BJS,

NCS-X will leverage the FBI's existing National Incident-Based Reporting System (NIBRS) by recruiting a sample of 400 law enforcement agencies to supplement the existing NIBRS data by providing their incident data to their state (or the federal) NIBRS data collection program. When data from these 400 agencies are combined with data from the more than 6,000 agencies that currently report NIBRS data to the FBI, NIBRS will be able to produce national estimates of crime that can be

National Crime Statistics Exchange (NCS-X): A collaborative effort between BJS and the FBI (and other organizations) that will produce nationally representative incident-based statistics on crimes using both data reported to law enforcement agencies and a sample.

Figure 2.2 ■ NIBRS and NCS-X Coverage

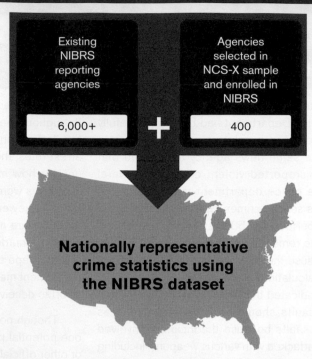

Existing NIBRS reporting agencies		Agencies selected in NCS-X sample and enrolled in NIBRS
6,000+	**+**	400

Nationally representative crime statistics using the NIBRS dataset

Given the coverage of NIBRS, do you feel it represents crime in the United States the same as, better than, or not as well as other data collection efforts?

Source: National Crime Statistics Exchange, Bureau of Justice Statistics.

disaggregated by victim-offender characteristics, the circumstances of the event, victim-offender relationship, and other important elements of criminal events. When completed, nationally-representative NIBRS data will increase our nation's ability to monitor, respond to, and prevent crime by allowing NIBRS to produce timely, detailed, and accurate national measures of crime incidents.[19]

CASE STUDY

Case Study Video 2.1: Interviews with case study participants

Case Studies and FBI Data

How would these crime data collection systems account for the crimes highlighted in our case studies? Would the criminal acts committed by Joshua Paul Benjamin be reflected in the FBI data? And what of the case of Chris Farias? How would the violence against Jennifer Schuett be reflected in the FBI data collection systems? Finally, would one find evidence of the offenses committed by Danny Madrid in the FBI data?

Let's begin with Joshua Paul Benjamin. In Chapter 1, we learned that as a child, Joshua was hit by a car, resulting in serious injuries. Initially, he was unable to communicate and his left side was paralyzed. Doctors believed that this near-fatal accident also stunted Joshua's cognitive and psychological development. Eventually, Joshua was again able to communicate, and he overcame his paralysis. One effect of the injuries sustained was Joshua's preference to play with younger boys. Joshua found that he just did not get along with adults or boys his own age.

When Joshua was 14, his uncle began molesting him. The molestation was not the cause of Joshua's introduction to the criminal justice system. Like many victims of molestation, he kept this abuse to himself. Rather, Joshua's introduction to the criminal justice system began with a police investigation into Joshua's alleged inappropriate interactions with two young boys. This criminal case remained open and unresolved for several years. During that time, Joshua moved and enrolled in college in another state. In 1992, when Joshua was a 22-year-old college student living in a Midwestern city, his roommate came across some videotapes believed to be of televisions shows. Joshua had asked his roommate not to watch the tapes, but the roommate disregarded Joshua's warning. In the middle of the show, personal videotaping by Joshua broke in abruptly. In it, Joshua is seen with a boy about age 7. The tape shows Joshua fondling the boy's genitals and raping him while the boy protests and cries. The alarmed and shaken roommate took the evidence directly to the police.

Would Joshua's crimes be recorded in FBI crime data? We know that his crimes were reported to the police, which is the first necessary step for the FBI to include the offenses in its data. The second necessary step is that the police agency learning of these crimes must have forwarded the crime reports to the FBI. If that happened, Joshua's crimes would be reflected in the FBI data. But how? What types of crimes would the FBI record? The UCR SRS would have reflected Joshua's crimes as a Part I crime: aggravated assault. Recall that the UCR SRS would not have recorded Joshua's crimes as rape, because in 1992 UCR SRS defined rape as a crime against a female victim only. The victims in Joshua's case were male. NIBRS was in place in 1992. It is unclear if the jurisdiction where Joshua committed his crimes participated in NIBRS. Assuming it did, Joshua's crime would have been recorded as the Group A crime of forcible rape. Since its inception, NIBRS has defined rape as a crime that can occur to a male or a female victim.

Recall Chris Farias, who had received several DUIs. His crime of drunk driving would also have been reflected in UCR data if the police agency that arrested him voluntarily reported his crime to the FBI. If the police reported Chris's crime to the FBI, both the UCR and NIBRS (if the jurisdiction was a NIBRS-certified reporter) would have recorded an incident of driving under the influence. This is a Part II crime in the UCR SRS and a Group B offense in NIBRS.

The crimes against Jennifer Schuett, the 8-year-old who was brutally assaulted, also came to the attention of the police. After raping and nearly decapitating her, Jennifer's assailant left her for dead on a fire ant mound in an overgrown field in Dickinson, Texas. Neighborhood kids playing hide-and-go-seek the morning after the attack discovered Jennifer when one little girl tripped over her apparently lifeless body. Officers responded to the dispatch call by sending an ambulance and then a helicopter. At the time, no one was certain if Jennifer was alive or not. Were the crimes committed against Jennifer recorded in the FBI's crime data? Assuming that Dickinson, Texas, voluntarily reported crimes to the FBI at that time, Jennifer's victimization would have been captured in UCR SRS data. But what type of crime would have been reflected? It is likely that Jennifer's victimization would have been recorded as a forcible rape in the UCR data. Because of the hierarchy rule in the UCR SRS, no other criminal aspect of her victimization would have been reflected in these data. If Dickinson was a certified NIBRS reporting agency at the time of this attack, Jennifer's victimization would have been recorded differently. Because NIBRS does not operate with a hierarchy rule, the extreme violence against Jennifer may have been recorded as a forcible rape, aggravated assault, attempted homicide, kidnapping/abduction, and possibly other crimes (at the time of her victimization, the FBI used the term *forcible rape* rather than the contemporary term *rape*). These crimes are all Group A offenses in NIBRS.

Danny Madrid was 13 years old when he joined the neighborhood gang, Clanton 14th Street. At the time, Clanton had a friendly relationship with Toonerville, a neighboring gang. Nonetheless, as a member of a gang, he experienced victimizations and committed crimes. About a year before being arrested for attempted murder, Danny was stabbed by a rival gang member from Rockwood Street. Danny retaliated for this stabbing and was sent to juvenile camp for 9 months. While Danny served time in juvenile camp, tension grew between Clanton and Toonerville. By the time Danny was released from camp, this feud was in full swing, and he was put on Toonerville's "hit list." Seven Toonerville members jumped Danny in the school locker room. Though he fought back, he ultimately was forced to flee. As a core member of Clanton, Danny began planning a response using even greater force—retaliation with a firearm.

Danny and a fellow gang member drove for hours throughout Toonerville's turf looking for members to harm. Danny initially carried the gun, and at one point jumped out of the car to attack a rival gang member. He failed to see a woman in the target's car, who could have identified him. Fortunately, his partner stopped him and chastised him for being careless. It was then that Danny's partner took the gun while they looked for other targets. Finally, a rival was sighted. Danny's partner exited the vehicle and shot the rival gang member nine times before returning to the car. Danny drove away. Amazingly, the victim of the shooting survived, but he was paralyzed and remains in a wheelchair today. Although Danny did not pull the trigger, he was as culpable as the shooter. As a result, when he was apprehended, Danny was charged with attempted murder.

Because the UCR SRS fails to record information on attempts and completions, the attempted murder of the rival gang member by Danny and his partner would have been recorded as an aggravated assault. In the SRS, this is a Part I crime. In NIBRS, attempts and completions are generally recorded in the data. However, an exception is found with attempted murder in NIBRS, and as in the SRS, an attempted murder is recorded as aggravated assault. This is a Group A offense in NIBRS.

These actual crimes and victimizations demonstrate how differently a crime measuring system—even one conducted by the same agency—may record the same offenses. Understanding the measurement of crime is important in order to fully appreciate the findings that come from these data.

Bureau of Justice Statistics Measurement of Crime

National Crime Panel

In 1965, the United States was experiencing high and increasing rates of crime. In response, President Johnson convened two Commissions on Law Enforcement and the Administration of Justice[20] to identify the causes and characteristics of crime as well as to recommend policies and programs. The commissions concluded that even with the UCR SRS, there were inadequate data available to develop needed policy recommendations. The need for additional crime data and the importance of alternative measures of crime are reflected in the commissions' quotation offered at the beginning of this chapter. At the time of the commissions' report, the only data available were the UCR SRS. The commissions identified four major limitations of the UCR, making fulfillment of their charge impossible. First, official crime data reflected only crime known to the police. Thus, an understanding of the nature and extent of the **dark figure of crime**—crime unknown to the police—remained a mystery. Without a better understanding of the dark figure, policy recommendations could not be developed. Second, the official crime data better reflected law enforcement activity, rather than actual changes in crime. Fluctuations seen in the UCR may have reflected changes in police activity and been divorced from actual changes in crime. Third, as noted above, these official crime data were vulnerable to manipulation and misrepresentation. And finally, at the time of the commissions, the available data failed to provide information on characteristics of the victim, offender, and incident. Recall that the commissions met prior to the advent of NIBRS. Clearly, an alternative but complementary

dark figure of crime:
Crimes that fail to come to the attention of the police, because they were unreported, it was unclear a crime occurred, or no one learned that a crime was committed.

measure of crime in the United States was needed to compensate for the limitations of the SRS. To collect these needed data, the commissions recommended the establishment of a national criminal justice statistics center. Thus in 1968, the Law Enforcement Assistance Administration was established.[21] This administration (later renamed the Office of Justice Programs) housed the National Criminal Justice Information and Statistics Service (NCJISS), which later became the BJS, was charged with conducting the first victimization survey in the United States. The mission of NCJISS and later BJS is to gather and analyze crime data, publish crime reports, and make available this information[22] to the public, policymakers, media, government officials, and researchers.

After extensive discussions, pilot studies, and preliminary research, the National Crime Panel was fielded in July 1972 by the NCJISS. The National Crime Panel was composed of four distinct samples: two household samples (known as the **National Crime Survey [NCS]**) and two commercial establishment samples (the Commercial Victimization Survey [CVS]).[23] The CVS originally included a sample of 2,000 commercial establishments in 26 large cities and a sample of 15,000 businesses across the nation. The NCS initially included a central city household sample in 26 large cities and a national probability sample of 72,000 households. Almost immediately, budgetary and methodological issues constrained these efforts, and the CVS and the central cities sample were halted. By 1976, only the national probability household sample portion of the National Crime Panel remained: the NCS.[24]

National Crime Survey

Although the other components of the National Crime Panel disappeared, the NCS continued collecting data focused on personal and property crimes from eligible respondents. The NCS provided two primary sets of crime statistics: those against persons and those against households. Unlike the UCR, which presents all crime rates based on the number of crimes per 100,000 persons, personal crime rates from the NCS were provided as the number of crimes per 1,000 persons. For property crimes, the rates provided by the NCS were given as the number of property crimes per 1,000 households. Because of the suspension of the business survey in the initial National Crime Panel, no business crimes were available in the NCS.

National Crime Victimization Survey

Shortly after the fielding of the NCS in mid-1972, work toward improving the survey began. In 1979, plans for a thorough redesign to improve the NCS's ability to measure victimization in general, and certain difficult-to-measure crimes, such as rape, sexual assault, and domestic violence, was started. In 1991, the NCS changed names to the NCVS, and in 1992 the redesign was implemented using a split sample design (i.e., during 1992, half of the victim surveys used the NCS methodology and instruments and half of the victim surveys used the NCVS methodology and instruments). Following the redesign, the NCVS measured an almost identical set of crimes as those gathered in the NCS. The only exception is that data on sexual assault (data on rape were always collected) started being collected following the redesign. While a complete accounting of the changes between the methodology of the NCS and NCVS is beyond the scope of this book, interested readers are encouraged to review this report available from the BJS: http://www.bjs.gov/content/pub/pdf/ERVE.PDF.

As anticipated, given the improved measurement implemented in the new NCVS, the number of crimes counted increased following the redesign.[25] Increases in crime measured varied across crime types, however. The number of crimes *not* reported to the police, for example, increased more than the number of crimes reported to the police. One reason for this occurrence is that improved cues for certain questions caused respondents to recall more of the less serious crimes—those that are also less likely to be reported to law enforcement officials. As a result of measuring additional, less serious crime, the percentage of crimes reported to police based on the redesigned survey is lower than the percentage calculated based on data collected with the previous survey design. This difference is particularly salient for crimes such as simple assault, which by definition does not involve an offender armed with a weapon or result in serious injury to the victim.[26]

Video 2.1:
Measurement tips

Web:
National Crime
Victimization Survey

National Crime Survey (NCS): The predecessor of the National Crime Victimization Survey. The NCS was first implemented in 1972.

Gathering information directly from crime victims offers advantages not found in police administration data. What advantages might victims offer? What disadvantages?

Today, the NCVS is the nation's primary source of information about the frequency, characteristics, and consequences of violent victimization against persons age 12 and older and property victimization against U.S. households. Extant understanding of nonfatal crime in the United States comes from more than 40 years of data collected from the NCS and the NCVS. Researchers use these data to identify amounts of and trends of victimization in general and for particular groups of victims, such as women, African Americans, the elderly, rural inhabitants, and the poor. Data from the surveys allow the identification of victim-offender relationships and how victimization differs across groups, over time, across characteristics, and by type of crime. The data provide an understanding of the extent of armed and unarmed violence, the rate of injuries resulting from violence, resistance used by victims, whether the resistance was helpful or harmful, the monetary value of items taken, service providers used following victimization, and interaction with the police and other elements of the criminal justice system, just to name a few.

NCVS crime data are gathered from surveys administered throughout the year in person and over the phone at a sample of housing units in the United States. Housing units are selected using a stratified, multistage, cluster sample. The NCVS also is characterized by a rotating panel design, in which persons are interviewed every 6 months for a total of seven interviews, and a very large sample size. For example, in 2014, 158,090 persons age 12 or older in 90,390 housing units were interviewed for the NCVS.[27] This methodology and proper use of the data mean that housing units in the sample are representative of all housing units in the nation, and the data provide a representative sample of noninstitutionalized individuals age 12 or older in the United States.

NCVS surveys are administered using two related instruments. The first instrument is the NCVS-1, which serves as a screening instrument.[28] This instrument asks questions to determine whether a respondent was a victim of a threatened, an attempted, or a completed crime during the preceding 6 months. If the screening instrument uncovers a possible victimization, a second incident-focused survey instrument is administered to gather detailed characteristics about each victimization revealed. These details include the victim characteristics, offender characteristics, and characteristics of each incident. Details include, for example, the outcome of the victimization (completed, attempted); the time and location of the incident; the numbers of victims, bystanders, and offenders; victim demographics; victim-offender relationship; offender demographics; offender drug and/or alcohol use; gang membership; weapon presences; injuries sustained; medical attention received; police contact; reasons for or against contacting the police; police response; victim retaliation; and success of retaliation.[29]

Aside from providing important information on victimization, details gathered using the NCVS-2,[30] the incident instrument (see Form 2.3 for an example), are used in two important ways. First, detailed incident information is used to determine *whether* the incident described by the respondent was a crime the survey was gathering information about (i.e., an in-scope crime). Second, if that incident was deemed an in-scope crime, the *type of crime* that occurred is established. Neither the field representative nor the survey respondent makes assessments about whether a crime occurred or about the type of crime. Rather, these determinations are made using incident details during data processing at the Census Bureau, the agency responsible for collecting the NCVS data on behalf of BJS. This methodology ensures consistency in identification of in-scope victimizations and the types of crimes across respondents and field representatives.

Because one of the major purposes of the NCVS was to serve as a benchmark for UCR SRS, in order to provide statistics on the proportion of crime not reported to police (i.e., the dark figure of crime), the victimizations measured by the NCVS are almost analogous to the Part I crimes measured by the traditional UCR SRS program in the early 1970s.[31] Currently, NCVS criminal offenses measured include the following:

- rape
- sexual assault (added during the major 1992 redesign)
- robbery
- aggravated assault
- simple assault
- pocket-picking and purse-snatching
- burglary
- motor vehicle theft
- property theft

Reporting crime to the police is a vitally important task, yet for most crime, only a small percentage is reported by individuals. The police learn of crimes in other ways given technology. For example, in many cities, police are informed of a possible crime involving a firearm through Shotspotter technology. Shotspotter uses highly sophisticated microphones to detect the sound of gunshots and send a signal to dispatchers.

The NCVS benefits from continual scrutiny.[32] During 2007 and 2008, for example, the Committee on National Statistics, in cooperation with the Committee on Law and Justice, reviewed the NCVS to consider options for improvement.[33] This need for review grew based on evidence that the effectiveness of the NCVS recently had been undermined given the demands of conducting an expensive survey in a continued flat-line budgetary environment. Based on this long-term environment, BJS had been forced to implement many cost-saving strategies, including multiple sample cuts over time. The committee noted that the result of repeated deep sample cuts (in conjunction with falling crime rates) created a sample size in which only a year-to-year change of 8% or greater was considered statistically different. The panel concluded that the NCVS as it existed at the time it was reviewed by the committee was unable to achieve its legislatively mandated goal of collecting and analyzing crime victimization data.[34] In addition, as technology moved forward, the NCVS was left behind and was the last paper-and-pencil survey collected by the Census Bureau. This outdated mode made changing and updating difficult. The review panel provided multiple recommendations regarding a redesign of the NCVS that are currently being studied and implemented. It remains unclear what a redesign of the NCVS will entail.

Though imperfect, NCVS data are valuable. An advantage of the NCVS is that it provides data on reported and unreported crimes. The survey continues to provide estimates of the proportion of crime that is and is not reported to the police. Furthermore, it allows the assessment of variation in the degree to which crime is committed against particular groups of victims. A second advantage of the NCVS is that its data offer a wide range of criminal victimization details, including information about crime victims (e.g., age, gender, race, Hispanic origin, marital status, income, educational level), criminal offenders (e.g., gender, race, approximate age, drug and alcohol use, victim-offender relationship), and the context of the crime (e.g., time and place of occurrence, use of weapons, nature of injury, economic consequences). A third advantage of the NCVS is its high response rates. In 2014, for example, NCVS response rates were 84% for housing units and 87% for persons. Obtaining such high response rates is exceedingly rare. A fourth advantage of the NCVS is that it has been ongoing for decades, allowing meaningful long-term trend analysis and the ability to aggregate data in an effort to study difficult-to-measure crimes such as rape and violence against relatively small populations, such as American Indians.

Form 2.3 ■ Page 1 of the NCVS-2 Survey Instrument

OMB No. 1121-0111: Approval Expires 7/31/2006

NOTICE – We are conducting this survey under the authority of Title 13, United States Code, Section 8. Section 9 of this law requires us to keep all information about you and your household strictly **confidential**. We may use this information only for statistical purposes. Also, Title 42, Section 3732, United States Code, authorizes the Bureau of Justice Statistics, Department of Justice, to collect information using this survey. Title 42, Sections 3789g and 3735, United States Code, also requires us to keep all information about you and your household strictly confidential. According to the Paperwork Reduction Act of 1995, no persons are required to respond to a collection of information unless such collection displays a valid OMB number.

FORM **NCVS-2**
(9-16-2004)

U.S. DEPARTMENT OF COMMERCE
Economics and Statistics Administration
U.S. CENSUS BUREAU
ACTING AS COLLECTING AGENT FOR THE
BUREAU OF JUSTICE STATISTICS
U.S. DEPARTMENT OF JUSTICE

CRIME INCIDENT REPORT
NATIONAL CRIME VICTIMIZATION SURVEY

Control number

PSU	Segment/Suffix	Sample designation/Suffix	Serial/ Suffix	HH No.	Spinoff Indicator

Notes

NCVS 2

INCIDENT REPORT

1a. LINE NUMBER OF RESPONDENT ———→ 601 ☐☐ Line number (ex., 01)

1b. SCREEN QUESTION NUMBER ———→ 602 ☐☐ Screen question number (ex., 39)

1c. INCIDENT NUMBER ———→ 603 ☐☐ Incident number (ex., 01)

CHECK ITEM A — Has the respondent lived at this address for more than 6 months? (If not sure, refer to 33a on the NCVS-1 or ASK.)
☐ Yes (more than 6 months) – **SKIP** to 3
☐ No (6 months or less) – Ask 2

2. **You said that during the last 6 months –** (Refer to appropriate screen question for description of crime.) **Did (this/the first) incident happen while you were living here or before you moved to this address?**
605 1 ☐ While living at this address
2 ☐ Before moving to this address

3. **You said that during the last 6 months –** (Refer to appropriate screen question for description of crime.)) **In what month did (this/the first) incident happen?** (Show calendar if necessary. Encourage respondent to give exact month.)
606 ☐☐ ☐☐   Month   Year

4. If known, mark without asking. If not sure, ASK – **Altogether, how many times did this type of incident happen during the last 6 months?**
607 _____ Number of incidents

CHECK ITEM B — How many incidents? (Refer to 4.)
608 1 ☐ 1–5 incidents (not a "series") – **SKIP** to 6
2 ☐ 6 or more incidents – Fill Check Item C

CHECK ITEM C — Are these incidents similar to each other in detail, or are they for different types of crimes? (If not sure, ASK.)
609 1 ☐ Similar – Fill Check Item D
2 ☐ Different (not a "series") – **SKIP** to 6

CHECK ITEM D — Can you (respondent) recall enough details of each incident to distinguish them from each other? (If not sure, ASK.)
610 1 ☐ Yes (not a "series") – **SKIP** to 6
2 ☐ No (is a "series") – Reduce entry in screen question if necessary – Read 5

5. **The following questions refer only to the most recent incident.** (ASK item 6.)

6. **About what time did (this/the most recent) incident happen?**

During day
612 1 ☐ After 6 a.m. – 12 noon
2 ☐ After 12 noon – 3 p.m.
3 ☐ After 3 p.m. – 6 p.m.
4 ☐ Don't know what time of day

At night
5 ☐ After 6 p.m. – 9 p.m.
6 ☐ After 9 p.m. – 12 midnight
7 ☐ After 12 midnight – 6 a.m.
8 ☐ Don't know what time of night

OR
9 ☐ Don't know whether day or night

U S C E N S U S B U R E A U

The NCVS uses field representatives to administer the survey. Considering the complexity of the survey, do you think this is the best approach? Or should respondents be required to fill it out by themselves? Could respondents fill it out by themselves?

Source: Bureau of Justice Statistics.

The NCVS performs well for the purposes for which it was designed; however, as with all data, there are limitations.[35] First, the NCVS is designed to generate *national* estimates of victimization. Because of this, the data cannot be used to estimate crime at the state, county, or local level. In 1996, a region variable was added to the NCVS data, enabling crime estimates for the Northeast, South, West, and Midwest. Furthermore, on rare occasions, special releases of NCVS data have provided insight into crime in major cities. Limited age coverage is a second limitation of the NCVS data, as eligible respondents must be age 12 or older. Because of this limitation, findings based on NCVS data are not generalizable to persons age 11 or younger. A third limitation relates to population coverage because those eligible to participate must live in a housing unit or group quarters. Persons who are crews of vessels, in institutions (e.g., prisons), members of the armed

The homeless are not represented in the NCVS. How might this limitation affect NCVS victimization rates? What is an efficient and cost-effective way to measure their level of victimization?

forces living in military barracks, and the homeless are excluded from the sample. This means that findings using NCVS data cannot be generalized to these populations. The fourth drawback is limited crime coverage. The NCVS collects data on the personal and property crimes listed above and excludes many other types of crimes. NCVS crimes tend to weigh heavily toward street crimes, excluding other crimes such as arson, crimes against businesses, stalking, vagrancy, embezzlement, and kidnapping.

NCVS data also are limited because of the sample. Like all surveys, the NCVS is subject to sampling and nonsampling error. Though every effort is taken to reduce error, some is inevitable. One source of nonsampling error stems from the inability of some respondents to recall in detail the crimes that occurred during the 6-month reference period. Some victims also may not report crimes committed by certain offenders (e.g., spouses). Others may simply forget about their victimizations. And still others may experience violence on a frequent basis and may not view each instance as important enough to report to an NCVS field representative. A final limitation is associated with series victimizations.[36] **Series victimizations** are defined as six or more similar but separate victimizations that a victim is unable to recall individually or describe individually in detail. Without detailed information on each incident, crime classification cannot occur, and the crime cannot be counted. In the past, series victimizations—regardless of how many times the victim stated they occurred—were counted as one crime. Clearly, this series protocol underestimates the actual rate of victimization. In 2012, the protocol for addressing series victimizations changed.[37] Currently, it is standard to count as many crimes as the victim states occurred, up to a maximum of 10. The characteristics of the most recent crime are used to identify the nature of all of the crimes. This method may offer a better quantification of crimes, but it is unclear whether it reduces the accuracy of the qualitative nature of the crimes.

In the future, the NCVS may change dramatically. In 2008, a National Research Council panel recommended that the methodology be reviewed to identify changes that continue to provide cost-effective and reliable estimates. Although identifying what exactly will change would be premature, some ongoing methodological research hints at areas likely to change. Changes may include a redesign of the instruments to (a) improve information gathered on victims (e.g., citizenship, sexual orientation); (b) better measure crimes, including a long overdue improvement to questions focused on sexual violence; and (c) address issues related to topics such as fear of crime, perceptions of neighborhood disorder, and police performance. Another change may provide state-level estimates of victimization, using modeling.

series victimizations: Victimizations not discrete in nature, but ongoing with no defined starting and stopping point. Series victimizations present a conundrum in terms of the best way to count them. Common examples of series victimizations are intimate partner violence, bullying, and sex trafficking of minors.

POLICY ISSUES

Difficulties in Counting Crime

A notoriously difficult aspect of counting crime is what is termed *series victimizations.* Most crimes are discrete events—that is, there is a clear beginning and end of the incident. A man comes into the store, pulls a gun on the clerk, demands money, and leaves. A robbery has just taken place. Identification of a single robbery is easy. Other types of crime, however, are not as easily counted. Imagine a child who goes to school where every day he is ferociously bullied. The bullying begins while he is walking to school, it occurs in class, between classes, at lunch, and on his way home. The bullying is a daily occurrence that never seems to stop. Or imagine a woman who is savagely beaten every day and night by her intimate partner. She lives in a rural area, and he has taken her car, her money, and her phone. He also has isolated her from friends and family. She is a prisoner in her home, with no way to leave. Every day, all day, her tormentor abuses her.

If asked, "How many times in the past 6 months have you been a victim?" how should the bullied boy or the abused woman respond? Is 1 the correct answer, as it reflects that each victimization has been part of one long, ongoing event? Would then using 1 to calculate crime rates accurately reflect the amount of violent crime? Or should the boy and the woman answer 180, given that in a 6-month period (the NCVS reference period) there are about 180 days? Is capping the number of victimizations at 10 for each a better approach? Is this a more accurate count of the crimes that occurred? What if each beating was different in nature? Would this change your ideas how about to count them?

Series victimizations refer to those crimes that are difficult to quantify because they are ongoing in nature. Each of the possible ways to answer is not precise and, as such, crime estimates will lack some precision.

Think About It

1. **How would you handle series victimizations if you were in charge of counting victimization?**

2. **What are the advantages and disadvantages of the approach you suggest?**

Journal:
Trends in conflict

Further attention is focused on better measurement of crimes such as rape and sexual assault. Given the scope of methodological research currently under way, improvements and changes to the NCVS may exceed any seen in the past.

CASE STUDY

Case Studies and NCVS Data

Returning to our case studies, how would the NCVS record these crimes and victimizations? Joshua Paul Benjamin's act of sexual assault would not be recorded in the NCVS. Why? This is because his victims were younger than age 12, and the NCVS is restricted to victimizations against noninstitutionalized persons *age 12 or older.* The drunk driving offense of Chris Farias also would not be reflected in NCVS data. Recall that the NCVS interviews persons about their experiences as crime victims, and more specifically, street crime victims. Drunk driving is a so-called victimless crime and not an in-scope crime in the NCVS. Even had Chris crashed his vehicle and injured someone else while driving drunk, the incident would not have been recorded as a criminal act in the NCVS. Jennifer Schuett's brutal attack and rape would not be reflected in the NCVS data either.

She was 8 years old when the crimes occurred, so she would have been ineligible to be interviewed for the NCVS. Finally, Danny Madrid's retaliatory attempted murder of a rival gang member would have been recorded in the NCVS. The victim was older than age 12, and he resided in a housing unit. Given this situation, the shooting victim's assault would have been recorded as an aggravated assault (i.e., it involved a weapon and resulted in a serious injury) in the NCVS.

The UCR SRS, SHR, NIBRS, and NCVS all gather data on a broad range of crimes, though none captures all offenses. Furthermore, the same criminal act may be measured differently across data collection systems, while some criminal acts may go unmeasured in some or all data collection systems. What was a rape in 2010 in one data collection system (i.e., NCVS) would have been an aggravated assault in another (i.e., SRS). Understanding the nuances, advantages, and disadvantages of each national data collection system is important. Together, information from all of the data sources is needed to make an informed judgment about crime in the United States (see Figures 2.3 and 2.4). Though different, each is a valuable tool in better understanding the nature and extent of crime in the United States.

Figure 2.3 ■ U.S. Violent Crime Rates, 2014, According to the FBI's Uniform Crime Reports

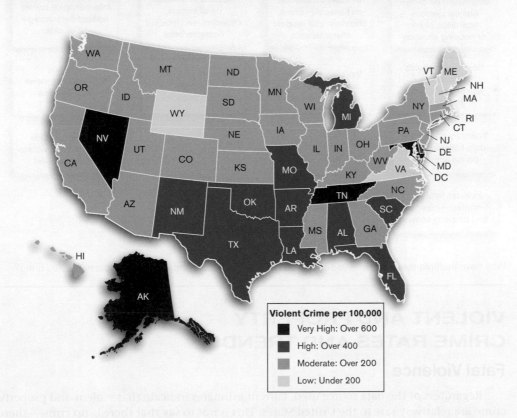

Violent Crime per 100,000
- Very High: Over 600
- High: Over 400
- Moderate: Over 200
- Low: Under 200

Source: Federal Bureau of Investigation, Uniform Crime Reporting Statistics.

Content

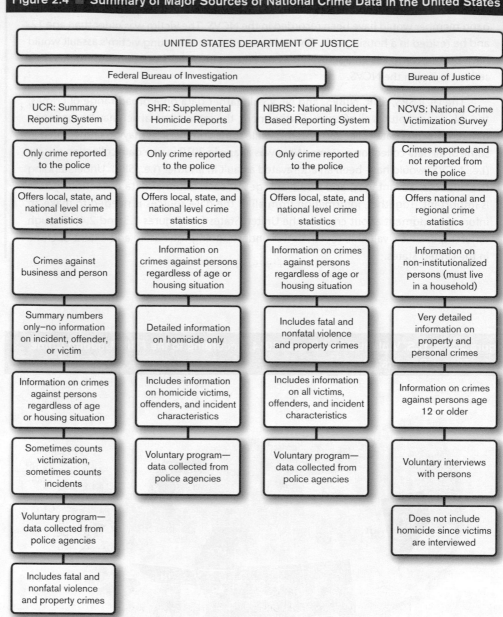

Figure 2.4 ■ Summary of Major Sources of National Crime Data in the United States

Why have multiple measures of crime? What advantages and disadvantages do multiple measures bring?

VIOLENT AND PROPERTY CRIME RATES AND TRENDS

Fatal Violence

Regardless of the data source used, current estimates indicate that violent and property crime are relatively rare in the United States. This is not to say that there is no crime—there is. The United States, however, has been enjoying a period of relatively low violent and property crime rates since they peaked in the early 1990s. Consider, for example, murder and nonnegligent manslaughter. The public fears this type of violence for obvious reasons. In 2014, the FBI's SHR estimated that 13,472 individuals in the United States were murdered.[38] This represents a 2.0% decrease in the number of people murdered in the

Audio:
California cops frustrated with 'catch-and-release' crimefighting

Table 2.2 ■ Murder: Race, Hispanic Origin, and Gender of Victims in the United States, SHR Data, 2014

		Gender			Race				Hispanic Origin		
	Total	Male	Female	Unknown	White	Black or African American	Other[a]	Unknown	Hispanic or Latino	Not Hispanic or Latino	Unknown
Total	11,961	9,246	2,681	34	5,397	6,095	309	160	1,871	6,764	1,913
Percentage distribution	100.0	77.3	22.4	0.3	45.1	51.0	2.6	1.3	17.7	64.1	18.1

Source: Federal Bureau of Investigation, adapted from "Expanded Homicide Data Table 2," *Crime in the United States 2014.*

[a]Includes American Indian or Alaska Native, Asian, and Native Hawaiian or Other Pacific Islander.

United States since 2013.[39] In terms of a rate, 4.5 per 100,000 persons were murdered in the United States during 2014.[40]

Gender, Race, Hispanic Origin, and Murder

No crime, including murder, is distributed randomly throughout the population. Rather, particular personal characteristics are associated with higher rates of murder. Among victims for whom age was known, boys and men are murdered at greater rates and in higher numbers than girls and women: In 2014, 77.3% of murder victims were male, and 22.4% were female (0.3% were of unknown gender).[41] Whites are murdered at lower rates, though in higher numbers, than blacks. Fewer than half of all murder victims in 2014 (45.1%) were white, 51.0% were black, and 2.6% were some other race. In total among those with known ages, 17.7% of murder victims were Hispanic, and 64.1% were not (Table 2.2).[42]

Murder tends to involve particular incident characteristics. FBI data for 2014 show that the majority of murders are committed by an acquaintance[43] and by offenders with firearms[44] (primarily handguns). Furthermore, an examination of victim and offender race indicates that murder is primarily intraracial.[45] In addition to being victims at higher rates, boys and men are most frequently the offenders[46] (Table 2.3).

Nonfatal Violence

The NCVS shows clearly that nonfatal violence continues to be low compared with its peak in the early 1990s (Figure 2.5). This decline is found across crime types and victimization characteristics. Estimates from 2014 NCVS data indicate that 20.1 per 1,000 persons age 12 and older were victims of nonfatal violence (rape, sexual assault, robbery, aggravated and simple assault; Table 2.4).[47] This rate represents an 11.1% drop in the 2011 rate of 22.6 victimizations per 1,000.[48] Evidence shows that simple assault is the most common form of violent crime in the United States (Table 2.4). Simple assaults are characterized by no or minor injuries and do not involve weapons. In 2014, more than 3.3 million simple assaults took place, which corresponds to a rate of 12.4 simple assaults per 1,000 persons.[49] This represents a 19.5% decrease from the rate of 15.4 in 2011.

In contrast, rape and sexual assault as currently measured in the NCVS is the least common form of nonfatal violence. Like other forms of violence, rates of rape and sexual assault have primarily declined over the past decade. In 2014, the rate of rape and sexual assault was 1.1 per 1,000 persons. This rate is equal to the 2013 victimization rate.[50]

The NCVS estimates that robbery is slightly more common than rape and sexual assault in the United States. In 2014, there were 2.5 robberies per 1,000 persons, which is statistically equal to the 2013 rate of 2.4 per 1,000.[51] Finally, aggravated assault is the second most common form of nonfatal violence measured by the NCVS, as more than 1 million aggravated

Table 2.3 ■ Race, Hispanic Origin, and Gender of Victim and Offender, 2014

Race/Hispanic Origin of Victim	Total	Race of Offender				Gender of Offender			Hispanic Origin of Offender		
		White	Black or African American	Other	Unknown	Male	Female	Unknown	Hispanic/ Latino	Not Hispanic/ Latino	Unknown
White	3,021	2,488	446	35	52	2,663	306	52	595	1,061	1,365
Black or African American	2,451	187	2,205	15	44	2,160	247	44	81	1,040	1,330
Other race[a]	168	47	25	93	3	148	17	3	10	90	68
Unknown race	63	34	17	3	9	41	13	9	6	10	47

Gender of Victim	Total	Race of Offender				Gender of Offender			Hispanic Origin of Offender		
		White	Black or African American	Other	Unknown	Male	Female	Unknown	Hispanic/ Latino	Not Hispanic/ Latino	Unknown
Male	3,949	1,708	2,070	91	80	3,448	421	80	511	1,517	1,921
Female	1,691	1,014	606	52	19	1,523	149	19	175	674	842
Unknown sex	63	34	17	3	9	41	13	9	5	11	47

Hispanic origin of Victim	Race of Offender					Gender of Offender					Hispanic Origin of Offender
	Total	White	Black or African American	Other	Gender of Victim	Total	White	Black or African American	Other	Gender of Victim	Total
Hispanic or Latino	720	578	119	8	15	654	51	15	519	162	39
Not Hispanic or Latino	2,213	956	1,148	84	25	1,977	211	25	151	1,996	66
Unknown	2,770	1,222	1,426	54	68	2,381	321	68	21	44	2,705

Source: Federal Bureau of Investigation, "Expanded Homicide Data Table 6," *Crime in the United States 2014*.

Note: This table is based on incidents in which some information about the offender is known by law enforcement; therefore, when offender age, sex, and race are all reported as unknown, these data are excluded from the table.

[a]Includes American Indian or Alaska Native, Asian, and Native Hawaiian or Other Pacific Islander.

assaults were measured in 2014. In 2014, the aggravated assault rate was 4.1 per 1,000,[52] which is identical to the 2011 rate of 4.1 per 1,000.[53] Aggravated assault is characterized by an armed offender and/or a serious injury to the victim (e.g., gunshot wound, stabbing, broken bones, concussion).

Gender, Race, and Hispanic Origin: Characteristics of Nonfatal Violent Crime

Estimates from the NCVS show that violent crime characteristics differ by victim characteristics. The relationship between the victim and offender, for example, varies by the gender of the victim. In 2014, about half (51.3%) of all nonfatal violent victimizations against boys and men were committed by strangers.[54] In contrast, during the same period, 24.6% of all nonfatal violent victimizations against girls and women were committed by strangers. Victim-offender relationship differs for male and female victims for the individual types

Figure 2.5 ▪ Percentage Changes in Nonfatal Violence Crime Rates From 1993 to 2014

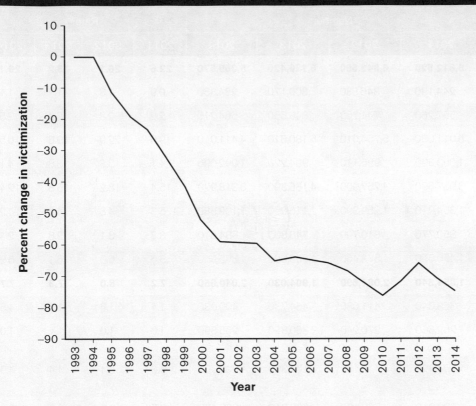

The total violent crime rate has plummeted since the early 1990s. Why might that be? What policies do you think may have been responsible, if any, for this decrease?

Percentage changes calculated from annual estimates in Truman and Langton, *Criminal Victimization, 2014.*

Source: Truman, J., & Langton, L. (2014). *Criminal victimization, 2014.* Bureau of Justice Statistics, Office of Justice Programs, U.S. Department of Justice.

of crime as well. In 2014, strangers committed 54.9% of robberies against male victims and 30.0% of robberies against female victims. During the same year, 14.2% of rapes and sexual assaults against female victims were committed by strangers, while 31.9% of rapes and sexual assaults against male victims were perpetrated by strangers. These findings show that unlike boys and men, girls and women are more likely to be violently victimized by someone they know.

In 2014, a greater percentage of strangers victimized blacks (50.4%) compared with whites (34.8%).[55] About 4 in 10 Hispanics (41.4%) were victims of violence by strangers. Blacks also were robbed by strangers at higher percentages than their white counterparts. During 2014, 64.3% of all robberies against blacks were committed by strangers. In contrast, 30.8% of all robberies against whites were perpetrated by strangers. About 6 in 10 (58.5%) Hispanics who were robbed were robbed by strangers. The percentage of individuals experiencing simple assault by strangers was similar across the groups. During 2014, simple assault by strangers was committed against 39.7% of blacks, 31.9% of whites, and 38.9% of Hispanics.

Estimates from NCVS data also show that most nonfatal violence is committed by armed offenders.[56] In 2014, 71.7% of all nonfatal violence involved armed offenders (Table 2.5). In the same year, 8.1% involved offenders armed with firearms, and 4.0% involved offenders armed with knives. The percentage of nonfatal violent crime involving armed offenders

Table 2.4 ■ Counts and Rates of Nonfatal Criminal Victimization, by Type of Crime, 2011, 2012, 2013, and 2014

Type of Crime	Number				Rate[a]			
	2011	2012	2013	2014	2011	2012	2013	2014
Violent crime[b]	**5,812,520**	**6,842,590**	**6,126,420**	**5,359,570**	**22.6**	**26.1**	**23.2**	**20.1**
Rape/sexual assault	244,190	346,830	300,170	284,350	0.9	1.3	1.1	1.1
Robbery	557,260	741,760	645,650	664,210	2.2	2.8	2.4	2.5
Assault	5,011,080	5,754,010	5,180,610	4,411,010	19.5	22.0	19.6	16.5
Aggravated assault	1,053,390	996,110	994,220	1,092,090	4.1	3.8	3.8	4.1
Simple assault	3,957,690	4,757,900	4,186,390	3,318,920	15.4	18.2	15.8	12.4
Domestic violence[c]	1,354,910	1,259,390	1,116,090	1,109,880	5.3	4.8	4.2	4.2
Intimate partner violence[d]	850,770	810,790	748,800	634,610	3.3	3.1	2.8	2.4
Violent crime involving injury	1,450,650	1,573,460	1,603,960	1,375,950	5.6	6.0	6.1	5.2
Serious violent crime	**1,854,840**	**2,084,690**	**1,904,030**	**2,040,650**	**7.2**	**8.0**	**7.3**	**7.7**
Serious domestic violence[c]	369,040	411,080	464,730	400,030	1.4	1.6	1.8	1.5
Serious intimate partner violence[d]	262,660	270,240	360,820	265,890	1.0	1.0	1.4	1.0
Serious violent crime involving weapons	1,194,420	1,415,120	1,174,370	1,306,900	4.6	5.4	4.4	4.9
Serious violent crime involving injury	689,810	762,170	739,210	692,470	2.7	2.9	2.8	2.6

Note: Detail may not sum to total because of rounding errors. If the offender was armed with more than one weapon, the crime was classified based on the most serious weapon present.

[a]Per 1,000 persons age 12 or older.

[c]Includes victimization committed by intimate partners (current or former spouses, boyfriends, or girlfriends) and family members.

[d]Includes victimization committed by current or former spouses, boyfriends, or girlfriends.

Source: Adapted from Truman, J. L. (2010). *Criminal victimization 2010.* Bureau of Justice Statistics, Office of Justice Programs, U.S. Department of Justice, and Truman, J. L., & Langton, L. (2015). *Criminal victimization 2014.* Bureau of Justice Statistics, Office of Justice Programs, U.S. Department of Justice.

differs by type of crime examined. For instance, a relatively small percentage of rape and sexual assault involves armed offenders; in 2014, armed offenders committed 5.9% of rape and sexual assault. About 1 in 50 (2.3%) rapes and sexual assaults during 2014 involved firearms. Robbery is the nonfatal violent crime most likely to involve armed offenders. Offenders with some type of weapon committed almost half of all robberies (44.3%). Almost 1 in 5 (20.9%) robberies involved firearms during 2014.

Contrary to popular perception, nonfatal violence infrequently results in an injured victim (Table 2.6).[57] NCVS data show, for example, that 62.7% of robberies resulted in injured victims in 2014. About 4 in 10 (42.4%) male victims and 3 in 10 (30.5%) female victims of robbery were injured. During robberies in 2014, those ages 25 to 34 were injured in the highest percentage (65.6%). Blacks are more likely than whites to be injured during robberies (61.7% and 33.2%, respectively). Victims are more likely to be injured when family members or strangers commits the robberies (41.1% and 39.1%,

Table 2.5 ■ **Nonfatal Violent Victimizations and Weapon Presence, by Gender, and Race/Hispanic Origin of Victim, and Type of Violence, 2014**

		Victim Gender		Victim Race/Hispanic Origin				Type of Violence			
	Total	Male	Female	White	Black	Other	Hispanic	Rape/ Sexual Assault	Robbery	Aggravated Assault	Simple Assault
No weapon	71.7%	63.9%	79.2%	73.5%	65.2%	74.7%	68.1%	94.2%	55.7%	8.6%	90.2%
Firearm	8.1%	12.3%	4.1%	6.2%	15.6%	6.4%	10.8%	2.3%	20.9%	30.6%	0.0%
Knife	4.0%	5.1%	2.9%	2.9%	7.0%	2.8%	6.9%	1.6%	8.2%	16.2%	0.0%
Other type of weapon	7.3%	7.5%	7.1%	8.1%	2.9%	8.9%	6.7%	0.0%	6.0%	36.7%	0.0%
Type weapon unknown	1.5%	2.6%	0.5%	2.0%	0.3%	0.5%	0.7%	0.0%	1.3%	7.5%	0.0%
Do not know if offender had weapon	7.4%	8.7%	6.3%	7.4%	9.0%	6.7%	6.7%	2.0%	7.9%	0.4%	9.8%

Most violence is committed without a weapon. Does this change your feelings regarding the need to arm yourself in the event of a violent crime? Why or why not?

Note: Includes violent incidents and victimization in which offenders had, showed, or used firearms.

Source: Data from Bureau of Justice Statistics.

respectively). About one third of all victims (32.6%) who were robbed by intimate partners were injured.

In 2014, 46.0% of all nonfatal violent crime was reported to the police (Figure 2.6).[58] The police were notified regarding 33.6% of rape and sexual assault during that year.[59] More than half of domestic violence (56.1%) was reported.[60] Using data from the NCVS, variation in reporting of violence against victims based on characteristics is evident. During 2014, nonfatal violence against a female victim (53.2%) was reported to the police in higher percentages than was nonfatal violence against a male victim (45.7%). Violence against blacks was reported at higher percentages (58.1%) than was violence against whites (44.4%), Hispanics (43.4%), and "other" races (36.4%).

Property Crime Rates and Trends

The NCVS gathers information on three types of property crime: burglary, motor vehicle theft, and property theft (also known as larceny). NCVS-based rates of property crimes are expressed in terms of number of property crimes per 1,000 *households* (not persons). The overall property crime rate (i.e., burglary + motor vehicle theft + property crime) in 2014 was estimated at 118.1 per 1,000 households (Figure 2.7).[61] Property offenses, like personal crime, has seen dramatic declines since the early 1990s. Recently, rates have fluctuated year to year. The 2014 rate of 118.5 property crimes per 1,000 households represents a 17.4% decrease from the 2011 rate of 138.7.[62] Furthermore, the 2014 rate of 118.1 is 46.8% lower than the 2003 property crime rate of 173.4 per 1,000 households.[63]

Theft is the most common form of property crime measured by the NCVS. In 2014, the property theft rate was estimated at 90.8 per 1,000 households.[64] This figure represents a 31.4% decrease from the 2003 rate of 132.4 property thefts per 1,000 households.[65] The second most common form of property crime is burglary. In 2014, there were an estimated

hear are conservative estimates? Or do you believe your exposure to crime is representative of the rate of offenses committed? If you were in charge of policy-making, what crimes would you want to estimate and why? What would be the best way to collect each of these types of data?

2. **Ethics and Crime Measurement.** Some researchers and advocates suggest that asking victims about their experiences is unethical, as it revictimizes them. That is, by asking about a traumatic event, the victim experiences trauma again. For example, a rape victim questioned by the police may be retraumatized. Some now find that victims are willing to convey information about their victimization. Do you believe that victimization surveys like the NCS and NCVS revictimize individuals? Is it an ethical way to proceed? If not, how would you go about getting information about traumatic events such as rape, robbery, or witnessing a homicide?

3. **Deciding Which Data Set Is Best.** You are charged with estimating the robbery rate in California. Which data set would you use to get the best estimate? Why did you choose that data set versus the others available? You are charged with estimating the rate of abuse experienced by children ages 2 to 10 in the United States. Which data set would you use to get the best estimate? Why did you choose that data set versus the others available? You are charged with estimating the rate of assault against homeless people in cities throughout the United States. Which data set would you use? Why did you choose that data set versus the others available?

4. **Why Crime Is Declining.** Both violent and property crime fell from the early 1990s to 2009. While researchers cannot definitively state why that is, there are many theories. Some suggest that the aging population is responsible. Others find that increased incarceration is at play. Some argue that the decline in the market for crack cocaine has driven the dramatic drops in crime in the United States. And some suggest that better policing is at play. Do you agree or disagree with these possibilities? Why or why not? What are some reasons you feel crime has declined that have not been discussed here? What are the policy implications of better understanding what causes crime to increase and decrease?

5. **Including Case Studies in Data Collection.** As the chapter showed, the degree to which Jennifer Schuett's victimization would be found in national sources of crime data varies by data collection system. The violence committed by Danny Madrid would have been recorded in all systems as an aggravated assault. In contrast, the chapter indicated that the crimes of Joshua Paul Benjamin and Chris Farias vary in terms of which sources they would be recorded in and how. What sort of changes to national data collection efforts do you suggest to better capture crimes like those found in our case studies?

6. **Crime Measurement and Crimes Against Children.** Many argue for more information about violence against juveniles, such as that experienced by Jennifer Schuett or the young victims of Joshua Paul Benjamin. Gathering more detailed information for use by researchers and ultimately policymakers will provide greater insight into crimes against children. Furthermore, this enhanced understanding may ultimately lead to superior policies that prevent future violence against children. Is this need for more details on violence against children more important than consideration of questions about juveniles like Jennifer? Or is this no different than investigators gathering information to solve the crime? Do the needs of many outweigh the needs of few? Why or why not? Does it matter that these victims are young people? Or do concerns extend to all victims regardless of age?

DIGITAL RESOURCES

$SAGE edge™

Sharpen your skills with SAGE edge at edge.sagepub.com/rennison2e. SAGE edge for Students provides a personalized approach to help you accomplish your coursework goals in an easy-to-use learning environment. You'll find action plans, mobile-friendly eFlashcards, and quizzes as well as video and web resources and links to SAGE journal articles to support and expand on the concepts presented in this chapter.

3 CRIMINAL JUSTICE AND THE LAW

"It is better for all the world, if instead of waiting to execute degenerate offspring for crime, or to let them starve for their imbecility, society can prevent those who are manifestly unfit from continuing their kind. The principle that sustains compulsory vaccination is broad enough to cover cutting the Fallopian tubes. Three generations of imbeciles are enough."

—Oliver Wendell Holmes (1927)

"A child born to a Black mother in a state like Mississippi . . . has exactly the same rights as a white baby born to the wealthiest person in the United States. It's not true, but I challenge anyone to say it is not a goal worth working for."

—Thurgood Marshall (1980)

LEARNING OBJECTIVES

After finishing this chapter, you should be able to:

3.1 Summarize the historical development of the law and explain the reforms introduced by the Classical School.

3.2 Identify the basic principles associated with the rule of law.

3.3 Compare the two main sources of criminal law: common law and constitutional law.

3.4 Explain the goals of the law and distinguish between the different types of law.

3.5 Definite the elements of a crime and two main classifications of crime.

3.6 Differentiate misdemeanors and felonies.

3.7 Review the types of criminal defenses available to defendants.

3.8 Discuss how legal standards and practices have evolved in recent history.

3.9 Distinguish the importance of victim rights and their role in the criminal justice system.

INTRODUCTION: THE DEVELOPMENT OF LAW

Understanding the development and use of law is a challenging endeavor; however, the rich history and evolution of court decisions, legislation, and policies are more interesting than a great episode of *Law and Order*. At the forefront of the law are the concepts of justice and equality, though as you will read in this chapter these ideals often fall short of reality. "Equal Justice Under the Law," a phrase inscribed on the front of the U.S. Supreme Court building in Washington, DC, is a part of our common language. Justice and laws differ and change according to societal norms, cultural shifts, and technology. Retrospective examinations of the law show the fallibility of the system and, at times, indicate that justice is not always achieved. As Supreme Court justice Thurgood Marshall (1908–1993), who devoted his life and career to equal treatment under the law, noted in his famous quotation at the beginning of the chapter, discrimination against blacks in the United States is ever present, despite important strides since the passage of the Civil Rights Act of 1964. In contrast, Supreme Court justice Oliver Wendell Holmes (1841–1935) undermined fair treatment when he supported the sterilization of the developmentally disabled in his biting decision in the case of *Buck v. Bell* (1927). As you explore the intricacies of jurisprudence, you will see that the law on the books and the law in action may defy logic, fairness, and compassion, though no better system of justice exists in the world.

The U.S. Supreme Court strives to provide equality for all, although history shows this can be a difficult task. Describe some historic and current cases that demonstrate the inherent difficulties the Court faces when making tough decisions.

HISTORY OF LAW

Ideas about appropriate behavior date back thousands of years, with codes of conduct and definitions of deviance traced to the Bible, the **Code of Hammurabi** (established by Hammurabi during his rule from 1792 to 1750 BCE), the Mosaic Code of the Israelites (1200 BCE), and the Roman Twelve Tables (451 BCE). No doubt codes and edicts throughout history influence what we currently deem as criminal and deviant behavior. The widely told biblical story of Cain and Abel is the first well-known case of homicide. Cain killed his brother Abel in anger after God rejected his crop sacrifice. Apparently not a vegetarian, God favored Abel's animal offerings, and Cain was sent into exile as punishment. The Code of Hammurabi, the oldest known legal code, established approximately 300 provisions for family, trade, real property, personal property, and labor. The code included civil matters such as marriage and divorce and criminal laws covering, for example, murder and arson—all with severe, though at the time considered proportional, consequences:

- If a man has accused another of laying a *kispu* [spell] upon him, but has not proved it, the accused shall go to the sacred river, he shall plunge into the sacred river, and if the river shall conquer him, he that accused him shall take possession of his house. If the sacred river shall show his innocence and he is saved, his accuser shall be put to death. He that plunged into the sacred river shall appropriate the house of him that accused.

- If a man has bought or received on deposit from a minor or a slave, either silver or gold, male or female slave, ox, ass, or sheep, or anything else, except by consent of elders, or power of attorney, he shall be put to death for theft.

- If a fire has broken out in a man's house and one who has come to put it out has coveted the property of the householder and appropriated any of it, that man shall be cast into the self-same fire.

- If a woman has hated her husband and has said, "You shall not possess me," her past shall be inquired into, as to what she lacks. If she has been discreet, and has no vice, and her husband has gone out, and has greatly belittled her, that woman has no blame, she shall take her marriage-portion and go off to her father's house.

- If a son has struck his father, his hands shall be cut off.[1]

Throughout history illegal behavior has resulted in harsh and strange punishments. Michel Foucault (1926–1984), a French philosopher, noted the bizarre nature of punishment in his book *Discipline and Punish*.[2] In the book, Foucault described the case of Damiens, who was found guilty of killing his parents. Damiens was "taken and conveyed in a cart, wearing nothing but a shirt, holding a torch of burning wax weighing two pounds" and moved to a plaza where "the flesh will be torn from his breasts, arms, thighs, and calves with red-hot pincers, his right hand, holding the knife with which he committed the said parricide, burnt with sulphur, and, on those places where the flesh will be torn away, poured molten lead, boiling oil, burning resin, wax and sulphur melted together and then his body drawn and quartered by four horses and his limbs and body consumed by fire, reduced to ashes."[3] Methods of punishment were gruesome and included acts such as drowning, burying alive, beheading, stoning, whipping, mutilating, and branding offenders.

Barbaric punishments and strange trials were common in early world history. In fact, people accused of crime often faced **trial by ordeal**. Ordeals were a primitive form of trial in which the outcome rested in the hands of God to determine guilt or innocence

Code of Hammurabi: The oldest known legal code, it established approximately 300 provisions for family, trade, real property, personal property, and labor.

trial by ordeal: Primitive form of trial in which the outcome rested in the hands of God to determine guilt or innocence by protecting an innocent person from some or all the consequences of the test.

by protecting an innocent person from some or all the consequences of the test. Placing a heated piece of iron, for example, in the accused person's hand was called trial by fire. The outcome was determined by how quickly the accused healed. Three days after the trial an examination was conducted to check for festers. If sores were present from the burning, the person was considered guilty. An ordeal by water involved binding the accused and throwing the person in a lake. Strangely, if the person sank, he or she was presumed innocent, though likely drowned. If the accused floated, he or she was considered guilty. Obviously, trials by water created a no-win situation and established a presumption of guilt. Clearly, the trials and punishments would be considered cruel and unusual by our standards.

A New Age of Reason

The **Age of Enlightenment** brought about new ways of thinking in numerous fields, and many of the reforms were thoughtful reactions of outrage against the barbaric system of law and punishment just before the French Revolution in the late 18th century. The Classical School and associated theorists critiqued the existing approach to law and punishment and sought reform in the system. Cesare Beccaria (1738–1794) became famous for his persistence in transforming the legal system, despite attacks from traditional jurists and religious zealots who believed he was an enemy of Christianity, a wicked man, and a poor philosopher.[4] He received his law degree at the age of 20, and his most famous tome, *On Crime and Punishment,* was published in 1764 when he was 26 years old. No stranger to arbitrary punishments, Beccaria was placed under house arrest for 3 months because his father objected to the woman he wanted to marry.[5] The Catholic Church condemned his work until 1962.

Cesare Beccaria emphasized the importance of free will and rationality in the legal system. When offenders decide to commit a crime, are they acting out of free will? Why or why not? What other factors may influence their decisions?

Case Study Video 3.1: Interviews with case study participants

Web: Deterrence

Beccaria emphasized rationalism, intellectualism, and humanitarianism. His reform of the system focused on three major premises. First, he believed that free will, logic, and rationality were central in decisions to commit or not commit crimes. Second, he promoted the idea of deterrence and establishing punishments proportional to the crime. Third, he asserted that it is better to prevent crimes than to punish. Specific and general deterrence are important foundations for prevention and punishment in our criminal justice system. **Specific deterrence** is directed toward the individual offender to stop bad behavior, which may be accomplished through restitution or incapacitation. In contrast, **general deterrence** is based on the perceived negative consequences of being caught and, thus, the threat of punishment will inhibit criminal behavior in all members of society.

Beccaria believed in the importance of the social contract; in other words, citizens should be willing to sacrifice a minimum amount of liberty to help prevent anarchy and chaos. His three principles of punishment are widely cited. In order to be effective, punishment must be certain, swift, and proportional. Other basic principles put forth by Beccaria include the following:

- Laws should maintain the social contract.
- Legislators should create laws.
- Judges should impose punishment in accordance with the law.
- Judges should not interpret the law.
- Punishment should be based on the pleasure/pain principle.
- Punishment should be based on the act, not the actor.
- Punishment should be determined by the crime.
- Punishment should be prompt and effective.
- All people should be treated equally.
- Capital punishment should be abolished except for a few crimes.

Age of Enlightenment: Brought about new ways of thinking including reforms arising from outrage against the barbaric system of law and punishment just before the French Revolution in the late 18th century.

specific deterrence: The notion that punishment serves to deter the individual being punished from committing crime in the future.

general deterrence: The notion that the general populace will be deterred from committing crimes based on the perceived negative consequences of being caught.

The legacy of Jeremy Bentham emphasized utilitarianism. How can the legal system best accomplish the greatest good for the greatest number?

felicitous or **hedonistic calculus:** A measure indicating how much pleasure an individual gains from a specific act.

utilitarianism: A doctrine stating that an action is morally right as long as the behavior is a benefit for the majority of a society. This is the concept of the "greatest good for the greatest number."

panopticon: An architectural design developed by Jeremy Bentham that allows a single person to watch others in a prison setting without those incarcerated knowing they are being watched.

Jeremy Bentham (1748–1832) also stressed rationality in the legal system and opposed the primitive and brutal methods of punishment. Bentham, who was born in London, could read Latin at the age of 4. He studied law at Oxford when he was 12 years old. He proposed that all citizens should have their names tattooed on their wrists for facilitating police identification. In one of Bentham's more astonishing mandates, he requested that after his death his body be dissected and put on display at the University College London. Bentham still sits in the hall, though his head has been reconstructed in wax.[6]

Despite certain odd proclivities, Bentham focused on important concepts of fairness and rationality. He argued for a legal system designed to provide consistent and equitable approaches. He espoused views that punishment could, in fact, serve as deterrence and wrote of the **felicitous** or **hedonistic calculus.** He believed that people would weigh the costs of their actions in order to maximize pleasure and minimize pain. He also grounded his work in the concept of **utilitarianism**—the greatest good for the greatest number.

Bentham's ideas, though often unrecognized, are ever present in the criminal justice system and law today. Bentham's **panopticon** prison design serves as a blueprint for current incarceration facilities. His ideas about using tattoos as a means of identification also came to fruition. Though not mandatory, tattoos now are commonly used by law enforcement to facilitate identification. A recently convicted offender, nicknamed the Band-Aid robber, was sentenced to 520 years. His moniker resulted from the bandages he used on his face and hands to cover tattoos that might have revealed his identity to the police. Police easily recognize the many gang tattoos that represent unique symbols of membership or past behavior. A spider web, for example, generally indicates that the wearer has served time in prison. A teardrop tattoo under the eye can be open, indicating that the person has killed someone, or closed to show the loss of a friend or relative. Bentham's influential ideas related to reform and practices in the criminal justice system have resulted in enduring practices.

Classical theorists focused on free will and rational choice, with an overarching goal of reforming the legal system. In historic and current theories, many scholars argue that the decision to engage in crime is a rational choice in which the offender weighs the benefits versus the cost. Overall, why people commit crime matters little in the law, except, perhaps, in defense arguments. Criminological theories of why people commit crime, whether biological, psychological, or sociological, are beyond the intricacies of legal versus illegal behavior used by the criminal justice system, although they play a major role in understanding all types of behavior.

THE ROLE AND PURPOSE OF LAW

The Rule of Law

The **rule of law** mandates the application of known legal principles in governmental decision making and establishes the premise that every citizen should obey laws. Without the rule of law as a framework for a legitimate legal system, government officials might become dictators and citizens might engage in acts that cause great harm. The World Justice Project identified four principles associated with the rule of law:

Bentham's design is still used in modern prisons. What types of policies are in place today in the criminal justice system that resemble Bentham's suggestions?

1. Members of the government are accountable under the law.

2. Laws must be clear, publicized, stable, and fair, and they must protect fundamental rights.

3. Laws are enacted, administered, and enforced in a fair and efficient manner.

4. Access to justice is denied to no one.[7]

In order to achieve the ideals set forth in the concept of the rule of law, scholars have identified basic principles to guide behavior by citizens and the government:

- Laws must be prospective rather than retroactive.

- Laws should remain stable.

- Rules and procedures for making the law need to be well defined.

- The judiciary must remain independent of outside influences and political agendas.

- Discretion in the system must be used fairly.[8]

The rule of law means many things, but in short it is envisioned as a legal concept that sets boundaries for the government to establish stable, clear rules, regulations, and statutes. Without the rule of law the government might find that a particular act you engaged in yesterday is illegal today and, therefore, deserving of punishment.

Goals of the Law

The law has four primary goals: retribution, restitution, rehabilitation, and incapacitation. Deterrence (both specific and general) may also be considered a goal because the law is created to prevent people from committing crimes by using the threat of punishment. In most cases, however, the goals of law are associated with deterrence. Offenders placed in prison or drug treatment facilities are, under the best of circumstances, deterred from committing additional crimes.

Web:
Wells Fargo restitution

rule of law: A fundamental principle in the criminal justice system in the United States that all government officers—including those in the criminal justice system—pledge to uphold the Constitution and to follow the Constitution, not any particular human leader.

Deterrence and how it applies to Danny Madrid's case is a perfect example. According to Danny, "In terms of a deterrence effect I can definitely say that as a juvenile, being thought of as a dangerous juvenile had quite the opposite effect. Indeed, when one juvenile judge commented on me being 'too dangerous' to be around others my age, I recall feeling a sense of pride and accomplishment . . . I really was a tough kid." Initially, deterrence had little effect on Danny. The court and correctional system were unable to deter Danny from further criminal activities through rehabilitation in juvenile facilities and incapacitation in prison. In fact, he notes that his time housed in California youth authority system was even more conducive to gang violence.

Retribution may be best described as an "eye for an eye, a tooth for a tooth" (also referred to as *lex talionis*). In many sentencing decisions, for example, offenders are court-ordered to pay fines (i.e., restitution) to help compensate victims. **Restitution** for the harm committed by an offender is essential to notions of justice. Sentencing to specialty courts is a means of providing treatment or other forms of **rehabilitation**. Drug courts are popular methods of offering treatment in legal procedures. Overseen by the judiciary, specialized courts (examined in greater detail in Chapter 7) help nonviolent offenders recover from drug and alcohol addictions and avoid further entanglement with the law. In contrast, **incapacitation** is based on the philosophy that removing the offender from society protects citizens from further victimization. Incapacitation serves as a method of specific deterrence.

SOURCES OF CRIMINAL LAW

Common Law

The U.S. legal tradition arises from English common law. **Common law** in Britain, ironically, was not developed for the common man, but served as a tool for English noblemen. Consequently, the common man had no rights at law. Common law was developed by case law; courts wrote their decisions in opinions that were applied to subsequent similar cases. Later, as common law developed along with new governments, what existed was codified or written as statutes by legislative bodies. Critical legal study scholars argue that laws continue to be used by the rich and powerful to control the behavior of the lower classes.

William Chambliss, a famous sociologist, offered an analysis of the rule of law serving the powerful in his article on vagrancy.[9] Chambliss traced one of the first uses of vagrancy laws back to the 12th century. Landowners were faced with a severely reduced labor force after the Black Death, which was a plague that occurred in England in the mid-1300s. In order to rectify the situation, a law was passed that made it illegal to refuse work or quit a job. Landowners depended on having a supply of cheap laborers. Then in the 16th century the law shifted to help the merchant class control criminal activity. Vagrancy laws focused on "rogues," "vagabonds," and "highwaymen" who preyed on citizens transporting goods. Additionally, the punishment for vagrancy became harsher, including whippings; later the death penalty was applied. According to Chambliss, "shifts and changes in the law of vagrancy show a clear pattern of reflecting the interests and needs of the groups who control the economic institutions of the society."[10] Other scholars posit that the same shift in law occurred in the United States against black slaves. Kennedy argued, "When white employers faced labor scarcities, police would often arrest unemployed blacks to create pools of cheap, exploitable labor."[11]

Legal critics argue that the law discriminates against minority groups, and retrospective analyses suggest that this occurs with some frequency. The history of legal decisions enslaving African Americans and disparate sentencing for crack cocaine versus powder cocaine are powerful examples. The law, however, changes to reflect social norms and can be corrected by legislators and judges. In 2010, Congress passed, and President Obama signed, new legislation to address the disparity that largely targeted African Americans, who were serving

Video 3.1:
How I defend the rule of law

retribution: A goal of law that states that punishment is deserved or morally right. In addition, it is a goal of sentencing that seeks to punish the offender for criminal behavior.

lex talionis: Latin for "the law of retribution" and commonly referred to as "an eye for an eye." This philosophy calls for retaliation in which the punishment received should fit the crime committed.

restitution: Repayment as part of a punishment for injury or loss.

rehabilitation: Sentencing goal that seeks to reduce chances of future offenders through education, alcohol or drug programs, psychological programs, and other treatments.

incapacitation: Sentencing goal that isolates the offender from the public and takes away one's ability to commit a crime against those in the public.

common law: A type of legal system originally developed in England, whereby the courts define the law and determine how to apply the law. This is the body of law derived from judicial opinions.

much longer sentences for the possession and distribution of crack cocaine. Similarly, in 2001, sentencing guidelines were changed to provide for harsher punishment for white-collar offenses. The lengths of many prison terms for financial crimes are now comparable with those for violent offenses. Sentencing in the past 5 years for financial and environmental crimes has been far more punitive compared with the past. Bernard Madoff, for example, received a 150-year prison sentence after he was found guilty of running a Ponzi scheme and defrauding investors of billions of dollars.

Rod Blagojevich, former governor of Illinois, was impeached after accusations of corruption and bribery became public. He was convicted and sentenced to 14 years in federal prison. What reasons can you think of for political white-collar criminals being given long prison sentences?

Constitutional Law

The other major source of law is **constitutional law**, which establishes the fundamental rules and relationships among the judicial, legislative, and executive branches at the state and federal levels. This large area of law deals primarily with governmental powers, civil rights, and civil liberties. Interpretations of the U.S. Constitution and each state constitution by the judiciary have established precedents that apply and explain the meaning of provisions and principles in constitutions. The courts uphold state and federal laws as constitutional if they adhere to written provisions and previous judicial interpretations.

Video 3.2:
Four ways to fix a broken legal system

TYPES OF LAW

Criminal Law

Criminal law is divided into two primary areas, procedural and substantive. **Procedural law** determines how people are treated in the system. The **Bill of Rights** (the first 10 amendments to the U.S. Constitution) guides procedural law pertaining to issues such as arrests, warrants, search and seizure, and trials. Procedural law asks, How does the process work? What are the defendant's protections? In the criminal context the laws protect defendants' rights to due process and a fair trial. In contrast, **substantive law** designates what conduct is considered criminal. For example, it defines what constitutes first-degree homicide as opposed to manslaughter. Substantive law is designed to put people on notice as to what types of conduct can be charged criminally. In other words, the law must be specific to let the accused know in advance what behavior is considered legally criminal. Both procedural and substantive laws generally are written statutory laws adopted by legislatures.

Procedural criminal law in the United States also has a basis in federal and state constitutions. The U.S. Constitution sets the guiding principles, which must be adhered to by states, though state laws sometimes come into conflict with federal laws. State laws in death penalty cases using gas chambers as the method of execution, for example, were considered cruel and unusual punishment prohibited by the U.S. Constitution, according to the federal courts. After the U.S. Supreme Court ruling on the use of gas chambers, several states were required to change laws related to the method of execution. The **preemption doctrine** designates federal law as the "Supreme Law of the Land."[12] In other words, usually federal law overrides conflicting state laws. The U.S. Constitution first established this mandate. The Supremacy Clause (Article VI) states that federal laws and treaties "made under its authority, constitute the supreme law of the land."

constitutional law: A major source of law that establishes the fundamental rules and relationships among the judiciary, legislative, and executive branches at the state and federal levels.

procedural law: Rules governing court proceedings.

Bill of Rights: The first 10 amendments to the U.S. Constitution, which guide procedural law pertaining to issues such as arrests, warrants, search/seizure, and trials.

substantive law: Rules that are used to determine the rights of individuals and collective bodies.

preemption doctrine: The idea put forth in the Constitution that federal law is the "Supreme Law of the Land." In other words, usually federal law overrides conflicting state laws.

ETHICAL ISSUES

The Use of Marijuana and Working in the Criminal Justice System

The sale of marijuana in Colorado and other states is creating novel legal and ethical issues. As of January 1, 2014, when the first retail marijuana shop opened, anyone was allowed to purchase pot from a licensed store without fear of citations or arrest, although public use is still banned. Marijuana sales in the first month that they were legal reached millions of dollars. In 2015, marijuana sales in Colorado reached $996 million. Although the marijuana industry offers a wide variety of employment opportunities, and in some cases the jobs are quite lucrative, positions in the field may limit opportunities to work in the criminal justice system.

The past or previous use of marijuana is a contentious matter when applying for jobs in the criminal justice system. The standards for law enforcement agencies vary. In some police departments a job candidate may be disqualified if he or she ever smoked marijuana, while others depend on the number of times a drug has been used across the life span, or if the last incident was 1 to 5 years ago. Many police departments consider the use of marijuana a justification for disqualification as long as it remains a federal crime. Also, an employee's use of medical or recreational marijuana while on the job gives an employer the right to fire the user, according to the Colorado Supreme Court.

Think About It

1. Should an otherwise qualified candidate for a law enforcement job be disqualified when he or she reveals the legal use of marijuana?

2. Should you tell the truth about alcohol and drug use when applying for a criminal justice position?

3. What are the possible long-term consequences for students who smoke pot legally and want to work in the criminal justice system?

Mary Dodge

How should federal law enforcement agencies handle state legalization of recreational marijuana?

Medical and personal use of marijuana in several states exemplifies the conflict between state and federal laws (see Figure 3.1). Federal law regulates the drug as a controlled substance. Recently, the Drug Enforcement Administration (DEA) contemplated changing marijuana from a Schedule I to a Schedule II drug. Schedule I drugs are designated as having no medical use and a high potential for abuse (e.g., heroin, lysergic acid diethylamide, ecstasy, peyote). In August 2016, the DEA rejected any change in the status of marijuana, and it remains illegal under federal law. The final report noted, however, that marijuana is no longer considered a "gateway drug." The possession, cultivation, and distribution of marijuana are federal crimes with serious penalties. State laws allowing the personal use of marijuana have pitted state and federal authorities against each other in a legal battle that remains unresolved as an increasing number of states consider expanding the use of recreational and medicinal marijuana.

Figure 3.1 ■ State Differences in Marijuana Laws and Policies

How does the state you live in regulate marijuana use?

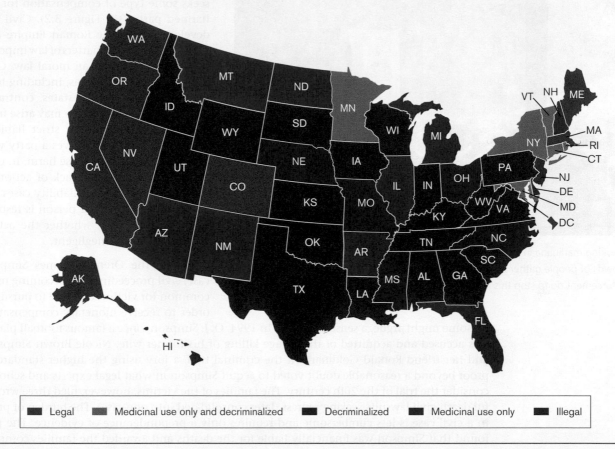

■ Legal   ■ Medicinal use only and decriminalized   ■ Decriminalized   ■ Medicinal use only   ■ Illegal

Source: 6 facts about marijuana. Pew Research Center, Washington, DC (April, 2015) http://www.pewresearch.org/fact-tank/2015/04/14/6-facts-about-marijuana/.

Criminal law also includes **statutes** passed by the U.S. Congress or state legislatures. In short, statutory law is written and enacted by the legislature. A statute, for example, provides penalties for attempted tax evasion or price fixing. Statutes contain procedural and substantive law and, in some cases, may address legal procedure. In some jurisdictions, courts have passed rules of criminal procedure allowing jurors to ask questions during criminal trials. While this is a common procedure in civil court, defense and prosecution lawyers object to jury participation in criminal trials. **Ordinances** are municipalities' statutes and include the written legislative enactments of counties, cities, and towns. Ordinances are limited and cannot invade the providence of the state in larger concerns. Driving under the influence is a statewide concern, and municipality ordinances are limited statutes enacted by smaller jurisdictions. Ordinances typically deal with matters of local concern, such as zoning, disturbing the peace, dogs without leashes, and traffic control within the municipality.

Case law is based on previous court decisions, also known as **precedent**. The legal principle of **stare decisis**, Latin for "let the decision stand," establishes prior case decisions as binding precedent. The important, though at times hindering, aspects of precedent are often portrayed in **landmark cases** decided by the U.S. Supreme Court. A landmark case establishes precedent that markedly changes the interpretation of the law or establishes new case law. In 1857, the Supreme Court's decision in the *Dred Scott* case found that people of African descent were neither U.S. citizens nor protected by the Constitution.[13] This precedent held until the Fourteenth Amendment was adopted in 1868, which established equal protection under the law.

statutes: Formal rules, or law, adopted by a governing body such as a state legislature.

ordinances: Municipal or city rules.

case law: Law that is based on previous court decisions or precedents.

precedent: The legal principle of *stare decisis*, Latin for "let the decision stand," it establishes prior case decisions as binding precedent.

stare decisis: Latin for "let the decision stand," meaning that judges must respect precedents set in previous court cases.

landmark cases: Establish precedent that markedly changes the interpretation of a prior law or establishes new case law.

Smoking marijuana in public remains illegal in Colorado. Across the United States, crowds of people gather to smoke pot on April 20 at 4:20 p.m. What should law enforcement do to stop this illegal behavior?

Civil Law

Civil law deals with disputes between individuals or organizations and typically seeks some type of compensation for the harmed party (see Figure 3.2). Civil law developed from the Roman Empire and typically deals with matters of law imposed by the state rather than moral law. Civil law addresses many areas, including torts (e.g., personal injury), estates, contracts, and property. A tort action may arise from intention, negligence, or strict liability. An intentional tort involves a party who acted purposefully to cause harm. In contrast, negligence is the lack of action to prevent harm. In strict liability cases the corporation, agency, or person is responsible for any harm, whether the action was intentional or negligent.

Since the Orenthal James Simpson case, civil proceedings are becoming more common for victims of crime to pursue in order to receive monetary compensation or, some might argue, a sense of justice. In 1994, O. J. Simpson, once a famous football player, was accused and acquitted of the savage killing of his former wife, Nicole Brown Simpson, and her friend Ronald Goldman. At the criminal trial, a jury using the higher standard of proof beyond a reasonable doubt voted to acquit Simpson in what legal experts and scholars consider the trial of the 20th century. The families of the victims, however, filed three wrongful death civil lawsuits seeking redress (later consolidated into one case). The burden of proof in a civil case is less cumbersome and requires only a preponderance of evidence. The jury found that Simpson was financially liable for the deaths and awarded the families compensatory damages of over $8 million and punitive damages of $25 million.[14] **Compensatory damages** are awarded to replace the loss suffered by the victim, whereas **punitive damages** are punishment for the wrongful action and may serve as a deterrent for future bad behavior.

Class action lawsuits are civil cases involving large numbers of victims. In a class action suit, the court authorizes a single or small faction to represent the interests of the larger group. Class actions often are undertaken when a large corporation or industry engages in wrongdoing harmful to so many victims that individual actions are impractical. The harm caused by white-collar crimes frequently is resolved through class action lawsuits. In 2002, a nationwide class action suit was filed against Wyeth Pharmaceuticals. The drug Prempro, manufactured by Wyeth, was designed to treat menopausal symptoms, such as hot flashes and mood swings, using a combination of hormones. Prempro was prescribed to more than 6 million women, despite research evidence that its use is linked to breast cancer. Beginning in the 1990s, hundreds or perhaps thousands of class action lawsuits were filed against big tobacco firms such as Philip Morris and R. J. Reynolds seeking billions of dollars in compensation for wrongful deaths and health-related harms. Plaintiff attorneys argue that tobacco companies intentionally manipulated the amount of nicotine in cigarettes to cause addiction.

The problems in pursuing civil cases, despite the lower burden of proof, are numerous. The high cost of legal representation, the investment of time away from work and family, and the idea that class action lawsuits will result in adequate compensation for losses represent major obstacles. Settlements with federal agencies offer some sense of restitution to victims of financial crime. In April 2013, news sources reported an agreement among federal agencies and some of the largest banks in the United States designed to compensate the millions of Americans who were targeted in wrongful foreclosures during the housing crisis. The settlements place no guilt on the banks and require no admission of criminal conduct. Bank of

civil law: Law that deals with disputes between individuals or organizations and typically seeks some type of compensation for the harmed party.

compensatory damages: Money awarded in a civil lawsuit for loss or injury suffered as a result of unlawful conduct.

punitive damages: Money awarded in addition to compensatory damages to punish the defendant for recklessness, malice, or deceit.

class action lawsuits: Civil cases involving large numbers of victims in which courts authorize a single individual or small faction to represent the interests of the larger group.

Figure 3.2 ■ Differences Between Civil and Criminal Law

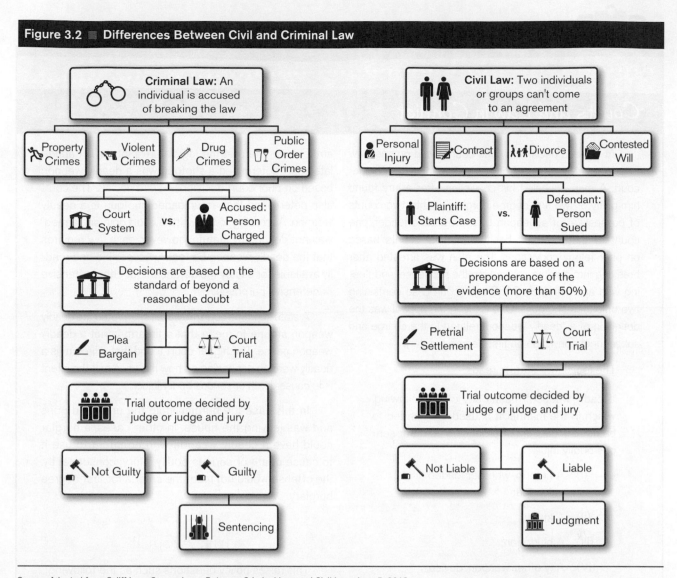

Source: Adapted from Scliff Law, Comparisons Between Criminal Law and Civil Law, June 5, 2013.

America, Chase, Wells Fargo, and Citigroup, for example, agreed to pay $9.3 billion in cash and in reductions of mortgage balances. From the total settlement, only $3.6 billion will go directly to borrowers who lost their homes or faced foreclosure. The 4.2 million victims will receive payments ranging from $300 to $125,000 as compensation.

Victims of white-collar crime often are involved in class action lawsuits. Litigation in these cases presents difficult obstacles. First, victims are difficult to identify because of their reluctance to report the crimes to authorities. Many people taken in by fraudsters do not report the crimes, because of feelings of shame and self-blame.[15] They may also be unaware of their victimization. Second, the victims may include organizations, businesses, and individuals, which complicates settlements. White-collar crime targets all groups regardless of age, race, ethnicity, socioeconomic status, and gender, although some evidence suggests that unsafe drugs and medical devices disproportionately victimize women.[16] Third, particularly in medical crimes, victims often are blamed for agreeing to the procedures or use of drugs, which may include elective cosmetic surgery or birth control devices.

Administrative Law

Administrative law derives from a legislative body's delegation of authority over commissions or boards to regulate activities controlled by written statutes. The Workers

administrative law:
Derives from a legislative body's delegation of authority over commissions or boards to regulate activities controlled by written statutes.

POLICY ISSUES

Courts and Law in Conflict

At times, a decision by one court based on case law fails to receive support from or is extended by a higher court. A man appealed his conviction after a jury found him guilty of two first-degree burglary counts, two counts of possession of a weapon by a previous offender, one count of theft, and six habitual criminal counts based on prior felony convictions. The man was arrested after breaking into a home, ransacking the residence, and fleeing with approximately $150 and a gun case containing two unloaded shotguns. One issue in the appeal was the definition of a "deadly weapon" related to the charge and subsequent conviction on first-degree burglary.

The legislative statute reads:

"Deadly weapon" means any of the following, which in the manner it is used or intended to be used is capable of producing death or serious bodily injury:

(I) A firearm, whether loaded or unloaded;

(II) A knife;

(III) A bludgeon;

(IV) Any other weapon, device, instrument, material, or substance, whether animate or inanimate.

In this example, a state statute provides a definition of a deadly weapon; however, if the meaning of the statute is questioned by the accused, courts are given the authority to interpret the legislature's intent. An appellate court determined a shotgun was a deadly weapon based on prior court decisions—*stare decisis*. The court also determined that an unloaded shotgun is a deadly weapon. According to the written court opinion, "armed" was not defined by statute; however, case law requires that the deadly weapon be "easily accessible and readily available for use by the defendant for either offensive or defensive purposes."

A state supreme court, however, interpreted the deadly weapon statute to mean that a firearm is not a deadly weapon per se. The higher court found that a firearm is a deadly weapon depending on how it is used or if the intent is to cause death or serious bodily injury.

In this case the burglar stole the unloaded guns and was leaving the house. In other cases, a burglar could have a deadly weapon with no intent to use it to cause death or serious bodily injury; consequently, the offense would not meet the criteria for first-degree burglary.

Think About It

This raises policy questions such as the following:

1. **If a gun is unloaded, does that mean there is no intent to harm?**

2. **If a robber enters a store, points an unloaded weapon, and says, "Give me all your money," would this be enough to show intent?**

Compensation Act, for example, is regulated and enforced by a state's division of workers compensation through administrative rules and regulations that it promulgates pursuant to the administrative authority granted by the legislature. Administrative statutes enumerate the legal rules and establish agencies to adopt and enforce the regulations.

Federal agencies are tasked with ensuring compliance with legislative enactments. Agencies such as the Occupational Safety and Health Administration, the Food and Drug Administration, the Equal Employment Opportunity Commission, the Environmental Protection Agency, and the Federal Trade Commission are given authority to develop rules and regulations to ensure compliance with the law. Licensing agencies deal with the regulatory enforcement of professional licensing requirements such as those for psychologists, social workers, dentists, chiropractors, and real estate brokers. In some states, statutes may prohibit a person with a felony conviction from receiving any type of license. Other states have statutes that may take the felony into consideration, though the conviction must not be used solely as a reason for licensure rejection or revocation. An administrative law judge can rule, for example, that a car salesperson that was convicted of selling a machine gun to an undercover officer pretending to be a collector can be licensed because the felony is not related to defrauding customers.

LEGAL DEFINITIONS

Elements of a Crime

Legal definitions of a crime delineate certain elements, including *actus reus* (the act), *mens rea* (the intent), and causation. These elements must be proved by the prosecution beyond a reasonable doubt and found to exist by the jury in order to convict the accused. Substantive law might state that a person commits the crime of first-degree murder by causing the death of another person after deliberation with the intent to kill that person, although specific elements vary by state. The federal government also has substantive law defining first-degree murder, with different elements. Typically, the accused must be found to have engaged in the act and committed the act, and both elements were present at the same time. Additionally, proximate cause of the injury must be established; that is, the state must show that the harm was caused by the defendant's actions.

White-collar crime cases, particularly those involving corporations, often are tried in civil court. Volkswagen denied knowledge in an emissions-cheating scandal and agreed to a $14.7 billion settlement. The global recall of vehicles involves numerous jurisdictions and regulatory agencies. How can this case best be handled?

In addition to the two basic elements of act and intent, prosecutors trying to prove their case beyond a reasonable doubt also contend with concurrence, harm, and attendant circumstances. Concurrence requires that the guilty act and mind occurred simultaneously, which is sometimes referred to as temporal. In some instances motivational concurrence occurs, which indicates that the guilty mind or *mens rea* motivated the resulting action. Additionally, causation and harm are connected to the bad results. Consider a bank robber who draws a gun on a teller and demands money. An hour later the bank teller dies of a heart attack. A prosecutor may argue that the trauma of the robbery and the gun threat caused the employee to die, despite the time difference between the actual criminal offense and death. An additional element may be attendant circumstances. This element includes external factors surrounding the case such at the time when the crime occurred.

Consider the elements of first-degree homicide under federal law:

- The defendant unlawfully killed.
- The defendant killed with malice aforethought.
- The killing was premeditated.
- The killing occurred at the known location.

According to these elements the prosecution must show that the accused killed with extreme disregard for human life and planned or deliberated in order to form the intent to kill. First-degree murder is distinguished from second-degree murder, which lacks the element of premeditation. Manslaughter lacks the element of premeditation and requires that the intent was not to kill but to harm. The police investigated but were unable to quickly identify an offender in the attack on Jennifer Schuett. If apprehended, the offender could face a multitude of charges, including attempted capital murder, kidnapping, and rape. During the trial, the burden of proof would be on the prosecution to show that all the elements of the three crimes were present. In the Texas Penal Code, under whose jurisdiction the Schuett case occurred, capital murder is the only crime that allows for the death penalty.

actus reus: Latin term meaning "guilty act," used to indicate the physical act of the crime. Usually paired with *mens rea* to show criminal liability.

mens rea: Latin for "guilty mind," used in court to prove criminal intent.

The elements of a crime often vary and depend on the wording of the specific statute(s) that may apply. In 1978, California passed the first hate crime law. Since its passage, 45 states now have some version of a hate or bias-motivated criminal statute. Many of the laws used the federal legislation as a model. The federal legislation was expanded in 2009, when President Obama signed the Matthew Shepard and James Byrd Jr. Hate Crime Prevention Act (HCPA or Matthew Shepard Act; U.S.C. § 249). The primary intent of hate crime laws was to establish protection for race, ethnicity, and religion. The HCPA and many states later included biased categories such as sexual orientation, gender, and disability. Only 30 of the states with criminal laws delineated sexual orientation as a protected status in their hate crime laws.[17] Additionally, hate crime laws may address stand-alone crimes or sentencing enhancement. In California, under Penal Code Section 422.6, the stand-alone crime includes violations of civil rights and destruction of property based on group or individual characteristics. California Penal Code Sections 422.7 and 422.75, the crimes of assault and vandalism, for example, must include motivation that the victim falls under one of the protected groups. In contrast, other states may exclude sexual orientation as an element of the law. Under Alabama's hate crime laws crimes motivated by anti-LGBT bias cannot be prosecuted.[18]

CASE STUDY

Hate crime was not among the charges against Danny Madrid, although California's law identifies race and ethnicity as a characteristic. The California Penal Code, however, includes proving that motivation was part of the crime. Gang activity presents prosecutors with many difficulties, and an offense like Danny's crime is more likely retaliation for perceived wrongs by other groups.

Federal and state constitutions give legislators the authority to adopt and enact substantive criminal laws. In many states, for example, a prosecutor must prove the elements of the crime in order to charge an individual with *felony* driving while intoxicated (DWI or DUI) rather than a less serious misdemeanor. The elements of the crime may include, for example:

1. The accused was driving or operating a motor vehicle.

2. The vehicle was on a public roadway.

3. The driver or operator was intoxicated.

4. The driver or operator has prior convictions for driving while intoxicated.

5. The driving results in injury to another party.

6. The violation of a statute such as speeding or running a traffic light.

7. The bodily injury must be proximately caused by the driver's violation of the statute.

The specific form of DUI elements varies by state (and in some cases by county). In New Mexico, for instance, the prosecutor must demonstrate that the driver or operator of the motor vehicle was previously convicted three times for driving while intoxicated. In contrast, in Texas, the prosecutor need demonstrate only that the driver or operator of the motor vehicle was previously convicted twice. In Florida, DUI elements include operating a motor vehicle, being under the influence of alcohol or controlled substance, and the extent of impairment. In the case of Chris Farias, the circumstances and evidence show that all the elements of a felony were present.

States vary on the elements of a felony DWI, though most consider the level of blood alcohol concentration, bodily harm to another, prior convictions, the presence of children in the vehicle, and driving on a restricted, suspended, or revoked license. Additionally, some states apply DUI laws to drunk biking, and offenders may face the same penalties as people driving cars, trucks, or motorcycles. If a state statute applies to "all vehicles," then a court may determine that bicycles are included in the category. California law, for example, includes cyclists, which means that intoxicated riders may be charged with a DUI.

CONTEMPLATING CAREERS

Paralegals

A career in the legal field often requires a person who pays attention to detail and has organizational skills. In addition to an educational background in criminology and criminal justice, expertise in technology, law, and psychology is beneficial. Students interested in becoming an attorney will generally follow prelaw programs as undergraduates. Also, paralegal studies are available at many community colleges and offer numerous opportunities in the court system.

Do you possess any of these characteristics? Many criminal justice students plan to continue their studies in law school, though jobs as paralegals, interpreters, or court administrators do not require advanced degrees. Paralegal or legal assistant positions are ranked among the fastest growing professions because of the high cost of legal fees. These jobs include many tasks, such as supporting attorneys, conducting research, and drafting documents. The average salary for a paralegal is about $48,000 annually. Positions for paralegals, according the Bureau of Labor Statistics, are projected to grow by 8% until 2024. Paralegals may work in law firms, corporations, and government agencies. Many legal careers draw from a liberal arts education (e.g., behavioral science, sociology, political science, psychology, criminology).

Career Video:
A state court law librarian discusses his experience and current issues in the field.

Classifying Crimes: Misdemeanor and Felony

Crimes also are distinguished in the law by seriousness. A **misdemeanor** is a less serious crime punishable by fine, forfeiture, or short-term confinement, though in some jurisdictions gross, aggravated, or serious misdemeanors may be charged. The misdemeanor manslaughter rule established doctrine that a death occurring during the commission of a misdemeanor is involuntary manslaughter, though many states and the Model Penal Code have abolished the rule.[19] In most cases, however, a misdemeanor is punished by less than a year in jail, and a felony conviction may include a year or more in prison. **Wobblers** are felony crimes that may be reduced to misdemeanors. Hitting someone with a bottle is an assault (a felony), but a prosecutor or judge may decide that the case should be charged as a misdemeanor with jail time during a plea bargaining, at the preliminary hearing, or during sentencing. A **felony** offense (e.g., murder, robbery, rape) is more serious and generally results in more severe punishment.

Audio:
Anti-abortion activists indicted on felony charges in Planned Parenthood case

CRIMINAL DEFENSES

Ignorance of the law is no defense for wrongdoing. Law enforcement and courts rarely accept the excuse "I didn't know it was illegal." Mistake of law, however, may be used as a legitimate criminal defense. A defendant may claim that a law was unpublished or unknown to the public. Also, a mistake of fact may be used as a defense if the mental state necessary to commit a crime is absent. There are legitimate defenses at law—some more persuasive than others.

Legal Defenses

In a criminal trial a defendant may present an excuse or a justification for committing a crime. An excuse for a crime provides mitigating factors that explain why the person engaged in criminal activity and relates to the status or capacity (or lack thereof) of the accused. An event in which someone forced you to commit a crime may be excused by a duress defense. Justification refers to the quality of the act. An easy method of distinguishing between an excuse and

misdemeanor: A less serious crime punishable by fine, forfeiture, or short-term confinement, though in some jurisdictions gross, aggravated, or serious misdemeanors may be charged.

wobblers: Crimes that can be charged as either felonies or misdemeanors.

felony: A criminal offense (e.g., murder, robbery, rape) that is more serious and generally results in more severe punishment than a misdemeanor.

A 16-year-old high school student stabbed his prom date in the neck, chest, and face. What arguments would you present to waive him to adult court? The offender pled not guilty based on an insanity plea. If you were his defense attorney, what would you argue to support your client's defense?

Journal:
The insanity defense

a justification is to remember that insanity is an excuse (e.g., "Evil spirits commanded me to kill") and self-defense is a justification (e.g., "I was protecting my family by shooting the intruder"). Legal defenses include, for example, alibi, consent, duress, infancy, and necessity. Many types of defenses have been used in criminal cases, and in some cases, critics have labeled them abuse excuses, although the latter's perspective is controversial.[20] Defenses to criminal acts may include legitimate, more recognizable claims: lawful capacity of office, legal duty, provocation, and legitimate purpose. Specific criminal defenses, such as the Twinkie defense, the Mario Brothers video game made me do it, and the idiot defense, have been but are rarely successful. The following represent some of the more commonly used criminal defenses.

Alibi. An alibi defense is a claim that the defendant was not present at the scene and therefore could not be the person who committed the crime. During a criminal trial, witnesses may testify to support the defendant's alibi. Consider a defendant who is charged with committing a burglary that occurred on Friday at 9 p.m. but claims she was at a restaurant at the time with friends. Her lawyer may consider an alibi defense. Her friends, wait staff, and other employees can testify regarding her whereabouts at the time of the incident. Family members, friends, or someone close to the defendant may testify for the defendant, which means the jury must decide the veracity of the testimony.

Automatism. Dreamlike states, posttraumatic stress, or severe mental disability may result in a criminal action that is unavoidable. This type of defense may include states in which a person's muscle control is lost and he or she acts with no consciousness. John the sleepwalker, for example, who shoots at someone while in a trance, has no control over his actions or is in a state of mind in which he failed to recognize that his actions were wrong or illegal. Because of the mental disability that often accompanies this defense, many states distinguish between noninsane automatism and insane automatism.

Consent. The defense of consent almost always requires the testimony of the victim, because the victim gave permission to the defendant to act in an illegal manner against him or her. Courts recognize this defense if the act did not involve serious bodily injury, if there is acceptance of the risk, and if the conduct led to a beneficial result. The defense is legitimate in cases of sporting events where excessive physical actions may result in death or injury, such as boxing and hockey. Consent is not a valid defense in mercy killing or assisted suicide in most states. Also, in murder-suicide, if one party survives he or she cannot use the consent defense.

Double Jeopardy. Once a person is tried and acquitted of a criminal act, he or she cannot be taken to trial again. Double jeopardy, in other words, prevents a prosecutor from charging the person with a different offense for the same action or for behaviors that were not illegal at the time the act took place. In the case of O. J. Simpson, who was acquitted of killing two people, even if new evidence were discovered that he committed the crimes, he could not be tried again under the double jeopardy defense.

Duress. A person who is forced or coerced into committing a crime may claim duress as an excuse for criminal liability. A person acting under duress must possess a reasonable fear of harm, and the perceived harm must be death or serious bodily injury. The use of a duress defense usually is limited to situations in which someone threatens to kill you or another person if you fail to commit the crime. Duress would apply if someone put a gun to your head and ordered you to rob a bank or be killed.

Entrapment. Entrapment typically occurs when a law enforcement officer convinces someone, whether through trickery or manipulation, to commit a criminal act he or she would not otherwise have committed. The most famous case of entrapment involved John DeLorean, who designed the car with a stainless steel body and gull-wing doors that was featured in the *Back to the Future* movies. DeLorean, who was experiencing serious financial problems, was arrested after undercover agents presented him with the opportunity to distribute cocaine. DeLorean, who had no prior criminal record, was viewed as susceptible to the offer to traffic drugs because he was desperate to save his company. He was found not guilty.

Infancy. Infancy is a defense in criminal law for children who are unable to grasp the consequence of their actions, usually under the age of 7. Children are viewed as incapable of forming mens rea and are not held responsible for crimes. If an 8-year-old child shot her friend, it is unlikely she would be charged with manslaughter, and the case would be handled in the juvenile system. Age limits vary by jurisdiction, and in most states older youth can be waived to adult court depending on the nature of the crime. If a 17-year-old shot her friend, the case may be handled in adult court, and an age or infancy defense would not apply.

Insanity. The **insanity defense** has a long and controversial past in criminal trials. Considering a defendant not guilty by reason of insanity is based on the belief that a select group of people who suffer from mental illness are unable to control their actions to such an extent that they cannot be held accountable for their crimes. As such, these individuals deserve treatment rather than punishment, though insanity is a legal, not medical, term.

Intoxication. An intoxication defense may be voluntary or involuntary. Involuntary intoxication may result when a person is forced to consume or inject alcohol or drugs or unknowingly takes a substance. Involuntary intoxication may also occur as a result of side effects from a legal prescription. Numerous cases of violent behavior have been linked to psychotropic drugs such as Zoloft, Prozac, and Luvox. Voluntary intoxication may be used to excuse certain actions. A defense attorney can argue that the accused was so drunk and high that he or she lacked the capacity to form mens rea. Many states are reluctant to recognize the voluntary intoxication defense and have eliminated this option. A defense of getting drunk, blacking out, and committing murder is unlikely to win an acquittal in a criminal trial.

Mistake of Fact. Ignorance of the law is not a defense, although ignorance of the facts may be used as a defense, particularly if used in conjunction with another defense that the actions were justifiable. A defendant may argue, for example, that he or she had no intent to commit a crime and that the resulting offense was a misunderstanding.

Necessity. The defense of necessity is recognized under common law. This defense argues that a person is forced into a no-win situation and must pick the "lesser of two evils." Cases in which necessity may be raised as a defense, for example, include trespassing on private property to save a person's life or a prisoner escaping from prison to avoid being killed by cellmates.

Restraint. In some cases, defendants may claim that external forces prevented them from controlling their actions. Consider the case of driver who runs over several people because a landslide or tsunami pushes the car into a crowd.

Self-Defense. Self-defense means that a person is acting to protect himself or herself (or a third party) from harm with a reasonable use of force. This claim may be raised, for example, when a store clerk shoots an armed robber or a homeowner kills an intruder. The use of deadly force for purposes of self-defense requires a reasonable belief of imminent death or bodily harm. A person also generally has a duty to retreat in public spaces, meaning that he or she must avoid a confrontation or conflict when the opportunity presents itself. Some states, as discussed in Chapter 1, have established the Castle Doctrine, which no longer requires the duty to retreat.

insanity defense: A defense based on the belief that a select group of people who suffer from mental illness are unable to control their actions to such an extent that they cannot be held accountable for their crimes.

COMMON MISCONCEPTIONS

The Success of the Insanity Plea

Many people believe the insanity defense is abused in the courtroom. In reality, the use of the insanity defense is rare. The majority of research suggests that the defense is used in fewer than 1% of felony cases. Additionally, insanity pleas rarely are successful. Highly publicized trials give the false impression that the insanity defense is an effective way to avoid punishment.

Other defenses, such as intoxication and diminished capacity, are used as mitigating factors in sentencing. Defense lawyers will argue that factors that interfered with a person's ability to appreciate his or her actions should result in a more lenient sentence. They can also be used as

a defense if the defendant contends that the intoxication or other mental state prevented him or her from forming the intent to commit the charged offense.

Think About It

1. Have you ever known someone who was so drunk that he or she forgot what happened the night before?

2. Do you feel that being intoxicated and blacking out should be excused by the courts? Why or why not?

3. If someone who is sleepwalking commits a crime, should he or she be held culpable?

M'Naghten standard: Also called the "right-wrong" test, requires a jury to consider two questions: Did the defendant understand what he or she was doing when the crime was committed? Did the defendant know that his or her actions were wrong?

Durham test: Determines if a criminal act was a product of mental disease or defect. This requires that jurors determine if a defendant had a mental disease or defect and if the condition was the reason for the criminal behavior.

Brawner rule: Also called the ALI rule, it reduced "knowing right from wrong" to the capacity to appreciate the difference between the two. In other words, a defendant must possess an "understanding of his conduct" and be able to "control his actions."

irresistible impulse test: A defense that fails to find a person criminally responsible if mental disease prevents the person from controlling his or her behavior.

battered woman syndrome: A criminal defense developed to excuse or mitigate the actions of women who kill their abusers in cases of domestic violence despite a lack of imminent danger.

The insanity defense was recognized in 1843 after the attempted assassination of British Prime Minister Robert Peel and murder of his private secretary. Daniel M'Naghten (also spelled McNaughton) suffered from paranoid delusions and believed Peel was involved in a conspiracy against him.[21] Based primarily on the testimony of medical experts, the jury found M'Naghten not guilty by reason of insanity without even engaging in deliberation. The **M'Naghten standard**, also called the "right-wrong" test, requires a jury to consider two questions: Did the defendant understand what he or she was doing when he or she committed the crime? Did the defendant know that his or her actions were wrong?

Other standards for establishing insanity include the **Durham test** and the **Brawner rule**. Under Durham, a person cannot be held criminally responsible if an unlawful act was a product of mental disease or defect. According to the Durham test, jurors are required to determine whether a defendant had a mental disease or defect and whether the condition was the reason for the criminal behavior. In response to the disagreement over what insanity means at law, the American Law Institute (ALI) test was created. The Brawner rule (also called the ALI rule) reduced "knowing right from wrong" to the capacity to appreciate the difference between the two. In other words, the defendant must possess an "understanding of his conduct" and be able "control his actions."

Public opposition to the insanity defense resulted in many states' adopting the option of a "guilty but mentally ill" verdict. This approach allows jurors a middle ground to determine that a person committed the act, but also is in need of psychological or psychiatric treatment.[22]

Courts also adopted the **irresistible impulse test** as a defense. Under these circumstances a person is not criminally responsible if mental disease prevents the person from controlling his or her behavior. In other words, a person will steal an item from Wal-Mart even though a police officer is standing directly behind him; this is also called the *policeman at the elbow* test. A widely publicized case of irresistible impulse involved an incident with Lorena Bobbitt in 1993. Bobbitt was acquitted of cutting off her husband's penis after he allegedly raped her. With the severed penis in hand, Bobbitt drove to an empty field and threw the appendage out the car window. The body part was later found by the police and reattached at the hospital.

Other defenses, or what some legal experts call excuses for criminal behavior, also are used in criminal trials. Lenore Walker introduced **battered woman syndrome** (BWS) in the 1970s.[23] This defense was developed from Walker's work to excuse or mitigate the actions of

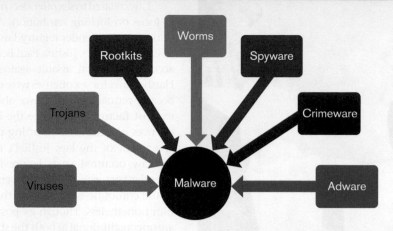

Figure 3.3 ■ Cybercrime

The law typically lags behind rapid technology changes. In what ways could the legislative process be streamlined to keep pace with technology?

Source: Data from Hyphenet, Inc.

women who kill their abusers in cases of domestic violence, despite a lack of imminent danger. The classic portrayal of BWS was seen in the movie *The Burning Bed*. In this adaptation of a true story, actress Farah Fawcett, who portrayed Francine Hughes, waited until her abusive husband was asleep and set his bed on fire. Hughes, who had been abused by her husband for 13 years, was found not guilty because of temporary insanity. Premenstrual syndrome (PMS) has also been used at trial as a defense. During the 1970s and 1980s, several women in the United Kingdom were exonerated of violent crimes. One woman claimed she was suffering from PMS when she crushed a former lover against a lamppost with her car. The charge was reduced to manslaughter based on her diminished capacity. In a U.S. case, a woman claimed she was suffering from PMS when she violently attacked her 4-year-old daughter. Ultimately, her attorney dropped the defense in exchange for a plea bargain on the lesser charge of harassment.[24]

EVOLVING STANDARDS AND PRACTICES

Technology

As previously mentioned, laws change and evolve, sometimes at a slow pace compared with societal expectations and technological advances. Laws governing cybercrime are forming rapidly, though technology outpaces our legal system (see Figure 3.3). Computers are tools for crimes such as identity theft, child pornography, surveillance, gambling, sex trafficking, and fraud. These new and innovative methods to commit crimes evolve with yet undefined statutes or precedent. Some computer hackers, or malgrammers, are focused on destruction or mayhem through the use of viruses, Trojans, and worms. Phrauders are introducing phishing, pharming, and phlawing to engage in larceny and identity theft. Sex offenders and traffickers also are using the Internet to recruit potential victims, distribute child pornography, and traffic children and adults. Voyeurs and extortionists use cameras to spy on and record people in their own homes. Often the laws around these types of behavior are unclear or ill defined. Adjudication of the cases involving violation of copyright laws using the online music-sharing website Napster took 7 years. Napster, now defunct, allowed millions of people to download free music. In a related case in Norway, a student was ordered by the courts to compensate the music industry $15,900 for his Napster web page that provided links to music files for free download.

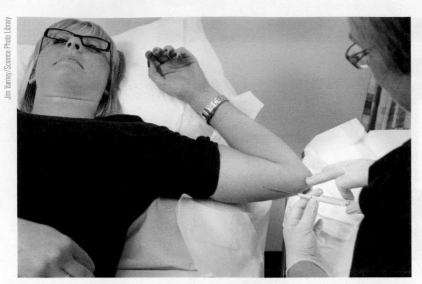

Some of the most serious offenders of white-collar crime are pharmaceutical companies. Despite numerous class action lawsuits, risky birth control devices are still being used on young women. Would you describe the harm caused by unsafe drugs as criminal or civil matters? Why?

Ex Post Facto Laws

Laws related to sex offenders have evolved to focus on lifelong retribution. An example of this is sex offender registry laws. As noted in earlier chapters, Joshua Paul Benjamin was accused of sexual assault against a minor. Harsher laws for sex offenses were enacted and became retroactive. Such laws, also known as **ex post facto laws**, change the legal consequences of behaviors occurring prior to the enactment of the law. Joshua's run-in with the law occurred years before harsher sex offender laws were in place. Given the nature of the crimes he is accused of, they apply to him nonetheless. Though ex post facto laws are unconstitutional at both the state and federal levels, some sex offender registry laws are not considered ex post facto laws. The Adam Walsh Child Protection and Safety Act of 2006 enacted new registration requirements on convicted sex offenders and applied the requirements to individuals who committed the crimes before the law was enacted. In *Smith v. Doe* (2003),[25] the Supreme Court ruled that posting sex offender registry information on the Internet is not a case of an ex post facto law because these laws, in theory, are not designed as punishment. Many practitioners and legal experts believe that sex offenders cannot be cured, which they say justifies severe legal action, long-term incapacitation, and lifetime registration.

White-Collar Crimes

White-collar criminals often are charged with mail fraud, wire fraud, or tax evasion when prosecutors lack specific laws related to a certain case. This legal maneuver also is seen in organized crime cases. Al Capone, an infamous mobster, likely killed or ordered the execution of many people during his criminal career, but in the end he was convicted of tax evasion. Martha Stewart was believed to have engaged in insider trading over the sale of her ImClone stock but was never charged with that offense. Instead, she was convicted of obstructing justice and making false statements. Doctors in California who allegedly misused women's eggs in fertility treatments were charged with wire and mail fraud, in addition to insurance fraud. In 1995, when the case was discovered, California had no written laws related to the theft of human eggs. In many cases, technology outpaces legal mandates.

Punitive laws are common and often are based on the need to invoke harsher punishments for certain crimes. In the early 1990s, three-strikes laws became a popular method of incapacitating career criminals. California's statute serves as the most punitive example. California law included any misdemeanor as justification for invoking a third strike. In one case, a man with two previous felonies received life in prison without parole for stealing a pair of jeans. Research is now examining the unintended consequences of policies such as three-strikes laws to develop more effective and efficient means to deal with career criminals.

Outdated Laws

ex post facto law:
A law that a legislature passed after a crime was committed. At the time the person committed the action, it was legal, and only later was the act deemed criminal.

In some instances, the reach of criminal law overextends its utility, particularly related to an outdated or inappropriate court decision or statute. Laws are difficult to change, especially when precedent has been established. *Plessy v. Ferguson* (1896),[26] for example, established the separate-but-equal doctrine that upheld the constitutionality of state laws on racial segregation. The *Plessy* case was precedent until 1954, when the Supreme Court issued a ruling in

Figure 3.4 ■ Data Supporting Why We Need the Violence Against Women Act

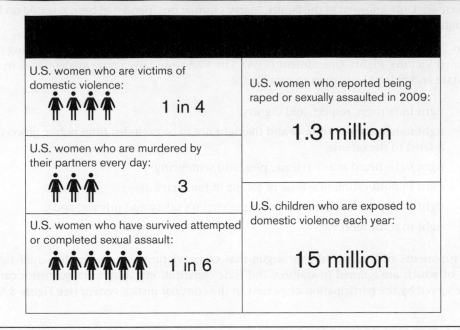

U.S. women who are victims of domestic violence: **1 in 4**	U.S. women who reported being raped or sexually assaulted in 2009: **1.3 million**
U.S. women who are murdered by their partners every day: **3**	U.S. children who are exposed to domestic violence each year: **15 million**
U.S. women who have survived attempted or completed sexual assault: **1 in 6**	

Source: National Task Force to End Sexual and Domestic Violence.

Brown v. Board of Education[27] and unanimously determined that racial segregation violated the equal protection clause of the Fourteenth Amendment.

Bowers v. Hardwick (1986)[28] is another example of a landmark decision that influenced the laws of states for many years. The Supreme Court upheld Georgia's sodomy law that made oral and anal sex in private between consenting adults criminal. The underlying goal of the law was to prevent homosexuals from engaging in what was perceived as deviant behavior. The Supreme Court finally overruled this decision 17 years later in *Lawrence v. Texas* (2003).[29] The Court's ruling invalidated the sodomy laws in 14 states.

THE RIGHTS OF VICTIMS

More recent legal trends have moved toward including victim rights under the law. Historically, victims had few legal rights in the criminal justice system. Currently, most states have created statutes defining basic rights and protections for crime victims, including the following:

- The right to attend criminal justice proceedings
- The right to apply for compensation
- The right to be heard and participate in criminal justice proceedings
- The right to be informed of proceedings and events in the process
- The right to protection from intimidation and harassment
- The right to restitution from the offender
- The right to prompt return of personal property seized as evidence
- The right to a speedy trial
- The right to enforcement of these rights[30]

Voters in California approved the Victims' Bill of Rights Act of 2008 to ensure victims' rights and due process. This bill of rights, also known as Marsy's law, was named in honor of Marsalee Nicholas, a student at the University of California, Santa Barbara. In 1983, she was stalked and killed by her ex-boyfriend. Only a week after her murder, her mother, Marcella

Journal:
Compensation for victims

Video 3.3:
The rights of victims

Leach, encountered the accused murderer in a grocery store. At the time, law enforcement and the courts had no legal obligation to keep the victim's family informed of the status of the accused. Unbeknownst to the family, Marsy's former boyfriend had been released on bail. The rights of victims are now widely recognized in the law.

In 2013, the House of Representatives Committee on the Judiciary held a hearing on a proposed Victims' Rights Amendment (VRA). The VRA would overcome inadequacies in current state and federal legislation to provide the

- right to fairness, respect, and dignity;
- right to reasonable notice of and the right not to be excluded from public proceeding related to the offense;
- right to be heard at any release, plea, and sentencing;
- right to notification of release or escape of the accused;
- right to due consideration of the crime victim's safety and privacy; and
- right to restitution.[31]

Author Video: Discrimination in criminal justice

Proponents of the amendment argue that crime victims deserve fundamental rights, some of which are ignored in statutes and state constitutions. Additionally, justice can be better served by the participation of victims in the criminal justice system (see Figure 3.4).[32]

CHAPTER WRAP-UP

Law represents one of the most important topics in the criminal justice system. Laws define and delineate appropriate and inappropriate behavior by citizens, police, attorneys, and judges. The goal of the law to provide equal and just treatment is an ideal that the U.S. legal system strives to achieve. Humans, however, are fallible and influenced by social context, technological changes, and individual or group prejudices. Ultimately, under the rule of law good decision making wins out over discrimination and injustice. Reform efforts are continuously under way to make a great system better.

KEY POINTS

- The development of law has a complex and lengthy historical background.

- The law and criminal justice systems are based on principles of fairness and justice.

- Free will and rational choice were emphasized during the Age of Enlightenment.

- The primary goals of the law are deterrence, retribution, restitution, rehabilitation, and incapacitation.

- Criminal and civil law have developed from many sources, including English common law, legislative statutes, constitutions, and ordinances.

- Landmark decisions by the U.S. Supreme Court clarify due process rights under the Bill of Rights and establish legal precedent.

- *Actus reus* and *mens rea* are important elements in proving a defendant committed a crime in a criminal case.

- Misdemeanor crimes are less serious compared with felonies.

- Defenses used at trial include justification, insanity, mistake of fact, mistake of law, intoxication, duress, entrapment, and infancy.

KEY TERMS

Actus Reus 85

Administrative Law 83

Age of Enlightenment 75

Battered Woman
    Syndrome 90

Bill of Rights 79

Brawner Rule 90

Case Law 81

Civil Law 82

Class Action Lawsuits 82

Code of Hammurabi 74

Common Law 78

Compensatory Damages 82

Constitutional Law 79

Durham Test 90

Ex Post Facto Law 92

Felicitous or Hedonistic
    Calculus 76

Felony 87

General Deterrence 75

Incapacitation 78

Insanity Defense 89

Irresistible Impulse Test 90

Landmark Cases 81

Lex Talionis 78

M'Naghten Standard 90

Mens Rea 85

Misdemeanor 87

Ordinances 81

Panopticon 76

Precedent 81

Preemption Doctrine 79

Procedural Law 79

Punitive Damages 82

Rehabilitation 78

Restitution 78

Retribution 78

Rule of Law 77

Specific Deterrence 75

Stare Decisis 81

Statutes 81

Substantive Law 79

Trial by Ordeal 74

Utilitarianism 76

Wobblers 87

REVIEW QUESTIONS

1. What types of criminal behavior and misconduct did the Code of Hammurabi cover?

2. What are trials by ordeal?

3. What are some examples of cruel and unusual punishment?

4. Name the three basic tenets of reform suggested by Beccaria.

5. What is the difference between specific and general deterrence?

6. What are the differences between proof beyond a reasonable doubt and preponderance of evidence?

7. How are *actus reus* and *mens rea* related?

8. What is the difference between procedural law and substantive law?

9. Compare and contrast the M'Naghten, Durham, and ALI tests of insanity.

10. Is the retroactive nature of sex offender registry laws an example of ex post facto law?

11. Why are the rights of victims important?

CRITICAL THINKING MATTERS

1. **Applying the Five Goals of Law.** Joshua Paul Benjamin sought out and engaged in intensive sex therapy treatment following his arrest and being charged with sexual exploitation of a minor and sexual abuse in the third degree, a forcible felony. How can the five goals of the law (i.e., deterrence, retribution, restitution, rehabilitation, and incapacitation) be applied to Joshua's case? Are they applicable in the case of Chris Farias or Danny Madrid? If you were a judge and Jennifer Schuett's offender were before you, what would you recommend to satisfy these five goals?

2. **Deterrence and Crime Prevention.** How many students broke the law today or last night? What kinds

of offenses? Often, students willingly admit to driving over the speed limit. And many acknowledge that they have driven while intoxicated. Why is it so easy to ignore a familiar law designed to protect public safety? In order to eliminate speeding violations and drunk driving, how severe would the potential punishment need to be for specific deterrence? Harsh consequences for violations of the law might serve as deterrence, but are they appropriate and proportional?

3. **Crime Prevention and Rational Choice.** In the early 1980s, Derek Cornish and Ronald Clarke emphasized the rational choice perspective in their theoretical framework on criminal behavior. They argued that a decision-making approach to criminal behavior, particularly burglary, depended on making a choice to satisfy needs based on possible rewards and punishments. Individuals decide to become involved in crime to satisfy needs influenced by background and personal characteristics. What situational factors in the environment can be changed to prevent or reduce crime? Are there methods of "inconveniencing" potential lawbreakers? What situational factors should have been used to stop the perpetrator in the crimes against Jennifer Schuett? Do you think that Joshua Paul Benjamin used rational choice in his decision to sexually assault young boys? What situational factors may have prevented Joshua from committing his crimes?

4. **Citizen and Criminal Identification.** The widespread use of DNA evidence has changed many aspects of the criminal justice system. Efforts to establish local and national DNA databases come with costs, despite the potential to combat crime. Should all offenders be typed according to their DNA? Should all citizens be subjected to DNA testing and added to data banks? In what ways could the use of DNA represent a threat to personal liberties? How do you think DNA may influence the outcome of Jennifer Schuett's case?

DIGITAL RESOURCES

$SAGE edge™

Sharpen your skills with SAGE edge at edge.sagepub.com/rennison2e. SAGE edge for Students provides a personalized approach to help you accomplish your coursework goals in an easy-to-use learning environment. You'll find action plans, mobile-friendly eFlashcards, and quizzes as well as video and web resources and links to SAGE journal articles to support and expand on the concepts presented in this chapter.

PART II

© Klaus Larsen

LAW ENFORCEMENT

4 THE HISTORY OF POLICING

> "The myth of the unchanging police dominates much of our thinking about the American police. In both popular discourse and academic scholarship one continually encounters references to the 'tradition-bound' police who are resistant to change. Nothing could be further from the truth. The history of the American police over the past one hundred years is a story of drastic, if not radical change."
>
> —Samuel Walker (1977)

> "You never can tell what a man is able to do, but even though I recommend ten, and nine of them may disappoint me and fail, the tenth one may surprise me. That percentage is good enough for me, because it is in developing people that we make real progress in our own society."
>
> —August Vollmer (n.d.)

LEARNING OBJECTIVES

After finishing this chapter, you should be able to:

4.1 Summarize the influence of early English policing on policing and the increasing professionalization of policing in the United States over time.

4.2 Identify how the nature of policing in the United States has changed over time.

4.3 Evaluate the contributions of August Vollmer and the International Association of Chiefs of Police to policing in the United States.

4.4 Review the role of women and minorities in early policing.

4.5 Identify the sources and consequences of the unrest in policing during the 1960s and 1970s.

4.6 Summarize how policing has become more than just law enforcement, and offer ideas as to the direction of the future of policing in the United States.

INTRODUCTION: POLICING AS A DYNAMIC ENTITY

Policing as we know it today is relatively new. The notion of a professional uniformed police officer receiving specialized training on the law, weapon use, and self-defense is taken for granted. In fact, policing has evolved from a system in which officers initially were appointed by friends, were given no training, were provided power to arrest without warrants, engaged in taking bribes from criminals, and carried revolvers. More contemporary police officers are screened, educated, and trained to serve and protect the public. As Walker's quotation above indicates, the change in American policing over time is nothing short of radical.[1] Policing has progressed and is not highly tradition bound—to the luck of society! The purpose of this chapter is to offer historical information about policing in the United States in order to better understand and appreciate law enforcement as we know it today.

EARLY ENGLISH POLICING

The history of British policing directly influenced the development of policing in the American colonies. Earliest records indicate that initially England had no regular formal police force and that policing and security responsibilities fell to a social unit referred to as the **borh**. This collective of 12 individuals stood surety for one another's good behavior. Membership in any borh was voluntary, and members were free to come and go among borhs of their

POLICY ISSUES

The Appropriate Role of a Police Officer

Historically, police officers performed a variety of tasks, such as tax collection, street sanitation, public health, and law enforcement. Today, many believe that all police should be tasked with additional law enforcement policies—namely immigration responsibilities. Some argue that police officers should be able to stop and ask citizens about their citizenship status, request papers, and arrest those they believe are undocumented.

A photo of an officer from the past. How is he different from officers of today? In what ways has policing changed over time? What changes do you feel remain to be made in our police agencies? Why?

Think About It

1. What is the appropriate role of a police officer? Should it change over time as it has?

2. Would a policy in which police officers have immigration duties have an effect on the relationship between police and the public? Would such a policy endanger the public or make it safer? Why? How might a policy giving police immigration powers affect a citizen's likelihood to report crime or victimization to the police?

3. Would a policy like this allow criminals to remain free, but target Hispanics or others commonly thought to be undocumented? Now that you have thought about the issue of immigration policies and the use of police to enforce them, imagine you are the new chief of police who gets to establish policy in Houston, Texas.

constables were large landowners who were appointed by colonial governors to enforce the law in the areas they controlled and to protect their lands.

Colonial sheriffs were responsible for capturing criminals, serving subpoenas, supervising elections, dealing with religious nonconformists, and collecting taxes. At the time, sheriffs worked reactively, focusing on citizen complaints after crimes had occurred, rather than patrolling to deter crime. Sheriffs were paid with fees based on tasks performed. Because tax collection offered the highest fees, sheriffs focused on the profitable task of tax collection. The fees were only one method used by sheriffs to enriched themselves. They were frequently engaged in embezzlement and other irregularities associated with tax collection. Law enforcement responsibilities such as apprehending criminals—while offering monetary rewards—were not financially worthwhile enough to become a focus of their daily activities. Rather, law enforcement responsibilities were a low priority, and predictably this system was inefficient in terms of crime fighting.

Initially, constables and sheriffs could contend with crime in their respective areas. Criminal activity increased in conjunction with the population, requiring new policing actors. Mayors were considered the chief law enforcement officers in some locations, though they rarely acted in this capacity. The mayor appointed town marshals, who had powers similar to those of sheriffs. Following the British system, night watchmen, operating during the night and later in the day, were also used to supplement law enforcement. The first night watch was implemented in Boston in the 1630s and consisted of an officer and six other men (some were soldiers and others citizens). This group of citizens patrolled the towns and cities to watch for suspicious actors, maintained street lamps, called the hour, gave weather reports, raised the hue and cry (i.e., alerting people to a problem or difficulty), and reported fires or any sort of mayhem. If something suspicious was noted, the watchman reported this activity to the constable.

Vigilantes

In some locales, **vigilantes** performed law enforcement duties with no legal authority. Vigilantes are self-appointed distributors of justice—at least justice as they see it. Charles Lynch, a Virginia farmer, was an early vigilante during the revolutionary period who led a group of men that tracked down and punished outlaws and other assorted criminals.[5] His acts as a vigilante resulted in the adoption of the term *lynching*. Another early example of vigilantism beginning in about 1765 and lasting almost 6 years was in colonial North Carolina with the Regulator Movement. This movement featured armed citizens turning on corrupt colonial officials such as sheriffs. Citizens believed that sheriffs, the courts, and others in power were using collected taxes for personal gain. Citizens complained that sheriffs collected and pocketed taxes only to return to citizens and demand taxes already paid. The colonial governor supported this corrupt system. The citizens—primarily lower class individuals—rebelled against those in power—primarily higher class individuals—to establish an honest government and reduce taxation. Elites in power brought in the militia to crush the uprising of the citizens and hung its leaders.

In South Carolina in the 1760s, citizen vigilantes went into action for a different cause. Unlike the uprising in North Carolina, the events in South Carolina occurred to protect citizens from outlaw gangs that had been terrorizing citizens. Because funding for peace officers had never materialized, citizens took law enforcement (policing and courts) into their own hands. This episode of vigilantism resulted in the funding of needed criminal justice improvements by the governor of South Carolina.

Slave Patrols

Another type of policing entity that emerged in the South was the **slave patrol**. Slave patrols originated in 1704 in South Carolina and consisted of a group of three to six white men whose purpose was to regulate the behavior of slaves and to hunt down and punish escaped slaves. Some argue that slave patrols were the first organized police organizations in America. Patrol members were frequently selected from state militias, and members were armed with and freely used firearms and whips. Apprehended slaves were not privy to any due process such as a jury trial or testifying on their own behalf. Slave patrols spread throughout the South and eventually became a national law. The **Fugitive Slave Law of 1850** was passed by the U.S. Congress to address fears of a "slave power conspiracy" as the population of slaves grew. This law required that runaway slaves be returned to their masters and that law enforcement agents arrest anyone *thought* to be a runaway slave. Persons who aided runaway slaves by offering food or shelter were subject to 6 months in prison and a $1,000 fine. Slave patrols created difficulty for both free and enslaved black persons, as all were subjected to questions, general harassment, requirements to disperse, and searches of their persons and homes by slave patrols. Often the patrols meted out punishment such as maiming and death regardless of whether a law had been broken.

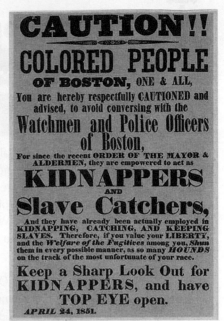

Slave patrol poster used in Boston during an early period in the United States. Many are surprised to learn that such writing was tolerated in the United States. Some argue that such views exist today, though they are less clearly articulated. Do you agree? Why or why not?

Video 4.1:
Drug war

vigilantes:
Self-appointed distributors of justice according to their own rules.

slave patrol: Policing group that originated in 1704 in South Carolina and consisted of a group of three to six white men who regulated the behavior of slaves and hunted down and punished escaped slaves.

Fugitive Slave Law of 1850: A law passed by the U.S. Congress that addressed fears of a "slave power conspiracy" as the number of slaves grew. This law created the need for slave patrols, which became the purview of police officers.

CONTEMPLATING CAREERS

Police Officer

Policing is a rewarding and challenging career. Do you handle stress well? Do you find that others seek out your perspectives when they are troubled? Are you adept at problem solving? Can you piece together what happened by available evidence? Working well with a diverse group of people and being a problem solver are key characteristics for policing.

Policing is a varied profession. One can apply to be a local, state, or federal law enforcement officer. Training requirements vary by agency, though many agencies, such as the Denver Police Department, require a high school education. Do not be fooled, though; while many departments require a high school education, hiring is competitive. Having a college degree makes a candidate more attractive and increases the chances of being hired.

In addition, serving as an officer requires passing a written and physical exam. Having excellent writing and spelling skills is also important, and report writing is a part of the job. Being bilingual offers greater opportunities in this growing profession. According to the Bureau of Labor Statistics, the 2015 median pay for a police officer was $60,270, or a median hourly wage of $28.979.[6] Demand for police officers is expected to increase by 4% from 2014 to 2024.

Career Video:
A police officer discusses her experience and current issues in the field.

Ineffective Policing Reigns

Overall, policing was a mishmash of citizens and part-time watchmen who functioned poorly and were plagued by corruption. Samuel Walker, a highly regarded police expert, offers some reasons for the ineffectiveness of early policing in America.[7] First, policing was a reactive endeavor. No attempt to patrol or proactively deter crime was made by any of the agents of policing. Furthermore, that the law was selectively applied and crimes were selectively dealt with did not escape the notice of citizens. This lack of equal justice was especially troubling given the recent promise of the Declaration of Independence and the Constitution, which touted the protection of life, liberty, and property, and the promise of fair and equal administration of criminal justice.[8] The lack of equal justice for all was abundantly clear. Second, citizens did not respect law enforcement agents. All too often, these men were as criminally motivated as the outlaws they were charged with apprehending. Third, the corruption of agents, lack of respect by the populace, and reactive nature (or lack of action altogether) by police resulted in poor reporting of crime to the police. If crimes are not reported to the police, then offenders may act with impunity, and law enforcement agents may believe that criminality is not an issue requiring their attention. An additional reason for the poor operation of the law is that many in the population did not want the laws enforced. During this period, sin and crime were synonymous. While theoretically citizens stated that they were against sin, in reality many engaged in and enjoyed illegal or illicit behaviors such as drinking and illicit sex and prostitution. This environment was not conducive to professional and efficient law enforcement.

Professionalism Enters American Policing

Initially, a modern police force was unsupported, and the citizenry preferred reliance on a community consensus model. The growth of cities and increasing heterogeneity of the population revealed the insufficiency of these approaches to policing. In the 1830s citizen opinions changed. The population viewed crime as being out of control, and they saw the mass immigration movement as contributing to increased poverty, crime, vice, disease, and lowered quality of life. Cities such as New York experienced riots, major fires, and economic depressions as a result of the strife. A new approach to law enforcement was needed: formal and professional police forces.

The early 19th century was characterized by several policing improvements and the organization of the first police departments. While it is difficult to distinguish which city was the first to implement an organized police agency, many identify Boston and New York as leading the charge. In 1838, Boston was the first major city to require by statute the maintenance of a permanent night watch patrol.[9] In 1854–1855, this night watch was joined with the Boston Police (the day patrol) to form a united entity. Boston also created the first detective division in 1851. New York City organized a police force with three separate components supervised by different authorities, and rivalries existed among the factions. In 1844, the forces were united in a centrally directed police department that was based on Peel's English Bobbies. In the 1830s, using funds left by a philanthropist, Philadelphia organized a 24-member police force and a night force with 120 watchmen. This force was short-lived, so most note that Philadelphia created its first formal police department in 1854. A civilian patrol unit was initially implemented in New Orleans, and in 1818, it was replaced by paid watchmen and a professional force.[10] Cincinnati required all adult men to serve in rotations (with no salary) as night watchmen. By the 1870s, unified police forces could be found in most U.S. cities.[11]

Being an officer was a highly desirable job because it paid about $900 annually, which was about twice the amount paid to blue-collar workers at the time. Initially many police departments required officers to engage in tasks that surprise people today. For instance, Boston police officers were charged with maintaining public health. New York City police officers were required to sweep the city streets. Other responsibilities included walking beats, finding lost children, rescuing people from accidents, regulating markets, putting out fires, hauling drunks to the station, moderating domestic fights, and untangling traffic jams of horse-drawn vehicles. While these were important tasks, the major responsibility of officers was to maintain order, which represented a significant change.

Web:
Remembering August Vollmer

While these professionalization efforts were a step forward, many serious problems remained as officer powers were unchecked and corruption continued to be a problem. Officers could arrest persons without a warrant, and controversy surrounded the type of weapons they carried. Initially, officers carried only clubs, which they used freely. Given the increasing violence of criminals, officers argued for the ability to carry revolvers. In contrast, many police chiefs described the carrying of revolvers as "unmanly." Eventually this issue was resolved, and officers carried revolvers by the end of the 1850s, although they did so without any firearm training. Controversy also surrounded whether officers should be uniformed. In 1693, when the first uniformed police officer was appointed in New York, the use of police uniforms was uncommon.[12] Some noted that police sloppiness in appearance was problematic and that uniforms might command more respect for officers as the citizens continued to disrespect them. In contrast, citizens were apprehensive because uniforms were linked to standing armies. The uniform debate was settled and the use of uniforms increased beginning in 1853. An additional controversy focused on to whom the police reported. Policing was highly biased because politicians in power selected officers, meaning that they served politicians first and the public second. When an incumbent was removed from power, officers were replaced by those favored by the new politician. This issue was settled in places such as St. Louis, Chicago, Detroit, and Cleveland as full control of policing agencies was moved to the state level. State-controlled policing agencies were short-lived in some places and lasted much

August Vollmer, Father of American Policing. How might policing look today without the influence of Vollmer? Would you be sitting in a criminal justice class if it weren't for his foresight?

Wikimedia Commons

longer in others. Additional controversies surrounding policing included ascertaining which laws to enforce, how to select officers, and the role of officers in the community. Interestingly, these are questions that are relevant today, centuries later.

ADVANCING PROFESSIONALISM IN POLICING: 20TH-CENTURY REFORM

August Vollmer: The Father of American Policing

While many improvements had been made in policing since the colonial era, police agencies at the turn of the 20th century were still disorganized and rife with political corruption, incompetence, and brutality. Police officers continued to be underpaid, poorly trained, and often pressured to enforce the laws that benefited those in political power. This changed with the contributions of August Vollmer, the Father of American Policing.

Vollmer was elected town marshal of Berkeley, California, in 1905 and believed that police officers should be free from political pressure and be highly educated, trained, and well paid.[13] Through the use of science and technology, and the education and professionalization of policing, Vollmer argued that officers could better protect the public and their property. Some of his first actions as leader of the Berkeley police force were to implement a code of ethics for officers, ban political corruption and gifts, and outlaw the **third degree**.[14] The third degree was a brutal activity used by officers to gather information from a citizen. Vollmer was a tireless advocate who believed that officers should function as social workers and do more than arrest offenders.

Technology

Vollmer was directly responsible for the adoption of many innovative police techniques and technologies that are still in use today. He had telephone boxes with electric flashing signal alarms installed throughout town that allowed headquarters to summon and dispatch officers more efficiently. As technology advanced, he outfitted officers with radios to further facilitate communication. Vollmer started patrols on bicycles (and later motorcycles and patrol cars), which increased officer mobility and decreased response times. Vollmer implemented one of the first centralized police records systems in the nation. His emphasis on well-kept police records was a central theme in his strategy—one eventually taken to the national level in the form of the Uniform Crime Reports. Vollmer also implemented the first use of the **modus operandi** system to classify offenders and crimes, and facilitated the identification of crime patterns to solve crimes.[15] Vollmer was the first to make use of the scientific analysis of evidence such as blood, fibers, and soil in crime investigation. Another significant technological innovation implemented by Vollmer, in 1920, was a lie detector–type instrument developed at the University of California for use in crime investigations. Vollmer also introduced scientifically based screening methods for hiring officers and weeding out emotionally unsuitable individuals among policing candidates.

third degree: Early (now outlawed) method used by police officers that included brutalizing an individual in order to gather information.

modus operandi: A system for solving crimes that facilitated the identification of crime patterns. This system was first implemented by August Vollmer.

Keystone-France/Gamma-Keystone/Getty Images

Polygraphs are still used today in the criminal justice field. Leonarde Keeler began work on his Keeler polygraph in 1923 while helping August Vollmer clean up crime and police corruption in Los Angeles, where Vollmer was serving as temporary chief of police. The Keeler polygraph shown here resides in the Smithsonian Institution. What other types of technology did Vollmer influence?

Education and Professionalization

Vollmer's influence extended beyond improvements for street-level policing. He strongly believed in the need for an educated police force, and he required that Berkeley police officers earn college degrees. To this end, in 1908 Vollmer established the Berkeley Police School, where all officers were required to complete course work while off duty. Courses taught by academics and experienced police professionals covered topics such as police methods and procedures, marksmanship, laws of evidence, fingerprinting, and first aid. This recognition of the importance of a well-educated police force is astonishing considering that more than 100 years later, only 1% of police agencies in the United States require that their officers hold 4-year degrees, and only 9% require the completion of 2-year degrees.[16]

In 1916, Vollmer began offering a series of summer courses at the University of California, Berkeley, which police officers and university students attended. These summer courses constitute the beginning of criminal justice and criminology as an academic field, leading directly to the 1951 establishment of the School of Criminology on the Berkeley campus. This was the first school in the nation to offer graduate degrees in criminology.[17] Even after his official retirement, Vollmer contributed to the field. He and several colleagues formed what is known today as the American Society of Criminology, a professional organization of criminologists around the world.

Boston police officer on the Bicycle Squad in 1910. Some may not view the bicycle as an improvement in policing. How might it have helped with policing? How may it have hindered it? How do agencies use bicycle patrol today?

It is difficult to imagine policing without the influence of August Vollmer. Imagine, for example, trying to investigate the crimes against Jennifer Schuett without the tools and technologies we take for granted today. Would police have ever been able to identify a suspect in the Schuett case? Without the improvements in policing that began with Vollmer and others like him, how difficult would it have been to identify and prosecute a suspect in the Schuett case? Without these advances, an innocent person may have been identified and convicted in Schuett's case and then punished severely or executed. What of Chris Farias? Would he have been caught had he been driving while intoxicated during the early part of the 20th century? Possibly, but it would have depended on where he was driving. It was illegal to drive while intoxicated in New York as early as 1910. Areas in Massachusetts viewed driving under the influence as a crime as early as 1907. Though laws existed regarding driving under the influence a century or more ago, they were not specific about blood alcohol content, so it remains unknown if Chris would have been interacting with the criminal justice system had he been caught driving drunk 100 years before. It is possible that the actions of Joshua Paul Benjamin would never have come to light had he committed these deeds in the early 1900s. Child sexual abuse was first recognized as a criminal act in 1973 in the United States. In addition, clearly Joshua's actions would not have been videotaped, as that technology was yet to be developed. In other words, he would have technically not committed a crime, and there would not have been video of these activities. Finally, what of the crimes of Danny Madrid? In Vollmer's time, as today, investigating and solving attempted murders were a priority. However, it is unclear how one may have identified Danny and his partner in the attempted murder of the rival gang member. While juvenile gangs have been a part of the landscape for centuries, gathering intelligence about gangs per se has been facilitated with greater technology. Clearly, improved policing is tied intimately to advances in and development of technology.

CASE STUDY

International Association of Chiefs of Police

An influential and important group in the United States also has contributed to the professionalization of policing in more contemporary times. This group, currently known as the International Association of Chiefs of Police (IACP), started taking form in 1871.[18] At this time, 112 police officials from across the nation gathered to discuss policing issues, including police telegraphing, detective information, social evil, abandoned youth, and an increase in crime. This gathering was organized largely through the efforts of officials in the St. Louis Police Department. A committee was established to plan the next meeting, which failed to materialize.

Twenty-two years later, the chief of police in Omaha suggested a meeting in Chicago to further advance policing. At this 1893 meeting the organization was officially launched as the National Chiefs of Police Union, with an emphasis on crime prevention and rehabilitation.[19] The meeting, however, was unsuccessful because those in attendance were more interested in partaking of the benefits of Chicago than in dealing with police business.[20] The next convention was held in 1895, and annual conventions have occurred since.

Initially, the goal of the organization was to apprehend and return criminal offenders who had absconded from jurisdictions in which they were wanted. Over time, the goals of the association have expanded to include advancing the art and science of police work, fostering cooperation, developing information exchange among police agencies, promoting best practices in law enforcement agencies (including recruitment and training of officers), and encouraging officers to behave with integrity and professional conduct.

The first president of the IACP was Richard Sylvester, the superintendent of the District of Columbia's police department.[21] He infused the organization with a professional spirit and ushered in the dawn of a new era of police administration in the United States as he served for 15 years. One contribution was the renaming of the association in 1902 to the International Association of Chiefs of Police, the name by which it is still known today. Sylvester was responsible for many other important changes in the organization, including ideas related to professionalism. This effort included criticizing the motion picture industry for depictions of police officers as bumbling Keystone Cops.

In 1921, Vollmer was elected president of the IACP.[22] As president, Vollmer advocated that officers act as social workers and intervene in citizens' lives before those individuals began committing crimes. In addition, Vollmer pushed for many of the advances he had implemented in the state of California and Berkeley specifically. Vollmer also advocated for a national fingerprint collection system. And just as Vollmer had called for shared uniform crime data in California, he also was instrumental in urging the adoption of a nationally uniform system for the classification and collection of crime data. This system was adopted by the IACP after his presidency. Shortly thereafter in 1935, the Bureau of Investigation (the precursor to the Federal Bureau of Investigation) took charge of the Uniform Crime Reports, as noted in Chapter 2.

Today, the IACP publishes *Police Chief Magazine*, which advertises police positions, manages centers such as the IACP Center for Officer Safety and Wellness, and provides information on a variety of topics, including school violence, victim response, training, and ethics. The organization continues to be an important leader in the continued professionalism of police officers and policing agencies.

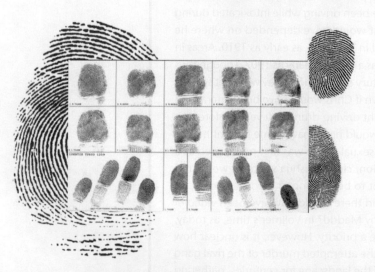

Fingerprinting is widely used in policing today. Imagine the criminal justice system without the use of fingerprints. What other ways would we have of tying an offender to a crime scene?

DIVERSITY IN POLICING

Female Police Officers

Historically, policing was viewed as a man's job. In fact, in many agencies women were not even considered for clerical work.[23] Identification of the first female officer is difficult because titles and responsibilities varied from place to place. One possibility is Lucy Gray. She was the first Los Angeles **police matron**, who in the 1880s created a position in the police department that aided children and women who were victims and offenders. While Gray was never referred to as a policewoman, she performed many of the same duties that male officers did while serving as police matron. Another possibility is Marie Owens, who in 1893 became the first woman appointed to perform police duties in Chicago. In this capacity, Owens held the rank of sergeant and enforced child labor and welfare laws. Others identify Lola Baldwin as the first female police officer. Appointed in 1905 in Portland, Oregon, Baldwin was given a temporary assignment with the Department of Public Safety for the Protection of Young Girls and Women. Initially, volunteers who staffed this group were not referred to as police officers. Rather, they were called operatives and workers, at the request of Baldwin. This group was so successful that they were given permanent positions in the Portland Police Department, though they were housed at the YMCA instead of the precinct. Alice Stebbins Wells is another whom some cite as the first female officer in the United States. In 1910, she became the first full-time paid policewoman with arrest powers in the Los Angeles Police Department. Importantly, she was identified as a police officer, as opposed to a matron, a worker, or an operative. Los Angeles also has the distinction of having hired the first female black police officer, in 1916: Georgia Robinson. Some

Alice Stebbins Wells, a Los Angeles police officer thought by many to be the first female police officer in the United States. What, if any, sort of work would Stebbins have been able to accomplish that male officers could not? Why does gender matter when it comes to policing?

police matron: Title frequently given to women who worked in the early days of policing.

Author Video: Women in the criminal justice system

Video 4.2: Police diversity lags in many cities

Figure 4.1 ■ **Percentage of Female Law Enforcement Officers in the United States, 1987–2013**

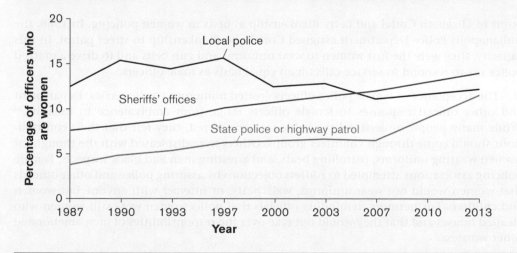

Sources: Langston, L. (2010). *Crime data brief: Women in law enforcement, 1987–2008*. Washington, DC: U.S. Department of Justice, Office of Justice Programs, Bureau of Justice Statistics. Burch, A. (2016). *Sheriffs' office personnel, 1993–2013*. Washington, DC: U.S. Department of Justice, Office of Justice Programs, Bureau of Justice Statistics. Reaves, B. (2015). *Local police departments, 2013: Personnel, policies, and practices*. Washington, DC: U.S. Department of Justice, Office of Justice Programs, Bureau of Justice Statistics. Federal Bureau of Investigation. (2013). *Crime in the United States 2013*. Retrieved from https://ucr.fbi.gov/crime-in-the-u.s/2013/crime-in-the-u.s.-2013.

Note: Most recent data available.

ETHICAL ISSUES

Different Criteria for Male and Female Police Officers

Overall, on average men are stronger than women, and in most cases men have superior upper body strength. Traditionally, female police recruits were held to the same physical testing standards as male recruits. After the passage of Title VII and the Equal Opportunity Act in 1972, law enforcement agencies were legally accountable if their hiring, training, and deployment of female and male officers were unequal. Even in the early 2000s, many agencies and citizens, however, believed that women lacked the strength and presence needed for policing and continued to subscribe to the myth that physical prowess was required for the job. Eventually, minimum height and weight criteria were eliminated, which allowed more women to join law enforcement. Additionally, unsubstantiated physical testing requirements were challenged because the standards failed to reflect valid job performance requirements. Eventually, some departments adopted new physical requirements, though a nationwide valid testing procedure remains elusive. New Hampshire, for example, requires female recruits to satisfy less rigorous physical standards than men when training in the police academy.

Think About It

This policy raises several questions.

1. **Is it ethical that women be held to lower physical standards than men? Will the smaller physical presence of female officers (on average) provoke attacks by offenders and therefore endanger the public?**

2. **Research suggests that women on average are more empathetic, better communicators, and less aggressive than men. Given the nature of most police work (which is not entirely physical), are greater communications skills among women an indicator that they are more suitable police officers?**

3. **As the new police chief of Peacefulville, you are charged with establishing police officer testing criteria. How will you address average differences between men and women in terms of requirements?**

Audio:
A look at women's role in policing

point to Elizabeth Coffal and Betty Blankenship as firsts in women policing. In 1968, the Indianapolis Police Department assigned Coffal and Blankenship to street patrol. In this capacity, they were the first women to wear uniforms and gun belts and to drive a marked police car to respond to service calls on an equal basis as male officers.

The acceptance of female police officers created numerous controversies. Department and other official responses to female officers range from ambivalence to hostility.[24] While many people understood the value women offered, they felt that their contributions should come through volunteer groups. Others were displeased with the thought of women wearing uniforms, patrolling beats, and arresting men and black suspects. Female policing associations attempted to address objections by assuring police and other officials that women would not wear uniforms, walk beats, or interact with anyone but women and children. Furthermore, reminding officials that policewomen were still women who cleaned houses and that they would not take over the responsibilities of men ameliorated other worries.

The responsibilities of policewomen differed from those of policemen. They patrolled areas where juveniles gathered, searched for missing persons, and suppressed inappropriate billboard displays. Not surprisingly, female officers were paid less than their male counterparts. Over time, enthusiasm for female officers diminished and fewer entered the profession. In the 1960s, attention on female officers reemerged (Figure 4.1). During this second era of policewomen, the first woman was killed in the line of duty. Officer Gail Cobb, who was black, was shot and killed while apprehending a bank robbery suspect in Washington, DC, in 1974.

Black Police Officers

Not only was policing viewed as men's work, but it was seen as *white* men's work. Identifying the first black police officer is difficult because many jurisdictions failed to name these men. Police expert and researcher Samuel Walker notes that a mayor in Chicago appointed the first African American officer in 1872.[25] Although never identified by name, this individual is considered to be the first black officer anywhere. In 1884, the mayor of Philadelphia appointed 35 black officers at one time.[26] Members of the public were passionately opposed to this move and assaulted the newly minted officers. In 1886, the Los Angeles Police Department hired two black officers, Robert William Stewart and Roy Green. Even in light of this, many sources give the distinction of the first African American police officer to Wiley Overton of the then Brooklyn Police Department (now part of the New York City Police Department). Overton was hired in 1891, shortly before the incorporation of the five boroughs into New York City.

In 1899, Julius Boyd Loving was hired as the first African American deputy in the Los Angeles County Sheriff's Department.[27] Loving was responsible for progressive programs in the Los Angeles jail system. Known to many as the father of jail programs, Loving started the jail store, craft programs, a carpenter shop, a shoe shop, and a tailor shop. These programs helped lower jail costs. Loving also was responsible for founding and supervising a prisoners' art exhibit, which displayed paintings and other creative works produced by inmates. And he designed a three-tier bunk system in the jail that alleviated crowding and reduced the number of inmates sleeping on the floor.

New York City hired its first black officer in 1905 (though some sources note 1911). Samuel Battle was hired to patrol Central Park West but was ostracized by other officers. Many officers wished to preserve the all-white nature of the New York Police Department and gave Battle the silent treatment. Still, he rose to become the department's first black sergeant, lieutenant, and parole commissioner. While these examples demonstrate early hiring of black officers, this activity was still an anomaly. Following this early period, few were hired. In 1965, for example, only five black officers worked for the Los Angeles Police Department.

As with women and men, the responsibilities of early black officers differed from those of their white male counterparts. Most early black officers worked in plain clothes because it was believed that having them in uniform would offend the white public. In addition, black officers generally worked

While there have been black law enforcement officers for some time, they continue to be underrepresented in most police agencies. What advantages does having a diverse police department offer? Would it matter if the officer who arrested you was black or white or Asian or female? Would it trouble you if all officers in a jurisdiction were black? Or women? Should it be troubling that in most places in early years, all officers were white men?

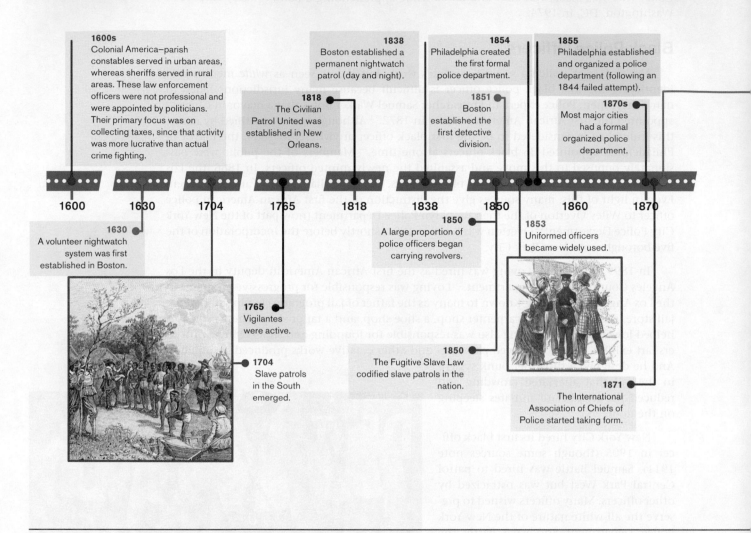

Figure 4.2 ■ Major Events in Policing History in the United States, 1600–1960

1600s
Colonial America–parish constables served in urban areas, whereas sheriffs served in rural areas. These law enforcement officers were not professional and were appointed by politicians. Their primary focus was on collecting taxes, since that activity was more lucrative than actual crime fighting.

1630
A volunteer nightwatch system was first established in Boston.

1765
Vigilantes were active.

1704
Slave patrols in the South emerged.

1818
The Civilian Patrol United was established in New Orleans.

1838
Boston established a permanent nightwatch patrol (day and night).

1850
A large proportion of police officers began carrying revolvers.

1850
The Fugitive Slave Law codified slave patrols in the nation.

1854
Philadelphia created the first formal police department.

1851
Boston established the first detective division.

1853
Uniformed officers became widely used.

1855
Philadelphia established and organized a police department (following an 1844 failed attempt).

1870s
Most major cities had a formal organized police department.

1871
The International Association of Chiefs of Police started taking form.

1600   1630   1704   1765   1818   1838   1850   1860   1870

Photo credits: 1704: © iStockphoto.com/wragg; 1850: Wikimedia Commons; 1853: Library of Congress; 1888: Courtesy of Guardians of Angels.

only in black neighborhoods and could not arrest white citizens. Eventually, more African Americans joined police forces. In 2013, about 58,000 black or African American officers were employed by local police departments. This corresponds to 12% of local police being black, a proportion that has remained stable since 2007, but is greater than the estimate of 9% black officers in 1987.[28] The percentage of officers who are black differs by jurisdiction. For example, about 36.4% of the Philadelphia police department is composed of black officers today.[29] This is less than found in Los Angeles, where as of 2013, 11.6% of police officers were black.[30] In New York City at the end of 2010, 53% of all patrol officers were non-Hispanic white (i.e., black, Latino, or Asian; no estimate on the proportion of officers who were black is offered).[31]

Hispanic Police Officers

Gathering information on the history of Hispanic police officers in the United States is challenging.[32] Hispanic police officers were long present in areas that are now part of the United States. Prior to the English arriving in what became the United States in 1609, Florida, Texas, New Mexico, and many other locales were home to Hispanics—and to Hispanic police officers. While there is information about often brutal policing against

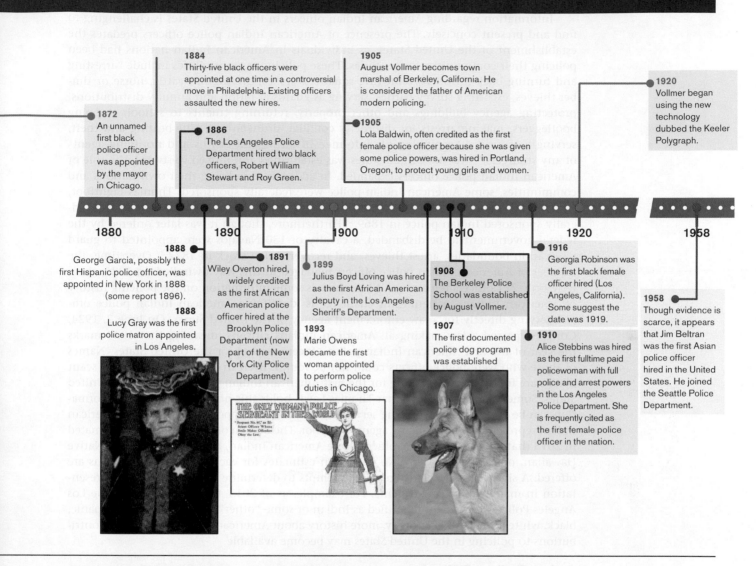

1872
An unnamed first black police officer was appointed by the mayor in Chicago.

1884
Thirty-five black officers were appointed at one time in a controversial move in Philadelphia. Existing officers assaulted the new hires.

1886
The Los Angeles Police Department hired two black officers, Robert William Stewart and Roy Green.

1905
August Vollmer becomes town marshal of Berkeley, California. He is considered the father of American modern policing.

1905
Lola Baldwin, often credited as the first female police officer because she was given some police powers, was hired in Portland, Oregon, to protect young girls and women.

1920
Vollmer began using the new technology dubbed the Keeler Polygraph.

1880

1890

1900

1910

1920

1958

1888
George Garcia, possibly the first Hispanic police officer, was appointed in New York in 1888 (some report 1896).

1888
Lucy Gray was the first police matron appointed in Los Angeles.

1891
Wiley Overton hired, widely credited as the first African American police officer hired at the Brooklyn Police Department (now part of the New York City Police Department).

1899
Julius Boyd Loving was hired as the first African American deputy in the Los Angeles Sheriff's Department.

1893
Marie Owens became the first woman appointed to perform police duties in Chicago.

1908
The Berkeley Police School was established by August Vollmer.

1907
The first documented police dog program was established

1916
Georgia Robinson was the first black female officer hired (Los Angeles, California). Some suggest the date was 1919.

1910
Alice Stebbins was hired as the first fulltime paid policewoman with full police and arrest powers in the Los Angeles Police Department. She is frequently cited as the first female police officer in the nation.

1958
Though evidence is scarce, it appears that Jim Beltran was the first Asian police officer hired in the United States. He joined the Seattle Police Department.

THE ONLY WOMAN POLICE SERGEANT IN THE WORLD
"Sergeant No. 917," an Efficient Officer Whose Smile Makes Offenders Obey the Law.

1907: © iStockphoto.com/anopdesignstock; 1920: Library of Congress.

Hispanics during the expansion of the United States,[33] there is less information about the first Hispanic police officers. Some report that the first Hispanic police officer was appointed to what is now the New York City Police Department. George Garcia became a police officer in New York in 1888 (some sources report it as 1896). No additional information regarding this officer can be located. A search suggests that the first Hispanic police officer killed in the line of duty was Manuel Garcia y Griego. He was shot and killed on June 24, 1868, in Albuquerque, New Mexico. New Mexico became a state in 1912; consequently, it remains unclear who was the first Hispanic officer killed in the line of duty in the United States proper. Sadly, searches for information about Hispanics and policing are rich with incidents of police brutality *against* Hispanics,[34] and less rich with information about Hispanics as officers. Nationally in 2013, 11.6% of all local police officers were Hispanic or Latino, which corresponds to an estimated 55,000 officers. In contrast, in 1987 only 4.5% of officers were Hispanic.[35] Still, the proportion of Latino officers varies by place. At last report, about 6.5% of Philadelphia police officers were Hispanic.[36] In contrast, as of 2013, 43.6% of officers in the Los Angeles Police Department were Latino.

American Indian Police Officers

Information regarding American Indian officers in the United States is challenging to find and present concisely. The presence of American Indian police officers predates the establishment of the United States, as individuals in American Indian nations had been policing their communities for centuries. These policing responsibilities include "arresting and turning back intruders, removing squatters' stakes, driving out cattle, horse or timber thieves, escorting survey parties, serving as guards at ration and annuity distributions, protecting agency buildings and other property, returning truants to school, stopping bootleggers, making arrests for disorderly conduct, drunkenness, wife-beating and theft, serving as couriers, keeping agents informed of births and deaths and notifying agents of any strangers."[37] As the United States was established and moved westward, the role of American Indian police officers expanded. In addition to policing their own nations and communities, some American Indian police were federally sponsored. Thomas Lightfoot, working in Nebraska as a United States Indian agent, reported the establishment of a federally sponsored Indian police in 1869.[38] Furthermore, though it was later ordered by the federal government to be disbanded, a cavalry of 130 Navajos were appointed to guard reservation boundaries, arrest thieves, and recover stolen stock in 1872.[39] Over time, the number of American Indian police officers managed in this way dwindled. In 1925, there were only 271 officers remaining. While there is some information on the policing history of American Indians, a significant challenge is identifying American Indian police officers serving directly for a law enforcement agency of the United States. On June 2, 1924, Congress passed a law making all American Indians citizens, meaning that 1924 marks the year of the first American Indian police officers serving for the United States. Names of those who were police officers could not be found. Even in contemporary times, scant details are found when searching for the first American Indian police officer in the United States. Some literature suggests that Thomas Lewis holds this honor. However, no information can be located as to where he served or when he was appointed. Currently American Indian representation in policing agencies is poor. The Bureau of Justice Statistics estimated in 2013 that about 14,000 local officers were American Indian, Alaska Native Asian, Native Hawaiian, or Pacific Islander.[40] No details on estimates for each of these populations are offered. A similar lack of clarity plagues attempts to determine American Indian representation in major police departments. For example, as of 2013, 0.8% of officers in the Los Angeles Police Department identified as Indian or some "other" race (other than Hispanic, black, white, or Asian). Eventually, more history about American Indian individuals contributions to policing in the United States may become available.

Asian Police Officers

Finding information about Asian police officers serving in the United States in the literature is challenging as well. Jim Beltran reportedly became the first Asian police officer in the United States when he joined the Seattle Police Department in 1958. Some report that Beltran served only a few years as an officer before moving on to other interests in life. No additional information on Officer Beltran and his accomplishments can be located. There are national organizations, such as the National Asian Peace Officers' Association (NAPOA), from which additional information about Asian officers is available.[41] This national organization serves members of the law enforcement community who identify with or share interest in Asian culture and heritage. According to NAPOA executive director Thomas Masters, Harry Lee, the son of Chinese immigrants, was the first Asian American sheriff of Jefferson Parish, Louisiana, when appointed in 1979.[42] Masters's information highlights the progressive nature of San Francisco, being one of the first cities to hire Asians as officers and for higher level positions. From 1996 until his retirement in 2002, Fred H. Lau served as chief of police in San Francisco, making him the first Asian American police chief of a major U.S. city. Lau had begun his career in 1970, when he entered the San Francisco Police Academy as the first Asian enrolled. As police chief, Lau oversaw a force of more than 2,000 members. Not long thereafter, San Francisco was also the first major city to appoint a female police chief, when Heather Fong served in this capacity from 2004 to 2009. In more recent times, the percentage of Asian police officers continues to be low, and poorly estimated, across the United States. As noted above, it was estimated in 2013 that about 14,000 local officers were American Indian, Alaska Native Asian, Native Hawaiian, or Pacific Islander, though details on each group are not offered.[43] During the same year, 9.4% of law enforcement officers in the Los Angeles Police Department were identified as Asian. Even fewer are found in the Philadelphia Police Department, which reports that Asians make up some unknown proportion of the 1.5% of their officers described as "other" (meaning not white, black, or Hispanic/Latino).

LGBTQ Police Officers

While there have always been lesbian, gay, bisexual, transgender, and queer/questioning (LGBTQ) police officers, being openly homosexual as an officer was unusual in the past, as law enforcement has been, and continues to be, characterized as homophobic (although slightly more tolerant of lesbian than gay officers). Signs of change are evident, and more recently LGBTQ officers are coming out in larger numbers. For example, an estimated 100 open and about 3,000 closeted LGBTQ police officers are employed in the New York City Police Department. Additionally, more than 200 primarily closeted LGBTQ officers work in Southern California. Clearly estimating the number of LGBTQ officers is extremely challenging, whether in a local police agency or nationally, given the stigmatization that continues to be attached to this identification. Still, the number of those coming out is growing.

LGBTQ officers, and support of the LGBTQ community is one way that policing has changed over time.

Several organizations have been established that cater to the needs of LGBTQ law enforcement officers. For example, there exists a Lesbian and Gay Peace Officers Association in Austin, Texas; the Southern California Chapter of the Golden State Peace Officers Association; Law Enforcement Gays and Lesbians in Florid; and chapters of the Gay Officers Action League in the New York Police Department, Chicago, Iowa, Michigan, and other locations. The first World LGBTQ Conference for Criminal Justice Professionals was held in August 2016. In addition to the support provided by these groups, several media outlets have been established to support LGBTQ officers. Prominent outlets include Blue Pride (www.bluepride.org). Gregory Miraglia is an openly gay former officer who is a frequent speaker about LGBTQ issues in policing. When Miraglia became an officer in the early 1980s, it was instantly clear to him that being an openly gay man would not be tolerated. He kept his identity hidden until 2004 and has since been active in media interviews, writing, and speaking on the topic. In addition, he continues his work to "inspire and support gay, lesbian, bisexual, and transgender members of law enforcement who are closeted or in the process of coming out."[44] His goal is to eradicate homophobia in law enforcement.

UNREST IN POLICING (1960s AND 1970s)

By the time the 1960s rolled around, professionalism in policing in the United States had improved dramatically (Figure 4.2). Officers were trained, and hiring was no longer based on the political patronage system. Still, this era showed that much remained to be accomplished in policing. The 1960s was a period of civil unrest in the United States. The civil rights movement was in full effect as African Americans worked toward securing equal rights through peaceful and sometimes not so peaceful demonstrations. Riots became more commonplace, and too frequently these gatherings led to violence with the police. African Americans had long been segregated into ghettos and forced to attend separate schools, had few employment opportunities, and were routinely discriminated against at the voting booth. The civil rights movement frequently was countered with excessive use of force by officers, resulting in violent interactions between police and citizens.

Legislative Changes

Several legislative changes directly affecting policing occurred during this decade. Rights were expanded through legislation including the Civil Rights Act of 1964 and the Voting Rights Act of 1965. The Civil Rights Act was initially called for by President John F. Kennedy. This important piece of legislation, signed by President Lyndon B. Johnson, outlawed discrimination against racial, ethnic, national, and religious minorities and women. The act stopped the unequal application of voter registration requirements and racial segregation in schools, the workplace, and general public facilities (e.g., separate white and black drinking fountains). Initially the powers available to enforce the Civil Rights Act were weak; however, later legislation supplemented them. The Voting Rights Act, also signed by President Johnson, outlawed discriminatory practices that led to widespread disenfranchisement of blacks. It specifically sought to end the use of **literacy tests** to register to vote. It established federal oversight of election administration, which meant that states with histories of discriminatory practices could not change anything that affected voting without the approval of the Department of Justice. Even today, states such as Texas are considered **covered jurisdictions** requiring federal oversight given historical discrimination.

Additional challenges presented themselves to policing following publication of *The Challenge of Crime in a Free Society* (1967).[45] This work called for increasing educational requirements to college levels and improved training programs, techniques, and facilities for policing. Recommendations included the modernization of recruitment and promotion to reflect education, personality, and performance. In addition, the need for improved community relationships with an emphasis on improving relations between the police and the poor, minorities, and juveniles was outlined. An effort to recruit more minorities and improve officer supervision and discipline was called for in this report in an effort to reduce crime rates.

Another problem characterizing the 1960s was high rates of crime and the perceived lack of control over the sale and possession of firearms. In response, Congress enacted the **Omnibus Crime Control and Safe Streets Act of 1968.** The act accomplished four primary criminal justice improvements. First, it established the Law Enforcement Assistance Administration and charged it with assisting states and local jurisdictions in preventing and reducing crime and improving the function of their criminal justice systems (Figure 4.3). Second, it addressed the admissibility of confessions in criminal trials. Third, the act established rules for obtaining wiretap orders by police agencies.[46] Finally, it included provisions that regulated firearm sales and possession. Clearly, these provisions affected policing and the interaction of officers with the public. By the end of the 1970s, significant progress in developing more efficient and professional policing had been made.

Canine Police Officers

Canines have served proud and important roles in law enforcement for centuries. While unofficially dogs have worked alongside human policing agents for thousands of years, history points to 1899 in Belgium as the beginning of canines' official relationship with law enforcement.[47] A dog training program was established in Ghent, and before the year ended, 37 trained dogs were working on police forces assisting officers on night patrols. Not long after, in 1907, the first documented police dog programs were established in the United States. One program was located in South Orange, New Jersey, and the other in New York City.[48] Like their predecessors, these trained dogs were used on night patrols with the goal of deterring burglaries and thefts. Though the canines proved successful, the use of dogs did not become widespread. Between 1907 and 1952, only 14 police dog programs operated (and many closed shortly thereafter) in the United States. Most of

Journal:
Canine sniffs and policing the drug war

literacy tests:
Tests used to deny African Americans the right to vote.

covered jurisdictions:
States, cities, or counties that must submit proposed voting changes to the U.S. Department of Justice because of their histories of discrimination against minority voters.

Omnibus Crime Control and Safe Streets Act of 1968: An act that established agencies and rules dealing with crime.

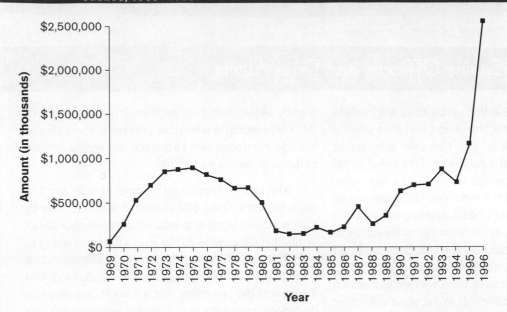

Figure 4.3 ■ Budgets for Law Enforcement Assistance Administration/Office of Justice, 1969–1996

Budgets since the creation of the Law Enforcement Assistance Administration/Office of Justice have increased to deal with criminal justice issues. Do you feel that using taxpayer dollars to fight crime is appropriate? Why or why not?

Source: *Preventing Crime: What Works, What Doesn't, What's Promising: A Report to the United States Congress.* Prepared for the National Institute of Justice by Lawrence W. Sherman, Denise Gottfredson, Doris MacKenzie, John Eck, Peter Reuter, and Shawn Bushway in collaboration with members of the Graduate Program Department of Criminology and Criminal Justice University of Maryland.

Note: most recent data available.

these training programs were located in the northeast corridor, though Berkeley, California, also trained and used police dogs.[49] Beginning in the mid-1900s, police dog programs gained in popularity. By 1960, there were 44 canine units that had been started, and by the end of the decade, 350 programs existed.[50]

During the civil rights movement of the 1960s, support for police dogs waned. For many people, canine officers came to represent aggressive and violent attitudes toward civil rights protesters and African Americans in general. One significant incident leading to decreased public support occurred in Wichita, Kansas, in 1961. Police released dogs during a riot by youth outside a theater. Perhaps the most iconic incident occurred in 1963 in Birmingham, Alabama, which at the time was one of the most racially divided cities in the nation. During a peaceful civil rights protest led by Dr. Martin Luther King, Jr., a young man in the crowd was "downed" by a police dog. Nearly 200 black protesters attempted to help the man, and in response, Birmingham Police Commissioner "Bull" Connor gave the order to use the dogs (and high-pressure water hoses) on the entire crowd, including children and bystanders.[51]

Today, general sentiment regarding police dogs is positive. Canine police officers offer an effective nonlethal method of deterring and detecting crime. Presently, police dogs are trained to search buildings and areas for explosives, evidence (such as firearms), narcotics, chemicals, illegally taken game, and human remains. Police dogs also help locate missing

Ostermann, retired ATF canine law enforcement officer. What role might other animals play in law enforcement?

Audio:
In the digital age, Connecticut state police K-9 unit trains Edogs

COMMON MISCONCEPTIONS

Infallibility of Canine Officers and Drug Alerts

Many people believe that police dogs are infallible when it comes to detecting drugs and that when a drug dog "hits" or "alerts," one has solid evidence of the presence of illegal substances. This belief is not surprising given the incredible sensitivity of a dog's nose, which is thought to be, at a minimum, 1,000 times more sensitive than a human's nose. Alerting by a canine officer is directly tied to law enforcement's ability to conduct warrantless searches. The U.S. Supreme Court has ruled that a canine's alert for narcotics is sufficient to establish probable cause for a warrantless search of a vehicle and the individuals in the vehicle. In other words, a dog's alert may mean the difference between having one's car, luggage, bags, pockets, and other items searched without warrant and not having these searched.

So how accurate are police dogs when it comes to alerting on drugs? Findings vary, but some research suggests that they are not terribly accurate. For example, in a 2007–2008 examination of the Illinois State Police canine unit, slightly fewer than 26% of the alerts by police dogs resulted in uncovering drugs. A similar study in the suburbs of Chicago revealed a slightly better outcome: an overall accuracy rate of 44%. Interestingly, when the officers in the Chicago suburbs interfaced with Hispanics, the accuracy rates of the dogs were a mere 27%.

Why is this happening? Some people say the dogs, though trained, often respond to subtle cues by their handlers. In other words, officers intentionally or unintentionally provide subtle cues prompting a dog to alert. This lack of accuracy and the ease with which one could subtly cue a drug dog to alert is disturbing. And it suggests the possibility that a few officers may use drug dogs improperly to provide law enforcement with legal cover to conduct a search.

Think About It

1. Given that dogs fall short of perfection in these situations, should they not be used? Why or why not?

2. What approach would be infallible?

3. Do you believe officers would intentionally provide cues to a dog to alert? Why or why not?

persons and track and capture criminals using minimal force. Canine units are often outfitted with their own bulletproof vests, identification, and police badges. Law enforcement agencies provide trading cards with police dogs' photos and their statistics. Intentionally injuring or killing a K-9 is a felony in most jurisdictions. Canine officers are retired if they become pregnant, are raising puppies, or are too old, sick, or seriously injured. When a canine officer is killed in the line of duty, he or she is given a police funeral with the same honors afforded a human officer killed.

POLICING AS MORE THAN LAW ENFORCEMENT

Author Video:
The role of police over time

Following the tumult of the 1960s and 1970s, policing became relatively calmer. Although since the 1980s, policing remained controversial, civil unrest was reduced and working conditions for officers improved. One reason for this improvement was the proliferation of police unions. Unions bargained and won greater benefits and salary for officers. They also forced policing administrators to negotiate with unions before making personnel decisions.

Another important change that occurred around this time was the renewed call that policing be more than a law enforcement role. Many argue that policing should become more connected to the community. Officers should focus on being polite, courteous, and helpful, not just on being social control agents. This perspective harks back to Vollmer's calls almost 100 years ago that officers be more than enforcers, that they be social workers as well. Regardless of the role law enforcement officers take, today there are many officers in the United States (Figure 4.4).

CHAPTER WRAP-UP

This chapter presented a history of policing in the United States through the early 1970s. This overview included discussion of the British system, which heavily influenced practices in the United States in its early history and today. We learned that policing began as an unprofessional, untrained, and all too often corrupt and cruel occupation. With the growth and increasing heterogeneity of the population, it became clear that policing by community consensus was untenable, and calls for training and education mounted. The influence of visionaries such as August Vollmer and those at the IACP, in addition

---

Figure 4.4 ■ Full-Time Sworn Personnel per 100,000 Residents Employed by State and Local Law Enforcement Agencies

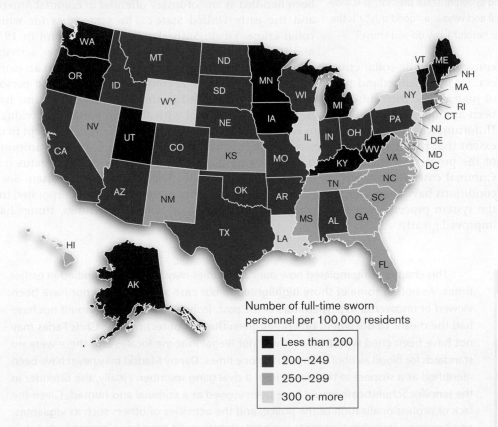

Number of full-time sworn personnel per 100,000 residents

- Less than 200
- 200–249
- 250–299
- 300 or more

When last estimated, Wyoming, Louisiana, Illinois, and New York had the highest rates of full-time sworn officers per 100,000 residents. What difference would more or fewer police officers make on crime rates? Or feelings of safety by residents? Why?

Source: Figure 4 from *Census of State and Local Law Enforcement Agencies, 2008.* Brian Reaves. July 2011. U.S. Department of Justice, Office of Justice Programs, Bureau of Justice Statistics.

Note: Most recent data available.

EPS 10

Policing cybercrime is one way policing has changed over time. What challenges does policing cybercriminals present? Is it easy to determine who is a criminal and who is a "good guy"? Is the group Anonymous criminal or heroic? How do you know?

Video 4.3:
Changes in law enforcement

to the availability of technology, resulted in continual professionalization of policing. The 1960s and 1970s demonstrated that while policing had become more professional and honorable than it once was, great progress was still needed. Through a variety of crime commissions, research, and the support of policymakers, policing has become professional and approaches now depend on serving the community and using intelligence to be efficient and effective.

Conspicuously missing from this chapter is direct attention to cybercrime, terrorism, white-collar crime, and victims. This is not an oversight, but rather reflects the history of policing though the 1970s. Much has changed in terms of society, technology, and the criminal justice system over time. The Internet and widespread use of personal computers were far in the future, meaning that cybercrime was unheard of in the early United States (and even later into the 20th century). Terrorism, as conceived of today, was also unimagined. These individuals lacked the access to technology (e.g., jetliners) to create the scale of terror possible today. An individual committing crimes who today would be considered a terrorist would have been handled as any ordinary offender in colonial America and the early United States. The same goes for white-collar crime. Edwin Sutherland coined the term in 1939, and those engaging in embezzlement or other activities considered white-collar crime likely were treated the same as other criminals in an earlier era. Or if, as Sutherland proposed, white-collar crime is committed by respected persons of high status, their misdeeds were entirely overlooked in the past. Clearly, victims have been around since colonial times. How did police deal with these important individuals? Unfortunately, in the past, victims were ignored by the criminal justice system except to the extent that they served as witnesses to crimes. They had no rights and were not informed of the progress of their cases. In fact, viewing it as "their case" was not the status quo. Criminal cases were viewed as crimes against the state. The victim was forgotten. Social conditions have changed in recent decades as victims are more integrally incorporated into the system process. While not perfect, at least compared with earlier times, things have improved greatly.

CASE STUDY

This chapter contemplated how our case studies may have been handled in earlier times. As noted, some of those highlighted in our case studies would not have been viewed or uncovered as perpetrators in the past. Joshua Paul Benjamin would not have had the means to document his crimes given the lack of technology. Chris Farias may not have been cited with DUI, as it was not illegal in some locales and there were no standards for blood alcohol content in bygone times. Danny Madrid may never have been identified as a suspect in the shooting of a rival gang member. Finally, the offender in the Jennifer Schuett case would have been viewed as a criminal and hunted. Given the lack of professionalization of the police, and the activities of others such as vigilantes, one can speculate about whether the perpetrator would have been apprehended. It is equally likely that an innocent individual would have been captured and made to pay the price for these crimes. All in all, the case studies highlight the incredible advances in the professionalization of the police and the use of technology in fighting crime. In the next chapter, we focus on policing in recent decades. During this time there has been a reinvigorated approach to policing as more than law enforcement, using approaches such as community-oriented and intelligence-driven policing.

KEY POINTS

- The development of policing has a complex and lengthy historical background that is based on a foundation of British policing.

- The earliest role of security was performed by men in the community and operated on a community consensus model.

- Early officers were appointed by the patronage system, required no training or skills, and were highly corrupt. At times it was difficult to distinguish the officer from the criminal.

- Early police officers performed many functions, such as tax collecting, street sanitation, and law enforcement. In general, tax collecting was their primary focus, as it was the most lucrative.

- Sir Robert Peel is considered the Father of Modern Policing, while August Vollmer is touted as the Father of American Policing.

- Though a few African Americans and women were hired as police officers in the late 1800s, they did not become a substantial portion of police agencies until later in the 20th century.

- The International Association of Chiefs of Police, while getting off to a rocky start, has been responsible for much of the professionalization of policing in the United States. Richard Sylvester was the first president of the IACP and contributed greatly to the professionalization of policing in the United States.

- The victim played virtually no role in the criminal justice system aside from that of witness until recent decades.

- Civil unrest in the 1960s contributed to a negative view of policing as officers were considered to have used excessive force against citizens, especially those engaging in civil rights demonstrations.

- Supreme Court rulings in the 1960s reinforced the right of citizens to be free and equal in the United States. Several rulings handed down during this time period curtailed police powers and enhanced citizen freedoms (e.g., search and seizure, personal rights).

- Government attention to unrest indicated the need for greater training of officers, so the federal government offered money and expertise to state and local jurisdictions to improve policing in their communities.

- Police unions improved policing conditions by improving benefits and salaries.

KEY TERMS

Bobbies 101

Borh 100

Covered Jurisdictions 116

Frankpledge 100

Fugitive Slave Law of 1850 103

Hundred 100

Literacy Tests 116

Metropolitan Police Act of 1829 101

Modus Operandi 106

Omnibus Crime Control and Safe Streets Act of 1968 116

Parish Constable 100

Peelers 101

Peelian Principles 101

Police Matron 109

Sheriffs 100

Shire Reeves 100

Slave Patrol 103

Thief Takers 100

Third Degree 106

Tything or Tithing 100

Vigilantes 103

Watchmen 100

REVIEW QUESTIONS

1. How is a shire reeve associated with a sheriff?

2. Who appointed police officers in colonial times?

3. How have training and the responsibilities of officers changed over time?

4. How have the uses of tools and weapons changed for police officers through history?

5. What cities were leaders in terms of the increasing professionalization of policing over time?

6. How did the civil rights movement influence policing in the United States?

7. What role did women and minorities play in early U.S. policing?

8. What role did canine officers play in early U.S. policing?

9. Where do you see policing going in the future in terms of recruitment, training, and roles?

CRITICAL THINKING MATTERS

1. **Role of Officers.** There is no agreement as to the role or responsibilities of police officers. August Vollmer argued that vice should not be the purview of police and that when police become involved in vice, it erodes public trust in policing. In early times, police gathered slaves and returned them to their captors, which some viewed as outside their responsibilities. Others disagree and believe that the role of police should extend beyond law enforcement responsibilities. What do you believe are the proper roles and responsibilities of police? Given the specific roles and responsibilities you have identified that officers have that they should not, or do not have that they should, how would the expansion and contraction of these policing roles have benefited or hindered officers dealing with the case of Jennifer Schuett? Chris Farias? Joshua Paul Benjamin? Danny Madrid?

2. **Educating Police Officers.** Initially, officers received no training and were frequently corrupt and ill prepared for the responsibilities of being an officer. If you were in charge, what policies would you implement to ensure that your officers were of sound mind and body? Would you require particular psychological exams? What would you seek to uncover that would make a candidate unsuitable? Or suitable? What type of education should be required of police officers? What are the three most important skills you believe your officers should possess? What specific training would you require? Is physical fitness mandatory? Would you pay more for officers trained according to your policies? Are there particular places you would recruit the type of officer you envision for your police agency? Which of these skills would be most important in dealing with the Schuett, Farias, Benjamin, and Madrid cases? Why? Which of these skills are least important in dealing with the case studies? Why?

3. **Minorities in Policing.** Diversity in policing is problematic. Is having a diverse police department important? Why or why not? If diversity should not be a concern, would you be okay with a police force that is 100% female? One hundred percent black? Or 100% Hispanic? Should we celebrate and seek diversity? Does it enhance the job of officers? Or create more trouble? What do you mean by diversity? Is it race, ethnicity, gender, age, income, able-bodiedness, socioeconomic class? Is being bilingual (or more) important? What accounts for the lack of parity in women and officers of color found in many departments today? What, if anything, should be done to remedy this? Do the highlighted case studies in the text influence your beliefs about having a diverse police force?

4. **Canine Officers.** Are canine police officers an appropriate tool in law enforcement? Has the way they have been used over time been appropriate? Is it appropriate to punish those who harm a canine officer severely? If you were a police chief, what policy would you implement regarding canine officers and penalties associated with their work?

5. **Proper Role of Victims.** In the past, victims were a forgotten part of the criminal justice system. More recently, they have been incorporated into the

process as more than just witnesses. Do you think victims should be treated any differently than other witnesses to crimes? Do you think that victims deserve special rights? Why or why not? Should the government assist victims of crime emotionally, psychologically, materially, and financially? Why or why not? Thinking about Jennifer Schuett, what, if anything, should the city, state, or federal government have done for her to help her cope with her victimization? Why? And what of offenders such as Joshua Paul Benjamin? What should the criminal justice system do for him to assist him in coping with his crimes? Why?

6. **Dealing With White-Collar Crime, Terrorism, and Cybercrime.** In colonial America there was no such thing as white-collar crime, terrorism, or cybercrime. Or was there? Were these sorts of crimes committed but viewed as ordinary crime? Or were such crimes impossible decades ago? Do you believe these sorts of crimes get special attention today? If so, is that special attention deserved? Should penalties for such crimes be enhanced, or should these criminals be treated as ordinary street criminals?

DIGITAL RESOURCES

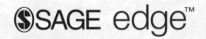

Sharpen your skills with SAGE edge at edge.sagepub.com/rennison2e. SAGE edge for Students provides a personalized approach to help you accomplish your coursework goals in an easy-to-use learning environment. You'll find action plans, mobile-friendly eFlashcards, and quizzes as well as video and web resources and links to SAGE journal articles to support and expand on the concepts presented in this chapter.

5

ON THE STREETS

ORGANIZATION, RESPONSIBILITIES, AND CHALLENGES

> "Considerable progress has been made in American policing since the great institution-building phase in the mid-1800s. Improved standards for the recruitment and selection of police officers, as well as their corresponding training have resulted in largely professional police officers who are asked to do what amounts to an impossible job."
>
> —Andrew Giacomazzi (2004)

LEARNING OBJECTIVES

After finishing this chapter, you should be able to:

5.1 Describe the organization and structure of a typical police department and summarize the responsibilities of patrol.

5.2 Discuss public perceptions of how and when police officers decide to use lethal force and how they differ from reality.

5.3 Identify unique characteristics of the subculture of policing.

5.4 Differentiate community policing from traditional approaches.

5.5 Discuss the main tenets of intelligence-led/evidence-based policing.

5.6 Summarize the relationship between the use of force by an officer and a suspect's behavior.

5.7 Prepare arguments for and against the use of new technologies in police work.

INTRODUCTION: CONTEMPORARY POLICING

Policing from the 1970s through the 1990s remained turbulent, and numerous attempts were made to improve the reputation of law enforcement across the country. Reform efforts included blue-ribbon panels assembled to examine problematic departmental practices. In 1972, the Knapp Commission reported that more than half of the police officers in the New York Police Department (NYPD) engaged in corruption. The commission developed primarily from the famous case of whistle-blower Frank Serpico, an NYPD officer who reported to the press evidence of widespread corruption in the agency that reached the highest ranks. The Knapp Commission dismissed the idea of the **rotten apple theory**, that is, that only a few officers were engaging in misconduct. The bad apple perspective, according to the commission, presented a problem easily remedied, and members of the panel saw serious issues requiring widespread reform. The infamous report identified **grass-eaters** as officers who were passive participants, accepting bribery and corruption, and those who knew but chose not to act. The **meat-eaters** were officers who actively engaged in corruption. Years later, the Christopher Commission was formed after the beating of Rodney King by officers from the Los Angeles Police Department (LAPD). That commission noted the rampant racism and bias in the LAPD and demanded that measures be taken at all levels to ensure accountability. The problems encountered in the major scandals in large city departments, however, fail to reflect the majority of urban and rural agencies that serve the public with integrity.

The primary mission of most police agencies is to enhance our quality of life by means of enforcing laws, preventing crimes, and arresting suspects while upholding core values. A quick glance at a police vehicle may show that it has "to serve and protect" emblazoned on the side. Organizational core values often focus on policing ideals such as *respect* for the law and community, *dedication* to service and professionalism, and *responsibility* for public safety and ethical conduct. We expect police officers to catch the "bad guys" and keep us safe from harm, which represents only a small segment of law enforcement duties.

Few people want to see flashing red and blue lights in their rearview mirrors. The instant reaction, for most of us, when a police car pulls in behind us is one of apprehension. "Oops, was I speeding? Are my brake lights working? Does the officer know I haven't paid my last 15 parking tickets?" Any number of worst-case scenarios may cause trepidation when we see a police officer. Rarely do we internalize feelings of pride and safety when followed by a police vehicle, which in an ideal world should be the case—unless, of course, you're breaking the law. Overall, the image of police officers as the enforcers of public order sanctioned by the government to use force is a small part of the goals and mission of law enforcement. In fact, patrol officers devote an estimated 80% of their time to duties other than what we view as traditional law enforcement.

In the late 1980s, policing underwent significant transformation as the philosophy of community policing spread among law enforcement agencies throughout the United States. An increase in professionalism in policing, as noted in the quotation at the beginning of this chapter, recognized law enforcement as more than just an occupation. The changes in policing increased citizen expectations of what local law enforcement can and should provide in terms of crime prevention. As criminologist and policing expert Andrew Giacomazzi notes, we have high expectations of line-level officers: They must provide efficient and effective responses to calls, settle disputes, partner with the community in problem-solving efforts, educate the public, and prevent crime. As you will see in this chapter, technology and new approaches offer the means and methods for accomplishing law enforcement goals in the 21st century.

THE POLICE ORGANIZATION

Web:
Department of Justice organization, mission, and functions manual

State and local law enforcement agencies provide a variety of services to large cities, small towns, counties, and all areas in between. Additionally, a huge variety of federal law enforcement agencies are housed in the Department of Homeland Security and the Department of Justice (DOJ) (see Figures 5.1 and 5.2), for example:

- Department of Homeland Security
  - U.S. Customs and Border Protection
  - U.S. Immigration and Customs Enforcement
  - U.S. Secret Service
- Department of Justice
  - Federal Bureau of Investigation
  - Drug Enforcement Administration
  - Bureau of Alcohol, Tobacco, Firearms, and Explosives
  - U.S. Marshals Service

rotten apple theory:
The idea that corruption in most police departments can be traced to just a few officers.

grass-eaters: Identified by the Knapp Commission as officers who acted as passive participants when others were engaging in bribery and corruption.

meat-eaters:
Identified by the Knapp Commission as officers who actively engaged in corrupt activities.

The number and types of state and local law enforcement agencies vary by jurisdiction and may include sheriff's offices, state highway patrols, university campus police, and city police departments. Typically, images of policing focus on large, well-known departments like those in New York, Chicago, Philadelphia, Los Angeles, and Baltimore. In fact, the NYPD is the largest department in the United States, with more than 37,000 officers.

Figure 5.1 ■ Homeland Security Organizational Chart

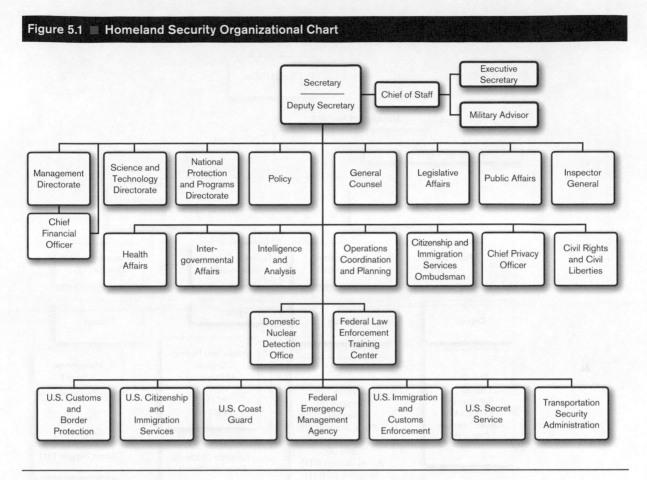

Source: U.S. Department of Homeland Security.

The Los Angeles County Sheriff's Department employs more than 8,000 sworn officers and about 7,000 nonsworn positions. The majority of agencies, however, are small. In the United States, local police departments represent more than two thirds of the approximately 18,000 state and local law enforcement agencies. Almost 50% of these agencies employ 10 or fewer full-time officers.[1]

The organization of each department varies, although almost all are structured under a paramilitary framework with a distinct chain of command. Though command structures vary, the police chief ultimately is responsible for everything that occurs in a department. Higher-level staff, depending on the organization, may include ranks such as deputy chiefs, division chiefs, commanders, and lieutenants. Figure 5.2 shows a basic organizational chart with positions and divisions for a small department. Many departments are organized with the following command and control structure from the top down: chief of police, deputy chief, captain, lieutenant, sergeant, corporal or technician, and officer.

Police departments are civil service organizations, and promotional opportunities usually require rising through the ranks. In other words, time-in-rank systems require an officer to experience lower level positions before moving up the ladder. A patrol officer, for example, will not become a lieutenant until he or she serves at the lower rank of sergeant. The promotional process may include written and oral testing, further background checks, and interviews.

Figure 5.2 ■ Police Department Organizational Chart

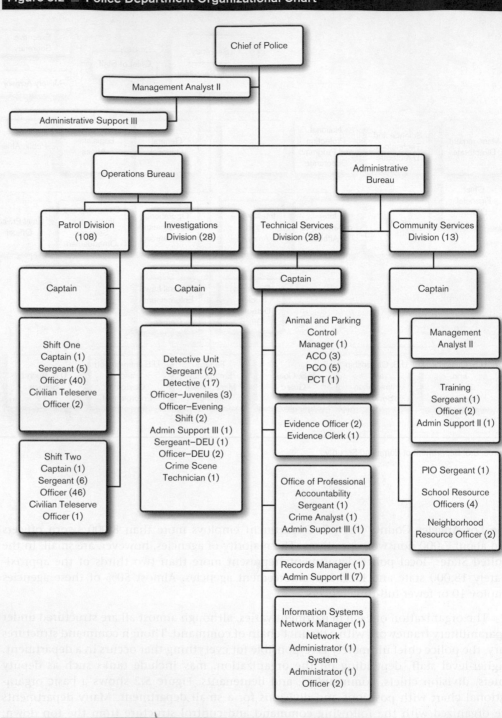

Source: Reprinted with permission from the City of Lawrence, Kansas, Police Department.

Becoming a Police Officer

Video 5.1:
Police officer recruitment and work

The process of becoming a police officer involves many steps as candidates go through interviewing, testing, and screening. Applicants must meet all minimum qualifications, such as age, education, and background (e.g., no history of illegal behavior). Almost all departments require a high school diploma, and some require a 2- or 4-year college degree. A more recent movement in education involves creating specialized police graduate programs that focus on professionalism, research, and leadership.[2] Testing includes written examination focusing on reasoning, basic math, and language. Applicants also must complete physical fitness testing, oral exams, polygraphs, and character investigations. Other procedures involve medical and drug screenings and psychological evaluations. Selected applicants attend a police academy for Police Officer Standards and Training certification and then enter a field-training program. The process may take several months before an actual hire is made.

THE POLICE ROLE

Police officers are considered the gatekeepers of the criminal justice system. In other words, they are given a high level of **discretion** on when to write a ticket or make an arrest. In cases of serious crimes when offenders are present or known, undoubtedly officers will make arrests. In the case of a minor illegal act (e.g., loitering, drinking in public, possessing a small amount of marijuana), an officer may decide to issue a warning or ignore the behavior. Discretion is found throughout the criminal justice system and can be a useful tool for police officers when applied properly.

New York City's top cop: James P. O'Neill, police commissioner. What special challenges does the chief of a large urban department face compared with the chief of a smaller agency?

Journal:
Organizational-level
police discretion

Patrol

Patrol is the backbone of all police agencies. Patrol officers are responsible for preventing crime, apprehending suspects, and assisting community members. A typical day may include any or all of the following:

- maintaining police presence
- ensuring public order
- providing help to individuals who may need assistance
- identifying and apprehending suspects
- finding lost children
- directing traffic
- issuing traffic tickets
- chasing fleeing felons
- responding to criminal events

Officers assigned to patrol are engaging in numerous activities and different styles of policing. Activities may be *proactive* or *reactive*, terms first introduced by researchers Albert Reiss and David Bordua.[3] **Reactive policing** is generally a response to a call for service rather than a self-initiated action. Typically, officers patrol the streets in their vehicles until they receive a dispatch call (call for service) to respond to a crime scene or problematic incident. In many communities, because of a large influx of federal money in the early 1990s, **proactive policing** efforts that involve crime prevention activities are popular.

discretion: It allows police and others throughout the criminal justice system the latitude to make an arrest (or other action) or not.

patrol: Patrol officers are responsible for preventing crime, apprehending suspects, and assisting community members.

reactive policing: A traditional style of policing relying on responding to calls for services.

proactive policing: Self-initiated officer activities to prevent and detect crime.

In the case of Chris Farias, patrol officers stopped him for driving his motorcycle slowly on a cold night. His driving behavior established the initial probable cause for the police stop. After a brief conversation, the officers believed Chris was intoxicated and asked him to take a field sobriety test. Chris, who had previous charges, knew that he was within his rights to refuse the voluntary test, which is true in the majority of states. His refusal to take the test resulted in his arrest for the suspicion of driving while intoxicated, and he was read his Miranda rights. At the police station he was booked and required to undergo a chemical test. This type of test may be conducted through blood or urine analysis. The penalties for driving under the influence, as we will see when Chris goes to court, are severe. Overall, a common DUI stop involves many procedures, lots of paperwork, and considerable time investment for officers. For the suspect, a DUI entails a costly entanglement with the criminal justice system and the potential loss of many freedoms. These losses, however, are minimal compared with the potential of dealing with the knowledge that a person was injured or killed because of an offender's lack of judgment.

Gina Ferazzi/Los Angeles Times via Getty Images

Extended training opportunities make SWAT a popular assignment. Should qualifications for SWAT positions be different for men and women? Why or why not?

Video 5.2:
Patrol duties and challenges

Police officers' activities go beyond routine patrol and require a wide range of skills. Officers assist community members, write citations, direct traffic, and serve as escorts. Radio calls may involve investigating complaints, interceding in disturbances, dealing with traffic collisions, and administering first aid. Police officers also watch for suspicious activities, search for wanted persons, and make arrests. Officers assist in criminal investigation, collect and preserve evidence, serve warrants, and appear in court proceedings. An officer's duties vary and may be demanding physically and psychologically. Report writing and desk work use other important skills taught in college criminal justice programs and police academies.

A large number of job opportunities exist in small and large police departments: training and firearms instructors, mounted horseback, motorcycle, bicycle patrols, canine units, and special weapons and tactics (SWAT) teams. Many departments have created positions for school resource officers, who work directly with students in partnership with public schools. Also, the increased use of nonsworn personnel has opened positions in statistical analysis, victim advocacy, and certain types of investigative functions.

Investigation

Investigative positions and special assignments in policing are highly sought after and generally require several years of experience on patrol. These assignments often are rotated and may require testing and interviewing. Special assignments for sworn officers include, for example, detectives, vice and narcotics, sexual assault, and cybercrime investigation. Detectives work as plainclothes officers in a variety of tasks and may specialize in a particular area. A homicide detective, for example, oversees and conducts an entire murder investigation from the initial crime scene investigation to solving the case through interviews, forensics, and arrest. Detectives also work closely with district attorney's offices when prosecuting a case.

Each crime scene is unique, and law enforcement and first responders protect and preserve physical evidence that can be collected and scientifically analyzed. According to a report from the National Institute of Justice, the initial on-scene officer(s) is responsible for the following:

1. Logging dispatch information
2. Watching for persons or vehicles leaving the crime scene

COMMON MISCONCEPTIONS

Understanding Police Use of Force

Public perception of how and when police officers decide to use lethal force is often skewed. Citizens may wonder why an officer involved in a lethal force incident "didn't just shoot the person in the leg, arm, or hand." Officers are trained to shoot center mass. Attempts to "wound" an armed dangerous suspect would endanger officers and, at times, the public. Most officers end their careers without ever using a service revolver, and the decision to shoot a suspect is extremely difficult. The media or videos of police shootings influence public perceptions of the use of force, although the representations often fail to reflect what really happened. Often, what we see is edited or framed in a way to make the officer look bad. The other missing aspect is what is seen from the officer's perspective. Police officers facing encounters with armed suspects, including guns and knives, must make split-second decisions on how to best handle the situations.

Think About It

1. How might body cameras worn by officers change our perceptions of police shootings?

2. Police officers in the United Kingdom are generally unarmed. How do you feel this influences the public's view of police officers? Why?

3. How would you explain to a friend why police officers shoot center mass instead of attempting to wound a suspect? Do you think this is the best policy? What policy would you implement?

3. Approaching cautiously and scanning the entire area and noting possible secondary crime scenes

4. Making initial observations to assess the scene and ensure officer safety

5. Remaining alert and attentive (i.e., assume the crime is ongoing until determined otherwise)[4]

CASE STUDY

The investigation of Jennifer Schuett's case presented numerous challenges for the initial detectives and later for the cold case investigation. Patrol officers responded to the dispatch call, which included an ambulance, then a helicopter, though no one knew if Jennifer was alive or dead. The field where she was found became the primary crime scene, though a patrol officer later found the suspect's soiled underwear in a roadside ditch several miles away from where Jennifer's battered body was discovered. The original detectives' case files, fortunately, were complete and offered enormous assistance to the investigation years later. In addition, the evidence was handled and preserved properly. These elements were key in solving the case eventually.

The first concern in Jennifer's case was ensuring that she received medical attention while minimizing contamination of the scene. The processing of the scene begins after the initial response, documentation, and evaluation. Detectives, patrol, forensic specialists, and other nonsworn personnel engaged in specialized tasks during the investigation, such as photography and fingerprinting. While in the hospital, Jennifer was able to give her description of the suspect and the car he was driving to a sketch artist. Her assistance with the investigation was

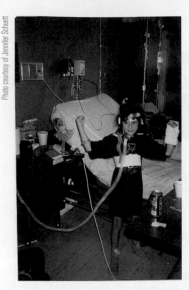

especially remarkable because doctors originally believed she would never speak again. During the attack the assailant had severed her vocal chords. In Jennifer's case, blood and sperm evidence was collected from the clothing, including the suspect's underwear. Unfortunately, DNA technology at the time of the crime was basic, and little more than an identification of the blood type of the assailant could be determined. While this narrowed the list of suspects, it could not identify a primary suspect.

Investigating Joshua Paul Benjamin's crimes was relatively easy. When taken to the police station and questioned, Joshua admitted to his actions and gave officers permission to search his home, where they found videotape evidence of sexual assault against several young male victims. Given Joshua's full cooperation with law enforcement, the investigative phase was simple, although his future entanglements with the criminal justice system were not.

Danny was initially surprised that the police did not contact him immediately following the shooting. In the past when he had committed a crime, they would arrive at his home quickly and aggressively. This time was different. Finally, about five days after the shooting, Danny received a phone call from the police asking him to come to the station. He complied and was interviewed about the shooting. Danny lied his way through that interview and again was surprised when he was allowed to leave. Little did he know, the next day his co-conspirator made a confession and implicated Danny. A few days after that, police officers arrived at his home very early in the morning with a search warrant related to the shooting. Danny was arrested and taken into custody.

Jennifer, though young and unable to speak because her vocal chords had been cut, was able to help the police doing the initial investigation.

First concerns: Preserving the scene and protecting the victim in the Schuett case.

Other special assignments in policing involve undercover work. Vice squads often conduct undercover stings, and plainclothes officers work closely with patrol in the organization and implementation of the operations. Undercover officers may work with confidential informants to set up drug buys. Other stings use minors to buy alcohol and tobacco products. Male vice officers often cruise in unmarked cars in areas known for prostitution and pretend to be johns (i.e., clients) wanting to make financial transactions for sex. In reverse sting operations, female officers pose as prostitutes.[5] During most john stings, decoys stand on street corners waiting for customers to approach and arrange motel deals or around-the-corner rendezvous. When a john drives to a meeting spot or enters a motel room, a patrol officer or special response team makes the arrest. Sting operations are controversial because luring a person into committing a crime may be considered entrapment. Additionally, especially for female officers pretending to be prostitutes, sting operations present a heightened level of danger.

Command

As previously mentioned, the top cop is the chief of police. Strong leadership by the chief and other commanders is essential in establishing respect and high-level organizational functioning. Police chiefs face numerous challenges and must "successfully meet the demands of community members, politicians, members of the organization, unions and police associations, interest groups, and their own executive staff members."[6] Police chiefs often are tasked with negotiating and intervening in tough situations with politicians, citizens, and the rank and file. In most cities, the mayor or city council appoints the police chief, whereas sheriffs are elected. The chief often "serves at the pleasure of the mayor," and his or her employment term is undefined. The tenure of a police chief varies, but the average is about 5 years, though some research shows the average is only 3 years.[7]

Usually, the chief appoints a deputy chief or an assistant chief from high-ranking personnel. In many departments, commanders are appointed positions. Midlevel administrator positions are under the auspices of civil service and include majors and captains, followed by lieutenants. Sergeants are first-level supervisors. The majority of command positions require climbing up through the ranks and completing vigorous testing procedures.

WHO ARE THE POLICE?

Culture

Policing is characterized by a unique subculture. Early research identified several key aspects of the policing subculture related to secrecy, group solidarity, violence, cynicism, masculinity, isolation, and authoritarianism.[8] Some scholars argue that police are acculturated or socialized into the subculture, though other evidence exists that officers bring their own characteristics and values to the job.[9] The policing culture often is criticized for the code of silence, which is said to foster a secretive world that excludes outsiders and interferes with reform efforts. Police culture shapes, drives, and sustains choices and actions—both good and bad.[10]

Web:
Police culture

Police corruption and misconduct is an area that receives a great deal of attention because of the serious implications for departments and communities. Police officers who engage in misbehavior or criminal activities undermine community trust and break their oath to uphold the law on and off duty. Their actions also damage the integrity and legitimacy of the agencies they work for.[11] Research studies have examined and documented cases of perjury, bribery, extortion, robbery, burglary, domestic assault, and brutality.[12] The classifications of misconduct include corruption (illegal abuse of authority), misconduct (breach of department policy), and criminal activity. The amount of misconduct across departments in the United States is impossible to determine, and most of the violations are likely minor infractions. Police corruption is also considered a white-collar

The militarization of policing is causing great concerns among citizens. How does the use of military equipment by local police make the community safer? What are the concerns?

ETHICAL ISSUES

Off-Duty Versus On-Duty Misconduct

Police officers take an oath to uphold the law. Officers swear to be above reproach, both on and off duty, obeying all laws and showing integrity in all aspects of their lives. In many ways, officers' lives are not their own. Proper personal conduct may apply to finances, the use of drugs and alcohol, and Internet postings.

Think About It

Our view that officers uphold the law both on and off duty raises questions.

1. Should an officer who engages in acts of domestic violence be allowed to remain on the force?

2. In some cities, officers maintain the code of silence when a fellow officer is stopped for drunk driving. Should their actions be considered unethical and/or illegal?

3. If you worked in law enforcement, would you report a conduct violation of a fellow officer who is off duty?

4. What types and how serious would the misconduct need to be?

Author Video:
Police culture, victims, and female police officers

crime similar to political corruption when an offender uses official authority for personal gain.[13] Police corruption may include activities involving kickbacks, shakedowns, opportunistic theft, and protection of illegal activities.[14]

The acceptance of gratuities by police officers is a common problem. When an officer accepts a free cup of coffee or meal, is he or she engaging in misconduct? The International Association of Chiefs of Police and many departments view the practice as unethical and prohibit the acceptance of gratuities. Another argument against accepting gratuities is the concept of the slippery slope. In other words, minor acts of deviance may lead to more serious acts. Business owners, however, appreciate the presence of police officers because they offer a sense of protection to employees and customers.

The motivations for working as a police officer and job satisfaction are well researched. Early research discovered that the motivations of white male officers were linked to authoritarian personalities and a desire for power, authority, and control.[15] These characteristics are particularly pronounced in male-dominated agencies. More recent research shows that other motivations for pursuing a law enforcement career include job security, the opportunity to help people, and the importance and excitement of the work. In most studies, the majority of police officers express a great deal of job satisfaction when they believe they are making meaningful contributions, and dissatisfaction with overwhelming policies, procedures, and lack of advancement.[16] Overall, motivation and job satisfaction in policing are related to salary, benefits, career opportunities, job security, and excitement.[17]

The literature on policing shows that high levels of stress are common among police officers. The pressures of law enforcement place officers at risk for high blood pressure, heart problems, posttraumatic stress disorder, and suicide. A study conducted at the University of Buffalo shows that officers over 40 years old have a higher risk for a coronary event compared with national standards. Among the officers who participated in the study, 72% of female officers and 43% of male officers had high cholesterol levels and higher than average pulse rates and diastolic blood pressure.[18] The stressful nature of policing often is associated with increased suicides, divorce, drug use, and alcoholism. The National Study of Police Suicides, however, reported a noticeable drop in deaths during 2012. This study found that 91% of suicides were by men between the ages of 40 and 44 with 15 to 19 years on the job. Sixty-three percent of suicide victims were single.[19] Successful interventions to help officers cope with stress and trauma include peer support programs and professional resources targeting the unique circumstances of policing.

Gender

The subculture of policing emphasizes the notion of hypermasculinity. In other words, policing is a man's job that requires physical strength. Currently, female officers are found in most departments, though their numbers remain low. Female police officers represent approximately 14% of all sworn officers and face stereotyping and marginalization. Many scholars and researchers argue that gender discrimination and inequality continue to exist in policing, despite reform efforts.[20] A great deal of empirical research has focused on how men and women may differ in their approaches while on duty and why so few women become police officers. Perceived differences between policewomen and policemen are based on both biological and psychological factors thought to hinder or help performance. These differences rest primarily in size, strength, and communications skills.

Physical size and strength were seen as necessary attributes for making arrests and handling uncooperative suspects.[21] Even in the late 1970s, agencies maintained minimum height and weight criteria for new recruits, which applied to both genders but favored male applicants. A slew of lawsuits, however, ended this practice when agency officials were unable to show that size mattered in doing the work.[22] Physical strength and agility testing remain in place in some departments, with different performance standards required for different applicants. Departments without physical agility testing typically employ greater numbers of women. In one large department, researchers discovered that only 28% of female recruits were passing the tests, compared with 93% of the male recruits.[23] Masculine physical strength, however, is not the defining characteristic of being a police officer or being able to perform the job. Perceived differences between how male and female officers approach policing duties are controversial and equivocal.

Many researchers argue that male officers engage in more use of force compared with female officers.[24] One explanation for these findings is the ability of policewomen to use communication skills to de-escalate potentially violent incidents. Many officers, however, believe that "blue is blue" after training and indoctrination. Despite known differences in attitudes and approaches, stereotyping based on gender is a sensitive subject and, in some cases, prone to exaggeration or overgeneralization.[25] Differences in behavior and skills can be attributed to any variety of physical abilities or personality traits.

Whether or not a "glass ceiling" exists in law enforcement in the United States is debatable. Female officers, on one hand, are encouraged to engage in promotional processes, though some have expressed feelings that these requests are made solely on the basis of gender as departments strive to meet diversity quotas.[26] On the other hand, many policewomen show little interest in promoting or seeking special assignments. Choice assignments such as special task forces, undercover narcotics, and SWAT remain male dominated.[27] Commonly, female officers are happy with shifts and assignments that allow them to attend to family or childcare obligations. Overall, family and childcare responsibilities are more prevalent for female compared with male officers.[28] While women have increased their presence in policing, they continue to be underrepresented at the uppermost ranks, particularly supervisory and command positions. In the United States, only 1% of police chiefs are women.[29]

Journal: Are female officers at a greater risk?

Female police chiefs, though still underrepresented, are becoming more common. How does gender make a difference in leadership?

Photo courtesy of Police Chief Michelle Tovrea

The reality of integrating diversity in policing is an area that has received substantial attention from criminologists, although many scholars argue that equality in policing is still lacking. Susan Miller's extensive research on women and policing was based on the following questions:

1. How can a paramilitary and masculine profession be changed to "honor the values of care, connection, empathy, and informality"?

2. How can the contradictions between "masculine" and "feminine" police activities be changed?

3. What matters more, the gender of an officer or the integration of "feminine" traits into social control and policing ideology?

4. Will male and female officers be evaluated differently because of gender? (This question also applies to race and ethnicity.)[30]

Research on women and policing shows the following:

- Female officers are as competent as their male peers.
- Female officers are less likely to use deadly force.
- Female officers use communication, problem solving, and cooperation to enhance community policing efforts.
- Female officers de-escalate violent situations by using interpersonal skills.
- A greater number of female officers in an agency reduces incidents of sexual harassment and discrimination.[31]

While law enforcement remains primarily masculine, community policing has integrated values and norms beyond the stereotypical male police officer by requiring a wide range of social skills. Also, organizations such as the National Association of Women Law Enforcement Executives, the National Center for Women and Policing, and Women in Federal Law Enforcement offer mentoring, training, and support for female officers. The most salient barriers women continue to face include "good old boys" networks and negative attitudes toward women, despite increased numbers and equivalent on-the-job performance.[32]

Race and Hispanic Origin

As was seen in Chapter 4, historically, minority officers have been uncommon. Today, police departments continue to lack minority representation in their ranks, though since the 1970s the number of African Americans, Hispanics, and members of other ethnic/racial groups has increased. In 2013, the Bureau of Labor Statistics reported that the number of minorities employed as police and sheriff's patrol officers remained low: 15% Hispanic or Latino, 14% black, and 2% Asian.[33] Minorities in policing face unique stressors, including social distance from the white, male-dominated workforce. Research also shows that the intersectionality of gender and race poses additional problems for black policewomen, who may lack acceptance from both female and male peers.[34] Under these circumstances black women hold limited expectations of becoming members of the in-group.[35]

COMMUNITY POLICING

Proactive policing is conceptually tied to working with community members, though many officers have long engaged in self-initiated neighborhood efforts to curtail crime and help citizens. In 1994, after the Violent Crime Control and Law Enforcement Act passed, the DOJ created the Office of Community Oriented Policing Services (COPS). COPS distributed almost $9 billion to fund community-based programs and increase the number of police officers in agencies across the United States. The majority of police departments engage in some type of **community policing**, although, on the downside, officers sometimes view these efforts as more appropriate for social workers.

Author Video:
Women in policing and SWAT

Author Video:
Crime theory

Video 5.3:
I love being a police officer, but we need reform

community policing:
A philosophy and style of policing that adopts proactive measures and collaborates with community members.

Working With Victims

More than ever, police are trained to respond to and support crime victims. Over time, policing agencies have recognized that this emphasis on the appropriate treatment of victims not only is the right thing to do, but also serves to reduce future crime and victimization. Victims are critical in solving committed and future crimes. Research demonstrates that victims who are treated with respect and dignity by the police are significantly more likely to willingly participate in current criminal investigations. This positive interaction with victims maximizes the likelihood that an offender is arrested and successfully prosecuted. A second reason that police are trained to work with victims is because these collaborative relationships reduce future crime. When police treat victims with respect, victims are more willing to report future victimizations, which increase the probability that offenders are removed from the street. Third, future crime can be reduced because victims treated well in the past are more willing to act on crime prevention advice they receive from law enforcement. This activity can reduce offending and victimization in the future. As crimes and technology change, training of police officers is essential to ensure their relationship with victims remains positive. Through collaborative relationships with victims, crime and victimization can be reduced.

Police officers are an important part of the community, and as part of the job they keep people safe and ensure their safety. Describe ways in which an officer may offer comfort to victims.

Community policing, according to the DOJ, is a philosophy that encourages organizational strategies designed to partner and problem-solve in a proactive manner. Community policing efforts often focus on public safety issues (e.g., high–crime rate areas, social disorder, fear of crime). The three key components of community policing are partnerships, organizational transformation, and problem solving. Community partnerships involve collaborative efforts to solve problems and increase trust in police. Organizational transformation requires a structure of management, personnel, and information systems that support the community partners and proactive initiatives. Finally, problem solving promotes systematic examinations of crime-related issues to provide for effective responses. The four dimensions and elements of community policing identified by police expert Gary Cordner for the DOJ are philosophical, strategic, tactical, and organizational (see Table 5.1).

Exact definitions of community policing are elusive, and programs may include school resource officers, bicycle patrol, and educational interventions. In 1997, scholar Wesley Skogan described community policing as goals that defy easy characterization. General

Audio:
New NYPD commissioner led shift toward "community policing"

Philosophical	Tactical
Citizen input	Positive interaction
Broad function	Partnerships
Personal services	Problem solving
Strategic	**Organizational**
Reoriented operations	Structure
Prevention emphasis	Management
Focus on geographical area	Information

Table 5.1 ■ The Dimensions of Community Policing

features of community policing, according to Skogan, include decentralization and communication between police and the public that requires focusing on solving local problems and establishing crime prevention programs.[36] COPS describes community policing as a philosophy that embraces "partnerships and problem-solving techniques, to proactively [address] conditions that give rise to public safety issues such as crime, social disorder, and fear of crime."[37]

Problem-oriented policing (POP), as developed by Herman Goldstein, requires the identification and analysis of crime and disorder problems in order to construct an effective response. The process depends on rank-and-file officers to identify problems and develop solutions. POP often makes use of the scan, analysis, response, and assessment model (**SARA model**). This method requires officers to do the following:

Scan: Identify and prioritize problems.

Analyze: Research the problems.

Respond: Develop long-lasting solutions.

Assess: Evaluate the success of the responses.

In addition to SARA, police officers may use the **crime triangle**, also referred to as the problem analysis triangle, to focus on immediate concerns present in the environment in order to confront difficult issues. The concept originated from work by Lawrence Cohen and Marcus Felson called **routine activity theory**.[38] A comparison of the similarities of the two models is seen in Figure 5.3. According to Cohen and Felson, who developed this theory to understand changes in crime rates across areas and over time, when a likely offender and suitable target come together in time and place, without a capable guardian present, the necessary components needed for crime are in place. In other words, the convergence in space and time of motivated offenders, suitable targets, and the absence of capable guardians increases the risk of criminal incidents. In the triangle scenario, a capable guardian may be a family member, friend, neighbor, or law enforcement officer—that is, someone who can provide protection. The crime triangle and routine activity theory are closely connected.

problem-oriented policing: A policing style that emphasizes the use of data analysis and assessment to address crime problems.

SARA model: The scan, analysis, response, and assessment model, used in problem-oriented policing.

crime triangle: Also referred to as the problem analysis triangle, a strategy that focuses on immediate concerns present in the environment in order to confront difficult issues.

routine activity theory: Cohen and Felson's theory that posits that the convergence in space and time of motivated offenders, suitable targets, and the absence of capable guardians increases the risk of criminal incidents.

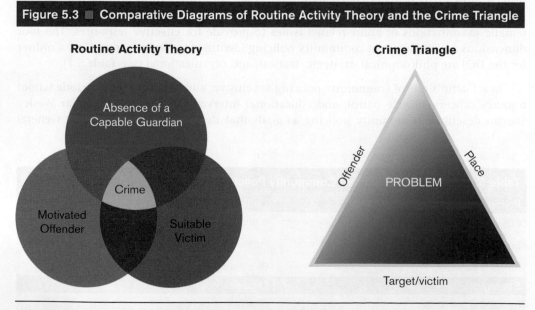

Figure 5.3 ■ Comparative Diagrams of Routine Activity Theory and the Crime Triangle

Routine Activity Theory

Absence of a Capable Guardian

Crime

Motivated Offender

Suitable Victim

Crime Triangle

Offender

Place

PROBLEM

Target/victim

Sources: Caskey, T. R. (n.d.). *Decision support in POP: Understanding crime displacement and diffusion via agent-based models.* Retrieved from http://slides.com/trevorcaskey/swarmfest#/. Lopez, A. (2014, October 28). *Routine activity theory elements of crime.* Retrieved from http://lemoncenter.com/routine-activity-theory-elements-crime.

Community policing efforts also evolved from the **broken windows theory** developed by George Kelling and James Q. Wilson. Their work offered an applied approach to social disorganization and was adopted by many law enforcement agencies.[39] Broken windows suggests that "untended areas, blight, graffiti and signs of disorder decrease neighborhood residents' willingness to enforce social order, which in turn leads to more serious crime. If police target minor transgressions, they may prevent serious crime from developing in those places."[40]

Advances in mapping efforts revealed crime is clustered in small areas, also called **hot spots**. In the late 1980s, researcher and policing expert Lawrence Sherman explored call patterns for police service in Minneapolis and discovered that 3% of the city's addresses were responsible for over half of the calls for law enforcement assistance. The crime mapping offered information on where to concentrate patrols depending on the hot spot patterns.[41] Similarly, Sherman and colleagues' Kansas City Gun Experiment concentrated patrol (hot spotting) on gun crime, which resulted in an increase of weapon seizures and a decrease in gun-related violence.[42]

The use of technology for crime mapping is essential for identifying crime trends and reducing crime. How might potential offenders react to the use of increased patrols in an area?

Hot spotting became controversial when research revealed that the practice might lead to displacement of crime problems.[43] In other words, many were concerned that criminals under close police surveillance moved to a new area to perpetrate crimes. Other research, however, shows crime will drop in small hot spot areas without displacement.[44] Reducing crime is connected to things other than policing presence and includes many environmental factors, as posited by the broken windows theory.

Another controversial method of policing derived from the broken windows approach is **zero tolerance**. The premise is based on focusing enforcement efforts on quality-of-life issues such as disorder and minor crime. The partnership between policing and community is absent in this approach. Enforcement efforts are applied to low-level crime in specific neighborhoods. Zero tolerance, a more traditional style of policing, means that officers issue tickets and make arrests for less serious transgressions such as jaywalking, loitering, prostitution, and panhandling.

The best example of zero-tolerance policing occurred in New York City. In the 1990s, Police Commissioner William Bratton and Mayor Rudolph Giuliani used computer statistics (often referred to as COMPSTAT or CompSTAT) as a management tool to organize and identify crime trends and develop solutions. In New York City, CompSTAT and zero-tolerance models were blended to address crime and disorder. The approach appeared to be successful in reducing disorder and minor offenses, but one unforeseen consequence was the increased number of citizen complaints.[45] Complaints seemed to be most prevalent in minority neighborhoods, and the link to "hyperaggressive crime-control tactics" undermined community relations.[46] While the zero-tolerance approach reduces low-level crimes, whether it is effective in reducing serious crime is unknown.[47]

INTELLIGENCE-LED/EVIDENCE-BASED POLICING

Intelligence-led policing, first developed in the early 1990s in the United Kingdom, was envisioned as a means of creating efficiency and effectiveness in police agencies, particularly under conditions of rapid globalization and increased transnational organized

broken windows theory: Introduced by James Q. Wilson and George Kelling to describe the social disorder that occurs in run-down and neglected neighborhoods, which leads to higher crime rates.

hot spots: Specific geographical locations identified as high-crime areas.

zero tolerance: A policing approach that focuses enforcement efforts on quality-of-life issues such as disorder and minor crime. Enforcement efforts are applied to low-level crimes and minor infractions in specific neighborhoods.

intelligence-led policing: A means of creating efficiency and effectiveness in police agencies that emphasizes the importance of risk assessment and risk management.

Video 5.4:
Crime theory

crime.[48] Intelligence-led policing emphasizes the importance of risk assessment and risk management. This approach relies on accountability and the need to effectively use resources. Australian police scholar Jerry Ratcliffe identified four key elements:

- Targeting of offenders
- Management of crime and disorder hot spots
- Investigation of linked series of crimes and incidents
- Application of preventative measures[49]

Intelligence-led policing is a paradigm built on community policing and problem solving with an emphasis on information sharing. The implementation of intelligence-led policing requires interpreting the criminal environment and using strategic decisions based on a contextual analysis. The creation of a structure (analysis), process (implementation), and product (reduced crime) can be accomplished with coordination, in-depth data analysis, and intelligence sharing.

Fusion centers were developed under the National Criminal Intelligence Sharing Plan to facilitate information exchanges on intelligence gathered from confidential informants, surveillance, and crime data analyses. The concept is similar to POP, which requires officers to identify problems and develop solutions. Intelligence-led policing is a top-down approach that focuses less on the community and more on global perspectives. This policing model, however, is the target of critics who believe the concept is vague and ill defined. Intelligence-led policing is proactive and focuses on threats, similar to CompSTAT models.

Video 5.5:
CompStat: An inside look at the NYPD's crime fighting tool

CompSTAT was first introduced in the early 1990s in the NYPD. It uses computer technology to gather up-to-date and accurate information on crime within neighborhoods. Crime-mapping technology is a major tool used to identify problem areas and trends in illegal activity. The use of CompSTAT in New York City is credited with a dramatic decline in crime.[50] Evidence-based policing uses CompSTAT-like approaches to curtail criminal activity and enhance community relationships.

21st-CENTURY POLICING

Police agencies are viewed as slow to transform, and in some instances, new chiefs are hired as "change agents." Former police chief Gerald Williams described making changes in police departments as being similar to trying to turn the *Titanic*—difficult but possible. In reality, new technologies, better policies, and evidence-based practices are transforming law enforcement. As previously noted, many departments are increasingly driven by statistical analyses. Departments often depend on crime analysts to make data-driven decisions related to crime control based on trends and patterns. Also, many staffing deployment decisions result from crime analyses, which can assist departments in placing extra patrol in certain districts or precincts.

Procedural justice and policing is likely to become more predominant in the future. This approach to policing depends on communication and is being used as a method to achieve legitimacy. Yale law professor Tom Tyler identified the major principles of procedural justice. First, citizens need to be given a voice in the process to tell their side of the events surrounding incidents to officers. Second, officers must be neutral when dealing with people and events. In other words, policing depends on the consistent application of legal principles and neutral interpretation of incidents. Third, people want to be treated with dignity and politeness, which is incumbent on all officers. Finally, people react favorably to officers they view as trustworthy and caring; procedural justice requires officers to listen to accounts and explain their actions in a sensitive manner.[51] Procedural justice can be applied to leadership in organizations and officers at all levels of personnel.

Another approach becoming popular in policing is based on attribution theory. This framework is particularly important given recent highly publicized shootings involving

fusion centers:
Developed under the National Criminal Intelligence Sharing Plan to help in information exchanges on intelligence gathered from confidential informants, surveillance, and crime data analyses.

CompSTAT: A law enforcement strategy first adopted by the New York City Police Department that relies on crime mapping to identify hot spots and crime trends in order to effectively address problems.

minority suspects. One aspect of attribution theory, a social psychology perspective, posits that we interpret people and events based on past experiences and stereotypes. An event first catches our attention (i.e., we see something); then our perceptions about the person or event develop. Ultimately, cognition occurs and we make judgments about what we see. Attribution theory, according to researcher and scholar Lorie Fridell, is that stereotypes surrounding African Americans and crime may operate implicitly or explicitly and must be recognized and "unlearned."[52] When police officers and people recognize that their attributions about particular individuals, groups, or events are incorrect, stereotyping or labeling can perhaps be reduced.

The most comprehensive exploration of 21st-century policing developed from former President Barack Obama's task force.[53] Law enforcement leaders and researchers across the country collaborated to develop a best practice model of policing practices that would also help establish trust with citizens. The task force constructed a six-pillar model:

1. Building trust and legitimacy

2. Policy and oversight

3. Technology and social media

4. Community policing and crime reduction

5. Training and education

6. Officer wellness and safety

The results of the report suggest a number of initiatives in each area. First, trust and legitimacy require relationship building with the public and the adoption of a guardian mind-set instead of a warrior mentality. Second, the DOJ can assist departments in establishing best policies and procedures. Third, rapid technological developments and social media require national standards, in addition to local needs. Fourth, further focus on community policing as a guiding philosophy is strongly encouraged. Law enforcement agencies, in other words, must to continue to work with citizens to identify problems and engage in activities with vulnerable populations, especially at risk children and youth. Fifth, higher levels of training and education are essential to high quality police services. Finally, supporting and providing services to law enforcement officers (e.g., wearing seatbelts, training in first aid, financing education) are necessary components of officer wellness and safety.

CONTROVERSIAL ISSUES IN POLICING

Use of Force

The use of force by police officers represents a highly debated and often misunderstood aspect of law enforcement, though the ramifications of these events for departments and communities are significant and widespread. The use of force is distinctly different from excessive force. In the latter, a police officer exceeds the necessary force to control a suspect or contain a situation. Excessive force incidents are rare, but when they do occur they make great fodder for the media.

Officers are trained to use the appropriate level of force given the totality of the circumstances presented in the context of the situation. The type of arrest control tactic used by an officer is sometimes structured as a **continuum of force**, from physical restraints to firearms. The idea of an actual continuum of force offices should follow from mere presence to deadly force has fallen out of favor in the majority of agencies (see Figure 5.5). Any type of force can be used when appropriate and proportional, rather than the perspective that police should, for example, start at level three and then work up to level five. The amount of force used in an arrest depends on a large number of variables, including, for example, the suspect's demeanor, choice of weapon, and level of compliance. The goal is to

Audio:
Publicizing use-of-force videos included in Chicago-area sheriff's reforms

continuum of force:
Guideline for the degree of force and weapon an officer may use during an arrest, which is becoming outdated.

reasonably ensure suspect compliance with an appropriate response.[54] Figure 5.4 illustrates the many elements that play a part in decisions related to the use of force.

Early work examining police–citizen encounters by researcher David Bayley during an observational study in Denver, Colorado, targeted domestic disturbances and traffic stops.[55] Bayley discovered that officers' tactical choices change during the course of an encounter according to three stages: contact (beginning), processing (middle), and exit (end). In his study, officers used force in 5% of all initial contact in domestic disturbance calls, with verbal orders and threats being used 10% of the time. Physical force was used about 8% of the time during the processing stage. Research also shows that the type of call for service is related to the use of force and that domestic violence and robbery generally pose a greater risk to the responding officer and increases the probability of subsequent use of force.[56]

In the majority of law enforcement agencies, use-of-force incidents involve weaponless tactics and reasonable actions on the part of officers. It is the rare incident of "excessive" or "lethal" force, however, that captures the attention of the media and public. Lethal shootings and "beatings" are atypical events. The majority of police–citizen encounters in which force is used involve resistance by suspects and minor physical force tactics.[57] Nationally, research shows that use of force is involved in a small percentage of overall police–public interactions, despite what is frequently shown in the media. Recent police shootings that have captured media headlines often fail to reflect what really occurred during the incident. The police officer Darren Wilson shot and killed 18-year-old Michael Brown in Ferguson, Missouri. This incident led to community outrage and riots. The use of lethal force against

Figure 5.4 ■ Situational, Tactical, and Perception Considerations in Use of Force

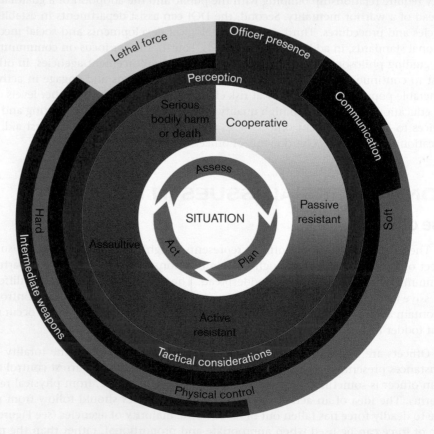

The officer continuously assesses the situation and selects the most reasonable option relative to those circumstances as perceived at that point in time.

Source: Adapted from the Ottawa Police Service.

minorities, though rare, presents serious problems for law enforcement agencies. This incident appeared, on the surface, to represent an excessive use of force. Witnesses asserted that Brown, after running away from the police officers, was shot while holding up his hands to surrender, although all the aforementioned witnesses recanted this version of the event. In fact, the DOJ's report found "no credible evidence that Michael Brown was kneeling, shot execution-style, and was in a 'Hands up, don't shoot' position."[58] The grand jury and the DOJ found no probable cause or evidence to pursue charges against the officer.

Research studies suggest that some level of force is used in 8% to 10% of police–citizen encounters.[59] Overall, higher levels of force are used when police are attempting to arrest suspects who are actively resisting. The use of deadly force against a fleeing suspect was addressed in *Tennessee v. Garner* (1985). In the *Garner* decision, the U.S. Supreme Court ruled that the use of deadly force is appropriate in the pursuit of a fleeing suspect only to prevent escape if probable cause exists to believe that the suspect poses a significant threat that endangers officers or others.

Unequivocally, research evidence shows that the majority of use-of-force incidents involve grabbing, pushing, or shoving; weaponless tactics are used in 80% of use-of-force situations.[60] In Miami, 64% of use-of-force situations involved grabbing or holding suspects, and any injuries suffered by the suspects were minor.[61] In most cases, the arrest and control technique used by an officer directly correlates with a suspect's behavior. Most situations require a minimum amount of force; physical and defensive techniques are generally sufficient unless a suspect is uncooperative. Suspect resistance can be categorized into various behaviors toward arresting police officers, as shown in Table 5.2. Officers are trained to evaluate the situational context and escalate (i.e., choose from all the arrest and control techniques available) to an action level necessary and reasonable in order to control the situation (see Figure 5.5).

Racial Profiling

Racial profiling continues to be a major issue for policing, as seen in the recent legal problems in New York City over stop-and-frisk cases. In 2013, a federal judge issued a 198-page decision on New York's use of stop-and-frisk.[62] Clear evidence of racial bias and selective enforcement was evident in the city's policy. Over a period of 10 years, officers conducted more than 4 million stop-and-frisks that targeted minorities, in which 90% of the people stopped had engaged in no wrongdoing.

Profiling occurs when an officer questions or investigates an individual based on race, ethnicity, religion, or national origin.[63] "Driving while black" is a common phrase used to identify the practice of police officers' stopping, searching, and detaining people based on skin color. The issue of racial profiling is complex and involves many overt and covert influences, including perceptions, community demographics, and political factors. Research suggests that the majority of officers rarely consciously make a decision to conduct a stop

profiling: Occurs when officers question or investigate a person based on race, ethnicity, religion, or national origin.

Table 5.2 ■ Suspect Resistance Measures	
Psychological Intimidation	Nonverbal Cues in Attitude, Appearance, Demeanor, or Posture That Indicate Unwillingness to Cooperate or Desire to Threaten
Verbal noncompliance	Verbal responses indicating an unwillingness to comply with officer's directions or threat to injure a person
Passive resistance	Physical actions that prevent the officer's attempt to control, for example, a person who remains in a limp, prone position
Defensive resistance	Physical actions that attempt to prevent the officer's control, including flight or attempt to flee, but do not involve attempts to harm the officer
Active aggression	A threat or overt act of an assault, coupled with the present ability to carry out the threat or assault, which reasonably indicates that an assault or injury to any person is imminent
Aggravated active aggression	Deadly force encounter

based on race or ethnicity, though unconscious decisions may influence perceptions of a suspicious person.[64]

A long history of distrust between law enforcement and minority community members suggests that police shooting incidents are indicative of the overall mistreatment of African Americans in the community. In the Michael Brown case, for example, Ferguson, a suburb of St. Louis, maintains a population of about 21,000, and 70% of the population is black. In contrast, the police department has 53 employees, with only 3 black officers. The state attorney general issued a report in 2013 that found that Ferguson police stopped and arrested black drivers almost twice as often as whites, although they were less likely to find contraband among the black drivers.[65] Former U.S. attorney general Eric Holder ordered a DOJ investigation into the department's use of force, stops, searches, and arrests and into the treatment of jail inmates in the city. Additionally, the New York City Bar Association cautioned when interpreting the causal relationship between the number of stops and reduction in crime that isolating the effectiveness of one policy from that of another is extremely difficult.[66] In the New York stop-and-frisk case, the federal court judge ruled that the city violated the Fourth and Fourteenth Amendments, finding the department liable for racial profiling and unconstitutional stops.

Discretion and Mandatory Arrest Policies

mandatory arrest policies: Policies that limit police discretion in certain situations; they are frequently applied to incidents involving domestic violence.

private policing: Policing provided by private entities. Protection is extended to corporate executives and other high-profile individuals.

As previously mentioned, police officers have a great deal of discretion. They decide whom to pull over in traffic stops, when to issue citations, and when to make arrests. Discretion, according to policing expert Jeffery Ross, depends on a variety of contextual factors:

- *Personal disposition styles:* A police officer may feel more sympathy for a contrite suspect versus a "smart-mouth."

- *Situation:* An officer may ignore certain less serious criminal activities or avoid making an arrest at the end of a shift.

- *Departmental rules:* Written or unwritten organizational rules may encourage or discourage the use of discretion by individual officers.[67]

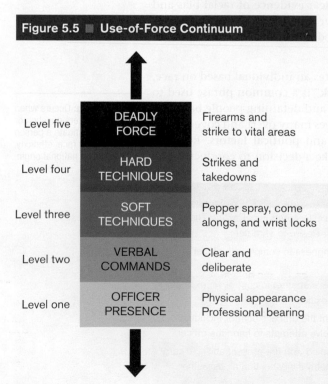

Figure 5.5 ■ Use-of-Force Continuum

Level five	DEADLY FORCE	Firearms and strike to vital areas
Level four	HARD TECHNIQUES	Strikes and takedowns
Level three	SOFT TECHNIQUES	Pepper spray, come alongs, and wrist locks
Level two	VERBAL COMMANDS	Clear and deliberate
Level one	OFFICER PRESENCE	Physical appearance Professional bearing

Source: Dunetos K-9.

The use of discretion (or the decision not to act) can be positive when police are dealing with vague laws and scarce resources.[68] In contrast, the improper use of discretion can result in unfair practices and discrimination.

Mandatory arrest policies limit police discretion in certain situations. These policies are frequently applied to incidents involving intimate partner violence. Historically, domestic violence was seen as a private matter outside the purview of law enforcement. Changes in how intimate partner violence is viewed resulted in many jurisdictions' passing mandatory arrest laws. *Thurman v. Torrington* (1984) promoted some of the movement toward mandatory arrests after a court ruling that extended police liability to acts of omission, that is, incidents when responding officers fail to take action against the primary aggressor. Additionally, the court determined that failure to protect victims of domestic violence could result in civil litigation against the department and the city.

Private Policing

Private policing is a large and lucrative area of law enforcement. Billions of dollars a year are spent on private security. As city, state, and federal resources dwindled, private policing expanded to address personal and company needs for protection. Private policing provides protection to corporate executives and other high-profile individuals. Private security companies respond to alarms and patrol gated communities. The National Association of Security Companies represents a large group of private security companies (e.g., Brinks, Pinkerton, Wells Fargo) that employ more than 250,000 officers. Private security is used, for example, to protect airports, hospitals, retail companies, banks, and factories. Private policing may include proprietary services (in-house security staff) or contract services that employ security to provide protection to specific clients. While private policing fills a void, many of the officers are undertrained. The industry often is criticized for a lack of regulations, and the requirements for each state vary, though most mandate minimal standards.

Social Media

Police departments across the nation are facing budget shortfalls and personnel shortages. One method of extending limited resources is the use of social media. Facebook, Twitter, and Google provide opportunities to reduce crime, communicate with citizens, and enhance media relations. Police departments can use social media to send crime reports,

POLICY ISSUES

Policing Intimate Partner Violence

Police officers sometimes comment on the difficulties, frustration, and dread they have when called to an incident of intimate partner violence. These incidents are viewed as particularly dangerous and can result in physical harm to responding officers. Also, departments face harsh public criticism for a perceived, or perhaps real, reluctance to make an arrest. Wayne Welsh and Philip Harris identified three reasons for the "hands-off" response:

1. Culture and training: Police are crime fighters, not social workers.

2. Disincentives: Police performance is measured on arrest and clearance rates, not mediation skills.

3. Perceived futility: There is a perception that few arrests result in prosecution.

Many state laws changed after the deaths of women who had called the police and received no response. In addition, a widely cited research experiment showed that mandatory arrest was the most effective means of deterring and stopping domestic violence. Mandatory arrest policies in domestic violence situations removed officers' discretion. One unintended consequence of the policy was an increased number of women arrested for

aggravated assault. When the primary aggressor was difficult to identify, officers discovered that it was much easier to arrest both parties. Another result of the policy was the unexpected manipulation of the criminal justice system by aggressors who use the threat of calling the police to further intimidate and control their partners. A devastating consequence is the removal of children from the home if the police have been called. As a result, victims may be less willing to call for help for fear of losing their children.

Think About It

Policing domestic violence raises multiple important questions.

1. Did passing mandatory arrest laws in domestic violence cases cause more harm than good? Why or why not?

2. How would you design a police training program to change the hands-off attitude?

3. In what ways can responding officers identify the primary aggressor in domestic violence calls?

Sources: Welsh, W. N., & Harris, P. W. (2008). *Criminal justice policy and planning* (3rd ed.). Newark, NJ: Anderson. Mallicoat, S. L. (2015). *Women and crime: A text/reader* (2nd ed.). Thousand Oaks, CA: Sage.

crime prevention tips, traffic updates, and safety advisories. Agencies are using websites and blogs to educate members of the public about services, take reports, and display crime data. Facebook pages are being used for recruitment. Existing research indicates three major areas where social media platforms may assist law enforcement.[69] First, social media appear to increase communication with citizens. Second, some forms of social media may increase positive police–community interaction and act as a form of community policing. Third, this type of technology can be used to increase organizational legitimacy.

Twitter is used by a large number of agencies. Over 300 million users are on Twitter, and approximately 500 million tweets are sent daily.[70] For policing agencies the outcome of tweets may be both positive and negative. After riots erupted over a police shooting in England in 2011, Twitter was allegedly used to incite further lawlessness and to promote the organization of cleanup efforts.[71] After the Boston Marathon attacks in April 2013, the police department used Twitter to provide reliable information to the public and to assist in its investigation.[72] An estimated 75% of large police departments in the United States use some type of social media to reach out to citizens.[73]

In one department, the use of social media assisted police in the rapid detection of a series of burglaries. The social media campaign using Facebook and Twitter notified citizens of burglars posing as salesmen. The department requested that citizens report suspicious people in their neighborhoods, and dispatchers broadcasted the calls to patrol officers. Within a day, because of the public response, the suspects were apprehended.

Technology

Technological advances have changed the landscape of policing. The most dramatic changes occurred in the early 20th century with the automobile, telephone, and two-way radios.[74] Currently, an increased reliance on information systems, nonlethal weapons, intelligence sharing, and state-of-the-art technology is redefining policing.

CopLink is an information technology system first funded by the National Institute of Justice in 1997. Developed by Knowledge Computing Corporation, CopLink supports more than 1,600 jurisdictions across the United States. The software offers tactical lead generation, crime analysis, and information sharing among local, regional, state, and national law enforcement agencies. CopLink also assists in the rapid identification of criminal suspects and offers analysis of relationships and crime trends to stop or prevent crime and terrorism. A CopLink training video demonstrating how the system works shows an officer responding to a child abduction call. According to the eyewitness on the scene, two men asked a young girl to help them find their dog at a park. The young girl, who refused the men's advances, described the suspects as Hispanic or white. One man was named "Lipo." Within minutes the officer begins the search in CopLink with the reported information, and the system provides 29 names with 18 available mug shots of possible suspects. The officer is then able to create and print a mug book for witness identification.

Cameras have changed policing in significant ways and offer several advantages. First, videos and pictures of police–citizen interactions are easily recorded by anyone with a smart phone. Under these circumstances officers may be less likely to engage in use of force, and suspects may act more cooperatively, knowing how easily the event can become public. Second,

CopLink: An information technology system that offers tactical lead generation, crime analysis, and information sharing among local, regional, state, and national law enforcement agencies.

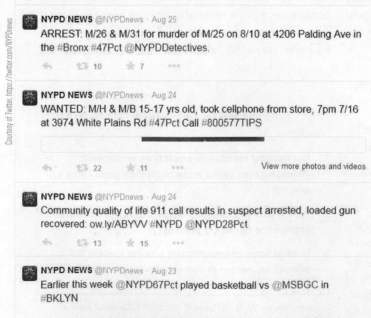

Courtesy of Twitter, https://twitter.com/NYPDnews

NYPD NEWS @NYPDnews · Aug 25
ARREST: M/26 & M/31 for murder of M/25 on 8/10 at 4206 Palding Ave in the #Bronx #47Pct @NYPDDetectives.
10   7

NYPD NEWS @NYPDnews · Aug 24
WANTED: M/H & M/B 15-17 yrs old, took cellphone from store, 7pm 7/16 at 3974 White Plains Rd #47Pct Call #800577TIPS

22   11   View more photos and videos

NYPD NEWS @NYPDnews · Aug 24
Community quality of life 911 call results in suspect arrested, loaded gun recovered: ow.ly/ABYVV #NYPD @NYPD28Pct
13   15

NYPD NEWS @NYPDnews · Aug 23
Earlier this week @NYPD67Pct played basketball vs @MSBGC in #BKLYN

The use of Twitter by police departments helps solve crimes and protect the public. What crimes and announcements appear on your police department's Twitter page?

police body-worn cameras are being used to protect officers from false accusations of being discourteous or using inappropriate force. Critics of body cams believe the technology may inhibit officers from stopping possible suspects, though departments are finding many positive outcomes. One agency using police body cams showed increased officer–citizen contacts and decreased formal complaints against officers. Additionally, use-of-force incidents in the agency dropped by almost 60%.

High-activity location observation (HALO) cameras, also called police observation devices (PODs), are used in many cities. PODs were installed in Chicago to help prevent crime, collect evidence, reduce gang loitering, and conduct drug stings. HALO cameras were first installed in Denver in preparation for the 2008 Democratic National Convention and continue to be used to document crime, conduct drug stings, and serve as a deterrent. Concerns over the use of these cameras focus on security versus privacy, though signs are posted informing people of the presence of the cameras. Police departments describe the cameras as crime-fighting tools. Cameras are monitored in a central control room 24 hours a day.

Nonlethal technology has changed police use of force. Instances of neck or choke holds to control suspects are now rare, though these were once widely used by law enforcement. Most agencies have banned this method of control because of the high likelihood of death. **Nonlethal force** (many people believe this term is a misnomer), or more accurately **less-than-lethal weapons**, provides viable options for dealing with resisting suspects. Police now use pepper spray, rubber bullets, beanbag guns, and sedative darts to control combative suspects. The most controversial less-than-lethal weapons are **Tasers**, which is a brand name commonly used to refer to conductive energy devices or electronic control devices. First introduced by Taser International, a Phoenix-based company, the device offers a means of controlling suspects while saving lives and offering officers protection from injuries.

At the extreme end of technology is the use of **military drones** by police agencies. Drones are being tested as possible crime-fighting tools in some parts of the country. A test project in Los Angeles County used three drones to track a gun tossed by a fleeing suspect, find lost hikers, and locate the source of a fire. The use of drones in policing has a huge market potential, which is estimated at $90 billion in the next 10 years. Draganfly Innovations is marketing drones for law enforcement to aid in accident investigations, traffic patrol, and crowd control.

high-activity location observation (HALO) cameras: Remote-controlled cameras that can view 360 degrees, zoom, and tilt. This technology enables law enforcement to observe and monitor areas of interest for criminal investigations and crime prevention.

nonlethal force: Type of force (including weapons) that provides viable options for dealing with resisting suspects such as pepper spray, rubber bullets, beanbag guns, and sedative darts. Also called less-than-lethal weapons.

less-than-lethal weapons: Weapons that provide viable options for dealing with resisting suspects; they include pepper spray, rubber bullets, beanbag guns, and sedative darts.

Tasers: A type of conductive energy device or electronic control device. These devices offer a means of controlling suspects while saving lives and offering officers protection from injuries.

military drones: Technology increasingly used as possible crime-fighting tools in some parts of the country.

Photos courtesy of Denver Police Department

HALO cameras monitor streets for crimes and are used in undercover sting operations. Why might the use of cameras be considered an invasion of privacy?

The use of drones by police departments is controversial, and in this case, technology has outpaced the law. In North Dakota, a local police agency borrowed a Predator drone from border patrol to collect photographic evidence without a warrant. The *Brossart* case is the first of its kind to reach the courts and will likely continue to make its way higher in the court system.[75] The Supreme Court has yet to determine if the use of drones violates the Fourth Amendment, though in 2013 a bill was introduced in Congress to ban the use of drones for targeted surveillance of people and property without a warrant.

CHAPTER WRAP-UP

This chapter focused on contemporary local and state policing, which represents only a small part of law enforcement. From the 1970s through the 1990s, policing remained turbulent, and numerous attempts were made to improve the reputation of law enforcement across the country. Since that time, improvements in policing have continued. The chapter examined the role of police officers and the culture of policing. Special attention was given to gender, race, and Hispanic origin and the strides made in these areas in recent decades. Technological advances have changed much of policing in recent decades. With these advances come ethical and policy questions. Furthermore, advances in technology often outpace laws, making for quandaries.

The 2014 shooting of Michael Brown by police officer Darren Wilson exemplifies many of the issues facing law enforcement beyond the use of lethal force and illustrates the important role technology plays in policing. Although no one captured the shooting of Brown, many cell phone videos were in the news and on YouTube showing the scene and spectators. Also, a surveillance tape of Brown stealing a box of cigarillos and bullying a store clerk was released. Shortly after the incident, private companies donated body cameras, which offer a clearer picture compared with car dashboard cameras, to the Ferguson Police Department. The cameras allow live streaming of police interactions with citizens and suspects for $19.99 a month. Approximately 1,200 law enforcement agencies across the

CONTEMPLATING CAREERS

Victim Advocate

Are you understanding? Are you nonjudgmental? Are you an excellent communicator? Can you be discrete and trustworthy? Can you be supportive to others and emotionally strong? Are you a problem solver?

If you answered yes to these questions, then a career as a victim advocate may be an ideal choice for you. Victim advocates assist crime victims in obtaining emergency medical treatment and other treatment needed immediately. Once a victim's immediate needs are met, the advocate ensures the victim has a safe place to stay, food, transportation, and other basic needs met.

The tasks of a victim advocate are numerous and may include educating the victim of his or her rights, assisting in interactions with law enforcement, supporting the victim during investigations, accompany

the victim to court, and other supporting roles. Each situation is different, and advocates must be nimble enough to address specific needs of victims.

Advocates are employed by a number of agencies, including police agencies, legal offices, hospitals, shelters, and the courts. Advocates frequently work with police even if they are not employed by police agencies. Education required is at least an associate's degree, but more likely a bachelor's degree in criminal justice, psychology, victimology, or social work.

Career Video:
A victim advocate discusses her experience and current issues in the field.

country have purchased body cameras, and the Denver Police Department plans to buy 800 cameras next year.[76] Police chiefs believe the cameras will provide documentation, accountability, and transparency. Even in the Brown case, eyewitness testimony varies. Several witnesses claim Brown was turning around to face the police officer with his hands in the air. In contrast, another witness described Brown as charging toward the officer. Social media and Facebook offered graphic details of the ensuing riots, vandalism, and looting.

The videos of police in riot gear after the Ferguson shooting raised questions about law enforcement using military-grade tactical equipment. Author and researcher Peter Kraska explored the militarization of policing in a 2001 book.[77] He noted the increased emphasis on the paramilitary hierarchy and hypermasculinity in police departments, including the military weapons transfer programs, the use of National Guard units, and an increase in the number of SWAT teams. An article in the *Wall Street Journal*, "Rise of the Warrior Cop," questions the use of police recruitment videos that show police officers "rappelling from helicopters, shooting big guns, kicking down doors and tackling suspects."[78] Federal grants and programs have provided military equipment to local law enforcement, including, for example, bomb suits, armored vehicles, helicopters, battering rams, and assault rifles. Now policymakers are questioning the usefulness of providing this type of equipment and whether officers have received proper training on when and how to use the military weapons.

CASE STUDY

Case Study Video 5.1:
Interviews with case study participants

The chapter discussed the interaction of police with our case studies. It identified Chris Farias's interactions with police from his initial stop to his arrest. Joshua Paul Benjamin also interacted with police when he was brought in for questioning. He gave the police consent to search his apartment for evidence and admitted to his crimes. Jennifer Schuett had an especially long history with police given that her case lasted 19 years. She worked with them and prompted the continued attention to her case, which eventually paid off. Danny Madrid's case showed how the use of search warrants and confessions lead to arrest. During Danny's arrest he noted that the police respected his rights, which he claimed were not violated during the process. The next chapter covers policing and the rule of law, including information on police and the courts, search and seizure, and issues related to warrants.

KEY POINTS

- Scandals in major police departments promulgate perceptions of widespread corruption.

- The bad apple theory of policing, though discounted by the Christopher Commission, is supported by research.

- Police officers struggle to overcome negative public opinions often fueled by media coverage.

- Large police organizations have a complex chain of command.

- Patrol officers are the gatekeepers to the criminal justice system.

- Community policing is a partnership that embraces problem solving.

- Policing styles include community policing, problem-oriented policing, intelligence-led policing, and zero tolerance.

- Use of force is based on a variety of tools and is dependent on a suspect's behavior during an arrest.

- Computers, cameras, and weapon technologies are redefining methods of policing.

- Law enforcement agencies face future challenges adapting to service consolidation and working with restricted budgets.

KEY TERMS

REVIEW QUESTIONS

1. What major issues did law enforcement face during the 1960s through the 1990s?

2. What are the different types of police agencies?

3. What is the primary mission of policing?

4. Why is the police chief responsible for anything that occurs in his or her department?

5. What types of job positions are available in policing organizations?

6. How are community and intelligence-led policing the same or different?

7. What is the SARA model?

8. How does the broken windows theory influence different styles of policing?

9. Explain why so much attention is paid to individual use-of-force incidents.

10. What are the major challenges with implementing new technology for law enforcement agencies?

CRITICAL THINKING MATTERS

1. **Cold Case Investigations.** Unsolved cases are a challenge for police departments, and many victims are still seeking closure years after crimes were committed. Now investigators are solving crimes using DNA and other recently developed technology and methods. Jennifer Schuett's abduction was a cold case, and no arrest was made until 19 years later, when a detective and special agent from the Federal Bureau of Investigation reopened the case in 2008. Is solving cold cases a good use of police resources? Develop arguments for and against cold case investigations.

2. **Public Labeling of Repeat Offenders.** Chris Farias was a repeat offender and had several past offenses for driving while intoxicated. California legislators considered the use of special vehicle license

plates to identify convicted drunk drivers. How would this law aid police officers in doing their job? What are the possible negative consequences for the police and the offender? What crimes, if any, should include public notification and shaming? How would such a strategy work with the goals of the criminal justice system identified in earlier chapters?

3. **Unrealistic Expectations.** Community policing often requires officers to participate in undertakings outside of traditional law enforcement duties. In one small city, parents called the police when they were unable to get their child to attend school. In the same city, officers also were expected to move trash cans from the street and assist homeowners with their pets. Do these cases fit within the community policing perspective? In what situations should a police officer just say no to a citizen? Do community members have unrealistic expectations for police officers?

4. **The Decision-Making Process and the Law.** Marijuana is legal in several states. These states' laws allow possession of a limited amount of pot for personal use in private. When the legislation was enacted in Colorado, people stood on the steps of the capital and lit up joints. Should the police have arrested the demonstrators? Is it better for public relations to ignore small infractions of the law? Across the nation on April 20, thousands of people gather to smoke marijuana at 4:20 p.m. as a protest. How should the police handle these situations?

5. **Diversity in Policing.** Diversity in policing is a highly sought after characteristic. Why is that? Should the diversity of interest focus on gender, race, and ethnicity only? Or are there other important characteristics, such as LGBTQ status, religion, or income? Why or why not? What advantages do diverse officers bring to law enforcement? How does it affect the way victims are dealt with?

DIGITAL RESOURCES

$SAGE edge™

Sharpen your skills with SAGE edge at edge.sagepub.com/rennison2e. SAGE edge for Students provides a personalized approach to help you accomplish your coursework goals in an easy-to-use learning environment. You'll find action plans, mobile-friendly eFlashcards, and quizzes as well as video and web resources and links to SAGE journal articles to support and expand on the concepts presented in this chapter.

6 POLICE AND THE RULE OF LAW

> "Justice is incidental to law and order."
>
> —J. Edgar Hoover

> "Justice may be blind, but she has very sophisticated listening devices."
>
> —Edgar Argo

LEARNING OBJECTIVES

After finishing this chapter, you should be able to:

6.1 Explain the importance of law enforcement interactions with the courts.

6.2 Describe the major issues related to due process, especially as it relates to search and seizure.

6.3 Identify how technology has changed law enforcement tactics.

6.4 Identify how and when a search or arrest warrant can be obtained.

6.5 Provide examples of court decisions that have limited police searches and seizures and the associated concepts, such as probable cause, reasonable suspicion, and the exclusionary rule.

6.6 Identify the major landmark cases related directly to how police conduct searches, with an emphasis on warrants.

6.7 Summarize cases related to the right to counsel at trial.

INTRODUCTION: THE IMPORTANCE OF JUSTICE, LAW, AND ORDER

The rule of law is a fundamental principle in the criminal justice system in the United States. It is based on the belief that all government officers, including those in the criminal justice system, pledge to uphold and follow the Constitution, not any particular human leader. Law enforcement interacts with all the components of the criminal justice system, especially the courts, and must follow the rule of law to maintain legitimacy and trust. Judges, prosecutors, and defense attorneys depend on the police to follow the myriad laws in arresting, detaining, and questioning suspects. Law enforcement is held to historical and evolving legal mandates when dealing with suspects. As noted previously, police officers are the gatekeepers to the criminal justice system and often are exposed to the highest level of scrutiny and legal standards, beginning with the initial citizen contact and ending at trial. The judiciary depends on police administrators and officers to add valuable testimony when a case goes to trial. All evidence gathered and introduced by a law enforcement agency must conform to established legal standards.

Law and order is not just a popular television show; the phrase represents two significant underlying themes in the criminal justice system. The conflict between law and order often creates an inherent clash between the protection of citizens and individual freedoms.[1] The need for law and order is fundamental,

COMMON MISCONCEPTIONS

Federal, State, and Local Policing Perform the Same Duties

State and local governments are responsible for fighting ordinary crime. Local police departments patrol and respond to calls for service in communities. State police typically handle highways and many rural areas that lack police departments or sheriff's offices. The duties of federal law enforcement vary according to the agency. Dozens of federal law enforcement agencies exist, including the Library of Congress Police, the Defense Criminal Investigative Service, and the FBI. The FBI, for example, is a bureau in the Department of Justice and is responsible for law enforcement in the areas of domestic and international terrorism, counterintelligence, public corruption, civil rights, organized crime, white-collar crime, and cybercrime. The FBI is considered a national security and intelligence organization, not a national police force. A law enforcement agency is any agency empowered to enforce U.S. laws.

Think About It

1. In what ways do the jurisdictions of law enforcement agencies overlap? Is this beneficial to the criminal justice system and members of the public? Why or why not?

2. Is there really a need for all these levels of law enforcement? Why or why not?

3. How would you structure jurisdictions in law enforcement if you were in charge? What advantages does your plan have over existing structures?

though what is defined as criminal may change according to political agendas that influence our nation's policies. When J. Edgar Hoover, who served as the director of the Federal Bureau of Investigation (FBI) for 48 years, remarked in the quotation at the beginning of the chapter that justice may or may not occur as a consequence of law and order, he undermined the most fundamental belief of our system, though his words ring true in some cases. When law enforcement officers fail to do the right thing or violate individual freedoms guaranteed by the Constitution, the courts should intercede. In the early 1900s, the U.S. Supreme Court began to establish rules on individual freedoms guaranteed by the Constitution. In *Weeks v. United States* (1914), for example, the Court unanimously ruled that repeated warrantless searches of Fremont Weeks's home and seizure of private possessions violated his rights under the Fourth Amendment, which is the right to be secure from unreasonable searches and seizures. The *Weeks* decision set the precedent for future court decisions by ruling that a warrantless seizure of property from a private home is a violation of the Fourth Amendment.

POLICE AND THE COURTS

Due process is one of the most important concepts in our Constitution. The Fifth Amendment addresses due process at the federal level, protecting citizens against the abuse of government authority. The Fourteenth Amendment guarantees equal protection and due process to all citizens at the state levels. The full text of these important amendments is provided in the Appendix. The U.S. Supreme Court broadly defines the due process clause of the Constitution as comprising protections including procedural due process, substantive due process, protection against unclear laws, and application of the Bill of Rights to include the states (Fourteenth Amendment). Due process is a legal requirement, though the meaning is fluid and may change if the Supreme Court establishes a new precedent by overturning existing case law. The rule of law, however, requires that citizens be guaranteed fairness,

due process: Established rules and principles designed to protect private rights found in the Fifth and Fourteenth Amendments that prevent the government from unfairly or arbitrarily depriving anyone of life, liberty, or property.

justice, and liberty. Procedural due process is applicable to arrest and trial procedures. Most important, the Supreme Court and the Constitution place limits on police powers to ensure procedural due process. This includes guarantees against double jeopardy, proper arrest procedures, the right to silence (nonincrimination), the right to not be subject to unreasonable search and seizure, and the right to an attorney, to name a few.

Due Process and the Schuett Case

CASE STUDY

Due process is important in handling suspects in all cases, even suspects committing crimes as brutal as those perpetrated against Jennifer Schuett. In 2008, Dickinson police detective Tim Cromie and FBI special agent Richard Rennison decided to try to analyze evidence from the Schuett cold case given new developments in using DNA. This approach paid off as analysis of evidence matched a DNA sample entered into the FBI's Combined DNA Index System (CODIS) system. Their suspect's name was Dennis Earl Bradford. His DNA was catalogued in CODIS because several years earlier he had been convicted of kidnapping a woman he met in a bar in Arkansas. Bradford picked up the woman, and while driving her home he attacked her. He threatened to kill her, and he raped her. Similar to the Jennifer Schuett attack almost two decades before, Bradford slit the woman's throat and left her for dead. Like Schuett, the victim survived. She was able to give authorities his license plate number, which led to his arrest.

Bradford was initially charged with attempted first-degree murder, kidnapping, and rape for his assault on the woman. Using prosecutorial discretion, prosecutors dropped the attempted murder charge, though the remaining charges proceeded to trial. At the trial, the jury found Bradford guilty of kidnapping, but not guilty of the assault (i.e., not guilty of cutting her throat) or the rape. He was sentenced to 12 years in prison. Ultimately, he served only 3 years and was then released. Because Bradford was incarcerated, his DNA was taken and catalogued in CODIS.

Dennis Earl Bradford's driver's license photo and police sketch at the time of the assault. How accurate was Jennifer's description of a suspect? Given her young age and the trauma she experienced, how reliable was she as a witness immediately following the crime?

The CODIS match in the Schuett case meant that law enforcement was able to identify the suspect's name. With that, they could compare the police sketch of Jennifer's attacker that was made while Jennifer was in the hospital with Bradford's driver's license photo. The similarity was astonishing. When questioned about Schuett by law enforcement, Bradford admitted to his nearly deadly assault of her (at one point claiming that he thought he had killed her) and agreed to be returned to Texas to face the consequences of his actions. During this time, great care was made to ensure that none of Bradford's constitutional rights were violated. He had the right to remain silent, though he opted to speak. He had the right to an attorney, though he decided to discuss the case and ultimately confess without an attorney present. Once back in Texas, he was placed in a solitary cell, where he was on suicide watch awaiting the next steps in this case.

Case Study Video 6.1:
Interviews with case study participants

DUE PROCESS AND POLICE ACTIVITIES

Due process rights related to search and seizure are based on a rich body of court rulings. These rulings focus on arrest, warrants, and searches and address many important interrelated concepts, including probable cause, reasonable suspicion, stop and frisk, racial profiling,

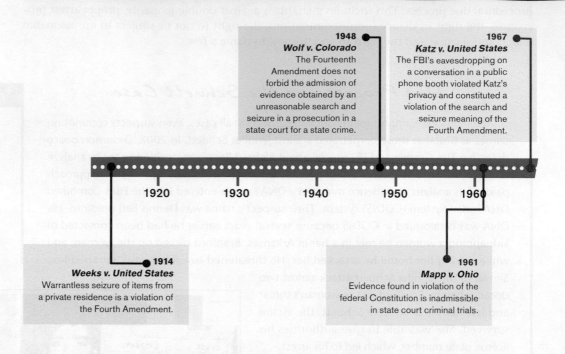

Figure 6.1 ■ U.S. Supreme Court Rulings on Due Process

1948
Wolf v. Colorado
The Fourteenth Amendment does not forbid the admission of evidence obtained by an unreasonable search and seizure in a prosecution in a state court for a state crime.

1967
Katz v. United States
The FBI's eavesdropping on a conversation in a public phone booth violated Katz's privacy and constituted a violation of the search and seizure meaning of the Fourth Amendment.

1920   1930   1940   1950   1960

1914
Weeks v. United States
Warrantless seizure of items from a private residence is a violation of the Fourth Amendment.

1961
Mapp v. Ohio
Evidence found in violation of the federal Constitution is inadmissible in state court criminal trials.

Sources: Case citations in order of appearance: *Weeks v. United States,* 232 U.S. 383 (1914); *Wolf v. Colorado,* 338 U.S. 25 (1949); *Mapp v. Ohio,* 367 U.S. 643 (1961); *Katz v. United States,* 389 U.S. 347 (1967); *Terry v. Ohio,* 392 U.S. 1 (1968);

searches, the exclusionary rule, seizures, and privacy. The number of court decisions at the state and federal levels on just search and seizure related to persons, homes, and cars is large, and the details of each decision are painstakingly reviewed in criminal law books and Court opinions. Figure 6.1 provides a few examples of related U.S. Supreme Court cases.

Probable Cause

Probable cause is the standard established by criminal law to make an arrest, obtain a warrant, or conduct a search. A widely cited definition of probable cause is "a reasonable amount of suspicion, supported by circumstances sufficiently strong to justify a prudent and cautious person's belief that certain facts are probably true."[2] An example of probable cause would be an officer who can plainly see or smell contraband such as drugs or stolen merchandise. Another example would be the admission of committing a crime. The terminology of "probable cause" is derived from the Fourth Amendment:

Journal:
Probable cause

> The right of the people to be secure in their persons, houses, papers, and effects, against unreasonable searches and seizures, shall not be violated, and no warrants shall issue, but upon probable cause, supported by oath or affirmation, and particularly describing the place to be searched, and the persons or things to be seized.

The exact definition and parameters of what constitutes probable cause have evolved through numerous court decisions. Consider a motorist who is pulled over for speeding. Under what circumstances may a police officer have probable cause to search the vehicle? Often, when officers are suspicious of a person's behavior, they may simply ask to search the car.

probable cause: In criminal law, the existence of more than a suspicion that a person has committed an illegal act.

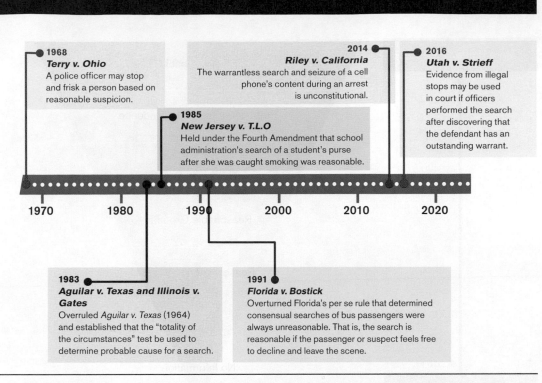

1968
Terry v. Ohio
A police officer may stop and frisk a person based on reasonable suspicion.

2014
Riley v. California
The warrantless search and seizure of a cell phone's content during an arrest is unconstitutional.

2016
Utah v. Strieff
Evidence from illegal stops may be used in court if officers performed the search after discovering that the defendant has an outstanding warrant.

1985
New Jersey v. T.L.O
Held under the Fourth Amendment that school administration's search of a student's purse after she was caught smoking was reasonable.

1970   1980   1990   2000   2010   2020

1983
Aguilar v. Texas and Illinois v. Gates
Overruled *Aguilar v. Texas* (1964) and established that the "totality of the circumstances" test be used to determine probable cause for a search.

1991
Florida v. Bostick
Overturned Florida's per se rule that determined consensual searches of bus passengers were always unreasonable. That is, the search is reasonable if the passenger or suspect feels free to decline and leave the scene.

Illinois v. Gates, 462 U.S. 213 (1983); *Aguilar v. Texas,* 378 U.S. 108 (1964); *New Jersey v. T.L.O.,* 469 U.S. 325 (1985); *Florida v. Bostick,* 501 U.S. 419 (1991); *Riley v. California,* 573 U.S. ___ (2014); *Utah v. Strieff,* 579 U.S. ___ (2016).

CASE STUDY

When Joshua Paul Benjamin was questioned about suspected sex offenses, he gave law enforcement consent to search his house, where they discovered pornographic photographs and video of underage children being sexually assaulted. Under the rights granted by the courts and Constitution, a person may say no to warrantless searches. It is unclear whether Joshua, who did not consult an attorney when questioned, recognized this right or opted to proceed nonetheless.

In order to conduct a search, officers must show probable cause (see Figure 6.2). In 1983, the Supreme Court ruled that probable cause is established by "substantial chance" or a "fair probability" of illegal activity.[3] The court determined that a reasonable person, in this case law enforcement, must believe that "there is a fair probability that contraband or evidence of a crime will be found."[4] In the case of a traffic violation, a motorist's surly attitude is not enough to constitute probable cause, though the trace aroma of marijuana and erratic driving may lead a reasonable person to believe that drugs will be found in the car.

CASE STUDY

Turning to one of our case studies, Chris Farias's slow driving of a motorcycle in extremely cold weather established the initial reason for the police stop. After his arrest, Chris was booked and required to undergo a chemical test. At the time of his test, it was legal to force defendants to submit. In April 2013, the Supreme Court ruled in *Missouri v. NcNeely*[5] that police must obtain a warrant for blood testing without consent, though the opinion leaves open the option to conduct a warrantless blood test under circumstances on a case-by-case basis. While in jail, Chris summoned his attorney to ensure that his rights were protected.

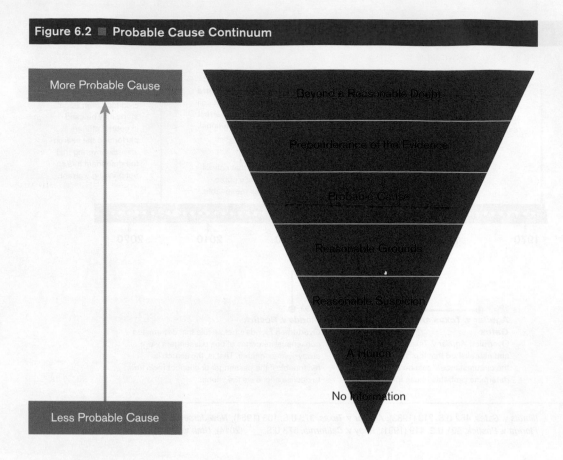

Figure 6.2 ■ Probable Cause Continuum

More Probable Cause

Beyond a Reasonable Doubt

Preponderance of the Evidence

Probable Cause

Reasonable Grounds

Reasonable Suspicion

A Hunch

No Information

Less Probable Cause

Reasonable Suspicion

Probable cause is based on a reasonable assumption that a crime is being committed and circumstances that support this belief. In some cases, an officer may have a handful of relatively weak arguments for the search, but the totality of the circumstances bolsters the case. In other words, added together, the minor suppositions in the context of the situation may warrant a search. Most standards of probable cause require more than reasonable suspicion but less evidence than necessary for a conviction.[6] **Reasonable suspicion**, like probable cause, is considered an objective measure but is based on minimal or no evidence. According to the U.S. Supreme Court in the landmark case *Terry v. Ohio* (1968), reasonable suspicion may be enough for an officer to stop and frisk a suspect.

In *Terry v. Ohio*, the Supreme Court ruled that a police officer might stop and frisk a person based on reasonable suspicion. The case began on the streets when Detective Martin McFadden observed two men acting suspiciously near a neighborhood jewelry store. The officer, who believed that the men were "casing the place for a stick-up job," decided to stop John Terry and Richard Tilton and conducted a pat-down search, also commonly referred to as a stop and frisk. The case raised two important Fourth Amendment issues: What constitutes an unreasonable search and seizure? And how is probable cause or reasonable suspicion determined, and under what circumstances? Detective McFadden, who had worked for the Cleveland Police Department for over 35 years, was wearing civilian clothes and patrolling the area for shoplifters and pickpockets. According to the transcript of the court case, McFadden stated, "They didn't look right to me." He observed two black men walking back and forth, looking in store windows, and allegedly conspiring with a third white man. He approached the three men and asked for their names. He described the incident with Terry that immediately followed: "I spun him around, holding him in front of me. I then began to pat him down. I felt inside of his topcoat what felt to be the handle of a gun." The discovery of a gun in Terry's coat resulted in the immediate arrest of

reasonable suspicion:
An objective basis supported by specific facts for believing that someone committed a crime.

all three men. McFadden argued that his search was based partly on an intuitive sixth sense acquired during his long tenure as a police officer. The Court agreed that police officers, based on their previous experiences, may "sense" whether someone is up to no good. *Terry v. Ohio* provided the guiding framework related to the constitutionality of stop and frisk, though its scope and limits continue to be addressed by the Court.

The Court heard two other cases concurrently with *Terry* that further detailed the limits of the ruling. In *Sibron v. New York* (1968), a police officer followed the defendant for several hours and observed his conversations with several known heroin addicts. The officer finally stopped, questioned, and frisked Sibron. During the initial questioning, the officer placed his hand in the suspect's pocket and discovered envelopes containing heroin. The Court ruled that the mere observation of Sibron, without hearing any of his conversations with the addicts, failed to provide probable cause for a warrantless search. In *Peters v. New York* (1968), the defendant also appealed his conviction and challenged the constitutionality of stop and frisk. In his case, the officer gave chase to the suspect after observing him sneaking around an apartment building. The officer patted down the suspect and found burglary tools. In this case, the Court upheld the stop and frisk as constitutional.

A police officer must have probable cause to search a vehicle. What types of situations may give police probable cause to search a car?

Stop and Frisk

The *Terry* decision represented the first in a series of cases related to the intricate issues involved in **stop and frisk**. In *Adams v. Williams* (1972), for example, the Court ruled that reasonable cause for a stop and frisk may be based on information supplied by another person, such as a police informant. In *Alabama v. White* (1995), the Court decided that an anonymous tip to the police provided reasonable suspicion for a Terry stop. In *Florida v. J. L.* (2000), the court debated a "firearms exception" to *Terry v. Ohio*. In other words, any anonymous tip about a person carrying firearms would justify a stop and frisk. The courts refused to recognize this exception because such a ruling could promote false tips to law enforcement and harassment of innocent people. The body of law related to stop and frisk is substantial. Numerous other cases tied to *Terry*, for example, have examined the reasonable suspicion standard, the meaning of seizure, and the limitations of pat-down searches.

In 2013, the ongoing debates and court decisions about Terry stops drew national attention. The New York Police Department received harsh criticism for its stop-and-frisk tactics (see Figure 6.3). Reportedly, almost 700,000 people were stopped in 2011, and the majority of suspects were African American or Latino. Despite complaints made by the New York Civil Liberties Union, then mayor Michael Bloomberg and the police department reported a reduction in murders over the past 10 years and documented the confiscation of more than 8,000 weapons, including just over 800 guns, partly attributable to the stop and frisks (see Figure 6.3). The department argued that stop and frisk represented part of a community-wide effort to detect crime before it happens; others saw the practice as racial profiling. In August 2013, a federal district court judge ruled that the department's tactics were unconstitutional and represented a method of "indirect racial profiling."[7] In January 2014, Mayor Bill de Blasio agreed to the reforms proposed by the court and announced an agreement to settle the civil rights lawsuits (see also Chapter 5).

Video 6.1:
Stop and frisk

stop and frisk:
Also known as a Terry stop or field stop, this allows a police officer to detain and search a person when he or she reasonably suspects that a crime has been or will be committed.

Video 6.2:
Protections against
unreasonable searches

Web:
Exclusionary rule

---

exclusionary rule:
The rule excludes from
trial evidence that was
obtained unlawfully,
which violates a person's
constitutional rights.

Searches

Several landmark Supreme Court rulings have changed the way police interact with the public and expanded the rights of citizens. In 1961, in *Mapp v. Ohio* the Court found that evidence obtained in the midst of unreasonable searches and seizures may not be used in criminal prosecutions in state courts. Police officers in Cleveland, Ohio, received information about a suspect in a bombing case and intelligence that Dollree Mapp harbored illegal betting equipment in her house. The officers arrived at the home without a warrant and requested permission to search. Mapp refused. Several hours later the officers returned to the home with a piece of paper they portrayed to be a search warrant (it was not), but refused to show Mapp the document. Mapp grabbed the paper and stuffed it into her dress. The officers then engaged in a struggle with Mapp, took the paper, and handcuffed her. Although the police found nothing in the house related to the intelligence they had received, they discovered pornographic materials. Mapp was arrested, found guilty, and sentenced for possessing these illicit photos. No search warrant was produced during the trial. The Supreme Court, in a 6–3 decision, ruled that the search and seizure of materials at Mapp's home was unconstitutional and that any evidence obtained in an illegal search was inadmissible at trial. Prior to the *Mapp* decision, this protection had already been granted citizens at the federal level.

Exclusionary Rule

The **exclusionary rule** was applied to the states in *Mapp v. Ohio*. In this case, the Supreme Court ruled that any evidence obtained during an illegal search would be disallowed at trial. Subsequent Court decisions modified the *Mapp* decision and now allow for an inevitable discovery rule and good faith exceptions.[8] The original intent of the exclusionary rule was to deter police misconduct, though legal experts often argue that the Court's decision hampered investigation, arrest, and conviction. Perhaps in response to the criticism and the need for flexibility, the Supreme Court has established exceptions to the *Mapp* ruling. In the case of *United States v. Leon* (1984),[9] the court found the need for a good faith exception to the

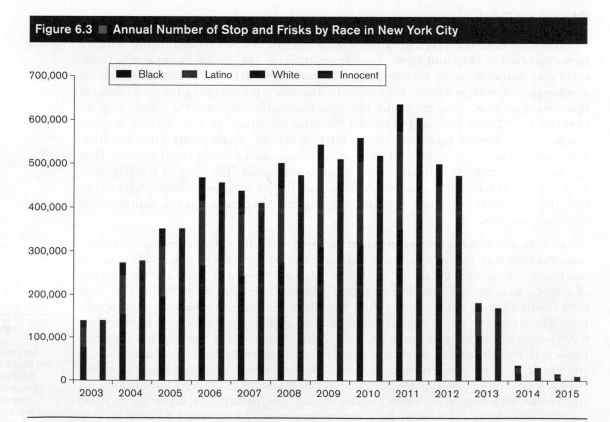

Figure 6.3 ■ Annual Number of Stop and Frisks by Race in New York City

Source: Adapted from Stop-and-Frisk Data, New York Civil Liberties Union.

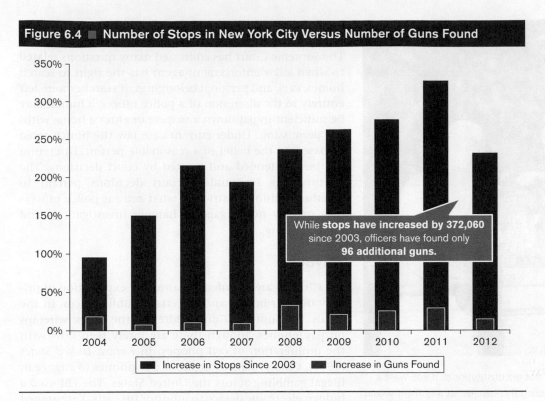

Figure 6.4 ■ Number of Stops in New York City Versus Number of Guns Found

While **stops have increased by 372,060** since 2003, officers have found only **96 additional guns.**

■ Increase in Stops Since 2003   ■ Increase in Guns Found

Source: Stop-and-Frisk Graph is reprinted with permission from the New York Civil Liberties Union (www.nyclu.org).

exclusionary rule. Alberto Leon was arrested for possessing a large stash of drugs after police received intelligence from an informant. In this case, police obtained a warrant, but another judge determined that the reasons for the search were weak and failed to establish probable cause. As a result, the evidence could not be introduced at trial. The Supreme Court, however, held that police officers trying to do the right thing by obtaining a search warrant should be allowed an exception to the rule if they acted in good faith. The six justices who issued the majority opinion believed that strict adherence to the exclusionary rule without consideration of the costs and benefits would hinder truth finding and justice.

The **fruit of the poisonous tree** doctrine is an extension of the exclusionary rule.[10] Under this doctrine, any additional evidence discovered as a result of the initial illegal police activity also may be excluded. If the police, for example, conducted an illegal search of a suspected marijuana growing operation (i.e., they lacked a warrant) and discovered evidence that methamphetamine was being cooked at the site, the latter evidence would fall under the fruit of the poisonous tree and likely be ruled inadmissible. The legal metaphor denotes that if the source (tree) is diseased, then any gains (fruit) are tainted. In other words, the marijuana evidence would be suppressed under the exclusionary rule, and the evidence of methamphetamine would fall under the poisonous tree doctrine.

Another exception to the exclusionary rule is **inevitable discovery**. In other words, with or without a search warrant, the police would have discovered the evidence. This doctrine holds that evidence, though obtained unconstitutionally without a search warrant, can be used in court if by a preponderance of evidence it can be established that police would have clearly discovered it no matter what the circumstances.

Seizures

The Fourth Amendment protects "the right of the people to be secure in their persons, houses, papers, and effects, against unreasonable searches and seizures." Seizures may include the arrest of a suspect and the confiscation of physical evidence. The laws

fruit of the poisonous tree: Also called the exclusionary rule, this doctrine was applied to the states in *Mapp v. Ohio*. This case ruled that any evidence obtained during an illegal search would be disallowed at trial.

inevitable discovery: In criminal law, the rule makes an exception to the fruit of the poisonous tree doctrine. Illegally obtained evidence may be used if eventually it would have been found legally.

Private trash searches are not unconstitutional. If you were a member of the court deciding this case, what argument would you use for and against the right to search through trash?

surrounding searches and seizures have become more clearly defined, particularly as a result of court decisions. The Supreme Court has addressed many questions related to when a law enforcement agent has the right to search homes, cars, and personal belongings. If searches were left entirely to the discretion of a police officer, a hunch may be sufficient to pat down a suspect or enter a home without permission. Under current case law the hunch must be based on the belief of a reasonable person. Discretion has been extended and limited by court decisions. The controversies surrounding court decisions pertain to whether decisions restricting what actions police officers may or may not engage in hamper investigations and crime fighting.

Privacy

Citizens are afforded a reasonable expectation of privacy in their homes and in certain public places. In the 1960s, the Supreme Court addressed the use of wiretaps on pay phones, though these are rarely seen now with the proliferation of cell phones. In *Katz v. United States* (1967), Charles Katz used public pay phones to engage in illegal gambling across the United States. The FBI used a hidden electronic device to monitor his calls. Katz argued that this phone tapping was a violation of his Fourth Amendment rights. Katz claimed that the FBI listening device represented a search without a warrant. The FBI case rested on the assumption that no search took place because the glass booth allowed complete visibility, though an electronic device was needed to listen to the conversations. The Court determined that a search is a search when the state violates a reasonable expectation of privacy, which in the case of a phone applies because a person expects to conduct a private conversation. The decision, however, opened further exploration related to defining a search and notions of privacy.

When people place garbage outside for pickup, do they have an expectation of privacy that police will not search their trash for evidence? In the case of *California v. Greenwood* (1988), the Laguna Beach Police Department suspected Billy Greenwood of drug trafficking. In an effort to find evidence, officers searched his trash and found enough information to obtain a search warrant for his house. The higher courts in California dismissed the charges against Greenwood after deciding that the trash searches were a violation of the Fourth Amendment. The U.S. Supreme Court, however, ruled that no warrant was necessary to search trash. According to the ruling, everyone realizes that garbage is "readily accessible to animals, children, scavengers, snoops, and other members of the public."[11] Two justices, however, dissented in the case, noting, "most of us . . . would be incensed to discover a meddler—whether a neighbor, a reporter, or a detective—scrutinizing our sealed trash containers to discover some detail of our personal lives."[12]

TECHNOLOGY

Technology has changed law enforcement tactics, and monitoring activities and behaviors is now easier. Many commentators note that we are involved in the second law enforcement technology revolution.[13] The first revolution fundamentally altered the way police were organized given the advent of the telephone, the two-way radio, and the car in law enforcement. The current revolution is bringing even greater change with the introduction and use of innovations such as record management systems, automated fingerprint identification systems (commonly referred to as AFIS), computer-assisted dispatch, less-than-lethal force

CONTEMPLATING CAREERS

Public Policy Work

Are you familiar with or interested in parliamentary procedure? Are you pragmatic and able to compromise? Are you able to build strong relationships? Do you take things personally? These are some of the questions to ask yourself if you are considering a career in public policy. Those successful in this field understand process, are pragmatic and able to compromise without abandoning ideology, and do not take things personally.

The criminal justice system looks to legislators to write and pass laws, though students in the field rarely see this as a career choice. Having members of the legislature, at either the federal or state level, familiar with the intricacies of the criminal justice system is vital to maintaining and protecting our rights. A double major in criminal justice and political science or public affairs provides a background for seeking political office and for a wide variety of jobs. Many career paths are available in legislative work, including conducting policy research, drafting bills, writing legal opinions, and, perhaps, ultimately running for office (see www .legislativecareers.org).

Career Video:
A former former lawyer and legislator discusses her experience and current issues in the field.

technologies, gunshot location technology, and many others. Much has changed with the use of these and other technologies.

Surveillance

Cameras take pictures if we run a red light or stop our cars in a pedestrian walkway. Most departments use photo radar to catch people driving over the speed limit. Security cameras (public and private) monitor and record our movements, and GPS tracking devices follow our driving routes. Even toll road payment boxes in automobiles can be used to track a citizen's movement. The increased use of technology by law enforcement and the ability to monitor our movements changes expectations of privacy. Issues of privacy related to technology are especially troublesome, as many companies providing technology are privately owned.

The use of technology has created troubling situations for police and the courts. In 2001, the Supreme Court ruled that heat-sensing thermal imaging technology to observe activity in a person's house could not be used without a warrant. In this case, thermal imaging was used to monitor Danny Lee Kyllo's home for radiant heat. Federal agents believed Kyllo, who lived in Oregon, was growing marijuana, and the imaging device showed high levels of heat being emitted from several areas in the house, which was assumed to show grow lights for the crops. The agents used this information to obtain a search warrant and found 100 marijuana plants. The Court, in a close decision (5–4), determined that the thermal imaging was

Red light cameras are an efficient way of identifying speeding vehicles. Should the public be warned of the presence of a camera? Why or why not?

a search, which required a warrant. The decision was based on a reasonable expectation of privacy even with the availability of technology outside the home.

Law enforcement surveillance is essential to criminal investigations and may be conducted, for example, through computers, satellites, and mobile phones. The **Communications Assistance for Law Enforcement Act** (1994) allows federal agencies to more easily monitor phone calls and Internet messages (see Figure 6.5). After the September 11 terrorist attacks, sophisticated monitoring devices were designed to search suspicious terms in emails, texts, and phone conversations. In contrast, the Electronic Communication Privacy Act (ECPA; 1986) established stricter standards and requirements for search warrants. The ECPA, however, allows agencies access to emails older than 180 days without a search warrant. In 2010, an appellate court held that email was protected under Fourth Amendment rights and government agencies must establish probable cause before forcing Internet providers to reveal users' messages.[14]

Communications Assistance for Law Enforcement Act: A 1994 law that allows federal agencies to more easily monitor an individual's phone calls and Internet messages.

Currently, courts are struggling over the issue of monitoring cell phones and whether a warrant is needed in nonemergency situations. In Rhode Island, a judge determined that cell phone evidence collected without a warrant could not be used in the trial of a man charged with murdering a 6-year-old. In contrast, a Washington court ruled that text messages and voicemail messages are not protected under state privacy laws. In California, police may examine information on a cell phone if found on a suspect at the time of arrest. The U.S. Supreme Court has yet to hear a case dealing with cell phones, though in 2012 it ruled that a search warrant is needed to install a GPS tracking device on private property such as vehicles.[15]

83%

of Law Enforcement Personnel Use **Social Media** to Conduct Investigations

Canine Searches

While often not thought of as technology, a dog is an investigative tool—a form of technology—used to investigate crime. The Supreme Court also is tasked with determining the limits of search and seizure with police dogs. In most cases, the Court has determined that canine sniffs are allowed under the Fourth Amendment. Trained drug-sniffing dogs are commonly used in airports, and any alerts by the canines may establish probable cause for a search warrant. In 2012, the Court examined the actions of Franky, a Labrador Retriever, and Aldo, a German Shepherd. The cases began in Florida when state courts determined that the detection of drugs by police dogs constituted unreasonable search and seizure under the Fourth Amendment. The two primary questions in the case involved the use and qualifications of the dogs. Can a dog sniff outside a home without a warrant? What qualifications are necessary for a dog to conduct a sniff and search?

In Franky's case, an anonymous informant reported a marijuana growing operation inside a particular house. Franky and a detective went to the door, and the dog alerted his handler to the odor of drugs. The decision in the Florida court noted this tactic was an "unreasonable governmental intrusion into the sanctity of the home." In other words, the expectation of privacy is higher in your home compared with an airport or a public street. In Aldo's case, an officer pulled over Clayton Harris for an expired license plate. Harris, who appeared nervous, refused the officer's request to search the truck after the latter noticed an open beer can. Aldo circled the truck in a "free air sniff" and gave the officer his alert sign for drugs. The subsequent search revealed 200

Courtesy of Ventura County Star

This police dog became sick after inhaling methamphetamine during a search in Ventura County, California. Under what circumstances should law enforcement agencies be allowed to use canines?

ETHICAL ISSUES

The T-Ray Machine and Personal Privacy

In January 2013, newspapers announced the New York Police Department's use of the T-Ray machine. The machine detects terahertz radiation, described as high-frequency electromagnetic natural energy emitted by the human body. The T-Ray penetrates almost all materials except metal. The scanner image can show the outline of a hidden object such as a gun. In a public demonstration, the T-Ray scanner highlighted a plainclothes officer, who appeared neon green with a black gun shape. The machine, developed in collaboration with a security and surveillance company and the London Metropolitan Police, can be mounted on a truck and taken into violence-prone neighborhoods. This first-generation prototype is a multimillion dollar device, but future technological advances may provide for a handheld, less costly model.

New York City has engaged in an aggressive and apparently successful campaign to reduce criminal behavior. One method has been to employ stop-and-frisk searches.

Think About It

Technology such as the T-Ray machine raises important ethical issues.

1. What due process concerns might arise because of the T-Ray?

2. Should the police be able to scan everyone on the streets as a means of reducing gun violence?

3. Does this crime-fighting tool violate expectations of privacy? Why or why not?

Source: El-Ghobashy, T. (2013, January 23). Police tool targets guns. *The Wall Street Journal.* Retrieved from http://www.wsj.com/articles/SB10001424127887323539804578260261579068182.

---

pseudoephedrine pills and 8,000 matches, both ingredients used to manufacture methamphetamine. Aldo's reliability, however, was called into question by the state court, whereas Franky's career included almost 400 documented positive alerts.

In 2013, the Supreme Court's decision limited the use of dogs to sniff outside a home for illegal drugs. The 5–4 decision determined that using trained police dogs to investigate a home or the surrounding area constituted a search and required a warrant under the Fourth Amendment.[16] In the case of the search of Harris's vehicle, however, the Court ruled that the use of the dog's alert for drugs was constitutional.

WARRANT REQUIREMENTS AND SERVING WARRANTS

The Fourth Amendment requires a warrant before police can conduct a search, though some exceptions exist. The key issue in obtaining a warrant is probable cause. An officer seeking a warrant must be able to articulate probable cause in an affidavit to the issuing judge. In *Katz v. United States*, the Supreme Court determined that searches conducted outside the judicial process are a violation of the Fourth Amendment,[17] which protects citizens against unreasonable searches and seizures and requires probable cause for a warrant. Search warrant requests must define a reasonable amount of time (e.g., not more than 10 days). Also, the warrant must contain specific information on the place and items police expect to find. When a person's home is the target, the correct address and related information are vital to the safety of the officers and citizens; otherwise the results can be tragic.

Police search the home of New England Patriot Aaron Hernandez. The information a police officer uses to request a search warrant must be accurate to avoid litigation. What additional requirements might be developed to avoid mistakes in search warrants?

Mistakes on search warrants have been known to occur.[18] Mistakes such as searching the incorrect residence result in negative consequences; innocent people are harassed, public trust of law enforcement is eroded, and citizen confidence in the criminal justice system diminishes. Consider an actual case in which a police officer shot a 61-year-old man and handcuffed his wife after conducting a drug raid on the wrong house. According to the department, the informant in the case gave the officers the incorrect address; the suspected drug activity was next door. In Delaware, a SWAT (special weapons and tactics) team entered the wrong house at 6 a.m. looking for a suspect to collect DNA evidence. In another case, the chief of police was forced to resign after an officer allegedly lied about the address of a crack house under surveillance. The officer obtained the search warrant based on intelligence from an informant who claimed to have purchased drugs at the house and swore that he had seen people loitering and drinking on the front lawn. The SWAT team shot and killed the resident.

POLICY ISSUES

Combating Terrorism Versus Protecting Civil Liberties

After the 9/11 attacks, Congress passed legislation to assist law enforcement agencies in the war on terror. The USA PATRIOT Act consists of more than 150 sections and changed about 15 federal statues involving criminal procedure, intelligence gathering, and wiretapping. Covert searches, for example, can be conducted without notification in homes and other private places. Information from computers can be downloaded in secret. Wiretaps can be used without warrants, although probable cause and review within the Department of Justice are necessary. Other parts of the act allow

- tracing electronic communications,
- access to stored voicemail,
- "sneak and peek" search warrants,
- nationwide execution of warrants in terrorism cases,
- easier access to confidential information, and
- collection of DNA samples from prisoners convicted of any federal crimes of violence or terrorism.

Proponents of the act argue that the expanded powers given law enforcement provide the tools necessary to identify terrorist threats and prevent further attacks.

Opponents believe the expanded power of the government will harm freedoms. The American Civil Liberties Union believes the act is a "surveillance monster." Many people argue that the USA PATRIOT Act threatens our First, Fourth, Fifth, Sixth, Eighth, and Fourteenth Amendment rights.

Think About It

Several questions are raised regarding the tension between combatting terrorism and protecting civil liberties.

1. **What limits should be placed on investigating and arresting suspects at the federal and local levels?**

2. **What conditions in the PATRIOT Act may violate our rights to privacy?**

3. **Does the act offer protection or intrude on civil freedom?**

Most search warrants are executed during the day and require the police to identify themselves. A knock-and-announce warrant commonly is used by the police. In these cases, law enforcement must wait a reasonable amount of time for anyone in the house to answer before using a forced entry. A no-knock warrant allows officers to enter a house forcibly without identifying themselves as law enforcement if justified by the circumstances. No-knock warrants remain controversial, but the increase in the use of this type of warrant is substantial. Research estimates that in 1981, about 3,000 no-knock warrants were conducted, compared with more than 50,000 in 2005.[19]

> **CASE STUDY**
>
> Danny's experience with the police and the criminal justice system has not been positive in general. The many times he was arrested, or stopped by police, he felt his civil rights and due process were not always honored. However, given who he was — a gang banger — he did not feel he had any recourse and took these as inevitable punches from the police. Like these interactions, Danny noted that his earlier arrests happened in a similar way: The police would kick in his family's door during the wee hours of the morning. He would be arrested and his apartment would be searched.
>
> Interestingly, he noted that the way the retaliatory shooting case was handled was quite different. The day of the shooting, Danny went home and assumed the police would be there during the early hours to arrest him. They never arrived. Days went by and the police never came. Almost a week later, Danny heard the phone at his apartment ring. He answered it, and a police officer introduced himself and asked if Danny would come to the station to answer some questions involving a shooting, noting that he thought one of the members of Danny's gang might be involved. Danny agreed, went to the station, and lied about his involvement. The police thanked him and he went home. Again, several days went by. During this time, the police interviewed his collaborator — the actual shooter. This individual confessed and provided damning evidence against Danny. One early morning after that, the police kicked in his family's apartment door and arrested him. Danny noted that during this arrest, unlike so many earlier arrests, they did their jobs well. They were polite (as one can be when arresting someone), and they took care to ensure Danny's rights were not violated.

Exceptions to Warrants

Court rulings have carved out six exceptions that justify warrantless searches.[20] The six exceptions are consent, plain view, exigent circumstances, incident to a lawful arrest, automobiles, and regulatory searches. If police officers ask for permission to search, and you voluntarily say yes, they can proceed. The key to **consent** is that the agreement must be made without any coercion such as a threat of arrest.

The **plain view doctrine** allows police to seize illegal materials or evidence without a warrant. If an officer enters a house and sees illegal contraband on the table, it would be silly to think he or she would need to contact a judge for a search warrant, though the Supreme Court ruled in *Arizona v. Hicks* (1987) that evidence must be in plain view. In other words, the police are not allowed to open drawers or move belongings to find evidence.

Exigent circumstances, or emergency circumstances, are narrowly defined by the Court to provide for searches when warrants cannot be obtained. Exigent circumstances are present to prevent (a) escape, (b) harm to the officer or others, and (c) destruction of evidence. For example, if an officer holds some reasonable belief that someone's safety is at risk or evidence of criminal activity may be destroyed, then entrance without a warrant is justified. In other words, the time it may take to obtain a warrant would give the suspect the opportunity to destroy the evidence or perhaps in a worst-case scenario cause physical harm to another person. Other circumstances include hot pursuit of a criminal suspect and the need to render immediate aid to a person in trouble.

consent: When police officers ask for permission to search, and you voluntarily say yes, they can proceed without a warrant.

plain view doctrine: The rule that permits police officers to seize evidence without a warrant if it is easily seen.

exigent circumstances: One of six exceptions that allow a warrantless search. These are emergency circumstances that are present to prevent (a) escape, (b) harm to the officer or others, and (c) destruction of evidence.

Incident to a lawful arrest allows law enforcement to search any person without a warrant once that person is lawfully arrested. The Supreme Court decision in *Chimel v. California* (1969) established the arm's length doctrine. According to the Court, a police officer may search a suspect and the area surrounding the suspect to prevent injury to the officer and the destruction of any evidence. The **automobile exception** states that should police have probable cause to believe that a vehicle (including boats) contains contraband, fruits of a crime, or evidence and/or instrumentalities of crime, the vehicle can be searched. The stop-and-frisk exception, as previously discussed, allows police to stop a person given a reasonable suspicion of a criminal act. In addition, this exception allows the police to frisk the suspect if they believe the person is armed and dangerous. Finally, **regulatory searches** by government officials, such as restaurant health inspections, inspections of vehicles crossing borders, airport screenings, and fire inspections, may be conducted without warrants (see Figure 6.5).

Arrests

An individual walking down the street is stopped by the police for questioning. Is this individual under arrest? A driver is pulled over by the police. Is this individual under arrest? Most courts agree that someone is under arrest when a reasonable person believes that she or he is not free to leave. In an investigatory stop a person is still free to leave, and the incident likely involves a brief time period. Once a person is placed under arrest, he or she may be detained for an extended period of time. If you were stopped for speeding and asked to step out of the car to answer questions, a reasonable person might or might not assume you were not under arrest. When an officer handcuffs you, however, the assumption is that you are under arrest, though physical restraints are not the defining factor. The courts remain

incident to a lawful arrest: This exception allows law enforcement to search any person without a warrant once that person is lawfully arrested.

automobile exception: States that, should police have probable cause to believe that a vehicle (including boats) contains contraband, fruits of a crime, evidence, and/or instrumentalities of crime, the vehicle can be searched.

regulatory searches: Searches by government officials, such as restaurant health inspections, inspection of vehicles crossing borders, airport screenings, and fire inspections, that may be conducted without a warrant.

Video 6.3:
Arrest warrant

Figure 6.5 ■ Evidentiary Search Overview

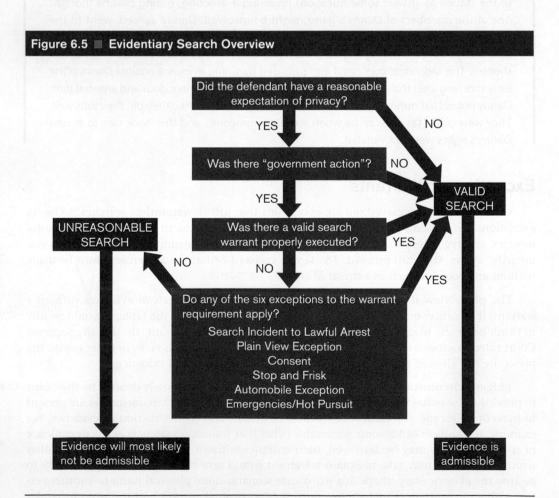

Did the defendant have a reasonable expectation of privacy?

YES → NO → VALID SEARCH

Was there "government action"? NO → VALID SEARCH

YES

Was there a valid search warrant properly executed? YES → VALID SEARCH

NO

Do any of the six exceptions to the warrant requirement apply?
Search Incident to Lawful Arrest
Plain View Exception
Consent
Stop and Frisk
Automobile Exception
Emergencies/Hot Pursuit

NO → UNREASONABLE SEARCH → Evidence will most likely not be admissible

YES → VALID SEARCH → Evidence is admissible

Source: Reprinted with permission from National Paralegal College.

unclear about whether the words "you are under arrest" are necessary and sufficient, but a person must be informed within a reasonable time period of a formal arrest.

On the surface, it appears that being under arrest is a simple idea; however, the actuality is much more complex. The question of being under arrest requires probable cause and may be obvious when handcuffs are used, guns are pointed, or the words are stated. A lawful arrest entails taking a person into legal custody either under a valid warrant or based on probable cause the person committed a crime.[21]

Being Informed of Rights: Mirandized

A person must be informed of certain rights if taken into custody and interrogated. An arrest, in and of itself, does not require that Miranda rights be read and applies only when suspects are questioned. In 1966, the Supreme Court considered the case of *Miranda v. Arizona*. Ernesto Miranda was arrested in Phoenix and during a 2-hour interrogation confessed to kidnapping and raping a woman. The police recorded the interrogation, though Miranda was never fully informed of his rights prior to the questioning. Miranda, who was uneducated and had a history of mental illness, made his confession without an attorney being present and without realizing that the information he provided to the police was self-incriminating. After his conviction, he appealed to the Arizona Supreme Court, arguing that the confession was obtained unconstitutionally. The state-level appeal was unsuccessful. The U.S. Supreme Court, however, overturned his conviction because he had not been informed of his Fifth Amendment right against self-incrimination and his Sixth Amendment right guaranteeing an attorney in a criminal case.[22] Miranda's conviction was overturned, but he was retried and convicted without the use of the confession. The case resulted in the establishment of guidelines that must be followed when informing a suspect of her or his rights. That ruling stated:

> The person in custody must, prior to interrogation, be clearly informed that he/she has the right to remain silent, and that anything the person says will be used against that person in court; the person must be clearly informed that he/she has the right to consult with an attorney and to have that attorney present during questioning, and that, if he/she is indigent, an attorney will be provided at no cost to represent him/her.

Contrary to common beliefs, there is no specific required wording that must be read to the suspect, although many people are familiar with this wording:

> You have the right to remain silent. Anything you say can and will be used against you in a court of law. You have the right to an attorney. If you cannot afford an attorney, one will be provided for you. Do you understand the rights I have just read to you? With these rights in mind, do you wish to speak to me?

The exact moment of arrest can be difficult to determine. If you were interacting with a police officer during a traffic stop, at what points in the encounter might you believe you were under arrest? Why?

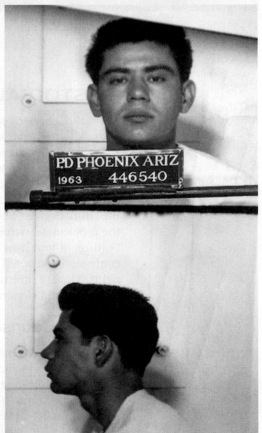

Ernesto Miranda following his arrest in Phoenix, Arizona. Explain why the *Miranda* case is so important and receives so much attention.

Danny Escobedo. Should an arrestee ever talk to the police without an attorney? Why or why not?

While *Miranda* is the most widely known decision related to this topic, it is important to recognize that Miranda warnings today represent the culmination of many similar cases related to individual rights presented to the Supreme Court. Some legal scholars argue, for example, that since the actual *Miranda* ruling, courts have made a number of decisions that have weakened the original intent of the landmark decision. Exceptions to *Miranda* became more common during the 1970s and 1980s under Chief Justice Warren Burger's stewardship of the Supreme Court. The ruling in *Harris v. New York* (1971)[23] held that defendants could be impeached based on statements made before they were Mirandized. In 1984, the Court also established a public safety exception in cases in which the police lacked sufficient time to read Miranda rights. In 2010, the Supreme Court ruled in *Berghuis v. Thompkins* that defendants who have been Mirandized, understood this warning, and not waived these rights must explicitly declare during or before an interrogation that they want to remain silent and not speak to the police for that protection against self-incrimination to take effect.[24] Since 2010, anything shared with the police prior to this declaration can be used against them.

CUSTODIAL INTERROGATION

Journal:
Interrogation technique

Although many forms of interrogation exist, this section focuses on one particular type: custodial interrogation. After arrest, a suspect is questioned, or interrogated, by police about the crime under investigation. Police often believe they can obtain confessions, which can be used at trial to bolster conviction rates. Before the early 1930s, police were known to use multiple unsavory tactics to persuade suspects to confess, including beatings, torture, tricks, and threats. The brutality and violence associated with the interrogations became known as the "third degree," as described in Chapter 4. As early as 1936, the Supreme Court recognized the problematic nature of gaining information through violent or coercive means. After the beatings of four men by police attempting to obtain a confession, the Court suppressed the confession and ruled that the interrogation was a violation of the defendants' due process rights. Though difficult to believe, many suspects have been known to give false confessions under stressful circumstances.[25]

Right to Counsel

Audio:
Need a public defender in New Orleans? Get in line

The Sixth Amendment guarantees the right to counsel during questioning. This right was confirmed in *Escobedo v. Illinois* (1964). In January 1960, Manuel Valtierra was murdered. The following morning, Danny Escobedo, Valtierra's brother-in-law, was arrested without a warrant and questioned by police. During the interrogation, Escobedo remained silent and was released. Shortly thereafter, an additional suspect in custody told police that Escobedo had murdered Valtierra following the mistreatment of his wife, Escobedo's sister. Escobedo (and his sister Grace) were then arrested. When police questioned Escobedo in custody, they were met with silence except for his repeated requests to speak to an attorney. At the same time, Escobedo's attorney was attempting to gain access to his client. Ignoring Escobedo's recurrent requests to communicate with his attorney, police continued the custodial interrogation for 14 hours. Finally, Escobedo made statements signifying his knowledge of the crime, which led to his eventual conviction for murder. Escobedo appealed the conviction to the Illinois Supreme Court, arguing that he was denied his constitutional right to an attorney during questioning. The Court ruled in his favor. Illinois then petitioned for a rehearing, which resulted in a second murder conviction. Escobedo appealed to the U.S. Supreme Court, which ultimately ruled that the actions by the police were a violation of Escobedo's Sixth Amendment right to counsel and his Fifth Amendment right against self-incrimination.

CHAPTER WRAP-UP

The laws and cases related to a citizen's rights under the Constitution are numerous and often involve subtle distinctions. Police are responsible for maintaining public order and ensuring public safety, in addition to preventing and detecting crime. The onus on law enforcement is to accomplish these tasks without violating the rights of the individual and to act within the boundaries of the law. Laws establish police power to control and regulate the behavior of citizens and law enforcement. Case law, as seen in court precedents, provides further definition on the exceptions of what rights to privacy are protected. Federal and state legislators also enact laws to protect our constitutional freedoms.

Not all laws have the intended effect, and some become burdensome. Some legal commentators and researchers, for example, argue that the myriad laws passed to harshly punish sex offenders created a moral panic, which stigmatizes a person as evil for life.[26] Sex offender registry laws and resident restrictions isolate offenders and limit their employment and opportunities. In other instances, the law has failed to keep up, especially in cases of white-collar crime. Often, professional and occupational white-collar crime is unethical behavior, and whether these actions should be considered criminal is debatable.[27] In these cases, laws are implemented after the crimes occur and cannot be applied retroactively. The rule of law evolves according to perceived and actual societal needs, and the consequences may be good or bad.

CASE STUDY

In this chapter, we discussed how the rule of law influenced how our case studies were handled. In the case of Joshua Paul Benjamin, he consented to a request by the police to search his home. With his consent, the police were not required to obtain a warrant to search his apartment, where they found video evidence of his crimes. The rule of law also played an important role in the Schuett case. When law enforcement identified the perpetrator, they took care to ensure that the rights of the accused were respected.

This chapter concludes our attention to policing in the criminal justice system. In the next chapter we begin our consideration of the courts. This is the first in a series of chapters devoted to courts and the judicial process. In it, we discuss federal and state courses, court congestion, problem-solving courts, and the role of judges.

KEY POINTS

- Maintaining law and order protects individuals and their freedoms.

- The due process clause protects against unclear laws and applies the Bill of Rights to the states.

- Probable cause is the standard needed in criminal law to arrest, obtain a warrant, or conduct a search.

- Standards of probable cause require more than reasonable suspicion.

- The U.S. Supreme Court ruled stop and frisk as a lawful action by police officers.

- The exclusionary rule prohibits the use of illegally obtained evidence in court.

- Evidence discovered by officers in plain sight can be used at trial.

- U.S. citizens are afforded a reasonable expectation of privacy.

- New technology continues to change expectations of privacy.

- The courts provide specific guidelines for obtaining search warrants and have identified certain circumstances that justify a warrantless search.

KEY TERMS

Automobile Exception 168

Communications Assistance for Law Enforcement Act 164

Consent 167

Due Process 154

Exclusionary Rule 160

Exigent Circumstances 167

Fruit of the Poisonous Tree 161

Incident to a Lawful Arrest 168

Inevitable Discovery 161

Plain View Doctrine 167

Probable Cause 156

Reasonable Suspicion 158

Regulatory Searches 168

Stop and Frisk 159

REVIEW QUESTIONS

1. Why was *Weeks v. United States* (1914) an important precedent?

2. How has the U.S. Supreme Court defined due process?

3. How is probable cause established according to the U.S. Supreme Court?

4. When can a police officer stop and frisk a person?

5. What is the exclusionary rule, and what are some exceptions to it?

6. Describe how technology has changed expectations of privacy.

7. When can a drug-sniffing dog be used without a search warrant?

8. What is the difference between a knock-and-announce and a no-knock search warrant?

9. What are the exceptions to justify warrantless searches?

10. What is responsible for our right to counsel in state and federal court?

CRITICAL THINKING MATTERS

1. **Reasonable Suspicion Versus Probable Cause.** When Chris Farias was stopped for drunk driving, were the police officers acting on reasonable suspicion or did they have probable cause? What is the difference between reasonable suspicion and probable cause? Once Chris was stopped, what actions were available to the police officers? In other words, how could they have used their discretion in this particular case? Should the standard be lowered to allow police officers to search cars and homes more easily in order to arrest more criminals?

2. **The Use of Drug-Sniffing Canines.** Imagine that one of the officers involved in Chris's arrest had a police dog in his car. After Chris refused to be tested for alcohol, the officer brought the dog out. The dog circled the motorcycle and gave the alert sign for drugs. The officer then searched the compartments on the motorcycle, despite Chris's insistence that he would not consent. Is the officer's action an invasion of Chris's privacy in this fictional scenario? If Chris had cooperated with the police and allowed the dog to search, how might the given scenario have been different?

3. **Miranda Rights and Policing.** Critics of the *Miranda* decision argue that the ruling hampers police investigations. How do the defined rights in the Miranda warning limit police officers? Does the Miranda warning prevent unethical police behavior? What types of behavior and in what ways? When is the most appropriate time to read a suspect his or her Miranda rights? Should we have exceptions to *Miranda*? Are the more recent changes to *Miranda* a positive step for police? Or do the more recent changes hamper police? What does it mean for citizens?

4. **Changes to Expectations of Privacy Because of Technology.** Many states have enacted laws preventing texting while driving. Imagine you were involved in an accident and the officer on the scene wanted to check your last text message, thinking perhaps that you were to blame for the incident. How would you react? Should police have access to our personal texts or email messages, and under what conditions? Should police be able to access and read everyone's Facebook pages to ferret out criminal behavior?

5. **The Reliability of Police Informants.** Is information from a police informant enough to justify a search warrant? Why might an informant give the police bad information, intentionally or unintentionally? If an innocent person is harmed during a no-knock search, who is to blame and why? The police in Joshua Paul Benjamin's case were alerted by his roommate. Do you think that the word of a roommate is enough to prompt the police to gain a search warrant in a case like Joshua's? Do you think the roommate's word—with no other evidence—was enough for the police to bring Joshua in for questioning?

6. **Cold Cases.** The crimes against Jennifer Schuett were eventually found to have been committed by Dennis Bradford. This was one of many cold cases selected to use scarce resources and updated technology. What about Jennifer's case may have prompted the police and the FBI to focus on it? What other cases may not be given this scrutiny? In a time of limited resources and manpower, all cases cannot be given equivalent attention. If you were a detective, what cases would you focus these limited resources on? To which cases would you give less attention? What are the advantages and disadvantages of your proposed strategy?

DIGITAL RESOURCES

Sharpen your skills with SAGE edge at edge.sagepub.com/rennison2e. SAGE edge for Students provides a personalized approach to help you accomplish your coursework goals in an easy-to-use learning environment. You'll find action plans, mobile-friendly eFlashcards, and quizzes as well as video and web resources and links to SAGE journal articles to support and expand on the concepts presented in this chapter.

PART III

COURTS

© Bart Sadowski

7 THE COURTS AND JUDICIARY

> "My sense is that jurists from other nations around the world understand that our court occupies a very special place in the American system, and that the court is rather well regarded in comparison, perhaps, to their own."

> —Sandra Day O'Connor

LEARNING OBJECTIVES

After finishing this chapter, you should be able to:

7.1 Identify the basic federal and state court structures and jurisdictions.

7.2 Discuss the purpose and procedures of the U.S. Supreme Court.

7.3 Distinguish between limited and general jurisdiction courts.

7.4 Identify the problems associated with court congestion.

7.5 Describe the types and objectives of problem-solving courts.

7.6 Summarize the selection and role of judges.

7.7 Discuss the history and importance of diversity in the judiciary.

7.8 Name the positive and negative aspects of delayed trials.

INTRODUCTION: THE COURT PROCESS

The reenactments or docudramas of criminal and civil trials in film and television portray the process as an exciting battle of wits between attorneys to convince a judge and jury of the innocence or guilt of a defendant. The evidence and arguments might be described as surprising or shocking as each side advocates for the accused or the state. The reality of criminal trials, though fascinating, is much more mundane and must follow a multitude of rules and procedures. Additionally, court systems are complex at the federal and state levels, with varying structures and jurisdictions. The functioning of the courts, despite the difficult subject matter, is perhaps the most intriguing part of the criminal justice system, which explains why the media devote enormous attention to many criminal trials.

The U.S. court system, though flawed in some respects, is recognized throughout the world as one of the most legitimate means of determining guilt and innocence. As noted in the chapter's beginning quotation by former Supreme Court justice Sandra Day O'Connor, U.S. courts stand out as the best means of achieving justice and have garnered worldwide respect. Despite periodic mistakes and mind-boggling minutiae, the judicial system attempts to ensure fairness, equality, and justice.

Figure 7.1 ■ Diagram of the U.S. Courts

U.S. Supreme Court

State Supreme Court

U.S. Court of Appeals | **State Court of Appeals**

U.S. District Courts | **State District Courts**

en banc: A case heard by all judges of the court, or the full court. Cases are typically heard en banc when a significant issue is presented or if both parties request it and the court agrees.

Source: National Abortion Federation. (2010). *Federal court system.*

The diversity of the U.S. Supreme Court has progressively changed to include women and minorities. Why is diversity on the court such an important issue?

is, when four justices agree to hear the case. The court then reviews written arguments submitted by the attorneys and may hear oral arguments presented in Washington, DC. The Court can affirm or reverse the decision of the lower court. The chief justice typically assigns a colleague to write the majority opinion. In cases in which the justices disagree, a dissent or minority opinion may be written.

Each year the U.S. Supreme Court hears a limited number of cases, which involve constitutional issues or federal law. The majority of cases are appealed from lower federal courts or state supreme courts. According to the Federal Judicial Center, the Supreme Court receives 8,000 to 10,000 petitions to review annually. The Court has the authority to decide which cases to address and hears 80 to 90 cases; of those, about 50 or 60 cases are decided without oral arguments.[4] The U.S. Supreme Court sits **en banc**; in other words, all members participate in the decision-making process unless a justice recuses himself or herself from the case because of a conflict of interest.

The U.S. Court of Appeals covers 12 regional circuits, with an appellate court for each area, and one U.S. Court of Appeals for the Federal Circuit with nationwide jurisdiction. The majority of cases are criminal, prisoner petitions, and administrative decisions. Appeals of

Figure 7.2 ■ U.S. Courts of Appeals: Appeals Filed and Cases per Panel, 2009–2014

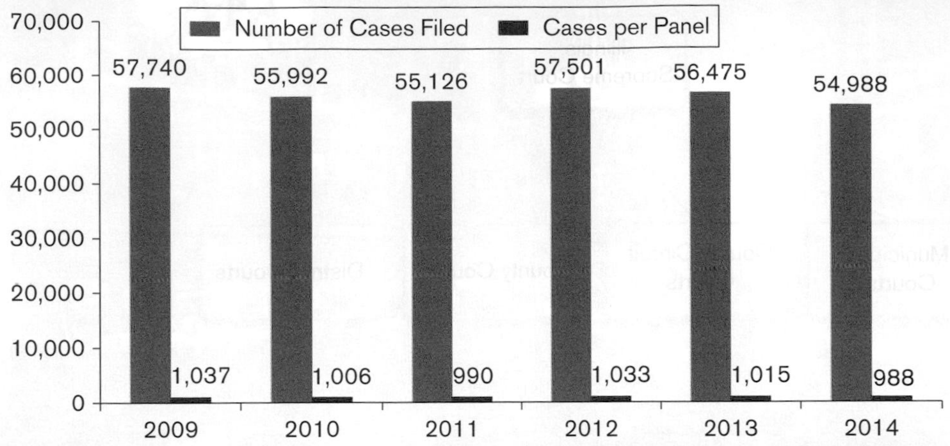

Source: Adapted from United States Courts, *U.S. Courts of Appeals.*

decisions by district courts represent the greatest number of cases (77%), followed by administrative (15%), original proceedings (7%), and bankruptcy (1%). An appellate court often is referred to as the **court of last resort**, and these courts review a high volume of cases (Figure 7.2). Cases decided by federal appellate courts rarely travel to the U.S. Supreme Court. These courts make decisions by using three-judge panels. In rare cases, all the judges on a U.S. Court of Appeals may hear a case en banc.

In 2012, the U.S. Appeals Courts experienced a 12% increase in the number of criminal appeals. This increase is attributed to appeals related to crack cocaine offenses for sentence reductions because of a change in the federal guidelines. Defendants sentenced to long prison terms because of charges of possessing crack were able to request shorter sentences in proportion with offenders whose crimes related to powder cocaine.

The U.S. Courts of Appeals hear cases involving patent laws and appealed decisions from the Court of International Trade, the Court of Federal Claims, and the U.S. Court of Appeals for Veterans Claims.

Federal district courts have jurisdiction over civil and criminal cases. The First through Eleventh and D.C. Circuits have the same jurisdiction except for civil cases involving patent laws. The federal trial courts consist of 94 judicial districts, including the District of Columbia and Puerto Rico, and the U.S. Bankruptcy Court. The Virgin Islands, Guam, and the Northern Mariana Islands, all U.S. territories, have district courts. The federal system also includes two specialized courts: the U.S. Court of International Trade and the U.S. Court of Federal Claims. The former hears cases on international trade and customs issues. The latter has jurisdiction over claims for monetary damages against the United States, disputes over federal contracts, and unlawful confiscation of private property by the federal government.

State Courts

State court structures vary, though most follow a pattern similar to the federal system, including a supreme court, an intermediate appellate court, and trial courts. Figure 7.3 offers an illustration of the Illinois court structure. In contrast, Figure 7.4 illustrates the Colorado court structure.

The structure of each state court system differs to various degrees, though the roles and jurisdictions are fundamentally the same. The New York Supreme Court conducts felony trials; other states call this intermediate level the superior or district court. Each state has a separate court system typically comprising three levels. You can compare your state with

court of last resort: The final court with appellate authority in a given court system. In the United States at the federal level, the Supreme Court is the court of last resort.

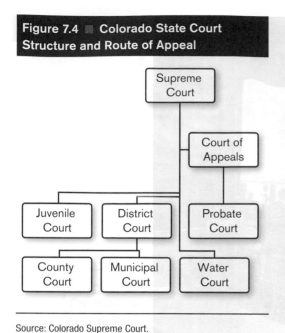

Figure 7.4 ■ Colorado State Court Structure and Route of Appeal

Source: Colorado Supreme Court.

In all criminal prosecutions, the accused shall enjoy the right to a speedy and public trial, by an impartial jury of the State and district wherein the crime shall have been committed, which district shall have been previously ascertained by law, and to be informed of the nature and cause of the accusation; to be confronted with the witnesses against him; to have compulsory process for obtaining witnesses in his favor, and to have the Assistance of Counsel for his defense.

The definition of *speedy* varies, although the Federal Speedy Trial Act, passed in 1974, requires that those charged with crimes be indicted within 30 days of arrest and that trial occur within 70 days after the indictment. Many states followed the federal model and enacted similar statutes with varying times for setting a trial date. In some jurisdictions, a trial must occur within 6 months if the defendant is in jail and within 12 months if the accused has been released on bail. Congestion is common because of the large number of cases and scarce resources. Delays also happen in complicated trials or at the request of defense attorneys. Delays can create both positive and negative circumstances for involved parties. Many defendants waive their right to a speedy trial, as it is frequently in their best interest to do so.

The judiciary's inability to efficiently process cases is problematic for a number of reasons. First, victims and defendants are forced to wait too long for resolution. Second, scarce resources in the criminal justice system are wasted if defendants are in jail waiting for the trial. Defendants may pay a high price, particularly given the presumption of innocence, and those who are not released on bail are unable to work and care for families. Finally, to the extent that those on bail may commit additional crimes, these delays can harm victims and communities.

Attorneys and defendants may benefit from delayed trials. Defense attorneys often like delays, hoping to weaken prosecutors' cases. The longer a case takes to go to trial, the more likely victim and witness testimony will be less accurate. Also, the passage of time may reduce highly charged emotions in victims and witnesses. Prosecutors may gain an advantage in being able to arrive at a plea bargain. In fact, judges prefer that cases be settled by plea bargains, rather than facing potentially lengthy and expensive trials.

Scholars and commentators have called for policy changes to reduce court delays.[5] The appointment of additional judges or more streamlined decisions on federal judges can reduce overbooked court dockets. Additional public prosecutors would create more efficiency in the system. Also, reducing the number of continuances before a case goes to trial is a possible reform. Many people argue for limiting the number of appeals, particularly in capital cases.

Video 7.1:
Cosby court delay rejected

Video 7.2:
Court delays

SPECIALIZED AND PROBLEM-SOLVING COURTS

Specialized courts, also called problem-solving courts, have developed as a means of addressing particular types of offenses and offenders. These courts differ from traditional proceedings in several respects. First, judges play a major supervisory role and collaborate with representatives from other criminal justice agencies and social services. Second, the courts' goal is to provide treatment alternatives in lieu of incarceration. Third, the courts typically focus on first-time nonviolent misdemeanor and, in some cases, felony offenders. Fourth, the outcomes are focused on reduced recidivism and rehabilitation. Finally, the courts are designed to be nonadversarial. Specialized courts emphasize collaboration among public and

specialized courts:
Also called problem-solving courts, they work with particular types of offenses and offenders.

POLICY ISSUES

Limits on Death Penalty Appeals

A great deal of controversy exists surrounding the use of the death penalty in the United States. One area of contention is the amount of time from conviction and sentencing to actually carrying out the penalty. In the United States, the average stay on death row is 10 to 12 years. Some inmates have been on death row for more than 20 years.

All defendants sentenced to death have a right to an automatic direct appeal, whether voluntary or mandatory. The direct appeal is limited to trial issues. The second type of appeal is referred to as postconviction remedies. Petitions are filed first with the original trial court and then appealed to an intermediate court. At this point the defendant can challenge events at trial, such as ineffective assistance of counsel, juror misconduct, and new evidence. Federal habeas corpus is the final appeal that allows death row inmates to challenge issues outside the trial record. This process may include up to three courts: U.S. District Court, U.S. Court of Appeals, and the U.S. Supreme Court.

One argument for a more efficient and cost-effective system is to reform the appeals process to prevent repeated and frivolous petitions. Proponents of the death penalty argue that a more streamlined process will enhance effectiveness, save taxpayers money, and promote justice. Postconviction appeals can cost taxpayers nearly $1 million per death row inmate. California has more than 650 death row inmates, and appeals have created a backlog in the state supreme court. Florida's Timely Justice Act of 2013 was introduced to reduce the legal challenges of death row inmates, though the measure may create a number of problems. On one hand, Florida's death row currently houses just over 400 condemned prisoners, and 40% have been there for 20 years or more. On the other hand, Florida leads the country in the number of death row inmates who were later found innocent: A total of 24 men have been released from the state's death row.

Think About It

1. Should state or federal courts limit the number of appeals made by death row inmates? What are the advantages and disadvantages of limiting appeals?

2. How would a more efficient process for carrying out the sentence better serve victims of violent crime?

3. Should the risk of killing an innocent person be considered in determining how many appeals are allowed?

4. If a death row inmate has exhausted his or her appeals, what happens when new DNA evidence exonerates him or her?

private agencies in order to create a nonpunitive approach and serve a variety of populations (see Table 7.1).

Drug Courts

Drug courts were first implemented in 1989 and have grown in popularity as alternatives to traditional proceedings. The National Institute of Justice reported more than 2,600 drug courts in the United States at the end of 2011. Over half the courts target adult offenders, and 10 types were identified: adult, juvenile, family, tribal, designated DUI, campus, reentry, federal reentry, veterans, and co-occurring disorders.[6] The drug court model includes the following elements:

- offender assessment
- judicial interaction
- monitoring and supervision
- graduated sanctions and incentives
- treatment services[7]

Journal:
Juvenile drug court operations

Table 7.1 ■ Problem-Solving Court Programs

Type	Offender/Offenses Description
Treatment Court Drug Court	First-time nonviolent misdemeanor and felony drug offenders
Community Family Court Family Recovery Court	Parents with substance abuse problems who have children placed with human services
DUI Court Sobriety Court	DUI and DWI offenders
Culturally Focused Batterer	Designed for African American men arrested for domestic violence
Behavioral Health Court	Defendants who suffer from serious mental health issues
Engaging Moms Program	Gender-specific, family-based intervention to assist mothers with substance abuse problems retain child custody

Source: CrimeSolutions.gov, National Institute of Justice, Office of Justice Programs.

Video 7.3:
Drug court

One key to successful management of offenders in drug courts is collaboration among members of a multidisciplinary team. Drug court teams may consist of judges, social workers, psychologists, attorneys, probation officers, police officers, rehabilitation counselors, and other representatives from the criminal justice and treatment communities.[8] After an offender is identified as eligible for drug court, the case management model commonly provides intensive treatment, random drug testing, appearances in court before the judge to review progress, and accountability with reward for doing well or sanctions for mistakes.

CASE STUDY

While many supporters argue that drug courts are the most effective justice intervention for addicts, their success continues to be evaluated. Proponents of the model argue that the courts reduce drug use, decrease crime, save money, restore lives, and reunite families.[9] Chris Farias, a nonviolent offender, volunteered to participate in the specialized court because of his background with alcohol abuse. Under the court's strict supervision, Chris received successful case management and was able to avoid serving a long period of time in jail. He was held accountable through frequent appearances before the same judge; mandatory frequent testing for alcohol (at his own cost); rehabilitation services, including personal counseling, group counseling, and alcohol counseling (all at his own cost); and intensive supervision by a case worker while in the community. Critics of the approach claim that the courts have failed to provide evidence of cost savings, lower incarceration, or improved public safety.[10] Others argue that the potential savings and benefits of this approach are minimized as more behaviors become criminalized and subject to greater criminal justice oversight. This "net-widening" is discussed in greater detail in Chapter 10.

Domestic Violence Courts

Specialized courts for cases involving intimate partner or domestic violence were created in the 1990s. A report prepared for the Center for Court Innovation in 2009 showed 208 domestic violence courts operating across the United States. The courts were established to process cases more efficiently by focusing on rehabilitation and deterrence.[11] Collaborations in these courts occur among judges, health care workers, police, prosecutors, and treatment providers. The two primary goals focus on victim safety and offender accountability.[12]

Though these courts are concerned with offender deterrence and rehabilitation, many focus on the victim and provide advocacy services, assistance with obtaining orders of protection, and some assurance of physical safety in the courtroom.

Veterans' Treatment Courts

In 2008, the first Veterans court was introduced in Buffalo, New York.[13] As an increasing number of veterans returned home from combat duty, an increase in crime among men and women returning from war appeared to occur. Many veterans experience symptoms associated with mental health disorders or cognitive impairment.[14] Veterans who experience post-traumatic stress disorder and other issues assimilating to life after wartime experience often find themselves compensating by abusing drugs and alcohol. These situations and other behaviors have resulted in criminal offenses. Veterans courts, like other specialized courts, are designed to treat the unique underlying problems by using one judge, who listens to all cases, and works with an interdisciplinary team to engage in a more holistic approach. Specialized courts work beyond the courtroom workgroup. The traditional courtroom workgroup includes defense attorneys, prosecutors, and judges. These workgroups also may include clerks, administrators, security, legal staff, court reporters, and representatives from criminal justice agencies such as probation, parole, and correction. In many specialty courts the involvement of mental health professionals or peers, for instance, is crucial to success.

Alternative Dispute Resolution

Although not a specialized court, **alternative dispute resolution** (ADR) offers a means of settling cases without costly litigation. This approach uses a variety of methods to assist the disputing parties in finding a solution without relying on more expensive procedures. ADR was initially developed as a means of expediting court cases and saving money. ADR has increased in popularity for several reasons, including congested caseloads, the notion that it is cheaper than litigation, the capability to keep the proceedings confidential, and the ability of the participants to maintain greater control over the proceedings. Most courts endorse and support these alternative proceedings, and in some situations the use of ADR is mandatory. ADR comes in many forms, although negotiation, mediation, and arbitration are the primary approaches used in the United States. Negotiation is simply the meeting of the disagreeing parties to work toward a solution. The advantage of negotiation is that the quarreling parties control both the process and the solution. Mediation is an informal process using a neutral third party that encourages parties to settle their dispute to everyone's satisfaction. A mediator trained in negotiation works with the two parties to achieve a settlement or agreement. The parties may or may not come to a solution. Arbitration is similar to a trial proceeding, with less discovery and fewer rules of evidence. Like a trial, arbitration ends with a binding ruling.

THE JUDICIARY

The Role of Judges

The public often views judges as powerful, authoritarian figures with little tolerance for illegal behavior or courtroom misbehavior. Judges commonly are ranked among doctors, astronauts, and firefighters as one of the most respected professions. Judges are, perhaps, the most visible and prominent figures in the courtroom, making decisions that affect our everyday lives. Given their importance, it is surprising that so few people can name but a few state or federal court judges. For the most part, they remain unknown figures in black robes presiding over trials.

Judges, who attempt to be tolerant and fair, perform a variety of tasks, and their role is crucial in the criminal justice system. Judges interact with the entire spectrum of agencies, working with probation personnel, public defenders, prosecutors, and law enforcement on items related to bail, sentencing, and treatment recommendations. During hearings and trials, judges are responsible for the functioning of the courtroom. They determine appropriate conduct, what evidence may be introduced, and correct procedure. Judges also conduct

alternative dispute resolution: An approach to settle cases using a variety of methods to assist the disputing parties in finding a solution without relying on costly litigation.

Judge Janis Roberts Brown. Diversity in judicial selection is improving. How might a higher level of diversity help improve the image of judges?

bench trials, in which they hear the evidence without a jury present and make a ruling on guilt or innocence.

Judges oversee trial proceedings. At the conclusion of a trial, the judge reads the jury instructions before the panel deliberates, which includes a statement of the law. In some instances, judges oversee sentencing. Over time, many more constraints and limitations to sentencing have been implemented. For example, mandatory minimum sentencing, determinant sentences, and policies such as three strikes became more prevalent. These constraints are discussed in detail in Chapter 9. For now it is important to recognize that judges play different roles in sentencing and that they are constrained to degrees that limit their discretion.

Decisions by a judge during a trial may be appealed. The grounds for an appeal include any error related to a legal issue that the litigant or defendant believes the judge has made during the trial. In most instances, those appeals go to the intermediate appellate court, which is obligated to respond to the case in either a published or an unpublished opinion, unless it lacks jurisdiction. Remember, intermediate appellate courts are not afforded the luxury of picking certain cases. Errors that might be appealed are matters concerning selection of the jury during *voir dire* (e.g., the judge denies a challenge for cause), pretrial motions regarding the admissibility of evidence (e.g., the defendant's confession was incorrectly admitted at trial), evidentiary rulings made during trial (e.g., hearsay testimony), or objections to the content of closing arguments. Litigants also can appeal final judgments they feel are unfair. In contrast, prosecutors are not allowed to appeal a not guilty verdict; doing so would be a violation of **double jeopardy**.

Selection of Judges

In general, the qualifications necessary to be a judge include state residency, a license to practice law, membership in the state bar, and age ranging from 25 to 70. Specific qualifications may differ depending on the jurisdiction. A municipal judge might have no legal background, whereas all appellate court judges must have law degrees.

A great deal of controversy and debate exists over the selection of judges. Some states appoint judges to the bench, while others hold elections. Elections are a competitive process. Proponents of elections argue that the electorate should have a voice in selecting judges and that elected judges are more likely to serve the needs of the citizens. Those in favor of elections also contend that this process promotes accountability. Opponents express concern that campaign contributions may influence a judge's ability to remain impartial. In elections, judges raise money from constituents to run for office and once elected may pander to the voting public. Judges should not be swayed by public sentiment and are obligated to fairly and equally apply the law. Opponents of judicial elections include the American Bar Association and the American Judicature Society.

The **Missouri Plan**, also called the merit selection system, attempts to eliminate politics from the selection process. Proponents of this selection method argue that the appointment of judges is fair and impartial, though the process has failed to fully remove political influences. The governor is responsible for the initial appointment of a judge, typically based on the recommendation of a nominating committee. After appointment, retention elections allow voters to determine whether the judge should remain on the bench. State and public officials who might have political agendas appoint the nominating committee. Additionally, the governor's appointment may be based partly on political affiliation.

double jeopardy: Constitutional protection under the Fifth Amendment that prevents the accused from facing charges or trial by the same sovereign after an acquittal or conviction for the same offense.

Missouri Plan: Also called the merit selection system, it is a process to elect judges that attempts to eliminate politics.

⚖ CONTEMPLATING CAREERS

Case Administrator

Are you motivated, articulate, and detail oriented? Can you interact professionally with judges, attorneys, government agencies, and the public? Are you professional, discrete, flexible, and committed?

If you answered yes to these questions, you might consider a career as a case administrator. Case administrators work closely with a judge's caseload and maintain the official case records on the docket from opening to final disposition. As a case administrator, you will be responsible for the accurate and timely entry of both civil and criminal orders to the docket, performing quality control, and notifying interested parties when orders are docketed. Though salary varies, one can expect to make between $46,000 and $66,000 depending on experience.

If a case administrator is not quite what you are looking for, remember that federal and state courts offer a wide variety of job opportunities. Careers in the courts range from information technology to librarian. Here is a short list of possible positions:

- Probation and pretrial services
- Information technology
- Judicial executive
- Courtroom deputy
- Court interpreter
- Court reporter
- Human resources
- Jury administrator
- Librarian

You can see videos about working in the judiciary at www.uscourts.gov/Careers.aspx.

 Career Video: A manager of a court interpretation program discusses his experience and current issues in the field.

Previous research shows little difference in performance quality or legitimacy between elected and appointed judges. Elected judges are viewed as being just as legitimate, and public perceptions of both remain positive. Judges have varying opinions among themselves about which process works best. Some judges are cynical about both approaches because of the political influence in selection, whether elected or nominated. In other words, elections involve the politics of mass voting, and the merit system involves the politics of public officials.

DIVERSITY IN THE JUDICIARY

Women in the Judiciary

Before becoming active in the judiciary, women had to fight for several rights. This battle included the right to attend law school (where applicable), to be admitted to the bar, and to serve as judges. During the late 1800s, women worked to change policy to gain these rights. A leader in these efforts was Myra Bradwell. Although she had the knowledge and experience from clerking in her husband's successful firm, Bradwell was denied entrance to the Illinois state bar. At this time, training in law occurred via apprenticeship, not law school. Bradwell sued, contending that the refusal to admit her to the Illinois bar violated her Fourteenth Amendment rights.

In *Bradwell v. State of Illinois* the U.S. Supreme Court disagreed and found that the right to practice a profession is not addressed in the Fourteenth Amendment's privileges and immunities clause. This clause states, "No State shall make or enforce any law which shall abridge the privileges or immunities of citizens of the United States." This case is one of several that narrowly interpreted this clause, rendering it virtually meaningless. The Court based its ruling in part on the notion that "the paramount destiny and mission of woman are to fulfil [*sic*] the noble and benign offices of wife and mother. This is the law of the Creator."[15]

Journal: Race and gender of the judiciary

Myra Bradwell. What challenges did Bradwell face in trying to enter a male-dominated profession?

Across the nation, other women were fighting for these rights. In several court cases, rulings that women were too tender and gentle, lacked intelligence, and were properly fit only to serve the needs of their husbands and children were used to prohibit women from participating in the judiciary. In 1873, Belva Lockwood became the first woman accepted to the bar in Washington, DC. Other states followed slowly. California admitted its first woman, Clara Shortridge, to the bar in 1878. Bradwell eventually was admitted to the Illinois bar in 1890.

Progress continued, albeit slowly. In 1879, Belva Lockwood successfully lobbied Congress to change Supreme Court admissions rules to allow a woman to argue before the Court. Her efforts paid off. She was the first female member of the Supreme Court bar, and in 1880 she became the first female lawyer to argue a case before the Supreme Court.

Today, though a large number of women attend law school, the majority of elected and appointed judges are men. And women are grossly underrepresented among those arguing before the U.S. Supreme Court. In 2014, 22 members of the U.S. Supreme Court bar were women. This corresponds to 16% of all appearances in 2014.[16] Findings show that the majority of female bar members were from the solicitor general's office. Only 8 of the 22 members arguing before the Court in 2014 were not Justice Department attorneys. Clearly, much work remains to be done to achieve gender parity at the highest level of the judiciary.

The appointment of women as judges may improve the quality of justice by offering better understanding of the diverse populations served. Though the number of female judicial nominees has increased under the Obama administration, representation on the bench is still unequal (Figure 7.5). The National Women's Law Center notes the following facts:

- Of the 112 justices who have served on the U.S. Supreme Court, only 4 have been women.
- Women make up only 10% of the Tenth Circuit's active members.
- About 30% of active U.S. district judges are women.
- Only 68 women of color are serving as active federal judges across the United States.
- Seven federal courts of appeals have no active female judges.[17]

Race in the Judiciary

Initially in the United States, there was no standardized method to admit someone to serve in the judiciary. The steps to becoming an attorney differed across states, but most required some type of an oral examination. The first black attorney in the United States was Macon Bolling Allen, who was admitted in Maine in 1844. This victory was short-lived because Allen was unable to find work in Maine as prejudice prevented whites from hiring a black attorney. Few blacks lived in Maine, making client prospects bleak. Allen then moved to Boston, where he encountered the same prejudice and difficulty in making a living. To counter this, he passed a difficult exam to serve as a justice of the peace to supplement his meager earnings. This position, achieved in 1848, earned Allen the title of the first African American judge in the United States. Note that at this time, he was not considered a citizen under the U.S. Constitution because he was black.

The first black man to be allowed to argue before the U.S. Supreme Court was John Rock, from Massachusetts. This accomplished physician and dentist is credited with coining the phrase "black is beautiful" in 1858. The day after Congress ended slavery with the approval of the Thirteenth Amendment, a motion to make Rock the first black lawyer to be admitted to the bar of the Supreme Court was passed. The first black woman admitted to the Supreme Court bar was Violette Anderson. An alumna of Chicago Law School, Anderson also was first to practice law in the U.S. District Court, Eastern Division, and later was the first female prosecutor in the city of Chicago.

Other black firsts followed higher in the judiciary. In 1945, the first black judge to serve at the federal level was appointed by President Harry Truman. Irvin Mollison served in the U.S. Customs Court in New York City beginning in 1945.[18] Shortly thereafter, in 1950, Truman appointed William Hastie to the Circuit Court of Appeals, making him the first African American to serve in this capacity. James Parsons was the first African American appointed to sit on a federal district court. Parsons was appointed by President John F. Kennedy in 1961 to serve in the Northern District of Illinois, and he served until his retirement in 1992. Perhaps one of the most widely known black judges is Thurgood Marshall. Marshall held many important judicial positions, including the U.S. Court of Appeals for the Second Circuit and as solicitor general of the United States. Marshall is also recognized for his position as chief counsel of the NAACP Legal Defense Fund. In that role he argued the landmark case of *Brown v. Board of Education* before the Supreme Court. In 1967 Marshall was nominated and appointed as an associate justice on the U.S. Supreme Court by President Lyndon B. Johnson. Marshall served in this capacity until retiring in 1991.

In 1861, John Rock passed the state bar of Massachusetts, and, in 1865, the very day after Congress approved the 13th Amendment ending slavery, he became the first Black person to be admitted to the bar of the Supreme Court of the United States.

Hispanics in the Judiciary

Gathering information on Hispanic firsts in the judiciary proves more difficult. As noted by Professor Michael Olivas, "identification of Latino ethnicity is, as always, problematic. This type of identification is an art, not a science."[19] Olivas had written that the attorneys arguing the landmark case of *Hernandez v. Texas* in 1954 were the first Latinos to appear before the U.S. Supreme Court. This important case established that Mexican Americans and racial groups had equal protections under the Fourteenth Amendment of the Constitution. Newer information suggests that this may be incorrect, as there is evidence that Pedro Capo-Rodriquez argued cases before the Supreme Court in 1950. In addition, the first Latina to argue before the Supreme Court may well have been Miriam Neveira de Rodon, who argued *Examining Board v. Flores de Otero* before the Court in 1975.[20] This case held that state law could not exclude aliens from practicing civil engineering in Puerto Rico.

Other Hispanic firsts occurred recently. The first Hispanic attorney general to serve the United States was Alberto Gonzalez, who was appointed by President George W. Bush in 2005. Gonzalez served for 2 years before resigning. His time at the Department of Justice was controversial. It was alleged by some individuals that Gonzalez fired many U.S. attorneys for political reasons. Also, during his tenure as attorney general, the United States engaged in warrantless wiretapping to fight the war on terror. This program allowed the monitoring of phone calls, email, web browsing, text messaging, and other communication without a warrant. This controversial tactic remains a point of contention today. Finally, Gonzalez's tenure was marked with controversy surrounding "enhanced interrogation techniques," referred to by many people as "torture." Gonzalez allegedly supported these techniques. Though serving only 2 years, his tenure involved many difficult issues. Today, he serves as dean of Belmont University's College of Law.

Figure 7.5 ■ Federal Judges and Gender, 1998–2009

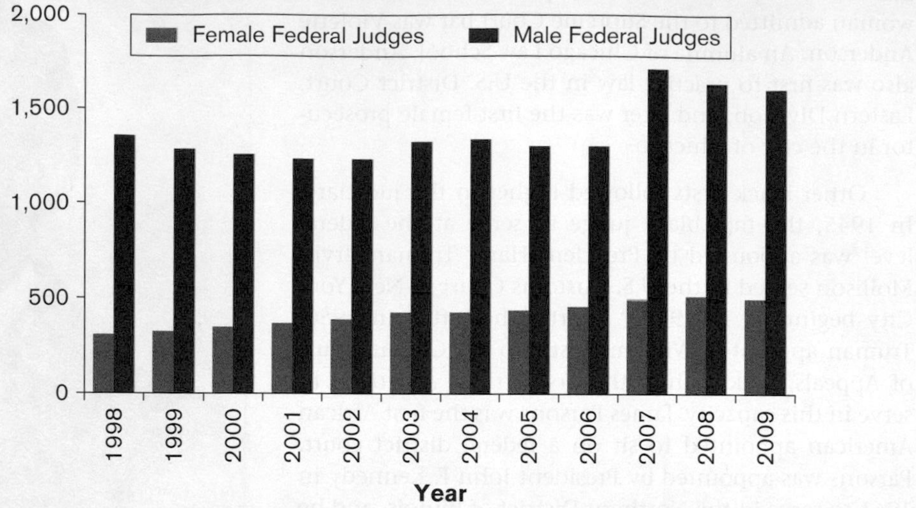

Source: United States Courts.

Note: Most recent data available.

Appointed in 2009 by President Obama, Sonia Sotomayor is the first Hispanic associate justice on the U.S. Supreme Court. Some notable cases in which she was part of the majority decision include *Arizona v. United States* and *National Federation of Independent Business v. Sebelius*. The issue before the court in the *Arizona* case was whether an Arizona statute appropriated the federal government's authority to regulate immigration laws and enforcement. The Supreme Court struck down much of the Arizona statute but allowed the ability of law enforcement to investigate a person's immigration status. The *National Federation* case is more widely known as the Obamacare case. In this ruling, the Supreme Court upheld much of Obamacare.

As with women, the appointment of people of color and a variety of ethnicities as judges can improve the quality of justice through better understanding of the diverse populations served.

COURT ADMINISTRATION AND MANAGEMENT

Courts are busy places and employ court administrators to manage scheduling for overloaded dockets. Cases move through the court system in different ways, following different paths. The initial involvement of the court may begin at the moment a search or arrest warrant is requested by the police and issued by a judge. After arrest, suspects are brought before a judge for an initial appearance. Defendants are informed of charges, considered for release on bail, and given legal representation when needed. In a misdemeanor case the defendant may plead guilty to the charge and be sentenced immediately. Felony offenders are not allowed to plead at this stage and will enter into plea bargain agreements or go to trial.

Technology and the Judiciary

Technology is ubiquitous, including in the judiciary. Though used in varying degrees at the state and federal levels, technology improves the efficiency, effectiveness, and timeliness of the court system. Some common technologies used to improve the judiciary are electronic filings, electronic documents, online dockets, electronic evidence, and electronic case management systems. These systems allow courts to maintain case documents in electronic form and allow the filing of case documents (such as pleadings, motions, and petitions) to be done

ETHICAL ISSUES

What Should Happen When a Judge Engages in Misconduct?

Because federal judges receive lifetime appointments, they leave the bench only under four circumstances: resignation, retirement, death, or impeachment. Initial complaints of misconduct were alleged against Chief U.S. District Judge Edward Nottingham in 2007. President George H. W. Bush had appointed Nottingham to the bench in 1989. Nottingham's former wife made several of the allegations during their divorce proceedings. She claimed he spent thousands of dollars in a strip club. A subsequent news investigation discovered his association with a known prostitution ring. A prostitute claimed Nottingham asked her to mislead investigators about their relationship. In another incident, the judge parked illegally in a handicapped space and engaged in a shouting match with a woman who challenged his behavior. The woman, a former lawyer who had been shot and paralyzed by an angry litigant, blocked his vehicle using her wheelchair. Nottingham reacted by putting the car into reverse to make her move and then threatened to have her forcibly removed by federal marshals. Nottingham denied the allegations, though he did admit to being a patron at strip clubs, which is not illegal.

The other side of the picture portrays a judge who is greatly admired by his colleagues. One U.S. district court judge noted Nottingham's great leadership skills and the advancements he implemented, including electronic courtroom evidence and case filings. A U.S. senator praised Nottingham's performance and commented on his skills as a lawyer and jurist. Nottingham was known for his fair treatment of parties in the courtroom and efficient case management practices.

In 2008, Nottingham resigned from the federal bench and issued an apology. An unsigned statement issued on Nottingham's behalf noted that he is deeply remorseful for his actions, and embarrassed and ashamed for the loss of confidence his behavior caused.

Think About It

1. In your opinion, what may have motivated this judge to engage in the alleged behavior?

2. Were the allegations unethical and/or illegal?

3. Does a lifetime appointment protect judges who engage in misconduct?

online. This strategy saves paper, money, and time as documents are available in virtual form to all parties of interest. Online dockets are used widely, including by the U.S. Supreme Court. This technology serves as a case tracking system and includes information on decided and pending cases. For the U.S. Supreme Court, searching for cases is made via case numbers, names, or key words. See www.supremecourt.gov/docket/docket.aspx to search for cases that interest you.

CHAPTER WRAP-UP

The courts play a leading role in the administration of justice and represent a major component of the criminal justice system. Unfortunately, few people pay attention to the decisions made by our judicial system. Even more disturbing is how we tend to ignore who is appointed or elected to serve as judges. In many respects, the complexities of the law (full of rules, procedures, and legalese) impede our ability to understand and fully participate. The intimidating atmosphere of the courtroom also inhibits full participation; whether a litigant faces a civil claim or felony charge, few people can navigate the intricacies of the system without adequate legal representation, which comes at a high cost. We all benefit from learning more about the courts and understanding how court decisions affect our daily lives.

Technology now allows suspects and offenders to appear on video before the court. Would you argue for or against this practice? What types of nuances might be missed in the communication?

CASE STUDY

Case Study Video 7.1:
Interviews with case study participants

Justice is rarely about one-size-fits-all solutions. The courts are designed to accommodate many types of people and offenders with options that serve rehabilitative goals for suspects caught in the system. Pretrial services arranged for Joshua Paul Benjamin to attend an inpatient sex offender treatment program while his attorney worked on his case. In addition, he sought out and was treated by a psychiatrist to minimize chances of future recidivism. While Joshua engaged in numerous therapeutic approaches, he was not spared the traditional punishment of prison, as later chapters outline. Legal mandates may prevent more therapeutic approaches for all offenders, but the trend toward a less punitive judicial approach may reduce jail and prison populations and result in enormous cost savings.

As we will see more fully in Chapter 10, Chris Farias was deeply involved with the judiciary for over a year as he worked closely with a judge and personnel assigned to a specialized court. Jennifer Schuett's opportunity to see her case go to trial was taken from her, as later chapters will detail.

In the following chapter, our discussion focuses on the prosecution, defense, and pretrial activities. In that chapter, vital information related to the important roles of prosecutors and defense attorneys, charging of the suspect, trial and pretrial events, and other elements of the trial is covered.

KEY POINTS

- Federal and state courts vary in structure and jurisdiction.

- The federal court system developed from the Judiciary Act of 1789.

- The courts rely on the U.S. Constitution and state constitutions to guarantee that our rights are protected.

- The right to privacy guaranteed by the Fourteenth Amendment has been expanded in important, though controversial, ways by the U.S. Supreme Court.

- The United States has a dual court system, and federal and state laws may come into conflict.

- The U.S. Supreme Court is the highest court.

- The role of judges is crucial to the functioning of the courtroom.

- Problem-solving courts play an important role in helping victims and offenders. Similar to problem-solving courts, alternative dispute resolution includes arbitration and mediation.

- Technologies such as e-filings and online dockets have improved the effectiveness and efficiency of the judicial system.

- Diversity in the judiciary is marginal at best. Although diversity in law schools has grown over time, diversity at the highest levels of the judiciary is still poor.

KEY TERMS

Alternative Dispute Resolution 189

Court of Last Resort 183

Double Jeopardy 190

Dual Court System 180

En Banc 182

Indictment 185

Information 185

Judicial Review 178

Judiciary Act of 1789 181

Jurisdiction 181

Missouri Plan 190

Pro Se 184

Separate-but-Equal Doctrine 178

Specialized Courts 186

Strict Interpretation 178

Writ of Certiorari 180

REVIEW QUESTIONS

1. How did the U.S. court system develop?

2. What role does political affiliation play in judicial decisions?

3. Why is judicial activism controversial?

4. How do the federal and state court systems differ?

5. What is the federal Speedy Trial Act?

6. Describe the positive and negative aspects of court delays.

7. What are the differences between arbitration and mediation?

8. What are the focus and purpose of problem-solving courts?

9. What are the responsibilities of judges?

10. What are the two methods for selecting state-level judges?

CRITICAL THINKING MATTERS

1. **Specialized Courts for Offenders.** In the cases of Chris Farias and Joshua Paul Benjamin, how would a specialized alcohol or sex offender court work? Would treatment rather than prison be a better approach for a repeat offender with multiple arrests such as Chris? Would treatment rather than prison be a better approach for a first-time offender such as Joshua? Many professionals argue that sex offenders cannot

be treated, only managed. How would you design a court that specializes in sex offenders? How would you respond to critics of such an approach?

2. **Equity in Punishment Part I.** How should the criminal justice system, specifically the courts, address issues of racial and gender inequality within the system? Should a judge or governor be permitted to intervene in a jury's decision if certain biases are suspected, specifically in death penalty cases? Should a jury have the power to determine death sentences considering that many members are not informed on current research and potentially untrained to avoid bias in decision making?

3. **Equity in Punishment Part II.** How should the criminal justice system, specifically the courts, address issues of victim characteristics in the system? In Jennifer Schuett's case, a minor was brutally assaulted by an adult. Should a judge or jury be able to rule more harshly when the victim is a minor versus an adult? Should a judge or jury be able to hand out a stiffer penalty when the victim is a stranger to the offender? What if the victim is mentally incapacitated? Or physically disabled? Should characteristics of the victim play a role in the way courts handle these cases? Is your decision based on the Constitution? If not, on what basis do you make your decision?

4. **Judges and Higher Ethical Standards.** Should the role of judge or magistrate require a high degree of ethics for continued appointment? Should judges be dismissed for breaches of ethical standards, even if the actions do not constitute crimes or break laws? What level of scrutiny should judges be placed under? Does the manner in which judges conduct themselves in their personal lives matter?

5. **The Logic of Specialized Courts.** While it is important to address special needs, should every court not be trained to address special needs, rather than segregating populations by judicial district, crime committed, or background information? What may the consequences be of judicial districts that do not use specialized courts compared with those that do? Could this be construed as an inequality in the criminal justice system? What other types of crimes currently referred to general courts may need a specialized court?

6. **Arguments for Local Control.** As an example, despite legalization in Colorado, Washington, Oregon, and the District of Columbia, the use of recreational marijuana remains illegal under federal law. How could lack of uniformity affect populations traveling through the states or relationships with neighboring states? How should the federal government react, specifically in terms of punishments for those who violate federal law but are in compliance with state law? Examples may include revocation of federal student aid or commercial driver's licenses.

DIGITAL RESOURCES

Sharpen your skills with SAGE edge at edge.sagepub.com/rennison2e. SAGE edge for Students provides a personalized approach to help you accomplish your coursework goals in an easy-to-use learning environment. You'll find action plans, mobile-friendly eFlashcards, and quizzes as well as video and web resources and links to SAGE journal articles to support and expand on the concepts presented in this chapter.

8

THE PROSECUTION, DEFENSE, AND PRETRIAL ACTIVITIES

> "People assume I'm OK with a young boy being murdered because I represent the defendant. To me, that's pretty vicious. They have to understand, I'm not all right with people being murdered or with crime. I'm all right with defending constitutional rights."
>
> —Jennifer L. McCann,
> criminal defense attorney, Garden City, New York, 2011

> "There is no client as scary as an innocent man."
>
> —J. Michael Haller,
> criminal defense attorney, Los Angeles, 1962

LEARNING OBJECTIVES

After finishing this chapter, you should be able to:

8.1 Explain the roles and responsibilities of prosecutors and defense attorneys.

8.2 Summarize the similarities and differences in the responsibilities of federal- and state-level prosecutors.

8.3 Identify how and why defense lawyers are able to defend a person who may be guilty.

8.4 Describe the positive and negative aspects of plea bargaining.

8.5 Summarize the considerations used by the court to determine if bail is appropriate.

8.6 Identify the procedures related to discovery, motions, and scheduling undertaken before trial.

8.7 Explain how jurors are selected and why the role of the jury is essential to the courts.

8.8 Summarize issues of diversity among defendants, jurors, and those sentenced for crimes.

INTRODUCTION: ACTORS AND PROCEDURES IN THE COURTROOM

Many activities occur prior to the start of a trial, and prosecutors and defense attorneys play a major role in determining the course of a defendant's future. Their decisions and efforts before, during, and after trial have great influence on everything that happens in the case. In the trial of George Zimmerman, who was charged with the murder of 17-year-old Trayvon Martin, the prosecutor and defense attorneys' roles were well defined by the law before they entered the courtroom. At first glance, many viewers watching pretrial and trial activities may have believed that the prosecutor represented the victim, Trayvon Martin. In reality, the prosecutor represented the people of the State of Florida, because criminal behavior causes societal harm. The defense attorney, who ultimately won this trial, played the role of advocate for his client, defending Zimmerman's constitutional rights. Whether Zimmerman's attorney believed the shooting was self-defense was immaterial to his goal of advocating for his client and winning the case. The adversarial system means that one side wins and the other, much to the chagrin of representing attorneys, loses. The arguments, the characters, and the stories told in the courtroom are at odds with one another, but the adversarial system is the fundamental aspect of determining the truth. Consequently, understanding the role of lawyers beyond what the media portrays is an important aspect of the criminal justice system.

Joe Burbank/Orlando Sentinel/MCT via Getty Images

The prosecutor in the George Zimmerman case represented the people of the State of Florida. What types of factors influenced the media coverage of the Zimmerman case?

Criminal attorneys operate using an **advocacy model** in an **adversarial system**.[1] Their goal is to "uphold the legal process," to offer effective, quality representation, and to "be a zealous advocate on behalf of a client."[2] Ideally, trials involve effective and ethical advocates doing their best to "win" for their clients. An adversarial system pits one side against the other to reveal the truth. Does an advocacy model in an adversarial system always lead to a just outcome? Not always. There are many examples of innocent people being found guilty, serving time in prison, and in some cases being executed.[3] There also are instances of guilty people being found not guilty.

THE PROSECUTOR

Prosecutors, who leverage a great deal of power (i.e., prosecutorial discretion), are major figures in and out of the courtroom. A prosecuting attorney, as noted above, represents the government, or the "people," and is responsible for presenting the state's case in criminal, civil, and administrative matters. Prosecutors include U.S. attorneys at the federal level and state, county, and local (city) attorneys. Prosecutors are appointed or elected to office and are licensed lawyers. They perform many tasks, including conducting crime investigations, establishing charges against the accused, presenting evidence in court, and assisting in determinations regarding appropriate punishment.

Federal Prosecutors

At the federal level, the Judiciary Act of 1789 created the U.S. Attorney General's Office. The **U.S. attorney general** is the chief law enforcement officer in the government and head of the Department of Justice (see Figure 8.1). As the chief federal law enforcement officer, the U.S. attorney general represents the United States in legal matters and serves as an adviser to the president.[4] Rarely does the U.S. attorney general appear in the courtroom to argue cases, though he or she may appear before the U.S. Supreme Court in matters of great importance. The president appoints the U.S. attorney general to serve a 4-year term.

Despite the importance of this position, relatively little attention is paid to the people who hold this office. While we know the name of the first president, identifying the first attorney general might challenge even the most skilled game show contestant. The anonymity of the attorney general may result from relatively short terms in office and because the press pays little attention to the position unless a scandal unfolds. The first U.S. attorney general was Reverdy Johnson (1849–1850), whose unique first name should be easily remembered. More famous attorneys general include Robert F. Kennedy (1961–1964); Janet Reno (1993–2001), the first woman appointed to the position; and Alberto R. Gonzales (2005–2007), the first Hispanic appointment. Gonzales, appointed by President George W. Bush in 2005, was forced to resign amid accusations of perjury in several political scandals, including warrantless wiretapping, innuendos that he condoned the torture of suspected terrorists, and the unprecedented and seemingly unfair dismissal of seven U.S. attorneys—a move that appeared to be motivated by partisan politics. Eric Holder, who was appointed by President Barack Obama in 2009, was the first black attorney general of the United States. He has also been a controversial figure because of his alleged knowledge about Operation Fast and Furious, which resulted in the smuggling of illegal firearms into Mexico and the death of a Border Patrol agent killed by a weapon involved in this

Video 8.1:
A prosecutor's vision for a better justice system

advocacy model: A model in which the defendant and the government are represented by advocates who act on behalf of their clients.

adversarial system: A system used in the United States in which prosecutors and defendants compete against each other to reveal the truth.

prosecutor: An attorney who represents the government or the "people" and is responsible for presenting the state's case in criminal, civil, and administrative matters.

U.S. attorney general: Chief law enforcement officer in the government and head of the Department of Justice.

Figure 8.1 ■ Office of the Attorney General Organizational Chart

Figure 8.1 ■ Office of the Attorney General Organizational Chart

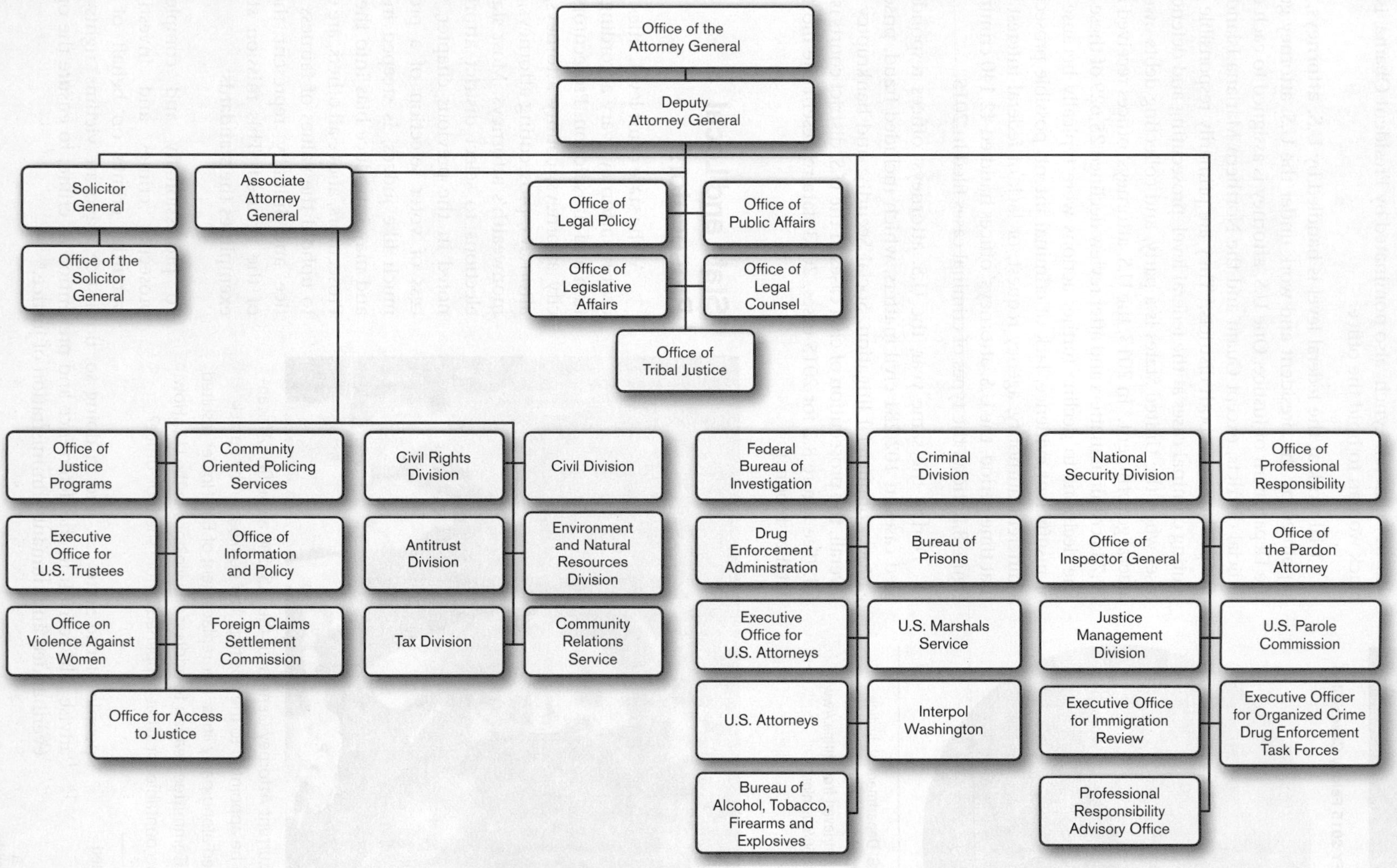

Source: U.S. Department of Justice. (2015). *Organization, mission and functions manual.* Retrieved from https://www.justice.gov/jmd/organization-mission-and-functions-manual.

Figure 8.2 ■ U.S. Attorneys' Offices Criminal Cases, by Type, 2015

Criminal Workload FY 2015 Felony Cases Filed

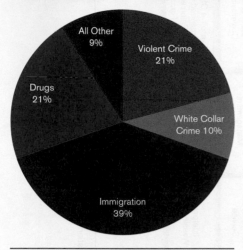

All Other 9%

Violent Crime 21%

Drugs 21%

White Collar Crime 10%

Immigration 39%

Source: Adapted from U.S. Department of Justice. (2015). *United States attorneys' annual statistical report: fiscal year 2015*. Retrieved from https://www.justice.gov/usao/file/831856/download.

program. Holder's testimony before Congress resulted in the dubious distinction of his being the first attorney general to be held in contempt of Congress. In April 2015, Loretta Lynch was sworn in as the 83rd U.S. attorney general. Lynch, also nominated by President Obama, is the first black woman to hold the office.

Trial work at the federal level is handled by **U.S. attorneys**, who are appointed by the president and work under the U.S. attorney general in the Department of Justice. One U.S. attorney is assigned to each of the 94 judicial districts, except Guam and the Northern Mariana Islands, where one person serves both districts.[5] They are primarily responsible for prosecuting criminal cases at the federal level, prosecuting and defending civil cases when the United States is a party, and collecting debts owed to the federal government.[6] In 2013, the U.S. attorneys' offices received notice of 79,735 criminal matters and after review declined 25,629 of these referrals. The decisions to decline further actions were typically because of weak or insufficient evidence, lack of criminal intent, possible prosecution by a different authority, agency request, or lack of federal interest.[7] During that time period, the U.S. attorneys' offices handled 42,140 criminal cases. Figure 8.2 shows the types of criminal cases filed in 2015.

During the same year, the U.S. attorneys' offices responded to or filed cases in 102,281 civil matters, which included fraud, prisoner litigation, commercial litigation, Social Security, and bankruptcy matters. Overall, the prosecution of civil cases in the U.S. district courts is successful. (See Figure 8.2 for 2015 cases. 2013 data represent the most current detailed report.)

Loretta Lynch is the current Attorney General of the U.S. She is the first African-American woman to be appointed to the position. Her nomination by Barack Obama was confirmed along party lines. Her replacement of Eric Holder resulted in a House Judiciary Committee hearing to address the violence in the U.S. How should she be held accountable for what happened before she took office?

U.S. attorney: Appointed by the president and supervised by the U.S. attorney general in the Department of Justice, a U.S. attorney is responsible for trying cases at the federal court level.

State and Local Prosecutors

At the state court level, titles for prosecuting attorneys vary according to position and jurisdiction. Prosecutors may be city attorneys, county attorneys, district attorneys, prosecuting attorneys, or commonwealth's attorneys. Most states hold elections to select district attorneys. As noted in the previous chapter, the process of voter selection of a prosecutor, much like judges, is steeped in politics and may introduce bias into the system. Prosecutors, above all others, are expected to uphold the values of fairness and justice and initially represent the rights of the accused. This mission statement exemplifies the standards:

To professionally and completely prosecute crimes and investigate potential crimes on behalf of the people of the State . . . and in doing so, do justice, advocate victims' rights and advise and consult in the deterrence and prevention of crime; to ensure the open, evenhanded and humane administration of justice.[8]

Prosecutors hold a great deal of discretionary power and make autonomous decisions about who will be charged, what will be charged, whether to engage in plea bargaining, and

Table 8.1 ■ Criminal Case Outcomes in United States District Courts, 2015

Offense	Number of Defendants	Dispositions			
		Guilty	Not Guilty	Dismissed	Other
Immigration	22,525	21,924	13	726	58
Violent crimes	13,214	11,780	63	696	163
Drug dealing	15,719	14,625	38	868	168
Counterfeiting	514	470	0	38	3
Bank fraud and embezzlement	998	910	7	55	23
Terrorism/national security critical infrastructure	236	206	1	21	6
Organized crime	434	345	2	26	61
Identity theft	500	455	1	34	5

Source: Adapted from *United States Attorneys' Annual Statistical Report: Fiscal Year 2015.*

when or whether to drop charges against the accused. This high level of discretion allows prosecutors to decide how to pursue cases based on the available evidence and other legal factors. The choice to file charges rests solely on the prosecutor, not on the wishes of the victim, family members, or law enforcement, although these perspectives are all part of the decision-making process. A prosecutor's decision to file a case hinges on a variety of factors:

Web:
Racist prosecutors

- the quality and quantity of evidence
- the seriousness of the crime
- the odds of winning the case
- court resources
- the wishes of the victim or family members
- public opinion

The decision to drop charges against a defendant either before or during a trial is referred to as *nolle prosequi* (Latin for "be unwilling to pursue"). In the Jennifer Schuett case, a Galveston County district attorney used his discretion and charged Dennis Bradford with attempted capital murder (among other crimes). Given this charge, if convicted, Bradford would have faced very severe sanctions in Texas.

Prosecutors also have the power to refile charges against a defendant after a mistrial or hung jury. Many commentators and people believe the high level of discretion makes prosecutors the most powerful figures in the criminal justice system. Not only are they making decisions about who and what will be charged, they are deciding who faces life or death in potential capital cases.

Like most professionals, prosecutors make mistakes, and this involves some innocent people being convicted. Erroneous convictions, often discovered after **exculpatory evidence** such as DNA emerges, have been documented in numerous death penalty, rape, and other cases. Specifically, exculpatory evidence is evidence that exonerates the defendant or is at least favorable to the defendant. Prosecutors, like judges, have absolute or partial immunity from being sued if they make mistakes. In some cases, however, prosecutors have engaged in deliberate misconduct, although the legal system is unlikely to hold them accountable. Overzealous prosecutors may ignore or suppress exculpatory evidence. Here are some legal and ethical concerns for prosecutors:

- communicating with defendants without a defense attorney
- failing to disclose evidence in discovery
- ignoring conflicts of interests
- allowing false witness testimony

exculpatory evidence: Evidence that may be favorable to a defendant in a criminal trial, often clearing some or all guilt during criminal proceedings.

COMMON MISCONCEPTIONS

Lawyers Are Unethical and Greedy

Many people view attorneys as fair game for jokes and may actually believe they are greedy, misbehaving opportunists. The perceived misbehavior justifies the generalization that "all lawyers are shysters." In reality, the vast majority of attorneys are professionals operating with high ethical standards.

In fact, the American Bar Association (ABA) developed the *Model Rules of Professional Responsibility* as a guide to navigate the moral and ethical dilemmas faced by attorneys. The document is extensive and includes guidance to attorneys on topics such as preserving the confidences and secrets of a client, exercising independent professional judgment on behalf of the client, and the requirement that the client be represented completely, zealously, fully, and within the bounds of the law.

Most prosecutors and public defenders acquire these positions to help people and improve the functioning of the legal system; rarely do the majority of lawyers make a lot of money. Harvard Law School states, for example, that assistant district attorneys earn between $35,000 and $90,000 annually. Criminal defense attorneys earn an average salary of $50,000 to $130,000. Keep in mind that many of these same individuals are paying back extensive educational debt.

Think About It

1. Would you complete 4 years of college and 3 years of law school to earn less than $100,000? Do you believe that attorneys are motivated by money only? What would motivate you?

2. What do you think would be the most just punishment for an unethical attorney? Why is that? Do you think it would deter other attorneys from acting unethically?

3. As an attorney you are required to represent a defendant who clearly committed multiple gruesome homicides. Given your professional duties as defined by the ABA, you must represent your client completely, zealously, fully, and within the confines of the law. How then do you respond to members of the public who want to know how you could possibly defend such a client?

Prosecutors, like many other professionals, have a duty to uphold ethical guidelines. Under what circumstances should prosecutors be allowed to discuss their case with the media? In what ways may this bias potential jurors?

Prosecutors are expected to provide defense attorneys with all evidence—even materials that may exonerate suspects. This expectation appears to be silly in our adversarial system, especially since each side sets out to win the case, but the process of **discovery** is instrumental in the fact-finding mission. Discovery is the process through which the defense learns about evidence held by the prosecution. This evidence may include reports, DNA, and witness statements. Prosecutors who withhold information in a case are engaging in a serious breach of ethics and acting illegally. In 1963, the U.S. Supreme Court noted several forms of prosecutorial misconduct in *Brady v. Maryland*:

POLICY ISSUES

The Duke Lacrosse Sexual Assault Case

In 2006, a criminal investigation was undertaken after allegations of sexual assault were made against three members of the lacrosse team at Duke University. Crystal Gail Mangum, an African American student at North Carolina Central University, accused the white players of raping her at a party. Mangum, who was hired to dance at the party, was said to have worked as a stripper, a dancer, and an escort. The investigation was turned over to District Attorney Michael Nifong, who publicly introduced the specter of a hate crime in more than 50 press conferences. In other words, the players not only raped the girl; they engaged in the crime because she was black.

After a series of unfortunate events the same evening, Mangum was picked up by the police and involuntarily committed. During the hospital admission, she claimed she had been raped and underwent a physical examination in which DNA samples were collected. Later, the prosecutor obtained DNA samples from 46 of the team's 47 members. The DNA samples taken from the victim failed to match any of the players. But part of this evidence was not shared with defense lawyers, who filed a motion claiming that the DNA report was incomplete and excluded specific information on the DNA of two unidentified men. Nifong asserted that the lack of DNA evidence was inconsequential in proving his case given the circumstantial evidence and testimony of the victim. As a result, two of the young men were arrested and indicted on charges of rape, sexual offenses, and kidnapping. Eventually, the charges against the young men were dropped and Nifong resigned from the case. Ultimately, Nifong's overzealous behavior became a leading example of prosecutorial misconduct as details of his behavior were discovered. Today he is retired.

Think About It

1. Given the structure of our legal system, what factors may motivate a prosecutor to engage in misconduct like this?

2. What are the advantages and disadvantages of restricting prosecutors from appearing in the press before trial?

3. Is it ethical to first try a case in the "court of public opinion"?

- using unreliable snitches
- coercing witnesses
- withholding information from the defense
- using questionable forensic science or scientists
- accepting coerced confessions
- misleading jurors[9]

The frequency with which prosecutorial misconduct occurs is unknown, though several studies indicate a large number of reported cases. The Northern California Innocence Project examined a total of 4,000 cases of alleged prosecutorial misconduct in California. The research showed that court rulings determined that only 707 of the cases involved misconduct; the courts determined that the majority of these cases (548) were "harmless" errors, and 159 cases were found to be harmful enough to set aside the conviction or declare a mistrial.[10]

THE DEFENSE ATTORNEY

The role of **defense attorneys** often is misunderstood, and the public commonly notes that their job is to put criminals back on the street. As is well illustrated by McCann's quotation that opened this chapter, defense attorneys are responsible for ensuring that the constitutional rights of a defendant are protected. Protecting rights is important regardless of the

discovery: The process through which the defense learns about evidence held by the prosecution. This may include reports and witness statements.

defense attorney: A lawyer who advocates for his or her client and protects the client's constitutional rights.

Defense Attorney Baez during a proceeding. Baez accused the prosecution of willingly withholding evidence. What should happen when a lawyer engages in misconduct as alleged here?

presumed guilt or innocence of the defendant. The public frequently forgets that not all people being accused of crimes are guilty. Imagine the burden on the defense attorney to ensure that an innocent victim is not prosecuted and that his or her rights are protected. The great burden is clearly noted in Haller's quotation that opened the chapter. As we know, everyone has the right to counsel in a criminal trial. The quality of legal representation for defendants can be controversial. Only a small percentage of defendants can afford to hire private counsel, who may have better education, more experience, or expertise in a particular area. The majority of criminal defendants rely on public defenders, legal aid groups, or private attorneys appointed by the court to represent them **pro bono**; that is, legal representation that is provided at no charge or a reduced fee.

A defense attorney may or may not know if a client is guilty or not guilty. The role of the defense lawyer is not to judge the client on his or her actions, but rather to focus on whether the prosecution can prove beyond a reasonable doubt that the accused knowingly committed the act while following the Constitution. While a lawyer may choose not to directly ask the client about guilt or innocence, any exchanges between the parties are protected by attorney–client confidentiality. Ethical mandates, however, prevent defense attorneys from lying to judges and juries or allowing clients to give perjured testimony. Defense lawyers rely on the facts of the case and focus on the weaknesses in the prosecution's case.

AFTER THE ARREST: CHARGING THE DEFENDANT

Before any court proceeding, a sequence of events occurs (see Figure 8.3). First, a crime is allegedly committed. Police respond by investigating, interviewing witnesses, gathering evidence, and identifying a suspect. Second, an arrest is made. A police officer, once probable cause is established, may arrest a suspect for a misdemeanor and/or felony offense. The case is then referred to the prosecutor's office for final decision on charges. After the prosecuting attorney reviews all the available information, he or she will then decide whether to file charges. The decision to file charges comes in the form of an information or complaint. The prosecutor files an information based on case-related materials and the belief that the accused may be guilty. In other words, the prosecutor decides to pursue a case after examining all the available evidence. Less commonly, a **complaint** is filed based on the complaining witnesses' affidavit or statement. The charges against the defendant are specified, and when multiple charges exist they are referred to as counts. Depending on the state, generally the information or complaint is filed in a lower court, such as a county court, where the defendant is initially advised of his or her first appearance to hear the charges.

The Grand Jury

Alternatively, in some states and at the federal level, the prosecutor may decide to seek an indictment from a grand jury. Grand juries, though selected from the same pool, differ from **petit juries** (i.e., trial juries) that determine guilt at the trial level. A federal or state grand jury hears evidence presented by the prosecution to determine whether a person should be charged with a crime (i.e., indicted). A grand jury consists of 16 to 23 jurors who are not determining guilt or innocence. In other words, the jury is determining

pro bono: Legal representation that is provided at no charge or a reduced fee.

complaint: The document that initiates legal proceedings by demonstrating facts and legal reasons the plaintiff believes the defendant owes remedy or has committed a crime.

petit juries: Juries that determine guilt or innocence by following the course of a criminal trial. Both prosecution and defense present to a petit jury in a trial.

if enough evidence exists to proceed to trial. Jurors on grand juries serve from 1 to 12 months, depending on the state, and meet two or three times a month. Federal grand jurors serve for 18 months.

Grand juries are controversial because they operate in secret with subpoena powers and are not bound by rules of evidence. Judges and defense lawyers are not allowed in the courtroom during the procedure—only the prosecutor. The jurors, witnesses, evidence, and related information are closely guarded in a grand jury for several reasons. First, the methods prevent outside parties from interfering or tampering with witnesses. Second, witnesses may feel safer testifying under the protection of secrecy. Third, suspects are less likely to flee if they are unaware of the prosecution's efforts to obtain an indictment and go to trial. Fourth, the grand jury offers protection for innocent or implicated people who may be involved in the investigation.[11]

Public defenders were assigned by the court to represent alleged mass murderer James Holmes. Two years later, the legal proceedings against Holmes have lingered because of his insanity defense. What types of problems are created for the victims and families of the shooting because of the delays?

CASE STUDY

Danny Madrid's case received little media attention, and the one article published about his crime in a local newspaper initially gave him a sense of pride and power. Danny remembers the multitude of pretrial hearings, including the arraignment and competency hearing. Like many other people caught in the criminal justice system, he recalls the entire ordeal as a "mysterious path." Because Danny was unable to afford a private attorney, a public defender was appointed to his case. Often, a public defender is an asset in negotiating pretrial motions and acting as an advocate for plea bargaining. In Danny's case, his attorney was able to arrange a plea deal for 10 years, which he accepted. His co-conspirator, who was able to hire a private attorney, made a similar plea bargain for about the same amount of time.

Figure 8.3 ■ The Bail Bond Process

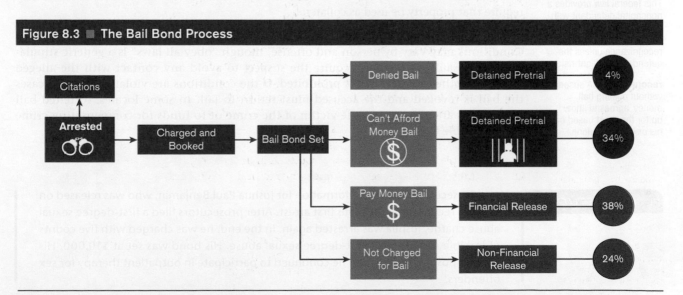

The use of a bond agent is common for defendants who are unable to afford bail. How fair is it to keep people in jail who are unable to afford bail?

Audio:
Ahead of pretrial hearing, Menendez defense points fingers at prosecutors

---

Bail Reform Act of 1966:
This federal law provides a noncapital defendant with the right to be released on bond or on personal recognizance unless the defendant is a flight risk.

recognizance: A suspect, without posting bail money, agrees to show up for the court based on his or her word alone.

BAIL AND PRETRIAL EVENTS

Generally, at the first appearance defendants are not asked to enter pleas, but are advised of their rights, and determinations about bail are made. Bail allows the arrested person, who is considered legally innocent, the opportunity to remain free until the case is resolved (see Figure 8.3). The Eighth Amendment of the Constitution is clear that excessive bail is prohibited. Specifically, the Eighth Amendment states, "Excessive bail shall not be required, nor excessive fines imposed, nor cruel and unusual punishments inflicted." While excessive bail is forbidden, the Constitution does not stipulate that a person has the right to bail. The right to bail for some individuals comes from the **Bail Reform Act of 1966**, which gives noncapital defendants the right to be released on bond or personal recognizance. When individuals are released on their own **recognizance**, this means that suspects, without posting bail money, agree to show up for court. In some cases, the Bail Reform Act provides the court with the discretion to deny bail. This is likely particularly if the person is a flight risk. Also, the judge may deny bail if he or she believes the suspect may commit additional crimes or interfere with witnesses. As previously mentioned, the court may consider a variety of factors in the decisions to grant bail, such as the type of offense (seriousness), the suspect's character, ties to the community, employment status, and/or past record. Given the characteristics of the Schuett victimization, prosecutors did not offer Bradford the opportunity to post bail. Rather, he was held in jail awaiting his preliminary hearing.

On a more practical note, bail reduces the population in overcrowded jails. Judges and magistrates determine the amount of bail. Bail bondsmen can be used for people who lack the financial resources to post bail. A bond usually is about 10% of the bail amount and may require that property be used as collateral.

A suspect released on bail must follow any conditions established by the courts. Conditions may vary by person and offense, though "obey all laws" is a generic stipulation. An assault charge may require the suspect to avoid any contact with the alleged victim. In other cases, travel is prohibited. If the conditions are violated, in most cases the bail is revoked and the accused must return to jail. In some locales, forfeited bail bond funds are dispersed to the victim of the crime or to funds for compensating crime victims (Table 8.2).

CASE STUDY

Prosecutors obtained information for Joshua Paul Benjamin, who was released on his own recognizance after his first arrest. After prosecutors filed a first-degree sexual abuse charge, Joshua was arrested again. In the end, he was charged with five counts of forcible sodomy and first-degree sexual abuse. His bond was set at $10,000. His mother posted the bail, and he continued to participate in outpatient therapy for sex offenders.

Table 8.2 ■ Forfeited Bail Bond Funds Disbursed to Victims	
State	Recipient of Forfeited Funds
Alaska	Victim
California	Victim
Illinois	Violent Crime Victims Assistance Fund
Indiana	Victim
Kansas	Crime Victims Assistance Fund and Victims Compensation Fund
Minnesota	Victim
Montana	Victim
Nevada	Fund for Compensation of Victims of Crime
Washington	Fund that supports local victim and witness programs
Wisconsin	Victim

Source: Adapted from National Conference of State Legislatures. (2015, May 12). *Victims pretrial release rights and protections.* Retrieved from http://www.ncsl.org/research/civil-and-criminal-justice/pretrial-release-victims-rights-and-protections.aspx.

Victims

Victims of crime have varying rights of notification and participation during pretrial activities. Statutes vary state to state, but currently most states require that the victim of a crime be notified when the defendant is released prior to trial. In about half of the states, victims are made aware of pretrial release hearings. In fewer states, victims have the right to participate in these pretrial proceedings by attending, being heard, and/or being consulted. The variation in victim rights by states is presented in the Table 8.3.

In addition to victim rights of notification and participation, in 19 states victims of particular crimes are given the option to use technology to allow them to monitor the location of the released defendant. The cases most often using this technology are those in which the crimes committed involved threats or harm to the victim, including stalking, domestic violence, and sexual offenses. This technology alerts the victim if the defendant is in close physical proximity. These devices not only offer greater peace of mind to victims, but also increase the safety of the victim while the defendant is in the community awaiting trial.

Journal:
Victim rights

Preliminary Hearing

The **preliminary hearing** commences after a criminal complaint is filed. The purpose of the preliminary hearing is to determine if there is enough evidence to believe a crime was committed and that the defendant may be responsible. At the hearing, evidence is presented by the prosecution to establish probable cause, and many of the rules of evidence applicable at a full trial may not apply, which gives the state more freedom in presenting possible evidence. Because the burden of proof at a preliminary hearing is probable cause, the prosecution does not need to prove anything beyond a reasonable doubt. Generally, the prosecution submits only that evidence deemed necessary to establish probable cause in order to show the crime likely was committed by the defendant. If the court finds that the prosecutor has established probable cause, then the defendant is bound over to the trial court of general jurisdiction. The proceedings are presented before a judge, and at this point the suspect is entitled to representation. When the defendant is bound over on felony charges, he or she then makes an appearance at the arraignment.

preliminary hearing:
This is typically held in criminal cases to determine the extent of evidence and whether enough exists to allow charges to be pressed against the defendant.

Table 8.3 ■ Victim Notification and Participation Rights in Pretrial Release

State and Citation	Right to Notification		Right to Participation
	Of Pretrial Release	Of Pretrial Release Hearing	
Alabama	X		
Alaska	X[a]	X	Attend and be heard
Arizona	X[a]	X	Attend and be heard
Arkansas		X	
California	X	X	Attend and be heard
Colorado	X	X	Attend
District of Columbia	X		
Florida	X	X	Be consulted and attend
Georgia	X	X	
Hawaii	X		
Idaho	X		
Illinois	X	X	
Indiana	X	X	
Iowa	X[a]		
Kentucky	X[a]	X	Be consulted
Louisiana	X	X	
Maine	X		
Massachusetts	X		
Michigan	X		
Minnesota	X[a]	X	Attend
Mississippi	X		
Missouri	X	X	Be consulted, attend, and be heard
Montana	X		Be consulted
Nebraska	X		
Nevada	X[a]		
New Jersey	X	X	
New York	X		Be consulted
North Dakota	X[a]	X	
Ohio	X		
Oklahoma	X		
Oregon		X	Attend and be heard
Pennsylvania	X		
Rhode Island	X	X	
South Carolina	X	X	Attend and be heard
South Dakota	X	X	
Tennessee	X[a]	X	Attend and be heard
Texas	X		
Utah	X[a]	X	Attend and be heard
Vermont	X[a]	X	Be consulted and attend
Virginia	X		Attend
Washington	X	X	Attend and be heard
West Virginia	X	X	Be consulted
Wyoming	X		

Source: National Conference of State Legislatures (2014). *Pretrial release: Victims' rights and protections.*

Note: No statutes were located for states not listed.

[a] State also requires that the victim be notified of the defendant's pretrial release conditions.

Arraignment

At **arraignments** defendants are readvised of the specific charges against them and asked to enter a plea: guilty, not guilty, or nolo contendere. *Nolo contendere* indicates that the defendant does not wish to contend or is offering no contest to the charges. In general, the plea of nolo contendere has the same consequence as a guilty plea. Nolo contendere is not a right and is restricted in some jurisdictions. At this point, a defendant may request a jury trial. Most likely before the arraignment is conducted, discovery and plea bargaining discussions are already under way between the prosecution and the defense counsel. Many felony cases are resolved at the arraignment, and if a plea bargain has been reached, the defendant enters a plea of guilty to the plea bargain disposition. In these cases, before the plea is entered the trial court judge conducts a full advisement of what rights the defendant is waiving by entering a plea. The judge also advises defendants that by entering pleas, they are admitting that there are sufficient facts and a basis to support guilt of the charge.

Author Video: Plea bargains

PLEA BARGAINS

The majority of criminal cases are resolved through **plea bargains**. In these cases, the prosecutor has the discretion to offer a lesser charge or reduce the number of charges. The defendant agrees to plead guilty in order to avoid a trial and a more severe sentence. In some plea bargains, the defendant is required to testify for the state in related cases going to trial. Plea bargains reduce the number of cases that go to trial and allow the prosecutor to allocate to other cases valuable resources that would have been used for trial. Typically, over 90% of felony criminal offenders plead guilty and are sentenced by judges.[12] While there are benefits to plea bargaining, it is not without controversy. On one hand, many believe it allows criminals to get away with minimal punishment. On the other hand, many argue that plea bargaining is coercive in that it strongly encourages innocent people to take a plea rather than risking a serious sentence. In this way, plea bargaining undermines constitutional rights. By plea bargaining, the defendant waives her or his right to a jury trial, right against self-incrimination, and right to confront witnesses.

arraignment: A formal reading of charges in a court of appropriate jurisdiction in front of the defendant.

plea bargain: When the prosecutor may offer a lesser charge or reduce the number of charges. The defendant agrees to plead guilty in order to avoid a trial and a more severe sentence.

CASE STUDY

Case Study Video 8.1: Interviews with case study participants

Joshua Paul Benjamin's case was settled in a plea bargain. While he was out on bond in another state receiving treatment for his sexual crimes, a plea agreement with the prosecutor was reached. His charges were reduced from second-degree to third-degree sexual abuse of a minor and sexual exploitation of a minor. Joshua flew home, appeared in court, and pleaded guilty. By doing so, the time and cost of a trial were saved and his victims were spared the ordeal of testifying. He was sentenced to two concurrent 10-year prison sentences. Nonetheless, he ended up serving his sentence in both states where the crimes occurred.

As is the outcome for most cases, Chris Farias's case did not go to trial. Rather, he pleaded guilty and was sentenced to serve time and participate in a specialized court devoted to dealing with his chronic DUIs.

Danny Madrid also took a plea bargain. He was facing the very real possibility of spending the rest of his life in prison. If he had selected to go to trial, he was looking at 25 years to life. Given his extensive juvenile record, it seemed likely he would get life. Rather, he opted to accept a plea bargain that put him in prison for 10 years. While he acknowledges that 10 years is a long time, it is far shorter than a life sentence.

In a plea bargain, the defendant is informed that he or she is waiving the right to a jury trial, the right to confront witnesses, the right to require the prosecution to prove the

Preliminary hearing. Why is the preliminary hearing important?

case against him or her, the right to challenge any evidentiary matters (e.g., search and seizure, Miranda), and the right to appeal the facts of the case. The judge must determine that the defendant entered his or her plea of guilty voluntarily, knowingly, and intelligently. During that advisement the judge will ask, "Have you been on medication, drugs, or alcohol? Do you fully understand what I'm saying? Do you speak, comprehend, and write the English language? Have you been subjected to any coercion or duress?" The judge also warns the defendant that any information about a sentence decided in the agreement is not binding on the court until the judge specifically accepts the terms of the plea bargain and sentence.

Once a judge accepts the plea, the sentence may be imposed immediately, particularly if an agreement was reached in the plea bargain. If sentencing is not agreed on by the parties, the court will schedule a sentencing hearing. In most cases, the probation department will conduct a presentence investigative report (commonly referred to as a PSI). The report may include information related to the circumstances of the offense, the defendant's background, and prior convictions. Recommendations for sentencing may be probation, intensive supervision probation, jail, or prison. In most plea bargains, the prosecution agrees to a range of sentencing options, and the probation department makes a recommendation. Judges have the final say on the sentencing and will exercise their discretion under the sentencing statutes.

Gender

Journal:
Women who plead guilty

There is a rich literature offering mixed findings on the influence of gender on bail and plea bargain decisions. Some research shows that the gender of the defendant does not influence decisions related to bail, while other findings indicate that women are treated less harshly than are men.[13] Research in the 1970s and 1980s by Goldkamp and Gottfredson as well as Nagel failed to find an effect of gender on bail decisions.[14] In contrast, work about 10 years later by Katz and Spohn found more leniency regarding bail for women compared with men, as women were much more likely to be released prior to the trial.[15] Katz and Spohn noted that the effect extended beyond gender and that race mattered as well. The researchers concluded that white women, white men, and black women were more likely to be released on bail compared with black men. Furthermore, when black men were offered the opportunity of bail, the amount of their bail was significantly higher than that required of other racial and gender groups.

Similar mixed results were obtained when considering gender and plea bargaining. Some research discovered that female defendants were offered more lenient plea deals than were men.[16] Other research found no influence of gender on decisions related to plea bargaining. Still other research showed that women are disadvantaged when it comes to plea bargaining. Work by Figueira-McDonough concluded that the terms of charge and sentence reductions in plea bargaining benefited men more than women.[17] The author concluded that lack of defense resources may be responsible for the findings that women are less likely to get sentence concessions than men committing the same offense. Clearly, the relationship between gender and plea bargaining is complex, as demonstrated by researchers Piehl and Bushway, who concluded the significance of extralegal factors (e.g., race, gender), legal characteristics, and where the case was prosecuted influenced the type of plea bargains offered.[18]

Race and Hispanic Origin

In contrast to gender, findings regarding the role of race on bail and plea bargain decisions are consistent: Black defendants are less likely to be offered bail or reduced charges through plea bargain than are white defendants. Furthermore, when a black defendant is offered a plea bargain, the sentence offered is harsher than that offered to a white defendant.[19] This disparity is compounded as some investigations find that plea bargain differences are also based on the type of crime committed: Drug-related offenses are less likely to be given lenient plea bargains. This is problematic, as black defendants are far more likely to be charged with drug-related crimes than are white defendants.[20] Like race, Hispanic origin plays a role in plea bargaining and bail. Research shows that Hispanics are less likely to be offered bail or lenient plea bargains compared with similar white and black defendants, and harsher treatment of drug-related crimes plays a role in these disparities.[21]

DISCOVERY AND MOTIONS

If no plea bargain occurs and the case is scheduled for trial, the process of discovery between the prosecution and the defendant begins in earnest. Under the rules of discovery, both sides must reveal the information they have that is pertinent to the case, though the rules for each side vary by state.

The judge will set a deadline for pretrial motions. The following include some of the more common motions filed with the court:

Plea bargains do not necessarily mean a light sentence. Are plea bargains helpful or harmful for achieving justice for the offender and the victims?

Motion to suppress: Defense attorneys often file this motion because of search and seizure issues or problems with a confession. In this motion, they are requesting that the court not allow illegally obtained evidence be presented at trial.

Motion in limine: This term is from Latin, meaning "threshold." The motion requests that the judge rule on whether particular evidence can be used at trial. Either side, for example, can file a motion claiming the anticipation of testimony from a witness they believe is hearsay or irrelevant.

Motion for a change of venue: A request for a change of venue, typically, is a pretrial motion asking for the trial to take place in a different geographical area (rules and procedures vary from state to state). In most cases the change is requested because of pretrial publicity or in the interests of justice. In a major case involving a great deal of media coverage, a defense attorney may file a motion to move the trial in order to avoid hostility or prejudice toward the defendant. In some cases, travel costs or locations of the witnesses, for example, may require a change of venue. Changing the location of a trial is at the judge's discretion.

Motion for discovery: As previously discussed, the rules of procedure establish a mandate for the prosecution to give the defense certain evidence. Defense lawyers may request everything the prosecution has gathered in the case, including statements from witnesses, DNA evidence, and names of expert witnesses.

Motion for recusal: A motion for the recusal (removal) of a trial judge or prosecutor is unusual, but it may arise if the defense has reason to believe one of the parties is unable to be fair or impartial.

Motion for expenses of experts: Public defenders may need additional financial resources to mount an effective defense. Retaining an expert psychiatrist is expensive, and this motion requests that the state pay expenses related to psychological evaluations or other types of expert testimony.

motion to suppress: A motion requesting that the court disallow illegally obtained evidence at trial.

motion in limine: A motion requesting that the judge rule on whether particular evidence can be used at trial.

motion for a change of venue: A pretrial motion requesting a geographical change of the trial.

motion for discovery: The rules of procedure establish a mandate for the prosecution to give the defense certain evidence.

motion for recusal: A motion for the recusal (removal) of a trial judge or prosecutor.

motion for expenses of experts: Defense can request that the state pay expenses related to psychological evaluations or other types of expert testimony.

ETHICAL ISSUES

How Does a Defense Attorney Represent an Admitted Mass Murderer?

Everyone, including prosecutors and defense attorneys, admits that James Holmes entered a movie theater in Aurora, Colorado, in July 2012 and opened fire, although he is still presumed innocent. Holmes, who killed 12 people and wounded 70, is charged with 166 felony counts of murder, attempted murder, and other related charges. The circumstances of the case show that he planned the crime for several months, collecting ammunition, gathering weapons, and setting explosive devices as booby traps in his apartment. Holmes was represented by two public defenders, who worked to ensure that he received a fair trial and vigorous defense. The attorneys argued that their client was not guilty by reason of insanity. Prosecutors were seeking the death penalty. Ultimately, Holmes was found guilty of 12 counts of murder and sentenced to 12 life sentences without parole and 3,318 years in prison.

Think About It

1. Imagine you are the public defender in this case. How would you justify defending someone you know is guilty?

2. What advantages do you see in the current legal strategy to prove that Holmes was suffering from a psychotic episode at the time of the shooting?

3. What are the moral and ethical issues you may face?

SCHEDULING AND THE RIGHT TO A SPEEDY TRIAL

A full schedule created by the court and the court participants is called a **trial management order**. This order designates what will happen and when as the parties work toward the trial date, though the goal of a speedy trial remains somewhat elusive. Prosecutors and defense attorneys may file other motions asking for a continuance before the trial begins. Delays may be related to difficulties getting expert witnesses, or DNA analysis backlogs, or illness. The extensive scheduling, however, is designed to meet the speedy trial deadline guarantee, which generally requires a trial to be conducted within 6 months of the date of the arraignment. In complicated cases, because of trial preparation time, the defense counsel may waive the right to a speedy trial. Whatever the defense does to delay the trial is not counted as violating the speedy trial clause, because defendants retain that right. In contrast, the prosecution does not have this option. As a prosecutor, if you run out of time the case is dismissed.

JURY SELECTION

Another vital component of pretrial activity is the selection of a jury (for jury cases). Jurors play a critical role in our criminal justice system, yet often individuals scheme to avoid this important responsibility. Juries act as fact finders in trials. They listen to evidence, deliberate, and deliver a verdict of guilty or not guilty. The number of jurors used in a criminal trial varies. Federal court requires 12 jurors be empaneled for criminal cases, and all states require that 12 jurors be empaneled for capital cases (i.e., death penalty trials). Beyond that, states differ in the number of jurors seated. In some cases, 12 members of the jury are seated, while in other cases (including felonies in some states), 6 jurors are required. In addition, alternate jurors are selected. Alternate jurors go through the same selection process and may replace jurors who become ill or are dismissed. The number of alternate jurors selected varies. In federal

trial management order: A full schedule created by the court and the court participants that designates what happens and when as the parties work toward the trial date.

🔨⚖️🔒 CONTEMPLATING CAREERS

Public Defenders

Do you like variation in your day-to-day routine? Is it important to you to help the underdog? Do you enjoy lots of client contact? Do you believe you would excel in a courtroom environment? Can you handle the ugliness that sometimes comes from poverty, homelessness, substance addiction, and violence?

If you answered yes to these questions, a public defender's career is one you might consider. Work as a public defender is neither as glamorous nor as unethical as many people believe. Not everyone has the fortitude to deal with clients who may be guilty, angry, or illiterate, but many lawyers find the experience challenging and rewarding. Public defenders are representing indigent defendants, not putting criminals back on the streets. Public defenders find themselves in the courtroom almost daily, and job opportunities are available at the local, state, and federal levels. New law school graduates often see defense work as a great opportunity and a chance to experience a wide range of cases, including specialization in juvenile, death penalty, or appellate litigation.

A law degree is necessary to work as a public defender. Public defenders have strong interpersonal skills and are characterized as bright, courageous, tenacious, persuasive, argumentative, tough, articulate, and empathetic. Entry-level salaries vary among states but generally range from $40,000 to $50,000. While this type of work is not for everyone, many law school graduates find public service work exciting and rewarding.

For additional information on becoming a public defender, see the following:

www.uscourts.gov/Careers/CareerProfiles/Assistant FederalPublicDefender.aspx

www.lawcrossing.com/article/95/Public-Defenders-Law-in-Action/#

 Career Video: A public defender discusses her experience and current issues in the field.

---

criminal cases, between 1 and 6 alternate jurors are selected. Alternate jurors participate in the trial, as do the other jurors; however, they do not actively deliberate. In some states, such as Connecticut, alternate jurors are dismissed before deliberation begins, whereas in others, they sit through deliberation proceedings.

The first step in the jury process is creating the **venire**, a list of potential jurors from which the jury is selected. Venires must represent a cross-section of the population in the jurisdiction where the trial will occur. To accomplish this, potential jurors' names are randomly selected from an assortment of sources, such as licensing rolls, tax rolls, motor vehicle records, utility user lists, and/or voting registration lists. There are few qualifications for jurors. In most jurisdictions, prospective jurors must be residents, 18 years of age or older, U.S. citizens, proficient in English, and not convicted of particular crimes. Jury summonses are mailed to those selected from the venire.

Prior to the selection of specific jurors, attorneys may make a challenge regarding the venire in total. This **challenge to the array** indicates that the venire, the full panel of prospective jurors, should be discharged because of a deficiency or illegality in the method in which the panel was selected.[22] The prosecutor or defense attorney presents this challenge to the judge, who may accept or deny this claim. The next step in jury selection is *voir dire*, in which prospective jurors are questioned in court under oath by the judge, prosecutor, and defense counsel. In some jurisdictions, jurors answer questions on a paper-and-pencil questionnaire designed to assess their suitability to serve.[23] During the *voir dire* examination, prosecutors and defense attorneys use two additional types of challenges to remove potential jurors: challenge for cause and peremptory challenge.

Web: Racial diversity in juries

venire: A list of potential jurors from which the jury is selected.

challenge to the array: An argument that the venire should be discharged because of a deficiency or an illegality in the way it was selected.

voir dire: Process in which prospective jurors are questioned in court under oath to attempt to uncover inappropriate jurors.

The jury system plays an important role in discovering the truth at trial. What types of biases may a juror hold that would influence the outcome of a trial?

Challenge for cause, also termed **strike for cause**, is used when the defense counsel, the prosecutor, or the judge identifies a potential juror he or she believes is unable to be unbiased, fair, or impartial. Legal reasons for making this challenge are required and can include the prospective juror's having a relationship with an individual involved in the trial (e.g., defendant, witness, judge, attorney), the prospective juror's attitude during *voir dire,* experience in a similar case, or admission of prejudice against race or religion pertinent to the case. There is no limit to the number of challenges for cause that may be made by either counsel.

The third type of challenge is the **peremptory challenge**. Unlike challenge for cause, attorneys are not required to offer a legal reason for removing the prospective juror from the jury pool. Though no cause is required, it is unconstitutional to remove a prospective juror based on her or his ethnicity, race, or gender.[24] Unlike with challenge for cause, attorneys are limited in the number of peremptory challenges they may use. In federal capital cases, each side may use up to 20 peremptory challenges. For lower level federal criminal cases, each side may be given as few as 3 peremptory challenges. The number of peremptory challenges allowed in state criminal court cases varies among states and cases.

The Sixth Amendment to the U.S. Constitution discusses rights as they relate to criminal juries:

In all criminal prosecutions, the accused shall enjoy the right to a speedy and public trial, by an impartial jury of the State and district wherein the crime shall have been committed, which district shall have been previously ascertained by law, and to be informed of the nature and cause of the accusation; to be confronted with the witnesses against him; to have compulsory process for obtaining witnesses in his favor, and to have the Assistance of Counsel for his defence.

The Sixth Amendment refers to the right of an impartial jury during criminal proceedings, but lacks any wording that a person is entitled to any particular jury composition. Precedents determined by the U.S. Supreme Court, however, have been interpreted to mean that one has the right to a selection, which does not systematically exclude any group from the venire. History indicates that this right has been ignored based on race/ethnicity and gender. The formal and informal exclusion of female, black, and Hispanic jury members is representative of this problem.

Female Jurors

Only recently, in 1975, were women called to serve on juries in the same capacity as men. Initially, women were legally prohibited from serving on juries. Later, while legally permitted to serve on juries, women were dissuaded from doing so because of bureaucratic complications. In many states, women, but not men, were required to register in writing at governmental offices stating their desire to serve on a jury. Given the U.S. Constitution's requirement that juries reflect a cross-section of the community, the prohibition and later discouragement of female jury participation appeared unconstitutional. Three major court cases considered this topic: *Hoyt v. Florida,*[25] *Taylor v. Louisiana,*[26] and *J. E. B. v. Alabama ex rel. T. B.*[27]

challenge for cause: A challenge during *voir dire* in which the defense counsel, the prosecutor, or the judge identifies a potential juror he or she believes cannot be unbiased, fair, or impartial. Also known as strike for cause.

strike for cause: A challenge during *voir dire* in which the defense counsel, the prosecutor, or the judge identifies a potential juror he or she believes cannot be unbiased, fair, or impartial. Also known as challenge for cause.

peremptory challenge: An attorney may remove a prospective juror from the venire without giving a legal reason.

In 1961, the U.S. Supreme Court heard *Hoyt v. Florida.* Hoyt was on trial for murdering her husband with a baseball bat following his act of infidelity. At the time of her trial, a Florida statute allowed women to serve on juries but only after registering in writing with the clerk of the circuit court. Jury duty was compulsory for men. A jury of 12 men convicted Hoyt. She appealed to the Supreme Court, claiming jury discrimination as women were effectively excluded from jury duty based on their sex only. The Supreme Court ruled unanimously against Hoyt, claiming that the exclusion of women was not discrimination and that no evidence was presented to demonstrate that Florida arbitrarily excluded women from jury duty.

An early female jury. It was only recently that women were allowed and selected to serve on juries in the same way as men. Why do you feel that this right was denied to women in the past? How might trials held during that time have been disadvantaged as a result?

The issue of female jurors came before the U.S. Supreme Court again in 1975 in *Taylor v. Louisiana.* Taylor was tried in Louisiana for kidnapping in a parish whose population was 53% female. Nonetheless, his jury included 12 men, who found him guilty and sentenced him to death. Taylor appealed to the Supreme Court that the selection of the venire, and subsequently the jury, was unconstitutional because women, but not men, were forced to register for jury duty. Taylor argued that this requirement resulted in a jury that failed to represent a cross-section of the community. The Court agreed with Taylor. Justice Byron White's statement echoed the feelings of almost the full court: "It is no longer tenable to hold that women as a class may be excluded or given automatic exemptions based solely on sex if the consequence is that criminal jury venires are almost totally male." In other words, this 1975 ruling struck down *Hoyt v. Florida,* which held that women's jury service was not mandatory. The *Taylor v. Louisiana* decision was nearly unanimous; only Justice William H. Rehnquist dissented.

The 1975 *Taylor* ruling guaranteed sex equality in jury service in theory. Still, the use of peremptory challenges continued to remove women from juries. Finally, in 1994, the Supreme Court ruled in *J. E. B. v. Alabama ex rel. T. B.* that it was unconstitutional to use peremptory challenges based on sex alone to remove women from the jury. Justices opined that to do so is a violation of the equal protection rights of the potential juror.[28] Chief Justice William Rehnquist, Justice Antonin Scalia, and Justice Clarence Thomas dissented from the majority opinion.

Black Jurors

With the end of the Civil War and the adoption of the Thirteenth, Fourteenth, and Fifteenth Amendments to the U.S. Constitution, basic rights were theoretically given to African Americans. In reality, additional legislation over a long period of time was required to ensure that basic rights were available. One such piece of legislation was the **Civil Rights Act of 1875,** which by a vote of 162 to 99 prohibited the exclusion of African Americans from public accommodations, including jury service. The specific text of the act pertaining to jury duty states,

Sec 4. That no citizen possessing all other qualification which are or may be prescribed by law shall be disqualified for service as grand or petit juror in any court of the United States, or of any State, on account of race, color, or previous condition of servitude; and any officer or other person charged with any duty in the selection or summoning of jurors who shall exclude or fail to summon any citizen for the cause aforesaid shall, on conviction thereof, be deemed guilty of a misdemeanor, and be fined not more than five thousand dollars.

Audio:
Blacks routinely excluded from juries

Civil Rights Act of 1875: One in a series of post–Civil War legislative acts, it prohibited the exclusion of African Americans from jury duty, among other things.

Unfortunately, the Civil Rights Act of 1875 failed to settle the question of whether black Americans could serve on juries. Some cases upheld this act, while others failed to do so. One important case was *Strauder v. West Virginia* (1880).[29] The case stemmed from the murder conviction of Taylor Strauder, a black man, by an all-white jury in West Virginia. At the time of Strauder's trial, West Virginia disallowed black persons from serving on juries. Strauder appealed his conviction on the grounds that his rights under the equal protection clause of the Fourteenth Amendment had been violated. The majority of the U.S. Supreme Court found that excluding black persons from juries violated the rights of black criminal defendants because the state had systematically excluded every black person from the jury pool.

This ruling was a victory for African Americans, but paradoxically it also upheld the right of states to prohibit women from juries because, as the Court noted, the Fourteenth Amendment was designed to prohibit discrimination against race or color only. It did not prohibit discrimination against sex.

Not long afterward, the gains made in the Civil Rights Act of 1875 and those established in cases such as *Strauder v. West Virginia* were reversed. This reversal stemmed from the Civil Rights Cases of 1883. This ruling was based on five similar cases that were jointly heard by the U.S. Supreme Court. The Court ruled the Civil Rights Act of 1875 unconstitutional because the federal government could not prohibit discrimination by a private individual and that the Constitution (specifically the Thirteenth Amendment) does not prohibit racial discrimination in public accommodations, public transportation, or jury duty. Thus, African Americans could be discriminated against and excluded from juries.

In 1935, *Norris v. Alabama* came before the U.S. Supreme Court after wending its way through the Alabama courts. This case centered on Clarence Norris and several other black men who had been accused of raping two white women. The appeal was based on (among other things) the fact that black individuals were excluded from juries in the county in which the indictment was generated. The Supreme Court concluded that the systematic exclusion of black persons from juries was a violation of the criminal defendant's due process rights.

In theory, *Norris* ended the wholesale exclusion of African Americans from jury service. In reality, just as was the case for women, African Americans were then dismissed systematically on the basis of peremptory challenges. This activity was addressed in 1986 in *Batson v. Kentucky*. In this case, James Batson, a black man, was convicted on criminal charges. The conviction was appealed because the prosecutor had removed all blacks from the jury pool in violation of the equal protection clause. A majority of the U.S. Supreme Court concluded that when there is the appearance that the state is using peremptory challenges to exclude a group of persons in violation of the equal protection clause, the state must provide a reason for the challenges. In theory, this ruling made illegal the removal of African Americans from the jury pool merely because they are black. In reality, many argue that the practice continues.

Hispanic Jurors

Less information on the treatment of Hispanics and other ethnicities in terms of jury duty is available. An extremely important case is the U.S. Supreme Court ruling in *Hernandez v. Texas* (1954). In this case, Pedro Hernandez argued that he had been denied an impartial jury because no ethnic minorities were included on the panel. In fact, not one Mexican American had served on a jury in more than 25 years in Jackson County, Texas, where his case was heard. Given these circumstances, Hernandez's conviction for murder was appealed, ultimately all the way to the Supreme Court.

The Court ruled unanimously that Hernandez's rights had been violated, and he was granted a new trial in which the jury was not selected on the basis of ethnicity. This case extended the rights guaranteed by the Fourteenth Amendment established for white and black individuals to other racial and ethnic categories.

American Indian/Alaskan Native Jurors

Although there is little to no literature focusing specifically on Asian, American Indian, and LGBTQ jurors, some evidence suggests that they have been prevented from serving on juries. For example, so-called "unassimilated" Indians (those retaining their tribal memberships) were excluded from serving on federal juries until Congress declared them citizens in June 1924.[30] This restriction prevented American Indians from serving, even after the 1868 ratification of the Fourteenth Amendment. This prohibition was codified by the Supreme Court, which ruled that Native Americans retaining their tribal membership were not citizens (and as such could not serve on juries).[31]

Asian Jurors

Asians faced barriers to serving on juries as well. The late 1800s were characterized by an influx of Asian, especially Chinese, immigration to the United States. These workers served as cheap labor on plantations, in mines, and on railroad construction projects. With increasing immigration, a xenophobic fear that Asian immigrants would take valuable resources and usurp the culture of white Americans grew. This "Yellow Peril" resulted in laws implemented to make difficult the day-to-day lives of Asians. The federal Naturalization Act of 1870, for example, created a system for the naturalization process in the United States, and that citizenship rights be given to Asians (and other nonwhite persons with the exception of black persons). Without citizenship, one cannot vote or serve on a jury. Anti-immigration sentiments were strong, and laws were passed that disallowed Chinese, Japanese, and other Asian immigration entirely.

LGBTQ Jurors

Unlike the previous groups discussed, no current federal law prevents removing persons from jury duty based on their LGBTQ status. The U.S. Supreme Court has not ruled on whether the equal protection clause of the Fourteenth Amendment prohibits the use of peremptory challenges to strike prospective jurors on the basis of sexual orientation or gender identity. Some states prohibit removing potential jurors based on their LGBTQ status (e.g., California); still others allow their removal from consideration. Some protection is available based on the precedent set in the 2014 case *SmithKline Beecham Corp. v. Abbott Labs.* Heard in the Ninth Circuit Court of Appeals, this ruling was the first at the federal level to find that jurors cannot be removed from consideration based on their sexual orientation. While this ruling does not cover the nation, it does apply to all federal courts in the Ninth Circuit as well as thousands of state courts. In addition, this ruling may provide precedent in other jurisdictions.

THE TRIAL DAY ARRIVES

In most cases, more motions will be filed on the day of the trial. The defense or prosecution may request sequestration of witnesses. This means that any person testifying cannot remain in the courtroom and hear the testimony of other witnesses. Additional motions *in limine* are filed when other evidence has been discovered and/or if the prosecutor or defense attempts to limit additional evidence. A defendant may decide to file a motion to fire his or her lawyer (a ploy sometimes used to delay the trial). Should the case proceed to trial, selection of the jury will begin. Chapter 9 covers material related to that and other aspects of the trial.

Figure 8.4 ■ Employment Among Law School Graduates

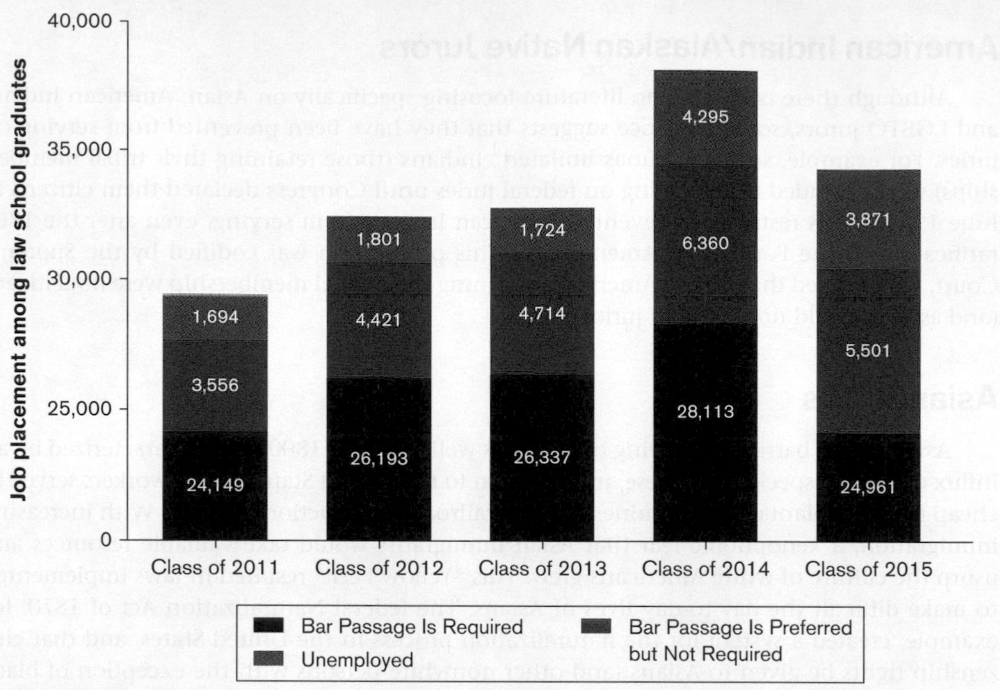

Source: American Bar Association, Section of Legal Education and Admissions to the Bar. (n.d.). *2015 law graduate employment data.* Retrieved from http://www.americanbar.org/content/dam/aba/administrative/legal_education_and_admissions_to_the_bar/reports/2015_law_graduate_employment_data.authcheckdam.pdf.

CHAPTER WRAP-UP

Certainly, the majority of lawyers practice law within the guidelines of professional ethics and adhere to codes of conduct. Studies of occupational crime under the umbrella of white-collar crime, for example, have focused on lawyers who engage in criminal conduct.

White-collar crime scholar David Friedrichs notes the "blind zeal to win cases" can result in violations of the law. Critics argue and some research shows the practice of law is particularly prone to misconduct involving, for example,

- overbilling;
- bribing judges, public officials, and witnesses;
- theft from clients;
- ethical violations; and
- aiding and abetting in criminal enterprises.

Prosecutors and defense attorneys play an important role in the criminal justice system, and their contributions, despite somewhat negative stereotypes associated with their profession, are instrumental in seeking the truth and obtaining justice. The structure of the court system ensures checks and balances on the behavior of lawyers, who are held to high standards, especially prosecutors. Additionally, the ABA and state and local bar associations provide resources and require continuing legal education for maintaining licensure for attorneys (see Figure 8.4). The ABA, established in 1878, is one of the largest voluntary professional organizations in the world, touting almost 400,000 members.[32]

Because most of the case studies described in this book failed to go to trial, there is little to note about pretrial activities. Joshua Paul Benjamin plea-bargained and avoided trial. He was sentenced to serve time in two states for his sexual crimes. Danny Madrid accepted a plea bargain that sentenced him to 10 years in prison, compared with the 25 years or life he would have been sentenced to should he have lost at trial.

Danny said, "One thing I would like to note though is that the day I was sentenced, I recall the adult court judge making a comment to me that still resonates. He said that despite the prison sentence, I would still be young enough (when I paroled) to change my life around . . . that not all was lost. What made this comment very powerful was that the judge did not give any such words of encouragement to my crime partner. He singled me out. In all, my experiences in juvenile court judge were different from adult court. In one I was viewed as dangerous, while in the other I was viewed as salvageable."

In the following chapter, we examine trials. Trials begin with opening statements and end in verdicts. As we will see, if the defendant is found guilty, sentencing follows. If the defendant is found not guilty, he or she is acquitted of the charges and is free to go.

KEY POINTS

- The U.S. attorney general is the chief law enforcement officer in the government.

- U.S. attorneys are assigned to judicial districts and are responsible for prosecuting cases at the federal level.

- Local- and state-level prosecutors are responsible for deciding who and what is charged.

- Prosecutors are powerful players in the courts and maintain a great deal of discretion.

- Defense attorneys ensure the constitutional rights of the accused.

- Prosecutors may file an information listing charges or use a grand jury to obtain an indictment.

- The right to bail is not present in the Constitution.

- During the preliminary hearing the court determines whether the case should proceed to trial.

- At arraignment defendants are readvised of the charges and asked to enter a plea.

- The majority of criminal cases are resolved through plea bargaining.

- Jury selection has changed greatly over time, as many groups were initially barred from sitting on juries. Ironically, now that the majority of the hurdles have been dismantled, many try to avoid this important responsibility when called.

KEY TERMS

REVIEW QUESTIONS

1. What are the responsibilities of the prosecutor?

2. What types of cases are handled by a U.S. attorney's office?

3. What factors are involved in a prosecutor's decision to file charges?

4. Why are plea bargains important to the criminal justice system?

5. List examples of conditions for bail. What happens if the defendant jumps bail?

6. What kinds of prosecutorial misconduct has the U.S. Supreme Court identified?

7. What is the role of a defense attorney?

8. What is the difference between an indictment and an information?

9. What happens at the preliminary hearing and the arraignment?

10. What are some victim rights during the pretrial phase? How do they differ across jurisdictions?

11. What are the steps in jury selection? May a prospective jury be removed based on gender, race, age, or LGBTQ status?

CRITICAL THINKING MATTERS

1. **Role of the Jury.** Many question whether the jury model is the best model for justice or if juries have stopped serving a beneficial purpose. Research shows that jury members often are unable to understand and apply the complex nuances of the law. It also shows jurors, when they do understand the law, often disregard it. And some argue those who end up on a jury are generally ignorant. Some have suggested other options for the dispensation of justice. One is that a panel of judges hear trials and renders verdicts. Another option is that professional jurors hear trials and render verdicts. These jurors would be trained in the law and impartiality, and paid for their work. What do you think are the advantages of moving away from juries toward one of these two (or both) alternatives? Would making these changes undermine democracy? Why or why not? How would the U.S. Constitution have to be changed to make such changes? If Dennis Earl Bradford had gone to trial, what do you think the outcome would have been? What would it have been

if you were in charge? Would that punishment be equitable and just?

2. **Prosecution in the Jennifer Schuett Case.** Imagine you are the prosecutor for the Schuett case. Who do you represent, and what is your most important goal? What type of evidence would you want to present to the jury in order to win your case? Would you consider a plea bargain, and if so, what sentence do you believe would be fair for Dennis Bradford?

3. **Differences in Bail.** Joshua Paul Benjamin was first released on his own recognizance, and then, after he was charged with five counts of forcible sodomy and first-degree sexual abuse, his bond was set at $10,000. Dennis Bradford had lived crime free for several years when he was arrested, yet he was denied bail. In what ways does the amount of bail or the lack of bail in these cases seem fair or unfair? What would you do if you were the judge?

4. **Balancing the Right to a Speedy Trial With Maintaining a Sense of Justice.** Some trials can take a significant amount of time to prepare evidence, assemble witnesses, and examine the details. In these scenarios, what should be considered a reasonable time frame for going to trial? What may the consequences be for the plaintiff and defendant for allowing a trial to commence too soon or waiting too long? What benefits may exist? What seems to be the ideal time to proceed to trial based on your analysis?

5. **Prosecutorial Misconduct.** Because of the power and respect afforded to prosecutors, should those who engage in misconduct face criminal charges? Are there ever any legitimate reasons a prosecutor may engage in conduct considered unethical? Does the end ever justify the means, or does such mentality simply undermine the entire justice system even if several guilty people are acquitted?

6. **Use of Plea Bargains.** What might happen to the criminal courts if plea bargaining were eliminated? Does the concept of a plea bargain encourage innocent people to plead guilty to lesser charges in order to avoid the risk of a trial and being sentenced to more severe punishment? Why are indigent defendants more likely to enter into plea bargains? What type of discrimination might this add to the system? How do these serve as important bargaining chips for prosecutors? Or defense attorneys? Do you think that Chris Farias, after his third DUI, should have been allowed to plea bargain? Do you think it will serve as specific deterrence to him if he believes he will always have that opportunity? What about Joshua—should a plea bargain have been an option for him? What about Danny Madrid—should a plea bargain be made available to crimes such as attempted murder?

DIGITAL RESOURCES

Sharpen your skills with SAGE edge at edge.sagepub.com/rennison2e. SAGE edge for Students provides a personalized approach to help you accomplish your coursework goals in an easy-to-use learning environment. You'll find action plans, mobile-friendly eFlashcards, and quizzes as well as video and web resources and links to SAGE journal articles to support and expand on the concepts presented in this chapter.

9

THE CRIMINAL TRIAL AND SENTENCING

"I continue to believe that sentence of 10 years imprisonment under the circumstances of this case is unconscionable and patently unjust. . . .
[The defendant] will be sacrificed on the altar of Congress' obsession with punishing crimes involving narcotics. This obsession is, in part, understandable, for narcotics pose a serious threat to the welfare of this country and its citizens. However, at the same time, mandatory minimum sentences—almost by definition—prevent the Court from passing judgment in a manner properly tailored to a defendant's particular circumstances."

—Paul A. Magnuson,
U.S. District Judge, Minnesota

"What we are paying for at such great cost is essentially our own ambivalence about capital punishment. We try to maintain the apparatus of state killing and another apparatus that almost guarantees that it won't happen. The public pays for both sides."

—Frank Zimring, JD,
William G. Simon
Professor of Law and
Wolfen Distinguished Scholar

LEARNING OBJECTIVES

After finishing this chapter, you should be able to:

9.1 Describe the purpose and process of criminal trials, including capital trials.

9.2 Summarize the purpose of juries, including the process by which they reach a verdict, as well as types of outcomes.

9.3 Summarize how sentencing has changed over time and the advantages and disadvantages of different methods of sentencing.

9.4 Differentiate the policy implications and costs of various sentencing alternatives in the United States.

9.5 Identify how capital cases differ from noncapital criminal cases, and explain why capital cases are more expensive than noncapital cases.

9.6 Identify the victim's role in criminal cases over time and rights gained by victims, specifically what victim impact statements are, how they are given, and the role they play in the criminal justice system.

INTRODUCTION: THE CRIMINAL TRIAL AND SENTENCING

Trials are rare. While estimates vary by type of case and other factors, it is safe to say that fewer than 10% of cases go to trial. By some estimates, only 2% to 3% of criminal cases go to trial. Most cases never go to trial; often they are settled when charges are dropped, when plea bargains are reached, or by other procedures during the pretrial phase. This chapter focuses on **criminal trials**, which are one type of trial conducted in the United States. **Civil trials** deal with issues between two private parties and do not involve criminal misconduct. These trials focus on issues such as divorce, child custody, physical injuries (e.g., slipping on ice on the front porch of someone's home or business), damage to one's reputation (e.g., libel, slander), disputes over money and payments, and contract breaches. **Traffic hearings** are the most common type of trial in the United States.

Criminal trials have a singular purpose: to ascertain the **legal guilt** or innocence of a person charged with a criminal act. Legal guilt is established when a prosecutor is able to persuade a judge or jury that the defendant is guilty of the criminal charges against him or her beyond a reasonable doubt. In criminal trials, the prosecutor has the burden of proof to demonstrate the defendant's legal guilt. Legal guilt differs from **factual guilt**, which refers to whether the defendant *actually* committed the crime. Ideally, trials will result in those who are factually guilty being found legally

Figure 9.1 ■ General Sequence of Events During a Criminal Trial

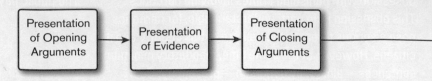

What other sequencing of trials do you feel may accomplish the task of justice better? Why?

criminal trials:
Trials to ascertain the guilt or lack of guilt of defendants charged with committing crimes.

civil trials: Trials used to settle disputes between two parties that do not involve criminal misconduct.

traffic hearings: Used to deal with traffic offenses.

legal guilt: Established when a prosecutor is able to persuade a judge or jury that the defendant is guilty of the criminal charges.

factual guilt: Refers to whether defendant actually committed a crime.

adjudicate: To render a formal judgment about a disputed matter.

guilty, or those who are factually innocent being found legally not guilty. Errors can and do happen in trials. If the prosecutor fails to persuade the judge or jury of the defendant's guilt, a factually guilty defendant may be found legally not guilty. And in the worst-case scenario, a trial may result in a factually innocent person's being found legally guilty.

Criminal trials include cases in which the criminal code was violated. These trials may include cybercrimes. Recently, 28-year-old Albert Gonzales was sentenced to 20 years in prison for stealing more than 90 million debit and credit card numbers from retailers. The theft resulted in a loss of $171.5 million. In addition, he has been ordered to pay a fine and will be required to pay restitution in the case. Like many traditional criminals, Gonzales was motivated by greed; his goal was to steal more than $15 million. Unlike most criminals, however, he had been earning $75,000 annually as an undercover informant for the U.S. Secret Service. Gonzales was hired by the Secret Service after being apprehended for making fraudulent ATM withdrawals in a hacking scheme. After the Secret Service learned of his role in the carding community, they had the charges against him dismissed and hired him. Gonzalez's sentence is the longest prison term to date for hacking. This may change, however, as he will be tried shortly for another case in which he allegedly stole more than 130 million debit and credit card numbers from another company. He is facing between 17 and 25 years for his crimes in that case. Gonzales's release from prison is scheduled for 2025.

CASE STUDY

Case Study Video 9.1:
Interviews with case study participants

Given the rarity of cases going to trial, it should come as no surprise that none of our case studies resulted in a trial. Chris Farias pleaded guilty before a judge before trial. Danny Madrid agreed to accept a plea bargain of 10 years' incarceration rather than risking a sentence of 25 years to life for his crime. Joshua Paul Benjamin plea-bargained and was sentenced to prison. The perpetrator in the Jennifer Schuett case, Dennis Earl Bradford, was scheduled to go to trial, but he never made it. Awaiting a hearing before the judge, Bradford was kept in a cell under suicide watch. He was later moved to another cell with less oversight. It was here that he fashioned a noose with his bed cover and hanged himself. He was discovered by a deputy on a routine round just after 1 a.m. and was pronounced dead later at a hospital. Detective Cromie then had to fulfill one role of being a law enforcement agent when dealing with victims: informing Jennifer Schuett of Bradford's suicide. Cromie had worked on the case and with Jennifer long enough to know that this news would be difficult to share. Nonetheless, he called her in the middle of the night and told her what had happened. Although some people may believe that Bradford's act was self-justified and ultimately saved taxpayer resources, his suicide was devastating to victim Jennifer Schuett and to Bradford's family. Jennifer had waited 20 years to use her voice and to tell him that he picked the wrong little girl to victimize. By killing himself, Bradford took the opportunity from Jennifer to face him and give her painstakingly crafted victim impact statement. Many victims want the opportunity to face their attackers in court. Some, like Jennifer, are robbed of that chance.

In both federal and state courts, the majority of criminal cases that go to trial are **adjudicated** or decided by juries. In lower criminal trial courts involving misdemeanors, a

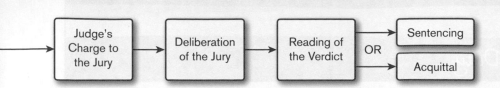

| Judge's Charge to the Jury | → | Deliberation of the Jury | → | Reading of the Verdict | OR | Sentencing |
| | | | | | | Acquittal |

defendant may opt for a **bench trial**. A bench trial (also known as a court trial or a nonjury trial) is possible if three criteria are met. First, the defendant must, in writing, voluntarily and knowingly waive his or her constitutional right to a trial by jury. Second, the government must consent to a bench trial. And third, the court must approve.[1] Bench trials may benefit defendants in cases that are complicated or technical, or those that involve stigmatizing events. In a bench trial the judge, or in some jurisdictions a panel of judges, serves as the fact finder by weighing the evidence presented. The judge, or panel, then renders a judgement of guilty or not guilty. Because bench trials do not require jury selection, charging the jury, and jury deliberation, they tend to be faster and less formal than jury trials. If a defendant chooses a **jury trial**, then the jury acts as the fact finder, weighs the evidence, deliberates, and renders a verdict.

A bench trial in progress. What are the advantages of bench trials to the offender? To the victim? And to the taxpayer? Should all trials be bench trials, or are jury trials vital?

Criminal trials are formal affairs guided by U.S. and state constitutions, statute, professional expectations, rules of evidence, ethics, and informal procedures.[2] Though varying by case and jurisdiction, criminal cases generally move through the following formal stages: presentation of opening statements, presentation of evidence, presentation of closing arguments, judge's charge to the jury, deliberation of the jury, reading of the verdict, and finally, sentencing (Figure 9.1).

PRESENTATION OF OPENING STATEMENTS

Following the selection of the jury (discussed in Chapter 8), opening statements are made. The purpose of the opening statements is to offer a summarized, logical, factual, and vivid mental picture of what actually transpired. These are called statements because counsel can only state what she or he expects the evidence to show. Counsel cannot argue what inferences should be drawn from the evidence during the opening statements. In general, judges instruct jurors that what they will hear in the opening statements is not evidence, but instead the attorneys' predictions of the evidence they will present. The prosecutor offers the first opening statement because he or she has the burden of proof in a criminal trial to demonstrate the defendant's guilt. This statement generally includes a summary of the criminal behavior the defendant committed and what evidence the prosecutor will be presenting during the trial to demonstrate beyond a reasonable doubt the guilt of the defendant.

Defense counsel offers their opening statement once the prosecutor's statement has concluded. The defense's goal in presenting an opening statement is to describe how the trial will demonstrate that the prosecution has failed to prove criminal conduct on the part of their

Author Video:
Evidence and the use of technology

Audio:
Judge allows criminal case against Bill Cosby to proceed

bench trial: A trial in which a judge (or panel of judges) acts as the fact finder, weighs the evidence, deliberates, and renders a judgement.

jury trial: A trial in which the jury acts as the fact finder, weighs the evidence, deliberates, and renders a verdict.

AP Photo/Mike Stone, Pool

ETHICAL ISSUES

Getting Out of Jury Duty

Getting out of jury duty is more than that—it is getting out of serving as a critical part of the trial process. Yet, it is common to hear of someone receiving a jury summons scheming to get out of *voir dire.* Maybe that someone is you. So common is this behavior that there are websites advising how to avoid jury duty. Tips include not responding to the summons, being very verbal, claiming biases, stating that the same crime happened to your cousin's ex-boyfriend, or informing the court that you are mentally ill.

Will these acts work? Maybe. But keep in mind that lying under oath during *voir dire* is **perjury**, as Susan Cole learned. Cole pleaded guilty to attempting to influence a public servant and to second-degree perjury after lying under oath during *voir dire* in a district courtroom. She appeared in court purposively disheveled while acting bizarrely. When asked, she told the judge she had mental issues and was promptly dismissed. Cole then bragged about her cleverness on a call-in radio show. What she failed to realize was that the judge was listening to the radio station and remembered her. Charges were filed, and eventually Cole pleaded guilty. Beginning in 2011, she began serving a 2-year deferred judgment on one count and 2 years of probation on a second count. She was also ordered to perform 40 hours of community service.

Think About It

The duty to serve, and disdain for doing so, raises many important policy questions.

1. Serving on a jury is an opportunity, an entitlement, and an obligation to engage directly in our democracy. Serving as a juror in a trial is a critical part of a healthy criminal justice system. Why, then, do so many shun this opportunity and privilege?

2. If you were a policymaker, what policy would you implement to encourage widespread participation on juries? How would better participation affect trials and trial outcomes? Should greater monetary reward be given to jurors for serving? As a taxpayer, are you willing to pay more in taxes for that?

3. Should the jury system be abolished in lieu of having criminal disputes settled by panels of judges or professional jurors?

---

defendant and what evidence they will present to undermine the prosecution's evidence. In addition, defense counsel will portray their client, the defendant, in favorable ways. The defendant is presumed innocent; consequently, the defense attorney does not bear the burden of proof. Because the defense attorneys open second, they have some advantages. First, they are afforded the opportunity to hear what the prosecutor intends to present in terms of evidence before revealing what evidence they intend to present. Second, they can refer to statements made by the prosecutor during their opening statement. And finally, the defense is advantaged because the prosecutor does not get an opportunity to rebut following the defense's opening statements.

perjury: A spoken or written intentional swearing of a false oath or misrepresenting of an agreement to be truthful.

Federal Rules of Evidence: Federal rules guiding what is evidence and what can be introduced in a trial.

PRESENTATION OF EVIDENCE

The trial then moves to the introduction of evidence. Strict rules guide what is evidence and how it may be presented during a criminal trial. Most states have their own rules of evidence, which may have been modeled after the **Federal Rules of Evidence** and changed to fit each state's particular policies. The purpose of the Federal Rules of Evidence is to "administer every proceeding fairly, eliminate unjustifiable expense and delay, and promote the development of evidence law, to the end of ascertaining the truth and securing a just determination."[3] If there is a legal question concerning the rule, which has not been addressed by the state's appellate courts, the state courts may rely on cases decided by federal courts concerning the federal counterpart rule. All evidence introduced must be relevant (i.e., must have the ability to help prove or disprove a fact in the trial), material (i.e., must be offered to prove a fact in dispute in the trial), and competent (i.e., must be reliable). Evidence can come in many forms, including witness testimony, objects such as weapons, written or electronic documents and reports, DNA, ballistics, maps, diagrams, video, audio, and photographs. Fact finders in a trial use evidence presented to decide the guilt or lack of guilt of the defendant.

Types of Evidence

Evidence can be classified in several ways. Two major classifications of evidence are **direct evidence** and **circumstantial evidence**. Direct evidence offers proof of something without requiring the judge or jury to interpret its meaning. This could be a video of the defendant committing the crime or a photograph of the defendant holding a smoking gun over the victim's dead body. Direct evidence is also testimony from a witness who saw the defendant commit the crime. In contrast, circumstantial evidence requires the judge or jury to interpret the evidence and draw conclusions about its meaning. An example of circumstantial evidence is a set of fingerprints at the scene of a crime. Another example is a witness who testifies that he heard the victim scream "He's trying to kill me!" and then saw the defendant run away from the area in which the victim was found murdered. Forensic evidence such as ballistics or DNA analysis presented by an expert witness is a type of circumstantial evidence (Figure 9.2).

Hearsay

Hearsay is defined by the Federal Rules of Evidence as "an out-of-court statement introduced to prove the truth of the matter asserted." Such statements, made outside of court and not under oath, are problematic because people often misstate what they have heard or seen and because human memory is imperfect. In addition, hearsay introduced in a trial excludes any possibility of cross-examination. In general, the **hearsay rule** disallows people testifying from introducing hearsay. A witness, for example, would be prohibited from testifying in court that a friend told her or him that the defendant bought the weapon used in a crime. In contrast, a person can testify that she or he saw the defendant buy the weapon. If a witness offers testimony about something she or he does not have personal knowledge of, counsel will object, and the judge will determine if that statement is to be admitted as evidence. If the judge agrees with the objection, she or he will instruct the jury to disregard the use of secondhand information as evidence.

Almost 30 exceptions to the hearsay rule exist.[4] One example is the **dying declaration**. If someone who is dying exclaims to the paramedic treating her or some other witness, "My husband shot me!" that witness could testify in court what the deceased victim stated. Another exception is the **excited utterance**. This is a statement made by a person during a shocking or upsetting event. Words blurted out during the stress of excitement may be entered into court. And a final exception covered here is the **reputation concerning character**. This exception allows witnesses to testify under oath about the reputation of a person's friends and acquaintances. It also allows testimony regarding the person's character to be introduced during testimony.

Opening statement. Why is the opening statement critically important? Do you feel that a poor opening statement may doom the defendant? Should a poor opening statement be grounds for appeal?

direct evidence: Something introduced in a trial that does not require an inference to be drawn by the fact-finding body.

circumstantial evidence: Evidence that requires the fact-finding body to interpret it and draw conclusions about its meaning.

hearsay: An out-of-court statement offered in court to prove the truth of the matter asserted.

hearsay rule: A basic rule that hearsay is inadmissible in court.

dying declaration: An exception to the hearsay rule that allows the dying words of a witness to a crime to be used in court.

excited utterance: An exception to the hearsay rule—a statement made by a person during a shocking or upsetting event. Words blurted out during the stress of excitement may be entered into court.

reputation concerning character: An exception to the hearsay rule that allows witnesses to testify under oath about the reputation of a person's friends and acquaintances.

Figure 9.2 ■ Ballistics Report

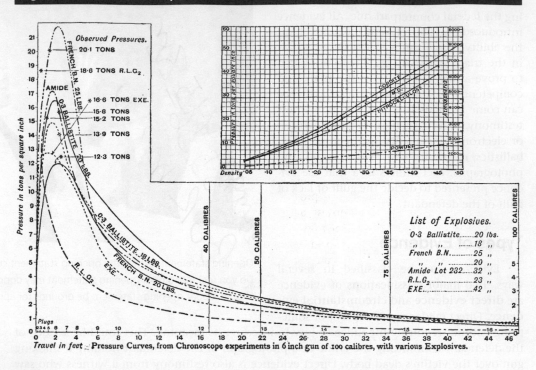

Juries are more likely to demand scientific evidence at trials today. Do you think that this relatively recent development has made it more or less difficult for a defendant to be found guilty? What evidence do you think juries of the past used when evidence such as ballistics reports was not available?

Author Video:
Eyewitnesses

Source: *Encyclopædia Britannica.*

Cross-examination of a witness. What advantages or disadvantages do you think being aggressive toward a witness may bring a defendant? Do you think the jury may view aggressiveness as bullying? Or do you feel the failure to be aggressive may be viewed differently by the jury? What would you do when presented with a witness and why?

In a criminal trial, the prosecutor presents evidence and calls witnesses to testify in an effort to support the state's case. At this time, the prosecutor engages in direct examination of the witnesses. The prosecutor cannot compel the defendant to testify, given the Fifth Amendment, which protects defendants from self-incrimination: "No person shall . . . be compelled in any criminal case to be a witness against himself." Furthermore, the prosecutor is forbidden from speculating why the defendant selects to remain silent (as most defendants do). Judges always direct jurors not to view the failure of the defendant to testify as evidence of guilt.

The defense attorney may then engage in cross-examination of the witnesses called by the prosecutor to raise doubt about their testimony. In general, the purpose of cross-examination is to test the credibility and memory of the witness. Following the cross-examination, the prosecutor may redirect and ask the witness final questions to clarify any confusing testimony for the fact-finding body. The prosecutor then rests the case, meaning that he or she may not call additional witnesses in an effort to support the charges against the defendant.

Following the prosecution's resting of the case, the defense has the opportunity to present evidence and call his or her own witnesses. Defense attorneys generally take advantage of this opportunity and present evidence and witnesses in support of and favorable to their client. Once a defense witness testifies, the prosecutor may cross-examine the witness, and the defense may redirect examine as well. This back-and-forth of redirect examination and re-cross-examination can continue until the prosecution and defense are satisfied or the judge limits the questioning. Once a defense attorney rests her or his case, the trial moves on to the next phase: presentation of closing arguments.

The judge charges the jury. Do you feel the judge's directions to the jury matter in terms of verdicts? Why or why not?

PRESENTATION OF CLOSING ARGUMENTS

Closing arguments, also called jury arguments, summation, or summing up, provide an opportunity for the defense and prosecution to summarize the evidence and arguments for the jury. In contrast to opening statements, counsel can state what inferences should be drawn from the evidence presented during the trial. No new evidence may be introduced during the closing arguments. While discrepancies exist, the prosecutor generally gives his or her closing arguments first to demonstrate how the evidence presented during the trial proved the defendant's guilt beyond a reasonable doubt. The prosecutor may directly ask that the jury find the defendant guilty of the charge(s). Once the prosecutor has completed his or her closing arguments, the defense counsel presents their own summary of the evidence, points to problems with the prosecutor's evidence and arguments, and then generally encourages the jury to find the defendant not guilty of the criminal charge(s). In federal criminal trials and in some other jurisdictions, the prosecutor gets the final opportunity to speak. During this, the **rebuttal**, the prosecutor may reiterate his or her argument, address comments made by the defense during their summation, and offer a final plea to find the defendant guilty as charged. Closing arguments are not mandatory for either party.

JUDGE'S CHARGE TO THE JURY

The next step in the criminal trial is for the judge to instruct the jury on the law they must follow in reaching their verdict. Judges' charges to the jury differ by jurisdiction and depend on factors of the crime as well as characteristics of the trial.[5] Most states have **pattern jury instructions**, which are templates of language to be used when charging the jury. While pattern jury instructions simplify the task of presenting instructions to the jury, the directives can still be complex and lengthy. Research suggests that with pattern jury instructions, most jurors have a poor understanding of the details.[6]

Charging instructions, while variable, may reiterate that the defendant is innocent until proven guilty and that the prosecution has the burden to prove the defendant's guilt beyond a reasonable doubt. **Beyond a reasonable doubt** means that the prosecutor must have proven the government's case such that a reasonable person would have no reasonable doubt that the defendant is guilty as charged. The judge may include in the instructions a reiteration of

rebuttal: In some criminal trials, the prosecutors have the last opportunity to speak during closing arguments. Other forms of rebuttal may include evidence or argument.

pattern jury instructions: Language template to be used when charging the jury.

beyond a reasonable doubt: The level of proof required for a criminal case conviction. Refers to a reasonable person having no reasonable doubt that the defendant is guilty as charged.

David Young-Wolff/Getty Images

A jury deliberates in private. In some cases, jurors go home each day. In others, jurors are sequestered until the end of the trial. What role do you think having a sequestered jury plays in the overall verdict, if any? How would you feel if you could not go home while on a jury? Would it affect your actions during the trial?

the disputed facts in the case as well as a description of the law related to those facts for the jurors. Judges may remind the jury of their duty to objectively consider only the evidence that has been presented and to remind jurors of their duty to be impartial. Following the charge, the jury is removed from the courtroom and begins its deliberations toward a verdict.

JURY DELIBERATION

Once removed from the courtroom, the jury is taken to a location to select a jury foreperson, deliberate, and reach a verdict. **Deliberation** is the process of deciding the guilt or lack of guilt of the defendant. While deliberating, the jury cannot be contacted by any individual involved in the trial. Should the jury have a question regarding the law during deliberations, they communicate it via a written note to the judge, who reads the question on the record with trial parties present (on the phone or in person). Jury deliberations can range from minutes to weeks or longer. Jurors must render verdicts on all charges before them. If the jurors are presented with several charges, they are required to render a verdict on each charge. In rare cases the jury may be **sequestered**. The goal of sequestering a jury is to prevent its members from hearing details about the case from, for example, the media, friends, family, and social media. Typically, only highly publicized cases with national media coverage result in decisions to keep a jury isolated. In such cases, food and housing are provided.

Guilty

The jury may reach any of several outcomes for each charge following deliberations. First, the jury may find the defendant guilty as charged on any, some, or all charges. Guilt is the outcome reached in the majority of criminal trials. Unanimity among the jury members is not universally required to convict the defendant. The U.S. Supreme Court has ruled that 9 votes are permissible to secure a conviction in state criminal courts if the jury is composed of 12 members. Unanimity is required in state criminal courts when the jury consists of 6 persons.[7] Furthermore, unanimity among jury members is required for a conviction in federal criminal cases.[8] If the jury

deliberation: The jury process of deciding the guilt or lack of guilt of the defendant.

sequestered: When a jury is isolated to prevent contact from outside influences, which may influence the verdict.

finds the defendant guilty, the judge enters a judgment of conviction, which is the final order in a criminal case.

Hung Jury

The second possibility is that a jury fails to reach an agreement regarding the guilt of the defendant on a particular charge. A jury in this position is considered **deadlocked** and a **hung jury**. At the federal level, hung juries occur less than 4% of the time, while the percentage at state criminal trials varies considerably.[9] A hung jury is a common reason for a judge to declare a **mistrial**. A mistrial may occur at any time during the trial for reasons such as incorrect jury selection, improperly admitted evidence, death or illness of a juror or an attorney, disqualification or misconduct of a juror, or a significant prejudicial error that cannot be overcome using instructions to the jury to disregard. On occasion, a mistrial means that the defendant cannot be retried. This is the case if the mistrial is granted without the defendant's consent or over the defendant's objection. Furthermore, retrial is not possible if a mistrial results from judicial or prosecutor misconduct.[10]

Reggie Cole spent 16 years in prison before a judge declared a mistrial when jurors could not reach a unanimous verdict. Prosecutors pledge to retry him at a later date. How might a mistrial affect the defendant? Victims? And the community?

At the federal level and in some states, judges may encourage a verdict and avoid a mistrial using the **Allen charge**. Also known as the "dynamite charge" or the "hammer charge," the Allen charge attempts to dislodge jurors from entrenched positions and stems from the Supreme Court ruling in *Allen v. United States* (1896). This decision allows a judge to use additional jury instructions to encourage jurors not in agreement with the majority to reconsider their position. The Allen charge is an option in federal criminal cases, but not in all states. If the jury cannot reach the threshold needed for conviction, the judge declares a mistrial, and the prosecutor must decide if it is prudent to try the case again.

Acquittal

And third, the jury may conclude that the defendant is not guilty and **acquitted** on the charge(s), indicating that the prosecutor failed to demonstrate the defendant's guilt beyond a reasonable doubt. In other words, legal guilt was not proved, and the defendant is free to go. In rare cases, the jury will acquit the defendant even if they believe he or she committed the crime. This maneuver, **jury nullification**, is a little-known power of the jury that allows them to "disregard the law and acquit a guilty defendant."[11] Reasons for jury nullification may be that the jury believes the law overly harsh or an overreach of the government.

Two cases form the cornerstone of jury nullification.[12] In 1670, Bushell's Case (also spelled Bushel) established the legal framework for future jury nullification. The London case involved two Quaker preachers, William Penn and William Mead (also spelled Meade), who were arrested and charged with unlawful and tumultuous assembly. Approximately 300 people gathered to hear their speech, which was critical of the king. Throughout a continuous trial between the justice and the jury, the latter refused to find the defendants guilty of anything except speaking in the street. Even after being sequestrated and deprived of food, drink, fire, and a chamber pot, the jurors refused to bow to the king's exaggerated charges. Second, *Rex v. Zenger* (1735) involved John Zenger, who owned and published a newspaper that criticized William Crosby, the governor of New York.[13] Zenger was subsequently arrested and tried for seditious libel. Zenger's attorney, Andrew Hamilton, informed the jury of their power and duty to *judge the law as well as the facts*. The jury acquitted Mr. Zenger because they felt the law was unjust. Though not a Supreme Court case, this is a landmark example of jury nullification. *Georgia v. Brailsford* (1794), an unusual case in which the U.S. Supreme Court actually presided over a jury trial, established the precedent of jury nullification. During the trial, Chief Justice John Jay told the jurors that although

deadlocked: A hung jury that is unable to reach an agreement regarding the guilt or innocence of a defendant is said to be deadlocked.

hung jury: A jury that is unable to reach an agreement regarding the guilt or innocence of the defendant. Also known as a deadlocked jury.

mistrial: A courtroom trial that ends prior to its normal conclusion.

Allen charge: Additional instructions a judge may give to a deliberating jury to discourage a mistrial.

acquit: To free someone from a criminal charge following a not guilty verdict.

jury nullification: Ability of a jury to ignore the law and acquit a guilty defendant.

the justices agreed on the applicable law, the jury had the right to *judge on the law as well as the fact in controversy*.

No controversy exists regarding the ability of juries to nullify; however, controversy does surround whether courts should explicitly instruct juries of their ability to disregard the law and acquit defendants regardless of the evidence presented. Currently, federal judges are not obligated to inform jurors of their full rights and powers to judge both the facts and also the law. *United States v. Dougherty* (1972) approved a lower court's refusal to instruct the jury regarding jury nullification. The court affirmed the de facto power of a jury to nullify the law but upheld the denial of the defense's chance to instruct the jury about the power to nullify. In *United States v. Thomas* (1977), the Second Circuit Court of Appeals ruled that judges can and actually have the duty to dismiss jurors who intend to nullify.

A defendant acquitted of a charge cannot be tried for the same charge again, even if new evidence pointing to his or her guilt surfaces in the future. Being tried again after acquittal is considered double jeopardy and prohibited per the Fifth Amendment of the U.S. Constitution, which states, "Nor shall any person be subject for the same offence to be twice put in jeopardy of life or limb." Specifically prohibited are the following:

1.   A second prosecution for the same offense after conviction

2.   A second prosecution for the same offense after acquittal

3.   Multiple punishments for the same offense

There are exceptions to double jeopardy. An individual can be tried twice based on the same facts as long as the elements of each crime are different. Different jurisdictions (cities in the same state excepted) may charge and try an individual with the same crime based on the same facts without violating double jeopardy. For example, a defendant may be tried in state court and again later in federal court. A member of the military may be retried by court martial in a military court after being tried in a civilian court. And because double jeopardy prohibits only more than one *criminal* prosecution based on the same facts and same crime, a defendant may be tried in civil court after being tried in a criminal court.

READING OF THE VERDICT

Once a verdict has been reached, the jury alerts the judge, and participants in the trial are gathered in the courtroom for a **reading of the verdict**. The precise language used at the reading of the verdict differs, but it is generally scripted. For example, in Massachusetts, the reading of the verdict begins with the court clerk, who asks, "Will the jury please rise. Will the defendant also please rise and face the jury. Mr. Foreman (Madam Forelady), has your jury agreed upon a verdict (your verdicts)?"[14]

In response, the foreperson states that the jury has reached a verdict or verdicts. The clerk then asks, "What say you, Mr. Foreman (Madam Forelady), as to complaint number _____, wherein the defendant is charged with _____, is he (she) guilty or not guilty?"

The foreperson then states for the record the verdict reached by the jury (guilty or not guilty). The language of the reading of the verdict differs based on the verdict reached by the jury and the number of charges. The judge may poll the members of the jury as to their particular votes on the verdict at this time. In general, with the verdict communicated, the judge discharges the jury.

SENTENCING

Following a guilty verdict, sentencing occurs. Sentencing may happen immediately after the trial, though in some cases, it is scheduled for a later date. Sentencing is the application of a criminal sanction to a legally guilty individual. Punishment meted out can include any combination of fines, restitution, probation, intermediate punishments (e.g., intensive

reading of the verdict:
Following jury deliberation, a formal event in the courtroom in which the jury offers their verdict on the charge(s).

supervision, substance abuse treatment, electronic monitoring, boot camp, halfway houses), imprisonment in a jail or prison, state hospital commitment, or death. Following a guilty verdict in a criminal trial, the judge generally sentences the offender. In some jurisdictions, if the jury has not been discharged, the jury may make sentencing recommendations or ask for leniency on behalf of the defendant.

Sentencing is guided by three essential concepts: proportionality, equity, and social debt. **Proportionality** indicates that the severity of sentencing should correspond to the severity of the crime committed. An individual who shoplifts a bag of candy bars should not be sentenced to life in prison. **Equity** focuses on the desire that similar crimes be punished in similar ways and with similar severity. If a man is convicted of a robbery with a firearm, his sentence should be similar to others who committed robbery with a firearm. Finally, **social debt** indicates the need to take into account the prior behavior of the offender. A career criminal owes a greater social debt to society than a first-time offender and therefore should be sanctioned more severely.

Jerry Sandusky was sentenced to 30 to 60 years in prison for child sexual abuse. What factors should go into a sentence? Should victim characteristics be considered? Why or why not?

There are five primary goals in sentencing: retribution, incapacitation, deterrence, rehabilitation, and restoration. Sentencing seeks to perform the dual function of punishing for past behavior and discouraging future criminal acts. The predominant form of sentencing varies over time, though some elements of each goal tend to be present at any given time. Retribution in sentencing seeks punishment for the criminal act committed and is based on the notion that the sentence is a deserved, justified, and necessary action against the criminal to punish him or her. Sentencing also seeks to incapacitate offenders and isolate them from society to protect the public from future criminal wrongdoing. Incapacitation is accomplished via imprisonment as well as several forms of intermediate or alternative sanctions. Another aim of punishment is **deterrence**, with the goal of convincing the offender (specific deterrence) and members of society (general deterrence) that future criminal acts will result in punishment. Punishment also serves to rehabilitate the offender through education, job training, drug or alcohol treatment, and psychological treatment to reduce future criminality. And finally, sentencing has the goal of **restoration**. While the acts of criminals cannot be undone, effort is made to address the harm done to victims, family and friends of victims, and the community. Restoration may come in the form of paying restitution, paying fines, and/or doing community service.

Aside from these guiding concepts and principles when sentencing, the judge is also required to abide by statutory sanctioning requirements. The judge may use recommendations from the jury as well as information from the **presentence investigation** of the defendant in determining the severity of the sentence. Presentence investigations include information on extenuating circumstances and the defendant's criminal history.

Indeterminate Sentencing

Sentencing has changed over the past four decades as the nation has moved away from indeterminate sentencing to structured sentencing. Prior to the 1970s, the federal government and all states used **indeterminate sentencing**. Under this system, judges had greater discretion to craft an individualized sentence with an emphasis on rehabilitation. In indeterminate sentencing, offenders were sentenced to a range of years with a stated minimum and maximum, based on the specifics of the case. Maximums were established by legislatures.[15]

proportionality: A sentencing concept that indicates that the severity of sentencing should correspond to the severity of the crime committed.

equity: A sentencing concept that emphasizes that similar crimes be punished in similar ways and with similar severity.

social debt: A sentencing concept that takes into account an offender's criminal past.

deterrence: Sentencing goal that seeks to dissuade the offender and others in the public from committing crime.

restoration: Sentencing goal that addresses the harm done to victims, family and friends of victims, and the community.

presentence investigation: An investigation that gathers information on extenuating circumstances and the criminal history of the defendant to be used when determining the severity of the sentence.

indeterminate sentencing: System of sentencing that allowed greater judicial discretion.

POLICY ISSUES

Discretion in Sentencing

Indeterminate sentencing was harshly criticized for allowing too much judicial discretion, which in part resulted in unequal sentences being handed out. In addition, it was criticized for parole board discretion, which in part resulted in radically different sentence lengths being served. Structured sentencing removed much judicial discretion and in most cases abolished parole boards altogether.

A result of structured sentencing has been prison overcrowding, at great expense to the taxpayer. Today, the United States has more people incarcerated than any other country—even countries much more populous than our own. Some states are now backing off of some elements of structured sentencing as a result of the costs associated with it.

As a policymaker, what policies would you implement that follow the three essential concepts of punishment (proportionality, equity, and social debt) as well as the five goals of sentencing (retribution, incapacitation, deterrence, rehabilitation, and restoration)?

Think About It

1. **Would your policies be overly costly to taxpayers?**
2. **Would your policies require statutory or constitutional changes?**
3. **What do you think would be the outcome of the policies you recommend?**
4. **Would your policies affect a particular segment of the population more than others?**

A convicted criminal, for example, may have received an indeterminate sentence of no less than 5 years and no more than 20 years in prison. **Parole boards** would make the actual determination as to when the prisoner was released from prison. Under this system, prisoners could earn "good time" and reduce their time served.

While an individualized approach to sentencing offers some advantages, an unintended consequence of this approach was that it resulted in inequity in sentencing. Two persons committing the exact same crime, for instance, might spend different amounts of time in prison. Research demonstrated that these inequities were associated with characteristics of the offender. Young compared with old, male compared with female, unemployed compared with employed, and black or Hispanic compared with white non-Hispanic offenders were more likely to be sentenced to prison. Furthermore, these groups were more likely to be sentenced to longer terms in prison than their counterparts.[16] Additional criticism of indeterminate sentencing included that this approach led to coddling criminals who could not be reformed. Others noted that the uncertain nature of indeterminate sentences amounted to cruel and unusual punishment for the prisoner.[17] Together, these criticisms resulted in calls for greater equity and proportionality in sentencing,[18] and changes were made.

Structured Sentencing

Today most states have adopted some forms of structured sentencing. Under a structured approach sentences are generally given in the form of fixed terms with an anticipated date of release, meaning that parole boards became obsolete and were largely disbanded.[19] Structured sentencing is far more impersonal, removes or greatly curtails judicial discretion, and reflects a shift away from rehabilitation toward greater retribution. One consequence of structured sentencing is it removes offenders' motivation to participate in rehabilitative programs as a means to shorten their sentence while in prison. Though structured sentencing is more prevalent, elements of indeterminate sentencing remain.[20] For example, some states continue to use parole release, while others have abolished it. Some states eliminated good time served,

Journal:
Prosecutors and mandatory minimum sentencing

parole board: A board that reviews the prior acts and behavior of an inmate to determine when the prisoner is to be released from prison.

Figure 9.3 ■ Adult Correctional Populations, 1980–2014

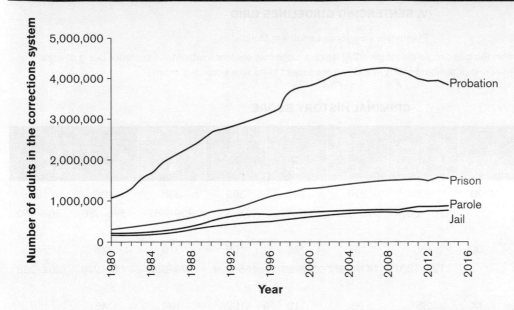

As seen in earlier chapters, violent crime has decreased since the early 1990s. Yet, during the same period, the population of persons under the control of the criminal justice system continues to rise.

Source: Kaeble, D., Glaze, L. E., Tsoutis, A., & Minton, T. (2015, December). *Correctional populations in the United States, 2014* (NCJ 249513). Washington, DC: Bureau of Justice Statistics. Retrieved from http://www.bjs.gov/content/pub/pdf/cpus14.pdf.

but most states simply minimized how much good time could be earned. A result of this shift is that sentencing across the nation varies greatly and is composed of a hodgepodge of structured sentencing components and features of indeterminate sentencing.

Determinate sentencing is a common part of structured sentencing. Determinate sentences are established by legislative statute and can rule out the possibility of alternatives to prison. Determinate sentencing increases the likelihood that offenders will be imprisoned and increases the length of their sentences. The increase in length is based on the **Violent Crime Control and Law Enforcement Act** of 1994, which requires prisoners to serve at least 85% of their sentences in order for states to qualify for federal financial aid. Determinate sentencing has clearly resulted in an increase in the prison population. While criminal offending has decreased since the early 1990s, the prison population has grown during the same time, at great cost to society (Figure 9.3).

Structured sentencing often includes an element of **mandatory minimums**, which are statute-based minimum sanctions that are to be applied to particular types of crime (e.g., drunk driving) and/or when particular elements of a crime exist (e.g., use of a firearm). Mandatory minimums do not allow judges discretion in sentencing and prevent them from imposing alternative sanctions when they are reasonable. As noted by Judge Paul A. Magnuson's statement that opened this chapter, some relatively minor drug crimes are now resulting in harsh prison sentences. Joshua Paul Benjamin's case was one involving a mandatory prison sentence. His plea of guilty to the felony of forcible sexual abuse of a child under age 14 required him to serve two terms of 10 years to run concurrently in prison.

Sentencing guidelines are a common component of structured sentencing as well. These guidelines are usually presented in the form of a grid that identifies the appropriate sentence for the offender based on the severity of the crime and the offender's criminal history (see Table 9.1). Federal sentencing is based on the **Federal Sentencing Guidelines Act** of 1984, which eliminated federal parole release for prisoners and abolished almost all good time earned (at least for prisoners sentenced after October 1987). While federal parole

determinate sentencing: A type of structured sentencing that is established by legislative statute and rules out the possibility of alternatives to prison. Prisoners are given fixed sentences.

Violent Crime Control and Law Enforcement Act: A 1994 law that requires prisoners to serve at least 85% of their sentences in order for states to qualify for federal financial aid.

mandatory minimum: A form of structured sentencing that applies statute-based minimum sanctions to particular types of crime and/or when particular elements of a crime exist.

sentencing guidelines: A type of structured sentencing based on criminal history and severity of the crime, usually presented in a grid format that dictates the sentence served.

Federal Sentencing Guidelines Act: A 1984 law that eliminated parole release for federal prisoners and abolished almost all good time earned by a prisoner.

Table 9.1 ■ Minnesota Sentencing Guidelines

IV. SENTENCING GUIDELINES GRID

Presumptive Sentence Lengths in Months

Italicized numbers within the grid denote the range within which a judge may sentence without the sentence being deemed a departure. Offenders with non-imprisonment felony sentences are subject to jail time according to law.

CRIMINAL HISTORY SCORE

SEVERITY LEVEL OF CONVICTION OFFENSE (Common offenses listed in italics)		0	1	2	3	4	5	6 or more
Murder, 2nd Degree (intentional murder; drive-by-shootings)	XI	306 *261–367*	326 *278–391*	346 *295–415*	366 *312–439*	386 *329–463*	406 *346–480*	426 *363–480*
Murder, 3rd Degree Murder, 2nd Degree (unintentional murder)	X	150 128–180	165 *141–198*	180 *153–216*	195 *166–234*	210 *179–252*	225 *192–270*	240 *204–288*
Assault, 1st Degree Controlled Substance Crime, 1st Degree	IX	86 *74–103*	98 *84–117*	110 *94–132*	122 *104–146*	134 *114–160*	146 *125–175*	158 *135–189*
Aggravated Robbery, 1st Degree Controlled Substance Crime, 2nd Degree	VIII	48 *41–57*	58 *50–69*	68 *58–81*	78 *67–93*	88 *75–105*	98 *84–117*	108 *92–129*
Felony DWI	VII	36	42	48	54 *46–64*	60 *51–72*	66 *57–79*	72 *62–84*
Controlled Substance Crime, 3rd Degree	VI	21	27	33	39 *34–46*	45 *39–54*	51 *44–61*	57 *49–68*
Residential Burglary Simple Robbery	V	18	23	28	33 *29–39*	38 *33–45*	43 *37–51*	48 *41–57*
Nonresidential Burglary	IV	12	15	18	21	24 *21–28*	27 *23–32*	30 *26–36*
Theft Crimes (Over $5,000)	III	12	13	15	17	19 *17–22*	21 *18–25*	23 *20–27*
Theft Crimes ($5,000 or less) Check Forgery ($251-$2,500)	II	12	12	13	15	17	19	21 *18–25*
Sale of Simulated Controlled Substance	I	12	12	12	13	15	17	19 *17–22*

☐ Presumptive commitment to state imprisonment. First degree murder has a mandatory life sentence and is excluded from the guidelines by law. See Guidelines Section II.E. Mandatory Sentences, for policy regarding those sentences controlled by law.

☐ Presumptive stayed sentence, at the discretion of the judge, up to a year in jail and other non-jail sanctions can be imposed as conditions of probation. However, certain offenses in the section of the grid always carry a presumptive commitment to state prison. See Guidelines Sections II.C. Presumptive Sentence and II.E. Mandatory Sentences.

Sentencing guidelines are widely used today. What advantages and disadvantages do they offer? If you were a policymaker, would you require them?

Source: Data from Minnesota State Courts.

Figure 9.4 ■ States With Three-Strikes Statutes for Habitual Offenders as of 2015

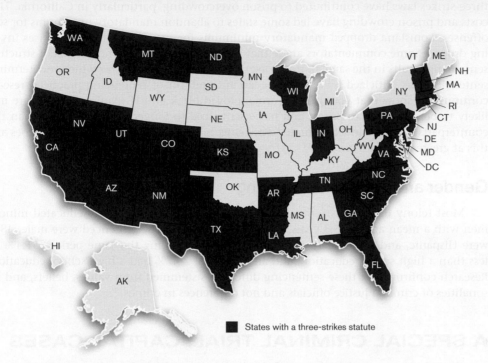

■ States with a three-strikes statute

Policies such as three-strikes statutes have increased the number of persons under control of the criminal justice system. Is this a positive or negative outcome of this policy? If you were a policymaker, would you argue that these are needed even if they are expensive? Why or why not?

Sources: *Other States Have Dialed Back Three-Strikes Law.* Boston University College of Communication, State House Program; Shoener, N. (2015, January 21). *Three strikes laws in different states.* Retrieved from http://www.legalmatch.com/law-library/article/three-strikes-laws-in-different-states.html.

was abolished, Congress replaced it with supervised release. When federal defendants are released from prison they are placed on supervised release under the control of the U.S. Probation Office. Supervised release can be thought of as postincarceration probation; violations are addressed by the sentencing judge, who might revoke supervised release and send the defendant back to prison. At the time of sentencing, the U.S. district judge imposes the specific period of supervised release so that the defendant knows how much supervision time follows the incarceration period. As a result, those convicted in federal criminal court served the time they were given. In general, state and federal judges cannot deviate from sentencing guidelines, though these guidelines are technically considered advisory in nature. Another consequence of structured sentencing and sentencing guidelines is that prisons have a larger population of nonviolent offenders who may be better handled and more efficiently dealt with using alternative sanctions. The larger populations are partly because inmates are serving longer sentences (with parole and good time abolished) rather than an increase in criminal behavior. While not perfect, the validity of sentencing guidelines has been reviewed in court cases in light of claims that some incorporate the consideration of information not reviewed during the earlier trial.

Three-strikes laws are an example of mandatory minimums (Figure 9.4). These laws require long prison sentences, including life without parole, for persons convicted of a third felony. While this policy has removed violent habitual offenders from the street, it has also incarcerated nonviolent offenders better suited for alternative corrections to life in prison. In California, a person with burglary convictions in the 1970s who then is caught with a small

Audio:
Brock Turner's sentencing revives mandatory minimums debate

Web:
California's new Three-Strikes law

---

three-strikes law:
A type of mandatory minimum that mandates long (including life) prison terms for a third offense.

amount of drugs for personal consumption is defined by the three-strikes law as a habitual criminal and sentenced to life in prison. Like other structured sentencing approaches, three-strikes laws have contributed to prison overcrowding, particularly in California. These costs and prison crowding have led some states to abandon mandatory minimums for some offenses. Louisiana dropped mandatory minimums for many nonviolent offenses involving drugs.[21] Some commentators argue that the interaction between elements of structured sentencing results in the same (if not worse) inequity of sentencing for which indeterminate sentencing was criticized.[22] Worse yet, even after reform of sentencing practices, research continues to show that young, male, unemployed black and Hispanic offenders are more likely to be sentenced to prison and to be sentenced to longer terms in prison than their counterparts.[23] Unlike indeterminate sentencing, however, structured sentencing does all of this at greater cost to society.

Gender and Race in Sentencing

Most felony defendants sentenced in the United States are poorly educated minority men with a mean age of 35.3 years.[24] In 2010, 86.8% of those sentenced were male, 48.1% were Hispanic, and 20.7% were non-Hispanic black.[25] During the same period, 51.4% had less than a high school education, and an additional 28.7% had a high school education.[26] Research confirms that these sentencing differences stemmed from values, beliefs, and personalities of criminal justice officials and not differences in crimes.[27]

A SPECIAL CRIMINAL TRIAL: CAPITAL CASES

Journal:
Information and death penalty support

Capital cases are a special type of criminal case in which defendants face execution if convicted. The federal government and several states try capital cases, which tend to involve premeditated or first-degree murder, treason, murder of federal agents and politicians, and some crimes against children. While capital cases largely follow the steps of noncapital criminal trials presented in this chapter, there are important differences.

Video 9.1:
Capital trial

First, in a capital case, prosecutors are required to file a notice of their intent to seek the death penalty in the case.[28] Second, during *voir dire*, attorneys ascertain whether prospective jurors are **death qualified**. That is, they determine if prospective jurors are suitable to serve on a case in which the punishment may be execution. A third difference is that capital juries are more likely to be sequestered. That is, the jury may be isolated during the trial. A fourth distinction is that capital cases involve **bifurcated trials**. That is, there are two trials: The first establishes the guilt of the defendant, while the second establishes the penalty. During the penalty phase of the trial, rules regarding evidence are not as stringent, and jurors review aggravating and mitigating circumstances surrounding the crime and the defendant. Following their deliberation, the jury provides a recommended sentence to the judge. In some states, the judge must follow the recommendation of the jury, while in other states a judge may sentence the defendant without a jury or override a jury's recommendation of capital punishment (a judge cannot override a jury's determination of life imprisonment and impose a death sentence). A fifth distinction between noncapital and capital criminal cases is that the latter require a unanimous verdict from the jury. Without unanimity, the defendant will not be found guilty and cannot be executed. And finally, a mandatory appeals process almost always characterizes capital cases.[29] The appeals required for capital cases are lengthy and increase the costs of these trials. As noted by Frank Zimring in the quotation that opens this chapter, as a nation we are conflicted about capital punishment, and this ambivalence costs us in several ways.

death qualified: A part of *voir dire* in capital cases in which attorneys ascertain whether the prospective juror is suitable to sit on a case that may result in the death penalty. A juror who will not impose death under any circumstances is removed from the panel.

bifurcated trials: A double trial system used for capital cases. The first trial is the guilt trial, while the second determines punishment.

Gender, Race, and Hispanic Origin on Death Row

At the end of 2013, 2,979 persons were on death row in 36 states, and an additional 56 persons sat on death row in the Federal Bureau of Prisons.[30] In 2013, 39 inmates were executed, 70 died of natural causes, 6 committed suicide, and 45 were removed from death row

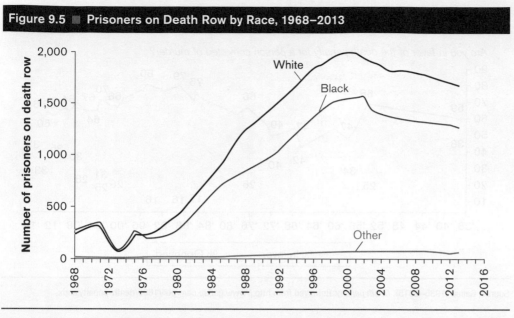

Figure 9.5 ■ Prisoners on Death Row by Race, 1968–2013

Source: Snell, *Capital Punishment, 2013—Statistical Tables*. Bureau of Justice Statistics.

as a result of courts overturning sentences (e.g., 20 in Texas, 19 in Florida). Research suggests gender disparity among those sitting on death row. Historically, few women have received the death penalty. Since the reinstatement of the death penalty in 1976, only 14 women have been put to death in the United States. In 2013, 98% of death row inmates were male, and only 2% were women.[31] A portion of this gender disparity occurs because women commit fewer crimes that make them eligible for capital punishment. Research findings also show, however, that women are less likely to receive the death penalty even when they commit crimes equivalent to men who end up on death row.

Disparity is also evident when considering the race of those on death row. According to the Bureau of Justice about half of death row inmates are non-Hispanic white (56%), and 42% are black (Figure 9.5). These proportions diverge from populations in society in general, as black inmates are overrepresented and white inmates underrepresented on death row. An examination of Hispanic inmates on death row indicates less disparity. In 2013, according to the Bureau of Justice Statistics, 14% of those sitting on death row were Hispanic.[32] This distribution is similar to the general population.

A portion of this disparity stems from differential offending rates. Yet much of it is based on the race of the victim and the offender. Research conducted in Harris County, Texas, by Scott Phillips[33] discovered that, even after controlling for relevant factors such as severity of the crime, prosecutors were more likely to pursue the death penalty against black defendants than when the victims were white. An interesting aspect of this research was the finding that although the district attorney was more likely to pursue a capital conviction in cases involving black defendants and white victims, juries were more likely to impose death penalties against white versus black defendants. Philips concluded that juries minimized the racially charged behavior of district attorneys, but not to the degree that black defendants benefited.

In contrast, the work of Katherine Beckett examined race and the death penalty in cases of aggravated murder in Washington State.[34] She found that jurors were more than three times more likely to recommend the death penalty for black defendants than for white defendants committing the same crime. In contrast to Phillips's findings, Beckett concluded that prosecutors in Washington were more likely to seek the death penalty against white defendants. These findings emerged even with controls for previous criminal records, the number of victims, aggravating factors, and other relevant correlates.

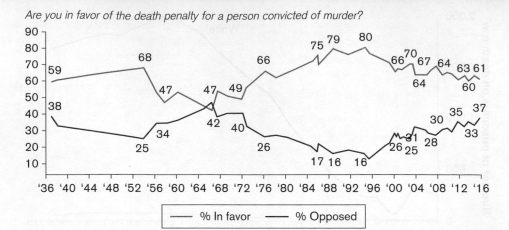

Figure 9.6 ■ Death Penalty for Murder and Public Opinion

Are you in favor of the death penalty for a person convicted of murder?

— % In favor   — % Opposed

Source: Gallup (1936–2015). *Death penalty.* Retrieved from http://www.gallup.com/poll/1606/death-penalty.aspx.

Public Opinion and the Death Penalty

Web:
Costs of the death penalty

Capital cases are controversial. In 2015, 61% of the public stated that they were in favor of the death penalty for someone convicted of murder. Public support of the death penalty has declined slightly over the past decade (Figure 9.6). Attitudes and opinions regarding the pros and cons of capital punishment tend to be emotional rather than rational.[35] Among those reasons given for maintaining capital punishment is that once executed, an offender is unable to commit another crime. Those supporting the death penalty also believe that execution deters would-be criminals from committing crimes (i.e., general deterrence). And finally, the death penalty is argued to be a just and moral response to the actions of an individual convicted of murder and other brutal crimes. Retribution is the most often cited reason used by people in favor of the death penalty.[36]

On the opposite side, there are several arguments for eliminating the death penalty. First, executing someone as a means of deterring others from murdering is contradictory and morally inconsistent. Second, though research findings are mixed, most studies fail to find a general deterrent effect of capital punishment. Professionals in the field, including researchers, practitioners, and law enforcement, agree that the death penalty does not offer a deterrent effect.[37] Third, although many safeguards are in place to prevent the execution of an innocent person, many innocent people have been executed.[38] Fourth, sentences of death are unfairly administered. In 2013, three states carried out about three quarters of all executions in the nations: Texas, Florida, and Oklahoma.[39] Thus, a person committing a crime in Texas is more likely to be executed than a person committing a similar crime in Alabama. Inequity has also been identified according to the victim's race. Killers of white individuals are more likely to be sentenced to death than those who murder black persons.[40] Others contend that those of low socioeconomic status are more likely to receive the sentence of death. Another argument against capital punishment is its expense. A capital case is far more costly than a noncapital case. In California alone, more than $4 billion has been spent on death penalty cases since 1978.[41] In Maryland, capital cases cost $3 million each, which is three times more than noncapital cases.[42] While those in favor of the death penalty suggest that the greater cost results from the appeals process, research suggests that the greatest costs come before postconviction proceedings.[43] Given the bifurcated nature of a capital case, and given that these trials require more preparation, more investigation, more evidence, more testimony, more attorneys, and more motions, it is easy to see why capital cases are costly even before the appeals process begins. As a result of the financial burden, some states have started moving away from capital punishment in order to reduce costs.[44]

VICTIMS OF CRIME AND THE CRIMINAL TRIAL

The victim plays a vital role in most criminal trials. In the past, victims were relegated to mere witnesses in trials and were largely forgotten in the criminal justice system. While a victim's role as a witness continues to be enormously important today, much has changed about the participation of the victim in the criminal justice system in recent decades. In order to maximize the success of convicting an offender, the initial actions of the victim are critical—the victim or his or her representative must report the crime to the police. Without this, the police are less likely to know about the crime and less likely to bring the offender to justice, meaning that the offender remains among the public, able to offend with impunity. At best, only 49% of all violent crimes and about 36% of property crimes are reported to the police.[45]

Victims also play a key role during the investigation and gathering of evidence. During the investigation, multiple criminal justice representatives interview the victim regarding the victimization. The information gathered from these interviews, as well as other evidence gathered during the investigation (including findings from a medical examination), provides important evidence to be used against the accused. The more evidence and better quality of evidence made available to the prosecutor, the greater the likelihood that the offender will plead guilty prior to a trial. Without the cooperation of the victim during the investigation, an offender will be less likely to plead guilty and will be more likely to avoid a guilty verdict at trial.

In some cases a trial is conducted, and the victim will need to testify. While this is a scary proposition, prosecutors and victim advocates and/or witness coordinators generally work with the victim in advance of the trial to educate her or him regarding what to expect. As with any witness in a trial, the victim will first be asked questions by the prosecutor and then cross-examined by the defense attorney, who will attempt to challenge the victim's credibility. Once defense counsel is satisfied, the prosecutor will have an opportunity to again question the victim in order to clarify any testimony given during cross-examination. While testifying can be frightening and intimidating, many victims also find that it is an important part of the healing process.

Integration of the Victim Into the Process

The important role of the victim has not changed over time. What has changed has been the way victims have been handled by the criminal justice system. In the past, victims were not informed of the status of their cases, and they were not alerted as to the whereabouts of the defendants. They had no voice in the plea-bargaining process, and were denied the opportunity to describe to the judge the impact the crimes had on them and their families. In general, victims felt neglected and abandoned by the criminal justice system.[46] More than 25 years ago, changes were made to include victims in the criminal justice process as more than just witnesses. In 1988, the federal government established the Office for Victims of Crimes (OVC) through an amendment to the Victims of Crime Act of 1984. The goal of the OVC is to assist crime victims through funding, leadership, policies, and practices.[47] Another change designed to assist victims was the implementation in 2004 of the **Crime Victims' Rights Act**. This law established the following rights for victims in federal criminal cases[48]:

- the right to be reasonably protected from the accused
- the right to reasonable, accurate, and timely notice of any public court proceeding or any parole proceeding involving the crime, or of any release or escape of the accused
- the right not to be excluded from any such public court proceeding, unless the court, after receiving clear and convincing evidence, determines that testimony by the victim would be materially altered if the victim heard other testimony at that proceeding

Video 9.2:
Victim impact statements

Crime Victims' Rights Act: A 2004 law that established numerous rights for crime victims in federal cases.

COMMON MISCONCEPTIONS

Defendants Get Off on Technicalities All the Time

We often hear someone complain about how criminals get off on technicalities all the time. By *technicality*, that person usually means that the government violated a constitutional right of the suspect or defendant. For example, an error may have been that the Miranda warnings were improperly given, a search warrant was not obtained, or a suspect was coerced and beaten into an admission. As a result of these improper procedures, important evidence is deemed inadmissible in court by the judge and the chances of a successful conviction are reduced or obliterated.

"Getting off on a technicality" is a popular story line in the media, but it is not a reality. In real life there is no legal definition of a technicality. Rather, our system is composed of constitutionally based rules and procedures that require strict adherence to ensure a just and fair criminal justice system. Law enforcement agents, prosecutors, and others in the criminal justice system are trained on proper procedures, so errors—or technicalities, as they are referred to in the media—are uncommon.

Still, there are documented cases in which an individual is retried because of a breach in procedure. In 2008, Timothy Becktel was sentenced for assault with the intent to commit murder. It turned out that the judge failed to administer the jury oath to members of the panel who subsequently found Becktel guilty. As a result of this error, Becktel was awarded a second trial.

Think About It

1. Why do you think so many people believe that criminals get off on technicalities? How do you respond to someone who states this given what you know of the criminal justice system now?

2. Should defendants be able to get off on a technicality more than they do now? Why or why not?

3. If the criminal justice system is not required to honor the constitutional rights of its citizens, why should citizens have those rights? If they are important, shouldn't the system be required to honor them?

- the right to be reasonably heard at any public proceeding in the district court involving release, plea, sentencing, or any parole proceeding
- the reasonable right to confer with the attorney for the government in the case
- the right to full and timely restitution as provided in law
- the right to proceedings free from unreasonable delay
- the right to be treated with fairness and with respect for the victim's dignity and privacy

victim bill of rights: Adopted in many states, it offers rights to crime victims.

victim impact statement: A statement prepared by the victim or his or her family to inform the judge how the crime affected them physically, financially, emotionally, and psychologically.

Many states also increased the rights of victims with state constitutional amendments and a **victim bill of rights**.[49] An important right of crime victims provided by these changes is the **victim impact statement**, which allows the victim (and others) to tell the judge how the crime affected the victim and the victim's family physically, financially, emotionally, and psychologically, and it ensures the victim's right to be heard. The statement may include the medical and psychological treatment needed by the victim as a result of the crime. The victim may also convey to the judge what punishment he or she would like the defendant to receive. Jurisdictions vary in terms of whether the statement must be made in person or in writing, whether it is given directly by the victim (or his or her family) or the prosecutor, and exactly when the statement may be given. Statements are included in the presentence report given to the judge, and they influence the criminal justice system beyond the trial or guilty plea. The statement is placed in the offender's file for consideration at any parole hearings (if applicable).

CONTEMPLATING CAREERS

Attorney

Are you detail oriented, ethical, and organized? Do you honor deadlines, write impeccably, and follow directions well? Are you just a little bit competitive? If you answer yes to these questions, you may want to consider a career as an attorney.

While it is fashionable (and boring) to crack jokes about attorneys, attorneys are hard-working, precise, and intelligent, and they use these skills to ensure that the rights of people are honored. The information in this chapter shows many roles an attorney can take: private defense counsel, public defender, prosecutor, and even judge. Not mentioned in this chapter are the many roles an attorney may hold outside of criminal trials. To become an attorney, students need to graduate with a 4-year college degree. Next, students study for the LSAT, which is a standardized exam required for admission to all American Bar Association–approved law schools. After acceptance into law school, students work hard reading, researching case law, writing legal briefs, and attending classes. This diligent work pays off after 3 years, when students are awarded law degrees. The next step is to take and pass the state bar exam. Once passed, one is a certified lawyer.

The Bureau of Labor Statistics (BLS) estimates that the 2015 median pay for lawyers is $115,820 annually, or $55.69 per hour. The job outlook for lawyers from 2014 to 2024 is about average, as BLS estimates 6% growth in the field.

Career Video:
A clerk for the court of appeals discusses his experience and current issues in the field.

Victim Impact Statement by Jennifer Schuett

CASE STUDY

Jennifer Schuett was denied the possibility of giving a victim impact statement when Dennis Bradford hanged himself in jail before he was scheduled to appear before a judge. Jennifer waited close to 20 years to give her prepared statement and was emotionally devastated when Bradford's suicide robbed her of that chance. For Jennifer, it was as if he had victimized her one last time. Though she did not have the opportunity to read her statement in court, on August 10, 2010, the 20th anniversary of her victimization, Jennifer read her victim impact statement at Bradford's gravesite. The text of her statement follows. (This statement is reprinted with permission from Jennifer Schuett. For more information, visit www.justiceforjennifer.com.)

Dennis Bradford

I waited nineteen years, 2 months, and 3 days to find out your last name and for you to be caught. I knew your first name was Dennis, because you told me before you raped and attempted to murder me on August 10, 1990. When you cut my throat from ear to ear, you assumed that I'd die, or if I lived, I wouldn't be able to talk. Well, you chose the wrong little forty-five pound, eight-year-old girl to try and murder because for nineteen years, I've thought of you every single day and helped in searching for you. Every year that's passed has given me more strength and drive for when I finally would be face to face with you as I am today. Some may feel sad for me that it took nineteen years to track you down, but I'm only sad for the others that have fallen victim to you. Wondering how you could be capable of committing such horrendous acts on such an innocent and frail little girl as I was back on August 10, 1990, and knowing others could be harmed by you are what has bothered me the most all of these years. I didn't know who you were, or where you were, but in my heart, I KNEW you were out there, alive, either in prison or living a lie, and now I know listening to my heart all of these years, and never giving up on finding you, I was right. All of this time, you've been living a lie, keeping your secret of who you really are . . . to yourself. Every year I spent trying to find you and bring you to justice, you spent thinking that you got away with what you did to me. You thought you got away with creeping into the window of an apartment, lived in by a single mother and daughter, and then kidnapping, raping, and almost succeeding at murdering me, just an innocent little girl, peacefully sleeping in the middle of the night, on the first night in my life I had gone to sleep in my own bed . . . when I couldn't fight to get away from you. What a cowardly way to commit a crime. I hope you had sleepless nights filled with nightmares, and spent every day looking over your shoulder all of these years.

After telling me you were an undercover police officer, and telling me your gun was in the back seat of your vehicle, and me curiously leaning over the front seat to look into the back. . . . I can still think back and feel the fear I had inside of me at that very moment when you ripped my panties off of me and laid me down in the front seat of that vehicle and started to lick me. As an eight-year-old child, I didn't know what you were doing, but I knew it was wrong. I knew at that moment that you didn't know my family, and I knew that you were NOT a police officer like you had said. I, in my mind, tried to

Courtesy of Jennifer Schuett

imagine what I could do to escape you, because I feared for my life, but knew that I wouldn't be able to get away because I wouldn't be strong enough or fast enough. As if putting your grown-man hands around my little neck and choking me repeatedly and raping me wasn't enough, you continued to play out your nightmarish fantasy. You slit my throat and as you dragged me by my ankles through brush and thorns, I did what came as first instinct to me . . . I played dead. You thought you killed me. You thought you had won this sick game you started. But, again, you were wrong. You left me there, in a fire ant pile, like I was nothing. Like I was an old rag-doll you had discarded in a field as trash after having your fun torturing her. We all know the details, but as a reminder, for over fourteen hours, I laid there, in that field, bleeding to death, helpless but NOT ALONE. I had angels sitting next to me. Even though I could not scream, I could not get up, I couldn't do anything physically as fire ants stung me all over my body . . . there was one thing I could do: pray for strength and survive. Luckily, those prayers were answered.

A victorious Jennifer Schuett.

The choices you made in the early morning hours of August 10, 1990, have impacted my life, and changed me forever. Before August 10, 1990, I was a free-spirited little girl. I can't remember ever even being afraid or living in fear besides always being afraid of the dark, as most children are at that age. You changed that. By the time I was released from the hospital, we didn't even live in our own home anymore. You put such a fear into myself and family, that I didn't get to go home to the home that I had known for almost five years. My mother and I had to move in with my grandparents, I had to be escorted to and from school, and instead of being my usual carefree self, I lived with anxiety and what I know now as post-traumatic stress disorder. I didn't know what those things were then, I don't even know if anyone ever explained it to me, for sure . . . but looking back on it, I realize now that me not sleeping in my own bed until fifteen, me living in fear of you coming back and hurting myself or my mother, and me not wanting to do anything without my mother, I wasn't like other "normal" children, even though my mother tried to make our life as normal as possible. When I would go in public, to the grocery store, doctor's appointments, or the mall, everyone, in my eyes, was a suspect, and it's remained that way until October 13, 2009. For years, I've studied the faces of every male that would pass by, because I was sure had I seen you, I'd recognize you. I was scared of my own bed, scared of sleeping . . . scared of the dark, as a child and teenager, but during the day, I was constantly looking for you, trying to save others from being attacked by the person that had so viciously attacked me. The only fear I DIDN'T have was doing anything and everything in my power to help in capturing you.

I had nightmares for a year or so after you attacked me, and for a short period of time can remember being afraid of men. I felt like myself and my family had been violated, but the drive and determination in me to find you has kept me going. Knowing one day I'd face you and know you'd never hurt another person, has kept me going. Also, from the age of five, my dream was to grow up, and be a mommy of eight boys. You also have changed that dream. For years after you attacked me, I knew something was medically wrong with me and I have gone to various doctors and I finally found out two years ago, after undergoing tests and surgery, that my medical issues are a result of you brutally attacking me and that it is medically impossible for me to conceive children without help of an infertility doctor and treatments. As a child, I can also remember locking myself in the restroom and sitting on the bathroom counter, staring at the long, ugly, red scar on my neck, left by you taking a knife and cutting me from one ear to another, and asking myself what I had done for someone to do such horrible things to me. As an elementary student at the time, and having to have a tube down my throat for part of my 3rd grade year, children and adults were curious and I was constantly asked questions of what happened to me and why. How was I, as an eight-year-old, supposed to answer questions that I didn't have the answers to? Because of the tube in my throat, I couldn't participate in physical education like all of the other children, but instead would sit in the nurse's office for an hour every day while the other children played. As a college student, I was nervous walking to and from classes in the parking lots, always frightened and worried about someone attacking or following me. I have suffered anxiety attacks at night in past years so bad that I cannot breathe, and sit up for hours trying to calm myself down.

But today, I sit in front of you as a twenty-eight-year-old woman, and would like you to know that I am not a victim because of what happened twenty years ago. Your plan the night of August 10, 1990, was not the same plan that God had for me. You may have taken away my voice for a short period of time, and you may have taken away a piece of my being and innocence I will never get back, but you've never taken away my strength or my will to survive. I have waited for this day for twenty years of my life, and hope you now feel as weak as you made me feel all of those years ago as a child. While you played out your fantasy on my tiny body, and attacked me, you made me feel "this" small. Today I hope you feel "this" small sitting in front of me, because I definitely feel like the strong one. In life we have choices, and I made a choice early on to not let this negative and traumatic experience define me. Instead, I turned the attack into something positive for not only myself, but others by using my voice to speak out against crime in hopes that myself and other survivors will conquer crime, one voice at a time.

Dennis Bradford, I am not your victim. I am Victorious.

CHAPTER WRAP-UP

The materials in this chapter offered a brief introduction to the complex topics of criminal trials and sentencing. Trials come in many forms, and even when focused on criminal trials only, great variation exists. In general, though, criminal trials pass through several standard stages: jury selection, presentation of opening statements, presentation of evidence, presentation of closing arguments, the judge's charge to the jury, jury deliberation, reading of the verdict, and sentencing. The chapter offered ways in which capital trials are special forms of criminal trials. They follow many of the same steps, though some elements in the *voir dire*, the need for unanimity, and these trials' bifurcated nature are distinct. Sentencing has undergone massive changes in the past several decades, resulting in a patchwork of policies from jurisdiction to jurisdiction. Though changes were made with an eye toward equity, proportionality, and social debt, it is unclear that the resulting system reflects any of these principles well. Evidence shows that many disadvantaged people continue to pay higher prices when entangled in the criminal justice system than do others. This chapter also identified the expense of current sentencing policies. People are being incarcerated at higher rates, inmates are serving longer sentences, and the cost to fund the expanding system continues to grow. An important element covered in this chapter is the victim. The text identified the growing role that victims play in criminal investigations and trials and outlined the increase in rights afforded them. No longer are victims treated as "just another witness." Rather, offices, funds, and policies are in place to assist victims of crime and their families.

CASE STUDY

Case Study Video 9.2: Interviews with case study participants

None of the case studies covered in this book resulted in a trial. This is not surprising given how relatively rare it is for criminal cases to end up at trial. Still, we contemplated how they may have been handled at trial. Imagine Chris Farias at trial for his third DUI, none of which resulted in an accident or injury. Would a jury have convicted him given the unfortunate reality that many can relate to having driven drunk? And what of Joshua Paul Benjamin? He avoided trial by pleading guilty. Given the videotape evidence and his own confession, it seems unlikely that any jury (or judge) would have rendered a verdict of not guilty. Do you think his sentence would have been the same, worse, or better had he gone to trial? We can only imagine what would have become of Dennis Bradford had he not taken his life. His crimes were committed in Texas against a child. While we can never know, it seems likely that had he gone to trial, his case may have been an attempted capital murder case. What of Danny Madrid? He started having run-ins with law enforcement, arrests, and time in the correctional system (juvenile initially, adult later) at the age of 10. Would he, a young Latino gang member, with a long rap sheet, who had pride in his being viewed as tough, have been viewed sympathetically by a jury? Would he have gotten the 25-years-to-life sentence? Danny certainly thought he'd face life in prison so he accepted the plea bargain of ten years. In the next chapter, we turn to correctional responses in the community. Such responses are where most persons who are found guilty find themselves. In fact, it is a community corrections and work release program in which Chris Farias served his sentence.

KEY POINTS

- The vast majority of charges brought against a person are settled prior to a trial. Fewer than 10% of cases go to trial.

- Criminal trials, though variable, proceed through several formal stages.

- Responding to a jury summons is an obligation and a right, and lying during *voir dire* is perjury and punishable by fines and other sanctions.

- Juries vary in size, and the number of jurors required for a guilty verdict varies by type of trial and the place.

- Prosecutors have the burden of proving guilt beyond a reasonable doubt. Defense counsel has no requirement to prove the defendant's innocence.

- Sentencing has changed dramatically in the past four decades.

- Sentencing changes are responsible for increases in the prison population due to mandatory sentences and longer sentences.

- It is questionable whether structured sentencing has led to a more equitable and proportional sentencing system.

- Victim rights have grown tremendously in the past few decades.

KEY TERMS

Acquit 235

Adjudicate 228

Allen Charge 235

Bench Trial 229

Beyond a Reasonable
    Doubt 233

Bifurcated Trials 242

Circumstantial
    Evidence 231

Civil Trials 228

Crime Victims' Rights
    Act 245

Criminal Trials 228

Deadlocked 235

Death Qualified 242

Deliberation 234

Determinate
    Sentencing 239

Deterrence 237

Direct Evidence 231

Dying Declaration 231

Equity 237

Excited Utterance 231

Factual Guilt 228

Federal Rules of
    Evidence 230

Federal Sentencing
    Guidelines Act 239

Hearsay 231

Hearsay Rule 231

Hung Jury 235

Indeterminate
    Sentencing 237

Jury Nullification 235

Jury Trial 229

Legal Guilt 228

Mandatory Minimum 239

Mistrial 235

Parole Board 238

Pattern Jury
    Instructions 233

Perjury 230

Presentence
    Investigation 237

Proportionality 237

Reading of the Verdict 236

Rebuttal 233

Reputation Concerning
    Character 231

Restoration 237

Sentencing Guidelines 239

Sequestered 234

Social Debt 237

Three-Strikes Law 241

Traffic Hearings 228

Victim Bill of Rights 246

Victim Impact
    Statement 246

Violent Crime Control and
    Law Enforcement
    Act 239

REVIEW QUESTIONS

1. What are the major types of trials held in the United States?

2. What percentage of cases go to trial?

3. What is the difference between a bench trial and a jury trial?

4. What are the basic steps in a criminal trial?

5. What percentage of criminal cases result in a guilty verdict?

6. What is double jeopardy and what are exceptions to it?

7. What role does a judge play in sentencing?

8. What are the main goals of sentencing?

9. What rights to victims now have that they did not before?

CRITICAL THINKING MATTERS

1. **Sentencing.** Changes in sentencing over time have resulted in more people going to prison and longer prison terms. This has happened alongside a reduction in criminal offending. It is clear that incarceration is expensive, but what of the social costs of this policy? In a two-parent household, how does imprisonment of one adult affect the children in that family? Are these children more likely to commit crimes and end up in prison themselves? Are they less likely to finish school with the reduced supervision of the incarcerated parent? Is the family more likely to be on public welfare because of the incarcerated parent? Do you think the children are stigmatized due to the parent's situation? How do you think any stigma may affect the children? What are the overall consequences for us as a nation of increasing incarceration?

2. **Victims' Rights.** The U.S. Constitution is rife with offenders' rights. For example, offenders have the right to remain silent, the right to counsel, the right to face their accuser, the right to an impartial jury, the right to bail, the right to the presumption of innocence, and so on. In contrast, the Constitution is silent on the rights of victims. Why is this? Do the newly gained victims' rights conflict with offenders' right to a fair trial? If so, how? Is it fair that victims are subject to repeated cross-examination by at times aggressive defense attorneys while the offender is not obligated to undergo the same? Is it fair that the mother of a child killed by a drunk driver is barred in some circumstances from giving a victim impact statement, yet the defendant can offer a parade of character witnesses? If you were a policymaker, what policies would you enact to ensure the constitutional rights of offenders were honored as well as honoring the victims of crime? What would you do in the case of Joshua Paul Benjamin had he opted to go to trial? What accommodations would you make for his minor victims as they testified? What rights do these young victims need that are not covered in recent legislation? Would these new rights conflict with Joshua's rights as the accused?

3. **Victim Wishes and the Death Penalty.** Dennis Earl Bradford committed his crimes against Jennifer Schuett in Texas during a period in which the state engaged in the death penalty. While we can never know, there is a good chance that Bradford would be sitting in prison for the rest of his life had he not hanged himself in jail. What if Jennifer as a victim did not believe that Bradford should remain in prison for the remainder of his life? Should her wishes be heeded by a judge or jury who makes this determination?

4. **Sentencing and Victim Characteristics.** Joshua committed terrible crimes against young boys. Bradford committed terrible crimes against a young girl. Pretend you are a judge operating under an indeterminate sentencing framework. If you had to render a sentence for the crimes committed by Joshua and by Bradford, would they differ? Why or why not? What if you were a judge operating in a structured sentencing environment? Do you think it would be appropriate if both Joshua and Bradford received similar sentences for their crimes? What if the mandatory minimums, determinate sentences, and sentencing guidelines required that they be given the identical sentence? Would this be appropriate based on the goals and concepts underlying sentencing?

DIGITAL RESOURCES

$SAGE edge™

Sharpen your skills with SAGE edge at edge.sagepub.com/rennison2e. SAGE edge for Students provides a personalized approach to help you accomplish your coursework goals in an easy-to-use learning environment. You'll find action plans, mobile-friendly eFlashcards, and quizzes as well as video and web resources and links to SAGE journal articles to support and expand on the concepts presented in this chapter.

PART IV

© Roberto A Sanchez

CORRECTIONS

10

CORRECTIONAL RESPONSES IN THE COMMUNITY

> "A crime-control strategy of locking up more people, and keeping them locked up longer, isn't working."
>
> —Bruce Western,
> professor and faculty chair of the
> Harvard Kennedy School Program in
> Criminal Justice Policy and Management (2013)[1]

LEARNING OBJECTIVES

After finishing this chapter, you should be able to:

10.1 Summarize the history and current state of corrections in the community, including identifying recent innovations.

10.2 Identify the purpose, goals, and different types of community corrections.

10.3 Critique the benefits of corrections in the community over incarceration for offenders, family members of the offenders, victims, and the overall community.

10.4 Critically examine net widening and understand detrimental issues associated with it.

10.5 Evaluate the rights of victims regarding offenders serving corrections in the community.

10.6 Assess the role of a probation officer.

10.7 Demonstrate an understanding of the role of technology in community corrections.

INTRODUCTION: CORRECTIONS IN THE COMMUNITY

As the previous chapter noted, sentencing is the application of sanctions or punishment to a legally guilty individual. Punishments or sanctions range from less severe to more severe. On the most severe end of that continuum is capital punishment. Less severe than capital punishment is full-time incarceration in prison or jail. Still less severe are types of punishment that involve offenders' spending at least some time in the community while serving out their sentences. Collectively, these sanctions are known as **correctional responses in the community**. These programs often are considered more cost effective and better at reducing future crime, while at the same time minimizing the negative and stigmatizing consequences of interaction with the criminal justice system experienced by the offender. Community corrections are increasingly necessary because our traditional strategy of locking up more people for longer periods of time is not working, as Bruce Western notes in the quotation at the beginning of the chapter. States such as California now spend more money on the criminal justice system than on the educational system. Not only is it prohibitively expensive, but the social costs are significant.

Most people think of full-time incarceration in jail or prison when considering criminal sanctions; however, this form of punishment is reserved for a relatively small fraction of offenders (Figure 10.1). In 2014, 23% of adult offenders in the correctional

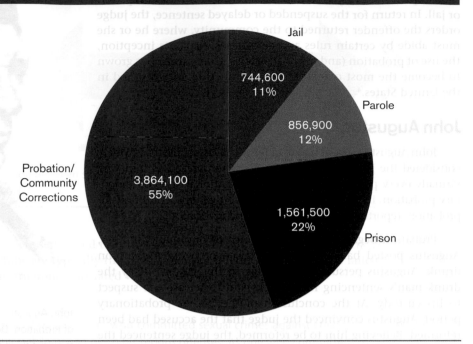

Figure 10.2 ■ Adults in the Correctional System in the United States, 2014

Jail
744,600
11%

Parole
856,900
12%

Probation/
Community
Corrections
3,864,100
55%

1,561,500
22%

Prison

Source: Adapted from Kaeble, D., Glaze, L. E., Tsoutis, A., & Minton, T. (2015). *Correctional populations in the United States, 2014* (NCJ 249513). Washington, DC: Bureau of Justice Statistics, Table 4.

Though community corrections has grown since its inception, from the 1980s to 2008 the use of corrections in the community proliferated. That growth recently reversed, from 2007 through 2014, as the number of adults under the supervision of correctional responses in the United States declined annually.[7] In 2014 (the most current year for which data are available), 2,240 adult offenders per 100,000 adults in the United States were serving probationary sentences. This corresponds to 4,708,100 adult offenders in the United States. In 2014, the average time in community supervision was 22 months.

While declines characterize the national estimates, there is variation at the state level. Estimates from the Bureau of Justice Statistics indicate that the national decline in the number of adults under supervision in the community resulted primarily from declines in the probation populations concentrated in California, Texas, Michigan, Florida, and Georgia. Together, these five states were responsible for 56% of the total decrease of community corrections at the national level. But not all states experienced decreases in the number of adults on probation from 2010 to 2011. Maryland, Mississippi, Alaska, Tennessee, and Alabama are among states that recorded increases in the number of adults under supervision in the community.

Gender and Race Among Those Serving Corrections in the Community

Information on the degree to which women are sentenced to community corrections is scarce. The literature offers information on women and *incarceration* showing that they make up a low proportion of the incarcerated population relative to their presence in the population. Furthermore, these findings show that the number of women being incarcerated has grown dramatically in the past two decades. A large part of this growth stems largely from increased prosecutions generally, and drug convictions specifically. Given the less serious nature of these charges, it seems plausible that the female presence in community corrections would also be growing rapidly. Estimates indicate that in 2000, 2013, and

Figure 10.3 ■ Adults on Probation at Year End, 1980–2014

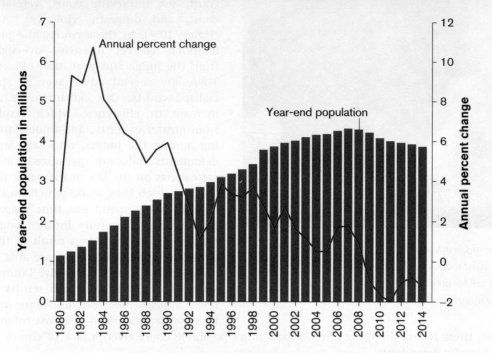

In recent years, the population serving a probationary status has decreased. What advantages does this bring to the taxpayer? What disadvantages? If you were a policymaker, would you sing the praises of this trend? Or would you campaign to change it?

Source: Adapted from Kaeble, D., Glaze, L. E., Tsoutis, A., & Minton, T. (2015). *Correctional populations in the United States, 2014* (NCJ 249513). Washington, DC: Bureau of Justice Statistics, Table 1.

2014, women made up 22%, 25%, and 25% of adults on probation or in community corrections.[8] These estimates and other factors suggest that women may be underrepresented in community corrections. Because there are relatively few women in the system, it may mean that offering particular community corrections to women is costlier and difficult. This is the position of Zaitow and Thomas, who argue that for women there are fewer community sanctions and treatment options available.[9] Only additional research can clearly identify the presence and trends of women being sentenced to community corrections.

There is a similar paucity of information about race and Hispanic origin with regard to correctional sanctions in the community. The literature is rife with information on race, Hispanic origin, and arrest, sentencing, incarceration, and recidivism. In contrast, it is virtually silent on race, Hispanic origin, and community corrections. What can be located suggests that in 2014, 54% of those serving community corrections or probation were non-Hispanic white, 30% were black, 13% were Latino/Hispanic, 1% were American Indian/Alaskan Native, and 1% were Asian (Figure 10.3). These percentages appear stable over time, as similar proportions were measured in 2013 and 2000.[10] One would think that with the increase in black and Hispanic individuals entering the criminal justice system that this same increase would be present in community corrections, but that is not the case given this evidence.

Problem-Solving Courts

Many offenders are sentenced to community corrections by a **problem-solving court** (see Chapter 7 for additional details). These specialized courts are intended to better meet the needs of particular groups of offenders. Some specialized courts include

Video 10.1:
Special courts

problem-solving court:
A specialized court designed to better meet the needs of a particular group of offenders.

A probationer stands before the judge in Veterans' Court. How do specialized courts such as Veterans' Court assist special populations such as veterans? If you were a policymaker, would you call for other types of specialized courts? If so, what would they focus on? What advantages do you believe these courts offer, if any?

Web:
Domestic violence courts

drug court, mental health court, reentry court, DUI/DWI court, prostitution court, sex trafficking court, veterans' court, and domestic violence court (Figure 10.4). In these courts, the probationer receives intensive oversight from the judge and probation officers. There are several advantages to specialized courts. One advantage is an increase in efficiency, which results from greater expertise and understanding among the judges, attorneys, and defendants. Judges in specialized courts are experts on the law in the particular area in which they work, which means that attorneys spend less time preparing documents to fully inform judges on the topical area. As a result of this expertise, specialized courts are able to handle more cases effectively. Tailored sentences are crafted, which results in fewer appeals filed. Because more uniform sentences are used across offenders, there is less shopping around for a more favorable court given a lack of choice of courts by defendants.

Privatized Community Corrections Services

In some jurisdictions, budget shortages in conjunction with rapid growth in the number of probationers have forced officials to consider alternatives to probation departments

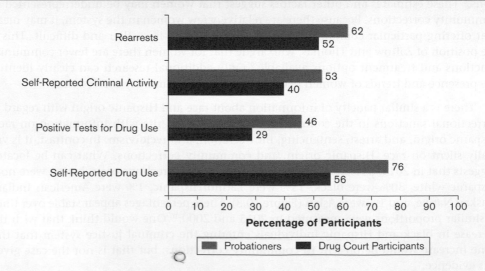

Figure 10.4 ■ Comparison of Drug Court Participants and Probationers on Certain Outcomes

Outcome	Probationers	Drug Court Participants
Rearrests	62	52
Self-Reported Criminal Activity	53	40
Positive Tests for Drug Use	46	29
Self-Reported Drug Use	76	56

Percentage of Participants

Some research shows that drug court participants have positive outcomes at higher rates than those who do not participate in drug courts. Under what circumstances would you as a judge assign an offender to one or the other group?

Source: Roman, J. (2013). *Cost-benefit analysis of criminal justice reforms.* National Institute of Justice. Retrieved from https://ncjrs.gov/pdffiles1/nij/241929.pdf.

overseeing probationers. Probation departments are increasingly strained to adequately monitor and supervise probationers due to growth in caseloads. A common alternative is the use of privatized probation services (Figure 10.5). Private probation agencies operate by requiring probationers to post a bond as insurance for their compliance with community corrections standards. If probationers fail to comply with conditions of their sentences, the bond money is lost. In some jurisdictions, privatizing probation services includes the use of privately commissioned presentence reports. Some find that privatized presentence reports tend to be favorable to offenders and costlier (up to $5,000) than those written by state probation officers. In addition, the use of privatized probation services introduces yet another aspect of potential economic discrimination into the criminal justice system. Private probation agencies generally focus on probationers of specific types. For example, in many states, private probation services supervise those convicted of DUI or driving while ability impaired.

GOALS OF CORRECTIONAL RESPONSES IN THE COMMUNITY

The goals of correctional responses in the community align with the perspectives and purposes of the overall criminal justice system. In Chapter 1, we identified the five overlapping perspectives of the criminal justice system: crime control, rehabilitation, due process, restorative justice, and nonintervention. Community correction sentences are in many ways an improvement over traditional incarceration.

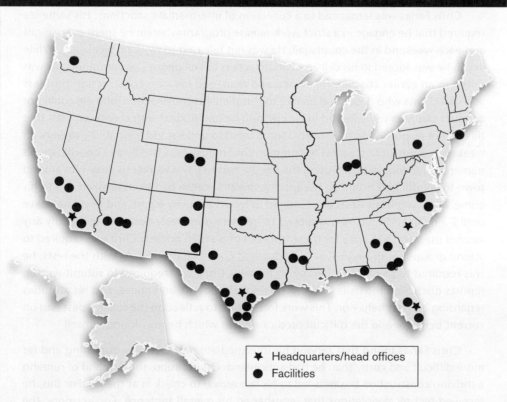

Figure 10.5 ■ Private Prison Facilities Owned or Controlled by GEO Group

★ Headquarters/head offices
● Facilities

What advantages and disadvantages do private prisons offer? In August 2016, the federal government announced its intention to end the use of private prisons, because they are less safe and less effective. If you were governor of a state, would you use them? Why or why not? Why do you feel there are more of these facilities in the South than the North?

Source: SourceWatch, The Center for Media and Democracy.

Barry Lewis/Getty Images

Community corrections in action. How might community corrections be beneficial to society? Or to the victim? If you were a judge, would you be willing to sentence offenders to community corrections? If so, under what conditions?

Punishment

One goal of community-based responses is to **punish** offenders for their lawbreaking behavior and to do so in a way that may deter future criminal acts. Contrary to popular stereotypes, community corrections are not a "walk in the park," and when given a choice some people convicted of crimes choose prison over corrections in the community. The approach taken by corrections in the community is thought to reduce rates of **recidivism**, which is a measure that identifies relapse into criminal offending behavior. Not only does corrections in the community deter future criminal acts by the offender (specific deterrence), but it also is a form of general deterrence to those around the offender.

CASE STUDY

punish: This is one goal of community-based corrections, designed to deter future criminal acts.

recidivism: A measure that identifies relapse into criminal offending behavior.

Chris Farias was sentenced to a collection of intermediate sanctions. His sentence required that he engage in a strict work-release program wherein he spent every night and each weekend in the county jail. He was not released to work on weekends. While in jail, he was locked in his cell and had no access to cell phones or computers. As was noted in an earlier chapter, he owned and managed his own construction business and had clients who depended on him to complete his construction jobs. He could not conduct business while locked in his cell, and he had to deal with clients who felt that he was not responsive to their needs. Some failed to understand his inability to work on weekends. With limited access to communication devices, Chris had to coordinate his numerous subcontractors. During the day, he had to pay a worker to drive him around town to conduct his business, because his driver's license had been revoked due to his crime. Every weekday, Chris was required to report to jail by 6 p.m. and could not leave until 7 a.m. In addition, he was subject to frequent urine tests designed to identify any alcohol use. He had to pay for these tests out of his own pocket. Chris was required to attend group therapy as well as individualized cognitive therapy. As with the tests, he was required to pay for his therapy. In therapy, Chris was required to submit written reports discussing the issue of drunk driving, alcohol use and abuse, and his attitudes regarding his past behavior. This work forced him to reflect on the role his past had on current behavior and the difficult predicament in which he now found himself.

Chris Farias found that serving his intermediate sentence was punishing and far more difficult and costly than he had anticipated. On occasion, the demand of running a thriving construction business led to his late arrival to check in at the jail. For this, he received technical violations that lengthened his overall sentence. Furthermore, the technical violations resulted in additional punishment that required Chris to spend weekdays in jail as well. Aside from the logistical and financial difficulties presented by his sentence, there were emotional costs. He worried that his aging mother would pass away before his sentence was complete. He worried that she would pass away knowing that her son was serving work release. Because he was unable to leave the state during his sentence, he was especially fearful that she would pass away before he was able to travel to see her again. Additional emotional loss came as Chris's long-time girlfriend ended their relationship because of the difficulties associated with serving the sentence. Chris's finances were devastated because of his diminished, though not completely eradicated, ability to earn a living. He lost many friends who learned that he was serving a community corrections sentence for his DUI.

Ensuring Safety

A second goal of community corrections is to keep society safe. The incarceration of nonviolent and/or petty criminals creates great cost to taxpayers, offenders, and the community when alternative safe solutions are available. When community corrections are used with the appropriate offenders, these sanctions do not jeopardize the safety of individuals in the community. Chris Farias is an example of an ideal candidate for corrections in the community. He was not a violent offender, and as long as he followed the conditions of his probation, society was not endangered.

Rehabilitation and Nonintervention

A third goal of community corrections is rehabilitating offenders, whether through better coping skills, help with drug or alcohol addictions, or gaining education or other occupational skills needed to become productive, law-abiding citizens. By avoiding full-time incarceration, reintegration is not an issue as the offender remains in the community. Avoiding incarceration also enables the offender to avoid the stigma and real limitations of becoming an ex-convict. Some research finds that withholding the label of "ex-con" through probation is associated with a lower likelihood of recidivism.[11] This more nonintervention approach enables offenders to better maintain employment, develop new skills through therapy and training, and remain engaged with their families. Furthermore, keeping nonviolent offenders from full-time incarceration in jail or prison lessens the risk of criminal socialization.

> By his own admission, Chris Farias's life was changed for the better as a result of his community sentence. While his sentence was punishing and costly, he willingly acknowledges that the sentence was what he needed. It was, he stated, the first time he recognized how his attitudes and beliefs—and not just his alcohol consumption—contributed to his unlawful behavior. He took seriously his need to abstain from alcohol and learn a new way to live. He enrolled in a local university to further his education, and he is mentoring others who are serving in the same program that he did.

CASE STUDY

Author Video:
Restorative justice

Journal:
Effectiveness of restorative justice

Restorative Justice

The fourth goal of community corrections is **restorative justice**. Corrections in the community often includes restorative justice elements designed to emphasize that crime is more than criminal behavior. Rather, lawbreaking disturbs and harms individuals and the community, especially the primary victim. Many elements of corrections in the community emphasize the need for offenders to take responsibility for their actions and to repair the harm caused by these actions. Restoration is accomplished when the victim, the offender, and the community work together to develop an appropriate response to the criminal behavior.[12] This restorative justice approach has long-lasting and far-reaching effects given that the majority of victims of violence know the offenders as either intimate family members or friends. Offenders locked away in prison or jail cannot as easily or effectively engage in restorative justice activities that benefit many.

restorative justice: A goal of community corrections that emphasizes that crime is more than criminal behavior. Rather, lawbreaking disturbs and harms individuals and the community, especially the primary victim.

COMMON MISCONCEPTIONS

Corrections in the Community Is Too Light a Punishment

Many people believe that probation is a "slap on the hand" and comparable to no punishment when compared with a prison sentence. Yet the reality is that some offenders who are convicted of crimes opt to be sentenced to prison rather than to serve their terms in the community because community sentences can be far more onerous.

Take, for example, Mark William Ivey, who was arrested in Texas for DUI. As reported in the *Texas Tribune* (see www.texastribune.org/2010/09/28/many-choosing-jail-time-over-probation), Ivey was arrested with a blood alcohol level more than double the legal limit. His case went to jury, and Ivey declined a provision that allows a jury to sentence him to probation. He did not want probation but preferred being sentenced to jail. Ivey was found guilty, and the jury sentenced him to 35 days in jail and a $2,000 fine. The judge felt that Ivey needed treatment he would not get in jail, so she suspended the jury's sentence and sentenced Ivey to 2 years of probation, a $500 fine, 30 days in jail, 60 hours of community service, and mandatory counseling. Ivey appealed the ruling but lost, and the judge's sentence stood.

According to Harris County Criminal Court at Law judge Sherman Ross, the "hassle factor" prompts some to choose prison over community corrections sentences, as time in the community can be harsh.[13] First, community corrections is financially costly to the offender. The offender must pay fines, fees, and for mandated counseling and testing. For some, prison is less expensive for the offender (and more expensive for the taxpayer). Second, some offenders want to avoid expectations regarding their behavior while serving corrections in the community. Often the offender is required to be employed, increase his or her education, and perform community service. These actions are not required while incarcerated. And third, the probationer must frequently submit to alcohol or drug testing. Some offenders wish to continue using drugs or alcohol. In prison they are not tested for these substances and can continue using to the extent they can gain access to these substances.

In summary, while in some cases, jail or prison may be a harsher sentence, to others, community corrections is viewed as the more severe penalty.

Think About It

1. If you were faced with the option of community corrections or jail or prison for an offense you committed, what would you select? Why?

2. Describe the types of offenses you believe are appropriate for community corrections. What are offenses you believe should always or never be dealt with using community corrections. Why is that?

3. Do you think extralegal factors should be considered when sentencing a person to community corrections? For example, should those who are employed get the opportunity when those who are unemployed should not? Should those who are married with children be given this chance when single individuals, or those who are homeless should not? Why or why not?

TYPES OF CORRECTIONAL RESPONSES IN THE COMMUNITY

Correctional responses in the community encompass a variety of sanctions. The two primary categories of correctional responses in the community are probation and intermediate responses. While these two primary types are presented as discrete categories, in reality, community correctional sanctions frequently include a mix of sanctions. This multifaceted approach allows customization of penalties for each individual offender based on her or his unique circumstances. Individualized and customized approaches are thought to better promote change, enable superior offender monitoring, address the dynamic risk factors that contributed to the offender's initial criminal behavior, and reduce the risk of recidivism.

Parole is also a type of correctional response that takes place when an offender is living in the community. Parole differs from probation and intermediate sanctions in that parole is granted to offenders who have served time in prison. Parolees are given the opportunity to serve the remaining portions of their sentences in the community. While in the community, these ex-prisoners are subject to a number of conditions. Failure to meet these conditions may result in a return to prison, where they will be required to serve out the remainder of their sentences. Chapter 12, which focuses on life after prison, offers more information on parole.

Probation

As noted above, probation is a sentence that suspends or delays a term of full-time incarceration in prison or jail. In return for the suspended or delayed sentence, the judge orders the offender returned to the community, where he or she must abide by certain rules and conditions. The term *probation* is derived from the Latin word *probare*, which means "to prove." An individual on probation is not incarcerated, but rather is placed in the community (in varying degrees) where the person must *prove* he or she can live within the constraints of the law and conditions set forth by the judge. During the probationary period, the probationer is supervised by a probation officer. If the probation officer finds that the offender has violated the rules and conditions of probation, probation may be terminated and the offender can be remanded to prison or jail to complete his or her sentence.

Intermediate Responses

The second primary category of correctional responses in the community is **intermediate responses and sanctions**. Intermediate sanctions, also called probation plus, involve probation plus additional community sanctions, which are usually administered by probation departments. As with people serving traditional probation, probation officers generally supervise those serving intermediate sanctions. This approach is based on a variety of sanctions that are more restrictive and severe than traditional probation. These punishments involve more intensive supervision and more restrictions on a probationer's ability to move freely in the community. Intermediate responses and sanctions, for example, may require that the offender be subjected to daily curfews, report to day-reporting centers, be subject to house arrest, or live in a halfway house or other residential facility. Intermediate sanctions may entail that the offender submit to random and frequent drug and alcohol testing and/or participate in cognitive therapy, anger management, and other forms of behavior modification programs. Intermediate sanctions can include work release, whereby the offender is employed during the day but is required to report to the local jail for weekends and nights. Many types of intermediate sanctions are being used in the United States. The most commonly used ones are described next.

Courts frequently **fine** offenders. One common form of fine is "day fines," which operate on a scale so that probationers are able to pay fines while working in the community. With greater emphasis on acknowledging victims and bringing them into the process, the requirements of restitution and community service have become more widespread. Restitution refers to paying money to the victim, victim's family, or a crime victims fund in response to a crime committed. Community service is related and includes performing service in the community in response to a crime. The nature of community service varies widely and may include, for example, helping the homeless, picking up litter, or removing graffiti. Research indicates that restitution reduces recidivism to some degree. Following a criminal conviction, material possessions of the criminal may be seized through **forfeiture** if these items were related to the commission or outcome of a criminal offense. For instance, the state may seize vehicles, cash, homes, and boats. Forfeiture is not restricted to tangible items. For example, federal employees engaged in corruption can lose their pensions through forfeiture.

Audio:
Juvenile probation

intermediate responses and sanctions:
A type of correctional response in the community that includes probation plus additional community sanctions, which are generally administered by probation departments.

fine: A type of community correction sanction.

forfeiture: A community correction sanction in which the criminal's material possessions may be seized if the items were related to the commission or outcome of a criminal offense.

One form of electronic monitoring. Electronic monitoring has facilitated monitoring offenders in the community. Under what circumstances, if any, would you as a judge use this type of technology? Why?

electronic monitoring: An intermediate sanction in which the probationer wears an ankle, wrist, or neck monitor that identifies his or her location.

intensive supervised probation: A type of probation in which offenders undergo extreme supervision and monitoring.

home confinement/ house arrest: A type of intermediate sanction that restricts offenders from leaving their homes.

split sentence or shock probation: A form of intermediate sanction in which the offender initially spends some time in jail or prison (usually 30 days) and then is released into corrections in the community.

boot camps: A type of intermediate sanction in which offenders are mandated to military settings, where they are required to follow orders, march, run drills, and engage in physical training.

A well-known type of intermediate sanction is **electronic monitoring**, which involves the probationer wearing an ankle, wrist, or neck monitor that identifies (either passively or actively) where the person is located. Probation officers use this information to monitor the whereabouts of the offender and to ensure that conditions of community corrections have not been violated.

Intensive supervised probation (ISP) is a type of probation in which offenders undergo extreme supervision and monitoring. Offenders are expected to meet frequently with their probation officer and have their homes and workplaces searched frequently. Probation officers who are assigned ISP caseloads have fewer clients in order to allow more intense scrutiny. ISP programs are implemented in a variety of ways and vary in terms of quality. For these reasons, evaluations of this approach are complex. While findings disagree, much research fails to point to greater effectiveness of ISP over traditional probation.[14] **Home confinement/house arrest** is an intermediate sanction that restricts offenders from leaving their homes. In this way, an offender's home becomes the place in which she or he is incarcerated. For some offenders, intermediate sanctions take the form of a **split sentence or shock probation**. This means that the offender initially spends some time in jail or prison (usually 30 days) and then is released into corrections in the community. The principle behind split sentences is that once the offender experiences time in jail or prison, she or he will be less inclined to violate the conditions of the community corrections sentence. Those required to attend boot camps find themselves in military settings where they are required to follow orders, march, run drills, and engage in physical training. While the public likes the idea of **boot camps**, some research finds that they are counterproductive and associated with *increased* recidivism. Some sentenced to intermediate sanctions are mandated to live in special **residential community housing** facilities. The facilities (often called halfway houses) are more secure than an offender's home, but less secure than jail and prison. Residential community housing keeps offenders secured at night. During the day, the offender is released to work, attend school, and engage in treatment. And finally, a **work-release program** is another form of intermediate sanctions. This sentence requires probationers to live in a secure facility (frequently the jail) and allows their release only for work. While released for work, supervision is strict. Probationers must provide information on where they will be at all times. Probation officers call frequently and show up unannounced to verify the probationers' whereabouts. Chris Farias was engaged in a work-release program as a part of his sentence.

Conditions of Probation and Intermediate Sanctions

There are two basic types of community correction conditions: standard (also called general conditions) and special. Standard conditions are rules that all offenders on community corrections are required to follow. While there is some variation from jurisdiction to jurisdiction, **general conditions** tend to include prohibiting breaking any laws, informing the court and probation officer if there is a change in employment or residence, reporting regularly to the probation department, appearing at scheduled court appointments, allowing unannounced visits to home and work for searches by the probation officer, obtaining and maintaining employment and/or working toward a higher level of education, not possessing firearms, avoiding persons with criminal records, and staying in the state unless given approval by the probation officer. An increasingly applied general condition is the submission of DNA to a DNA data bank. At the federal level, submission to a DNA data bank is required. In other jurisdictions, requirements in terms of who must submit a DNA sample vary, but all 50 states require DNA submission from convicted sex offenders at a minimum.

Special conditions are those requirements applied to offenders based on the nature of the crime, the motivation of the crime, and characteristics of the offender. Special conditions take a wide range of forms and are designed to help probationers successfully complete their probationary periods. For example, a special condition for a person serving corrections in the community for drunk driving may be for him or her to attend alcohol abuse classes, be restricted from drinking or possessing alcohol, and be prohibited from entering establishments that serve alcohol. Special conditions of child predators serving community corrections may be the prohibition of visiting particular websites or chat rooms, restrictions on working in particular fields, and restrictions on having contact with children. Special conditions for domestic violence offenders may include being restricted from contact with particular individuals, such as their children or an ex-husband or ex-wife and the requirement that they attend rehabilitation programs. Another special condition used is probation fees. **Probation fees** are used to cover costs of services such as the preparation of the presentence report, work-release programs, electronic monitoring, and drug, alcohol, or anger management counseling. Fees vary but range from approximately $10 to $120 each month. Probation special conditions may also require the offender to enroll in an anger management program, apologize to the victim, engage in community service, or abide by the Sex Offender Registration and Notification Act.

Substance abuse treatment is expensive. Is it more or less expensive than failing to treat those with substance abuse issues? Here, a graduate of a substance abuse treatment program celebrates her hard work. If you were a judge, would you require participation in such a program of your defendants? Why or why not?

EFFECTIVENESS OF CORRECTIONS IN THE COMMUNITY

In the United States, there is a strong preference for tough-on-crime stances, as the public believes that more severe punishment is more effective punishment. How effective are community corrections approaches? The effectiveness of probation is difficult to measure and receives a great deal of research attention. One means of measuring effectiveness is by looking at recidivism. While variation exists, extant literature indicates that nationally, most probationers successfully complete their probationary sentences. In 2014, about 64% of all adults serving traditional probation successfully completed their sentences.[15]

Those failing to complete their probationary periods can violate probation rules in two ways: a **technical violation** or a **legal violation**. A technical violation occurs when the rules of the probation contract are violated. This may mean failing to submit to a drug test, being late for curfew, failing to pay required restitution or a fine, or consuming alcohol or drugs. In contrast, a legal violation is the commission of a new criminal act. If a probationer commits a technical or legal violation of the terms of her or his probation, the incident is handled at the discretion of the probation officer. The probation officer may handle the violation informally, including issuing a warning. Or the probation officer may handle the violation formally, electing to begin proceedings to revoke or modify the probation. If probation is revoked, the community sentence is terminated, and the original sentence of full-time incarceration is enforced. In addition, a probationer who commits a legal violation may be indicted, tried, and sentenced for the new offense. Revocation of the probationary sentence stems primarily from technical violations during the first 3 months of the probation sentence.

In 2014, 8% of probationers had their sentences revoked and were incarcerated for committing legal violations (i.e., new criminal offenses) or for violating conditions of

residential community housing: A facility where offenders are secured at night but released during the day to work, attend school, or receive treatment.

work-release program: An intermediate sanction that requires offenders to live in a secure facility but allows their release for work.

general conditions: Conditions of corrections in the community that are standard across convicted offenders.

special conditions: Conditions of one's community corrections that are specific to a particular offender.

probation fees: Fees paid by the offender to cover costs of services such as the preparation of the presentence report, work-release programs, electronic monitoring, and drug, alcohol, or anger management counseling.

technical violation: The failure to abide by certain conditions of community corrections that do not involve committing a new crime.

legal violation: The commission of a crime while serving corrections in the community.

ETHICAL ISSUES

Probation Officers Carrying Firearms

In 2012, Jeffery Matthew McCoy, a probation officer working for the Oklahoma Department of Corrections, was fatally shot while conducting a routine visit with a probationer. Beth Hicks, a probation officer in Kendall County, Texas, was found murdered outside her home. Her murder remains unsolved. And in 1997, Steven Tielker of Fort Wayne, Indiana, was murdered by a client he was counseling. The offender, who had been convicted of molesting children, was required to meet with the counselor. Before killing Tielker, the offender fatally shot his probation officer.

Think About It

Increasingly, probation officers are being armed, representing a move away from social worker toward law enforcement officer. The arming of probation officers raises many questions.

1. What types of ethical problems may develop if probation officers are allowed to carry firearms?

2. Should probation officers receive the same firearms training as police officers?

   If probation officers are armed with firearms, ultimately a client will be shot and possibly killed. This raises additional important questions to ponder.

3. What psychological assistance to the probation officer, if any, should be provided by the state?

4. What are the legal ramifications if a probation officer kills a client? For example, can probation officers possibly be brought up on homicide charges?

---

their probation. Only 1% of adults under probation absconded, leading to a revocation of corrections in the community. In 2014, about 2% of adults serving probation exited the system through a variety of mechanisms, such as being transferred to the custody of Immigration and Customs Enforcement, being transferred to other states, having their sentences overturned or dismissed by way of appeal, or any other sort of deferment or termination.[16]

While hardly ideal, probationary effectiveness in terms of recidivism is generally better than results from incarceration. Findings show that incarceration is associated with higher recidivism rates than is probation.[17] This difference may occur, in part, because probationers remain in the community, where they can work, obtain an education, and maintain prosocial and family ties. Chris Farias represents one success story because of intermediate sanctions. His sentence was completed, and since then he has lived in the community without committing another infraction. His business is thriving, he is enrolled at a university, and he is enjoying a long-term relationship.

Research also demonstrates that there is variation in rates of recidivism among those serving probation. Individuals serving misdemeanor probation sentences have higher success rates (i.e., lower recidivism rates) than offenders who committed felonies. This difference does not necessarily mean, however, that felons were less in compliance with conditions of their sentences than nonfelons. One reason for this differential may be the more intensive supervision given to felony versus misdemeanor probationers.[18] With greater scrutiny of felons, there is a greater likelihood that an infraction will be detected and the sentence revoked. Finally, success among probationers is linked to personal characteristics. Research shows that women, married individuals, and those with higher education levels were less likely to recidivate than were men, unmarried persons, and those with lower educational accomplishments. Findings also show that older, employed persons are less likely to recidivate.[19]

Table 10.1 ■ Rate per 100 Probationers Who Exited Supervision by Type of Exit, 2010–2014

Most probationers exit probation successfully. What do you think are the reasons for this? If you were a policymaker, what could you do to increase the successful completion rate?

	Rate per 100 Probationers				
	2010	2011	2012	2013	2014
Total exit rate	55	55	53	54	55
Completion	36	36	36	36	35
Incarceration	9	9	8	8	8
Absconder	1	1	1	1	1
Other unsatisfactory exits[a]	6	5	5	6	7
Other[b]	2	2	2	2	2
Mean length of stay on probation (in months)[c]	21.7	22.0	22.8	22.1	21.9

Source: Kaeble, L. Maruschak, M., and Bonczar, T. P. (2015). *Probation and Parole in the United States, 2014* (NCJ 249057). Washington, DC: U.S. Department of Justice, Bureau of Justice Statistics, Table 3 (p. 4).

Note: Details may not sum to total exit rate due to rounding.

[a]Includes probationers discharged from supervision who failed to meet all conditions of supervision, including some with only financial conditions remaining, some who had their probation sentences revoked but were not incarcerated because their sentences were immediately reinstated, and some early terminations and expirations of sentences.

[b]Includes probationers discharged from supervision through a legislative mandate, because they were deported or transferred to the jurisdiction of Immigration and Customs Enforcement, transferred to other states through interstate compact agreements, had their sentences dismissed or overturned by the court through appeals, had their sentences closed administratively, deferred, or terminated by the court, were awaiting hearings, or were released on bond, and other types of exits.

[c]Mean length of stay is calculated as the inverse of the exit rate times 12 months.

Research on the effectiveness of intermediate responses and sanctions is more difficult to summarize. Overall, research demonstrates that intermediate sanctions are costlier than traditional probation, but less expensive than incarceration. There are higher technical violations associated with these sanctions compared with probation, but there is also more oversight, meaning that these violations are more likely to be recognized. Research shows that programs that are successful at reducing recidivism provide offenders with information about what they *should* do in high-risk situations versus merely what they *should not* do. Furthermore, successful intermediate sanction programs share the following characteristics[20]:

- intensive services that are cognitive-behavioral in nature
- services that address factors associated with criminal behavior, including antisocial attitudes, inappropriate peer groups, substance abuse, marital problems, low educational attainment, and employment deficits
- responsiveness on the part of the offender
- programs delivered by competent therapists
- high level of advocacy for the offender

In contrast, the following are characteristics of ineffective programs that fail to reduce (and in some cases increase) recidivism:

- talking cures and nondirective relationship-oriented therapy
- traditional medical model approaches
- intensive services directed at low-risk offenders or those that focus on factors that are unrelated to criminal offending

Several popular approaches to punishing offenders have been shown *not* to reduce recidivism (and in some cases to increase it), according to research conducted by Latessa and Smith[21]:

- conventional boot camps using traditional military basic training
- drug prevention classes focusing on fear and other emotional appeals, including self-esteem, such as Drug Abuse Resistance Education (D.A.R.E., as it is commonly known)
- school-based leisure-time enrichment programs
- "scared straight" programs in which juvenile offenders visit adult prisons
- shock probation, shock parole, and split sentences adding time to probation or parole
- home detention with electronic monitoring
- intensive supervision
- rehabilitation programs using vague, unstructured counseling
- residential programs for juvenile offenders using challenging experiences in rural settings

Net Widening

Journal:
Net widening

Web:
Net widening

Evaluation research suggests that some community corrections programs fail to result in lower recidivism rates. There are important possibilities as to why recidivism is not lower for some programs. One possibility is that some forms of corrections in the community are simply not more effective than traditional probation at reducing recidivism. Another possible explanation is **net widening**. Many evaluations have shown that intermediate sanctions are likely to be successful and save money or prison beds *only if they are used primarily for offenders who otherwise would serve prison terms*. Yet findings show that many judges resist using new correctional programs for offenders who traditionally would have been sent to jail or prison. Instead, community correction sentences are more often used for those who would have been sentenced to traditional probation. This new approach has resulted in net widening that captures a larger or different population than what was originally intended to have been subjected to intermediate sanctions. This net widening in conjunction with more intensive supervision exposes offender behavior, leading to technical violations and more revocations. Without such stringent oversight supervisees failing to meet an officer on time or other activity that constitutes a technical violation would not have been recorded. This increased oversight leads to a higher rate of recidivism than traditional probation.

Net widening is problematic for at least three reasons. First, it increases rather than decreases the costs of the criminal justice system. An offender who historically would not face such intense scrutiny is instead subjected to more concentrated scrutiny. Second, closer supervision leads to higher uncovering of technical violations and ultimately revocations.[22] Offenders who historically would have been sentenced to traditional probation and would have successfully completed this less intensive program now end up in jail or prison because they failed to follow the conditions of the more intensive intermediate sanctions. Clearly, this increases the costs to the criminal justice system. Third, net widening is problematic in terms of social control. By sentencing individuals to more severe and intensive sanctions, the criminal justice system widened its sphere of control over people in the community.[23] Intervention has increased over those committing relatively minor infractions, resulting in abandonment of the criminal justice goal of nonintervention.

Advantages of Corrections in the Community

There are multiple advantages to corrections in the community compared with traditional incarceration. First, while difficult to precisely quantify, probation and intermediate responses are thought to be less expensive than traditional incarceration. Estimates vary, but it appears that probation costs taxpayers $700 to $1,000 annually. In contrast, incarceration costs taxpayers about $30,000 annually. The cost to incarcerate is estimated to be double or triple that amount for inmates who are elderly or have special needs. The savings of community responses compared with traditional incarceration are enormous. However, one must recognize that many costs are difficult to quantify. For example,

net widening: The increasing harshness of sentencing given to offenders who would have traditionally been sentenced to probation.

how to quantify the cost of a violent crime committed by a probationer serving a community sentence? How does one put a monetary value on pain and suffering? A second advantage concerns the *social* benefits that probation and intermediate sanctions offer. Because the individuals who were convicted are employed in the community, they are contributing to the tax base and supporting themselves and their families (if applicable) rather than going on public assistance. Furthermore, persons engaged in intermediate sanctions often pay for their own treatment (or at least portions of it) while on probation—another savings to taxpayers. For some, remaining in the community means that they can continue their education or training to become productive and law-abiding members of society. A third advantage of community corrections is that offenders can maintain prosocial relationships with friends, family, and children. These are vital social connections that benefit all members of the relationship. When these relationship ties are disrupted due to incarceration, the risk of negative outcomes for all parties increases.

Residential check conducted by a probation officer. Many think that serving a probationary status is "getting off easy." Yet how many of you would welcome visits and inspections from probation officers at any time? Would it bother you to have them rummage through your belongings and question you when they wanted? Do you feel this would have any deterrent effect? Why or why not?

TECHNOLOGY AND COMMUNITY CORRECTIONS

The use of technology has increased along with the growth of the population under community corrections. Many are familiar with older technology such as Breathalyzers to detect blood alcohol content and urinalysis to identify specific substance use. Lesser known are newer technologies such as GPS monitors and radiofrequency devices, which are the two most frequently used types of technology in community corrections. GPS monitoring identifies the location of an offender within 15 meters using 24 global positioning satellites owned by the Department of Defense. GPS is used primarily to track high-risk offenders, especially sex offenders. **GPS monitoring** comes in two forms: passive and active. Passive GPS monitoring gathers data on the whereabouts of an offender during a 24-hour period and then transmits these data through the phone to the probation officer. In contrast, active GPS monitoring uploads information on an offender's location throughout the day. In addition, the probation officer can ping the monitor at any time to get an instantaneous location of the offender. This form of technology also enables the immediate notification of any victims that the offender is located within a particular distance. This technology is reliable and less expensive than incarceration. Research suggests that it reduces offenders' risk of failure, although the reduction varies by type of offenders. One study, for instance, focused on offenders in Florida and discovered an overall reduction in risk of failure of 31% when using electronic monitoring. Findings also indicated that risk of failure differed by type of offender being monitored. That is, risk reduction was lower among violent offenders compared with sex, property, and drug offenders.[24]

Radiofrequency identification devices (RFID) were originally used by corporations as a means of inventory control. This technology was introduced to the criminal justice system in 1997 and today is used primarily to monitor those serving home confinement sentences via ankle or wrist bracelets. These devices locate and track individuals, enabling better supervision by probation officers using fewer resources. RFID devices are quite sophisticated and are able to detect body mass index, which alerts the probation officer if the bracelet or anklet is removed or is moved more than a finger width from the skin. The data gathered by these devices locate probationers on a 30-second interval. RFID devices use a technology similar to GPS monitoring to track the locations of probationers, but at far less expense.

Audio:
Electronic monitoring devices

GPS monitoring:
Used primarily to track high-risk offenders, especially sex offenders, and comes in two forms: passive and active.

radiofrequency identification devices (RFID): A type of community corrections used to monitor those serving home confinement sentences via ankle or wrist bracelets.

Even lesser known technologies used in community corrections include kiosk reporting, remote alcohol detection, and eye scanning. **Automated kiosk reporting** (AKR) is a type of reporting in which a probationer provides information to a freestanding machine. Probationers report to kiosks to pay fines, fees, or other financial requirements; to provide information; and to confirm their identities. AKR enables low-risk offenders to report in, per the conditions of their probation, without having to actually meet with their probation officers in person. This technology for low-risk offenders frees up resources and probationary staff, allowing them to instead focus on their high-risk caseload. AKR offers cost-effective monitoring and the ability to focus on probationers who require more attention in a time of limited resources.

Another promising technology is **remote alcohol detection** (RAD), which comes in the form of a bracelet that, when applied to the probationer's skin, can detect ethanol excreted in perspiration. Unlike the traditional technology of the Breathalyzer, which offers a less sensitive snapshot of one's blood alcohol content, RAD is far more precise and provides a continuous measurement of excreted ethanol. If ethanol is detected, the probation officer is alerted. In addition, RAD technology will alert the probation officer if the monitoring bracelet has been tampered with or removed in violation of the community sentence.

A biometric technology increasingly being used in community corrections involves **eye scans**. These are used to determine if a probationer has used drugs or alcohol or is fatigued. Measuring pupil responses to a flashing light-emitting diode, the device can determine if substance use or fatigue is present. If the eye scan alerts to a potential violation, a urinalysis is used to ascertain any type of substance used.

Effective technological approaches often are inexpensive and easy to use. An effective type of technology used in supervision is social media such as Twitter and Facebook. Probation officers can follow their caseloads on social media to see if they are bragging about or posting criminal acts, associating with gang members, traveling when it is forbidden, drinking or using illegal substances, interacting with children, or doing anything that violates their probation orders. Social media can also be used to locate those who have absconded.

As promising as these technologies are, they are imperfect. They cannot force offenders to behave lawfully or follow the rules of their sentences, but with a comprehensive sentencing strategy using therapy and other tools, technology can enhance community corrections. Nonetheless, technology can break, malfunction, or be misunderstood (in the case of social media). A competent and dedicated probation officer and a well-constructed community sentence are required and cannot be replaced by technology.

VICTIMS AND CORRECTIONS IN THE COMMUNITY

Victims have gained increasing rights during the period offenders are engaged with the criminal justice system. Only 30 years ago, victims were not informed of court proceedings, arrests, releases, trials, or any aspect of the offenders' criminal justice system experience. Much has changed since then, and today all states provide basic rights to crime victims. Rights of victims vary by jurisdiction, but in general for offenders being sentenced with community corrections, victims have the right to provide input during the presentence phase and the postconviction phase.

automated kiosk reporting: A type of community corrections in which a probationer provides information to a freestanding machine, often using eye-scanning technology.

remote alcohol detection (RAD): Technology used in community corrections; a bracelet that, when applied to the probationer's skin, can detect ethanol excreted in perspiration.

eye scans: Biometric technology increasingly being used in community corrections to determine if a probationer has used drugs or alcohol or is fatigued.

Mikael Karlsson/Alamy

Breathalyzer technology continues to play a greater role in working with those serving community corrections sentences. What technology would you like to see implemented that would benefit the victim, society, and the offender?

In some places, rights during the postconviction phase must be requested in writing to take effect. Victims have the right to provide information during the presentence investigation on how the victimization affected them. This information is included in reports based on these investigations. Information gathered includes the victim's views on restitution and on the offender being sentenced to community corrections. Victims have the right to be notified prior to sentencing of offenders. In addition, victims have the right to be safe while offenders are serving their community corrections sentences. Technology has enhanced this right by notifying victims if the perpetrators of the crimes against them are located near them (for some offenses). And finally, the victim has the right to be notified of changes in and violations of conditions of probation and the termination of the sentence.

Web:
Crime Victims' Rights Act

PROBATION OFFICERS

Supervising probationers are probation officers who operate with a great deal of discretion.[25] They work closely with court personnel, primarily the sentencing judge. A probation officer is the court's fact finder and is frequently referred to as the **arm of the court**. Probation officers are technically law enforcement officers (i.e., surveillance), but also operate from the perspective of a social worker (i.e., treatment). They are expected to both assist probationers and protect the public, which can lead to role conflict. Over time, probation officers have been assaulted by their clients at an increasing rate. In an increasing number of jurisdictions, such as New York City and St. Louis, Missouri, probation officers now carry weapons. In other locations, probation officers routinely wear body armor. As a result of these protective measures, some suggest that probation officers have become much more like law enforcement officers and are now indistinguishable from police officers.

Duties of Probation Officers

The duties of probation officers begin when an individual enters the criminal justice system. Unlike others working in the criminal justice system, a probation officer works with the accused from arrest through completion of a probationary sentence. While probation officers perform many important tasks, three are of primary importance: **probation investigation**, **risk assessment**, **classification**, and **supervision**.

Probation Investigation

Probation officers perform investigations focused on the offender. Investigations begin when the accused is introduced into the criminal justice system, and depending on each particular case, additional investigations occur over time. Information gathered on the offender is used throughout the process, and most important, it is used to prepare a **presentence report**. The presentence report is relied on heavily in sentencing hearings. The importance of a presentence report cannot be overstated, as it consumes about 25% of the workload of a probation officer and determines whether the offender will be granted probation and, if so, the conditions of the probationary period.[26] It is used to create an individualized community corrections sentence to address the needs of the offender and the community. While the judge makes the ultimate determination as to the exact sentencing conditions, the probation officer makes recommendations in the report that are followed by judges in the majority of cases.

While the precise content of the reports differs by jurisdiction, a great deal of information goes into the presentence report. In general, it contains contact information for the offender, information on the offense committed, the defendant's previous criminal record, defendant and family demographics (e.g., education, employment, substance abuse, mental health issues, finances), victim impact (including a victim statement), an evaluation, and probation officer recommendations. The evaluation portion of the report synthesizes earlier report materials regarding the nature of the crime, the needs of the defendant, and the safety and needs of the victim and the community. The evaluation informs the ultimate

arm of the court:
A phrase used to describe a probation officer who acts as the court's fact finder.

probation investigation:
The process of gathering information on offenders' lives and ties to the community, both positive and negative.

risk assessment:
A determination of offenders' propensity to harm themselves or others.

classification:
Determines the level of supervision appropriate for each offender based on probation investigation and risk assessment.

supervision: The duty of probation officers to watch over offenders on their caseloads.

presentence report:
An important aggregation of facts about the offender, usually prepared by the probation officer.

between 23% and 53% of probation officers (depending on their rank) were women. Some research indicates that female probation officers experience different levels of stress than their male counterparts. Wells, Colbert, and Slate (2006) concluded that female probation officers reported higher levels of physical stress, whereas male probation officers experienced higher internal, job, and personal stress. The authors concluded that although these differences were found, additional work is needed to ascertain if there are in fact *meaningful* differences.[29] Information on the first female probation officer in the United States is unavailable. Like many other topics associated with the field of correctional responses in the community, more research is warranted.

CHAPTER WRAP-UP

The information presented in this chapter offered an introduction to elements of correctional response in the community. This area is rapidly changing to better meet the needs of communities and offenders in an effective and safe manner. As the population remains enormous, and as the cost of incarceration (both financially and socially) increases, one should expect even greater growth and innovation in community corrections. Over time, the field should benefit from greater research attention, including evaluation studies to better identify community corrections that work and those that do not. In addition, with time, the public can become better educated about those programs that benefit them and those that do not.

Research indicates that roughly two thirds of persons sentenced to corrections in the community complete their sentence successfully. Findings show that, given net widening, some intermediate sanctions are characterized by higher recidivism rates. Whether this is a result of appropriate punishment or criminalizing benign behavior remains a matter of debate.

This chapter covered the basic and important responsibilities of probation officers: investigation, risk assessment and classification, and supervision. Probation officers often face a role conflict because of their requirements to act both as law enforcement officers and as social workers. Furthermore, the chapter discussed the growth in arming probation officers in response to more assaults suffered at the hands of their clients. How this arming of probation officers influences how they conduct their job continues to be an area of vigorous research.

CASE STUDY

Chris Farias's experience with his intermediate sanctions sentence was discussed in this chapter. He was sentenced not only to a very strict work-release program requiring that he spend time in the county jail, give up his driver's license, and attend alcohol treatment and cognitive therapy for his DUI. Like the majority of those serving intermediate sentences, Chris completed his sentence, although he did commit several technical violations along the way. He finds that the work he did during his sentence made a difference and means that he will not reoffend in the future.

Community corrections was not a part of Joshua Paul Benjamin's or Danny Madrid's case. Joshua served two prison sentences with no community corrections. Danny served 10 years prior to his release. Dennis Bradford committed suicide before community corrections was even a possibility.

In the following chapter, we cover life in prison and life following prison. Although the majority of those convicted of crime do not serve time in prison, it is important to consider this aspect of the criminal justice system.

KEY POINTS

- Corrections in the community are used for the majority of convicted offenders in the United States.

- Community corrections sentences are not necessarily easier than prison or jail sentences.

- The purpose of corrections in the community is to better address the needs of the offender, to minimize risk to the community, and to save resources.

- A community corrections sentence is tailored to the needs of the particular offender. Requirements or conditions of this sentence focus on dynamic risk predictors.

- Probation officers are expected to act as both social workers and law enforcement officers. They are involved in cases as they move through the criminal justice system and are responsible for investigation, risk assessment and classification, and supervision. Probation officers act with great discretion and report to the court.

- Net widening is a problem in community corrections that entails the increased severity of sentencing for traditionally minor offenses.

- Most offenders successfully complete their community sentences, although variation exists in type of sentence and other factors.

- Public policies established in response to crime and the criminal justice system influence every person's life. Evidence exists that policies may disproportionately affect the disadvantaged to a greater degree than others.

KEY TERMS

Arm of the Court 275

Automated Kiosk Reporting 274

Boot Camps 268

Classification 275

Correctional Responses in the Community 258

Dynamic Risk Predictors 276

Electronic Monitoring 268

Eye Scans 274

Fine 267

Forfeiture 267

General Conditions 269

GPS Monitoring 273

Home Confinement/ House Arrest 268

Intensive Supervised Probation 268

Intermediate Responses and Sanctions 267

Legal Violation 269

Net Widening 272

Presentence Report 275

Probation Fees 269

Probation Investigation 275

Problem-Solving Court 261

Punish 264

Radiofrequency Identification Devices (RFID) 273

Recidivism 264

Remote Alcohol Detection (RAD) 274

Residential Community Housing 269

Restorative Justice 265

Risk Assessment 275

Special Conditions 269

Split Sentence or Shock Probation 268

Static Risk Predictors 276

Supervision 275

Technical Violation 269

Work-Release Program 269

REVIEW QUESTIONS

1. Why do we need correctional responses in the community?

2. What are the goals and advantages of corrections in the community?

3. Who is John Augustus and why is he important?

4. What are the roles of the probation officer?

5. How successful are community corrections?

6. What is net widening and why is it important to consider?

CRITICAL THINKING MATTERS

1. **Send All Convicted Criminals to Prison or Jail?** The United States has an enormous criminal justice system, and the public demands that it be tough on crime. What are the advantages and disadvantages of incarcerating all convicted offenders? If you were a policymaker, for what criminal offenses, if any, would you make prison mandatory? For what criminal offenses would you make community corrections mandatory? Are there ethical considerations in terms of which crimes should or should not be eligible for community corrections? Should the cost of incarceration drive the use of community corrections? Should characteristics and the history of the offender inform the choice of community corrections?

2. **The Victim and Community Corrections.** Should the victim of a crime have a voice in whether the offender is sentenced to corrections in the community? What are the advantages and disadvantages of allowing the victim a say in this decision? Do community corrections pose a threat to specific victims? Do corrections in the community retraumatize the victim in any way? If so, how? What are options for cost-effectively sentencing convicted offenders while at the same time being sensitive to the needs of crime victims? What policies would you propose to balance these needs?

3. **Joshua Paul Benjamin After Prison.** Joshua Paul Benjamin served time in prison in two states for his crimes. When he was released, he did not serve parole and was a free man. Given his crimes against children, do you think he should have been assigned some community corrections, additional treatment, or other sanctions? Or had he paid his debt to society for his crimes? What are the advantages to more oversight of Joshua postrelease? What are disadvantages of applying intermediate sanctions to his case? Had he received a community corrections sentence postrelease, what do you think are the chances that he would have committed technical or legal violations?

4. **The Dual Role of a Probation Officer.** You are in charge of managing community corrections for the state. You are deeply troubled by the dual responsibilities of probation officers as both social worker and law enforcement agent. These roles, though equally important, come into conflict with each other. A subordinate suggests splitting the role and having two probation officers overseeing each probationer. One would take on the law enforcement role, checking to see if the offender commits a technical or criminal violation of his or her sentence. The other would take on the social work aspect, assisting the probationer with educational opportunities, employment assistance, and other needs. What are the advantages and disadvantages of this approach? As the leader of the community corrections division of your state, would you recommend implementing this style of overseeing community corrections? Why or why not?

5. **Net Widening—Good or Bad?** Following the establishment of many intermediate sanctions, people who would have otherwise been sentenced to traditional probation have been sentenced to harsher intermediate sanctions. This net widening has come at a greater cost to the offender, is associated with higher rates of recidivism, and is costlier to the public. Many view net widening as an unintended negative consequence of better oversight. Is it? Is net widening good for the betterment of society? If you were in charge, would you support a policy that prohibits

net widening? Or would you support the increased harshness of penalties although they are costlier to the community? What is the answer?

6. **Chris Farias—A Case of Net Widening?** Chris was sentenced for a DUI that did not involve a crash or an injury to anyone. It was only because he was driving his motorcycle slowly on a cold evening in his town that the officer pulled him over and arrested him for DUI.

Given the nature of his crime, do you think that Chris deserved his sentence of intermediate sanctions? Given the hardships it caused him, do you feel the sentence was overly punitive? Is his case representative of net widening? If so, how did Chris's sentence cost you, the taxpayer? What sentence do you feel is more appropriate for him, or do you feel the sentence was ideal?

DIGITAL RESOURCES

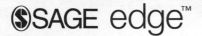

Sharpen your skills with SAGE edge at edge.sagepub.com/rennison2e. SAGE edge for Students provides a personalized approach to help you accomplish your coursework goals in an easy-to-use learning environment. You'll find action plans, mobile-friendly eFlashcards, and quizzes as well as video and web resources and links to SAGE journal articles to support and expand on the concepts presented in this chapter.

11 INSTITUTIONAL CORRECTIONS

"The treatment of criminals by society is for the protection of society. But since such treatment is directed to the criminal rather than to the crime, its great object should be his moral regeneration. Hence the supreme aim of prison discipline is the reformation of criminals, not the infliction of vindictive suffering."

—Declaration of Principles,
Congress of the National Prison Association (1870)

LEARNING OBJECTIVES

After finishing this chapter, you should be able to:

11.1 Summarize the history of institutional corrections.

11.2 Evaluate the current perspectives in institutional corrections.

11.3 Discuss the state of contemporary jails in the United States.

11.4 Differentiate how incarcerated women and minorities have been dealt with in the United States and how incarceration differs for male and female inmates and minorities.

11.5 Assess the differences in security levels in prisons and the institutions designed to deal with each.

11.6 Identify advances in technology in institutional corrections and the benefits technology offers.

INTRODUCTION: INSTITUTIONAL CORRECTIONS

Institutional corrections refers to facilities used to detain individuals in the criminal justice system. Many people are surprised to learn that being sentenced to an institutional correctional facility as a form of punishment was an idea developed in the United States only about 200 years ago. In early America, being detained in a jail or facility was not viewed as punishment in and of itself. Rather, jails served as holding pens for those waiting to go on trial, or those waiting to receive their **corporal punishment** sentences. Corporal punishment is physical punishment such as beating, whipping, caning, and the death penalty. In addition, jails served as holding pens used to coerce individuals to pay debts or fines and areas to detain people in an effort to accomplish religious proselytization. Unlike today's facilities, these holding pens confined all prisoners together regardless of sex, age, or the nature of the crimes (whether criminal, civil, or moral) for which they were being held. Jailhouses often were the sites of significant abuse of detainees by caretakers (who may or may not have been law enforcement agents) as well as filthy conditions and disease. While evidence shows a long history of the use of incarceration such as debtors' prison in Europe, the United States is credited with being the first country to use imprisonment as the *primary* means to punish and at times rehabilitate criminals.

Institutional corrections have changed in terms of purpose, philosophy, and structure of punishment.

In the past, offenders were punished via public floggings. We abandoned the use of flogging due to its barbaric nature. Some call for the reinstatement of this sort of punishment. If you were running for political office, would you advocate the use of flogging? Why or why not?

Even the way this aspect of the criminal justice system is referenced has changed. Initially, the term **penology** was used to describe the philosophy guiding how the nation punished criminal and immoral acts. This earlier period was marked by exposure of offenders to a variety of harsh and cruel corporal punishments. Public sentiment eventually turned against such cruelty, and the idea of reformation gained support. This change introduced the notion that criminals should be incarcerated as punishment for crimes they committed. Ultimately, reformation efforts were viewed as a failure as overcrowding hampered efforts and recidivism continued unchanged. Beginning in the early 1900s, emphasis turned back toward the use of harsher treatment to deal with inmates. When public opinion swung back away from increased punishment toward rehabilitation and reformation in the 1950s and 1960s, the term *corrections* was favored. This period focused on incarcerating offenders in hopes of rehabilitating them while at the same time punishing them for their criminal offenses. Since the 1980s, views about corrections have shifted back toward a get-tough-on-crime orientation, with some emphasis on rehabilitation, which reflects a new philosophy termed the **new penology**. New penology focuses on the use of correctional technology and reliance on statistical models to assess recidivism risk in a time of decreasing victimization and growth in incarceration. The discourse of institutional corrections now focuses more on management of warehoused humans and less on rehabilitation.

HISTORICAL PERSPECTIVES IN INSTITUTIONAL CORRECTIONS

The Brutal Early Years

From the earliest times in the American colonies, corrections was based on the philosophy of *lex talionis,* which calls for retaliation in which the punishment should fit the crime committed. This "eye for an eye" approach requires that someone who injures or wrongs another individual should be punished in a commensurate way. During these early years, punishment was cruel, barbaric, and often dispensed in a public setting to maximize public humiliation of the offender. Sentences included death, fines, physical punishment, and public shaming. **Hanging** was used as a penalty for the worst offenses, including sexual offenses. In 1642, 17-year-old Thomas Granger was convicted of buggery with a female horse, a cow, goats, sheep, calves, and a turkey. Having been found guilty, Granger was hanged. The victims of these crimes—the farm animals—were also executed for their participation in these acts. While hanging has been used in the United States for much of its history, in time, hangings stopped being public spectacles. In 1946, Rainey Bethea of Kentucky was the last offender to be publicly hanged, in this instance for having raped and murdered 70-year-old Lischa Edwards. Twenty thousand people traveled to Kentucky to witness this hanging. Hanging was the preferred method of capital punishment in the United States. The electric chair was developed as a more efficient method of execution. Capital punishment continued until the Supreme Court ruled it unconstitutional in 1972, resulting in a moratorium.[1] When capital punishment was reinstated by many states in 1976, offenders often were given limited options about how they met their demise. This was the case for William "Billy" Bailey of Delaware. When given a choice of lethal punishment, he refused to choose between hanging or lethal injection (he was given this choice because his crime was committed in 1979, prior to the 1986 law mandating execution by lethal injection only).

corporal punishment: Physical punishment in response to an offense designed to discipline and reform an offender.

penology: The study of principles of punishment for criminal (and in the past, immoral) acts.

new penology: The study of principles of punishment, often reflecting the contemporary turn toward the view that punishment is the primary role of prison.

hanging: A form of punishment used in the early days of the United States as a penalty for the worst offenses.

When an offender refused to choose the method of execution, the default sentence was hanging. Therefore, William "Billy" Bailey was hanged in January 1996, accounting for the last hanging of a criminal for an unlawful act in the United States.

Flogging was another form of punishment used against offenders in this nation until the middle of the 20th century. Floggings are serious beatings or whippings with a rod, whip, or cane that were generally conducted in public places. This painful punishment rarely resulted in the death of the offender. Flogging as a punishment continued until 1952, when the final state-sanctioned flogging occurred in the United States. **Mutilation** as punishment for criminal and moral offenses entailed the amputation of body parts to curtail a perpetrator's ability to reoffend. One form of mutilation was to sever the hand of a thief. Persons convicted of being spies would be blinded, while blasphemers would have their tongues removed. Those who nagged, slandered, or gossiped were sentenced to gagging while wearing a device that pinched the tongue, or they were required to wear the **gossip's bridle** or **scold's helm**. This heavy iron device covered the offender's head and included a flat tongue of iron (some with spikes) that was inserted into the offender's mouth over the tongue.

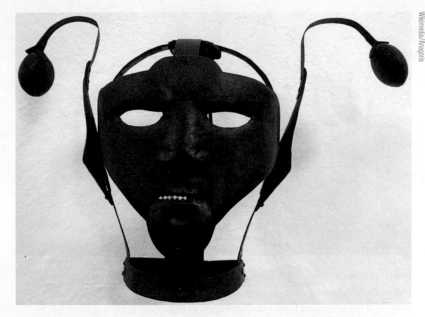

In the past, a scold's helm was used to punish gossips. Do you believe such an implement deterred people from gossiping? Why or why not?

Historically, offenders were frequently branded. **Branding** served many purposes. It punished an offender, provided a record of an individual's offenses, and warned members of the community of the specific potential danger the individual posed. In the American colonies, first-time offenders were generally branded on the hand, while repeat offenders were frequently branded on the forehead. Women were rarely physically branded but instead were forced to wear marked clothing. The letter branded or worn identified the offense committed. In colonial America burglary was punished by branding with a capital B on the right hand of the criminal for the first offense and on the left hand for the second offense. If the burglary occurred on a Sunday, the offender was branded on the forehead. A branded M indicated an individual who committed manslaughter, whereas a D identified a drunk. A branded T denoted a thief, an R was used to identify a rogue or a vagabond, and an F was used to indicate a forger.

The **stocks** and **pillory** were painful punishments primarily administered in conjunction with public humiliation. They were reserved for persons committing arson, witchcraft, perjury, wife beating, counterfeiting, cheating, forgery, fortune telling, and drunkenness. The pillory was a device that forced the offender into a standing position with hands, head, and ears commonly nailed to the pillory wood. The stocks operated similarly, although it restrained the offender into a seated position. While offenders were restrained in the stocks or pillory, members of the public would spit and throw a variety of things (including rocks and rotten produce) at them. The abuse of the public against the restrained offender was serious enough to lead to his or her death on occasion.

Moving Toward Humane Treatment: Penitentiaries

Early use of brutal and severe brandings, mutilations, and other punishments started being viewed as inhumane. Many argued that improvements to incarceration were needed, as harsh penalties failed to deter crime. In fact, there was evidence that in some cases, this

flogging: An early punishment that consisted of serious beatings or whippings.

mutilation: An early punishment that entailed the amputation of body parts to curtail a perpetrator's ability to reoffend.

gossip's bridle or scold's helm: A heavy iron device that covered an offender's head to punish and deter those who nagged, slandered, or gossiped.

branding: An early form of punishment that also served as a record to alert others of an individual's past offenses.

stocks: A painful punishment generally administered with public humiliation.

pillory: A painful punishment that forced the offender into a standing position with hands, head, and ears commonly nailed to the pillory wood.

Many approaches developed and used in in early prisons continue to be used today. Do you believe such approaches including isolation are valuable? Why or why not? Do you see a better way to imprison offenders knowing most will be returned to society eventually?

Video 11.1:
Inside Eastern State Penitentiary

penitentiary: A correctional facility used to imprison criminal offenders.

Pennsylvania System: A penitentiary system based on the guiding philosophy that isolation and silence are necessary for offender reflection, reformation, and rehabilitation. Also known as the separate system.

Auburn System: A style of incarceration based on reformation. Inmates were housed separately and not allowed to communicate. During the day inmates worked and ate in silence. Also known as the congregate system.

separate system: Another name for the Pennsylvania System, which reflects the lack of interpersonal interaction experienced by inmates.

barbaric system actually increased crime in perverse ways. Consider that offenses such as thievery and murder carried the same penalty—death—making it irrational to leave a witness when acting as a thief. It was during this period of reconsideration of punishment that the view of jails as actual punishment gained favor. Though viewed as punishment, jails and prisons offered more humane ways to deal with offenders than traditional brutal methods. Leading that charge was William Penn and the Quakers, who advocated for the abolishment of corporal punishment. Instead, Penn and the Quakers promoted humane imprisonment with a focus on rehabilitation of the offender. This change in philosophy started major changes in the early penal system, resulting in the **penitentiary**. Imprisonment as punishment for a criminal act began in the 1790s in the United States. Two approaches emerged that embodied Penn's philosophy of confinement for criminals: the **Pennsylvania System** and the **Auburn System**. While both penitentiary systems were based on the use of incarceration as punishment with the goal of reformation, each did so using distinctive approaches.

Pennsylvania System

The Walnut Street Jail in Philadelphia is credited with being the first public institution to use imprisonment as the primary means of punishing and reforming criminals. It served as a traditional holding facility from when it opened in 1773 until it was converted to a prison in 1790. Given the conversion, Walnut Street Jail is viewed by many as the first prison in the United States. The guiding philosophy—dubbed the Pennsylvania System—of the Walnut Street Jail was that isolation and silence were necessary for offenders' reflection, reformation, and rehabilitation. By being incarcerated in small, solitary cells, prisoners could reflect on their wrongdoings and be penitent (i.e., feel or show remorse and regret for crimes). It is from this philosophy that the word *penitentiary* emerged.

Later, a new Pennsylvania facility, the Eastern State Penitentiary in Philadelphia, was constructed to handle an increasing number of inmates. Like the Walnut Street facility, the Eastern State Penitentiary operated under the Pennsylvania System. Inmates ate, slept, worked, and studied the Bible in solitary silence. Inmates were not allowed to communicate with or see other inmates, they could have no visitors, and they had no access to information from news sources. In this system, offenders were blindfolded when moved through the facility. Given the lack of interpersonal interaction, this system is also known as the **separate system**. The architecture of the penitentiaries built under the separate system reflects its underlying philosophy. These prisons were built in a hub-and-spoke style. The center point, the hub, was octagonal with seven spokes radiating from it. Along each spoke or corridor were cells, 8 by 12 feet wide and 10 feet tall, with basic amenities. These cells were relatively large and facilitated the isolation needed for reformation and penitence. The design of the cells was important because inmates served their entire sentences in these solitary rooms. Each cell had a peephole so correctional officers could see prisoners, but prisoners could not see officers. As more and more individuals were sentenced to the penitentiary, it became difficult to maintain the necessary isolation, silence, and discipline required. It was only when overcrowding became an issue that problems with the Pennsylvania System appeared.

Auburn System

During the same period, the Auburn System emerged in New York. Like the Pennsylvania System, it was based on the notion of reformation. And like the Pennsylvania System, it housed inmates separately and did not allow any communication among them, verbal or otherwise. Auburn inmates were confined separately at night, but during the day they congregated in silence for work and meals. For this reason, this system is also known as the **congregate system**. Auburn inmates wore red and gray striped suits and walked in lockstep (a practice that continues in some prisons today). In contrast to the Pennsylvania System, work by inmates was a critical element in the Auburn System. Inmates silently worked and produced goods for private sector entities. The architecture of the Auburn System reflected the congregate philosophy. Cells were a mere 3.5 by 7.5 feet wide and 7 feet tall. Small cells facilitated the needed isolation of inmates as they reflected on their crimes during the evenings. Cells were arranged in two rows, stacked five tiers high, with the backs of cells adjoined. Prisoners in the Auburn System were used to build the infamous Rikers Island, which continues to serve as New York City's primary jail complex today. The Auburn System was the first prison to earn money from convict labor. Unlike the Pennsylvania System, the Auburn System used severe corporal punishment to maintain discipline. While the punishment used was slightly less cruel than the harshness that marked punishment in the previous era, routine rawhide whippings of inmates were common. The Auburn System functioned until overcrowding made it difficult for correctional officers to maintain discipline over the prisoners.

Contract and Convict Leasing Systems

Inmate labor was widespread, although not all prisons used it. Two systems of inmate labor dominated: the **contract system** and the **convict leasing system**. In both systems, convicts worked to develop skills and appropriate work habits as a means toward reformation. In both systems, monies gained from convict labor helped fund the facilities. Finally, in both systems, forced labor did not enrich the inmates. Differences between the two systems focused on supervision of the inmates and payment for their labor. In the contract system, prison officials sold inmate labor and services to private contractors for a fixed price per inmate per day; the inmates remained incarcerated and were supervised either by prison officials or by private sector officials at the prison. In contrast, under the convict leasing system, which was more widely used in the South, private businesses paid the state a fixed annual fee for control of inmates. When leased, the state forfeited supervision and control of the inmates. This lack of oversight and accountability led to abuses of these prisoners by their private sector "owners." The convict leasing system was especially prevalent following the emancipation of slaves as a result of the 1865 passage of the Thirteenth Amendment of the U.S. Constitution:

> Section 1. Neither slavery nor involuntary servitude, except as a punishment for crime whereof the party shall have been duly convicted, shall exist within the United States, or any place subject to their jurisdiction.

> Section 2. Congress shall have power to enforce this article by appropriate legislation.

The Abolition of Slavery and Black Codes

While the Thirteenth Amendment abolished slavery, an exception in this amendment was that persons convicted of crimes in the United States could be incarcerated. In the South, the lives of ex-slaves were criminalized by statutes following the Thirteenth Amendment that provided inexpensive labor for the convict leasing system.[2] These statutes, known as the **Black Codes**, differed by state. Some requirements included that black people contract with white farmers by the first day of the year or face charges of vagrancy and ultimately incarceration. Also criminalized was the use of obscene language, petty theft, and selling cotton after sunset by black persons only.

congregate system: Another name for the Auburn System, which reflects the silent congregation experienced by inmates during the day.

contract system: Penitentiary system in which prison officials sold the labor and services of inmates to private contractors for a fixed price per inmate per day.

convict leasing system: A system whereby private businesses paid the state a fixed annual fee for control of inmates.

Black Codes: Statutes that criminalized trivial behavior, such as obscene language, of newly freed slaves.

A Black Lives Matter protester peacefully protests in Ferguson. Do you believe peaceful protests like this are effective? Why or why not?

As a result of the criminalization of the lives of African Americans, there was a massive increase in the inmate population by black convicts in the South. Once convicted of these and other Black Code crimes, former slaves turned convicts were sold to farms, factories, mines, and other locations as laborers. Shelden estimated that from 1855 to 1867, the percentage of black inmates grew from 33% to 58%.[3] In Georgia, the prison population, which was dominated by black inmates, grew 10-fold from 1868 to 1908, and in North Carolina, the prison population grew more than 15-fold from 1870 to 1890.[4] Similar explosive growth in the number of black prison inmates was experienced in other southern states, offering substantial inexpensive convict labor.

The abolition of slavery in conjunction with convict leasing led to the same slave-type lives for many African Americans: one of forced servitude at the enrichment of others.[5] Convict leasing was lucrative to states and prisons and caused inhumane treatment of inmates, including death at the hands of whipping bosses. Convict leasing of inmates fell out of use in the South in the early 1900s: Texas stopped in 1910, Georgia halted its use in 1908, and Alabama ended this system in 1928. Some evidence suggests that convict leasing never ended, as the modern-day war on drugs, in conjunction with privatization of prisons, is nothing more than a contemporary convict leasing scheme.

The Reformation Movement

With problems of overcrowding in both Auburn- and Pennsylvania-style penitentiaries, a more humane approach to incarceration gained favor. The resulting **reformation movement** commenced at about the same period that slavery was abolished by the Thirteenth Amendment. During the 1870 meeting of the National Prison Association (renamed the American Correctional Association in 1954), a 37-paragraph **Declaration of Principles** was adopted that called for institutions focused on reformation and rejected the view that punishment was the definitive goal of imprisonment. This perspective is described in the quotation that opened this chapter, which calls for the moral regeneration and reformation of criminals in lieu of cruel suffering. The philosophy of reformation was largely captured in the 1924 words of Osborne[6]:

reformation movement: A movement born during the 1870 meeting of the National Prison Association, which called for institutions focused on reformation.

Declaration of Principles: A 37-paragraph document adopted at the 1870 meeting of the National Prison Association that called for institutions focused on reformation and rejected the notion that punishment was the ultimate goal of imprisonment.

1. Prisoners are human beings; for the most part remarkably like the rest of us.

2. They can be clubbed into submission—with occasional outbreaks; but they cannot be reformed by that process.

3. Neither can they be reformed by bribery in the shape of privileges.

4. They will not respond to sentimentality; they do not like gush.

5. They appreciate a "square deal"—when they get one.

6. There are not many of them mental defectives; on the contrary, the majority are embarrassingly clever.

7. All of these facts must be taken into consideration, if we want prisons which will protect society. Unless they are taken into consideration, our correctional institutions will continue to be what they have been in the past—costly schools of crime—monuments of wasted effort, of misguided service.

CONTEMPLATING CAREERS

Correctional Officer

Do you enjoy interacting with others? Are you able to effectively communicate orally and in writing? Can you be assertive yet diplomatic? Do you possess excellent grammar, spelling, and punctuation? Do you carry yourself with a sense of professionalism and discipline? Is moral integrity important to you? If these characteristics describe you, then a career as a correctional officer is one you might consider.

Correctional officers are charged with managing inmates in a jail, reformatory, prison, or penitentiary. In addition, correctional officers are charged with managing detained (but not convicted) persons waiting for or engaged in a trial. They interact with those confined, colleagues, those in the legal system, and visitors to the jail. Correctional officers also guard prisoners who are in transit between jails, courtrooms, prisons, or other locations. According to the Bureau of Labor Statistics, the 2015 median pay for a correctional officer was $40,530, or a median hourly wage of $19.49.[7] As in much of the criminal justice system, qualifications required for becoming a correctional officer vary. At a minimum, all jurisdictions require a high school diploma,

and attending a special training academy is routine. Demand for correctional officers differs by state. The Bureau of Labor Statistics identifies Texas, California, Florida, New York, and Georgia as the states with the highest employment levels in the nation in 2015.[8]

The environment in which correctional officers conduct their work can be difficult and dangerous, as this profession is characterized by one of the highest rates of on-the-job injuries. Correctional officers are responsible for enforcing rules, keeping order, supervising inmate activities, inspecting facilities, searching for contraband, and reporting on inmate conduct. Fitness requirements vary among agencies, although correctional officers need to be physically and psychologically fit. Correctional officers often report stress over role problems, work overload, demanding social contacts, and poor social status, although professionalization and better human resources are being used to reduce job stress and burnout.

 Career Video: A detentions division chief discusses her experience and current issues in the field.

Enoch Wines and Zebulon Brockway championed the Declaration of Principles. The new reformative approach was focused on younger, less serious criminals and used military regimentation as well as a focus on religion, work, academic achievement, and vocational training. The principles called for the rejection of determinate sentencing, the implementation of indeterminate sentencing, and the implementation of rewards for good behavior, positive deeds, and reformation by the offender. This philosophy recognized that indeterminate sentencing encourages good behavior through inmate incentives (e.g., early release) and provides correctional officers with greater control.

Elmira Reformatory

Elmira Reformatory is credited with many firsts. It was the first correctional institution operating under the 1870 Declaration of Principles. Zebulon Brockway served as its first warden when it opened in New York in 1876. Elmira focused on improving its inmates' skills, provided extracurricular activities (e.g., a prison band), and was first to pioneer the U.S. prototype of presenting forms of parole. The reformatory was designed to detain first-time male felony offenders between the ages of 16 and 30. Elmira's first inmates arrived from the established Auburn Prison.

Implementing the full philosophy of the Declaration of Principles was challenging, and Brockway eventually incorporated the use of corporal punishment. His free use of corporal punishment eventually earned him the nickname "Paddler Brockway." Some evidence shows that Brockway's use of the paddle was severe enough to send some inmates to mental asylums. While Elmira improved the day-to-day lives of most inmates, it did not improve recidivism rates.

correctional officers: People charged with managing inmates who are incarcerated in a jail, reformatory, prison, or penitentiary.

Contemporary all-female DUI chain gang in Arizona. Do you believe serving on a chain gang would deter DUIs in the future? Why or why not? What sort of treatment of those who drive drunk would be most effective to deter future DUIs? How about gang violence or other types of violence?

Historical Attention to Female Inmates

The reformation period improved the lives of inmates, including much-needed dedicated attention to female inmates. Prior to the reformation movement, there had been little (if any) effort to provide humane facilities for female inmates apart from male prisoners. When female inmates had been segregated from male inmates, it meant that they were kept in poorer conditions, where they were subjected to cruel treatment, including rampant rape and other sexual assault. Pregnancy as a result of this victimization during incarceration was common. While the treatment of white women was appalling, the treatment of black women was even worse. While white female inmates were routinely sexually victimized by prison officials and guards, the cells confining black female inmates were often intentionally left open so male prisoners *and* prison officials could gain access to sexually victimize these women freely. The Declaration of Principles called for separate establishments for women and, in doing so, not only improved conditions of incarcerated females but also feminized corrections.[9] The call for this separation is found in Principle XIX of the 1870 Declaration of Principles:

> Prisons, as well as prisoners, should be classified or graded so that there shall be prisons for the untried, for the incorrigible and for other degrees of depraved character, as well as separate establishments for women, and for criminals of the younger class.

Indiana Women's Reformatory was the first independently operating, all-female, maximum-security correctional facility managed using the Declaration of Principles. This reformatory, which opened in 1873 near Indianapolis, shared no staff or operations with a male prison, making it the first all-female, separate institution in the United States. Sarah Smith, an advocate calling for the end of sexual violence against women, served as the reformatory's first superintendent. In this role, Smith also became the first female superintendent of *any* prison in the United States. Fully implementing the principles outlined in the Declaration was challenging because finding willing and competent female staff for the reformatory proved difficult. Female staff members, known as **matrons**, were subjected to high demands in difficult circumstances with low pay. Given the lack of matrons, more traditional means of supervising female inmates, such as corporal punishment, were used. Like other reformatories, work was emphasized and female inmates were expected to develop useful skills to minimize recidivism upon release. These tasks included doing laundry, sewing, dealing with livestock, painting, and working on renovation projects.

By the early 1900s, most were disillusioned with the reformation movement. While reformation did much for improving the treatment of inmates and the conditions in which inmates—especially female inmates—were detained, little evidence of reformation among inmates emerged. After being released, inmates frequently reoffended. Public support grew for greater discipline, control, and punishment of inmates. The populace believed that criminals owed a debt to society and clamored for retributive incarceration. Reformatories continued to function, but they adopted more punitive policies as America's appetite for more discipline, punishment, and control was implemented.

Return to the Punitive Approach

matrons: Correctional officers in a women's prison or reformatory.

Since the end of the reformation period, a diversity of philosophies in incarceration has been adopted (and abandoned) in institutions across that nation. Some facilities used

POLICY ISSUES

Punishment Versus Rehabilitation

A historical examination of the purposes of prison indicates periods of severe punishment and harsh treatment as well as times when great efforts toward rehabilitation and reformation were made. Considering only recidivism rates, it appears neither approach results in a large percentage of inmates who live crime-free lives postincarceration.

Think About It

1. Given this information and the knowledge learned from this text, if you were a policymaker, which type of approach would you prefer and why?

2. We know that housing an ever increasing population of inmates is costly to taxpayers at the expense of other social programs such as education and transportation. What would you recommend to remedy this problem?

3. How could you save money for taxpayers without jeopardizing their safety?

4. Why would attempts made in the past work today?

5. Are there really only two approaches (punishment or reformation)? Or is there another novel approach you'd take? How might your new approach be better?

harsh corporal punishment, required convict uniforms (e.g., stripes), and even enforced codes of silence. Other facilities offered more options in terms of rehabilitation and reform, such as opportunities for education, work, and socializing. During the mid-1930s, some of the harshest conditions in correctional facilities were again abandoned, and while institutional corrections were still severe, they were greatly improved from pre-reformation times. Nonetheless, it has been recognized that rehabilitation or reformation of inmates is a failure if the measure of success is recidivism. Many of these inmates reoffend upon release. Furthermore, it is equally clear that merely warehousing inmates with a focus on punishment brings its own set of thorny issues. Widespread warehousing of inmates is expensive and has social ramifications that are detrimental to the inmates and the community. In addition, many of these inmates also reoffend upon release. Regardless of the specific approach used, in their 200-year history, correctional institutions have served as little more than facilities used to warehouse dangerous individuals with varying degrees of reformation opportunities.

CURRENT PERSPECTIVES IN INSTITUTIONAL CORRECTIONS

Just Deserts

Since about the 1980s, institutional corrections has been guided by the sentencing principle of **just deserts**, which focuses on proportionality vis-à-vis the crime and the ensuing punishment. Recall that in Chapter 9, proportionality was introduced as a sentencing concept in which the severity of sentencing should correspond to the severity of the crime committed. This perspective is evident, as today inmates have limited privileges and conditions are harsh, including the use of chain gangs, even for nonviolent offenders. Striped prison uniforms have reemerged and determinate, longer, and harsher sentencing is common. Parole has been abolished in almost half of the states and at the federal level. These and other get-tough initiatives have resulted in the growth in the population of inmates, little rehabilitation of those incarcerated, and crushing expense to the taxpayer.

just deserts:
Sentencing perspective that has dominated the purpose of incarceration since about the 1980s. It is focused foremost on proportionality vis-à-vis the crime and the ensuing punishment.

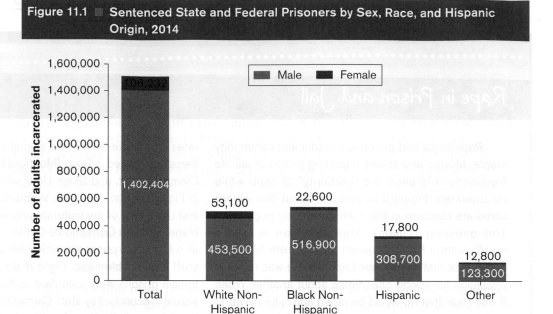

Figure 11.1 ■ Sentenced State and Federal Prisoners by Sex, Race, and Hispanic Origin, 2014

Men are far more likely to be imprisoned than are women. Why? Are they more violent? Are they simply more likely to be arrested and found guilty? What theory do you have about this huge discrepancy?

Source: Carson, E. A. (2015). *Prisoners in 2014*, September, 2014. Washington, DC: U.S. Department of Justice, Bureau of Justice Statistics. Retrieved from http://www.bjs.gov/content/pub/pdf/p14.pdf.

CASE STUDY

Case Study Video 11.1:
Interviews with case study participants

Being held prior to being tried for a crime is what placed Dennis Bradford, the individual who kidnapped, raped, and cut the throat of 8-year-old Jennifer Schuett in 1990, in jail. In 2008, Detective Tim Cromie and Federal Bureau of Investigation (FBI) agent Richard Rennison gathered evidence from this cold case. Using more contemporary technology, they retested the 20-year-old evidence for DNA. The outcome of the test linked Bradford to the Schuett case via the Combined DNA Index System (commonly known as CODIS).

Chris Farias was confined to a local county jail for little more than a year while on work release following his DUI. While in jail, he was kept in his cell, which he shared with another individual. Privileges were few, although socializing was not forbidden. Chris was fortunate enough to be housed in a location that offered this intermediate sanction privilege instead of strict lockup. Because of it, he could continue to run his business, although that was difficult. As a contractor, his lack of response frustrated his customers. What these customers did not recognize was that Chris frequently had no choice, as he was locked up without access to cell phones, computers, or other means to conduct work.

Jail Population

Author Video:
Women in jail

At the end of June 2014, 744,600 people were confined in city or county jails, a number that corresponds to a rate of 234 persons per 100,000 in the population.[11] The number of people held in jails had decreased slightly since 2007, when 780,174 people were held.[12]

When compared with 2000, when 621,149 were confined, the number and rate of inmates confined in local jails were up (a rate of 220 per 100,000). While jails housed about three quarters of a million people by midyear 2014, they had admitted approximately 11.4 million individuals during the 12-month period ending in June 2014.[13] These data reflect no statistical change since 2011, when about 11.8 million were admitted, but it is a decrease from the 13.6 million admitted in 2008. About 63% of people confined to county or city jails were not convicted of crimes; instead, these people were waiting for court activity on criminal charges.[14]

Audio:
Rikers Island jail population

Danny Madrid was incarcerated at both a local jail and a state prison as a result of his participation in the shooting of a rival gang member. Although he was a juvenile when he participated in the gang shooting, the judge noted that Danny was on "a dangerous path," and was "too dangerous and sophisticated" to be around other youth his age. The judge sent his case to adult criminal court. This meant that at the age of 16, Danny was transferred from the juvenile hall to the Los Angeles County Jail, where he spent the next 10 months. In the Los Angeles jail, he was one of approximately 15 other juveniles who were facing life sentences for gang-related crimes.

In the Los Angeles County Jail, Danny and the other juveniles were housed apart from the adult population. This segregated housing did not mean that they were always kept away from the adults, however. Whenever Danny and the others would go to the recreation yard, visiting room, or other areas, they would have to walk through the general population. In his words, Danny noted that the adult prisoners, although separated by metal bars, would get a kick out of him and the other juveniles and would whistle (in a sexually harassing way) and otherwise try to intimidate them. Also, whenever the inmates had court appearances, Danny and the other juveniles would have to ride on the same county bus as the adults, although as a juvenile, he was placed in a secure cage during the ride. This may have protected the juveniles physically (to some degree), but adults and juveniles could openly communicate. Although the sheriff's deputies were present during all of this mingling of adult and juvenile inmates, Danny acknowledges that these experiences were frightening. One thing that made his stay at the county jail better was that several adult members of his gang were in the same facility, which facilitated his reputation as a tough kid.

Women and Jail

Like prisons, jails are dominated by male inmates. According to BJS, at least 85% of the jail population since 2000 has consisted of men.[15] At midyear 2014, 109,100 women were held in city or county jails, a number that corresponds to 15% of the total jail population (Figure 11.2).[16] The proportion of women held in city and county jails grew about 1.6% each year between 2005 and 2014.[17] In contrast, the percentage of males held in jail has decreased by about 0.31% annually from 2005 to 2014.[18]

Race and Hispanic Origin in Jails

By now, it should come as no surprise to learn that a disproportionate number of African Americans are held in city and county jails compared with their presence in the general population. At midyear 2014, 47% of those confined to county or city jails were non-Hispanic white.[19] More than one third of those held in jails (35%) were black, and 15% were Hispanic (Figure 11.3).[20]

Video 11.2:
Prison culture

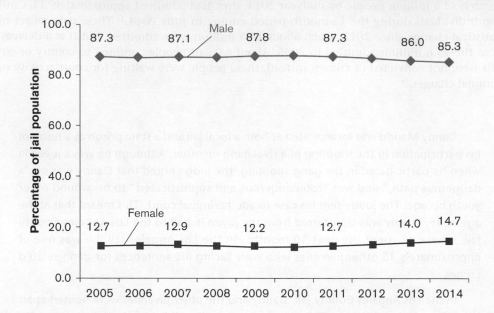

Figure 11.2 ■ Percentage of Jail Population by Gender, 2005–2014

Jails, like prisons, are dominated by men. How might the relatively fewer female jail inmates affect the facilities they are kept in? It means that there are likely fewer facilities, but does it mean that they are worse facilities? Are there likely to be fewer programs available for them? Are they more expensive to run as a result?

The gender disparity in jails has been in place for many years. Do you foresee this changing? Why or why not?

Source: Minton, T. D., & Zeng, Z. (2015). Jail inmates at midyear 2014. (NCJ 248629). Washington, DC: U.S. Department of Justice, Bureau of Justice Statistics.

Jail cells can be sparse and uncomfortable. Considering that a large proportion of those housed in jails have not been convicted of any crime, is this reasonable? Is it reasonable for those who have been convicted of a crime? Why or why not?

The percentage of non-Hispanic white individuals held in jail has increased over time. In 2005, 44% of individuals confined to jail were non-Hispanic white.[21] This percentage fell to 43% by 2008 and then increased to 47% by 2014.[22] In contrast, the percentage of black individuals held in city or county jails was stable from 2005 to 2009 (approximately 39%) and has since slowly decreased. At midyear 2014, 35% of persons in jail were black.[23] A similar pattern emerged for Hispanics/Latinos. In 2005, it was estimated that 15% of those held in jail were Hispanic/Latino. This percentage slowly increased to a high of 16% for 2006 through 2010.[24] Then the percentage of Hispanics held in jail fell to an estimated 15% in 2014.[25] The percentage of American Indians/Alaska Natives held in jail has remained low and stable over time. In 2005, 2014, and the intervening years, 1% of jail inmates were Asian. Similar estimates are found when considering Asians in local jails. From 2005 to 2014, slightly fewer than 1% of jail inmates were identified as Asian.[26]

Figure 11.3 ■ Percentage of Jail Population by Race and Hispanic Origin, 2005–2014

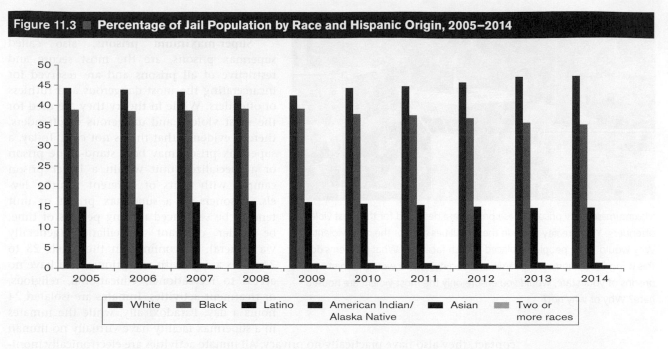

Legend: ■ White ■ Black ■ Latino ■ American Indian/Alaska Native ■ Asian ■ Two or more races

Unlike in prisons, a larger percentage of white men are found in jail than other racial and Hispanic-origin groups. Why does the distribution by race or Hispanic origin found in jail not translate to prison?

Over time, the percentage of white inmates found in jails has increased some. Why might that be? What policies might that be tied to? As a policymaker, what changes, if any, would you oversee to address this?

Source: Minton and Zeng, *Jail Inmates at Midyear 2014.*

CONTEMPORARY PRISONS

Prisons today are used to incapacitate offenders who have been sentenced to 1 year or more for felony offenses. Once an offender has been sentenced, an initial **classification review** of the offender is conducted to identify his or her risk level and needs based on information such as the offender's danger, escape risk, length of sentence, gang affiliation, mental or physical health needs, and treatment needs. Using this information, a determination of the most appropriate level of security and type of facility needed to detain the convict is made. Security levels used to describe incarceration facilities differ among states and the federal government. The federal system uses the following five-level security system, from highest to lowest security:

- administrative maximum (ADMAX), referred to as a penitentiary
- high security, referred to as a penitentiary
- medium security, referred to as a federal correctional institution (FCI)
- low security, referred to as an FCI
- minimum security, referred to as a federal prison camp

Institutional Corrections Security Levels

States use a variety of categorizations to describe prison security levels as well, but identifying one scheme that accurately describes security levels in all states is not possible. Nonetheless, the use of these security levels is found across most states: super-maximum, maximum-security, medium-security, and minimum-security prisons.

classification review:
An assessment made to determine an offender's risk level and needs.

Federal Bureau of Prisons

Maximum-security prison. These prisons are designed for the most violent offenders. Yet in reality many in these facilities are not the most violent. Why would these people be placed in such facilities? What problems does this bring for the inmates, guards, and society? If you were the chief of prisons of your state, would you ensure only the most violent are housed here? Why or why not?

Video 11.3:
Life in a supermax prison

Super-Maximum Prisons

Super-maximum prisons, also called supermax prisons, are the most secure and restrictive of all prisons and are reserved for incarcerating the most dangerous and ruthless of offenders. While in theory they are used for the most violent and dangerous of offenders, there is evidence that this is not case. Today, a supermax prison may be a stand-alone prison or a specialized unit within a larger prison campus with units of different security levels. Prisoners in a supermax prison or unit tend to be sentenced to long periods of time, be under constant surveillance (generally via camera), be confined in their cells 23 to 24 hours a day (with exceptions), and have no access to recreational, educational, religious, or treatment activities. Inmates are isolated 24 hours a day. Paradoxically, while the inmates in a supermax facility have virtually no human contact, they also have practically no privacy. All inmate activities are electronically monitored. Inmates eat in their cells after their food is slid through a "chuck hole" or "bean slot" on the door. These facilities are basic, and some argue that they violate the constitutional guarantee against cruel and unusual punishment.

In 2013, an estimated 25,000 prisoners were held in long-term solitary confinement in supermax prisons. The average stay in solitary confinement is almost 3 years. The supermax facility at the Pelican Bay prison has housed inmates in solitary for as long as 20 years. The majority of states use solitary confinement to promote staff and inmate safety, though it remains questionable if the practice reduces prison violence. In July 2013, more than 30,000 California prisoners staged a hunger strike to protest the use of solitary confinement.[27] Some describe the conditions in a super-maximum prison solitary unit as inhumane and torture.

Currently there is only one federally operated supermax (aka ADMAX) prison. This facility opened in 1994 in Florence, Colorado. Known as ADX or "Alcatraz of the Rockies," it houses more than 400 male inmates. As per Federal Bureau of Prisons policy, ADX should not house the seriously mentally ill, though some argue that this is simply not the case. Undoubtedly, living conditions at ADX are difficult, and the inmates live in extreme isolation. Inmates are locked in their cells alone 23 hours a day. When they are released from their cells for 5 hours of recreation each week (again, solitary), they are escorted by at least three officers. The facility is designed to prevent inmates from knowing where exactly they are located (to prevent escape). Communication with the outside world is not allowed. Force feedings have occurred. When an inmate misbehaves, he is place in the "Z-unit," otherwise known as the "black hole." This area can house up to 148 inmates in completely dark and fully soundproofed cells. Each black hole cell also has a full set of body restraints built into the concrete bed. Five plaintiffs (and six interested parties) housed in the Florence special housing unit (i.e., solitary confinement) filed a federal class action suit in 2012 against the Federal Bureau of Prisons and officials (*Bacote v. Federal Bureau of Prisons*, later renamed *Cunningham v. Federal Bureau of Prisons*) alleging "chronic abuse, failure to properly diagnose and neglect of prisoners who are seriously mentally ill."[28] As of early 2015, settlement negotiations were under way. ADX has housed notorious criminals, including Theodore Kaczynski (the Unabomber), Dzhokhar Tsarnaev (one of the two Boston Marathon bombers), John Walker Lindh (the American Taliban), Robert Hanssen (an FBI special agent turned Soviet spy), Zacarias Moussaoui (a conspirator in the 9/11 attacks), Eric Rudolph (the Olympic Park bomber), and Timothy McVeigh and Terry Nichols (the Oklahoma City bombers).

super-maximum prisons: The most secure and restrictive of all prisons, which are (in theory) reserved for the most dangerous of offenders.

Maximum-Security Prisons

Maximum-security prisons are the most secure facilities available in many states. Prisoners held in maximum security are generally sentenced to long sentences (i.e., 25 or more years) and are violent, disruptive offenders. Most inmates incarcerated in maximum-security facilities have committed violent crimes such as murder, rape, child abuse, and human trafficking. Alcatraz may be the most widely known maximum-security facility. Before it closed in 1963, Alcatraz housed criminals such as Al Capone, James "Whitey" Bulger, and Robert Franklin Stroud (otherwise known as the Birdman of Alcatraz). Inmates are housed in cells of their own where they spend 23 hours a day. Movement outside of the cells is made possible with remote-controlled sliding doors. Once outside of their cells, further movement by inmates is restricted by numerous checkpoints and gates. The exterior of these prisons also restrict movement, using large walls, razor wire, electrified fencing, motion detectors, and armed guards.

Medium-Security Prisons

Medium-security prisons are the next lower level of security. These facilities house inmates who have committed less serious crimes, such as theft and assault. Prisoners are generally housed in cage-like cells and allowed greater interpersonal interactions among inmates. While incarcerated, inmates may have access to work and treatment programs. Supervision in medium-security prisons is conducted using a lower officer-to-inmate ratio than found in higher security prisons. These prisons are frequently surrounded by double fencing, patrolled on a regular basis, and further protected using electronic detection equipment. Leavenworth, Kansas, is home to a medium-security federal prison for men. The facility in Leavenworth had previously been a maximum-security facility but was downgraded in 2005. Leavenworth has housed many offenders, including Phillip Garrido (who kidnapped Jaycee Dugard and held her for 18 years), James Earl Ray (who after his release for forgery assassinated Martin Luther King Jr.), and Michael Vick (a former National Football League quarterback who operated an interstate dogfighting enterprise).

maximum-security prisons: The most secure facilities available in many states. Most inmates incarcerated in maximum-security facilities have committed violent crimes such as murder, rape, child abuse, and human trafficking.

medium-security prisons: These facilities house inmates who have committed less serious crimes, such as theft and assault.

CASE STUDY

Facilities can differ greatly. An example of this is found in Joshua Paul Benjamin's case. Because he committed his crimes in two states, he was incarcerated in both states in a variety of facilities. In the first state, he first spent a year and a half in a classification center, which housed offenders who are considered a risk in a general prison. This includes child offenders, offenders under age 18, former police officers, and the disabled. After classification, Joshua was sent to a medium-security prison, where he spent 6 years. This particular medium-security institution used dormitory-style rooms housing four men in each cell. Indoors there was a library, a couple of TV areas, and many tables where inmates played dominos and cards. There was also an outdoor area where inmates could play basketball, pickleball, and other games. While incarcerated, Joshua was able to participate in sex offender treatment programs. He described this facility as a day camp surrounded by fences and razor wire.

In contrast, Danny Madrid found himself in adult prison after transferring from the Youth Training School (YTS) where he was housed following an initial 10-month stay in the Los Angeles County Jail. He was ultimately incarcerated at the Chino California Institute for Men. The reason for his transfer was assaulting a correctional officer at the YTS (Danny was sent to solitary confinement for 8 months for this action). After a year in the Chino prison, Danny spent additional time in solitary for participating in a race riot (6 months in solitary). Chino has experienced a number of race riots in its history. It was in this facility that Danny served the remainder of his sentence.

Following his incarceration at the medium-security facility, Joshua was paroled to the second state to a classification center. From there he was sent to a third facility where he was housed in a private prison for a short period. In Joshua's words, the private prison was truly pathetic, as they had 24 men in dorms with virtually no recreational activities and with incompetent staff: "I recall sending in a complaint that I wasn't getting my medicine and after five days I got the response back 'If you want your medicine, you should come to pill line.' Lost in the translation was that my complaint had been that I had been going to pill line and not getting my medicine, but given that the people who worked there were poorly educated and saw us as little more than a paycheck, it didn't do much good. I consider that to be among the most trying times for me in prison."

After 100 days there, Joshua was sent to a fourth state to be housed in what is considered a "higher medium-security" prison, which he found far more dangerous. This facility was set up like a penitentiary with two-man cells that contained a shared metal toilet. This facility purposely racially segregated cells (housing black inmates together and white inmates together) because of racial tensions in the prison. Joshua engaged in fewer self-improvement activities while housed here given the prevalent gang activity, white supremacists, and punks (weaker inmates who are sexually preyed upon) and their daddies (older men would assign younger inmates to be their punks). Joshua was assigned to the education department to be a tutor. It was here that he became a punk and was raped repeatedly.

Minimum-Security Prisons

Minimum-security prisons house mainly nonviolent white-collar criminals who are thought to pose little or no physical risk to members in the community. Housing in minimum-security settings is in the form of dormitories with communal bathrooms, which are regularly patrolled by correctional officers. The perimeter of a minimum-security facility may or may not have a fence, which may or may not be patrolled. Inmates frequently engage in community projects (e.g., litter cleanup) and supply labor to facilitate the operation of the prison.

When we think of prisons, we generally do not think of cybercriminals—a form of white-collar criminal. The majority of cybercrime is not reported to the police, yet prosecutors across the country frequently litigate these crimes, and offenders are convicted. Recent research indicates that cybercriminals, female offenders, and older offenders are more likely to receive harsher sentences.[29] Most frequently prosecuted are credit card fraud, identity theft, and other forms of crime involving financial losses. About half (52%) of those convicted of cybercrime received a relatively short prison sentence.[30] While not a large percentage of those incarcerated, from 2006 to 2010, 1,177 individuals were convicted and sentenced for cybercrime acts.[31] To date, Albert Gonzalez has the dubious distinction of being sentenced to the longest sentence for cybercrime. He was given a 20-year sentence for a massive credit card theft and the reselling of more than 170 million ATM card numbers. He currently is incarcerated at the FCI in Milan, Michigan, from which he is scheduled for release in 2025.

minimum-security prisons: These facilities house mainly nonviolent white-collar criminals who are thought to pose little or no physical risk to members of the community.

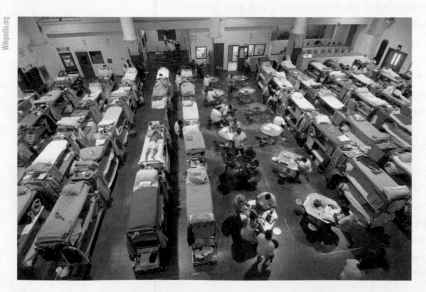

Minimum-security San Quentin Prison in California. Some view minimum-security prisons as "easy time." Do you believe living in a facility like the one pictured here looks "easy"? What sort of problems do you see with housing offenders in this density?

Wikipedia.org

Aside from Albert Gonzalez, some widely known minimum-security inmates include Martha Stewart, Leona Helmsley (a businesswoman convicted of tax evasion), Lauryn Hill (a recording artist convicted of tax evasion), Sun Myung Moon (a religious leader convicted of tax evasion), and Piper Kerman (woman convicted of money laundering who later authored *Orange Is the New Black*).

Prison Populations

The United States incarcerates a considerable proportion of its population (Figure 11.4). At year end in 2014, it is estimated that 1,561,500 people were confined in a state or federal prison in the United States.[32] In 2000, there were 1,394,200 persons held in prison.[33] The number of incarcerated in prison peaked in 2009 at 1,615,500 and has since declined. Variation in the prison population, and changes over time, is found among the states. Between 2013 and 2014, 24 states, and the federal system, experienced decreases in their prison populations. The largest percentage decline occurred in Mississippi (a 15% drop), as a result of policy changes that encourage community supervision versus prison for nonviolent offenders.[34] Vermont saw the second greatest percentage decrease in the prison population (a 4.8% decrease). Some other states experiencing declines included Texas, New Jersey, Louisiana, South Carolina, Oregon, Massachusetts, Alabama, and New York.[35] The prison population in California remained similar from 2013 to 2014 (a 0.1% increase). North Dakota's prison population grew the fastest (9.0%) and Nebraska the second fastest (8.3%) from 2013 to 2014. Growth in prison populations was measured in several states, including Washington, Tennessee, West Virginia, Minnesota, Arkansas, and Hawaii.[36]

In many states, the prison population has declined for two primary reasons: first, because sentences handed out for less serious offenders are getting shorter, and second, because fewer serious offenders are being diverted to corrections in the community. Given technology and risk assessment tools, public safety is not jeopardized, and enormous cost savings are available. These changes enjoy the support of some members of the public who are proponents of sentencing less serious offenders to community corrections or shorter

Figure 11.4 ■ Prisoners in State and Federal Prisons, 2002–2014

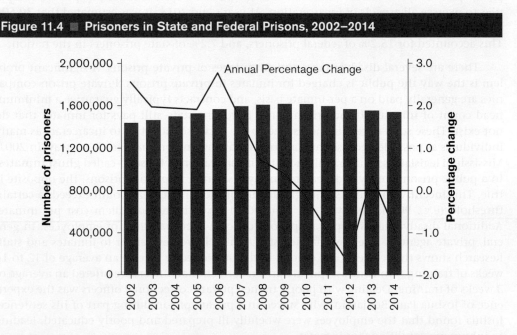

After increasing over time, in recent years the prisoner population has declined slightly. Do you believe this is good or bad news for offenders? For victims? And for society? Why or why not?

Sources: Carson, E. A., & Golinelli, D. (2013). *Prisoners in 2012—Advance counts.* Bureau of Justice Statistics, Office of Justice Programs, U.S. Department of Justice, Figure 1; and Carson, E. A. (2015) *Prisoners in 2014.* Bureau of Justice Statistics, Office of Justice Programs, U.S. Department of Justice. Figure 1.

Figure 11.5 ▓ Percentage of Men in State and Federal Prisons by Race and Hispanic Origin, 2014

Black Non-Hispanic,
37%

White Non-Hispanic,
32%

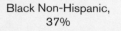

There was a larger percentage of non-Hispanic African Americans among male prisoners than any poverty? A lack of educational opportunities? Less opportunity overall? A racist criminal a priority for you? Why or why not?

Source: Carson, E. A. (2015). *Prisoners in 2014*, September, 2014. Bureau of Justice Statistics, Office of Justice Programs,

sentences.[37] And these changes are supported by the U.S. Congress, which has encouraged federal judges to make sentencing decisions keeping in mind that imprisonment is not "an appropriate means of promoting correction and rehabilitation."[38]

Privatization of Prisons

Journal:
Prison privatization

Although convict leasing systems in the United States theoretically ended approximately a century ago, a new form of incarceration benefiting from convict labor started in the 1980s: the privatization of prisons. Contracting out prison logistics such as food services, psychological testing, and health care is not new. Privatization of prisons simply takes small-scale privatization tasks a step further in that *all* aspects of a prison are managed by private agencies. In contrast to the convict leasing programs of the past, in which companies paid the state for use of inmate labor, in the new system states pay private companies to oversee all aspects of incarceration. At year's end 2014, it was estimated that 30,500 federal prison inmates and 91,200 state prison inmates are housed in private facilities.[39] This accounted for 15.2% of federal prisoners, and 7.2% of state prisoners in the nation.

There are several disadvantages and advantages of private prisons. A significant problem is the way the public is charged for inmates in private prisons. Private prison companies are generally paid on a per-inmate basis, and contracts typically guarantee a minimum head count of inmates. If the prison is not filled, the state still pays for inmates that do not exist. These sorts of requirements lead to the perverse incentive to incarcerate as many individuals as possible because the state or federal government pays for it anyway. In 2001, Mississippi legislators paid $6 million for the incarceration of these so-called **ghost inmates**. In a public prison, empty beds lead to taxpayer savings. In private prisons, the opposite is true. This incentive has limits, though, because if the inmate head count exceeds a certain threshold (e.g., 90%), taxpayers are required to pay a higher per diem cost per inmate. Additional disadvantages of private prisons concern their handling of employees. In general, private agencies hire less qualified staff, which increases danger to inmates and staff. Research shows that correctional officers in the public sector receive an average of 12 to 16 weeks of training.[40] In contrast, private prison correctional officers are offered an average of 3 weeks of training. Dealing with poorly trained private correctional officers was the experience of Joshua Paul Benjamin, who stayed in a private prison during part of his sentence. Joshua found that the employees were woefully ill prepared and poorly educated, leading to inhumane conditions for inmates.

Poor training for private prison staff translates to increased danger for the officers, the inmates, and the general public. In one case, the private Northeast Ohio Correctional Center dealt with stabbings, assaults, the use of tear gas, and ultimately the escape of six inmates who were serving long sentences in response to serious and violent offenses. An investigation following this event found that supervisors, officers, and staff were inexperienced and

ghost inmate:
A nonexistent inmate charged to the government (and taxpayer) by private prisons.

Latino/Hispanic,
22%

Other
Non-Hispanic,
9%

other group as of 2012. What could possibly account for this discrepancy? Is it greater levels of
justice system? If you were a policymaker, would better understanding why this discrepancy exists be

U.S. Department of Justice.

lacked training.[41] Likewise, an investigation into the private Santa Fe Detention Center in
New Mexico was launched as the U.S. government filed suit against the facility for violating
the constitutional rights of inmates housed there. Findings revealed more than 20 cases in
which negligence, indifference, poor training, and irresponsible cost cutting had resulted
in inmate deaths.[42] In almost every state, private institutions are not under the scrutiny of
each state's department of corrections, meaning much less accountability when compared
with public prisons. Consequently, in contrast to the examples described above, routine
instances of discrimination and abusive treatment are more likely to go unreported and
undetected in private compared with public prisons. An exception is New Mexico, which
ensures that private prisons meet the same standards as public facilities.

The purported benefits of private prisons are that these facilities are run more efficiently
and at less cost than public prisons and that they can reduce recidivism. Research fails to
offer support for either the lower cost or lower recidivism claim. There is little evidence
that public prisons have been run inefficiently and little evidence that private prisons do
any better. As noted above, given the per diem nature of charging the government, private
prisons are not necessarily less expensive. In addition, private companies have been caught
billing the government for **ghost employees**. The lower cost claim is difficult to reconcile
with the fact that private prison executives are paid 10 to 20 times the salary of those head-
ing state departments of corrections. Finally, there is no evidence that recidivism in private
prisons differs from that in public prisons.

In August 2016, the U.S. Department of Justice announced that it would end its use
of private prisons. Research has demonstrated that private federal prisons are less safe, are
less effective, offer fewer services and programs, and are not cost effective compared with
prisons run by the federal government. Importantly, they fail to provide equivalent levels
of safety for inmates and prison staff members. The end of private federal facilities will take
some time, as contracts with the private companies will not be renewed or will be greatly
reduced in scope.

The federal government is not the first to stop using private prisons. Some states
banned the privatization of facilities years ago. Both Illinois (in 1990) and New York (in
2000) made illegal the privatization of correctional facilities. Since 2001, Louisiana has
had a moratorium on private prisons. An early adopter of private prisons was Kentucky,
which initially established a 300-bed minimum-security prison in Marion. As of 2013,
for the first time in three decades, Kentucky completely abandoned the private prison
model. However, in 2016, with unanticipated growth in its inmate population, Kentucky
is again considering private prisons for approximately 1,600 inmates, on a temporary
basis only. Among its reasons for severing ties with the private prison world is that state
officials estimate that they could save the state $1.5 million to $2.5 million *annually* by
using only public facilities.

ghost employees:
Nonexistent employees
for whom private prisons
have illegally charged
the government (and
ultimately taxpayer).

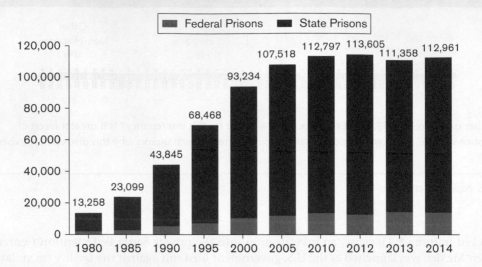

Figure 11.6 ■ Number of Women in State and Federal Prisons, 1980–2014

The number of women who are incarcerated has grown dramatically since the 1980s. Are women more dangerous than they once were? Or are women more likely to be arrested than they once were? What could account for the massive increase, and how does it affect our society?

Sources: Carson, E. A., & Golinelli, D. (2013). *Prisoners in 2012—Advance counts*. Bureau of Justice Statistics, Office of Justice Programs, U.S. Department of Justice; Carson, E. A. (2015) *Prisoners in 2014*. Bureau of Justice Statistics, Office of Justice Programs, U.S. Department of Justice.

Note: Estimates for 2014 include imputed counts for Alaska, which did not submit 2014 National Prisoner Statistics data.

Female Prisons and Prisoners

Journal:
Prison and female mental health

As noted earlier in the chapter, initially women were detained in the same facilities as men, suffering the same horrid conditions. Violence, especially rape and other sexual assault, was commonly perpetrated against female inmates, often resulting in pregnancy. The reformation period and the creation of separate facilities for women provided improved conditions. Since the opening of the Indiana Women's Reformatory, many other institutions to house female inmates have been built. As the number of incarcerated women grew, attention to female inmates increased. Currently, women continue to make up a relatively small portion of inmates in the nation. While relatively small compared with growth in the number of male inmates, growth in female inmates still has been explosive. In 2014, there were about 8.5 times more women in prison than in 1980 (Figure 11.6).

More than just facilities differ when considering incarcerated women. Research indicates that mental health issues, substance abuse, sexual victimization, drug use, and poverty are strong predictors of female incarceration. Most women are in prison for nonviolent crimes; one third of all women are incarcerated on drug-related offenses that were motivated by the desire to obtain more drugs. Most female inmates have been victims of childhood and adult physical and sexual abuse. Compared with men, female inmates are more likely to suffer from mental illness, including depression.[43] Findings show that about 73% of female prisoners suffer from mental health issues, compared with 55% of male prisoners.[44] Women are two times more likely than men to be HIV positive, and more likely to report that they were using drugs at the time of their first offenses. In 2004, the last year for which data are available, 60% of female prisoners (compared with 56% of male prisoners) had used drugs in the month before the offenses that resulted in their incarceration.[45]

ETHICAL ISSUES

Prison Isolation and Mental Health

Some prisoners are considered so dangerous that they are kept in isolation 23 to 24 hours a day. An example of this is John Jay Powers, who was convicted of robbing a bank in 1990 and was sentenced to prison. While incarcerated, Powers witnessed three inmates repeatedly stab and murder another inmate, which resulted in Powers's being diagnosed with severe and complex post-traumatic stress disorder. Powers then attempted to escape prison, which landed him in the federal government's ADX facility in Florence, Colorado, in 2001. In ADX, all approximately 450 inmates are deprived of almost any human interaction. Shortly after being sent to ADX, Powers became so deranged that he tried multiple times to kill himself. After some time at ADX, he also started engaging in mutilating behavior and successfully bit off several of his own fingers, severed his earlobes, and severed his own testicle and his scrotum. In his own words, he is damaged from this isolation.[46] Prior to being in ADX, Powers showed no signs of this degree of mental illness.

Advantages of isolating dangerous inmates include that it protects other inmates and correctional officers from danger, and it minimizes the risk of escape. A disadvantage of this approach is the severe deterioration of the mental health of inmates who find themselves in isolation for years. There is no doubt that mental illness is a major issue in correctional facilities. The Bureau of Justice Statistics estimated in mid-2005 that about 56% of state prisoners, 45% of federal prisoners, and 64% of local jail inmates had mental health problems.[47] Evidence suggests that extended time in isolation exacerbates mental illness and decreases the chance that these inmates will ever be able to reenter society. Yet thousands of inmates are kept in isolation in the United States each year, and some are released back into the population.

Think About It

1. Given evidence that such prolonged isolation is damaging, is it ethical to house humans in such extreme conditions?

2. Is this damage worth the protection of other inmates and staff?

3. Is it ethical that an inmate leave a prison in worse mental shape than when he or she entered as a result of the isolation?

4. What is the answer to housing dangerous inmates if not in isolation?

5. If you agree that such treatment of inmates is ethical, is it equally ethical that the United States end its condemnation of the treatment of prisoners in other countries doing similar things?

Race and Hispanic Origin in Prisons

Prison, race, and Hispanic origin are intimately tied together, as the history discussed in this chapter indicates. Today, prisons contain a disproportionate number of people of color. At the end of 2014, 34% of prisoners were non-Hispanic white, 36% were black, 22% were Hispanic, and 9% were non-Hispanic "other" (Figures 11.1, 11.5, and 11.7).[48] These percentages indicate a smaller proportion of white prisoners and larger proportions of black and Hispanic prisoners than would be expected based on the population alone. This difference suggests that white incarceration rates are lower than black and Hispanic rates. When considering only male prisoners in state or federal prison, the percentages are similar: 32% are non-Hispanic white, 37% are black, 22% are Hispanic, and 9% are non-Hispanic "other."[49] These differences suggest that black men were six times and Hispanic men more than two times more likely to be incarcerated than non-Hispanic white men in 2012. A focus on women tells an entirely different story: 50% of all female prisoners are non-Hispanic white, while 21% are black, 17% are Hispanic, and 12% are characterized as non-Hispanic "other."[50]

Figure 11.7 ■ Percentage of Women in State and Federal Prisons by Race and Hispanic Origin, December 2014

White Non-Hispanic, 50%

Source: Carson, E. A. (2015) *Prisoners in 2014*. Bureau of Justice Statistics, Office of Justice Programs, U.S.

LGBTQ Inmates

LGBTQ inmates face additional challenges whether housed in jails or prisons. Research shows that they are at far higher risk of sexual violence. Data from the 2011–2012 National Inmate Survey (the most recent data available) indicates that this population experiences sexual violence at the highest rates of all inmates.[51] Offenders include both other inmates and guards in the facilities. The report offers these major conclusions[52]:

- "Among non-heterosexual inmates, 12.2% of prisoners and 8.5% of jail inmates reported being sexually victimized by another inmate; 5.4% of prisoners and 4.3% of jail inmates reported being victimized by staff."

- "In each demographic subgroup (sex, race or Hispanic origin, age, and education), non-heterosexual prison and jail inmates reported higher rates of inmate-on-inmate sexual victimization than heterosexual inmates."

- "Among inmates with serious psychological distress, non-heterosexual inmates reported the highest rates of inmate-on-inmate sexual victimization (21.0% of prison inmates and 14.7% of jail inmates)."

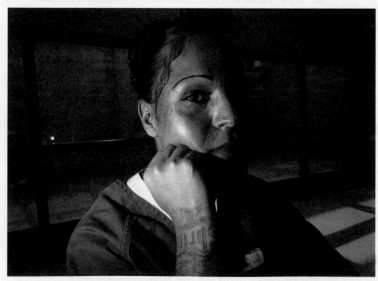

Transgender prisoners bring to light challenges in contemporary incarceration. How would you handle housing transgender prisoners in a fair and safe way? What other populations might require additional attention? Why?

Risk of physical and sexual victimization is one reason that LGBTQ inmates are frequently, and involuntarily, housed in solitary confinement settings. This treatment is undeserved and results in outcomes detrimental to the inmates. In addition, in this setting, inmates are deprived of educational, vocational, medical, recreational, and rehabilitative opportunities. Transgendered inmates are especially vulnerable when incarcerated. Think about an inmate who was at birth deemed male, but today identifies as, and has the physical appearance of, a woman. In general, in the United States, these individuals are incarcerated as men and are housed in male facilities. Dee Farmer, a black, transgender woman, lived this. She is a preoperative transsexual woman with breast implants who was incarcerated at a maximum-security male facility in Indiana. While in the general population, she was repeatedly raped and physically assaulted. One result of these victimizations is that Dee contracted HIV. Dee

| Black Non-Hispanic, 21% | Latino/Hispanic, 17% | Other Non-Hispanic, 12% |

Department of Justice.

sued prison officials for mental anguish, psychological damage, humiliation, and physical injuries. Her case eventually made its way to the U.S. Supreme Court, and in 1994, the Court ruled unanimously in *Farmer v. Brennan* that "deliberate indifference" to risk of serious harm to an inmate violates the cruel and unusual punishment right guaranteed by the Eighth Amendment.

In response, the Department of Justice issued regulations in 2012 to "prevent, detect and respond to sexual abuse in confinement facilities, in accordance with the Prison Rape Elimination Act of 2003 (PREA)."[53] Among the many regulations is the disallowing of the placement of LGBTQ inmates "in dedicated facilities, units, or wings in adult prisons, jails, or community confinement facilities solely on the basis of such identification or status, unless such placement is in a dedicated facility, unit, or wing established in connection with a consent decree, legal settlement, or legal judgment for the purpose of protecting such inmates."[54] The regulations also forbid a search or physical examination of a transgender or intersex inmate to determine genital status. Since 2012, a facility cannot simply assign an inmate to a facility based on genitals. Rather, a case-by-case decision must be made that takes into account what will maximize the inmate's health and safety, management and security issues, and the inmate's views regarding his or her own safety. Transgender and intersex inmates now must be given the opportunity to shower apart from others.

TECHNOLOGY AND INSTITUTIONAL CORRECTIONS

Technology is an increasingly important part of corrections. In earlier years, technologies such as locks, keys, firearms, basic forms of transportation, and simple communication devices were used to gain compliance and detain those incarcerated. As the criminal justice system has grown and changed, the responsibilities related to incarcerating individuals have increased. What has not changed is the purpose of all technology: ensuring the safety of individuals and the security of facilities. Today, providing food, clothing, shelter, health care, transportation, rehabilitation, banking, safety, and education are just some tasks prisons and jails must deal with. In addition, penal institutions are charged with keeping accurate records regarding inmate cases so that release, if possible, and other important moments during incarceration are accounted for.

In order to meet the demands of this broad range of needs, correctional facilities rely on a variety of technologies—far more than can be covered here. One important type of technology that enhances security for inmates and staff is controlled sliding doors. Using a centralized automated system, doors throughout prison and jail facilities are opened and closed. Automation allows an inmate to move in a controlled fashion through a facility

Web:
Using technology to make prisons and jails safer

without the need for staff and without jeopardizing the safety of correctional officers or other inmates.

Associated with controlled sliding doors is electronic surveillance, which is widely used to enhance the ability to survey a correctional institution. With electronic surveillance, correctional officers can view all areas of a facility without having to physically be present. Electronic surveillance (and other electronic detection devices) is not restricted to inside an institution. This technology is also used to monitor the perimeter of the facility. Newer cameras used for surveillance are bullet resistant and can survive the force of a sledgehammer. They also cannot be disabled during attempted escapes or fights in the facility.

Videoconferencing has changed much in institutional corrections. Prior to the use of this technology, inmates had to be personally escorted and transported to a variety of external locations such as the courthouse. Taking an inmate to a court appointment required staff, transportation, and time. Now, inmates can hold appointments without leaving the institution. This technology is also changing the way inmates visit with family and friends. Video visitation allows inmates to visit others remotely instead of in face-to-face visits. This technology enables visitation when distance prevents it, and it removes all possibility of smuggling of contraband by visitors.

Relatedly, **telemedicine** has gained traction in institutional corrections. Using telemedicine and remote medical tools, an inmate can be examined by medical staff via electronic conference. Physicians can look down an inmate's throat, listen to her or his heartbeat, and conduct a physical exam remotely.[55] In one decade, electronic health records and telemedicine saved the Texas prison system approximately $1 billion. Telemedicine means that inmates can be examined and treated without leaving a facility, traveling, or interacting with medical staff in person. Again, this results in efficiency, cost savings, and increased security.

As seen in Chapter 10, biometric devices are used in the correctional field. Some prisons have adopted the used of biometric entry points that scan irises or fingerprints. While not widely used due to cost, this technology offers great promise for efficiency and security.

videoconferencing: Technology used in correctional institutions to facilitate visitation, meetings, and medical care.

telemedicine: New technology used in correctional institutions to provide medical care to inmates remotely.

body-imaging scanners: Technology recently adopted in prisons to detect contraband.

A relatively new technology used by a growing number of correctional institutions is **body-imaging scanners**. These scanners, once used in airports, are used to scan visitors and sometimes correctional officers entering correctional facilities. Body-imaging scanners were removed from airports due to privacy concerns and are being relocated to prisons, where privacy is not an issue—at least for inmates. Controversy surrounds their use with correctional staff, but history shows that staff in these facilities have engaged in illegal acts of smuggling contraband. One California prison employee earned more than $100,000 by smuggling in and selling cell phones to inmates.[56] Body-imaging scanners are more sensitive than metal detectors and can identify weapons, cell phones, and illegal contraband being smuggled in through clothing. Preliminary uses of these scanners show

© Bill O'Leary/The Washington Post/Getty Images

Technology has influenced visitation in prison. In some cases, this is as close as inmates get to their family and friends. What are the advantages and disadvantages to electronic visitation? Why do you feel that way?

a reduced incidence of contraband. While body-imaging scanners are unable to detect items in body cavities, other technology can do so. Body orifice scanning devices have been used to detect swallowed contraband, items inserted into orifices, or items hidden between toes or in other locations. Handheld scanners are also available that assist in finding hidden weapons, cell phones, and other contraband. Increasingly, a major problem in prisons and jails is smuggled cell phones. A variety of technology is now available that is designed specifically to detect cell phones, phone calls, and text messages even if these devices are hidden in walls or elsewhere. Other technology can simply block cell phone signals. Using newer cell phone technology, the California prison system confiscated more than 4,000 phones in a single year.

Chapter 10 also discussed radiofrequency identification devices in conjunction with community corrections. This inmate-tracking technology is also used in prisons and jails to keep track of the locations of particular inmates. Using this technology, correctional officers can identify if inmates are in places they should or should not be or if a crowd of inmates is gathering when not appropriate.

CHAPTER WRAP-UP

This chapter outlined significant change in institutional corrections over several hundred years. Information presented identified both the birth and subsequent widespread rejection of parole. It described how the underlying perspective of correctional facilities oscillated from serious and harsh punishment, to reformation, to our current state that operates under a just deserts philosophy focusing primarily on punishment. A result of the public's demands for just deserts means that the United States continues to be the country with the largest population of persons under control of the criminal justice system in the world. This characteristic comes at great financial and social cost to the people in our nation. Technological advances have assisted in managing this enormous population.

CASE STUDY

This chapter described incarceration in general, and also our case studies' experience with it. Joshua Paul Benjamin's pathway through the criminal justice system placed him in a variety of facilities involving varying degrees of security. He even found himself in a private prison. Danny Madrid began amassing his juvenile record at the age of 10 and has been incarcerated in a variety of facilities as a juvenile (e.g., juvenile hall/camp) and an adult. He spent a lot of time in solitary, with the longest stay lasting 8 months. He describes his time in solitary as "very isolating and traumatic, given the deprivation and all." Dennis Bradford's final stay in a county jail was short-lived. While awaiting a hearing with the judge, he fashioned a sheet into a noose and hanged himself. We can only speculate where he may have ended up had he been convicted of his crimes. Chris Farias also spent a good deal of time in a county jail serving his work-release sentence. Although jail is considered the "easiest" of places to be incarcerated, Chris is quick to point out that his sentence was incredibly difficult.

In the next chapter, we move on to life in and after prison. That examination will delve into subcultures in prison, including gendered subcultures. Prison violence is addressed, including gang and sexual violence. Prisoner rights, rehabilitation, and education in prison are discussed. Finally, life after prison is described, with an emphasis on employment, marriage and relationships, sex offender registries, and recidivism.

KEY POINTS

- The early years of corrections used jails as holding tanks while the accused waited to find out his or her punishment. Only later did jails and prisons become viewed as punishment for an offense.

- Early forms of punishment were barbaric and excessively harsh, and they generally included public humiliation. These activities did not appear to affect recidivism.

- Institutional corrections has largely vacillated between harsh (and at times barbaric) punishment and reformation. Reformation has included attempts to reform prisoners by exposing them to religious doctrines, work, and education. Neither a punitive nor a reformative approach appears to influence recidivism. Currently, we are experiencing a period characterized by "just deserts" that focus more on punishment, though reformation is not totally absent.

- The contract and convict leasing systems were methods used by prisons in the past to benefit financially from inmate work. In the South, these systems were used to keep African Americans under the control of the state following the abolition of slavery.

- Initially, women were housed in the same facilities as men, where they were neglected and routinely victimized. The creation of separate facilities for women came out of the 1870 Declaration of Principles during the reformation period.

- Prisons function using a variety of security levels. At the most extreme—in super-maximum prisons— inmates have almost no human interaction and are kept in their cells 23 hours a day.

- The privatization of prisons has not proved to be more cost-effective or to lower recidivism rates. In some locales, private prisons are costlier and more dangerous. Currently, there is movement away from this practice in order to save taxpayer dollars.

- The United States now has the largest population of incarcerated women. With this comes the responsibility to provide medical care, including for those who are pregnant and give birth. To date, there is no national level of care mandated for these inmates and there is variation in the medical care available and treatment of infants born while their mothers are incarcerated.

KEY TERMS

Auburn System 286

Black Codes 287

Body-Imaging Scanners 308

Branding 285

Classification Review 297

Congregate System 287

Contract System 287

Convict Leasing System 287

Corporal Punishment 284

Correctional Officers 289

Declaration of Principles 288

Flogging 285

Ghost Employees 303

Ghost Inmate 302

Gossip's Bridle or Scold's Helm 285

Hanging 284

Jails 292

Just Deserts 291

Lockups 292

Matrons 290

Maximum-Security Prisons 299

Medium-Security Prisons 299

Minimum-Security Prisons 300

Mutilation 285

New Penology 284

Penitentiary 286

Pennsylvania System 286

Penology 284

Pillory 285

Reformation Movement 288

Separate System 286

Stocks 285

Super-Maximum Prisons 298

Telemedicine 308

Videoconferencing 308

REVIEW QUESTIONS

1. Why do we need institutional corrections? What other options exist or should exist to handle those in the criminal justice system?

2. What role has technology played in the field of corrections over time? Do you think the use of technology has enhanced or been problematic for the field of institutional corrections?

3. Should attention be given to differences in male and female inmates' trajectories, experiences, and needs in prison and jail? Why or why not?

4. What are the roles of correctional officers?

5. What are the advantages and disadvantages of private prisons?

6. What are the problems with segregation, and how does it affect inmates and society?

CRITICAL THINKING MATTERS

1. **Why Not Just Send All Convicted Criminals to Prison or Jail?** The United States has a vast criminal justice system, and the public demands toughness on crime. What are the advantages and disadvantages of incarcerating all convicted offenders? If you were a policymaker, for what criminal offenses, if any, would you make prison sentences mandatory? For what criminal offenses would you make community corrections mandatory? Are there ethical considerations in terms of which crimes should or should not be eligible for community corrections? Are there ethical considerations in terms of the offender characteristics (e.g., female, wealthy, older, ill) that should make them ineligible for prison? Should Danny Madrid, as a juvenile, have been subjected to the facilities and solitary confinement imposed upon him, given research showing the damaging effects of such treatment? Should the cost of incarceration drive the use of community corrections?

2. **Profiting From Prison Labor.** Should prison labor be a resource widely used by the community? If so, is this fair to local business owners who produce the same goods? Are private business owners being undermined if convicts make products more cheaply than they can? Or is the benefit of teaching offenders a new skill worth the pains it causes private business owners? What sorts of products should inmates produce? Lingerie for Victoria's Secret? Baseball caps? Recorded books for the blind? Military jackets and other military garb? Blue jeans? Silhouettes for target practice? These are all currently products made by prisoners—Is this good or bad policy?

3. **Pregnancy and Birth in Prison.** In large part due to the war on drugs, the United States now has the distinction of having the largest population of incarcerated women. Among them are thousands who are pregnant. A recent report indicated that there is no national standard of care in terms of dealing with pregnant prisoners. If you were a policymaker, what would your policy be in terms of prenatal care for the pregnant inmates, handling termination of pregnancy if desired by the inmates, shackling (by wrist, stomach, and ankle) of pregnant inmates (even during labor), and what to do with the baby after birth? Should the baby be sent to foster care immediately? Should the baby remain with the incarcerated mother for some time in prison, be put up for adoption, or be dealt with through some other option? Keep in mind the moral, ethical, and economic ramifications of your policy. Why is your policy better than alternative policies provided by classmates?

4. **Expending Resources to Understand Prison Rape.** President George W. Bush signed into law policies designed to minimize prison rape and hold prisons accountable for this violence. A great deal of resources are being used to identify the extent of this issue in the United States. Is this responsible spending of taxpayer money? Or is this wasteful? Should we care if prisoners are being raped? Should we care if prisoners rape one another or only if guards rape prisoners? What would you do if you were in charge of this issue? Why would your policy be a better way to deal with this than what is currently being done?

5. **Suicide While Incarcerated.** Dennis Bradford hanged himself while in the county jail. Who is responsible for this? What, if anything, should be done to those charged with watching Bradford? Do your thoughts incorporate the pains his suicide caused the victim of his crimes? Do you believe Dennis's family should be allowed to sue the county for damages? What about Jennifer? Should she be able to sue the county for damages? Should the public care about inmate suicide?

6. **Where to Serve the Sentence.** Joshua Paul Benjamin was sent to serve time in a state far from the state in which he committed his offenses. Is this practice ethical? This distance meant that Joshua received no visits from friends or family while he was incarcerated. Should inmates serve time as close to home as is possible? Or is it okay to send them far away, even if it creates excessive hardship on family members, including children? What is the best policy in terms of where inmates serve their time?

DIGITAL RESOURCES

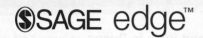

Sharpen your skills with SAGE edge at edge.sagepub.com/rennison2e. SAGE edge for Students provides a personalized approach to help you accomplish your coursework goals in an easy-to-use learning environment. You'll find action plans, mobile-friendly eFlashcards, and quizzes as well as video and web resources and links to SAGE journal articles to support and expand on the concepts presented in this chapter.

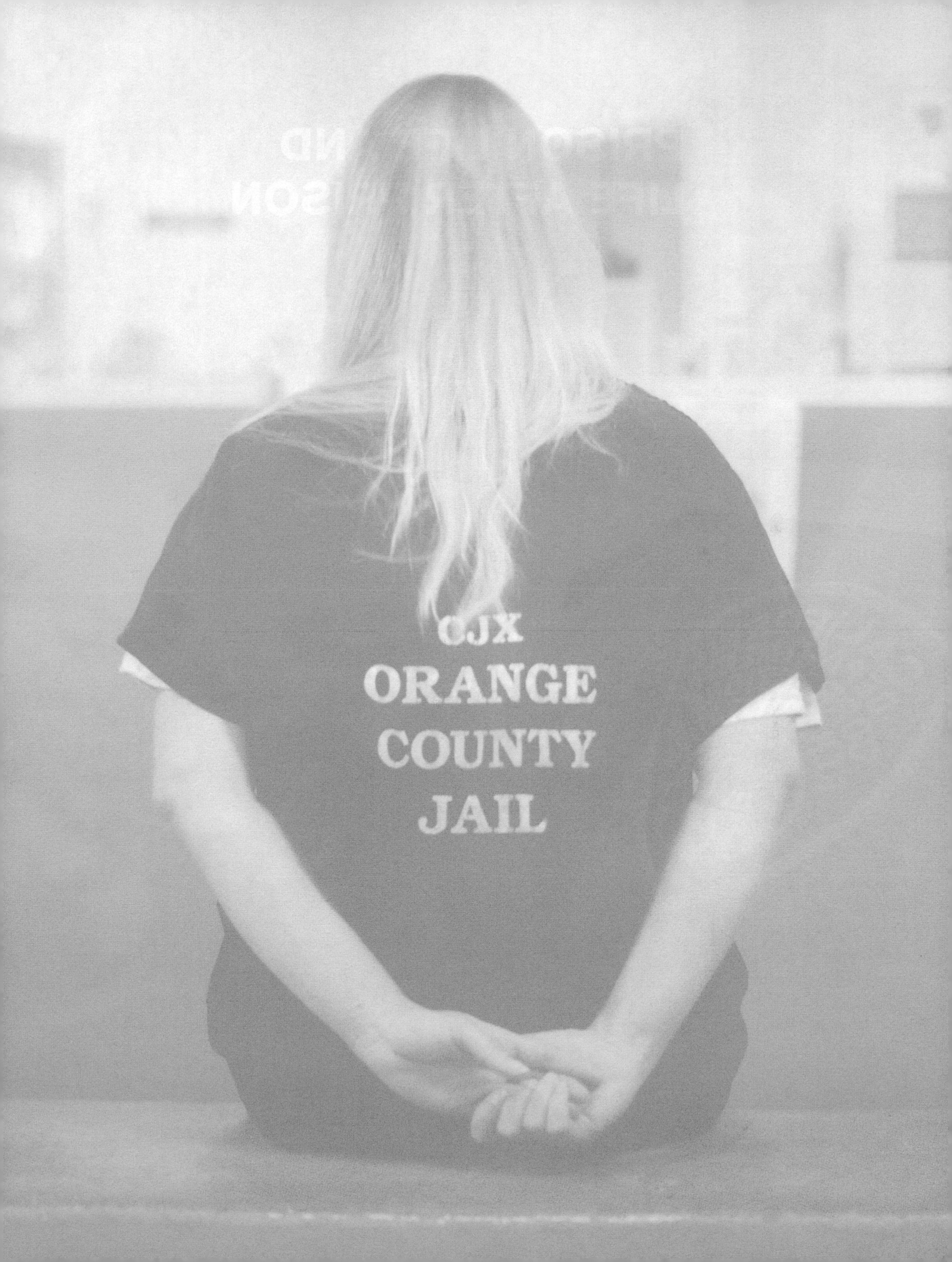
OJX
ORANGE
COUNTY
JAIL

12 PRISON LIFE AND LIFE AFTER PRISON

> "Incarceration, the best punishment we have been able to think up, has itself become a social problem. One of its unintended results is the growth of so-called prison culture."
>
> —Ted Conover

LEARNING OBJECTIVES

After finishing this chapter, you should be able to:

12.1 Describe the conditions and attitudes influencing prison subcultures.

12.2 Identify the five pains of imprisonment and explain how they shape inmate behavior.

12.3 List the advantages and disadvantages of solitary confinement.

12.4 Identify and propose measures that can be used to control prison violence.

12.5 Discuss challenges faced by inmates and prison staff.

12.6 Evaluate the methods through which successful reentry might be achieved.

INTRODUCTION: LIVING IN PRISON

When the state incarcerates someone, it becomes responsible for the safety and well-being of the person in jail or prison. The mission of many correctional institutions is to protect the public, ensure the safety of personnel, and provide care and supervision of offenders. An emphasis on reentry also is included in the majority of correctional mission statements, which note the importance of offering services and programs for successful life in the community after release. The prison environment presents a wide variety of challenges that are difficult to mitigate and overcome. Some prisons often are violent, hostile places plagued with inappropriate sexual behavior and gang activity. Many prisons are overcrowded and understaffed, and many have tight resources that limit the most realistic of rehabilitation goals. Ted Conover, author of *Newjack: Guarding Sing*, noted in the quotation at the beginning of the chapter that we have few alternatives to prison, and the environment gives rise to unique subcultures with mores and rules distinct and distant from our everyday lives.

More than 2.4 million Americans are incarcerated in state and federal prisons (see Figure 12.1). Spending time in prison achieves the goal of incapacitation and, in some cases, rehabilitation, and although recidivism rates for ex-convicts are high, attempts to facilitate reentry are a top priority in the criminal justice system. The prices of incarceration, without treatment and education, are high both in financial terms and regarding quality of life. Housing one inmate in federal prison costs an average of $21,000 annually in a minimum-security facility and $33,000 in a maximum-security institution. Prison comes at a high

Chino State Prison in California opened in 1941 and has a maximum capacity of almost 3,000 inmates. Describe what life may have been like for Danny Madrid while he was incarcerated.

Total institution is a concept developed by Erving Goffman, who is often referred to as the most influential American sociologist of the 20th century, to describe isolated, closed social systems designed to control people.[4] Goffman first used the term in his book *Asylums* (1961) for prisons and mental institutions; other total institutions include military schools, monasteries, and concentration camps. Imagine waking up in the morning without responsibility, making no decisions, and having no choices. Virtually everything you wear, eat, and do is determined and scheduled by someone else. Imagine every day getting up and following the exact same schedule with perhaps an hour outside (or an enclosed area with limited view of the sky); there are no weekend trips to the mountains or the beach, only the drudgery of the same events 24 hours a day, 7 days a week. Sleeping in an 8-by-10 cell with little or no privacy worsens this existence. The strictly regimented routine and isolation represent only some of the difficulties associated with serving time in prison. Total institutions also remove individuality, erase dignity, and are inescapable.

CASE STUDY

Danny Madrid retold a poignant story about his time in prison. He described the experiences as traumatic and monotonous—year after year doing the same thing every day. In fact, he still has nightmares about the confined space. Outside prison life he requires windows and is outside at every opportunity. Ironically, one of the lifelong consequences of being in prison was Danny's feeling of becoming a victim of the system. He also explained that federal prisons, compared with the state prisons he experienced, have better exercise yards, tennis courts, good food, and clothing.

While prison may serve as a deterrent up to a point, according to Danny, one turning point was an incident that occurred in Chino prison in the outside showers. While in the yard, Danny saw an older, wrinkled, white inmate with long gray hair in the shower. Danny described this scene as a "glimpse into the future." "Will that be me in the future?" His decision, after many years of believing he would either be dead or spend life in prison, was to take control of his life. Part of his coping mechanism was to begin drawing and creating art work that represented a potential for something better. Once Danny was released from prison, this became a turning point in his life was the opportunity to build social capital by leaving the gang life and relying on positive experiences and family.

total institution: Any isolated, closed social system designed to control people.

deprivation model: Where prisons require inmates to adapt to being deprived of basic rights and needs.

pains of imprisonment: The five primary pains that come from being incarcerated: deprivation of liberty, goods and services, heterosexual relationships, autonomy, and security.

Subcultures of Prison

Three models are commonly used to explain inmate subcultures: deprivation, importation, and situational. Research shows that all three models may work together to explain violent prison incidents and inmate behavior.[5] The **deprivation model** relies on the idea of a total institution where prisonization occurs as inmates adapt to being deprived of basic rights and needs. In other words, the prison environment shapes the inmates' society, and outside influences are soon forgotten. This deprivation may include, for example, the loss of heterosexual relationships. Gresham Sykes first identified the poverties associated with incarceration in the five **pains of imprisonment** in his famous book *The Society of Captives*[6]:

1. The deprivation of liberty

2. The deprivation of goods and services

3. The deprivation of heterosexual relationships
4. The deprivation of autonomy
5. The deprivation of security

Deprivation of liberty refers to the inmate's loss of freedom, which, according to Sykes, creates feelings of being a social outcast. Although basic needs such as food, clothing, and medical care are available, the standards of living are far below what we are accustomed to having in our daily lives. Without conjugal visits, Sykes described prisoners as being figuratively castrated by involuntary celibacy. The deprivation of autonomy is related to the total control of a prisoner's behavior, which may result in feelings of weakness and helplessness. Finally, the deprivation of security comes from living in a population of inmates and correctional officers whose actions, at times, may be intimidating and violent. As a result of the deprivations, the subculture is one of negativity, aggression, and resentment toward correctional administrators and officers, as well as other inmates.

The **importation model** proposed by John Irwin and Donald Cressey asserts that experiences and socialization from the outside are brought into prison. In other words, the characteristics and social backgrounds of inmates determine how they act in prison. Important in this model is the idea that different subgroups with different beliefs exist in a prison rather than it being a total institution with one subculture.[7] Inmates may, for instance, introduce their own special codes of behavior or subculture.

John Irwin's contributions to sociology and **convict criminology** offer a special perspective because, in addition to his research, he served time in prison. Reflecting on his pathway in life, Irwin described himself as a "thug, a drug addict and then—after being convicted of armed robbery—a convict," who later received a PhD at the University of California, Berkeley.[8] His work with Donald Cressey in the 1960s exploring prison culture and criminal subculture identified types of deviant prison subcultures: thief and convict.[9] The **thief subculture** includes professional thieves and career criminals who are "right guys" focusing on values such as in-group loyalties and being trustworthy and reliable. The **convict subculture** imports values from the outside and follows the inmate code. In most cases, these inmates have spent a great deal of time incarcerated. The other identified subculture is the group of prisoners Irwin and Cressey called **legitimate**. These inmates are one-time offenders who tend to identify with correctional officers and staff and take advantage of educational and rehabilitation opportunities.

> Joshua Paul Benjamin clearly aligned with the idea of a "legitimate" prisoner. In prison, he took advantage of educational and rehabilitation opportunities. He volunteered to assist other inmates with their own education and worked in the prison library. Not only did these activities align with his own interests and need to accept responsibility for his actions but they also protected him from the harsher elements of prison life. He was not as exposed to gang interactions, violence, and sexual assault (although he did not escape it entirely).

CASE STUDY

John Irwin also identified four methods of adapting to being in prison. Inmates may be **doing time** by accepting and following the rules. Doing time means that an inmate is working toward possible early parole or completing his or her jail sentence without any additional penalties for rule infractions or misbehavior. Some inmates engage in **jailing**. These individuals tend to be more comfortable in prison and have likely spent a substantial part of their lives in some type of institution. The **gleaning** group takes advantage of opportunities that may help future behavior, such as treatment and education. Finally, **disorganized** prisoners suffer from mental illness issues and/or low IQs. These inmates have severe difficulties adjusting to prison culture.

---

importation model: Experiences and socialization from the outside world are brought into prison and contribute to behavior while incarcerated.

convict criminology: The study of crime and correctional systems that challenges traditional viewpoints.

thief subculture: Prison subculture that includes professional thieves and values in-group loyalty, trust, and reliability. This subculture includes "right guys."

convict subculture: Imports values from the outside and follows the inmate code.

legitimate: A prison subculture wherein one-time offenders identify with correctional staff and take advantage of educational and rehabilitation opportunities.

doing time: Inmates who accept and follow the rules.

jailing: Inmates who have spent a substantial amount of time behind bars and tend to be comfortable in prison.

gleaning: Inmates who take advantage of rehabilitation, educational, and vocational opportunities while serving time.

disorganized: Inmates with mental illness and/or low IQs.

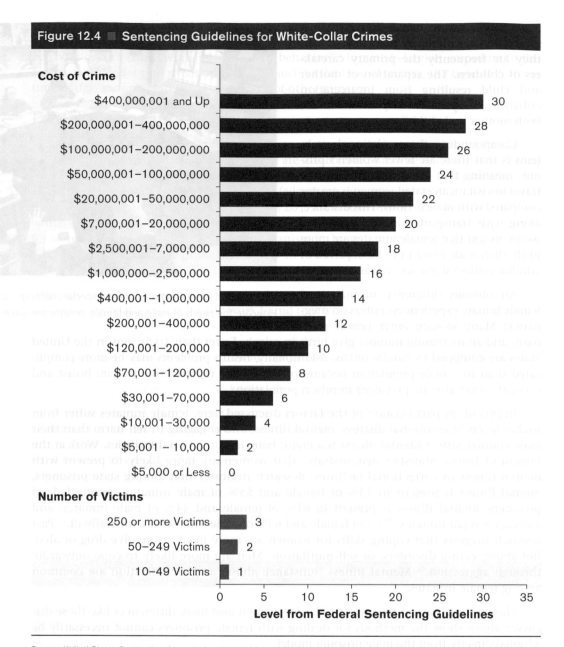

Figure 12.4 ▪ Sentencing Guidelines for White-Collar Crimes

Source: United States Sentencing Commission. (2015). *Amendments to the sentencing guidelines.* Retrieved from http://www.ussc.gov/sites/default/files/pdf/amendment-process/reader-friendly-amendments/20150430_RF_Amendments.pdf.

colleagues speculate that white-collar criminals adjust with greater ease because they understand how bureaucracies operate, appreciate the importance of rules, and have the support of family. Other inmates do not necessarily enter prison with these advantages. Still, while the transition may be the same, in the words of white-collar criminal Alfred Porro, prison is a "hellish place" and sentencing lengths have increased because of major financial scandals (see Figure 12.4).

CLASSIFICATION SYSTEMS AND SOLITARY CONFINEMENT

Classification systems are used to ensure staff and inmate safety. Prison administrators must accommodate a wide variety of offenders, including those who are violent, white-collar criminals, pedophiles, and the mentally ill. Grouping or separating certain types

Video 12.1:
Torment of solitary confinement

of offenders provides one method of control. Prison populations also can be controlled by incentives such as work, special privileges, or reduced sentences. Another method is the use of segregation to isolate problem inmates.

Often violent and mentally ill prisoners are placed in **solitary confinement**, also referred to as administrative segregation (see Chapter 11). These prisoners are isolated 23 to 24 hours a day. Many of the mentally ill suffer from schizophrenia and depression. The increased use of solitary confinement for mentally ill inmates occurs in some prisons because of the scarcity of psychiatrists and psychologists who are available to provide treatment. Solitary confinement, however, often exacerbates preexisting conditions. In 2012, the American Psychiatric Association noted that lengthy segregation (more than 3

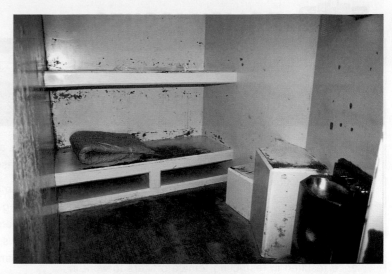

The ACLU challenges the use of lengthy periods of solitary confinement. What are the advantages and disadvantages of solitary confinement?

or 4 weeks) causes serious harm to ill prisoners and should be avoided.[24] Investigations by the American Civil Liberties Union (ACLU) have documented cases of mentally ill inmates in isolation attempting suicide, eating feces, and banging their heads against the wall.[25] From an administrator's or a correctional officer's perspective, keeping the mentally ill in the general population is problematic because of the disruptions, and without in-house special treatment facilities there are few alternative placements aside from solitary. Overcrowding and underfunding contribute to the lack of viable options, though the extended use of solitary confinement is detrimental to inmates' mental and physical health.

Numerous arguments are made against the use of solitary confinement. The practice, especially in a super-maximum facility, is expensive. The prisoners suffer from higher suicide rates, depression, decreased cognitive abilities, and sometimes hallucinations. A 2011 United Nations report noted that the practice is tantamount to torture and should be limited to 15 days.[26] Often, gang-affiliated prisoners are routinely placed in solitary confinement to avoid outbreaks of violence. All citizens should care about the plight of those in prison and those in solitary confinement, as many of these inmates are released back into the community. In 2013, after spending most of his 8 years in prison in solitary confinement, Evan Ebel was released on parole in Colorado. While in prison, he became affiliated with the racist 211 Crew gang. Almost immediately, he obtained a firearm and murdered a pizza deliveryman named Nathan Leon. Then, taking his pizza delivery uniform, he went to the home of Tom Clements. Clements was the Colorado prisons director. When Clements answered the door, Ebel assassinated him. Ebel was eventually found in Texas and died in a shoot-out with police. In his car, authorities found a hit list with 20 names of officials he intended to kill. Ebel's family contends that his long stay in solitary contributed to his increasing violence and erratic behavior. As a result of this incident, in 2014, Colorado banned the use of solitary confinement for mentally ill inmates and reduced the number of inmates released from solitary directly to the community (see Figure 12.5).

Audio:
Solitary confinement

PRISON VIOLENCE

Prison Gangs

Prison gangs have a long history, with their presence being traced back to the 1950s. Gangs represent serious problems for prison administrators and correctional officers. Members of gangs are a higher security risk and tend to be less compliant. Gangs in prison are known to engage in trafficking contraband (e.g., drugs, cigarettes, pornography) and running protection rackets. Many inmates use race or ethnicity to establish an identity,

solitary confinement: Also known as administrative segregation, it isolates violent or hard-to-manage prisoners from the general population.

POLICY ISSUES

Gender and Correctional Officers

Historically, male officers worked in men's prisons and female officers worked in women's prisons. Currently, correctional officers of both genders work in all types of institutions, though the practice remains controversial. Opponents of hiring female correctional officers for male prisons argue that they face greater danger. In the 1970s, for example, the incidence of violence resulted in restricting female officers to work in minimum-security prisons. This policy changed in the 1990s, though some female officers still experience harassment by male correctional officers and inmates. Critiques of the practice suggest that inmates are more likely to sexualize and fantasize female officers. Other arguments include lack of the physical strength needed to control violent inmates and contain confrontations. Female officers in men's prisons often report higher levels of stress compared with their male counterparts.

At the other end of the spectrum are problems related to male officers working in female prisons. A Department of Justice investigation of an Alabama prison discovered that male officers were forcing women into sexual acts and watching women shower and use the bathroom. Though widespread scandals are rare, any incident may suggest the need to restrict hiring based on gender.

Women work in many male-dominated fields, including policing. Though anecdotal instances of wrongdoing by correctional officers hint at possible problems, research shows that work performance is similar, and courts have determined that inmate and officer gender is superfluous to correctional work. In fact, several studies show lower assault rates in men's prisons with female officers, who tend to rely more on verbal skills to control tense situations.

Think About It

1. As a policymaker, what position would you take regarding gender and correctional officers?

2. What are some of the legitimate concerns about having male staff supervising female prisoners and female staff supervising male prisoners?

3. How would the exclusion of male or female officers be considered discrimination? Should this be a concern? Why or why not?

Figure 12.5 ■ Paroled From Solitary Confinement

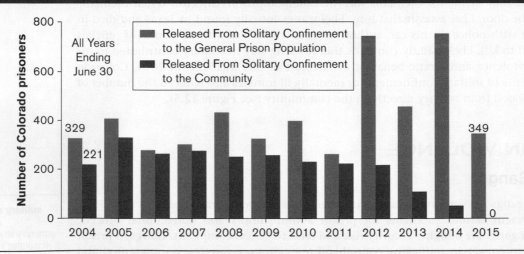

Source: Data from Colorado Department of Corrections.

and gang affiliation mirrors the world outside.[27] Known prison gangs include the Aryan Brotherhood, the Bloods, the Crips, La Nuestra Familia, the Latin Kings, and the Mexican Mafia. Each prison gang has unique characteristics and histories, and many were first formed to ensure protection.

The Aryan Brotherhood is believed to have formed in 1967 in California's San Quentin State Prison. Members of the gang are typically white supremacists and subscribe to a neo-Nazi ideology. These inmates spend their time in prison "getting high and getting over."[28] The Mexican Mafia was created in the late 1950s in California. The racial makeup of the gang is Mexican American/Hispanic, and it is known as one of the most active gangs in the Federal Bureau of Prisons.[29] The Mexican Mafia emphasizes ethnic solidarity and controls drug trafficking. La Nuestra Familia is the chief rival, and the two gangs are rumored to have a "kill on sight relationship."[30] The Black Guerrilla Family (BGF) is believed to be the most politically oriented prison gang, formed as an antigovernment group. Becoming a member of BGF includes taking a death oath of lifetime loyalty to the group.[31] The Barrio Aztec gang, with an estimated 2,000 members, is believed to be the most violent and active group in Texas prisons. Members are linked to the Mexican drug cartels and involved in smuggling, arson, extortion, kidnapping, and weapons violations.[32]

Gangs in prison are a serious safety risk for inmates and staff. What solutions would you propose to control gang activities in prisons?

Audio:
Prison gangs

Violence

Violence in prison takes many forms, including inmate on inmate, inmate on guard, and guard on inmate. Violence is common and may occur for a number of reasons:

- understaffing
- excessive or unreasonable force by correctional officers
- overcrowding
- poor living conditions
- gang activities
- physical design of the prison

Different types of violence may occur in prison related to fear, anger, acting out, and extortion.[33] Fear of violence can result in a prisoner turning the tables and becoming the aggressor before being harmed. Anger often occurs when an inmate perceives an injustice of some sort. Prisoners also act out in tantrum-like behavior to vent their frustrations. Finally, extortion occurs when a violent inmate threatens another inmate to obtain something of value. Prison violence includes incidents of bullying, physical and sexual assaults, stabbings, and murder.

Riots occur when violence among inmates is beyond the control of prison staff and administration. The Attica Prison riot in 1971, one of the most famous and deadly incidents, lasted 5 days. More than 1,000 inmates held some 40 correctional officers hostage while the inmates negotiated for rights and better living conditions. At the time, the prison was horribly overcrowded and housed more than 2,000, despite the maximum capacity of 1,200. Inmates complained, probably rightly so, about being able to shower only once a week, allocations of one roll of toilet paper per month, destruction of mail, bug-infested food, and abusive treatment. The riot finally ended when New York State Police troopers stormed the facility. A total of 39 inmates died and 88 were wounded. On the positive side, the riot and events stemming from the tragedy resulted in prison reform.

Prison riots often result in massive destruction and the loss of lives for both correctional officers and inmates. In 2009, a racially-motivated riot caused serious damage to the facility. What measures can be put in place to prevent prison riots?

Audio:
Prison rape

Sexual Violence

The exact amount of sexual violence that occurs in prison is difficult to ascertain, but the experiences of many inmates and empirical research suggest that it is a frequent and serious problem. In fact, as noted in the previous chapter, prison rape was perceived as important enough to warrant legislation and as early as the 1980s was labeled an epidemic.[34] In 2003, President George W. Bush signed the Prison Rape Elimination Act (commonly known as PREA), which was applauded by civil rights groups and inmate advocates. The act mandates that the Bureau of Justice Statistics (BJS) gather data on incidents and effects of rape each year. As noted in the last chapter, the most recent BJS report estimates that in 2011 and 2012, 4% of inmates housed in state and federal prisons were sexually victimized by another inmate.[35]

Inmates, not surprisingly, fail to report rapes out of concern for their own safety because they fear retaliation. Reporting a rape may result in the victim being labeled a snitch. Also, the shame and humiliation victims feel prevent them from reporting. Additionally, rapes may be ignored or the harm minimized by correctional staff or administrators, particularly when an officer is involved and responsible for reporting. Remember, not all rape is inmate on inmate, and women in prison are sexually assaulted by male correctional staff members.[36] One early research study noted that vulnerable targets in prison populations have also been identified and labeled according to prison argot: fags (homosexuals), queens (transsexuals), kids (young sex slaves), and punks (resistant but eventually give in) (Figure 12.6).[37]

A research project that surveyed 441 prison wardens explored the incidents of coerced and consensual sex.[38] Wardens were asked three questions: What percentage of inmate sexual assaults do you believe you personally know about? In the past 12 months what

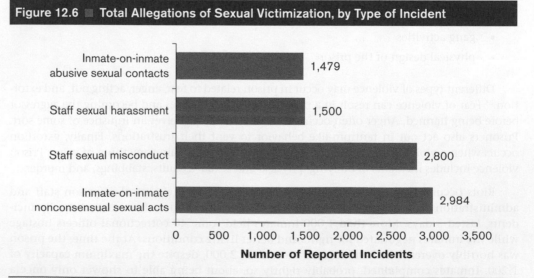

Figure 12.6 ■ Total Allegations of Sexual Victimization, by Type of Incident

Type of Incident	Number of Reported Incidents
Inmate-on-inmate abusive sexual contacts	1,479
Staff sexual harassment	1,500
Staff sexual misconduct	2,800
Inmate-on-inmate nonconsensual sexual acts	2,984

Number of Reported Incidents

Source: Beck, A. J., & Rantala, R. R. (2014, January). *Sexual victimization reported by adult correctional authorities, 2009–11,* (NCJ 243904). Washington, DC: U.S. Department of Justice, Bureau of Justice Statistics. Retrieved from http://www .bjs.gov/content/pub/pdf/svraca0911.pdf.

Note: Most recent data available.

percentage of the inmates in your institution do you believe have engaged in sexual activities with other inmates because of pressure and/or force? What percentage of inmates in your institution do you believe have engaged in sexual activities with other inmates consensually? The results showed that prison wardens do not believe that a high percentage of the inmates in their facilities engage in sexual activity, and they believe that only a few experience rape.

In 1994, in *Farmer v. Brennan,* the U.S. Supreme Court ruled that a prison's failure to protect inmates from sexual assault is a violation of the Eighth Amendment (cruel and unusual punishment). Prison rape is difficult to eliminate because of the cycle of violence.[39] Security-based methods to stop rape include controlling and restricting even consensual homosexual activity (a questionable method at best), using better classification to identify vulnerable inmates, offering victim treatment, prosecuting known incidents, and providing increased training for staff.[40] Experts also believe that the number of incidents can be lowered by screening inmates for high-risk factors for aggression and vulnerability: physical size, age, offense history, disability, sexual orientation, and prior sexual abuse.[41]

PRISON CHALLENGES

Medical Care and Death

Inmates enter prison with many physical and mental health issues. Though the majority of prisoners are young, during the 1990s an increase in older inmates occurred because of get-tough laws and mandatory sentencing. The increased elderly population also may be attributed to younger prisoners who are released and, without effective transition to the community, commit other crimes and return to prison. Prisoners over the age of 55 represent the fastest growing segment of the prison population.[42] An ACLU report estimates that by 2030 the population of elderly prisoners will approach 400,000. The aging prison population requires greater medical care and supervision as well as special geriatric wings.

Journal:
Treatment of the elderly in prison

Prison costs increase exponentially for elderly, ill inmates. State and federal prisons spend about $16 billion from taxes annually to house elderly convicts. Human Rights Watch reported that Georgia's annual average cost of medical care for prisoners over 65 years old is about $8,500, compared with $960 for younger inmates.[43] In North Carolina, the ACLU found that medical care costs for elderly prisoners were four times higher.[44] Older prisoners are more susceptible to health problems such as cancer, hypertension, asthma, hearing loss, and vision impairment. Often, lawsuits by prisoners are filed for substandard medical treatment. Some elderly inmates remain in prison in vegetative states even after their sentences, when outside placements are unavailable and they are no longer eligible for Medicaid or Medicare.

The number of inmates with HIV/AIDS who succumb to death from AIDS has dropped because of advances in medical treatment. The Centers for Disease Control and Prevention reports, however, that the prevalence of HIV infection in prison is nearly five times higher than in the general U.S. population.[45] These prisoners pose a risk for other inmates and correctional officers, but rights of privacy prohibit public identification of infected inmates. Female inmates are at a high risk for having or contacting HIV because of histories of prostitution

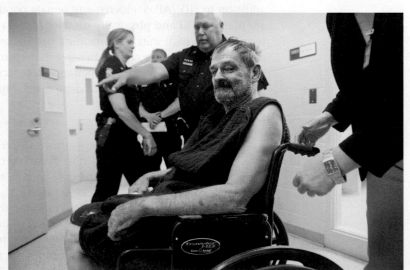

Billions of dollars are spent on the costs of medical care for older, ill prisoners. Should parole boards give special consideration to elderly prisoners? Why or why not?

Reuters/David Eulitt/The Kansas City Star/Pool

ETHICAL ISSUES

Shackled While Giving Birth

Women often are incarcerated while pregnant. A major controversy ignited when news reports emerged that women giving birth were shackled to their hospital beds. Over 30 states allow this practice. In 2012, California became widely recognized after officially banning this practice. The new law prevents the use of "leg irons, waist chains and handcuffs behind the body" on women undergoing labor, delivery, and recovery. Although some states may discourage shackling or have laws banning the practice, pregnant inmates continue to be shackled during delivery. A class action lawsuit in Illinois filed by 80 female inmates in Cook County Jail resulted in a $4.1 million settlement.

Prison officials fear that without restraints, women may escape from custody or may be violent prisoners who will harm others. Critics of the practice argue shackling women at any point during a pregnancy is dangerous. The American Medical Association also stated that the practice is "medically hazardous" and "barbaric." Other commentators suggest that shackling is a violation of the cruel and unusual punishment clause in the Eighth Amendment to the Constitution.

Think About It

1. Identify other reasons why pregnant inmates should or should not be shackled.

2. What arguments would you make for the discontinuation of shackling pregnant inmates while being taken to the hospital and while giving birth? What about recovery?

3. Describe a scenario in which a woman giving birth may attempt to escape from the hospital.

Sources: Sichel, D. L. (2008). Giving birth in shackles: A constitutional and human rights violation. *Journal of Gender, Social Policy & the Law*, 16(2), 223–255. Costantini, C. (2012, October 10). Should a woman be shackled while giving birth? Most states think so. *ABC News*. Retrieved from http://abcnews.go.com/ABC_Univision/News/woman-shackled-giving-birth-states/story?id=17436798.

and injection drug use, and a disproportionate number of racial minorities are infected.[46] Special populations are a challenge for prison administrators and correctional officers. In addition to HIV/AIDS, elderly, and female populations, prisons house many offenders who are mentally ill and physically disabled. Mentally ill inmates are often treated using short-term goals, which means controlling bad behavior and relying on medication, rather than developing long-term comprehensive management plans.[47] An estimated 3% to 11% of the jail and prison population experiences co-occurring substance use disorders and mental health issues, with high rates of depression, bipolar disorders, or schizophrenia.[48]

Prisoner Rights

Web:
Prisoners' rights

Until the 1960s, court interventions in prison cases were rare. In the case of *Cooper v. Pate* (1964) the U.S. Supreme Court began to take a closer look at prisoners' civil rights.[49] *Cooper v. Pate* represents the first case to give state prison inmates standing to sue in federal court under the Civil Rights Act of 1871. Thomas Cooper, an inmate in the Illinois State Penitentiary, argued that his religious beliefs were being denied. As a member of the Nation of Islam, he was denied permission to buy certain religious publications and denied other privileges, such as consulting with a minister and attending religious services. The Court determined that an inmate cannot be punished or disciplined based on religious beliefs; although some rights may be denied, an inmate does not relinquish all constitutional rights. In many cases, courts are faced with balancing the rights of the inmate with the security concerns of the facility.

COMMON MISCONCEPTIONS

Convicted Felons and Voting

There is a widely held misconception that while incarcerated, prisoners are not afforded the right to vote in elections. Two states allow voting while incarcerated, and the majority of states now allow convicted felons the right to vote once their sentences are completed. In the past 10 years, many states have reformed or repealed disenfranchisement provisions that limited voting, though some restrictions still exist. Kentucky and Virginia impose lifetime voting restrictions on almost all convicted felons. Maine and Vermont allow incarcerated felons to vote.

Think About It

1. **Would you give inmates the right to vote? Why or why not?**

2. **Under what circumstances would you institute a nationwide rule on inmates voting?**

3. **If an inmate has finished his or her sentence, should he or she be able to vote, and how does denying this right constitute additional punishment?**

In *Wolf v. McDonnell* (1974) inmates at a Nebraska prison argued that the disciplinary proceedings used by prison administrators, including a less than satisfactory legal assistance program and restrictive mail regulations, violated their due process rights. The U.S. Supreme Court determined that while prisoners are not entitled to full due process protections during disciplinary hearings, they must be given written notice of the charges, be provided a written statement of evidence, and be able to call witnesses and present evidence.[50] A more restrictive ruling was issued in 1995, in *Sandin v. Conner*, increasing the standards under which an inmate could present witnesses during a disciplinary hearing. The Court determined any deprivation of liberty must be "atypical and significant."[51]

Prisoners are granted the right to freedom of speech and religion, though officials may still search mail and deny certain types of reading material. Cruel and unusual punishment related to disciplinary tactics and prison conditions are prohibited. A 1994 federal court ruled in one case that a 150-year-old prison "infested with vermin, fire hazards, and bad plumbing" constituted cruel and unusual punishment.[52] Other rights include medical care for short-term and long-term conditions and adequate mental health treatment. Additionally, racial segregation is allowed only when necessary for prison security.

Prisoners, who have access to legal materials, may file appeals at the state and federal levels themselves or through attorneys. Inmates have access to courts, legal services, and legal representation. The proliferation of **jailhouse lawyer** lawsuits resulted in the **1996 Prison Litigation Reform Act**, which addressed five major issues:

1. Grievances must be processed internally before lawsuits are filed in federal court.

2. Prisoners are responsible for court filing fees.

3. Courts may dismiss lawsuits as frivolous or malicious.

4. Any prisoner claim for mental or emotional injury must include physical harm.

5. Prisoners may lose credit for good time if a judge determines that a lawsuit was filed for purposes of harassing or for presenting false information.[53]

jailhouse lawyer:
An inmate who has never received a degree or practiced law, but has become well versed in legal matters while in prison.

1996 Prison Litigation Reform Act:
A law resulting from the proliferation of jailhouse lawyers that addressed five issues related to prison litigation.

Vocational programs, like computer training, can help prisoners successfully reenter society. What other types of programs may help inmates stay out of prison?

Access to Technology

Technology is a challenging issue for many correctional facilities. One current debate is over a prisoner's right to have a Facebook page. The challenge for the courts is to determine if denial of social media, such as Facebook or Twitter, is a violation of an inmate's First Amendment rights. A current case involves a Facebook page created by the family of Elmer Wayne Henley, Jr. Henley is serving six life sentences in Texas for the abduction, rape, and murder of 28 boys and young men. The Facebook page also offered Henley's artwork for sale. Numerous problems are associated with these types of postings. First, families of Henley's victim are likely to experience strong negative emotions about the postings. Second, these pages may increase the infamy of offenders, particularly serial killers. Finally, Facebook officials have cooperated with official requests to remove the posts. In some states and cases, Facebook can be used to claim that a miscarriage of justice has occurred. Thus far, a California U.S. district court has upheld the rights of prisoners to have access to printed messages from the Internet, and in Arizona a judge allowed people to post information for inmates, who are unable to access social media. Certain released felons may also face problems with using Internet technology. Joshua Paul Benjamin, after years of having a Facebook page, was forced to delete his because he was a convicted sex offender.

Correctional Rehabilitation

Video 12.2:
Rehabilitation and transitions

Extremely limited rehabilitation and treatment programs are available in some prisons. Rehabilitation efforts focus on reform and attempt to help inmates live crime free once released. Prisons that maintain budgets for rehabilitation may offer counseling, educational and vocational programs, and drug treatment. An increasing number of prisons are discovering the benefits of dog training programs. Colorado Correctional Industries (CCI) allows inmates to train rescued dogs for adoption. The CCI website provides success stories of dogs that have been abandoned and saved. It also offers profiles of dogs available for adoption.

Rehabilitation programs vary among institutions (some methods are atypical and have little empirical support related to effectiveness) and include, for example, transcendental meditation, victim and offender mediation, dog training, yoga, Habitat for Humanity, baby care in prison, faith-based programs, conjugal visits, physical therapy, and GED classes.

LIFE AFTER PRISON: PAROLE AND REENTRY

It is estimated that approximately 65 million people currently have criminal records.[54] This is an enormous number given that in the middle of 2013, it was estimated there were about 316 million people (of all ages) living in the United States.[55] Being marked with a criminal record may mean great difficulty (and in some cases impossibility) in obtaining a job, securing housing, and even benefiting from educational or vocational training. The effects of this problem have worsened with the current "get tough on crime" sentiment, as restrictions and the stigma associated with a criminal record are more public and harsher than

Cellmates Tony Ward, left, and Brandon Rathbun bond quickly with their dog Burlesque during the meet and greet portion of the Puppies for Parole program, March 19, 2014, at the Missouri Eastern Correctional Center in Pacific.

ever before. This "collateral damage" from a criminal record persists decades following the arrest or conviction, and in some cases even after the conviction is vacated. What to do about this and the difficulties presented by a criminal record create many complications for reentry and rehabilitation efforts. The National Association of Criminal Defense Lawyers (NACDL) offers several recommendations toward restoration[56]:

1. The United States should embark on a national effort to end the second-class legal status and stigmatization of persons who have fulfilled the terms of a criminal sentence.

2. All mandatory collateral consequences should be disfavored and are never appropriate unless substantially justified by the specific offense conduct.

3. Discretionary collateral consequences should be imposed only when the offense conduct is recent and directly related to a particular benefit or opportunity.

4. Full restoration of rights and status should be available to convicted individuals upon completion of sentence.

5. Congress and federal agencies should provide individuals with federal convictions with meaningful opportunities to regain rights and status, and individuals with state convictions with mechanisms to avoid collateral consequences imposed by federal law.

6. Individuals charged with a crime should have an opportunity to avoid conviction and the collateral consequences that accompany it.

7. Employers, landlords, and other decision makers should be encouraged to offer opportunities to individuals with criminal records, and unwarranted discrimination based on a criminal record should be prohibited.

8. Jurisdictions should limit access to and use of criminal records for non–law enforcement purposes, and should ensure that records are complete and accurate.

9. Defense lawyers should consider avoiding, mitigating, and relieving collateral consequences to be an integral part of the representation of a client.

10. NACDL will initiate public education programs and advocacy aimed at curtailing collateral consequences and eliminating the social stigma that accompanies conviction.

Released inmates face significant barriers after release. How can community members help with the reentry of ex-offenders?

Video 12.3:
Prisoner reentry

Many inmates are released from prison on parole. Parole represents a provisional release of a prisoner, who is then expected to meet the expectations and conditions of the parole board. In most states, members of the parole board are appointed by the governor and confirmed by the senate. Initially, a parole hearing is held to determine if an offender has served the minimum terms of his or her incarceration and is ready for release. Not all inmates are released at parole hearings. Victims and relatives of victims have the option of attending the hearing and are allowed to make a statement. Also, victims or family members may offer statements through a representative, by video, in a written statement, or in person, and they have the right to be notified of the board's final decision.[57]

Inmates granted parole are required to fulfill conditions determined by the board, and any violations result in a parolee's being sent back to prison. Conditions for parole vary but most commonly include gaining employment, obeying the law, remaining in the state, and paying any required restitution to victims or the community. Also, parolees are not allowed to have firearms or any other deadly weapons. Violations of parole conditions may result in warnings, intermediate sanctions, or revocation of parole.

Community Reentry

Prisons may offer some transition programs to help released prisoners succeed, although many of these efforts fall short. For example, 40% of women released from prison commit new crimes within 3 years.[58] Many offenders exit prison with the best of intentions, but they face many challenges and hurdles. Prisonization often hinders reentry into the community because behaviors seen as acceptable in prison are seen by people outside of prison as offensive or strange. Prisoners face changes in society, technology, and economic trends. Released inmates must follow the conditions of parole. As with terms of probation, parolees must obey the law, maintain contact with parole officers, and avoid drug use. Any association with known felons is prohibited. Other conditions may be specific to the offender and the type of offense.

In 2011, the National Institute of Justice reported that 1,885 inmates per day were released from state and federal custody.[59] According to the Bureau of Justice Statistics, 637,400 inmates were released from state and federal prisons in 2012. The large number of released prisoners makes reentry a top priority. Reentry includes any efforts to prepare and assist ex-convicts to reenter and live in the community.[60] Partial funding for reentry comes from the Second Chance Act of 2007, which provides grants for programs and research on offender reentry. The Second Chance reentry program funds efforts such as California's Prisoner Reentry Employment Program, which offers a wide range of services and training for parolees for job readiness training, housing and life skills programs, and mental health treatment.

Reentry programs and services can be found nationwide. Services include help with food, housing, employment, health care, and education. A program in Houston, Texas, trains offenders in the culinary arts and warehouse certification.[61] The Colorado Criminal Justice Reform Coalition developed a comprehensive *Go Guide* that provides tips on working with case managers, guidelines for understanding parole, child support advice, and how to find medical and mental health treatment, employment, and financial assistance.[62] The California Reentry Program offers a comprehensive website with available resources; it also arranges meetings with prisoners at San Quentin State Prison before release.[63] National websites serve as clearinghouses for establishing and accessing successful programs (see http://csgjusticecenter.org/jc/category/reentry/nrrc and www.reentry.net).

The **intensive case management** approach represents an evidence-based practice that appears to be relatively successful. Programming includes low staff-to-client ratios; 24-hour coverage; and services and referrals for mental health treatment, housing, living skills, employment, and crisis intervention.[64] Addressing co-occurring disorders such as mental illness and drug abuse, especially among women, is essential to facilitating reentry.

Employment

Employment is recognized as one of the most crucial elements of successful reentry. Ex-convicts face barriers to obtaining jobs because of the stigma of having been in prison, and potential employers review applications for criminal backgrounds. On most job applications, ex-convicts must disclose convictions. In a tough job market, many other qualified applicants without prison records are available for hire. The lack of job opportunities often results in reoffending.

Often, ex-convicts have problems finding employment because of the stigmatization associated with having spent time in prison. A successful movement has started in the

intensive case management: An evidence-based practice that includes low staff-to-client ratios; 24-hour coverage; and services and referrals for mental health treatment, housing, living skills, employment, and crisis intervention.

United States to "ban the black box." The ban-the-box campaign argues that forcing convicted, recently released felons to check their status on a job application unfairly removes them from applicant pool. To date, 24 states and over 100 cities have adopted fair-chance policies, and the criminal history question is no longer included on job applications.[65]

Successful reentry requires job training, employment counseling, and placement programs.[66] In the Returning Home study, the Urban Institute highlighted the importance of employment and its role in reducing recidivism:

- Prisoners acknowledge the importance of a job for reducing the chances of future incarceration, but only one in five has a job lined up immediately after release.
- Work release jobs while still incarcerated improve chances of full-time employment after release.
- Case managers and regular contact increase the chance of finding and maintaining employment.
- Substance abuse treatment, including Alcoholics Anonymous and Narcotics Anonymous, increases the odds of working full-time.
- Transportation challenges often interfere with employment.[67]

Maintaining connections with family is an important aspect of prison life and reentry. Why is it important for inmates to remain in contact with their families?

Marriage and Relationships

Often ex-convicts have few friends and family members to rely on once they reenter the community, though a surprisingly large number maintain some level of contact with their children.[68] The lack of support and resources provided by family and friends makes successful transition difficult. The majority of former prisoners depend on family for housing immediately after release. As a result of spending time in prison, these relationships may be strained and often require major adjustments.

Maintaining family ties while still in prison can facilitate reentry. Families may represent the impetus to succeed in the community. In fact, as noted by criminologists John Laub and Robert Sampson, an investment in marriage (and work) represents a structural turning point that increases informal social control. A spouse and/or children are more likely to recognize deviant behavior, and stronger attachment bonds keep the offender from transgressing. Strong family relationships may result in "desistance by default" of criminal activities because offenders fear risking these connections.[69] Numerous research studies suggest that emotional support, housing and financial assistance, and acceptance and encouragement by family are essential to success.[70] Reentry is a stressful event for the released inmate, and ex-offenders with families benefit from programs or services to manage finances and secure employment.[71]

Sex Offender Registries

Sex offenders often face additional obstacles in reentry. Once these ex-convicts are released from prison, they are required to register as sex offenders. Sex offender registries track detailed information on offenders, including where they live and work. Finding housing is particularly difficult because of restrictions on living within a certain distance from a school and notices by law enforcement to neighbors (community notification laws). Many people believe that tracking the whereabouts of sex offenders is crucial to public safety because of the high risk of recidivism, though actual rates of reoffending are debatable.

A review of research studies suggests low rates of recidivism among sex offenders compared with other types of offenders, although accounting for the types of crimes, follow-up time frames, and underreporting undermines overall results.[72] Also, a wide variety of offenders must register (e.g., pedophiles, exhibitionists, rapists, child pornographers), and depending on the offense, they reoffend at different rates, which complicates research on recidivism.

Get-tough legislation to reduce the number of sexual crimes has occurred at the local, state, and federal levels. Federal legislation includes the following:

- The **Jacob Wetterling Crimes Against Children Act and Sexually Violent Offender Registration Act** requires convicted sex offenders to register with local law enforcement.
- **Megan's Law** requires registry information gathered in the Wetterling Act to be made public, including community notifications, photographs, names, and addresses of registered offenders.
- The **Adam Walsh Protection Act** mandates that states classify offenders based on type of offense; register sex offenders in jurisdictions where they live, work, or attend school; verify addresses according to yearly timelines; and make registries available on the Internet. Offenders may be registered for anywhere from 15 years to life.

States have passed legislation establishing safety zones (areas where sex offenders are not allowed), lifetime GPS monitoring, chemical castration using hormone injections, bans from the Internet, stamping "sex offender" on driver's licenses, and residency restrictions.[73] The collateral consequences of these laws produced fear in the community and protests in the yards of known offenders; harassment and evictions have become commonplace.

CASE STUDY

Case Study Video 12.1: Interviews with case study participants

Joshua Paul Benjamin continues to experience firsthand the hardships associated with sex offender registries. Although he served his time in prison and was released almost a decade before any law required sex offenders to register, Joshua was nonetheless required to register. A result of this registration was his removal from his apartment, his inability to live at his mother's home (her home was too close to a school), and the loss of his job. These events occurred, although he lived a crime-free life, had no issues at his apartment, and was considered a stellar employee. Many years later, his mother moved to a home in which Joshua would legally be able to live. Despite the completion of a PhD, he continues to be unable to secure work. Over the years, Joshua has received many excellent job offers, but when administrators of the organizations learn of his record, the jobs suddenly become unavailable.

Jacob Wetterling Crimes Against Children Act and Sexually Violent Offender Registration Act: Requires convicted sex offenders to register with local law enforcement.

Megan's Law: Requires that registry information gathered via the Wetterling Act be made public.

Adam Walsh Protection Act: Requires states to classify offenders based on type of offense; register sex offenders where they live, work, or attend school; and make registries available on the Internet.

Websites provide detailed information on sex offenders. MapSexOffenders.com and the U.S. Department of Justice's National Sex Offender Public website (www.nsopr.gov) are nationwide sex offender databases. Anyone can select a state and search for sexually violent predators, offenders with multiple offenses, and individuals who failed to register, and check for felony convictions. Information for each person includes his or her date of birth, type of conviction(s), race, gender, description, last known address, and picture. Whether registries keep the community safe or reduce recidivism is unknown.

Recidivism

For many years, prisons were said to have revolving doors because of high rates of recidivism. Once released, ex-convicts committed additional crimes or failed to meet the requirements of parole and were sent back to prison. The large number of ex-convicts would mean high reoffending. In 2012, according to the Bureau of Justice Statistics, nearly 1 million persons were either on parole or released from parole. Since 2005, however, the United States has experienced a decline in the rate of reincarceration for new sentences and revocations. Identifying specific factors for this reduction is difficult. Many offenders tend to age out of crime. Another explanation may be attributed to improved reentry methods such as intensive case management or an increase in legitimate employment opportunities for ex-offenders.

As noted above, recidivism among criminals is problematic. At least for our case studies, though, this has not been the case. Joshua Paul Benjamin continues to live a crime-free life (which is perhaps surprising given the hardships he continues to face). Chris Farias has been free of his work-release program and continues in therapy and refrains from drinking. Of course, Dennis Bradford, the offender in the Jennifer Schuett case, is not a recidivism risk given his suicide in jail while awaiting court proceedings. Danny Madrid returned to prison for 1 year after his release, though the incident was nonviolent and a parole violation. Using one definition of recidivism (i.e., committing any crime within a particular amount of time from release), Danny's act that sent him back to prison would be considered recidivism. Using a definition of recidivism requiring one to commit the *same* type of crime that resulted in the original sentence within a specified time period, Danny did not recidivate.

The majority of people incarcerated in jails and prisons are released back into the community. This includes individuals who committed heinous crimes such as murder, attempted murder, and rape. Often these individuals are released back into the same communities where their victims live. In the past, when an offender was released, the victim was not informed. Today, victims' rights have changed, and victim notification is a staple in the criminal justice system. Per 18 U.S.C. § 3771, crime victims' rights include (among others) being reasonably protected from offenders and the right to be notified in a timely and accurate fashion of any public court proceeding. Thus, a victim has the right to learn when

CONTEMPLATING CAREERS

Inmate Case Manager

Are you organized and objective? Are you able to work with individuals who may be dangerous? Do you have excellent vision and hearing? Are you emotionally and mentally stable? Are you able to communicate well in writing and orally? Do you have the temperament to work with inmates to minimize the risk that they'll commit new crimes? Are you happy working in the field and in an office? If this type of work in a varied environment is enticing, you may be cut out to be an inmate case manager.

Case managers, also known as correctional treatment specialists, evaluate the progress of incarcerated inmates as they serve their time. Managers are responsible for coordinating inmate training programs and analyzing program needs. As part of their work, case managers develop inmate social histories and must objectively identify both the strengths and weaknesses of inmates in order to create release plans.

This position requires a minimum of 24 hours of college courses in a field such as criminal justice, sociology, political science, psychology, social work, or counseling. While 24 hours is the minimum requirement, you will be far more competitive with a 4-year degree in one of the mentioned disciplines. Salary varies based on education and experience, although the Bureau of Labor Statistics notes that the 2015 median pay was $49,360 annually, which corresponds to $23.73 per hour.[74] According to the Bureau of Labor Statistics, correctional treatment specialist employment is anticipated to increase about four percent in the about the next decade.

Career Video:
A case manager discusses his experience and current issues in the field.

crimes are more violent and typically involve less victimization. How should white-collar offenders be treated differently than violent offenders in prison? Who may be more likely to reoffend when released from prison? Explain why.

5. **Solitary Confinement Versus Prisoner Safety.** Imagine Dennis Bradford had survived and been sentenced to prison. Given his crimes against a child, he may have been a target of violence from other offenders. One strategy to keep him safe would be to place him in solitary confinement. Yet we know that solitary confinement is problematic for inmates. Placing someone like Dennis Bradford in the general population may get him seriously injured or killed. Placing him in solitary confinement may produce devastating emotional and psychology outcomes. Danny Madrid did get placed in solitary confinement multiple times. Initially it was for his own protection, since he was young. Does that warrant such harsh treatment? What would you do if you were an administrator? What other choices are there? What is the best way to proceed for individuals such as Danny Madrid and Dennis Bradford?

DIGITAL RESOURCES

Sharpen your skills with SAGE edge at edge.sagepub.com/rennison2e. SAGE edge for Students provides a personalized approach to help you accomplish your coursework goals in an easy-to-use learning environment. You'll find action plans, mobile-friendly eFlashcards, and quizzes as well as video and web resources and links to SAGE journal articles to support and expand on the concepts presented in this chapter.

PART V

BEYOND THE BASICS

THE JUVENILE
JUSTICE SYSTEM

> "In the last 70 years many dedicated men and women have devoted their professional lives to the enlightened task of bringing us out of the dark world of Charles Dickens in meeting our responsibilities to the child in our society. The result has been the creation in this century of a *system* of *juvenile* and family courts in each of the 50 States."
>
> —U.S. Supreme Court Justice
> Potter Stewart

Matt McClain/The Washington Post via Getty Images

LEARNING OBJECTIVES

After finishing this chapter, you should be able to:

13.1 Describe the history of the juvenile justice system, and why the doctrine of *parens patriae* shapes and maintains the current system.

13.2 Define the important concepts and terminology found in the juvenile justice system, and summarize important Supreme Court cases with respect to juvenile rights.

13.3 Evaluate current rates of juvenile offenses and the differences in offending patterns for girls and minorities.

13.4 Describe the various steps in the juvenile justice system, and how they are similar to and different from steps in the adult system.

13.5 Identify the rights of victims of juvenile delinquency, and how they differ from victims of crimes committed by adults.

INTRODUCTION: THE JUVENILE JUSTICE SYSTEM

The contemporary juvenile system was built, in part, based on a commonsense approach that youth need protection and understanding. The juvenile justice system is distinct from the adult criminal justice system in that it reflects this perspective and has its own special terms and procedures. And unlike the adult system, the contemporary juvenile justice system strongly focuses on a rehabilitative goal and the best interests of the child. As in any legal system, errors occur and some failure is inevitable, but overall the juvenile system is relatively successful at determining the best interests of the child to promote positive change, despite what seems like an increasingly punitive approach. In most criminal justice programs, entire courses are devoted to the theories of delinquency and the juvenile justice system. This chapter is designed to give you an introduction and overview of the unique features of the juvenile justice system. And as you will see, the approach to dealing with wayward youth used today has not always been in place.

JUVENILE JUSTICE: A BRIEF HISTORY

The juvenile justice system is distinct from the structure, processes, and policies found in the adult system, although in some cases serious young

In the late 1900s, boys often were placed in workhouses in efforts to reform or rehabilitate. Describe how the juvenile justice system in the U.S. has changed its effort to help children.

Web:
Juvenile justice

Web:
Juvenile Justice history

offenders may be dealt with in the latter. The treatment of children in the legal system has a long and sordid history. The development of our juvenile justice system initially was grounded in English common law as jurists began to formally recognize and pass established standards related to a child's inability to form intent. Consider the actions of a young child compared with those of a young adult. Would a 7-year-old who kills his or her parents have a different understanding of this act compared with a 21-year-old? The most likely answer is yes, because biological, psychological, and social developmental stages are distinct and different for children and adults.

During the 18th and 19th centuries in England, juveniles were treated with harsh punishment and often placed in adult prisons, where they were easy targets for victimization. In the quotation opening this chapter, U.S. Supreme Court justice Potter Stewart referenced the dark world in the writings of Charles Dickens, whose novels portrayed the deplorable conditions for criminal and neglected children in London. In *Oliver Twist,* Dickens described the unfortunate plight of delinquent, unwanted children "to be cuffed and buffeted through the world, despised by all, and pitied by none." In England, abandoned and delinquent children were forced to labor long hours in terrible, abusive conditions at workhouses. Other children lived on the streets of London and scavenged for food and shelter, often engaging in petty crimes in order to survive, and were seen by royalty and members of the public as a scourge.[1]

In America, the first 13 colonies were influenced by the common law of England, much of which was grounded in the work of Sir William Blackstone, a famous lawyer whose widely celebrated legal tome, *Commentaries on the Laws of England,* was published in the late 1760s. On the topics of *mens rea* and *actus reus,* Blackstone argued that certain people were incapable of forming the intent or action of committing a crime and identified "infants" as children too young to understand their actions and consequences. Generally, children under the age of 7 were considered infants and viewed as incapable of forming the intent necessary for serious criminal offenses. Older children, especially those over 14 years old, were treated as adults, though accountability for the in-between ages depended on their ability to distinguish between right and wrong.

Development of a Different System for Juveniles

In the 18th century, children who engaged in wrongdoing were treated like adults in the penal system, and in the home, parents were responsible for controlling their behavior. *Patria postestas* established a father's right to use strict discipline for unruly children. By the 19th century, in the United States, increased birthrates, immigration, and industrialization resulted in large numbers of dependent and destitute children.[2] As a result, the U.S. juvenile justice system began to develop among numerous reform efforts.

During the 19th and 20th centuries the **child savers** emerged as progressive reformers who were determined to improve the treatment of juveniles. The child savers believed that children were not inherently bad or evil but were a product of their environments. This group was opposed to the imprisonment of children with adult offenders and the rancid conditions of workhouses. The child savers worked as advocates and fought for legislation, believing that the state had the right to intervene in family matters and the responsibility for taking care of children. Child saver reformers initiated efforts to build institutions designed to rehabilitate juveniles. The underlying model was to use treatment methods rather than punishment. These

patria postestas:
A father's right to use strict discipline for ill-behaved children.

child savers: Child advocates who fought to reform the brutal and harsh juvenile system.

houses of refuge, controlled by the state, provided shelter and structure for dependent, neglected, and delinquent children. In 1825, the Society for the Prevention of Juvenile Delinquency established one of the first reform houses in New York and worked to build a network of foster home placements. The Chicago Reform School opened in 1855. The first school for girls in Massachusetts opened in 1856.[3] Unfortunately, despite efforts to help educate and treat children, the reform schools failed to protect them from harsh punishment, abuse, and unfair labor practices.

The true age of reform for the system began in 1899 with the creation of **juvenile courts**. This period of change often is referred to as the Progressive Era. In 1899, Illinois passed the Juvenile Court Act, designed to "regulate the treatment and control of dependent, neglected, and delinquent children," and opened the first juvenile-specific court in Cook County (Chicago). By 1945, all states had implemented some type of juvenile court.[4] Like the child saver movement, the juvenile courts were based on a medical model (i.e., treatment) focused on rehabilitation rather than punishment. With the specialized judicial system in place, children 16 years old or younger were removed from the adult criminal court's jurisdiction.

The New York City House of Refuge opened in 1797. Many of these houses were criticized for their cruel practices. What reasons do you believe contributed to the legal system's decision to ignore the horrific conditions? What explanations would you offer for the failure of the child savers movement? Is forcing children to learn a vocation a good or bad method of treatment? Why?

Wikimedia Commons

Parens Patriae: In the Best Interest of the Child

The evolution and philosophical development of juvenile justice is firmly grounded on the principle of **parens patriae** (Latin for "parent of his country," also translated as "the state is the father"). This doctrine, which gives the state the power to act as a child's parent, represents an important aspect of the juvenile system, although the idea of the state assuming care of children is not without controversy. *Parens patriae,* however, establishes the most important foundation of the juvenile system. The most essential and fundamental question in the juvenile system is this: What is the best interest of the child?

The case of *Ex parte Crouse,* decided in 1838 by the Pennsylvania Supreme Court, expanded and reinforced the importance of *parens patriae.* The court determined that the state has a right and an obligation to remove children from questionable households lacking in appropriate parental supervision.[5] In this case, Mary Ann Crouse was taken from her home and committed to the Pennsylvania House of Refuge after her mother complained of her "vicious conduct." The girl's father, however, objected and argued the placement was a violation of the child's constitutional rights. The court ruled the state had the right to commit the young girl for her own protection based on the doctrine of *parens patriae.* The court decision found no violation of constitutional rights because Mary Ann was not imprisoned; in the house of refuge she could be protected and rehabilitated.[6]

The juvenile justice system, though continually evolving, has retained the basic philosophy that the protection and rehabilitation of children is fundamental to achieving its goal. The juvenile system has, in most cases, retained the idea of treatment and remained a non-adversarial process to help determine the best interests of the child. To maintain the informal nature of the system, the terms and procedures are markedly different from the adult criminal justice system (see Common Misconceptions). Juvenile delinquents are neither "tried" in a court of law nor found "guilty," though they are afforded many of the same due process rights as adult offenders.

houses of refuge: State shelters established to house dependent, neglected, and delinquent children.

juvenile courts: Courts designed specifically for juveniles to "regulate the treatment and control of dependent, neglected, and delinquent children."

parens patriae: Latin for "parent of his country" or "the state is the father." A doctrine that gives the state the power to act as a child's parent.

COMMON MISCONCEPTIONS

Distinguishing Concepts and Terminology Unique to the Juvenile Justice System

The terms used in the juvenile and adult systems help identify the distinction between the two. The terms are often misused in discussions of the juvenile system procedures. Use of appropriate terms for each system reflects the well-thought-out distinctions between the two systems. In addition, the differences in the systems reflect constitutional rights given adults not afforded to juveniles, including the right to trial by an impartial jury, a public trial, or rights associated with bail.

Juvenile System	Adult System
Focus on treatment	Focus on punishment
Informal proceedings	Formal proceedings
Taken into custody/detained	Arrested
Detention centers	Jails
Petition for delinquency	Criminal indictment
Respondent	Defendant
Adjudication	Conviction
Nonadversarial	Adversarial
Closed proceedings	Public/open proceedings
Nonjury "trials" or hearings	Jury trials
Disposition	Sentencing
Aftercare	Parole

Think About It

1. Do the differences in approaches used for juveniles and adults matter? Why is that? Would Danny Madrid have gone down a better or worse path in life had he been sent to the adult system after his first encounter with law enforcement?

2. Does the distinction in terms used between the juvenile and adult courts make a difference? Would you be more likely to offer a job to someone who was in an "aftercare program" versus on "parole"? Why or why not?

ESTABLISHING JUVENILE RIGHTS

Video 13.1:
Montgomery v. Louisiana

Because the juvenile justice system developed separately from the adult system, legislators and judges adopted a hands-off approach, for the most part, until a number of controversial issues about basic rights came to the courts' attention. In the 1960s, several U.S. Supreme Court decisions changed the treatment of juveniles in the system and granted them many of the same due process rights outlined in the Bill of Rights that adults already enjoyed. These court decisions changed the juvenile system in deep and meaningful ways.

Kent v. United States (1966) established procedural safeguards for juveniles charged with serious offenses. Sixteen-year-old Morris Kent, who had a history of burglary and attempted purse snatching, was identified as a potential suspect in a robbery and rape case. After interrogation by the police, Kent confessed to the behavior. Kent's mother retained a lawyer, and a psychological examination revealed that the young man suffered from "severe psychopathology."[7] Despite recommendations that Kent be transferred to a psychiatric facility for treatment, he was detained at a juvenile facility until the matter was transferred, without a hearing, to the jurisdiction of the adult court. The U.S. Supreme Court eventually addressed the constitutional issues involved in Kent's transfer to the adult court system.

The Court's majority opinion, written by Justice Abe Fortas, found that Kent was entitled to a hearing before the case was transferred to an adult court. The *Kent* decision established procedural safeguards for juveniles charged with serious delinquent acts. The Court ruling set the stage for informal hearings, which entitled a child to counsel before the case was transferred to an adult court.

In re Gault (1967), identified by many jurists and scholars as the most significant change in the juvenile justice system, altered the adjudication process and established due process rights. Gerald Gault, a 15-year-old living in Arizona, was taken into custody for allegedly making an obscene phone call to a neighbor. Gault was already on probation for stealing a wallet from a woman's purse. The sequence of events became instrumental in guiding the court's decision:

Michelle Carter, center, is shown at the Bristol County Juvenile Court in Taunton, Massachusetts, on Friday, July 29, 2016. Lawyers for Carter, charged with involuntary manslaughter for sending her boyfriend text messages encouraging him to take his own life, have asked a judge to suppress statements she made to police.

- At 10 a.m. the suspect, Gerald Gault, was picked up by the police and taken to a children's detention home. His parents were not contacted.

- At 6 p.m. his mother discovered her son missing and was told by the police that he was being held at a detention center until a scheduled hearing was conducted. Neither Gault nor his parents were informed of the charges.

- At the initial hearing Gault was not present, no sworn witnesses were called (including the neighbor who made the accusations), no legal representation for the accused was in the courtroom, and no record was made of the proceedings.

- The court failed to identify any specific charges except for accusing Gault of "delinquency."

After a second hearing, the judge committed 15-year-old Gault to Arizona's State Industrial School until he turned 21. Had the same circumstances been processed through an adult court, the penalty for using vulgar or obscene language would have been a $50 fine and imprisonment for a maximum of 2 months.[8]

The U.S. Supreme Court determined that Gault was denied due process and overturned his sentence. The *Gault* decision established the following rights for juveniles: notice of the charges, legal representation, confrontation and cross-examination of witnesses, and protection against self-incrimination.[9]

In re Winship (1970) changed the standard of evidence for juvenile courts. Twelve-year-old Samuel Winship was accused of stealing $112 from a purse and faced 6 years in a juvenile training school. Winship's guilt was based on a preponderance of evidence, and many of the involved parties believed that such a lengthy and punitive sentence should be based on the stricter standard of reasonable doubt. Supporters of using the lower standard of proof argued that his incarceration was a method of rehabilitation, not punishment. Though the appeal was rejected by the New York high courts, the U.S. Supreme Court granted *certiorari*. The 5–3 decision by the high court determined that the reasonable doubt standard applied to adults and juveniles.

One due process right not guaranteed in the juvenile system is the right to a jury trial. In *McKeiver v. Pennsylvania* (1971) the Supreme Court held that juveniles brought to trial had no right to a jury. Joseph McKeiver and Edward Terry were charged with robbery, larceny, and receiving stolen goods. The Juvenile Court of Philadelphia denied their requests for a jury trial. When the case reached the U.S. Supreme Court, the majority recognized that juveniles were afforded the protections related to accurate fact finding in order to ensure fundamental fairness, which could be determined by a judge. The majority opinion ruled that jury trials would create an adversarial system, ignoring a basic premise of the juvenile courts (i.e., the nonadversarial approach), and create substantial costs, delays, and unnecessary formality.

Juvenile facilities often are overcrowded. How have U.S. Supreme Court decisions added to or alleviated this problem?

In *Roper v. Simmons* (2005) the Supreme Court addressed the use of capital punishment for juvenile offenders. Christopher Simmons was sentenced to death in 1993 at the age of 17. Simmons, along with two friends, had entered Shirley Crook's home, kidnapped the woman, bound her with duct tape and electrical cord, and threw her into a river. The Court noted that Simmons was the instigator of the heinous act and previously had talked with friends about wanting to murder someone. In discussions with his co-conspirators, Simmons planned the brutal murder and noted that they could "get away with it" because they were minors. After the murder, Simmons bragged about the killing and commented he had killed a woman "because the bitch seen my face."[10] Simmons was tried as an adult and sentenced to death. During the penalty phase of the trial, the prosecutor argued that the murder "involved depravity of mind and was outrageously and wantonly vile, horrible, and inhuman."[11] In a 5–4 decision, the Supreme Court ruled that, based on standards of decency, the execution of minors violated the Eighth Amendment's cruel and unusual punishment clause. The majority opinion cited several reasons for the ruling, including a general consensus against the death penalty for minors among state legislatures, the disproportionate nature of the punishment, and international opposition to the juvenile death penalty (see Figure 13.1).

Five years later, *Graham v. Florida* (2010) addressed the question of juveniles serving life sentences without parole. In 2001, Graham, age 16, and two friends attempted to rob a restaurant in Florida. Graham was arrested and charged as an adult for a variety of acts: armed burglary with assault and battery, and armed robbery. He pleaded guilty, and 6 months later he was again arrested. This time Graham was arrested for a robbery and home invasion. This arrest placed him in violation of his earlier plea agreement, and the judge sentenced Graham to life in prison. Florida, where these offenses took place, had abolished parole, so the sentence was actually life without parole. The case was appealed on the grounds that a life sentence without parole for a juvenile who did not commit a homicide represented cruel and unusual punishment. The Supreme Court agreed and in doing so eliminated sentences of life without parole for nonhomicide cases involving juveniles. In 2012, Graham was resentenced to 25 years in prison.

Two years later, the Supreme Court extended the *Graham v. Florida* ruling in *Miller v. Alabama* (2012) when it decided that mandatory sentences of life without the possibility of parole for juvenile offenders are unconstitutional for crimes with the exception of murder. This decision was based on two cases in which juveniles were involved in violence. In one, a 14-year-old stayed outside while his friends robbed a video store, then shot and killed the clerk. Evidence shows the 14-year-old did enter the store shortly before the murder, but he was not the shooter. The second case involved a 14-year-old who with an accomplice became intoxicated with drugs and alcohol with a third party. When the third party passed out, the two boys robbed him. The juveniles beat the victim, and later returned to destroy evidence of the crime. They set fire to the man's trailer, where he ultimately died from the beating and smoke inhalation. Both 14-year-olds in these cases were given life sentences with no possibility of parole. The majority opinion noted that sentencing a juvenile to life without parole for crimes committed violates the Eight Amendment's prohibition on cruel and unusual punishment.

Author Video:
Life without parole for juveniles

In 2016, the Supreme Court ruled in *Montgomery v. Louisiana* that *Miller v. Alabama* must be applied retroactively, affecting more than 2,300 cases in the United States. The ruling means that individuals who as juveniles received automatic life sentences with no chance of parole must be resentenced or considered for parole. The Sentencing Project offers a map of

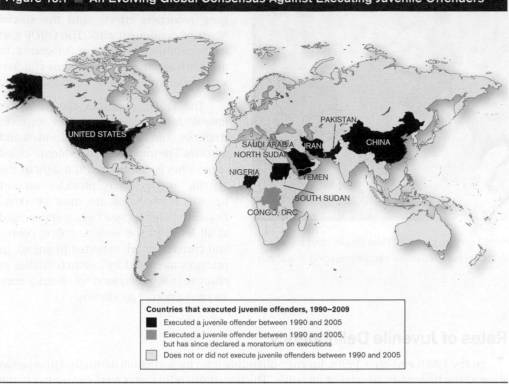

Figure 13.1 ■ An Evolving Global Consensus Against Executing Juvenile Offenders

Countries that executed juvenile offenders, 1990–2009

■ Executed a juvenile offender between 1990 and 2005

■ Executed a juvenile offender between 1990 and 2005, but has since declared a moratorium on executions

□ Does not or did not execute juvenile offenders between 1990 and 2005

Source: Prison Policy Initiative. Data from Amnesty International. (2011). *Indecent and internationally illegal: The death penalty against child offenders.* Retrieved from https://www.amnesty.org/download/Documents/116000/amr511432002en.pdf.

the United States that shows states that have banned or limited life without parole for juveniles: http://www.sentencingproject.org/publications/juvenile-life-without-parole/.

THE CONTEMPORARY JUVENILE JUSTICE SYSTEM

Youthful offenders are typically considered to be individuals who are 18 years old or younger, though age parameters vary by state. In Wyoming, a juvenile is considered someone age 19 or younger, while in Connecticut it is age 16 or younger, and in New York and North Carolina a juvenile is age 15 or younger. A lack of consensus is apparent among jurisdictions, and juvenile courts may supervise young adults until the age of 20 to 24.[12] For example, California, Montana, Oregon, and Wisconsin supervise young adults until age 24. In delinquency matters, some state juvenile courts may hold jurisdiction through the full term of the disposition, no matter what the age of the offender. Juvenile courts also handle children in need of supervision and dependent and neglected youth.

Juvenile **delinquency** refers to youthful offenders who engage in illegal acts, such as theft, burglary, robbery, property damage, or the sale or use of illegal drugs. In other words, these are the same types of criminal offenses adult offenders engage in. **Status offenses**, in comparison, are acts illegal only for juveniles: running away, truancy, possession of alcohol, smoking cigarettes, or curfew violations. There is no equivalent to status offenses among adults.

In 1974, Congress passed the **Juvenile Justice and Delinquency Prevention Act**, which was reauthorized in 2002. The legislation was designed to prevent delinquency and improve the juvenile justice system.[13] As a result, the Office of Juvenile Justice and Delinquency Prevention (OJJDP) was established to support community efforts to provide treatment and rehabilitation programs. The OJJDP's programs and efforts have addressed numerous issues in the system,

delinquency: Illegal actions by a youthful offender.

status offenses: Offenses that apply only to juveniles, such as smoking and curfew violations.

Juvenile Justice and Delinquency Prevention Act: A 1974 law that was designed to prevent delinquency and improve the juvenile justice system.

Status offenses are acts committed only by juveniles. How should children, who often imitate the actions of adults, be handled when caught engaging in a status offense?

including, for example, the disproportionate numbers of minorities in the system, gang reduction efforts, and the special needs of delinquent girls. The OJJDP also has established important programs to deal with Internet crimes against children and special interventions for tribal youth.[14]

The OJJDP publishes the *Journal of Juvenile Justice,* which provides research, strategies, and tactics for practitioners and scholars. The importance of evidence-based approaches is emphasized throughout the system, and research provides support for which programs are most effective. Evidence-based approaches are encouraged at all levels in the system. Police, courts, and corrections are expected to engage in practices identified by research studies as effective for prevention of delinquency and reduction of recidivism.

Rates of Juvenile Delinquency

In the 1980s and early 1990s, juvenile offending rates increased substantially. Urban areas showed the highest arrest rates of juveniles. The higher offending rates were connected to the accessibility of illegal firearms, crack, and increases in gang activity. Offending rates rose to their highest levels in the early to mid-1990s and then began to decline. In Denver, Colorado, the 1993 "Summer of Violence," which resulted in 74 homicides, created a climate of fear among the public and politicians. Ten bills to deal with youth violence were signed into law during a special legislative session, and Governor Roy Romer publicly announced, "These are very young people who have no code of conduct, no moral framework that teaches them to respect life."[15] As a result of the increasing violence, the movement toward a more punitive juvenile justice system swept across the entire country and remains in place today.

During the 1990s, members of the public and politicians believed the country was headed into a never-ending wave of juvenile violence that would spin out of control. Fear of juvenile violence was further promulgated by the introduction of the idea of the juvenile **superpredator** by John Dilulio, a political science professor at Princeton University. Dilulio coined the term *superpredator* and called attention to juveniles who recklessly engaged in violent, impulsive acts of murder, assault, robbery, and burglary.[16] His overblown rhetoric (picked up by some opportunistic politicians) warned of an impending storm of juveniles flooding the streets, creating a "crime bomb."[17] Despite research findings showing the notion of serious violence waves caused by superpredators to be untrue, the myth created and perpetrated by a few criminologists and the media led policymakers to enact more punitive laws to combat the projected (but never realized) rising tide of juvenile delinquency.[18] Many jurisdictions passed curfew, parental responsibility, and anti-gang laws. By the late 1990s, zero tolerance became the standard for dealing with juveniles as the get-tough approach took hold.

The Federal Bureau of Investigation's (FBI) Uniform Crime Reports (UCR) arrest data show decreases in juvenile offending and arrests over time. In 2014, the number of juvenile arrests (804,104) was 64% lower compared with 2001 (2,273,500 arrests).[19] Even compared with the adult system, arrests decreased dramatically over time, but have stabilized since.[20] Still, even with this decrease, FBI data show in 2014, there were 804,104 arrests of juveniles (under the age of 18) recorded in the UCR. During the same year, 590 juveniles were arrested for murder, 2,564 were arrested for rape, 15,312 were arrested for robbery, and 23,657 were arrested for aggravated assault. A total of 184,821 arrests of juveniles for property crimes were recorded in UCR arrest data, though based only on acts reported to the police, offer information on trends, demographics, and locations. The data are based on the

superpredator: A term coined by Princeton University's John Dilulio to describe the threat of increasing violent juvenile crime.

Table 13.1 ■ Uniform Crime Reports: Juvenile Arrests in 2014, Percentages and Rates per 100,000 for Select Offenses and Populations

Offense	Estimated Number of Juvenile Arrests	Percentage of Total Juvenile Arrests			Rate of Juvenile Arrests per 100,000			
		Female	Younger Than 15	Hispanic/ Latino (any race)	White (age 10–17 only)	Black (age 10–17 only)	American Indian (age 10–17 only)	Asian (age 10–17 only)
Murder and nonnegligent manslaughter	511	8	8	27	1.2	7.9	1.1	0.4
Rape	2,432	4	39	22	8.4	19.8	4.0	0.8
Robbery	13,260	10	20	21	21.2	253.4	18.1	9.2
Aggravated assault	22,211	25	33	27	65.7	233.4	53.6	19.4
Burglary	29,528	12	28	27	90.1	307.8	61.0	23.8
Vandalism	33,832	16	39	25	129.0	208.1	103.5	21.6
Weapons	14,798	11	34	32	47.3	150.5	23.2	15.3
Driving under the influence	5,234	25.8	2.2	25	24.7	7.5	21.7	6.0
Drug abuse violations	80,741	21	16	29	329.3	470.3	258.3	76.7
Liquor laws	40,231	40	9	17	183.1	70.1	274.7	34.8
Curfew and loitering	40,028	28	32	25	108.0	449.3	95.7	35.2

Source: Adapted from Federal Bureau of Investigation. (2015). Table 37: Current year over previous year arrest trends by sex, 2013–2014. In *Crime in the United States 2014*. Retrieved from https://www.fbi.gov/about-us/cjis/ucr/crime-in-the-u.s/2014/crime-in-the-u.s.-2014/tables/table-37. Federal Bureau of Investigation. (2015). Table 36: Current year over previous year arrest trends: totals, 2013–2014. In *Crime in the United States 2014*. Retrieved from https://www.fbi.gov/about-us/cjis/ucr/crime-in-the-u.s/2014/crime-in-the-u.s.-2014/tables/table-36. U.S. Department of Justice, Office of Justice Programs, Office of Juvenile Justice and Delinquency Prevention. (n.d.). *Statistical briefing book*. Retrieved from http://www.ojjdp.gov/ojstatbb/. Federal Bureau of Investigation. (2015). Table 43: Arrests by race, 2014. In *Crime in the United States 2014*. Retrieved from https://ucr.fbi.gov/crime-in-the-u.s/2014/crime-in-the-u.s.-2014/tables/table-43.

number of arrests reported by law enforcement agencies and may not reflect everyone arrested for every offense. Table 13.1, though not a full list of offenses, provides an overview of some offenses committed by gender, age, and race and Hispanic origin. Select findings show that male juveniles are arrested in higher percentages than female juveniles; children under the age of 15 commit a significant amount of delinquent acts; and American Indians are arrested at rates lower than other races and Hispanic origins for most offenses.

Female Offenders: Violence and Arrests

In 2014, 29% of the juvenile arrests involved female offenders.[21] The gender disparity in arrests is even more apparent when focused on violent crimes, as male juveniles are arrested for violence in higher percentages. In 2014, female juvenile arrests included 8.0% for murder, 18.6% for violence, and 34.6% for property crimes.[22]

A wave of juvenile delinquency in the 1990s resulted in more punitive laws. Why did the idea of the superpredator have such great appeal to politicians and the public?

Racial disparities in the juvenile system represent a complicated but crucial issue. What reasons would you develop to explain the high number of minorities in the juvenile justice system?

Historically, female juvenile delinquents were largely ignored, but as an increasing number of girls became involved in the system, research has expanded. Meda Chesney-Lind, the nation's leading expert on girls and delinquency, noted some common themes in the literature. First, girls compared with boys are more often arrested for less serious offenses. Second, girls caught up in the system are more likely to have been victims of sexual abuse (see Figure 13.2). Third, a large number of girls are involved in gangs. Fourth, judicial "double standards" result in girls,' more so than boys,' being detained and incarcerated for status offenses despite deinstitutionalization efforts.[23]

Many people fail to recognize that arrests are not necessarily proxies for offending, and more arrests do not necessarily reflect more serious violent behavior. These important distinctions are clear when considering rates of serious violence (versus arrest numbers) among female juveniles. Using victimization data, findings show that female juveniles are not committing more violent offenses such as robbery and aggravated assault. In fact, like all violence since the early to mid-1990s, serious female juvenile violence has decreased.[24] These findings demonstrate the popular media meme of "girls gone wild" in terms of violent behavior being misplaced and exaggerated. Rather, the more accurate and less titillating cultural characteristic may be "girls getting arrested for minor and status offenses" (see Figure 13.2).

Journal:
Juvenile female sex offenders

Audio:
Native Americans and juvenile justice

Racial Disparities: Violence and Arrests

Minorities represent a disproportionate number of arrested juvenile offenders. Black juveniles are arrested at higher rates than white, American Indian, and Asian juveniles for serious violent and property offenses and are more likely to be referred to the juvenile system. Law enforcement efforts to detect delinquent acts often focus on poor, minority neighborhoods, where crime rates tend to be higher. This approach contributes in part to the disproportionate number of minorities caught up in the system. In 2014, about six in ten of all arrests for juveniles were of whites (63%), 35% were of blacks, and 17% were of Latinos (any race). In cases of serious violence only, estimates show that 47% of arrests involved a white juvenile, 52.4% a black juvenile, and 17% a Latino juvenile.[25] Arrests for juvenile-perpetrated property crimes included 60% white, 38% black, and 17% Latino juveniles.[26] The racial disparities in arrests and commitment to detention facilities are a serious challenge for these communities, law enforcement, and courts.

More arrests do not necessarily indicate more delinquent or status behavior. Using data from the National Crime Victimization Survey, research shows that serious violence committed by juveniles has decreased over time (see Figure 13.3). Furthermore, these decreases are present among white, black, and "other" juveniles. Though serious violence by juveniles has decreased, there exists disparity in relative rates of serious violence offending among juveniles. There are many possible reasons for this disparity, including differences in prosocial opportunities, education, income, and family composition as well as greater scrutiny by the criminal justice system.

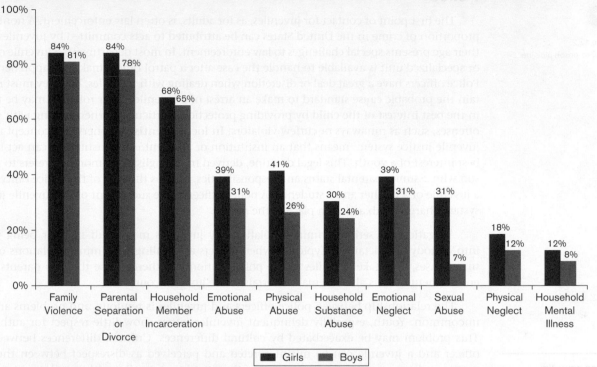

Figure 13.2 ■ Prevalence of Adverse Childhood Experiences Indicators by Gender

Girls compared with boys are more likely to experience emotional abuse and neglect. How can we explain the percentage of girls who experience higher levels of adverse childhood experiences?

Source: Baglivio, M. T., Epps, N., Swartz, K., Huq, M. S., Sheer, A., & Hardt, N. S. (2014). The prevalence of adverse childhood experiences (ACE) in the lives of juvenile offenders. *OJJDP Journal of Juvenile Justice, 3*(2), 1–23. U.S. Department of Justice.

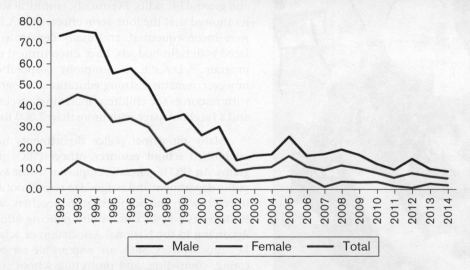

Figure 13.3 ■ Juvenile Offending Rates of Serious Violence per 1,000 Juveniles, 1992–2014

Serious juvenile offending has been declining while juvenile arrests have increased.

STEPS IN THE JUVENILE JUSTICE SYSTEM

Police

Video 13.2:
School-to-prison pipeline

The first point of contact for juveniles, as for adults, is often law enforcement. A nontrivial proportion of crime in the United States can be attributed to acts committed by juveniles, and their age presents special challenges to law enforcement. In most departments a juvenile officer or specialized unit is available to handle the case after a patrol officer makes an apprehension. Police officers have a great deal of discretion when dealing with juveniles, but they must maintain the probable cause standard to make an arrest of a juvenile. Their role also may be to act in the best interest of the child by providing protection, particularly when dealing with status offenses, such as runaways or curfew violators. **In loco parentis**, a cornerstone concept in the juvenile justice system, means that an institution or an agent of an institution can act in the best interest of a youth. This legal doctrine, derived from English common law, refers to a person who assumes parental status and responsibilities, such as the case of the police officer and a juvenile or a teacher and a student.[27] A police officer is one such agent of the juvenile justice system charged with acting in place of the parent.

Allegations of serious criminal violations by juveniles may result in their being taken into custody and detained. Typically, when officers are dealing with minor violations or status offenses, they take juveniles to the police station and then release them to parents. Law enforcement officers also can make referrals to the juvenile court.

The relationship between police officers and juveniles is tenuous, and problems are not uncommon. Youth, especially delinquent juveniles, often show little respect for authority. This problem may be exacerbated by cultural differences. Cultural differences between an officer and a juvenile can be misinterpreted and perceived as disrespect between the two parties and may escalate the seriousness of the situation. Juveniles with hostile or aggressive attitudes toward officers are more likely to be arrested, which may also contribute to the relatively large number of minorities in the juvenile justice system.

in loco parentis:
Actions taken in place of parents when dealing with juveniles.

school resource officer:
Generally an officer employed at the local police agency who is stationed in a school.

Law enforcement efforts to build community relationships have emerged in several popular programs. Police officers often volunteer time for police athletic leagues and diversion programs. In the 1990s, the Drug Awareness Resistance Education (D.A.R.E.) program was instituted in Los Angeles. D.A.R.E. was a police prevention program designed to educate schoolchildren about the dangers of drugs. The D.A.R.E. program was developed for fifth and sixth graders and teaches them resistance skills and general life skills. Eventually, empirical studies showed that the long-term effects of D.A.R.E. were inconsequential, and many departments, faced with tight budgets, have discontinued this program.[28] D.A.R.E, a nonprofit corporation, however, remains a strong educational program with resources for children, including a website and a Facebook page with more than 2,000 likes.

Many municipal police departments have established **school resource officer** (SRO) programs. An SRO is generally employed by the local police department and assigned to one school and interacts with the administrators, teachers, and students as part of community policing efforts. According to the National Association of School Resource Officers, SROs are responsible for educating, counseling, and protecting school communities. While SROs have been around since the early 1950s, they have become more widely recognized in recent decades. Though they are widely used, some schools have reduced the

Police officers often interact with youth to build positive relationships. Describe how community policing can build trust with juveniles. What programs would you develop to increase trust?

number of SROs over time given the drop in violence and reduced funding. This reduction concerns many who fear that a lack of SROs will mean more school violence. There is no doubt that SROs have saved lives. During the 2013 shooting at Arapahoe High School, in Colorado, the SRO saved many students after quickly encountering and facing off with the juvenile perpetrator, who died from a self-inflicted gunshot before being able to harm additional students. The presence of an SRO, however, does not guarantee student safety. Some of the deadliest school shootings, such as Columbine, occurred in schools with SROs on site. One aspect often lost in this discussion, and contrary to media portrayals, is that a robust body of literature demonstrates that schools are among the safest places for youth.

Police officers are assigned to many schools to help ensure safety. In what ways are schools becoming more like prisons? How have new security measures been negative and/or positive?

Many applaud the role of SROs, but the feeling is not universal. Opponents argue that having armed officers in schools creates a negative atmosphere that is not conducive to learning. Others find that SROs result in more juveniles' entering the juvenile justice system. Findings show that SROs make arrests for behavior that should be dealt with through school procedures versus the juvenile justice system.[29] The use of the juvenile justice system to deal with minor infractions has fueled the "**school-to-prison pipeline**," which diverts students from the educational system to the juvenile justice system to their detriment. Findings show that children of color and boys disproportionately suffer the consequences of this phenomenon. In one case, a 15-year-old boy engaged in a tug-of-war with a teacher. This resulted in detention and ultimately house arrest. In addition, this youth was expelled from all state public schools for a year. An important element of the growth in the school-to-prison pipeline is zero-tolerance policies. Schools that have adopted the zero-tolerance approach have been castigated in the media, and in some cases these policies are being reconsidered. In one widely publicized case, ninth grader Tracy J was suspended from school for giving Tylenol to a classmate. The school operated under a zero-tolerance policy, which banned the possession or use of Tylenol. For her transgression, Tracy J was expelled and treated like a drug dealer. In another case, a 6-year-old boy was banned from school and labeled a sex offender for kissing the hand of a female classmate. That school operated under a zero-tolerance sexual harassment policy.

Court

The process in the juvenile justice system roughly mirrors the adult system but takes a more informal path (see Figure 13.4). As in the adult system, the steps through the juvenile justice system vary from jurisdiction to jurisdiction, although some similarities are found among systems. Remember, a youthful offender may be engaged in a status offense (e.g., truancy) or delinquency (e.g., property theft). Law enforcement generally makes the first decision to either divert a juvenile outside of the formal juvenile justice system or process the juvenile within it. **Diversion** decisions are generally based on information gathered from the victim of the act, the parents of the juvenile, the children involved, and a review of previous contacts. The goal of diversion is to keep low-risk youth offenders from entering into the more formal processing of the juvenile system. Community-based programs for diversion include probation, treatment for medical or behavioral issues, education, drug and alcohol treatment, counseling (e.g., anger management), and restitution. About one quarter of juveniles arrested in 2009 were handled informally with law enforcement.[30] The remainder entered the formal juvenile justice system.

Audio:
Treatment of juveniles

school-to-prison pipeline: The diversion of juveniles from schools into the juvenile justice system for minor infractions.

diversion: The decision to keep low-risk youth offenders from entering into the more formal processing of the juvenile system.

Figure 13.4 ■ Generalized Juvenile Justice Flowchart

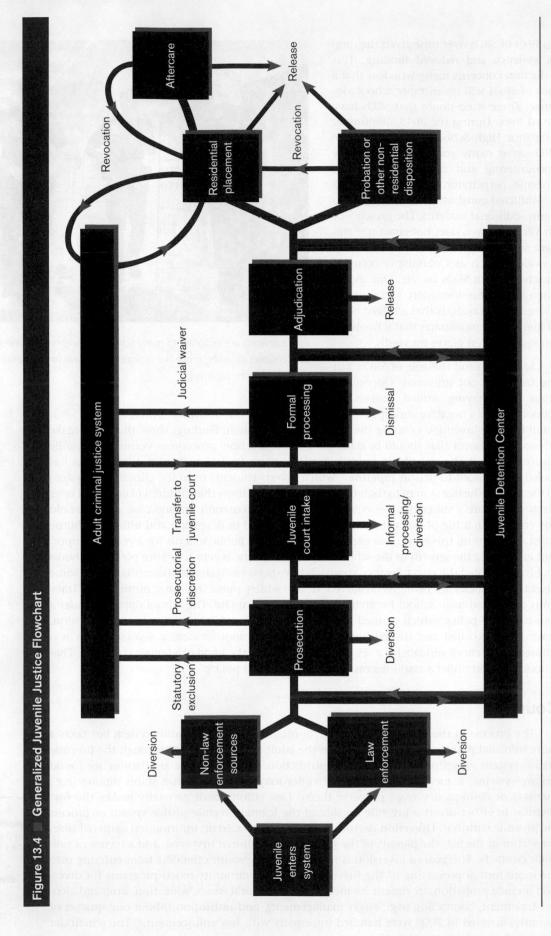

Source: Office of Juvenile Justice and Delinquency Prevention (n.d.). *Statistical briefing book: Case flow diagram.*

The majority of youth who enter the juvenile system are referred by law enforcement, though parents, school administrators, social workers, and probation officers refer a small percentage. In the cases in which the police elect to detain a juvenile, the first step in the process is **intake**. The intake process is similar to an initial hearing for adults. When juveniles are taken to detention centers by law enforcement, they meet with intake officers, juvenile probation officers, or prosecutors. At that point, several options are available. One option is to divert a juvenile from the system and dismiss the case; about 20% of all cases are dismissed at intake. A second option is to place the juvenile on **deferred status**, also called informal probation, which requires that he or she stay out of trouble for a certain length of time in order for the charges to be dismissed. The terms and conditions of deferred status are outlined in a document referred to as a **consent decree**. The third option is to file a petition for a court hearing. This delinquency petition is issued if the intake officer believes that the behavior of the juvenile warrants a more formal hearing and adjudication. A fourth option used in some instances is to file a waiver petition to transfer the youth to adult criminal court.

When juveniles are not released to their parents or legal guardians before adjudication by a judge, they may be detained in a secure facility. In these cases a **detention hearing** is held to determine probable cause and whether a child or juvenile should be held in a facility or released to a legal guardian. Much like setting bail in the adult system, the judge determines what will happen based on the best interest of the child and the community. When considering release to parents or a legal guardian, the judge must determine if the juvenile poses a danger to others, if the juvenile will return for the adjudication process, and if detention provides better protection for the child.

Adjudication is like a criminal court trial in the adult system, though the proceedings are less formal. An adjudicatory hearing ensures that the juvenile's due process rights have not been violated, including the right to counsel, the right to confront witnesses, and protection against self-incrimination. As noted earlier, currently adjudication provides no right to a jury trial for juveniles. The judge, working closely with information provided by law enforcement, attorneys, and probation officers, rules on the evidence and legal issues, and determines if the youth is delinquent and requires court supervision or dismisses the charges. The majority of cases handled in juvenile courts involve delinquency, followed by dependency and neglect (child victims), and status offenses.

Disposition

After adjudication, a judge will decide on the best placement of a delinquent youth during a **disposition hearing**. The probation department gathers background and current information on the juvenile and presents the material in a **predisposition report**. Disposition recommendations made by probation officers may include previous offenses, gang involvement, school performance, psychological evaluations, and/or interviews with parents, teachers, and school counselors. This report is somewhat analogous to the presentence report prepared in the adult system (see Chapter 10). Like the presentence report prepared for adults, the predisposition report prepared for juveniles offers extensive information about the juvenile (e.g., friends, family, school life, drug and alcohol use, medical issues), circumstances of the crime, and recommendations regarding disposition of the case. The report takes into account victim needs and wishes, community safety considerations, and offender needs and accountability. While similar, the predisposition report differs in important ways from the adult presentence report. Whereas the presentence report focuses on appropriate punishment, the predisposition report focuses on treatment options suitable for the juvenile and reintegration into the community. Judges determine whether the juvenile becomes a ward of the state and then assume responsibility for the child. Adjudicated delinquents may be placed, for example, in a secure institution or a nonsecure facility in the community. A wide variety of dispositions are available to juvenile court judges, including dismissal of the case or any number of alternative sanctions:

- restitution or fines
- therapy
- psychiatric treatment
- residential treatment facilities
- house arrest and electronic monitoring
- probation
- day treatment and reporting centers
- secure confinement

intake: The first step in the juvenile justice system for youth. The intake process is similar to an initial hearing for adults.

deferred status: Also known as informal probation, it requires that a youth stay out of trouble for a certain length of time in order for the charges to be dismissed.

consent decree: Document outlining the terms and conditions of deferred status.

detention hearing: Prosecutorial decisions to transfer a juvenile case to adult court.

adjudication: A hearing to ensure that a juvenile's due process rights have not been violated. Similar to a criminal court trial in the adult system.

disposition hearing: Hearing in which a judge decides the best placement of a delinquent.

predisposition report: Presents background and current information on a juvenile to help determine his or her disposition.

CONTEMPLATING CAREERS

Juvenile Court Counselor

Are you analytical? Are you of good moral character? Do you possess compassion and confidence, and are you able to handle stress? Are you in good physical shape? Are you drug free? Do you have strong written and oral communication skills? Is changing the lives of others for the better important to you?

If you answered yes to these questions and want to help youth become productive members of society, becoming a juvenile court counselor may be for you. A juvenile court counselor works both inside and outside of the criminal justice system to assist juveniles. The assistance may come in the form of finding employment, education, and training opportunities. Juvenile justice counselors also help youth deal with emotional, mental health, behavioral, and substance abuse issues.

Education required is a minimum of a 4-year degree in a field such as social work, psychology, or counseling. But many states require a master's degree to work in this capacity. The effort is worth it, as dealing with troubled youth offers a challenging but rewarding career. The Bureau of Labor Statistics shows that the average annual salary of a juvenile court counselor is dependent on education, but can be approximately $46,000.

Career Video:
A counselor for the division of youth corrections discusses her experience and current issues in the field.

Andrew Lichtenstein/Corbis via Getty Images

Juvenile boot camps are not all they are cracked up to be. What are the problems associated with boot camps? How would you design a boot camp to ensure effectiveness?

Probation is the most widely used though probably least effective disposition. Many juveniles are unable to meet the terms of their probation. Recidivism rates are high, particularly when intensive supervision probation is used. Juvenile facilities include residential or nonsecure placement such as foster care, group homes, long-term placement residential facilities, and secure lockup institutions.

Another disposition used for juveniles is boot camp. Boot camps (sometimes referred to as a form of shock probation), as discussed in an earlier chapter, are based on a military training model with regimented programming, including physical drills, hard labor, and job skills training. Boot camps operated by private companies have lost popularity as allegations of abusive treatment have emerged. A 2007 Government Accountability Office report detailed 10 deaths and more than 1,600 cases of abuse in the camps. One boot camp instructor was charged with child abuse and extortion for his disciplinary methods. Research on boot camps found them ineffective, and in one study, graduates of boot camps were more likely to commit new offenses compared with offenders who were on probation.[31]

The use of restorative justice has gained great momentum as a disposition in the juvenile system. Restorative justice brings victims and communities together with offenders. Working together, the process allows victims to take an active role in the healing process and offenders to take responsibility for the consequences of their actions.

Of the four case studies followed in this book, Joshua Paul Benjamin and Danny Madrid offended as juveniles. Joshua did not enter the juvenile justice system, because he was an adult when his offenses were discovered. If Joshua had entered the juvenile system as an offender, after adjudication the judge would have likely considered his earlier experiences—the head injury, the molestation, and school performance, for example—before determining the appropriate disposition. Although Joshua admitted to committing sexual offenses as a juvenile and later as an adult, his interactions with the criminal justice system occurred when he was an adult. In the past 20 years, specialized treatment programs have become available, though research on efficacy is lacking. In other words, whether a treatment program or intervention would have prevented Joshua from offending later in life is unknown. At least in his case, his participation in treatment programs after his arrest appears to play a part in his lack of criminal activity since then.

The majority of specialized programs for sex offender treatment use a cognitive-behavioral or relapse prevention model.[32] Core components of treatment programs require youth to take responsibility for their sexual offenses and work toward changing attitudes. According to the National Center on Sexual Behavior of Youth, Joshua might have served time on probation and received treatment. Predictions of risk to the community would be based on multiple sexual or nonsexual offenses, persistent sexual interest in children, failure to comply with a treatment program, and signs of out-of-control behavior.[33] On probation Joshua would have been prohibited from interacting with young children and possessing pornographic materials.

Danny Madrid, who engaged in stealing cars and gang violence as a youth, was first incarcerated at the age of 15. After spending 2½ years in a juvenile facility, he was arrested again for the gang-related shooting, and because he was almost 17 and labeled as a "menace to society," he was waived to adult court to face charges. When he was transferred to the Los Angeles County Jail, he was placed in a wing that held only juveniles. Ultimately, he was housed in one of the California Youth Authority facilities and then transferred to Chino State Prison.

Aftercare

After juveniles are released, either early or upon completing the disposition sentence, they are placed in **aftercare**. This is equivalent to adults' being placed on parole in the adult system. Aftercare programs are designed to reduce recidivism by offering support and monitoring juveniles through supervision. Aftercare is the final phase of completing a sentence. Conditions of release may include obeying curfews, attending school, obtaining counseling, and refraining from further criminal activities. Because of the abysmal failure of most aftercare efforts, the OJJDP funded intensive aftercare programs (IAPs) to help improve transitions and success. IAPs are designed to use both surveillance and treatment to facilitate the transition of high-risk youth from confinement back into the community. IAPs are based on five guiding principles:

1. Preparing the youth for increasing responsibility and freedom in the community

2. Facilitating interaction and involvement between the juvenile and the community

3. Working with the youth and the community support systems required for the youth's successful return to the community

4. Developing new resources and support for the juvenile as needed

5. Monitoring and investigating the ability of the youth and the community to work productively together

Video 13.3:
Goals and experiences of the juvenile system

aftercare: Programs designed to reduce recidivism by offering support and monitoring juveniles through supervision. Equivalent to adults' being placed on parole.

POLICY ISSUES

Specialized Teen Court

Teen courts, also called peer or youth courts, use a process similar to a juvenile court, but peers serve as judges, attorneys, jurors, and other members of the courtroom work group. Most teen courts hear cases for first-time, low-risk offenders typically engaged in minor offenses: vandalism, disorderly conduct, and petty theft. The majority of the courts require the defendant to admit to the charges in order to participate, although according to the Office of Juvenile Justice and Delinquency Prevention, some courts hold trials to determine guilt or innocence. Parents are required to be present for the trial. Defendants may be sentenced to community service, counseling, or restitution and/or may be required to make an apology to the victim.

Proponents believe that teen courts reduce future wrongdoing and increase respect for the law. Also, the process educates volunteers and defendants about the judicial system. Opponents argue that these courts create an additional sanction, which may pull more offenders into the system unnecessarily. Additionally, evaluation research is needed to determine whether the courts are effective.

Think About It

1. Explain how teen courts may be an effective method for reducing recidivism. What other types of diversion programs may be more effective than teen court?

2. How can the use of peer volunteers add bias to the system?

3. When defendants fail to comply with the peer sentence, what are the possible consequences?

Demonstration projects in Colorado, Nevada, and Virginia are halfway through 7 years of research, development, and training. The demonstration sites have been fine-tuning and expanding on elements of the programs. Juvenile participants in the IAP demonstration projects have recently begun graduating from aftercare, meaning that results about the long-term effects of these programs are currently unavailable.

Waiving Juveniles to Adult Courts

judicial waivers: Waivers sending a juvenile to the adult criminal justice system if the judge believes the youth cannot be helped through treatment efforts.

Waivers for juveniles to adult courts may occur at many points in the juvenile justice system. Waivers are controversial, partly because the practice undermines the doctrine of *parens patriae*. Jurisdictional transfers are punitive in nature and result in harsher punishment. Two groups of juveniles are identified as more likely to be transferred to adult criminal court: those who are beyond rehabilitation and those worthy of greater punishment.[34] Despite a large increase in the use of waivers in the late 1980s and early 1990s, a small percentage of cases end up in adult court. The Juvenile Law Center estimates that 250,000 youth are prosecuted annually in adult courts.[35]

direct files: When a prosecutor uses discretion to send a juvenile to the criminal justice system.

automatic waivers: By legislative action, transfers juveniles who committed serious crimes to the adult system. Designated in statutes for offenses such as murder, kidnapping, armed robbery, and carjacking.

Though state procedures vary, four types of waivers may be used in legal proceedings: judicial, prosecutorial (direct), automatic, and reverse. After a hearing in juvenile court, a judicial transfer may be initiated if the judge believes the youth cannot be helped through treatment efforts. **Judicial waivers** may occur when the offense is serious or the youth has a long history of involvement in the system. More controversial transfers are prosecutorial **direct files**. Prosecutors have the discretion to transfer a juvenile if they believe the offense and the offender warrant harsher punishment. **Automatic waivers** are determined by legislative action and transfer juveniles of certain ages designated in statutes for offenses such as murder, kidnapping, armed robbery, and carjacking. **Reverse transfers** allow a judge or prosecutor to send the case back to the juvenile court.

reverse transfers: Allows judges and prosecutors to send cases back to juvenile court.

What does the evidence suggest about the value of judicial waivers? Though not universal, findings point primarily to negative consequences of waivers. One major issue is that waivers appear to expose juveniles to disproportionately harsh punishment. For example, juveniles waived to adult court receive longer incarceration and/or longer parole sentences than their counterparts who remain in the juvenile system. A second way in which juveniles who are waived received harsher treatment is as victims. Findings show that juveniles housed in adult facilities are physically and sexually victimized at rates exceeding adults.[36] Although juveniles make up a small percentage of individuals housed in adult facilities, about one in five inmate-on-inmate sexually violent incidents involves a juvenile victim. One way some facilities try to protect juveniles is by placing them in protective solitary confinement. While this may protect them from predatory inmates, it results in a host of negative consequences such as psychological harm, increased risk of suicide, and developmental damage. Finally, research suggests waivers fail to have a general deterrence effect. While more research may reveal positive consequences of waivers, our current understanding points more to the negative outcomes. In sum, while waiving a juvenile to the adult system may feel good to some, evidence does not point to positive consequences of this action for the juvenile or society in general.

Journal:
Juveniles committing
adult crimes

CASE STUDY

Danny Madrid was a juvenile when he participated in the shooting of a rival gang member. Nonetheless, he was tried for this crime as an adult in the State of California. In other words, the judge issued a waiver in his case. The judge's decision was based primarily on two of Danny's prior juvenile convictions. Danny commented that the time spent in the juvenile facility was perhaps the most conducive to further engagement in gang violence. The first conviction was for grand theft auto in 1988 (stealing a car), which was logged as gang related because the arresting officers incorrectly indicated that Danny had stolen the car to make a profit for his gang. For this offense, Danny spent a year in a juvenile camp. The second conviction that convinced the judge to try Danny in the adult system was for a gang-related assault with a deadly weapon in 1989. Danny had been stabbed and spent a month in the hospital as a result. He retaliated after he recuperated and for that was sentenced to juvenile camp for a year. While this represents only two convictions, Danny openly admits to having been amassing arrests since age 10 and so was well known in the law enforcement community as a serious gang member.

When faced with Danny following the shooting, the judge commented that he was on "a dangerous path," and was "too dangerous and sophisticated" to be around other youth his age. For these reasons, Danny's case was waived to adult criminal court.

As a result of this (and some additional misbehavior on his part), Danny spent time in protective solitary confinement (up to 8 months at a time). Still, he also spent time with adults who had been in the system for a long time.

Critics of the prosecutorial waiver argue that extraneous factors, such as political pressures or get-tough attitudes, may influence these decisions. The American Bar Association also opposes the use of transfers. Research shows that juveniles tried and convicted in adult courts are more likely to commit offenses in the future compared with adjudicated youth.[37] Other studies found that juveniles in adult prisons are more likely to be abused by staff and be attacked with a weapon, and are at greater risk of death compared with other prisoners.[38]

VICTIMS

Throughout this text, you have learned that victims of crime have rights. The rights described vary from place to place and include (among other things) the rights to be treated with dignity and respect, to receive practical and emotional support, to receive restitution, to be heard, and to be involved and notified throughout the process. Today, most states provide

ETHICAL ISSUES

Police Use of Juvenile Informants

In 1998, three suspected drug dealers killed Chad MacDonald, 17 years old, after he agreed to work undercover with the Brea, California, police to buy methamphetamine. Chad's mother agreed to allow her son to act as an informant so that he could avoid prosecution on possession charges, though she later claimed that she was coerced into signing a waiver of liability. Police officials claim that MacDonald's role as informant had been terminated before he was kidnapped, tortured, and murdered. The MacDonald case highlights controversial issues that arise when juveniles become involved in police investigations as informants.

MacDonald's first encounter with the police occurred near the beginning of 1998. The taped conversation between police officer Keith Watson and MacDonald indicates that Watson had an agenda when he began questioning the youth during what seemingly was a routine traffic stop. During the arrest, Watson discovered 11 grams of methamphetamine in MacDonald's car. This episode launched a sequence of events that labeled a young man, who struggled with his own drug problem, as a "snitch."

MacDonald, who was 3 months shy of his 18th birthday, faced possible short-term detainment in a juvenile facility that may have included some type of treatment program. Law enforcement agents instead offered to dismiss MacDonald's possession charges if he

agreed to assist in their investigative efforts. Chad wore a wire and purchased methamphetamine at a suspected drug house. Police raided the house a few days later, but no drugs were found. The woman who sold the drugs confronted MacDonald and accused him of being a "narc."

On March 1, MacDonald disappeared. He and his 16-year-old girlfriend had been kidnapped, held hostage, and tortured. MacDonald's body was found in an alley in South Los Angeles on March 3. His girlfriend was raped and shot in the face, but she survived. Witnesses reported that the killers called MacDonald a snitch and a narc. Police officials claim that MacDonald was no longer acting as an informant at the time of his death.

Think About It

1. What are the advantages and disadvantages of using juveniles as confidential informants?

2. Are juveniles or their parents able to consent to participating in a drug sting when they face possible charges or incarceration?

3. Should juveniles be used in sting operations to buy alcohol or cigarettes? Should children under the age of 12 be used as informants?

Source: Dodge, M. (2006). Juvenile police informants: Friendship, persuasion, and pretense. *Youth Violence and Juvenile Justice, 4,* 234–246. Reprinted with permission from SAGE.

victims of juvenile delinquency with some or all of the rights afforded to those victimized by adults. This has not always been the case, though. Initial legislation aimed at victims' rights applied only to adult crimes. The juvenile justice system continued to operate by preserving the privacy of juveniles. In the early 1990s, with the increase in juvenile offenses and arrest, a shift in perspective occurred. The change in philosophy turned more toward holding juvenile offenders accountable for their actions, encouraging them to take personal responsibility for their egregious behavior and the consequences of their actions. A result of these changes was the removal of confidentiality of traditional juvenile proceedings, the facilitation of accessing juvenile records, the opening to the public of proceedings, and the inclusion of victims in the process. States quickly began introducing legislation that extended the same victim rights to juvenile-perpetrated offenses.

Today, some states provide rights to victims of juvenile violence. In general, though, victims of juvenile delinquency are afforded many or most of the same rights given to victims of adult violence. Given the differences in the criminal justice and juvenile justice systems, some language used to describe notification events may differ. In the juvenile justice system, for example, a victim has the right to be notified when a juvenile is being detained or released, if a petition of delinquency is filed, and if a detained juvenile escapes or is later captured. Unlike in the adult system, juvenile statutes include language requiring the parents of the delinquent to pay restitution to the victim(s). While many applaud the inroads made by victims, some find providing victims with rights in the juvenile justice system has changed the focus of the system. Whereas once the primary goal in the juvenile justice system was the best interest of the delinquent youth, with the inclusion of victims in the process, judges now consider the competing needs of the victim. In some cases, this work is diametrically against what is in the best interest of the youth. The tension between the needs of the victim and those of the offender is one that will surely continue.

CHAPTER WRAP-UP

This chapter considered the juvenile justice system. A brief history of the system was provided, indicating that the juvenile justice system developed from the criminal justice system. As a result, it follows a similar process though it is more informal. Furthermore, the juvenile justice system has been grounded primarily in doing what is in the best interest of the youth, although in recent years it has taken a decidedly more punitive approach. The chapter covered several important court rulings that extended due process rights to juveniles. Even with this expansion of due process to juveniles, they still do not have the right to a jury trial. The chapter identified the differences between status offenses and delinquency and offered some rates and trends of juvenile misdeeds in recent years. It dispelled the myth of the superpredator and "girls gone wild." Of import is that the juvenile justice system is characterized by disparities in youth in terms of gender and race. Reasons for these differences are varied, including differential offending and greater scrutiny by the juvenile justice system of particular groups of juveniles. Finally, the chapter noted the role of victims in the juvenile justice system. Today victims enjoy similar rights as victims in the criminal justice system. Yet in the juvenile justice system, doing what is in the best interest of the youth often exists in tension with victims' rights. In the following chapter we present information on several important but often overlooked criminal justice topics, such as violence against college students, sex trafficking of minors, hate crimes, and the CSI effect.

KEY POINTS

- The juvenile justice system has evolved from harsh and unfair treatment to a system of rehabilitation.

- The late 1800s marked the true age of reform in the system with the creation of the juvenile court system.

- Juvenile justice is grounded in the principle of *parens patriae* (the state as the father).

- Important U.S. Supreme Court rulings established procedural and substantive due process rights for juveniles.

- A youth adjudicated as delinquent has committed a criminal offense.

- Status offenses apply to acts illegal only for juveniles.

- The Juvenile Justice and Delinquency Prevention Act was passed to prevent delinquency and improve the system.

- The concept of the juvenile superpredator failed to come to fruition according to crime data.

- The notion of "girls gone wild" is based on arrest data for minor offenses.

- Youth of color are more likely to enter into the juvenile justice system.

- The court process for juveniles is distinct from the adult system, although in serious cases a juvenile may be waived to the latter.

- In general, victims of juvenile delinquency have the same rights as those victimized by an adult offender.

KEY TERMS

REVIEW QUESTIONS

1. What role did the child savers play in changing the treatment of youth?

2. What is *parens patriae* and why is the concept so important in the juvenile system? What role did the decision in *Ex parte Crouse* play?

3. What landmark U.S. Supreme Court cases played major roles in due process rights for children?

4. What reasons did the U.S. Supreme Court cite for stopping executions of juveniles?

5. What is the difference between delinquency and status offenses?

6. What is the crime bomb, and how did the notion of a superpredator change legislative decisions on juvenile crime?

7. Why are minority youth more likely to enter the system compared with white youth, and in what ways do delinquent girls differ from their male counterparts?

8. Why is there tension between the needs of juvenile delinquents and victims of juvenile delinquency? Has it always been that way?

9. How do police and juveniles interact? Why is this important for the juvenile justice system?

10. What are the steps in the adjudication of a juvenile case? What dispositions are available?

CRITICAL THINKING MATTERS

1. **Sex Offenders in the Juvenile System.** Imagine that Joshua Paul Benjamin had first entered the system as a juvenile. How might his experience have been the same or different compared with the adult system? Describe possible scenarios of positive and negative outcomes if Joshua had received a disposition in the juvenile system. Given the tendency for sex offenders to recidivate, should these cases be transferred to adult courts? Why or why not?

2. **Juveniles and the Death Penalty.** In 2005, the U.S. Supreme Court ruled that the death penalty was cruel and unusual punishment for juveniles. What arguments would you present for and against using the death penalty against juveniles?

3. **Victims in the Juvenile Justice System.** There is an inherent tension between providing victim rights and addressing what is needed for youthful offenders. By opening up proceedings and removing the cloak of confidentiality from juvenile proceedings, these cases may follow the juvenile offender decades into the future. However, removing the need for confidentiality facilitates victim participation in the process.

Does the presence of victims in the juvenile justice system help the offenders? Why or why not? Would the youth be better served with no interaction with the victims? Why or why not? What of the victims? Are victims' needs more important than the offenders' needs? Less important? Of equal importance? Why or why not?

4. **Reducing Discrimination in the Juvenile System.** Arrest data show youth of color are more likely to enter the system. Do you believe that because Danny Madrid is Latino, he was arrested more often than others may have been? Was that possibly discrimination? Danny mentioned that he felt many Latino officers treated him worse than non-Latino officers. What measures or programs would you design to reduce all discrimination by police officers? Is it possible? How would your proposal affect arrest data? Arrest data also show that male juveniles are more likely to be arrested than female juveniles. Would your policy address this difference? Why or why not?

5. **Juvenile Versus Adult Offenders.** Imagine Dennis Bradford had been a juvenile when he nearly killed Jennifer Schuett. If that were the case, do you feel his actions should have been viewed differently? Does the fact that he was an adult make the crime more heinous? Less heinous? Why or why not? Imagine Danny Madrid had been tried in the juvenile system for his attempted murder charge. Do you feel his actions would have been viewed differently? Why or why not? Should characteristics of the offender or the victim matter?

DIGITAL RESOURCES

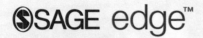

Sharpen your skills with SAGE edge at edge.sagepub.com/rennison2e. SAGE edge for Students provides a personalized approach to help you accomplish your coursework goals in an easy-to-use learning environment. You'll find action plans, mobile-friendly eFlashcards, and quizzes as well as video and web resources and links to SAGE journal articles to support and expand on the concepts presented in this chapter.

14 EXPLORING SPECIALIZED AND TOPICAL ISSUES

> "The expansion and sophistication of transnational crime represents one of the most dangerous threats we confront in the next millennium."

> —Rand Beers,
> acting Secretary of
> Homeland Security

LEARNING OBJECTIVES

After finishing this chapter, you should be able to:

14.1 Summarize terrorism, human and sex trafficking, and hate crimes and explain how these crimes differ from other types of violence.

14.2 Differentiate between international and domestic terrorism, and provide examples.

14.3 Assess the differences in hate crimes and other types of crimes and why this difference is important.

14.4 Differentiate transnational crime from other types of crime.

14.5 Consider the relationship between forensic science and the criminal justice system.

14.6 Criticize the influence of the CSI effect and tech effect and how they influence policy and the public's perceptions about crime, victims, offenders, and members of the criminal justice system.

14.7 Demonstrate an understanding about violence against college students, and how it differs from college campus violence.

INTRODUCTION: OVERVIEW OF SPECIALIZED AND TOPICAL ISSUES

One theme of this text is that the criminal justice system is dynamic. Most elements of the criminal justice system are in constant flux. In addition, our attention to elements of the system changes over time. Some topics fail to maintain the interest of the public, while others capture and hold that attention. This chapter offers some information on topics related to the criminal justice system that have been receiving greater attention in recent years: terrorism, homeland security, human and sex trafficking, hate crimes, college student victimization, transnational crime, forensic science, and the CSI effect. The chapter closes with a discussion devoted to updating the reader regarding our case studies: Where are Jennifer Schuett, Chris Farias, Joshua Paul Benjamin, and Danny Madrid today? Are they still involved in the criminal justice system? Can they ever be free from it?

TERRORISM AND HOMELAND SECURITY

Many erroneously believe that terrorism is new to the United States. This belief is simply incorrect. What is relatively new is that greater attention is being paid to terrorism occurring in the United States. Many definitions of terrorism can be found in the literature, and those definitions change over time. One definition is

Department of Homeland Security (DHS) seal. The DHS was created by cobbling together many existing U.S. government agencies. What advantages does the aggregating of multiple agencies provide? What disadvantages might it entail? If you were president, would you support continuing the DHS as is? Or do you see it in another format? If so, what format is that?

Audio:
Friend of San Bernardino shooter charged with aiding terror plot

international terrorism: Terrorism that occurs outside the territorial jurisdiction of the United States.

domestic terrorism: Terrorism that occurs within the territorial jurisdiction of the United States.

Homeland Security Act of 2002: An act by Congress that made the Department of Homeland Security a cabinet-level department in the U.S. government.

that terrorism is the completed or threatened use of coercion and/or violence against a population of people with the goal of changing political, religious, or ideological positions. In other words, completed or attempted violence against innocent civilians is used to force political, religious, or ideological change. Two major types of terrorism are generally identified: **international terrorism** and **domestic terrorism**.[1]

According to the Federal Bureau of Investigation (FBI) and some statutes, international terrorism includes three specific elements. First, the act must violate federal or state law and involve violence or acts that are dangerous to humans. Second, the purpose of the act must be to intimidate or coerce a civilian population, to influence government policy by intimidation or coercion, or to influence the conduct of a government by mass destruction, assassination, or kidnapping. And the third element of international terrorist acts is that they must occur primarily "outside the territorial jurisdiction of the U.S., or transcend national boundaries in terms of the means by which they are accomplished, the persons they appear intended to intimidate or coerce, or the locale in which their perpetrators operate or seek asylum."[2] Domestic terrorism shares the first two elements of international terrorism, but differs in that the terrorist act occurs primarily within the jurisdiction of the United States.[3]

There have been many cases of both international and domestic terrorism in the United States over time. The most recent memorable act of domestic terrorism may be the September 11 attacks in New York, Virginia, and Pennsylvania. Perhaps due to the scale of this attack, many falsely believe it to be the first to take place on U.S. soil. While the destruction and murder resulting from the September 11 attacks was enormous, it is not the first act of domestic terrorism in the United States. One earlier case of domestic terrorism was the Oklahoma City federal building bombing by Timothy McVeigh and accomplices, which killed 168 people (including 19 children). Other incidents of domestic terrorism are a 1983 U.S. Senate bombing by a militant leftist group, a 1980 bombing at the Statue of Liberty, a 1975 LaGuardia Airport bombing that killed 11 and injured 75 people, the 1960 Sunday Bomber, who detonated bombs in the New York City subways and ferries (1 killed, 51 injured), a 1920 Wall Street bombing, the 1901 assassination of President William McKinley, the 1865 assassination of President Abraham Lincoln, and the 1837 killing of abolitionist Elijah Lovejoy by a proslavery mob. A complete list of domestic terrorism is beyond the scope of this text.

Also, the 9/11 domestic terrorist attack was not the last one that occurred in the United States. Since 9/11, cases of domestic terrorism include the 2001 anthrax attacks, which killed 5 people, the 2009 Fort Hood shooting by U.S. Army major Nidal Hasan, the 2009 assassination of Dr. George Tiller by an antiabortion terrorist, and the 2013 Boston Marathon bombings, which killed 3 and injured more than 180 people. In pursuit of these bombers, a police officer was killed. In 2015 in Charleston, South Carolina, 9 people were killed at the Emanuel African Methodist Episcopal Church as they conducted a Bible study. Also in 2015, 7 people (6 members of the armed forces and 1 police officer) were killed at two locations in Chattanooga, Tennessee. Fourteen people were killed and 21 injured when a San Bernardino, California, county employee opened fire during a Christmas party. This list is not comprehensive, but offers just a few of the many terrorism incidents occurring in the United States since 9/11.

While the 9/11 terrorist attacks were neither the first nor the last incidents of domestic terrorism in the United States, they were important because they led to the founding of the U.S. Department of Homeland Security (DHS). Eleven days after the 9/11 attacks, the White House's Office of Homeland Security was created by President George W. Bush to "coordinate a national comprehensive strategy to safeguard the country against terrorism and respond to any future attack."[4] In November 2002, Congress passed the **Homeland Security Act of 2002**, which made DHS a cabinet-level department. This department officially began operations on March 1, 2003. Some inaccurately believe that DHS was staffed by a multitude of new government employees and resulted in a massive growth in the government bureaucracy.

In reality, DHS was created by integrating all or part of 22 existing federal departments and agencies. To create DHS, employees were taken from departments and agencies such as the Secret Service, Coast Guard, FBI, Federal Emergency Management Agency (FEMA), and the Departments of Defense, Energy, Health and Human Services, Justice, Treasury, and Transportation. In fact, "the creation of [the Department of Homeland Security] was the largest reorganization of the federal government in half a century."[5] The aggregation of these individuals in DHS offered a centralized location where traditionally secretive federal agencies could theoretically share information to the benefit of the nation. Prior to the establishment of DHS, information sharing was considered problematic.

Domestic terrorism and hate crimes are nothing new in the United States. What would cause Dylann Roof to murder several church congregants? The investigation into this violence considered both domestic terrorism and hate crimes, but ultimately indicted Dylann on 33 hate crime charges. What would you have done if you were an investigator? Why?

The purpose of DHS is to secure the United States and keep it safe from a variety of threats using more than 240,000 employees in a variety of contexts. DHS's specific mission is to "lead the unified national effort to secure America. We will prevent and deter terrorist attacks and protect against and respond to threats and hazards to the nation. We will ensure safe and secure borders, welcome lawful immigrants and visitors and promote the free-flow of commerce."[6] Using risk-based, intelligence-driven, multilayered detection, DHS works to prevent terrorism and other security threats. Among its detection responsibilities are the screening of about 2 million domestic airport passengers daily; training of state, local, rural, tribal, territorial, and international officers and agents regarding risk; and conducting vulnerability assessments of key locales. The work conducted by DHS is expensive. In fiscal year 2016, the department's total budget authority was almost $65 billion (not counting billions in grant money).[7] The largest proportion (21%) of the DHS budget is committed to Customs and Border Protection, and the second largest portion of the budget (20%) is used for FEMA (not including grants) activities (Figure 14.1).

There is vigorous debate as to whether DHS and other antiterrorism activities have made the United States safer. Some argue that these efforts are a huge waste of taxpayer dollars, created an ever expanding bureaucracy, are a huge problem for the public, which has given up its privacy and freedom for nothing in return, and in the end have not made Americans safer. Many commentators maintain that the creation of DHS was an overreaction to the 9/11 attacks.[8] Still others find that the creation of DHS and the work done there has made the United States safer through enhanced information sharing. DHS proponents point to dozens of instances in which planned terrorism events were uncovered and prevented. One example revealed in 2002 involved Jose Padilla, a New York City resident and citizen of the United States who was arrested at Chicago's O'Hare Airport. He had just returned from Pakistan following terrorist training. He was arrested and charged as an enemy combatant for his plans to use a **dirty bomb**—an explosive using radioactive material—in the United States. Padilla was ultimately sentenced to just over 17 years in prison for his activities. In 2011, Jose Pimental, a naturalized U.S. citizen, was arrested based on his holy war plans to use homemade pipe bombs at police stations and post offices and to specifically target U.S. troops returning home from Iraq and Afghanistan throughout New York City. In February 2014, Pimental pleaded guilty and was sentenced to 16 years in prison days before his scheduled trial on terrorism charges.

In 2013, DHS uncovered a plan by terrorists to use lethal doses of ricin and cyanide to poison salad bars in restaurants and hotels over one weekend throughout a wide geographic area. Few additional details of this alleged plot are available.

Web:
Department of Homeland Security

Video 14.1:
Agencies and missions

---

dirty bomb:
An explosive device using radioactive material.

Figure 14.1 ■ 2016 U.S. Department of Homeland Security Budget Distribution

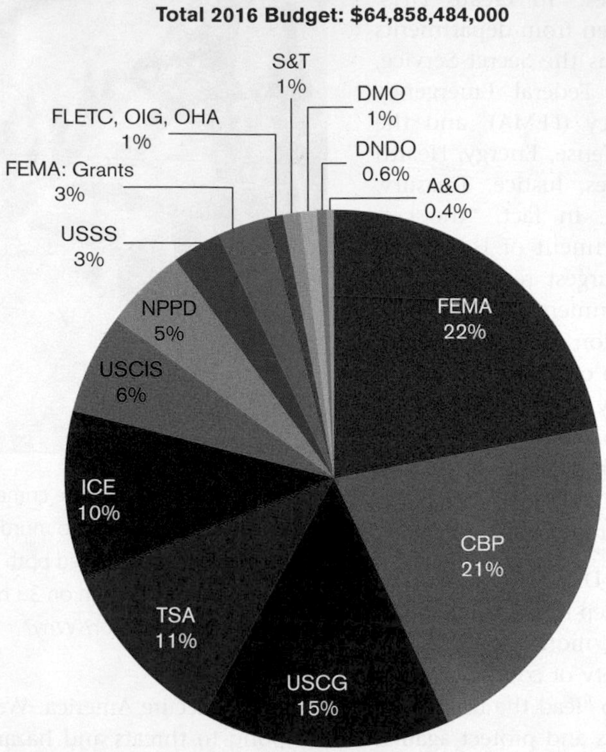

Total 2016 Budget: $64,858,484,000

S&T 1%
DMO 1%
DNDO 0.6%
A&O 0.4%
FLETC, OIG, OHA 1%
FEMA: Grants 3%
USSS 3%
NPPD 5%
USCIS 6%
ICE 10%
TSA 11%
USCG 15%
FEMA 22%
CBP 21%

Source: U.S. Department of Homeland Security, *Budget-in-brief: Fiscal year 2016.*

Note: A&O = Analysis and Operations; CBP = U.S. Customs and Border Protection; DMO = Departmental Management and Operations; DNDO = Domestic Nuclear Detection Office; FEMA = Federal Emergency Management Agency; FLETC = Federal Law Enforcement Training Center; ICE = U.S. Immigration and Customs Enforcement; NPPD = National Protection and Programs Directorate; OHA = Office of Health Affairs; OIG = Office of the Inspector General; S&T = Science and Technology Directorate; TSA = Transportation Security Administration; USCG = U.S. Coast Guard; USCIS = U.S. Citizenship and Immigration Services; USSS = U.S. Secret Service.

TERRORISM AND THE CRIMINAL TRIAL

In the past, terrorists were tried in federal criminal courts. For example, Timothy McVeigh, the Oklahoma City bomber, was tried, found guilty, and ultimately executed as a result of his terrorist attack. Scott Roeder, the domestic terrorist who murdered Dr. George Tiller, was tried and sentenced to life in prison by a federal criminal court. A variety of other domestic terrorists have pleaded guilty or been tried and sentenced in this way as well. The terrorist attacks on September 11, 2001, raised questions about whether federal courts were the best way to handle terror suspects in the United States. These questions are based on the rules of evidence and how these procedures conflict with national security issues.

To deal with this difficult issue, President Bush issued a 2001 military order requiring **military commissions** to try non-U.S. citizens who are or were affiliated with Al Qaida, or those who harbor suspected terrorists.[9] Military commissions have a long history in the United States. Since the Revolutionary War they have provided "fair and transparent trials of those persons subject to trial by military commissions while protecting national security interests."[10] While military commissions have a long history, the form of these commissions and persons eligible to be tried by them has varied over time. The 2001 directive represented a change in who could be tried by military commissions in that it allowed persons captured (primarily) outside of the United States to be taken to a prison camp in Guantánamo Bay, Cuba, for trial. The 2001 order also implemented major shifts in the procedures used to try these detainees.[11] President Bush's directive noted the impracticality of applying the laws and rules regarding evidence required by federal criminal courts in the cases of terrorists. In contrast to federal

military commission:
A type of military tribunal that offers a detainee a fair and transparent trial while protecting national security interests.

criminal court rules of evidence, the 2001 order allowed military commissions to use evidence against a detainee that he or she has never seen, hearsay testimony, unsworn testimony, and evidence obtained through coercion, and it limits appellate review.

In 2004, the first charges under the new military commission were filed against Osama bin Laden's driver, Salim Hamdan. Hamdan challenged these charges on the basis of the commission's jurisdiction by way of a writ of habeas corpus in the Federal District Court in Washington, DC. The District Criminal Court granted Hamdan's petition, and the case ultimately ended up in the U.S. Supreme Court in 2006. The Supreme Court ruled in favor of Hamdan and invalidated the military commission established by President Bush's 2001 military order.[12]

Labor trafficking victims. Many in the United States are surprised to learn that trafficking occurs here. Why should this come as a surprise to us? Why would someone feel the United States is immune to such crimes? What can the United States do to stop trafficking domestically?

In response, Congress enacted the Military Commissions Act of 2006, which allowed the president to designate individuals as unlawful enemy combatants subject to military commissions. While this act expanded detainee rights, military commissions continued to offer fewer civil rights than federal courts. Military commissions still limited a detainee's right to seek a writ of habeas corpus, limited rights to counsel, and allowed the use of evidence gathered via coercion. In 2009, the 2006 law was amended. The new Military Commissions Act of 2009, which is in effect today,[13] established additional rights of detainees, aligning them more with those available in federal criminal cases. The 2009 act prohibits the use of evidence gained through torture, inhumane treatment, and degrading methods.[14] Still, elements of the 2009 act exposed the commission to legal challenges. As a result, additional changes and challenges to the use of military commissions for terrorist suspects are likely.

DOMESTIC HUMAN AND SEX TRAFFICKING

Human trafficking crimes, which include sex trafficking, have a long history in the United States. In contrast, attention to domestic trafficking has exploded in recent years. While human and sex trafficking occur within and between other countries, many people inaccurately believe that trafficking does not occur in the United States. This belief is false; both human and sex trafficking occur in the United States. **Human trafficking** is a broad term that includes the trade in humans for labor and/or sex, and the extraction of organs or tissues (including ova removal).

The United Nations Protocol to Prevent, Suppress and Punish Trafficking in Persons, Especially Women and Children, offers the following definition of human trafficking[15]:

(a) The recruitment, transportation, transfer, harbouring or receipt of persons, by means of threat or use of force or other forms of coercion, of abduction, of fraud, of deception, of the abuse of power or of a position of vulnerability or of the giving or receiving of payments or benefits to achieve the consent of a person having control over another person, for the purpose of exploitation. Exploitation shall include, at a minimum, the exploitation of the prostitution of others or other forms of sexual exploitation, forced labour or services, slavery or practices similar to slavery, servitude or the removal of organs;

(b) The consent of a victim of trafficking in persons to the intended exploitation set forth in subparagraph (a) of this article shall be irrelevant where any of the means set forth in subparagraph (a) have been used;

Video 14.2:
U.S. releases human trafficking report

Author Video:
Sex trafficking

human trafficking:
The trade in humans for labor and/or sex, and the extraction of organs or tissues. Sex trafficking is one form of human trafficking.

Reuters/Attorney General's Office/Handout

COMMON MISCONCEPTIONS

There Are No Child Prostitutes, but There Are Prostituted Children

Minors are unable to legally consent. This is true for all behaviors, including prostitution. There is an effort to end the use of the phrase *child prostitutes* because it implies that the child is responsible for this behavior. Rather, a more accurate phrase is *children who are prostituted*. Further strides are being made to educate people that no child can consent to being prostituted and that prostituting children is a form of child abuse and a form of violence against children.

Think About It

1. Why do you think that children who have been prostituted have long been (and in many cases still are) treated like criminals rather than victims? What do you think is responsible for that?

2. Do you believe that there is a difference between the terms *child prostitute* and *prostituted child*? Does this language difference matter in other ways? Consider the terms *child sex partner* and *sexually assaulted child*? Does that matter in the same way? Why or why not?

(c) The recruitment, transportation, transfer, harbouring or receipt of a child for the purpose of exploitation shall be considered "trafficking in persons" even if this does not involve any of the means set forth in subparagraph (a) of this article;

(d) "Child" shall mean any person under eighteen years of age.

Some victims claim to have voluntarily entered the world of human trafficking; however, most involved are tricked, threatened, and otherwise coerced into this practice. Furthermore, those who do so "voluntarily" frequently have no other choice, bringing into question whether being trafficked can really be voluntary. This is especially true when considering victims of trafficking who are minors. Minors cannot give consent under any circumstances, meaning that their participation in human or sex trafficking is never voluntary.

In the United States, common types of domestic human trafficking include persons forced to work as domestic servants, farmworkers, factory workers, and sex labor.[16] Domestic human trafficking most often occurs around international travel hubs, especially where large immigrant populations exist. Several major U.S. government departments compile reports on human trafficking in the United States. For example, in 2011, the Department of Justice released a report for activity from 2008 to 2010 and concluded that during this period, federally funded antitrafficking task forces opened 2,515 cases to investigate suspected cases of human trafficking, the bulk of which (82%) were sex trafficking cases.[17] About 1 in 10 of these focused on suspected cases of labor trafficking. Findings show that U.S. citizens were more likely to be victims of sex trafficking, while aliens were more likely to be victims of labor trafficking. During this period, the Department of Justice estimates that 144 offenders were arrested for this crime. A total of 2,515 cases may seem unlikely, and that's because these cases represent only some of those that come to the attention of the criminal justice system. Trafficking is a hidden crime, making it difficult to recognize and act on. While no one can say with certainty the precise number of human trafficking cases ongoing in the United States, it is certain that 2,515 is an underestimate.

Sex trafficking, a subset of human trafficking, has received renewed attention in recent years. As with many concepts in the criminal justice system, there is no universally agreed upon definition of domestic sex trafficking. Nonetheless, commonalities among definitions

sex trafficking:
The trade in sexual acts or exploitation.

do exist and generally include the following elements: a lawful permanent resident who is under the age of 18 who gives or receives anything of value (money, drugs, shelter, food, clothes) to some other in exchange for prostitution, pornography, or other sexual entertainment. This includes acts of **survival sex**. Survival sex is a type of trafficking in which the victim is frequently homeless or gravely disadvantaged and trades sex for food, shelter, and other basic needs. Like domestic human trafficking, an estimate of the number of minors who are domestically sex trafficked and exploited is extraordinarily difficult to ascertain. Nonetheless, the best estimates available indicate that this crime victimizes a nontrivial number of minors in the United States. Like human trafficking—or perhaps even more so than human trafficking—domestic sex trafficking of minors in the United States is frequently overlooked and misunderstood, and the needs of the victims of this crime go unaddressed. Research shows that many victims of this crime and abuse are runaways and kids thrown out of their parents' home. In addition, some victims of domestic sex trafficking live in their parents' homes. These minors may be victimized without their parents' knowledge, or their parents may be the individuals who are trafficking these children.

Prostituting children is a crime and a form of child abuse. Why do many believe a prostituted child is a criminal offender? What about a child being abused in this way makes some feel that blaming the victim is okay? What would you do as a policymaker to end the prostitution of all children?

A frequent method of ensnaring minors into sex trafficking involves the initial tricking of victims into taking photos or videos that increasingly become more sexual and pornographic. Minors may engage in this activity willingly to please someone they erroneously feel cares about them. Once the trafficker has these photos or videos, he or she can then blackmail the victims to engage in sex work. Whether by trickery, coercion, and/or force, once involved in this scheme, the victims find it difficult and even dangerous to escape.

A recently released report by the Institute of Medicine and the National Research Council focuses specifically on domestic commercial sex trafficking and sexual exploitation of minors in the United States and correctly frames these crimes as child abuse.[18] The committee that compiled this report was guided by three principles: viewing the minor victims of domestic sex trafficking and sexual exploitation as having suffered acts of abuse and violence, no longer viewing victims as criminals, and making sure that any identification of the victims and intervention offered does no further harm to the victims of domestic sex trafficking. The report offers myriad findings, including that victims suffer immediate and long-term adverse consequences, that attempts to prevent sex trafficking and sexual exploitation of minors in the United States are largely absent, that efforts to identify victims and respond to their needs are woefully insufficient, that dealing with this violence requires collaborative approaches, and finally that confronting demand for the sexual abuse and exploitation of minors must be a priority. All indications suggest that in the future, even greater attention to identifying and responding to the needs of victims of this form of child abuse will proliferate. Furthermore, this attention will require even greater resources of the criminal justice system in terms of both dealing with victims and addressing the behaviors of offenders and those who facilitate these crimes.

HATE CRIMES AND BIAS-MOTIVATED CRIMES

Hate crimes, also known as bias-motivated crimes, have been a topic of great concern in recent years. Hate crimes occur when an offender targets a victim and/or her or his property due to the victim's *perceived* membership in a specific group. Groups frequently targeted for hate crimes include racial, ethnic, religious, sexual orientation, and gender identity groups. Some people argue that "all crimes are hate crimes" and abhor the notion of a specific label of "hate crime." Such a stance reflects a failure to fully understand the definition of a hate

survival sex: A type of trafficking in which the victim is frequently homeless or gravely disadvantaged and trades sex for food, shelter, and other basic needs.

hate crimes: Crimes committed that target victims and/or their property due to their perceived membership in a particular group. Also known as bias-motivated crimes.

Robert Nickelsberg/Getty Images

ETHICAL ISSUES

Can Sex Trafficking Ever Be Ethical?

Karyn is a 16-year-old who is being prostituted. She contends that she does this work because she wants to, and it earns her enough money to live comfortably. In addition, she earns enough to support her partner, who introduced her to this way of life. Earning money is important since her parents kicked her out when she told them she was a lesbian. Karyn contends that no one is making her do it and that she should be able to if she wants to. Still, she notes that her partner gets angry and sometimes a little physical if she does not bring home enough cash.

Think About It

1. Karyn is younger than 18 and claims to voluntarily engage in this prostitution. Many youth engage in this behavior to survive because it helps them obtain food, shelter, clothes, and other needed basics. Is it unethical for Karyn to engage in this activity given her circumstances?

2. Should the age of the people being prostituted matter? Should it matter if someone lured them into this activity when they were minors? If their trafficker violently abuses them but they choose not to leave, should it matter?

3. If people state that they are engaged in sex trafficking but have no skills or education and have no other opportunities, is their participation by free choice? What policies would you implement to deal with this thorny issue?

Gerardo Mora/Getty Images

The United States is marked by a long and violent history of hate crimes and terrorist attacks. Recently, Omar Mateen murdered 49 people and wounded 53 others in a brutal attack on the Pulse Nightclub in Orlando, Florida. This attack was the deadliest terrorist event since 9/11. What will it take, in addition to statutes, to end this type of violence?

Civil Rights Act of 1871: Federal legislation passed to give federal protection to Fourteenth Amendment rights that were violated by private persons, including those in the Ku Klux Klan.

crime. A hate crime is not just any crime that is committed against someone in a protected group. A hate crime is one *motivated by bias* regardless of whether the victim is a member of the specific group. Hate crimes are such that if there was no perception that the victim belonged to a particular group, no crime would have occurred. The motivation for committing hate crimes differs from the motivation to commit other crimes. A person convicted of committing a hate crime is subject to a harsher penalty.

Not everyone is in favor of hate crime legislation. Some commentators argue that the hate crimes are already crimes and do not benefit from the additional "hate" moniker. Others suggested that hate crimes are no more harmful to society than are "regular" crimes so distinguishing them is unnecessary. Establishing a crime as a hate crime can be difficult because there must be evidence that the offender's discriminatory attitude or bias is responsible in part or whole for the commission of the crime. Because it is more challenging to prove a crime was motivated by bias or hate, greater costs in the criminal justice system are incurred. Others find the criminalization of thought (i.e., hate, bias, prejudice) troubling. In sum, some believe that hate crime legislation causes more harm than good.

Like crime in general, hate crime is not new in the United States. An obvious example is the long history of violence against black persons by groups such as the Ku Klux Klan. In response to this violence, the first hate crime law was the **Civil Rights Act of 1871**. This act extended federal protection to individuals whose Fourteenth Amendment voting rights were being violated by private persons, including those in the Klan. This statute made it illegal to, "by force or by threat of force, injure, intimidate, or interfere with anyone" engaged in protected voting activities "by reason of their race, color, religion, or national origin." More than a century later states began extending these protections to other groups. California was the first to pass a hate crime statute, in 1978, which designated penalty enhancement for hate crimes based on race, religion, color, and national origin. Over time, states adopted their own hate crime laws with a variety of protected groups. Among those protected by these laws were ancestry, age, creed, marital status, sex, and membership in collectives such as the armed forces and civil rights groups. In 2009, the federal law was updated to include protection for persons based on actual or perceived gender, gender identity, sexual orientation, and disability. These most recent changes were prompted by the unrelated brutal murders in 1998 of James Byrd and Matthew Shepard.

James Byrd Jr., a native Texan, was murdered in June 1998 in Jasper, Texas. On the day he was murdered, Byrd had accepted a ride from Shawn Berry, Lawrence Brewer, and John William "Bill" King. Berry, the driver, and Byrd were acquainted from past interactions around town. Rather than drive Byrd home as promised, the three took him to a remote rural area, beat him severely, urinated on him, and chained him by the ankles to the pickup truck. The three then hopped in the truck and drove off, dragging Byrd behind the truck for several miles down Huff Creek Road. The autopsy indicated that Byrd remained conscious during this event and was killed only when his body hit a culvert, which severed his right arm and decapitated him. The three murderers then scattered Byrd's body parts along a rarely used road and deposited his torso at an African American cemetery. At the time of Byrd's torture, mutilation, and death, Texas did not have a hate crime law. Nonetheless, the three murderers were tried and convicted for Byrd's murder. Brewer, an established white supremacist, received the death penalty and was executed in 2011. King, an established white supremacist, also received the death penalty and sits on Texas's death row. He has two levels of appeals to navigate. In 2013, King's attorney raised claims about evidence he stated was not presented at trial. Specifically, the attorney claimed that there is evidence that King was not at the scene of the crime and that King did not intend to start a racist group in Jasper. The prosecutor rejected these claims, stating that these topics were indeed presented to the jury, which ultimately discredited them. Berry, the driver of the truck, was sentenced to life in prison and is eligible for release in 2038.[19]

Matthew Shepard, a native of Wyoming, was a University of Wyoming student who was tortured and murdered in 1998 because he was a homosexual. On the night of October 6, 1998, Matthew met with Aaron McKinney and Russell Henderson at the Fireside Lounge in Laramie. There, McKinney and Henderson pretended to be gay to gain Shepard's trust. As the evening concluded, McKinney and Henderson offered to give Shepard a ride home. Instead of going home, they drove Shepard to a remote location, robbed him, pistol-whipped him, and tortured him. The attackers' final act was to tie Shepard to a fence, where he was left to die. Still alive, Shepard was found by a cyclist 18 hours later. He was taken to a hospital, where his injuries included brain stem damage and numerous fractures to the skull. Shepard was in a coma, but his injuries were so grave that doctors were unable to operate. Shepard never regained consciousness and was pronounced dead on October 12, 1998. At the time of his torturing and murder, Wyoming did not recognize gays as a protected class under its hate crime statute and has yet to add this category. Only because of the pleading of Shepard's parents, both McKinney and Henderson were spared the death penalty. Instead, both were given life sentences without the possibility of parole.

One outcome of the murders of Byrd and Shepard was that the **Matthew Shepard and James Byrd, Jr. Hate Crimes Prevention Act** was passed by Congress and signed into law by President Barack Obama in 2009. This act expanded established federal hate crime laws to include crimes

James Byrd Jr. met a torturous and grisly death at the hands of three men who were motivated to kill him because he was black. Can murderers like this be rehabilitated? If so, how? If you were a judge overseeing the trial of these perpetrators, what do you feel would be the appropriate sentence for them and why?

Video 14.3:
Hate crime

Matthew Shepard and James Byrd, Jr. Hate Crimes Prevention Act: Federal legislation signed into law in 2009 that expanded earlier federal hate crime laws to include crimes motivated based on the victim's gender, sexual orientation, gender identity, or disability.

Matthew Shepard was also tortured and suffered terribly before he was killed simply because he was gay. Can murderers motivated by one's sexual orientation be rehabilitated? Or are some perpetrators lost causes? Why?

This photo shows a University of Maryland Police Department vehicle patrolling the extended jurisdiction area of the University of Maryland. Do more college police make students safer? Do they make students feel less safe? What do you think?

motivated by the victim's gender, sexual orientation, gender identity, or disability. Another outcome was the requirement that the extent and nature of hate crime in the United States be reported by a variety of government agencies. For example, the Bureau of Justice Statistics provides estimates on hate crime. Estimates show that from 2003 to 2011, 259,700 nonfatal violent and property hate crimes were perpetrated against individuals age 12 or older in the United States.[20] This level of hate crime was unchanged from earlier estimates for 2003 through 2006. Findings showed that about 4% of all violent crime in the United States takes the form of hate crime and that most of these crimes were committed based on the victim's race.[21] The same findings also show that most hate crimes are violent in nature (as opposed to being property crime) and that during the study period, white, black, and Hispanic persons experienced similar rates of hate crime victimization in the United States.

VIOLENCE AGAINST COLLEGE STUDENTS

Violence against college students has become a topic of intense interest in recent years. High-profile cases such as Stanford rapist Brock Turner, who raped and assault an unconscious woman behind a waste bin at a fraternity party, have been plastered across the media. Before this horrific violence was known to the public, many had heard and repeated the "common knowledge" statistic that one in five college women is raped. These events have fueled the belief that college campuses are the epicenters of sexual violence where especially female students are at great risk. Not surprisingly, college students, especially women, express high levels of fear that they will be victimized.

While there is no doubt that college students are victimized, and that they are victimized at unacceptably high rates, this topic is subject to much misunderstanding. What does the research tell us about college student victimization?

First, research findings come primarily from two types of data sources: surveys administered at specific universities and national surveys gathering information from students across the nation. The source of the data makes a big difference in terms of the generalizability of the findings. Findings stemming from students attending specific colleges can be used to describe what happens to students only at *those specific colleges*. These findings are not generalizable to colleges, universities, or students elsewhere in the nation. In contrast, findings from national probability surveys can be used to describe what happens to college students across the nation. These findings are generalizable across the nation.

Perhaps the most widely known statistics is the one-in-five statistic, based on the work of Krebs and colleagues.[22] The one-in-five statistic, however, has been widely misappropriated. This estimate is not nationally representative of the prevalence of sexual assault, but rather it is an estimate that can be used to describe only the population of senior undergraduate women at the two universities where the data were collected. Furthermore, this statistic has been widely misidentified as referring to rape (penetration). In truth, it refers specifically to completed rape and completed sexual assault (e.g., forced kissing or unwanted groping of sexual body parts).

Research in 2015 by Cantor and colleagues gathered data from 27 universities and found 12% of the female students attending the 27 universities had experienced nonconsensual penetration (rape) or sexual touching (sexual battery) by force or incapacitation since enrolling.[23] Importantly, though, Cantor and colleagues found wide variation in the rates of sexual violence committed at each university. In other words, one number cannot adequately describe the extent and nature of victimization for all universities. This report finds that a singular one-in-five-type statistic is overly simplistic and misleading at best. If you are interested in the state of victimization at your university, you need to find out if a Campus Climate Study has been conducted. Knowing the nature and extent of sexual violence and sexual misconduct that has occurred elsewhere cannot tell you about your own institution.

National surveys also find unacceptably high rates of college student victimization. For example, Bonnie Fisher and her colleagues have used nationally representative samples of college women and found that 3% of their female sample had experienced completed rapes, and 1.9% had experienced attempted rapes in the past 12 months.[24] Findings from the National Crime Victimization Survey[25] offer additional important context to the topic of college student victimization (Figure 14.2). As shown in Figure 14.2, these nationally representative data show that college women are victims of violence at rates lower than their noncollege counterparts. Additional work demonstrates that college women are sexually victimized—completed rape, attempted rape, and sexual assault—at rates higher than among college men. In contrast, college men are victims of other types of violence (e.g., robbery) at higher rates than are college women. Other work shows that college men are more likely to be victimized with a third party present, and that college women are less likely to report their victimization to authorities than are noncollege women.

An important finding using all data available is that a higher percentage of college student victimization occurs off campus, compared with on campus.[26] Many times, one finds information about so-called campus violence, but upon careful reading, the information refers to violence against a college student *that occurs anywhere,* including a campus. Understanding how risk differs by location is important information for students to have. If students misunderstand where risk of victimization is greater, they can act accordingly. What do the data say about violence that occurs on versus off campus? Data from the National Crime Victimization Survey show that nationally, 4% of rapes and sexual assaults against college women occur on campus. Findings from Fisher and colleagues' National College Women Sexual Violence Survey (NCWSV) indicate that for nearly all of the 12 types of sexual victimization examined, off-campus victimization was more common. For example, NCWSV data show that 66% of completed rapes occurred off campus. The Campus Sexual Assault Study, which studied students at two universities (and focused on violence against college students occurring anywhere), found that 63% of instances of forced (in contrast to incapacitated) rape and sexual battery, and 61% of instances of incapacitated rape and sexual battery occurred off campus.

Research identifies characteristics of campus crime, and characteristic that are associated with higher rates of victimization.[27] A robust finding is that crime committed on campus is property in nature, and that violent crime is relatively rare. This literature also demonstrates

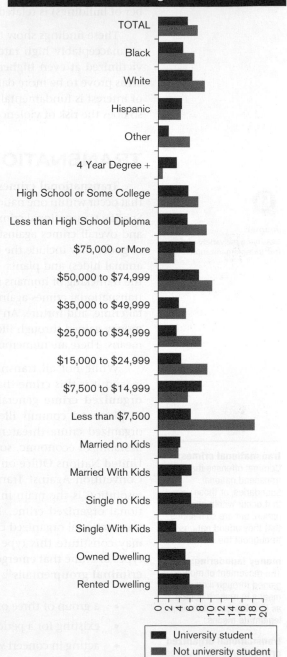

Figure 14.2 ■ Rape/Sexual Assault Victimization Rates (per 1,000): Comparison of College and Noncollege Women 18 to 24 Years of Age

Source: Author's calculations using NCVS data.

that a greater number of students living on campus in dormitories or other residences (especially male students) is related to higher crime rates on campus. Another finding pertains to the type of institution considered. Compared with students at 2-year colleges, students in medical schools and health science centers were three times more likely to be victims of violence on campus. Results also indicate that greater accessibility to and from campus (e.g., public transportation) and greater visibility of the campus (e.g., more acreage, greater number of buildings) is related to higher campus crime rates.

These findings show that violence does occur against college students and that it occurs at unacceptably high rates. But these findings also indicate that non–college students are victimized at even higher rates. Furthermore, research is clear that in general, off campus areas prove to be more dangerous than those on campus. Knowing the location and campus of interest is fundamental to understanding the risk of violence. Campuses vary greatly, and so does the risk of violence associated with them.

TRANSNATIONAL CRIME

Journal:
Classifying the variety of drug trafficking organizations

Transnational crimes are criminal offenses that transcend national boundaries or those that occur within one nation but are so heinous that they offend nations throughout the world. Specific transnational crimes vary and may include trafficking, illegal distribution of materials, and overall crimes against humanity. Transnational crimes involving the illegal distribution of goods may include the trading of endangered animals or animal parts (e.g., elephant ivory, animal hides) and plants. Transnational crimes that include trafficking may take the form of the trafficking of humans for labor or sex, or the trafficking of organs, weapons, or drugs. And transnational crimes against humanity may include genocide, terrorism, piracy, environmental crime, and torture. An associated crime is **money laundering**, which is the movement of money gained through illegal means to make it appear as if it was gained through legitimate means. There are numerous methods of money laundering, some of them quite complex.

While not all transnational crime is organized in nature, a substantial portion of it is, and it is this crime that garners the bulk of law enforcement attention. **Transnational organized crime** generally involves multiple people working in a coordinated fashion to plan and commit illegal business undertakings that span countries.[28] Transnational organized crime threatens individual and national security, violates human rights, and destabilizes economic, social, cultural, and political systems throughout the world.[29] The United Nations Office on Drugs and Crime adopted a resolution titled the United Nations Convention Against Transnational Organized Crime (UNTOC) in November 2000.[30] This resolution is the main international document addressing issues associated with transnational organized crime. The UNTOC purposefully does not offer a precise definition of transnational organized crime, and it does not offer a comprehensive listing of crimes that may constitute this type of crime. This lack of specificity allows the ability to add new types of crime that emerge globally. The UNTOC does, however, outline what an **organized criminal group** entails[31]:

transnational crimes:
Criminal offenses that transcend national boundaries, or those that occur within one nation, but are so heinous that they offend nations throughout the world.

money laundering:
The movement of money gained through illegal means to make it appear as if it was gained through legitimate means.

transnational organized crime: Crime that involves multiple people working in a coordinated fashion to plan and commit illegal business undertakings that span countries.

organized criminal group: A group of three or more persons that was not randomly formed, which acts in concert with the aim of committing crime.

- a group of three or more persons that was not randomly formed
- existing for a period of time
- acting in concert with the aim of committing at least one crime punishable by at least 4 years' incarceration
- in order to obtain, directly or indirectly, a financial or other material benefit

One example of transnational organized crime uncovered by law enforcement was the casing of emergency telephone systems, water storage and distribution facilities, nuclear power plants, gas facilities, and electrical facilities in the United States by Al Qaida, which took place over the course of several years. This surveillance could have been used for massive and devastating cyberattacks or more conventional terrorism. A second example, in 1998, involved the arrest of 12 people from an organized crime ring and the seizure

Transnationally trafficked elephant ivory and rhinoceros horns. Elephants and rhinos are killed for these products. This text has focused on crimes against humans. As these photos illustrate, crime victims also include animals. If you were the judge overseeing the trial of the offenders who mutilated and killed these animals, what sentence would you give? Why?

of drugs, cash, and jewelry following the cooperation of law enforcement in Canada, the United States, Mexico, and Italy. This 2-year investigation dismantled what at the time was an enormous drug smuggling and money laundering operation. A third transnational crime example occurred in 1994, when almost a ton of uranium en route to Saddam Hussein was intercepted by authorities working around the globe. Another case of transnational organized crime was uncovered when U.S. and Canadian law enforcement revealed an alien smuggling ring that had transported more than 3,600 illegal Chinese migrants into the northern United States during 1997 and 1998. At the time, it was considered one of the largest human smuggling efforts in the northern United States. And finally, in the late 1990s, authorities halted a transnational organized crime ring out of Florida that had been smuggling stolen motor vehicles with counterfeited vehicle identification numbers to South America. Transnational crimes result in tremendous losses annually. The current estimated cost of transnational crimes, according to Yury Fedotov, executive director of the United Nations Office on Drugs and Crime, is $870 billion.[32] This estimate, however, does not account for the emotional, physical, and psychological damage resulting from these crimes.

As noted by the quotation at the opening of the chapter, transnational crime is a critically important issue. This means that greater work is needed to better understand, identify, and respond to transnational crimes—organized or not. It is imperative that research programs offering information for the development of policies and programs to assess transnational threats improve threat assessments and stop these crimes.[33] Given the importance and prominence of transnational crimes, it is plausible that attention to this matter will increase over time.

FORENSIC SCIENCE

Forensic science (as used in the criminal justice system) is the use of science to solve crimes. In the field of criminal justice, forensic science is used to gather information using knowledge in several fields, such as geology, entomology, arson, firearms, explosives, audio and video investigations, and medical analyses, to understand criminal incidents. Interest in forensic science in criminal justice, largely due to the widespread media portrayal, has been robust in recent years. This attention has led to the mistaken belief that forensic science in the arena of criminal justice is new. In contrast, the use of forensic science in criminal justice has a long history. While there is no agreed-on first time that forensic science was used in criminal justice, one possibility stems from the assassination of Julius Caesar in 44 CE. Caesar was the dictator of the Roman Republic before he was stabbed to death by a group of Roman senators. Dubbed the Liberators, the group of murderous senators feared

Web:
Forensic science

forensic science: The use of science to solve crimes.

CONTEMPLATING CAREERS

Crime Scene Investigator

Does approaching problems with a linear, methodological, step-by-step approach appeal to you? Do you have patience and great attention to detail? Are you a team player, with excellent communication skills and a strong stomach? If you answered yes to these questions, a career as a **crime scene investigator**, also known as a forensic scientist, may be for you.

A forensic scientist or crime scene investigator is one member of a team of scientists and investigators who investigate crimes. Unlike the unrealistic portrayal of forensic scientists in the media, one person does not gather evidence, analyze evidence, track down offenders, and ultimately make an arrest. Rather, crime scene investigators engage in more narrow tasks. They may gather physical evidence in the field, or they may analyze a particular type of evidence in a laboratory. Regardless of the area one works in (field or laboratory), writing skills are important in this role. Forensic scientists write reports, which means that excellent writing skills are mandatory. There are relatively few people who work as forensic scientists. It is estimated that in 2010, 13,000 individuals were employed in this capacity in the United States. Most are employed by government agencies and work in law enforcement agencies, crime laboratories, or coroner's offices. According to the Bureau of Labor Statistics, in 2012, forensic scientists earned an average of about $53,000 annually.

Many people falsely believe that they need a criminal justice degree to work as a forensic scientist. This is incorrect. To become qualified for this position, one must earn a minimum of a bachelor's degree in a "hard" science such as biology or chemistry. Some universities now offer forensic science degrees, but it is important to ensure that this degree is "hard" science in nature. After earning the degree, one should expect to receive additional on-the-job training while employed. As one may imagine, forensic scientists are exposed to some gruesome scenes. For this reason, the job can be stressful. Still, the work done by these individuals is important and rewarding.

Career Video:
A crime scene investigator discusses her experience and current issues in the field.

that Caesar wanted to overthrow the Senate (although the Senate had just declared Caesar "dictator in perpetuity"). Following Caesar's murder, the Roman physician Antistius conducted his autopsy and ascertained that of the 23 stab wounds inflicted, only 1 resulted in his death.

Other examples of forensic sciences used in the criminal justice system include the use of fingerprints. While August Vollmer was responsible for the introduction of fingerprinting for use in the field of criminal justice, this science was used initially in 1880 by Henry Faulds and William Herschel, who published research in *Nature* that demonstrated the permanence and distinctiveness of human fingerprints. That is, one's fingerprints do not change over time, and each person has a unique set of fingerprints. Because of these characteristics, it was shown that fingerprint evidence could be used in crime investigations to implicate or rule out suspects of criminal acts.

crime scene investigator: Also known as a forensic scientist; a member of a team of scientists and investigators who investigate crimes.

DNA: Deoxyribonucleic acid. This is hereditary material found in the nuclei of human cells (and most organisms).

Deoxyribonucleic acid (**DNA**) receives the lion's share of attention with regard to forensic science in the criminal justice system. DNA is hereditary material found in the nuclei of human cells (and most organisms; Figure 14.3).[34] Each person's DNA is a combination of his or her parents' DNA. Each individual has unique DNA, except in the case of identical twins, who share the same DNA. The ability to use DNA to identify (or exclude) a suspect in a crime began in 1984 with the work of British geneticist Alec Jeffreys and his colleagues.[35] Jeffreys showed that if there is DNA left behind at a crime scene (e.g., hair, blood, saliva, skin, semen, sweat, mucus, earwax), this information can be used to

Figure 14.3 ■ DNA Molecule Illustration

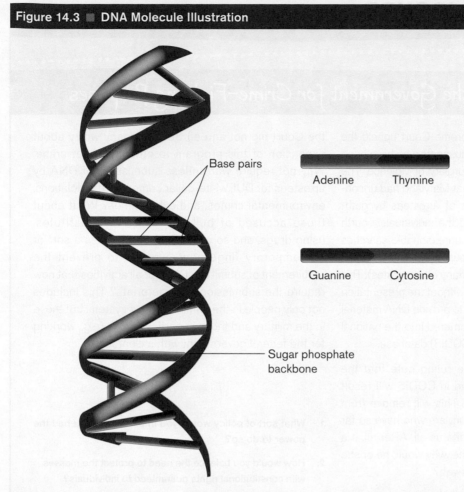

DNA has changed many aspects of the criminal justice system. In what ways has it benefited victims, offenders, and society? In what ways has it made operation of the criminal justice system more challenging?

Source: Genetics Home Reference. (2014). *What is DNA?* U.S. National Library of Medicine.

identify the offender through a process called DNA fingerprinting. In 1985, the procedures of DNA fingerprinting were improved, making the process more sensitive, reproducible, and easily cataloged in a computer database. This newer, more sensitive approach is termed DNA profiling.

The first use of DNA profiling in the criminal justice arena occurred in 1986, when Jeffreys was approached by law enforcement to see if, by using DNA, he could tie together two brutal crimes that occurred 3 years apart. The victims in each crime had been raped and murdered. The police had a suspect and needed evidence that he had committed these unrelated crimes. This approach was possible because in each case, the suspect left behind semen that could be tested using DNA profiling. Jeffreys agreed to generate DNA profiles, and what he found surprised everyone: The two girls were indeed raped and murdered by the same man. However, it was not the man the police had suspected![36] After verifying the results, in order to find the killer, the police conducted a campaign asking for blood samples from men in the community where the murder occurred. The perpetrator was found after he attempted to have a friend give blood as his proxy. The friend confessed to the police about the deception, and Colin Pitchfork was apprehended. Pitchfork's DNA was profiled, and it was a match for both rapes and murders. This first example of using DNA profiling in the criminal justice system demonstrates its significance. Not only does DNA profiling offer insight into the identity of actual offenders, but it also can exonerate those wrongly accused. With more precision,

POLICY ISSUES

Providing DNA to the Government for Crime-Fighting Purposes

In June 2013, the U.S. Supreme Court upheld the practice of gathering DNA from suspects who have been arrested, but not charged, for burglary or violence. The case before the Court claimed that Maryland had unconstitutionally conducted searches of arrestees by gathering DNA and that this violated the individuals' Fourth Amendment protections against unreasonable searches and seizures. In a 5–4 vote, the Court upheld the Maryland law (and in doing so, the laws in many others states). This means that one can be required, without the presentation of a warrant by law enforcement, to provide DNA material via a cheek swab, which will be entered into the national Combined DNA Index System (CODIS) database.

Those who agree with the ruling note that the enhancement of the data found in CODIS will result in the solution of many crimes. This will remove from society violent offenders and burglars who have so far escaped attention, which benefits us all. After all, if a person has not committed a crime, why would he or she worry about a harmless cheek swab?

In contrast, this ruling has alarmed many people for a variety of reasons. First, many view this activity as a violation of a citizen's Fourth Amendment protection against unreasonable search and seizure. (Clearly, the Court did not agree.) Second, many worry about expansion of this program to other types of crime. Why not require warrantless submission of DNA by arrestees for DUI, white-collar crimes, traffic violations, environmental crimes, and cybercrimes? What about those accused of bullying, soliciting prostitutes, using drugs, and so on? After all, if DNA is a sort of contemporary fingerprint, what is to prevent the requirement of submitting DNA for all activities that now require the submission of fingerprints? This includes not only people in the criminal justice system, but those in the military and those in particular jobs (e.g., working for the federal government with a clearance).

Think About It

1. What sort of policy would you implement if you had the power to do so?

2. How would you balance the need to protect the masses with constitutional rights guaranteed to individuals?

3. Would you be willing to sacrifice the rights of one person to ensure the safety of the majority? What laws would you be willing to undermine to prevent future terrorist attacks?

violent criminals can better be taken off the street, innocents not punished, and future suffering and death among the public avoided. For almost 30 years, DNA profiling has improved and proved to be a powerful forensic tool that can greatly increase fairness and accuracy in the criminal justice system. While improvements to this technology continue, DNA profiling continues to be the standard forensic DNA system used in the criminal justice system.[37]

CASE STUDY

An attractive element of DNA technology is that improvements to it today can be used to solve crimes from the past. It was DNA profiling that identified Dennis Bradford as the person who raped, assaulted, and nearly killed Jennifer Schuett almost 20 years before. Care had been taken to preserve evidence from the crime scene. At the time of the crime, DNA technology required more than a few cells for examination. This limitation meant that in 1990, no DNA match could be made. Law enforcement had the foresight to maintain the Schuett evidence for possible future technological advances. After assaulting and nearly killing Schuett, Bradford kidnapped, sexually assaulted, and threatened to murder another woman. He was tried, convicted, and sentenced to prison for 3 years in that case. In addition, this conviction meant that Bradford's DNA was entered into a database under the CODIS program. This program maintains the DNA profiles submitted by local, state, and federal systems and is available to law enforcement agencies throughout the United States. Bradford was paroled in 2008 and resided in Arkansas, where he worked as a welder. In 2009, new DNA technology meant that a DNA profile could be obtained from a single human cell. This meant that DNA from the almost 20-year-old evidence from Schuett's assault could be extracted and entered into CODIS. When this was done, a match was retrieved: Dennis Earl Bradford was the violent criminal responsible for Schuett's victimization.

More recently, the use of "fingerprinting" has been extended to nonliving items. The **National Integrated Ballistic Information Network** (NIBIN) is one example of relatively recent forensics progress that is based on "fingerprints" from shell casings. Since the 1990s, NIBIN, administered by the Bureau of Alcohol, Tobacco, Firearms and Explosives, has been linking shell casings, guns used in crimes, and scenes of crimes. This linking is accomplished using automatic imagining systems that identify the unique characteristics found on shell casings. Once imaged, data from each shell casing are entered into the **Integrated Ballistic Identification System**. Using these data, analysts can then identify any other crime scenes in which the firearm was used within or across jurisdictions. Before NIBIN, firearms examiners had to do this work manually, which was both time-consuming and labor-intensive. Evidence gathered in the NIBIN program has facilitated the conviction and incarceration of armed violent criminals. Furthermore, NIBIN evidence has linked crime scenes that were not recognized as being related. This technology has solved several crimes that were labeled as cold cases.

CSI EFFECT

The presentation of crime in the media has resulted in the **CSI effect**. While this term has a variety of related meanings, it generally refers to the distorted understanding held by the public of the role of forensic science in the criminal justice system. One example of the CSI effect is the public's perception that all crime scenes are littered with forensic evidence and that all of that evidence must be gathered—no matter how minor the crime. In reality, DNA, fingerprint, and other evidence is not available at all crime scenes. Regardless, the CSI effect has led to an increased demand by the public that forensic evidence be collected. These demands have detrimentally affected the workloads of criminal justice employees. The CSI effect also has manifested itself in that many in the public believe that evidence can be gathered in ways that is patently fictitious. For example, in one episode of a CSI crime show, a plaster mold of a stab wound was made to ascertain the type of knife used in the homicide. This type of evidence gathering is fantasy.[38] The CSI effect was evident when a jury member from an actual trial lamented the fact that police had not dusted a lawn for fingerprints. Dusting a lawn of grass for fingerprints is impossible.

One forensic scientist estimates that 40% of the techniques shown on CSI television shows are complete fiction.[39] Another result of the CSI effect is that many in the public believe that forensic evidence is available instantly, or nearly instantly. This perception, too, is unrealistic. Forensic evidence can take days, weeks, and even months to prepare. Trials are thought to have been affected by the CSI effect in two primary ways: Jurors expect more forensic evidence to be presented at trial, and jurors are more willing to uncritically accept any forensic evidence presented to them at trial. These beliefs are alleged to

National Integrated Ballistic Information Network: A system administered by the Bureau of Alcohol, Tobacco, Firearms and Explosives that links shell casings, guns used in crimes, and scenes of crimes.

Integrated Ballistic Identification System: The computer database that houses "fingerprints" for shell casings in the United States.

CSI effect: Distorted understanding held by the public of the role of forensic science in the criminal justice system.

The CSI effect has resulted in some unforeseen consequences in the criminal justice system. What would you do as a policymaker to minimize the CSI effect? Is it possible to neutralize it? Why or why not?

Illustration by Arthur Ball

Journal:
CSI effect and forensic backlog

lead to different outcomes of a trial. On one hand, if a jury fails to be presented with forensic evidence (even if it is unnecessary or not possible), jurors are more inclined to acquit the suspect. On the other hand, any forensic evidence presented to the jury tends to be believed uncritically and the defendant is more likely to be found guilty. These outcomes have real implications in terms of our criminal justice system. Former actor Robert Blake was acquitted of murdering his wife although two eyewitnesses were able to state that Blake had committed the murder. Jurors acquitted Blake, noting that no forensic evidence was presented at the trial. Many contend that the CSI effect allowed Blake to get away with murder.

Some people theorize that some of these associations stem not from the CSI effect, but rather from the **tech effect**. The tech effect refers to the public's awareness of modern technology and the expectation that it plays an important role in the contemporary criminal justice system, including trials. That is, it may not be watching a CSI crime show per se, but rather having a better understanding of the role of technology that leads to demands by jurors in a trial. This tech effect comes from the media environment, a small part of which includes the CSI shows.

tech effect: The phenomenon whereby the public's increased awareness of modern technology results in the expectation of unnecessary and at times unrealistic forensic evidence at trial.

CASE STUDY

Where Are They Now?

Jennifer is now the mother of two wonderful children.

In 2016, Joshua Paul Benjamin was hired to conduct statistical analyses for a governmental agency.

The text presented four actual encounters with the criminal justice system. This section shares with the reader where each of the persons highlighted in our case studies is today. Jennifer Schuett continues to live in Texas and works as an advocate and speaker on behalf of survivors everywhere. She has never stopped wanting to be a mother, although the attack left that looking very unlikely. After a story about her case was aired on a local television station, a fertility doctor contacted her to offer his services in the hope that she and her husband Jonathan could become parents. This effort was successful, and Jennifer and Jonathan welcomed a baby named Jenna into their lives in 2012. Jenna is a smart, happy, and beautiful child. Jenna now travels with her mom for her speaking engagements. Even more good news came in 2016, when Jennifer and Jonathan welcomed baby Jonah. Her work as a mother to two young children keeps Jennifer busy. Still she attends many events each year to share her story with others.

Chris Farias successfully completed his community corrections sentence and is no longer serving a work-release sentence. He enrolled in college courses to further his education and signed several new clients based on recommendations from past customers. He has more work than he can possibly take on. Chris met a woman and has been in a long-term, healthy relationship for some time. He is now able to travel out of state to see his extended family and is frequently returning from time on the slopes or at the beach. He continues to pay close attention to his behavior and has no desire to risk finding himself in trouble with the law again. He knows that the chance of receiving another community corrections sentence is unlikely.

Joshua Paul Benjamin continues to struggle with the stigma of the crimes he committed decades ago. After serving time in prison, he continued treatment on his own. He enrolled in graduate school to pursue a master's degree and then a PhD. He was an A student and completed both degrees. He is active in his church, and has earned an additional master's degree in theological studies. He has continued living a crime-free life. While Joshua was pursuing these degrees, the sex offender registry laws went into effect, and Joshua was required to register. This requirement generated many difficulties for him even though he'd completed his sentence more than a decade before. First, as a student, the university housing in which he lived informed him that he had to leave. Second, as a student, the university informed him that he could no longer serve as a teaching or research assistant. Furthermore, professors were prohibited from paying him out of pocket to work on research. Joshua completed his PhD and, after an extended job search, was hired in 2016 to conduct statistical analyses for a governmental agency.

And finally, Danny Madrid is enjoying a healthy and fulfilling life today. He is currently completing a PhD in criminology and criminal justice at a major state university. Soon, he'll be on the job market and beginning work as an assistant professor. This is a proud accomplishment given that Danny had only a GED when he began this journey in the criminal justice system in 2003. Danny has discovered that he finds great joy in teaching. He recalls being nervous and mindful about inadvertently revealing his "secret past" when he taught his first class—a gangs class—at California State University Dominguez Hills. He feared that if his secret past in the criminal justice system were revealed, he would be misunderstood, scare the students, or get in trouble with faculty. He laughs about it now because revealing his past to students turns out to be an advantage when teaching, as students love hearing his stories. Plus, he finds the ability to discuss social problems through a critical and informed perspective with his students therapeutic. Outside of education, Danny finds great pleasure in both fine art and graffiti painting. In terms of the future, Danny wants to collect original data, publish research, and eventually write books. He also intends to get involved in some type of outreach program with disenfranchised youth, particularly immigrant Latinos. He made a commitment long ago to sacrifice himself for the greater good, and he is more committed now to that ideal than ever before. He acknowledges that he is blessed to have survived the hell that was his youth, and he wants to use his experiences to spread the good word and help others.

When not studying in his PhD program, Danny Madrid spends time oil painting on canvas. This painting is titled *His Science is Nearly Complete* and is one of many he has completed.

Case Study Video 14.1:
Interviews with case study participants

CHAPTER WRAP-UP

This chapter outlined specific issues related to the criminal justice system that have received great attention in recent years. A main theme that guides this chapter, as well as the book as a whole, is that the criminal justice system is dynamic. Our perspectives toward issues change over time, and as a result, some topics receive extra attention. The topic of terrorism has received great attention, especially since the terrorist attacks of 9/11. While we strived to include information on terrorism and homeland security throughout the text, we felt it necessary to devote a special section in this chapter to this topic. It is a topic that will only gain in attention and resources received as time goes on.

Another topic that has recently been the focus of great research, attention, and debate is human and sex trafficking. In the past, most people have dismissed this crime as something that happens in other countries. More recently, attention has been given to the acknowledgment that these crimes occur within the borders of the United States.

A similar topic that has been a problem for centuries in this nation is hate or bias crimes. Though present in the United States since its inception, scrutiny and attention to these special crimes has increased over time. Given the changing notions about "special populations," we can only surmise that this topic is one that will continue to be of utmost interest in the future.

We also included a section devoted to violence against college students. While this category of crime has long been examined in the academic literature, only recently has the general public become concerned. This section outlines the realities of this type of violence, which contrasts in many ways with the media portrayals of it.

Transnational crimes, like the others, have been a problem in the United States for a long time. It is important that students be exposed to information on these crimes and why they are problematic. As noted in the text and by this chapter's opening quotation, they may be the greatest threat that faces our country today. For this reason, it is important that students be aware of these crimes.

No special topics section would be complete without attention given to forensic science and its role in the criminal justice system. As time marches on, there will be greater advances in this area, and greater ethical and policy questions will be raised. An understanding of this topic is critical for students of criminal justice.

The final portion of this chapter addressed our four case studies. Each was introduced to the criminal justice system unwillingly, and each will be connected to it throughout their lives. We have seen the variety of ways in which these cases moved through the criminal justice system and how it has affected these individuals and those around them. It is our hope that your journey with these people through the criminal justice system opened your eyes to the complexity and realities of the system.

KEY POINTS

- International and domestic terrorism has been going on for centuries.

- The Department of Homeland Security was established shortly after the 9/11 terrorist attacks in the United States; it consolidated existing groups within the federal government to enhance communication.

- Human and sex trafficking have a long history in the United States. Recently, renewed attention to these issues has arisen, especially in terms of sex trafficking of minors in the United States.

- Trafficking of minors is never voluntary, and their victimization is a form of child abuse. Minors are unable to consent and should be treated as victims and not criminals in cases of trafficking.

- Hate crimes are motivated by the offender's perception that the victim belongs to a particular group. If it weren't for the belief about this group membership, the crime likely would not occur.

- Findings show that the extent of hate crimes has been stable in recent years and that most hate crimes take the form of victimization based on religious affiliation.

- Violence against college students happens at unacceptably high rates, yet at rates lower than their non-college counterparts. Most violence against college students occurs off campus, and the rates of violence associated with campuses can vary greatly.

- Transnational crimes take many forms and transcend borders. Some believe that this type of crime is the most dangerous facing the United States today.

- Forensic science is the use of science to solve crimes. This includes fingerprints, DNA, fiber analysis, tread analysis, soil analysis, entomology, and myriad other methods. Not all crime scenes have forensic evidence available.

KEY TERMS

Civil Rights Act of 1871 372

Crime Scene
   Investigator 378

CSI Effect 381

Dirty Bomb 367

DNA 378

Domestic Terrorism 366

Forensic Science 377

Hate Crimes 371

Homeland Security Act
   of 2002 366

Human Trafficking 369

Integrated Ballistic
   Identification
   System 381

International Terrorism 366

Matthew Shepard and
   James Byrd, Jr. Hate
   Crimes Prevention
   Act 373

Military Commission 368

Money Laundering 376

National Integrated
   Ballistic Information
   Network 381

Organized Criminal
   Group 376

Sex Trafficking 370

Survival Sex 371

Tech Effect 382

Transnational Crimes 376

Transnational Organized
   Crime 376

REVIEW QUESTIONS

1. How does terrorism differ from nonterroristic crime?

2. Has the creation of the Department of Homeland Security made the nation safer?

3. For what purposes are humans trafficked? Should it matter if those trafficked are adults or minors?

4. Is it necessary to distinguish between hate crimes and other types of crimes?

5. Why does distinguishing between campus violence and violence against college students matter?

6. What other groups should be included as protected under hate crime or bias crime laws? What groups should not be protected?

7. What are the types of transnational crimes? Is the distinction between organized and nonorganized transnational crimes important? Is this type of crime especially difficult to fight? Why or why not?

8. Is forensic evidence available at every crime scene? Should forensic evidence be collected at the scene of minor crimes?

9. How do shows such as *CSI* influence the criminal justice system? Is the influence a positive one or a negative one?

CRITICAL THINKING MATTERS

1. **The Motivation of a Crime: Should It Matter?** Currently, some crimes are treated differently based on the motivation of the offender. For example, hate crimes are such because the offender is motivated by the perceived membership of the victim in some group. Terrorism is based on the motivation of the offender to terrorize innocent people because leadership holds a position the terrorists wish to change. Should crimes in which the motivation is based on membership or forcing change be treated differently than other crimes? Should the punishment differ if an offender kills in a fit of rage, the victim started a fight, the victim belongs to a religious organization, or the offender wanted to change policy and therefore killed an innocent bystander? Should the motivation of the criminal be taken into account? Why or why not?

2. **Violence Against College Students.** Given what you have learned about college student victimization, do you feel safer or less safe when you are on campus? Why do you think that there has been this recent explosion in interest about college student victimization, especially sexual and gender-based violence? Given the prevalence of sexual and gender-based violence in society in general, why the focus of this violence among college students only?

Are universities different from society in general? Should we expect them to be?

3. **Forensic Science and Exoneration.** If you were a policymaker, would you allow all incarcerated persons the opportunity to exonerate themselves using DNA if DNA is available? Why or why not? If so, who would pay for the testing? How would already overworked labs deal with the increase in workload that allowing this would cause? If an incarcerated person is found to be erroneously incarcerated as a result, what do you do? Do you offer financial assistance to allow them to get a start in life? Do you pay for the error and time lost in prison? Why do you think the U.S. Supreme Court will not allow incarcerated suspects to request DNA testing to show they are innocent?

4. **Joshua and Hope for the Future.** Joshua has lived a crime-free life, he continues treatment, and he has gained real skills and an advanced education. Still, he searched for an extended period of time before finding employment. He completed his sentence long before sex offender registries were implemented. Why should he have to register? How would you handle this case if you were a policymaker? What would you do if you were Joshua? How does hope for the future influence how he'll behave in the future?

DIGITAL RESOURCES

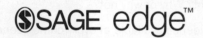

Sharpen your skills with SAGE edge at edge.sagepub.com/rennison2e. SAGE edge for Students provides a personalized approach to help you accomplish your coursework goals in an easy-to-use learning environment. You'll find action plans, mobile-friendly eFlashcards, and quizzes as well as video and web resources and links to SAGE journal articles to support and expand on the concepts presented in this chapter.

APPENDIX

THE BILL OF RIGHTS

I. Freedom of Religion, Press, Speech, and Petition

Congress shall make no law respecting an establishment of religion, or prohibiting the free exercise thereof; or abridging the freedom of speech, or of the press; or the right of the people peaceably to assemble, and to petition the Government for a redress of grievances.

II. Right to Bear Arms

A well-regulated militia, being necessary to the security of a free State, the right of the people to keep and bear arms, shall not be infringed.

III. Conditions for Quarters of Soldiers

No soldier shall, in time of peace be quartered in any house, without the consent of the owner, nor in time of war, but in a manner to be prescribed by law.

IV. Right of Search and Seizure Regulation

The right of the people to be secure in their persons, houses, papers, and effects, against unreasonable searches and seizures, shall not be violated, and no warrants shall issue, but upon probable cause, supported by oath or affirmation, and particularly describing the place to be searched, and the persons or things to be seized.

V. Prosecution Provisions

No person shall be held to answer for a capital, or otherwise infamous crime, unless on a presentment or indictment of a Grand Jury, except in cases arising in the land or naval forces, or in the militia, when in actual service in time of war or public danger; nor shall any person be subject for the same offense to be twice put in jeopardy of life or limb; nor shall be compelled in any criminal case to be a witness against himself, nor be deprived of life, liberty, or property, without due process of law; nor shall private property be taken for public use without just compensation.

VI. Right to a Speedy Trial

In all criminal prosecutions, the accused shall enjoy the right to a speedy and public trial, by an impartial jury of the State and district wherein the crime shall have been committed, which district shall have been previously ascertained by law, and to be informed of the nature and cause of the accusation; to be confronted with the witnesses against him; to have compulsory process for obtaining witnesses in his favor, and to have the assistance of counsel for his defense.

VII. Right to a Trial by Jury

In suits at common law, where the value in controversy shall exceed twenty dollars, the right of trial by jury shall be preserved, and no fact tried by a jury shall be otherwise reexamined in any court of the United States, than according to the rules of the common law.

VIII. Excessive Bail and Cruel Punishment

Excessive bail shall not be required, nor excessive fines imposed, nor cruel and unusual punishments inflicted.

IX. Constitutional Construction

The enumeration in the Constitution, of certain rights, shall not be construed to deny or disparage others retained by the people.

X. Constitutional States Rights

The powers not delegated to the United States by the Constitution, nor prohibited by it to the States, are reserved to the States respectively, or to the people.

GLOSSARY

1996 Prison Litigation Reform Act: A law resulting from the proliferation of jailhouse lawyers that addressed five issues related to prison litigation.

Acquit: To free someone from a criminal charge following a not guilty verdict.

Actus Reus: Latin term meaning "guilty act," used to indicate the physical act of the crime. Usually paired with *mens rea* to show criminal liability.

Adam Walsh Protection Act: Requires states to classify offenders based on type of offense; register sex offenders where they live, work, or attend school; and make registries available on the Internet.

Adjudicate: To render a formal judgment about a disputed matter.

Adjudication: A hearing to ensure that a juvenile's due process rights have not been violated. Similar to a criminal court trial in the adult system.

Administrative Law: Derives from a legislative body's delegation of authority over commissions or boards to regulate activities controlled by written statutes.

Adultery: In general, sex by a married person with someone other than his or her spouse; specific laws differ by state, as does the level of criminality associated with it.

Adversarial System: A system used in the United States in which prosecutors and defendants compete against each other to reveal the truth.

Advocacy Model: A model in which the defendant and the government are represented by advocates who act on behalf of their clients.

Aftercare: Programs designed to reduce recidivism by offering support and monitoring juveniles through supervision. Equivalent to adults' being placed on parole.

Age of Enlightenment: Brought about new ways of thinking including reforms arising from outrage against the barbaric system of law and punishment just before the French Revolution in the late 18th century.

Allen Charge: Additional instructions a judge may give to a deliberating jury to discourage a mistrial.

Alternative Dispute Resolution: An approach to settle cases using a variety of methods to assist the disputing parties in finding a solution without relying on costly litigation.

Arm of the Court: A phrase used to describe a probation officer who acts as the court's fact finder.

Arraignment: A formal reading of charges in a court of appropriate jurisdiction in front of the defendant.

Auburn System: A style of incarceration based on reformation. Inmates were housed separately and not allowed to communicate. During the day inmates worked and ate in silence. Also known as the congregate system.

Automated Kiosk Reporting: A type of community corrections in which a probationer provides information to a freestanding machine, often using eye-scanning technology.

Automatic Waivers: By legislative action, transfers juveniles who committed serious crimes to the adult system. Designated in statutes for offenses such as murder, kidnapping, armed robbery, and carjacking.

Automobile Exception: States that, should police have probable cause to believe that a vehicle (including boats) contains contraband, fruits of a crime, evidence, and/or instrumentalities of crime, the vehicle can be searched.

Bail Reform Act of 1966: This federal law provides a noncapital defendant with the right to be released on bond or on personal recognizance unless the defendant is a flight risk.

Battered Woman Syndrome: A criminal defense developed to excuse or mitigate the actions of women who kill their abusers in cases of domestic violence despite a lack of imminent danger.

Bench Trial: A trial in which a judge (or panel of judges) acts as the fact finder, weighs the evidence, deliberates, and renders a judgement.

Beyond a Reasonable Doubt: The level of proof required for a criminal case conviction. Refers to a reasonable person having no reasonable doubt that the defendant is guilty as charged.

Bifurcated Trials: A double trial system used for capital cases. The first trial is the guilt trial, while the second determines punishment.

Bill of Rights: The first 10 amendments to the U.S. Constitution, which guide procedural law pertaining to issues such as arrests, warrants, search/seizure, and trials.

Black Codes: Statutes that criminalized trivial behavior, such as obscene language, of newly freed slaves.

Blocked Opportunities Frame: This frame indicates that crime results from a lack of legal options. Offenders live in poverty, are uneducated, unemployed, and discriminated against, and because of that commit crime.

Bobbies: Nickname of officers in Britain named for Sir Robert Peel. Bobbies replaced the existing (and generally corrupt) system of parish constables and night watchmen.

Body-Imaging Scanners: Technology recently adopted in prisons to detect contraband.

Boot Camps: A type of intermediate sanction in which offenders are mandated to military settings, where they are required to follow orders, march, run drills, and engage in physical training.

Borh: Earliest known system of policing in England. The borh was a unit that was responsible for policing and security, which was generally a collective of 12 individuals who stood surety for one another's good behavior.

Branding: An early form of punishment that also served as a record to alert others of an individual's past offenses.

Brawner Rule: Also called the ALI rule, it reduced "knowing right from wrong" to the capacity to appreciate the difference between the two. In other words, a defendant must possess an "understanding of his conduct" and be able to "control his actions."

Broken Windows Theory: Introduced by James Q. Wilson and George Kelling to describe the social disorder that occurs in run-down and neglected neighborhoods, which leads to higher crime rates.

Case Law: Law that is based on previous court decisions or precedents.

Castle Doctrine: A legal doctrine that states that homeowners are no longer required to retreat if threatened by intruders. In some states it extends beyond homes.

Challenge for Cause: A challenge during *voir dire* in which the defense counsel, the prosecutor, or the judge identifies a potential juror he or she believes cannot be unbiased, fair, or impartial. Also known as strike for cause.

Challenge to the Array: An argument that the venire should be discharged because of a deficiency or an illegality in the way it was selected.

Child Savers: Child advocates who fought to reform the brutal and harsh juvenile system.

Circumstantial Evidence: Evidence that requires the fact-finding body to interpret it and draw conclusions about its meaning.

Civil Law: Law that deals with disputes between individuals or organizations and typically seeks some type of compensation for the harmed party.

Civil Rights Act of 1871: Federal legislation passed to give federal protection to Fourteenth Amendment rights that were violated by private persons, including those in the Ku Klux Klan.

Civil Rights Act of 1875: One in a series of post–Civil War legislative acts, it prohibited the exclusion of African Americans from jury duty, among other things.

Civil Trials: Trials used to settle disputes between two parties that do not involve criminal misconduct.

Class Action Lawsuits: Civil cases involving large numbers of victims in which courts authorize a single individual or small faction to represent the interests of the larger group.

Classification: Determines the level of supervision appropriate for each offender based on probation investigation and risk assessment.

Classification Review: An assessment made to determine an offender's risk level and needs.

Code of Hammurabi: The oldest known legal code, it established approximately 300 provisions for family, trade, real property, personal property, and labor.

Common Law: A type of legal system originally developed in England, whereby the courts define the law and determine how to apply the law. This is the body of law derived from judicial opinions.

Communications Assistance for Law Enforcement Act: A 1994 law that allows federal agencies to more easily monitor an individual's phone calls and Internet messages.

Community Policing: A philosophy and style of policing that adopts proactive measures and collaborates with community members.

Compensatory Damages: Money awarded in a civil lawsuit for loss or injury suffered as a result of unlawful conduct.

Complaint: The document that initiates legal proceedings by demonstrating facts and legal reasons the plaintiff believes the defendant owes remedy or has committed a crime.

CompSTAT: A law enforcement strategy first adopted by the New York City Police Department that relies on crime mapping to identify hot spots and crime trends in order to effectively address problems.

Conflict Model: A theoretical view of the criminal justice system that highlights the adversarial nature of the system. Components of the criminal justice system work in competition to produce a fair outcome or justice.

Congregate System: Another name for the Auburn System, which reflects the silent congregation experienced by inmates during the day.

Consensus Model: A theoretical view of the criminal justice system that highlights the collaborative nature of the system. The components of the criminal justice system work in unison to achieve justice.

Consent: When police officers ask for permission to search, and you voluntarily say yes, they can proceed without a warrant.

Consent Decree: Document outlining the terms and conditions of deferred status.

Constitutional Law: A major source of law that establishes the fundamental rules and relationships among the judiciary, legislative, and executive branches at the state and federal levels.

Continuum of Force: Guideline for the degree of force and weapon an officer may use during an arrest, which is becoming outdated.

Contract System: Penitentiary system in which prison officials sold the labor and services of inmates to private contractors for a fixed price per inmate per day.

Convict Criminology: The study of crime and correctional systems that challenges traditional viewpoints.

Convict Leasing System: A system whereby private businesses paid the state a fixed annual fee for control of inmates.

Convict Subculture: Imports values from the outside and follows the inmate code.

CopLink: An information technology system that offers tactical lead generation, crime analysis, and information sharing among local, regional, state, and national law enforcement agencies.

Corporal Punishment: Physical punishment in response to an offense designed to discipline and reform an offender.

Correctional Officers: People charged with managing inmates who are incarcerated in a jail, reformatory, prison, or penitentiary.

Correctional Responses in the Community: Sanctions for criminal acts that are less severe than full-time incarceration but more severe than probation.

Corrections: Functions to protect society from criminals through housing, monitoring, and other community-based programs.

Court of Last Resort: The final court with appellate authority in a given court system. In the United States at the federal level, the Supreme Court is the court of last resort.

Courts: One of the three main components of the criminal justice system. The courts are responsible for interpreting and applying the law.

Covered Jurisdictions: States, cities, or counties that must submit proposed voting changes to the U.S. Department of Justice because of their histories of discrimination against minority voters.

Crime: The breaking of a law for which the criminal justice system or some other governing authority prescribes punishment.

Crime Control Perspective: A popular view of the role of the criminal justice system. This perspective states that the goal of the system is to prevent crime by shrewdly and harshly punishing offenders.

Crime Multiplier: The saturated media presentation of crime that leads to a public that believes there is more crime than there is. In addition, this disproportionate and repetitive coverage leads to enhanced fear of crime among the public.

Crime Scene Investigator: Also known as a forensic scientist; a member of a team of scientists and investigators who investigate crimes.

Crime Triangle: Also referred to as the problem analysis triangle, a strategy that focuses on immediate concerns present in the environment in order to confront difficult issues.

Crime Victims' Rights Act: A 2004 law that established numerous rights for crime victims in federal cases.

Criminal Justice: The system of institutions, policies, and practices with the goal of maintaining social control and deterring crime through sanctions and rehabilitation.

Criminal Trials: Trials to ascertain the guilt or lack of guilt of defendants charged with committing crimes.

Criminology: An academic discipline that investigates the nature, extent, and causes of criminal offending and criminal victimization.

CSI Effect: Distorted understanding held by the public of the role of forensic science in the criminal justice system.

Cybercrime: A form of illegal activity using a computer or computer networks as the primary method of commission. Examples of cybercrime include network intrusions, dissemination of computer viruses, and phishing.

Dark Figure of Crime: Crimes that fail to come to the attention of the police, because they were unreported, it was unclear a crime occurred, or no one learned that a crime was committed.

Deadlocked: A hung jury that is unable to reach an agreement regarding the guilt or innocence of a defendant is said to be deadlocked.

Death Qualified: A part of *voir dire* in capital cases in which attorneys ascertain whether the prospective juror is suitable to sit on a case that may result in the death penalty. A juror who will not impose death under any circumstances is removed from the panel.

Declaration of Principles: A 37-paragraph document adopted at the 1870 meeting of the National Prison Association that called for institutions focused on reformation and rejected the notion that punishment was the ultimate goal of imprisonment.

Decriminalization: The act of ending or reducing criminal penalties associated with some behaviors.

Defense Attorney: A lawyer who advocates for his or her client and protects the client's constitutional rights.

Deferred Status: Also known as informal probation, it requires that a youth stay out of trouble for a certain length of time in order for the charges to be dismissed.

Deliberation: The jury process of deciding the guilt or lack of guilt of the defendant.

Delinquency: Illegal actions by a youthful offender.

Deprivation Model: Where prisons require inmates to adapt to being deprived of basic rights and needs.

Detention Hearing: Prosecutorial decisions to transfer a juvenile case to adult court.

Determinate Sentencing: A type of structured sentencing that is established by legislative statute and rules out the possibility of alternatives to prison. Prisoners are given fixed sentences.

Deterrence: Sentencing goal that seeks to dissuade the offender and others in the public from committing crime.

Direct Evidence: Something introduced in a trial that does not require an inference to be drawn by the fact-finding body.

Direct Files: When a prosecutor uses discretion to send a juvenile to the criminal justice system.

Dirty Bomb: An explosive device using radioactive material.

Discovery: The process through which the defense learns about evidence held by the prosecution. This may include reports and witness statements.

Discretion: It allows police and others throughout the criminal justice system the latitude to make an arrest (or other action) or not.

Disorganized: Inmates with mental illness and/or low IQs.

Disposition Hearing: Hearing in which a judge decides the best placement of a delinquent.

Diversion: The decision to keep low-risk youth offenders from entering into the more formal processing of the juvenile system.

DNA: Deoxyribonucleic acid. This is hereditary material found in the nuclei of human cells (and most organisms).

Doing Time: Inmates who accept and follow the rules.

Domestic Terrorism: Terrorism that occurs within the territorial jurisdiction of the United States.

Double Jeopardy: Constitutional protection under the Fifth Amendment that prevents the accused from facing charges or trial by the same sovereign after an acquittal or conviction for the same offense.

Dual Court System: U.S. court structure wherein the federal government has a court system and procedures distinct from the states.

Due Process: Established rules and principles designed to protect private rights found in the Fifth and Fourteenth Amendments that prevent the government from unfairly or arbitrarily depriving anyone of life, liberty, or property.

Due Process Perspective: A perspective that views the role of the criminal justice system to be to ensure that all people accused of crimes are treated fairly and equally in the system.

Durham Test: Determines if a criminal act was a product of mental disease or defect. This requires that jurors determine if a defendant had a mental disease or defect and if the condition was the reason for the criminal behavior.

Dying Declaration: An exception to the hearsay rule that allows the dying words of a witness to a crime to be used in court.

Dynamic Risk Predictors: Characteristics of offenders amenable to change, such as employment status, educational level, and peer groups.

Electronic Monitoring: An intermediate sanction in which the probationer wears an ankle, wrist, or neck monitor that identifies his or her location.

En Banc: A case heard by all judges of the court, or the full court. Cases are typically heard en banc when a significant issue is presented or if both parties request it and the court agrees.

Equity: A sentencing concept that emphasizes that similar crimes be punished in similar ways and with similar severity.

Ex Post Facto Law: A law that a legislature passed after a crime was committed. At the time the person committed the action, it was legal, and only later was the act deemed criminal.

Excited Utterance: An exception to the hearsay rule—a statement made by a person during a shocking or upsetting event. Words blurted out during the stress of excitement may be entered into court.

Exclusionary Rule: The rule excludes from trial evidence that was obtained unlawfully, which violates a person's constitutional rights.

Exculpatory Evidence: Evidence that may be favorable to a defendant in a criminal trial, often clearing some or all guilt during criminal proceedings.

Exigent Circumstances: One of six exceptions that allow a warrantless search. These are emergency circumstances that are present to prevent (a) escape, (b) harm to the officer or others, and (c) destruction of evidence.

Eye Scans: Biometric technology increasingly being used in community corrections to determine if a probationer has used drugs or alcohol or is fatigued.

Factual Guilt: Refers to whether defendant actually committed a crime.

Faulty Criminal Justice System Frame: Suggests that crime occurs because of a dearth of law and order in the country and that criminals offend because they feel they can get away with it.

Federal Rules of Evidence: Federal rules guiding what is evidence and what can be introduced in a trial.

Federal Sentencing Guidelines Act: A 1984 law that eliminated parole release for federal prisoners and abolished almost all good time earned by a prisoner.

Felicitous Calculus: A measure indicating how much pleasure an individual gains from a specific act.

Felony: A criminal offense (e.g., murder, robbery, rape) that is more serious and generally results in more severe punishment than a misdemeanor.

Fine: A type of community correction sanction.

Flogging: An early punishment that consisted of serious beatings or whippings.

Forensic Science: The use of science to solve crimes.

Forfeiture: A community correction sanction in which the criminal's material possessions may be seized if the items were related to the commission or outcome of a criminal offense.

Framing: The packaging of criminal events in the media into tidy presentations that make sharing the information easy.

Frankpledge: A system of policing that replaced the borh. A frankpledge included all boys and men age 12 or older from 10 households into groups referred to as tythings.

Fruit of the Poisonous Tree: Also called the exclusionary rule, this doctrine was applied to the states in *Mapp v. Ohio*. This case ruled that any evidence obtained during an illegal search would be disallowed at trial.

Fugitive Slave Law of 1850: A law passed by the U.S. Congress that addressed fears of a "slave power conspiracy" as the number of slaves grew. This law created the need for slave patrols, which became the purview of police officers.

Fusion Centers: Developed under the National Criminal Intelligence Sharing Plan to help in information exchanges on intelligence gathered from confidential informants, surveillance, and crime data analyses.

General Conditions: Conditions of corrections in the community that are standard across convicted offenders.

General Deterrence: The notion that the general populace will be deterred from committing crimes based on the perceived negative consequences of being caught.

Ghost Employee: Nonexistent employees for whom private prisons have

illegally charged the government (and ultimately taxpayer).

Ghost Inmate: A nonexistent inmate charged to the government (and taxpayer) by private prisons.

Gleaning: Inmates who take advantage of rehabilitation, educational, and vocational opportunities while serving time.

Global Terrorism Database: A database housed at the University of Maryland that contains a broad range of data on threatened, failed, and completed terrorist attacks since 1970.

Gossip's Bridle or Scold's Helm: A heavy iron device that covered an offender's head to punish and deter those who nagged, slandered, or gossiped.

GPS monitoring: Used primarily to track high-risk offenders, especially sex offenders, and comes in two forms: passive and active.

Grass-Eaters: Identified by the Knapp Commission as officers who acted as passive participants when others were engaging in bribery and corruption.

Group A and Group B Crimes: Two major clusters of crimes gathered by the FBI in NIBRS. Group A includes 22 crimes covering 46 offenses including homicide and robbery. Group B includes 11 offenses such as loitering and drunkenness.

Hanging: A form of punishment used in the early days of the United States as a penalty for the worst offenses.

Hate Crimes: Crimes committed that target victims and/or their property due to their perceived membership in a particular group. Also known as bias-motivated crimes.

Hearsay: An out-of-court statement offered in court to prove the truth of the matter asserted.

Hearsay Rule: A basic rule that hearsay is inadmissible in court.

Hedonistic Calculus: See Felicitous Calculus.

Hierarchy Rule: Used to facilitate counting crime, this rule ranks crimes from least to most serious. In a criminal incident, only the most serious crime committed during the incident is counted.

High-Activity Location Observation (HALO) Cameras: Remote-controlled cameras that can view 360 degrees, zoom, and tilt. This technology enables law enforcement to observe and monitor areas of interest for criminal investigations and crime prevention.

Home Confinement/House Arrest: A type of intermediate sanction that restricts offenders from leaving their homes.

Homeland Security Act of 2002: An act by Congress that made the Department of Homeland Security a cabinet-level department in the U.S. government.

Hot Spots: Specific geographical locations identified as high-crime areas.

Houses of Refuge: State shelters established to house dependent, neglected, and delinquent children.

Human Trafficking: The trade in humans for labor and/or sex, and the extraction of organs or tissues. Sex trafficking is one form of human trafficking.

Hundred: Ten tythings grouped together into a collective for police and security purposes. A hundred was supervised by a leader known as a hundredman.

Hung Jury: A jury that is unable to reach an agreement regarding the guilt or innocence of the defendant. Also known as a deadlocked jury.

Importation Model: Experiences and socialization from the outside world are brought into prison and contribute to behavior while incarcerated.

Inalienable Rights: Rights that are universal and not contingent on laws or beliefs specific to a particular government or culture.

Incapacitation: Sentencing goal that isolates the offender from the public and takes away one's ability to commit a crime against those in the public.

Incident to a Lawful Arrest: This exception allows law enforcement to search any person without a warrant once that person is lawfully arrested.

Indeterminate Sentence: Sentence given to a defendant in the form of a range of years to be served (e.g., 3 to 15 years).

Indeterminate Sentencing: System of sentencing that allowed greater judicial discretion. The sentence is given in the form of a range of years (e.g., 3 to 15 years).

Indictment: A formal accusation that an individual has committed an act punishable by law, typically presented by a grand jury.

Inevitable Discovery: In criminal law, the rule makes an exception to the fruit of the poisonous tree doctrine. Illegally obtained evidence may be used if eventually it would have been found legally.

Information: A formal charge against an individual suspected of committing a crime, typically presented by an authorized public official, such as the prosecutor. The purpose is to inform the accused of the charges so a defense may be prepared.

Infotainment: The marketing of a highly edited and distorted combination of entertainment and information purported to be truthful and comprehensive.

In Loco Parentis: Actions taken in place of parents when dealing with juveniles.

Insanity Defense: A defense based on the belief that a select group of people who suffer from mental illness are unable to control their actions to such an extent that they cannot be held accountable for their crimes.

Intake: The first step in the juvenile justice system for youth. The intake process is similar to an initial hearing for adults.

Integrated Ballistic Identification System: The computer database that houses "fingerprints" for shell casings in the United States.

Intelligence-Led Policing: A means of creating efficiency and effectiveness in police agencies that emphasizes the importance of risk assessment and risk management.

Intensive Case Management: An evidence-based practice that includes low staff-to-client ratios; 24-hour coverage; and services and referrals for mental health treatment, housing, living skills, employment, and crisis intervention.

Intensive Supervised Probation: A type of probation in which offenders undergo extreme supervision and monitoring.

Intermediate Responses and Sanctions: A type of correctional response in the community that includes probation plus additional community sanctions, which are generally administered by probation departments.

International Terrorism: Terrorism that occurs outside the territorial jurisdiction of the United States.

Irresistible Impulse Test: A defense that fails to find a person criminally responsible if mental disease prevents the person from controlling his or her behavior.

Jacob Wetterling Crimes Against Children Act and Sexually Violent Offender Registration Act: Requires convicted sex offenders to register with local law enforcement.

Jailhouse Lawyer: An inmate who has never received a degree or practiced law, but has become well versed in legal matters while in prison.

Jailing: Inmates who have spent a substantial amount of time behind bars and tend to be comfortable in prison.

Jails: Local facilities managed by cities and counties that perform an overlapping but distinct purpose from prisons and penitentiaries.

Judicial Activism: This refers to deviation from the literal meaning of the Constitution, to take into account the present situation, including complex societal advances.

Judicial Review: A doctrine that ensures checks and balances by allowing courts to review the actions of the executive and legislative branches of government.

Judicial Waivers: Waivers sending a juvenile to the adult criminal justice system if the judge believes the youth cannot be helped through treatment efforts.

Judiciary Act of 1789: Although the Constitution allows a Supreme Court, Congress established the federal court system and specified jurisdictions.

Jurisdiction: The extent of a particular court's power to make legal decisions and judgments.

Jury Nullification: Ability of a jury to ignore the law and acquit a guilty defendant.

Jury Trial: A trial in which the jury acts as the fact finder, weighs the evidence, deliberates, and renders a verdict.

Just Deserts: Sentencing perspective that has dominated the purpose of incarceration since about the 1980s. It is focused foremost on proportionality vis-à-vis the crime and the ensuing punishment.

Justifiable Homicide: The lawful killing of another person such as when a law enforcement officer or a citizen kills in self-defense or to defend another.

Juvenile Courts: Courts designed specifically for juveniles to "regulate the treatment and control of dependent, neglected, and delinquent children."

Juvenile Justice and Delinquency Prevention Act: A 1974 law that was designed to prevent delinquency and improve the juvenile justice system.

Landmark Cases: Establish precedent that markedly changes the interpretation of a prior law or establishes new case law.

Law Enforcement: One of the three main components of the criminal justice system. Law enforcement agencies are charged with investigating crimes and arresting individuals alleged to have committed crimes.

Legal Guilt: Established when a prosecutor is able to persuade a judge or jury that the defendant is guilty of the criminal charges.

Legal Violation: The commission of a crime while serving corrections in the community.

Legitimate: A prison subculture wherein one-time offenders identify with correctional staff and take advantage of educational and rehabilitation opportunities.

Less-Than-Lethal Weapons: Weapons that provide viable options for dealing with resisting suspects; they include pepper spray, rubber bullets, beanbag guns, and sedative darts.

Lex Talionis: Latin for "the law of retribution" and commonly referred to as "an eye for an eye." This philosophy calls for retaliation in which the punishment received should fit the crime committed.

Literacy Tests: Tests used to deny African Americans the right to vote.

Lockups: Local facilities that are used to detain individuals for 24 to 48 hours.

Mala in Se: One of two types of illegal behavior. *Mala in se* refers to behavior that is sinful and inherently wrong by nature.

Mala Prohibita: One of two types of illegal behavior. *Mala prohibita* describes behavior that is prohibited by law. What constitutes *mala prohibita* is dynamic and has changed over time.

Mandatory Arrest Policies: Policies that limit police discretion in certain situations; they are frequently applied to incidents involving domestic violence.

Mandatory Minimum: A form of structured sentencing that applies statute-based minimum sanctions to particular types of crime and/or when particular elements of a crime exist.

Matrons: Correctional officers in a women's prison or reformatory.

Matthew Shepard and James Byrd, Jr. Hate Crimes Prevention Act: Federal legislation signed into law in 2009 that expanded earlier federal hate crime laws to include crimes motivated based on the victim's gender, sexual orientation, gender identity, or disability.

Maximum-Security Prisons: The most secure facilities available in many states. Most inmates incarcerated in maximum-security facilities have committed violent crimes such as murder, rape, child abuse, and human trafficking.

M'Naghten Standard: Also called the "right-wrong" test, requires a jury to consider two questions: Did the defendant understand what he or she was doing when the crime was committed? Did the defendant know that his or her actions were wrong?

Meat-Eaters: Identified by the Knapp Commission as officers who actively engaged in corrupt activities.

Medium-Security Prisons: These facilities house inmates who have committed less serious crimes, such as theft and assault.

Megan's Law: Requires that registry information gathered via the Wetterling Act be made public.

Mens Rea: Latin for "guilty mind," used in court to prove criminal intent.

Metropolitan Police Act of 1829: An act introduced by Sir Robert Peel, which established London's Metropolitan Police Force. This is considered the beginning of modern public policing.

Military Commission: A type of military tribunal that offers a detainee a fair and transparent trial while protecting national security interests.

Military Drones: Technology increasingly used as possible crime-fighting tools in some parts of the country.

Minimum-Security Prisons: These facilities house mainly nonviolent white-collar criminals who are thought to pose little or no physical risk to members of the community.

Misdemeanor: A less serious crime punishable by fine, forfeiture, or short-term confinement, though in some jurisdictions gross, aggravated, or serious misdemeanors may be charged.

Missouri Plan: Also called the merit selection system, it is a process to elect judges that attempts to eliminate politics.

Mistrial: A courtroom trial that ends prior to its normal conclusion.

Modus Operandi: A system for solving crimes that facilitated the identification of crime patterns. This system was first implemented by August Vollmer.

Money Laundering: The movement of money gained through illegal means to make it appear as if it was gained through legitimate means.

Motion for a Change of Venue: A pretrial motion requesting a geographical change of the trial.

Motion for Discovery: The rules of procedure establish a mandate for the prosecution to give the defense certain evidence.

Motion for Expenses of Experts: Defense can request that the state pay expenses related to psychological evaluations or other types of expert testimony.

Motion for Recusal: A motion for the recusal (removal) of a trial judge or prosecutor.

Motion *in Limine:* A motion requesting that the judge rule on whether particular evidence can be used at trial.

Motion to Suppress: A motion requesting that the court disallow illegally obtained evidence at trial.

Mutilation: An early punishment that entailed the amputation of body parts to curtail a perpetrator's ability to reoffend.

Narrow-Casting: The presentation of a narrow view of information in the media to small homogeneous audiences.

National Crime Statistics Exchange (NCS-X): A collaborative effort between BJS and the FBI (and other organizations) that will produce nationally representative incident-based statistics on crimes using bother data reported to law enforcement agencies and a sample.

National Crime Survey (NCS): The predecessor of the National Crime Victimization Survey. The NCS was first implemented in 1972.

National Crime Victimization Survey (NCVS): A nationally representative survey of victims of property and personal violence in the United States.

National Incident-Based Reporting System (NIBRS): A large and complex national data collection system designed to gather incident-based crime information from law enforcement.

National Integrated Ballistic Information Network: A system administered by the Bureau of Alcohol, Tobacco, Firearms and Explosives that links shell casings, guns used in crimes, and scenes of crimes.

Net Widening: The increasing harshness of sentencing given to offenders who would have traditionally been sentenced to probation.

New Penology: The study of principles of punishment, often reflecting the contemporary turn toward the view that punishment is the primary role of prison.

No bill: A decision made by a grand jury that indicates that insufficient evidence is present to proceed with the case.

Nolle Prosequi: Latin for "be unwilling to pursue," this is commonly used by a prosecutor to willingly terminate legal proceedings before trial or before a verdict. The statement is often construed as an admission that the charges cannot be proven.

Nolo Contendere: A plea made by a defendant in which he or she neither admits nor disputes guilt. It is commonly referred to as a "no-contest" plea.

Nonintervention Perspective: A view that the appropriate role of the criminal justice system is to be as minimal and nonintrusive as possible.

Nonlethal Force: Type of force (including weapons) that provides viable options for dealing with resisting suspects such as pepper spray, rubber bullets, beanbag guns, and sedative darts. Also called less-than-lethal weapons.

Omnibus Crime Control and Safe Streets Act of 1968: An act that established agencies and rules dealing with crime.

Ordinances: Municipal or city rules.

Organized Criminal Group: A group of three or more persons that was not randomly formed, which acts in concert with the aim of committing crime.

Pains of Imprisonment: The five primary pains that come from being incarcerated: deprivation of liberty, goods and services, heterosexual relationships, autonomy, and security.

Panopticon: An architectural design developed by Jeremy Bentham that allows a single person to watch others in a prison setting without those incarcerated knowing they are being watched.

Parens Patriae: Latin for "parent of his country" and "the state is the father." A doctrine that gives the state the power to act as a child's parent.

Parish Constable: Policing agent who operated in smaller towns. Initially elected by the parishioners, the parish constable was generally unarmed, unpaid, and part-time.

Parole Board: A board that reviews the prior acts and behavior of an inmate to determine when the prisoner is to be released from prison.

Part I and Part II Crimes: Designation of crime types under the UCR's Summary Reporting System. Part I includes common and serious crimes, while Part II crimes are less common and less serious.

Patria Postestas: A father's right to use strict discipline for ill-behaved children.

Patrol: Patrol officers are responsible for preventing crime, apprehending suspects, and assisting community members.

Pattern Jury Instructions: Language template to be used when charging the jury.

Peelers: Nickname of officers in Ireland named for Sir Robert Peel. Peelers replaced the existing (and generally corrupt) system of parish constables and night watchmen.

Peelian Principles: Widely cited list that described Sir Robert Peel's philosophy of an ethical police force. Research shows that these excellent principles were never provided by Peel.

Penitentiary: A correctional facility used to imprison criminal offenders.

Pennsylvania System: A penitentiary system based on the guiding philosophy that isolation and silence are necessary for offender reflection, reformation, and rehabilitation. Also known as the separate system.

Penology: The study of principles of punishment for criminal (and in the past, immoral) acts.

Peremptory Challenge: An attorney may remove a prospective juror from the venire without giving a legal reason.

Perjury: A spoken or written intentional swearing of a false oath or misrepresenting of an agreement to be truthful.

Petit Juries: Juries that determine guilt or innocence by following the course of a criminal trial. Both prosecution and defense present to a petit jury in a trial.

Pillory: A painful punishment that forced the offender into a standing position with hands, head, and ears commonly nailed to the pillory wood.

Plain View Doctrine: The rule that permits police officers to seize evidence without a warrant if it is easily seen.

Plea Bargain: When the prosecutor may offer a lesser charge or reduce the number of charges. The defendant agrees to plead guilty in order to avoid a trial and a more severe sentence.

Police Matron: Title frequently given to women who worked in the early days of policing.

Precedent: The legal principle of *stare decisis,* Latin for "let the decision stand," it establishes prior case decisions as binding precedent.

Predisposition Report: Presents background and current information on a juvenile to help determine his or her disposition.

Preemption Doctrine: The idea put forth in the Constitution that federal law is the "Supreme Law of the Land." In other words, usually federal law overrides conflicting state laws.

Preliminary Hearing: This is typically held in criminal cases to determine the extent of evidence and whether enough exists to allow charges to be pressed against the defendant.

Presentence Investigation: An investigation that gathers information on extenuating circumstances and the criminal history of the defendant to be used when determining the severity of the sentence.

Presentence Report: An important aggregation of facts about the offender, usually prepared by the probation officer.

Prison Argot: Slang used in prison.

Prisonization: The socialization process in prison that requires accepting different values and customs.

Private Policing: Policing provided by private entities. Protection is extended to corporate executives and other high-profile individuals.

Problem-Solving Courts: See Specialized Courts.

Pro Bono: Legal representation that is provided at no charge or a reduced fee.

Pro Se: Latin for "for himself," meaning self-representation in legal proceedings without the aid of a legal representative.

Proactive Policing: Self-initiated officer activities to prevent and detect crime.

Probable Cause: In criminal law, the existence of more than a suspicion that a person has committed an illegal act.

Probation Fees: Fees paid by the offender to cover costs of services such as the preparation of the presentence report, work-release programs, electronic monitoring, and drug, alcohol, or anger management counseling.

Probation Investigation: The process of gathering information on offenders' lives and ties to the community, both positive and negative.

Problem-Oriented Policing: A policing style that emphasizes the use of data analysis and assessment to address crime problems.

Procedural Law: Rules governing court proceedings.

Profiling: Occurs when officers question or investigate a person based on race, ethnicity, religion, or national origin.

Property Crime: Crime against property. The most common forms of property crime include burglary, property theft (aka larceny), and motor vehicle theft.

Proportionality: A sentencing concept that indicates that the severity of sentencing should correspond to the severity of the crime committed.

Prosecutor: An attorney who represents the government or the "people" and is responsible for presenting the state's case in criminal, civil, and administrative matters.

Pseudofamily: Relationship structures built in female prisons to replicate family relationships left behind when incarcerated.

Punish: This is one goal of community-based corrections, designed to deter future criminal acts.

Punitive Damages: Money awarded in addition to compensatory damages to punish the defendant for recklessness, malice, or deceit.

Racist System Frame: Indicates that the problem is not crime, but rather that law enforcement, courts, and corrections are racist agents of oppression.

Radiofrequency Identification (RFID) Devices: A type of community corrections used to monitor those serving home confinement sentences via ankle or wrist bracelets.

Rape: A type of violent crime considered *mala in se* that includes "penetration, no matter how slight, of the vagina or anus with a body part or object, or oral penetration by a sex organ of another person, without the consent of the victim."

Reactive Policing: A traditional style of policing relying on responding to calls for services.

Reading of the Verdict: Following jury deliberation, a formal event in the courtroom in which the jury offers their verdict on the charge(s).

Reasonable Suspicion: An objective basis supported by specific facts for believing that someone committed a crime.

Rebuttal: In some criminal trials, the prosecutors have the last opportunity to speak during closing arguments. Other forms of rebuttal may include evidence or argument.

Recidivism: A measure that identifies relapse into criminal offending behavior.

Recognizance: A suspect, without posting bail money, agrees to show up for the court based on his or her word alone.

Reformation Movement: A movement born during the 1870 meeting of the National Prison Association, which called for institutions focused on reformation.

Regulatory Searches: Searches by government officials, such as restaurant health inspections, inspection of vehicles crossing borders, airport screenings, and fire inspections, that may be conducted without a warrant.

Rehabilitation: Sentencing goal that seeks to reduce chances of future offenders through education, alcohol or drug programs, psychological programs, and other treatments.

Rehabilitative Perspective: A view that the purpose of the criminal justice system is to rehabilitate offenders.

Remote Alcohol Detection (RAD): Technology used in community corrections; a bracelet that, when applied to the probationer's skin, can detect ethanol excreted in perspiration.

Reputation Concerning Character: An exception to the hearsay rule that allows witnesses to testify under oath about the reputation of a person's friends and acquaintances.

Residential Community Housing: A facility where offenders are secured at night but released during the day to work, attend school, or receive treatment.

Restitution: Repayment as part of a punishment for injury or loss.

Restoration: Sentencing goal that addresses the harm done to victims, family and friends of victims, and the community.

Restorative Justice: A goal of community corrections that emphasizes that crime is more than criminal behavior. Rather, lawbreaking disturbs and harms individuals and the community, especially the primary victim.

Restorative Justice Perspective: This perspective indicates that the appropriate role of the criminal justice system is to restore justice as best as possible through repairing the harm caused by criminal behavior.

Retribution: A goal of law that states that punishment is deserved or morally right. In addition, it is a goal of sentencing that seeks to punish the offender for criminal behavior.

Reverse Transfers: Allows judges and prosecutors to send cases back to juvenile court.

Risk Assessment: A determination of offenders' propensity to harm themselves or others.

Rotten Apple Theory: The idea that corruption in most police departments can be traced to just a few officers.

Routine Activity Theory: Cohen and Felson's theory that posits that the convergence in space and time of motivated offenders, suitable targets, and the absence of capable guardians increases the risk of criminal incidents.

Rule of Law: A fundamental principle in the criminal justice system in the United States that all government officers—including those in the criminal justice system—pledge to uphold the Constitution and to follow the Constitution, not any particular human leader.

SARA Model: The scan, analysis, response, and assessment model, used in problem-oriented policing.

School Resource Officer: Generally an officer employed at the local police agency who is stationed in a school.

School-to-Prison Pipeline: The diversion of juveniles from schools into the juvenile justice system for minor infractions.

Sentencing Guidelines: A type of structured sentencing based on criminal history and severity of the crime, usually presented in a grid format that dictates the sentence served.

Separate-but-Equal Doctrine: The concept that black and white individuals could legally be segregated under the Constitution given that the facilities and services available were comparable in quality for each race.

Separate System: Another name for the Pennsylvania System, which reflects the lack of interpersonal interaction experienced by inmates.

Sequestered: When a jury is isolated to prevent contact from outside influences, which may influence the verdict.

Series Victimizations: Victimizations not discrete in nature, but ongoing with no defined starting and stopping point. Series victimizations present a conundrum in terms of the best way to count them. Common examples of series victimizations are intimate partner violence, bullying, and sex trafficking of minors.

Sex Trafficking: The trade in sexual acts or exploitation.

Sheriffs: Early policing agents who were charged to pursue and apprehend criminals at great personal financial expense.

Shire Reeves: Precursors to sheriffs.

Situational Model: Emphasizes the place, time, and person to understand the behavior of inmates.

Slave Patrol: Policing group that originated in 1704 in South Carolina and consisted of a group of three to six white men who regulated the behavior of slaves and hunted down and punished escaped slaves.

Social Breakdown Frame: Indicates that crime is the result of a breakdown in family and community.

Social Debt: A sentencing concept that takes into account an offender's criminal past.

Solitary Confinement: Also known as administrative segregation, it isolates violent or hard-to-manage prisoners from the general population.

Special Conditions: Conditions of one's community corrections that are specific to a particular offender.

Specialized Courts: Also called problem-solving courts, they work with particular types of offenses and offenders.

Specific Deterrence: The notion that punishment serves to deter the individual being punished from committing crime in the future.

Split Sentence or Shock Probation: A form of intermediate sanction in which the offender initially spends some time in jail or prison (usually 30 days) and

then is released into corrections in the community.

Stare Decisis: Latin for "let the decision stand," meaning that judges must respect precedents set in previous court cases.

Static Risk Predictors: Characteristics of offenders that cannot be changed, such as the age at first arrest, the number of prior arrests, and the number of times the person has been incarcerated in the past.

Status Offenses: Offenses that apply only to juveniles, such as smoking and curfew violations.

Statutes: Formal rules, or law, adopted by a governing body such as a state legislature.

Stocks: A painful punishment generally administered with public humiliation.

Stop and Frisk: Also known as a Terry stop or field stop, this allows a police officer to detain and search a person when he or she reasonably suspects that a crime has been or will be committed.

Street Crimes: These crimes are relatively common and serious, involving a victim and an offender who come together in space and time.

Strict Interpretation: Typically deciphers the words of the Constitution as literal, discounting the current context socially, historically, or technologically, and focusing on the plain language contained in the document and how to apply the literal meaning.

Strike for Cause: A challenge during *voir dire* in which the defense counsel, the prosecutor, or the judge identifies a potential juror he or she believes cannot be unbiased, fair, or impartial. Also known as challenge for cause.

Substantive Law: Rules that are used to determine the rights of individuals and collective bodies.

Summary Reporting System (SRS): The original aggregated crime data collected under the FBI's Uniform Crime Reporting Program.

Super-Maximum Prisons: The most secure and restrictive of all prisons, which are (in theory) reserved for the most dangerous of offenders.

Superpredator: A term coined by Princeton University's John Dilulio to describe the threat of increasing violent juvenile crime.

Supervision: The duty of probation officers to watch over offenders on their caseloads.

Supplementary Homicide Reports (SHR): Supplemental reports to the FBI's Uniform Crime Reporting System that gather details about homicides in the United States, including information about offenders, victims, and incidents.

Survival Sex: A type of trafficking in which the victim is frequently homeless or gravely disadvantaged and trades sex for food, shelter, and other basic needs.

Tasers: A type of conductive energy device or electronic control device. These devices offer a means of controlling suspects while saving lives and offering officers protection from injuries.

Tech Effect: The phenomenon whereby the public's increased awareness of modern technology results in the expectation of unnecessary and at times unrealistic forensic evidence at trial.

Technical Violation: The failure to abide by certain conditions of community corrections that do not involve committing a new crime.

Telemedicine: New technology used in correctional institutions to provide medical care to inmates remotely.

Terrorism: The completed or threatened use of coercion and/or violence against a population of people with the goal of changing political, religious, or ideological positions.

Thief Subculture: Prison subculture that includes professional thieves and values in-group loyalty, trust, and reliability. This subculture includes "right guys."

Thief Takers: Men hired by victims to capture criminal offenders. Once an offender was captured, the thief taker was paid a bounty. Often these individuals were very corrupt.

Third Degree: Early (now outlawed) method used by police officers that included brutalizing an individual in order to gather information.

Three-Strikes Law: A type of mandatory minimum that mandates long (including life) prison terms for a third offense.

Total Institution: Any isolated, closed social system designed to control people.

Traffic Hearings: Used to deal with traffic offenses.

Transnational Crimes: Criminal offenses that transcend national boundaries, or those that occur within one nation, but are so heinous that they offend nations throughout the world.

Transnational Organized Crime: Crime that involves multiple people working in a coordinated fashion to plan and commit illegal business undertakings that span countries.

Trial by Ordeal: Primitive form of trial in which the outcome rested in the hands of God to determine guilt or innocence by protecting an innocent person from some or all the consequences of the test.

Trial Management Order: A full schedule created by the court and the court participants that designates what happens and when as the parties work toward the trial date.

Tything or Tithing: A system of policing that replaced the borh. A tithing was a group of all boys and men age 12 or older from 10 households.

Uniform Crime Reports (UCR): This program, started by the International Association of Chiefs of Police and then moved under the umbrella of the FBI in 1929, is a compilation of crime data.

U.S. Attorney: Appointed by the president and supervised by the U.S. attorney general in the Department of Justice, a U.S. attorney is responsible for trying cases at the federal court level.

U.S. Attorney General: Chief law enforcement officer in the government and head of the Department of Justice.

USA Freedom Act: A 2015 law that came into effect the day after the USA PATRIOT Act expired. This act restored many provisions of the PATRIOT Act but limited the collection of telecommunication metadata of citizens by the National Security Agency.

USA PATRIOT Act: The 2001 Uniting and Strengthening America by Providing Appropriate Tools Required to Intercept and Obstruct Terrorism Act was signed into law by President George W. Bush to strengthen security measures designed to protect the United States from attack.

Utilitarianism: A doctrine stating that an action is morally right as long as the behavior is a benefit for the majority of a society. This is the concept of the "greatest good for the greatest number."

Venire: A list of potential jurors from which the jury is selected.

Victim Advocates: Trained professionals who support crime victims as their cases move through the criminal justice system.

Victim Bill of Rights: Adopted in many states, it offers rights to crime victims.

Victim Impact Statement: A statement prepared by the victim or his or her family to inform the judge how the crime affected them physically, financially, emotionally, and psychologically.

Victimless Crimes: These criminal offenses are thought not to involve victims because they do not directly harm individuals other than the offenders.

Videoconferencing: Technology used in correctional institutions to facilitate visitation, meetings, and medical care.

Vigilantes: Self-appointed distributors of justice according to their own rules.

Violent Crime Control and Law Enforcement Act: A 1994 law that requires prisoners to serve at least 85% of their sentences in order for states to qualify for federal financial aid.

Violent Media Frame: This frame finds that crime is depicted as a direct result of the violent media present in television, movies, video games, and music.

Voir dire: Process in which prospective jurors are questioned in court under oath to attempt to uncover inappropriate jurors.

Watchmen: Used to protect property in England's larger cities and towns, and in colonial America. These individuals patrolled at night to protect the community from robberies, fires, and other disturbances.

Wobblers: Crimes that can be charged as either felonies or misdemeanors.

Work-Release Program: An intermediate sanction that requires offenders to live in a secure facility but allows their release for work.

Worldwide Incident Tracking System: An FBI database containing information on completed terrorist attacks since 1996.

Writ of Certiorari: Used by appellate courts that have discretion to review a lower court's opinion (e.g., the U.S. Supreme Court). The writ is an order to send all the documents of a case to be reviewed. (*Certiorari* is Latin for "to be more fully informed.")

Zero Tolerance: A policing approach that focuses enforcement efforts on quality-of-life issues such as disorder and minor crime. Enforcement efforts are applied to low-level crimes and minor infractions in specific neighborhoods.

NOTES

CHAPTER 1

1. Retrieved from Justice for Jennifer: http://justiceforjennifer.com.
2. See, for example, Amir, M. (1971). *Patterns in forcible rape*. Chicago: University of Chicago Press.
3. Though this account is true, the names of all persons have been changed.
4. Though this account is true, the names of all persons have been changed.
5. Or more colloquially, cops, courts, and corrections.
6. Kaeble, D., Glaze, L., Tsoutis, A., & Minton, T. (2016, January 21). *Correctional populations in the United States, 2014*. Retrieved from http://www.bjs.gov/content/pub/pdf/cpus14.pdf.
7. Pratt, T. (2009). *Addicted to incarceration: Corrections policy and the politics of misinformation in the United States*. Thousand Oaks, CA: Sage.
8. Carson, E. A. (2015, September). *Prisoners in 2014*. Retrieved from http://www.bjs.gov/content/pub/pdf/p14.pdf.
9. Ibid.
10. Ibid.
11. Pratt, *Addicted to Incarceration*.
12. gabe. (2013, June 24). Measuring justice. *The Crime Report*. Retrieved from http://thecrimereport.org/2013/06/24/2013–06-measuring-justice/.
13. Henrichson, C., & Delaney, R. (2012, July 20). *The price of prisons: What incarceration costs taxpayers*. Vera Institute of Justice, Center on Sentencing and Corrections. Retrieved from http://archive.vera.org/sites/default/files/resources/downloads/price-of-prisons-updated-version-021914.pdf.
14. Truman, J. L., & Langton, L. (2015, September). *Criminal victimization, 2014*. Department of Justice, Bureau of Justice Statistics. Retrieved from http://www.bjs.gov/content/pub/pdf/cv14.pdf.
15. For more about victims' rights, see the National Center for Victims of Crime, http://www.victimsofcrime.org/help-for-crime-victims/get-help-bulletins-for-crime-victims/victims%27-rights.
16. See U.S. Department of Justice. (n.d.). *The USA PATRIOT Act: Preserving life and liberty*. Retrieved from https://www.justice.gov/archive/11/what_is_the_patriot_act.pdf.
17. See, e.g., American Civil Liberties Union. (2016). *Surveillance under the USA PATRIOT Act*. Retrieved from https://www.aclu.org/surveillance-under-usapatriot-act.
18. Truman, J. L., & Langton, L. (2014, September). *Criminal victimization, 2014*. Retrieved from http://www.bjs.gov/index.cfm?ty=pbdetail&iid=5366. See Tables 1 and 3.
19. Meier, R., & Geis, G. (1997). *Victimless crime? Prostitution, drugs, homosexuality, abortion*. Los Angeles: Roxbury.
20. Geis, G. (2004). *White-collar and corporate crime*. Upper Saddle River, NJ: Prentice Hall.
21. Sutherland, E. H. (1945). Is "white collar crime" crime? *American Sociological Review, 10*, 132–139.
22. Friedrichs, D. O. (2010). *Trusted criminals: White collar crime in contemporary society* (4th ed.). Belmont, CA: Wadsworth Cengage Learning.
23. Federal Bureau of Investigation. (n.d.). *Xuyen Thi-Kim Nguyen: Failure to appear*. Retrieved from https://www.fbi.gov/wanted/wcc/xuyen-thi-kim-nguyen/view.
24. Sutherland, E. H. (1940). White-collar criminality. *American Sociological Review, 5*, 1–12. Tappan, P. W. (1947). Who is the criminal? *American Sociological Review, 5*, 96–102.
25. Sutherland, E. H. (1983). *White collar crime: The uncut version* (G. Geis & C. Goff, Eds.). New Haven, CT: Yale University Press. (Original work published 1949)
26. Geis, G., Meier, R. F., & Salinger, L. M. (1995). *White-collar crime: Classic and contemporary views* (3rd ed.). New York: Free Press. Tappan, "Who Is the Criminal?"
27. Federal Bureau of Investigation. (2011, February 24). Internet crime trends: The latest report. In *The FBI story*. Retrieved from https://www.fbi.gov/file-repository/stats-services-publications-fbi-story-fbistory2011.pdf.
28. See, e.g., the National Consortium for the Study of Terrorism and Responses to Terrorism, http://www.start.umd.edu/start.
29. See http://www.madd.org.
30. Federal Bureau of Investigation. (2012, January 6). *Attorney General Holder announces revisions to the Uniform Crime Report's definition of rape*. Retrieved from http://www.fbi.gov/news/pressrel/press-releases/attorney-general-eric-holder-announces-revisions-to-the-uniform-crime-reports-definition-of-rape.
31. See, e.g., Futter, S., & Mebane, W. R., Jr. (2001). The effects of rape law reform on rape case processing. *Berkeley Women's Law Journal, 16*, 72–131. Retrieved from http://www.d.umn.edu/cla/faculty/jhamlin/3925/Readings/RapeLawEffects.html.
32. National District Attorneys Association. (2011). *Rape shield statutes*. Retrieved from http://www.ndaa.org/pdf/NCPCA%20Rape%20Shield%202011.pdf.
33. Baker, K.J.M. (2012, November 28). Lawyer says 11-year-old gang rape victim was a "spider" luring men into web. *Jezebel*. Retrieved from http://jezebel.com/5964064/lawyer-says-11-year-old-gang-rape-victim-was-a-spider-luring-men-into-web.
34. Estrich, S. (1988). *Real rape*. Cambridge, MA: Harvard University Press. Brownmiller, S. (1975). *Against our will: Men, women, and rape*. New York: Ballantine.
35. Wilson, J. Q., & Petersilia, J. (1995). *Crime*. San Francisco, CA: ICS Press.
36. Surette, R. (2007). *Media, crime, and criminal justice* (3rd ed.). Belmont, CA: Wadsworth.
37. Sasson, T. (1995). *Crime talk*. Hawthorne, NY: Aldine de Gruyter.

CHAPTER 2

1. See http://www.fbi.gov.

2. See http://www.fbi.gov/about-us/cjis/ucr/ucr.

3. See http://ojjdp.gov/ojstatbb/ezashr.

4. See http://www.icpsr.umich.edu/icpsrweb/NACJD/NIBRS.

5. See http://www.bjs.gov.

6. See http://www.icpsr.umich.edu/icpsrweb/NACJD/NCVS.

7. Barnett-Ryan, C. (2007). Introduction to the Uniform Crime Reporting Program. In J. P. Lynch & L. A. Addington (Eds.), *Understanding crime incidence statistics: Revisiting the divergence of the NCVS and the UCR* (pp. 55–92). New York: Cambridge University Press.

8. See http://www.theiacp.org.

9. Note that until very recently, the SHR did not collect data on homicides against persons based on Hispanic origin. Another option is to use data from death certificates captured in the National Vital Statistics System. These data are collected by the Centers for Disease Control and Prevention and are available through the WISQARS system: http://www.cdc.gov/injury/wisqars/fatal_injury_reports.html.

10. See http://www.bjs.gov/index.cfm?ty=pbdetail&iid=3245.

11. Federal Bureau of Investigation. (n.d.). *UCR Program changes the definition of rape.* Retrieved from http://www.fbi.gov/about-us/cjis/cjis-link/march-2012/ucr-program-changes-definition-of-rape.

12. National Archive of Criminal Justice Data. (2010). *NIBRS concepts.* Retrieved from http://www.icpsr.umich.edu/icpsrweb/NACJD/NIBRS/concepts.jsp.

13. Addington, L. A. (2007). Using NIBRS to study sources of divergence. In J. P. Lynch & L. A. Addington (Eds.), *Understanding crime incidence statistics: Revisiting the divergence of the NCVS and the UCR* (pp. 225–250). New York: Cambridge University Press.

14. James, N., & Council, L. R. (2008, January 3). CRS *report for Congress: How crime in the United States is measured.* Retrieved from https://www.fas.org/sgp/crs/misc/RL34309.pdf.

15. Addington, "Using NIBRS to Study Sources of Divergence."

16. Ibid.

17. Maltz, M. D. (1999). *Bridging gaps in police crime data.* Retrieved from http://www.bjs.gov/content/pub/pdf/bgpcd.pdf.

18. Addington, "Using NIBRS to Study Sources of Divergence."

19. Bureau of Justice Statistics. (n.d.). *National Crime Statistics Exchange.* Retrieved from http://www.bjs.gov/content/ncsx.cfm.

20. President's Commissions on Law Enforcement and the Administration of Justice. (1967). *The challenge of crime in a free society.* Retrieved from https://www.ncjrs.gov/pdffiles1/nij/42.pdf.

21. National Archives. (n.d.). *Records of the Law Enforcement Assistance Administration.* Retrieved from http://www.archives.gov/research/guide-fed-records/groups/423.html.

22. Rennison, C. M., & Rand, M. (2007). Introduction to the National Crime Victimization Survey. In J. P. Lynch & L. A. Addington (Eds.), *Understanding crime incidence statistics: Revisiting the divergence of the NCVS and the UCR* (pp. 17–54). New York: Cambridge University Press.

23. Ibid.

24. Ibid.

25. Biderman, A. D., Cantor, D., Lynch, J. P., & Martin, E. (1986). *Final report of the National Crime Survey redesign.* Washington, DC: Bureau of Social Science Research.

26. Ibid.

27. Truman, J. L., & Langton, L. (2015, September). *Criminal victimization, 2014.* Retrieved from http://www.bjs.gov/content/pub/pdf/cv14.pdf.

28. See http://www.bjs.gov/content/pub/pdf/ncvs104.pdf.

29. See, e.g., Truman, J. L. (2011). *Criminal victimization, 2010.* Retrieved from http://www.bjs.gov/content/pub/pdf/cv10.pdf. Rennison, C. M. (2002). *Rape and sexual assault: Reporting to police and medical attention, 1992–2000.* Retrieved from http://www.bjs.gov/content/pub/pdf/rsarp00.pdf. Hart, T. C., & Rennison, C. (2003). *Reporting crime to the police, 1992–2000.* Retrieved from http://www.bjs.gov/content/pub/pdf/rcp00.pdf. Rennison, C. M., & Welchans, S. (2000). *Intimate partner violence.* Retrieved from http://www.bjs.gov/content/pub/pdf/ipv.pdf.

30. See http://www.bjs.gov/content/pub/pdf/ncvs204.pdf.

31. Rennison and Rand, "Introduction to the National Crime Victimization Survey."

32. If you are interested in learning about the many improvements and changes made to the NCS and NCVS over time, please see Rennison and Rand, "Introduction to the National Crime Victimization Survey."

33. Groves, R. M., & Cork, D. L. (2008). *Surveying victims: Options for conducting the National Crime Victimization Survey.* Washington, DC: National Academies Press. Retrieved from http://www.nap.edu/openbook.php?record_id=12090&page=R1.

34. Ibid.

35. Rennison and Rand, "Introduction to the National Crime Victimization Survey."

36. Rand, M. R., & Rennison, C. M. (2005). Bigger is not necessarily better: An analysis of violence against women estimates from the National Crime Victimization Survey and the National Violence Against Women Survey. *Journal of Quantitative Criminology, 21,* 267–291.

37. Lauritsen, J. L., Owens, J., Planty, M., Rand, M. R., & Truman, J. (2012). *Methods for counting high-frequency repeat victimizations in the National Crime Victimization Survey.* Washington, DC: U.S. Government Printing Office.

38. Federal Bureau of Investigation. (2014). Table 12: Crime trends by population group, 2013–2014. In *Crime in the United States 2014.* Retrieved from https://ucr.fbi.gov/crime-in-the-u.s/2014/crime-in-the-u.s.-2014/tables/table-12

39. Ibid.

40. Federal Bureau of Investigation. (2014). Table 16: Rate: Number of crimes per 100,000 inhabitants. In *Crime in the United States 2014.* Retrieved from https://ucr.fbi.gov/crime-in-the-u.s/2014/crime-in-the-u.s.-2014/tables/table-16

41. Federal Bureau of Investigation. (2014). Expanded Homicide Data Table 2: Murder victims by age, sex, race, and ethnicity, 2014. In *Crime in the United States 2014.* Retrieved from https://ucr.fbi.gov/crime-in-the-u.s/2014/crime-in-the-u.s.-2014/tables/expanded-homicide-data/expanded_homicide_data_table_2_murder_victims_by_age_sex_and_race_2014.xls

42. Ibid.

43. Federal Bureau of Investigation. (2014). Expanded Homicide Data Table 10: Murder circumstances by relationship, 2014. In *Crime in the United States 2014.* Retrieved from https://ucr.fbi.gov/crime-in-the-u.s/2014/crime-in-the-u.s.-2014/tables/expanded-homicide-data/expanded_homicide_data_table_10_murder_circumstances_by_relationship_2014.xls

44. Federal Bureau of Investigation. (2014). Expanded Homicide Data Table 11: Murder circumstances by weapon, 2014. In *Crime in the United States 2014.* Retrieved from https://ucr.fbi.gov/crime-in-the-u.s/2014/crime-in-the-u.s.-2014/tables/expanded-homicide-data/expanded_

homicide_data_table_11_murder_circumstances_by_weapon_2014.xls.

45. Federal Bureau of Investigation. (2014). Expanded Homicide Data Table 6: Murder: Race, ethnicity, and sex of victim by race, ethnicity, and sex of offender, 2014. In *Crime in the United States 2014*. Retrieved from https://ucr.fbi.gov/crime-in-the-u.s/2014/crime-in-the-u.s.-2014/tables/expanded-homicide-data/expanded_homicide_data_table_6_murder_race_and_sex_of_vicitm_by_race_and_sex_of_offender_2014.xls

46. Ibid.

47. Truman, J., Langton, L., & Planty, M. (2013). *Criminal victimization, 2012*. Retrieved from http://www.bjs.gov/content/pub/pdf/cv12.pdf. The 2013 and 2014 values can be found in Truman & Langton, *Criminal Victimization, 2014* (Table 1).

48. Ibid.

49. Truman & Langton, *Criminal Victimization, 2014*.

50. Ibid.

51. Ibid.

52. Ibid., see Table 1.

53. Truman et al., *Criminal victimization, 2012*.

54. All estimates in this paragraph were calculated by Rennison.

55. All estimates in this paragraph were calculated by Rennison.

56. All estimates in this paragraph were calculated by Rennison.

57. All estimates in this paragraph were calculated by Rennison.

58. Truman et al., *Criminal Victimization, 2012*; Truman & Langton, *Criminal Victimization, 2014* (see Table 6, in which 2013 and 2014 values are provided).

59. Truman & Langton, *Criminal Victimization, 2014*.

60. Ibid.

61. Truman et al., *Criminal Victimization, 2012*; Truman & Langton, *Criminal Victimization, 2014*.

62. Ibid.

63. Ibid.

64. Truman & Langton, *Criminal Victimization, 2014*.

65. Ibid.

66. Ibid.

67. Ibid.

68. Ibid.

69. Ibid.

70. U.S. Department of Justice. (2004). *The nation's two crime measures*. Retrieved from http://bjs.gov/content/pub/pdf/ntcm.pdf.

71. Internet Crime Complaint Center. (n.d.). *Internet crime schemes*. Retrieved from http://www.ic3.gov/crimeschemes.aspx.

72. See http://www.ic3.gov/default.aspx.

73. Internet Crime Complaint Center. (2015). *2015 Internet crime report*. Retrieved from https://pdf.ic3.gov/2015_IC3Report.pdf.

74. National Counterterrorism Center. (2011). Report on terrorism. Retrieved from http://www.defendingdissent.org/pdf/Gov Reports/2011NCTC.pdf.

75. See http://www.start.umd.edu/gtd/about.

76. Federal Bureau of Investigation. (n.d.). *Section V: Special report*. Retrieved from http://www.fbi.gov/about-us/cjis/ucr/crime-in-the-u.s/2001/01sec5.pdf.

77. Geis, G., Meier, B., & Salinger, L. (1995). *White-collar crime: Classic and contemporary views* (3rd ed.). New York: Free Press.

78. Steffensmeier, D. (1989). Causes of white-collar crime revisited: An assessment of the Hirschi and Gottfredson assertions. *Criminology, 27*, 345–358.

79. National White Collar Crime Center. (2014). *Research*. Retrieved from http://www.nw3c.org/services/research.

80. Huff, R., Desilets, C., & Kane, J. (2010). *The 2010 National Public Survey on White Collar Crime*. Retrieved from https://www.nw3c.org/docs/research/2010-national-public-survey-on-white-collar-crime.pdf?sfvrsn=8.

81. Peter Yeager, personal communication, 2011.

82. Ferraro, K. (1995). *Fear of crime: Interpreting victimization risk*. Albany: State University of New York Press.

83. *Miller v. Alabama*, 567 U.S. ___ (2012).

CHAPTER 3

1. King, L. W. (Trans.). (2008). *The Code of Hammurabi*. Retrieved from http://avalon.law.yale.edu/ancient/hamframe.asp. See also Assyrians: Cavalry and conquest. (2008–2016). In USHistory.org (Ed.), *Ancient civilizations*. Retrieved from http://www.ushistory.org/civ/4d.asp.

2. Foucault, M. (1977). *Discipline and punish: The birth of the prison* (A. Sheridan, Trans.). New York: Vintage. (Original work published 1975)

3. Ibid., p. 3.

4. Brown, S. E., Esbensen, F., & Geis, G. (2010). *Criminology: Explaining crime and its context* (7th ed.). New York: Anderson.

5. Ibid.

6. Geis, G. (1955). Pioneers in Criminology VII: Jeremy Bentham (1748–1832). *Journal of Criminal Law, Criminology, and Police Science, 46*, 159–171.

7. World Justice Project. (2008–2014). *What is the rule of law?* Retrieved from http://worldjusticeproject.org/what-rule-law.

8. Raz, J. (1977). The rule of law and its virtue. *Law Quarterly Review, 93*, 195.

9. Chambliss, W. (1960). A sociological analysis of the law of vagrancy. *Social Problems, 12*, 67–77.

10. Chambliss, W. (1973). Elites and the creation of criminal law. In W. Chambliss (Ed.), *Sociological readings in the conflict perspective* (p. 442). Reading, MA: Addison-Wesley.

11. Kennedy, R. (1997). *Race, crime and the law*. New York: Pantheon, p. 91.

12. U.S. Constitution, Article VI, Clause 2.

13. *Dred Scott v. Sandford*, 60 U.S. 393 (1857).

14. Geis, G., & Bienen, L. B. (1998). *Crimes of the century*. Boston: Northeastern University Press.

15. Dodge, M. (2009). *Women and white-collar crime*. Upper Saddle River, NJ: Prentice Hall.

16. Button, M., Tapley, J., & Lewis, C. (2013). The "fraud justice network" and the infra-structure of support for individual fraud victims in England and Wales. *Criminology and Criminal Justice, 13*, 37–61. Shover, N., Coffey, G. S., & Hobbs, D. (2003). Crime on the line: Telemarketing and the changing nature of professional crime. *British Journal of Criminology, 43*, 489–505.

17. Human Rights Campaign. (2015). *Maps of state laws and policies*. Retrieved from http://www.hrc.org/resources/entry/maps-of-state-laws-policies. Valcore, J., & Dodge, M. (2016). How hate crime legislation shapes gay and lesbian target groups: An analysis of social construction, law, and policy. *Criminal Justice Policy Review*. doi:10.1177/0887403416651924

18. Scott, A. (2016, March 20). *Murder of Dora teen shows need for LGBT hate crime law in Alabama*. Retrieved from http://www.al.com/opinion/index.ssf/2016/03/murder_of_dora_teen_shows_need.html.

19. *Black's law dictionary* (8th ed.). (2004). St. Paul, MN: West.

20. Dershowitz, A. M. (1994). *The abuse excuse: And other cop-outs, sob stories and evasions of responsibility*. Boston: Little, Brown.

21. Writers have spelled the name in a variety of ways: McNaughten, M'Naghten, and M'Naughten. We use M'Naghten here.

22. Bartol, C. R., & Bartol, A. M. (1994). *Psychology and law: Research and application* (2nd ed.). Pacific Grove, CA: Brooks/Cole.

23. Walker, L. (2009). *The battered woman syndrome* (3rd ed.). New York: Springer.

24. Dershowitz, *The Abuse Excuse*. Dodge, *Women and White-Collar Crime*.

25. *Smith v. Doe* (01–729), 538 U.S. 84 (2003).

26. *Plessy v. Ferguson* 163 U.S. 537 (1896).

27. *Brown v. Board of Education of Topeka*, 347 U.S. 483 (1954).

28. *Bowers v. Hardwick*, 478 U.S. 186 (1986).

29. *Lawrence v. Texas*, 539 U.S. 558 (2003).

30. VictimLaw. (n.d.). *About victims' rights*. Retrieved from https://www.victimlaw.org/victimlaw/pages/victimsRight.jsp.

31. Victims' Rights Amendment. (2013, April 25). Retrieved from http://www.gpo.gov/fdsys/pkg/CHRG-113hhrg80543/pdf/CHRG-113hhrg80543.pdf.

32. *Statement of David L. Voth*. (2002, May 9). Retrieved from http://www.crimevictimservices.org/page/victimsrights/43.

CHAPTER 4

1. Walker, S. (1977). *A critical history of police reform*. Lexington, MA: Lexington.

2. Inwood, S. (1998). *A history of London*. London: Macmillan.

3. Lentz, S. A., & Chaires, R. H. (2007). The invention of Peel's principles: A study of policing "textbook" history. *Journal of Criminal Justice*, *35*(1), 69–79.

4. Ibid.

5. Law Enforcement Assistance Administration (LEAA). (1976). *Two hundred years of American criminal justice: An LEAA bicentennial study*. Washington, DC: U.S. Department of Justice. Retrieved from https://www.ncjrs.gov/pdffiles1/Digitization/143157NCJRS.pdf.

6. Bureau of Labor Statistics. (2015, December 17). Police and detectives. In *Occupational outlook handbook*. Retrieved from http://www.bls.gov/ooh/protective-service/police-and-detectives.htm.

7. Walker, *A Critical History of Police Reform*.

8. LEAA, *Two Hundred Years of American Criminal Justice*.

9. Ibid.

10. Ibid.

11. Ibid.

12. Ibid.

13. Parker, A. E. (1972). *The Berkeley Police story*. Springfield, IL: Charles C Thomas.

14. Ibid.

15. Ibid.

16. Reeves, B. (2010). *Local police departments, 2007*. Washington, DC: U.S. Government Printing Office.

17. Walker, *A Critical History of Police Reform*.

18. LEAA, *Two Hundred Years of American Criminal Justice*.

19. International Association of Chiefs of Police. (n.d.). *History*. Retrieved from http://www.theiacp.org/History. Walker, *A Critical History of Police Reform*.

20. Walker, *A Critical History of Police Reform*.

21. LEAA, *Two Hundred Years of American Criminal Justice*.

22. Parker, *The Berkeley Police Story*.

23. Walker, *A Critical History of Police Reform*.

24. Ibid.

25. Ibid.

26. Ibid., although the Philadelphia Police Department's wiki page notes that the first black officer (unnamed) was hired in 1881. Some questionable webpages note that James Lee Wright, Sr., was his name.

27. Stanley, J. J. (2011–2012). Julius Boyd Loving: The first African American deputy on the Los Angeles County Sheriff's Department. *Southern California Quarterly, 93*, 459–493.

28. Reaves, Brian A. (2015, May). *Local police departments, 2013: Personnel, policies, and practices*. Retrieved from http://www.bjs.gov/content/pub/pdf/lpd13ppp.pdf.

29. *Philadelphia police department*. (2014). Retrieved from http://en.wikipedia.org/wiki/Philadelphia_Police_Department.

30. Romero, D. (2013, May 31). LAPD command is majority white even as the department has diversified. *LA Weekly*. Retrieved from http://www.laweekly.com/news/lapd-command-is-majority-white-even-as-the-department-has-diversified-4177529.

31. El-Ghobashy, T. (2011, January 7). Minorities gain in NYPD ranks. *The Wall Street Journal*. Retrieved from http://www.wsj.com/articles/SB10001424052748704415104576066302323002420.

32. See Taylor, P., Lopez, M. H., Martínez, J., & Velasco, G. (2012, April 4). *When labels don't fit: Hispanics and their views of identity*. Retrieved from http://www.pewhispanic.org/2012/04/04/when-labels-dont-fit-hispanics-and-their-views-of-identity/. We recognize differences in definitions between the terms *Latino* and *Hispanic*, as well as the bluntness of these terms in describing a heterogeneous population, but that here we are using the terms synonymously to reflect the broadest coverage.

33. For additional information, see Urbina, M. G., & Alvarez, S. E. (2015). *Latino police officers in the United States*. Springfield, IL: Charles C Thomas.

34. See, for example, Urbina & Alvarez, *Latino Police Officers in the United States*.

35. Reaves, *Local Police Departments, 2013*.

36. *Philadelphia Police Department*.

37. U.S. Department of the Interior, Bureau of Indian Affairs, Office of Law Enforcement Services. (n.d.) *A short history of Indian law enforcement*. Retrieved from http://web.archive.org/web/20000824055722/http://bialaw.fedworld.gov/history/history.htm.

38. Ibid.

39. United States, Office of Indian Affairs. (1869). *Annual report of the commissioner of Indian affairs, for the year 1869*. Retrieved from http://digicoll.library.wisc.edu/cgi-bin/History/History-idx?id=History.AnnRep69.

40. Reaves, *Local Police Departments, 2013*.

41. National Asian Peace Officers' Association. (2016). *About*. Retrieved from http://napoablue.org/about/.

42. Masters presented this information at the national conference of the National Organization of Black Women in Law Enforcement during its national conference in Gaithersburg, Maryland, on July 11, 2013. The theme of the conference was "Leadership, Diversity, Empowerment and Beyond." His presentation also noted that in United States, the history of Asian Americans' involvement in law enforcement is relatively short. His research indicates that Don S. Tokunaga was the first Asian American Federal Bureau of Investigation (FBI) special agent in charge, serving from 1968 to 1988. As recently as 1985, there were 44 Asian FBI agents among 11,000. By 2010, Asian agents numbered 1,420, or 4% of the agent population. FBI agents consisted of 839 Asian men and 531 Asian women.

43. Reaves, *Local Police Departments, 2013*.

44. Out to Protect, Inc. (2016). *Coming out from behind the badge*. Available at: http://www.comingoutfrombehindthebadge.com.

45. President's Commissions on Law Enforcement and the Administration of Justice. (1967). *The challenge of crime in a free society*. Retrieved from https://www.ncjrs.gov/pdffiles1/nij/42.pdf.

46. LEAA, *Two Hundred Years of American Criminal Justice*.

47. Chapman, S. (1990). *Police dogs in North America*. Springfield, IL: Charles C Thomas.
48. Ibid.
49. Dorriety, J. K. (2005). Police service dogs in the use-of-force continuum. *Criminal Justice Policy Review, 16*(1), 88–98.
50. Chapman, *Police Dogs in North America*.
51. Ibid.

CHAPTER 5

1. Retrieved from http://www.bjs.gov/index.cfm?ty=tp&tid=71.
2. Cordner, G. (2016). The unfortunate demise of police education. *Journal of Criminal Justice Education*. doi:10.1080/10511253.2016.1190134
3. Bordua, D. J., & Reiss, A. J. (1966). Command, control and charisma: Reflections on police bureaucracy. *American Journal of Sociology, 72*, 68–76. Reiss, A. J., & Bordua, D. J. (1967). Environment and organization: A perspective on the police. In D. Bordua (Ed.), *The police: Six sociological essays* (pp. 25–55). New York: John Wiley.
4. Technical Working Group on Crime Scene Investigation. (2000). *Crime scene investigation: A guide for law enforcement*. Washington, DC: U.S. Department of Justice. Retrieved from http://www.ncjrs.gov/pdffiles1/nij/178280.pdf.
5. Dodge, M., Starr-Gimeno, D., & Williams, T. (2005). Puttin' on the sting: Women police officers' perspectives on reverse prostitution assignments. *International Journal of Police Science & Management, 7*, 71–85.
6. Greenburg, S. F. (1992). *On the dotted line: Police executive contracts*. Washington, DC: Police Executive Research Forum.
7. Rainguet, F., & Dodge, M. (2001). The problems of police chiefs: An examination of the issues in tenure and turnover. *Police Quarterly, 4*(3), 268–288.
8. Niederhoffer, A. (1969). *Behind the shield: The police in urban society*. Garden City, NY: Doubleday. Skolnick, J. (1966). *Justice without trial*. New York: John Wiley. Westley, W. A. (1970). *Violence and the police: A sociological study of law, custom and morality*. Cambridge, MA: MIT Press.
9. Crank, J. P., & Caldero, M. A. (2010). *Police ethics: The corruption of noble cause*. New York: Elsevier. Herbert, S. (1998). Police subculture reconsidered. *Criminology, 36*, 343–370. Rokeach, M., Miller, M. G., & Synder, J. A. (1971). The value gap between the police and the policed. *Journal of Social Issues, 27*, 155–171.
10. Carlson, D. (2002). *When cultures clash: The divisive nature of police-community relations and suggestions for improvement*. Upper Saddle River, NJ: Prentice Hall.
11. Stinson, P. M., Liederbach, J., & Freiburger, T. L. (2010). Exit strategy: An exploration of late-stage police crime. *Police Quarterly, 13*, 413–435.
12. Barker, T., & Carter, D. L. (1994). A typology of police deviance. In T. Barker & D. L. Carter (Eds.), *Police deviance* (3rd ed., pp. 3–11). Cincinnati, OH: Anderson. Gorta, A. (2009). Illegal drug use by police officers: Using research and investigations to inform prevention strategies. *International Journal of Police Science & Management, 11*, 85–96. Kappeler, V. E., Sluder, R. D., & Alpert, G. (1998). *Forces of deviance: Understanding the dark side of policing*. Long Grove, IL: Waveland. Miller, L. S., & Braswell, M. C. (1985). Teaching police ethics: An experiential model. *American Journal of Criminal Justice, 11*, 27–46.
13. Rosoff, S., Pontell, H., & Tillman, R. (2007). *Profit without honor: White-collar crime and the looting of America*. Upper Saddle River, NJ: Prentice Hall.
14. Ibid. Barker, T., & Roebuck, J. (1973). *An empirical typology of police corruption: A study in organizational deviance*. Springfield, IL: Charles C Thomas.
15. Lester, D. (1983). Why do people become police officers? A study of reasons and their predictions of success. *Journal of Police Science and Administration, 11*, 170–174. McNamara, J. H. (1967). Uncertainties in police work: The relevance of police recruits' backgrounds and training. In D. J. Bordua (Ed.), *The police: Six sociological essays* (pp. 163–252). New York: John Wiley.
16. Miller, H. A., Mire, S., & Bitna, K. (2009). Predictors of job satisfaction among police officers: Does personality matter? *Journal of Criminal Justice, 37*, 419–426.
17. Seklecki, R., & Paynich, R. (2007). A national survey of female police officers: An overview of findings. *Police Practice and Research, 8*, 17–30.
18. University at Buffalo. (2008). Impact of stress on police officers' physical and mental health. *ScienceDaily*. Retrieved from http://www.sciencedaily.com/releases/2008/09/080926105029.htm.
19. Clark, R., & O'Hara, A. (2013). *2012 police suicides: The NSOPS Study*. Retrieved from http://www.policesuicidestudy.com/id16.html.
20. Archbold, C. A., & Schulz, D. M. (2008). Making rank: The lingering effects of tokenism on female police officers' promotion aspirations. *Police Quarterly, 11*, 50–73. Brown, J., & Heidensohn, F. (2000). *Gender and policing: Comparative perspectives*. New York: St. Martin's. Parsons, D., & Jesilow, P. (2001). *In the same voice: Women and men in law enforcement*. Minneapolis, MN: Seven Locks. Rabe-Hemp, C. E. (2007). Survival in an "all boys club": Policewomen and their fight for acceptance. *Policing: An International Journal of Police Strategies and Management, 31*, 251–270.
21. Garcia, V. (2003). "Difference" in the police department: Women, policing, and "doing gender." *Journal of Contemporary Criminal Justice, 19*, 330–344.
22. Birzer, M. L., & Craig, D. E. (1996). Gender differences in police physical ability test performance. *American Journal of Police, 15*(2), 93–108. Gaines, L. K., Falkenburg, S., & Gambino, J. A. (1993). Police physical agility testing: An historical and legal analysis. *American Journal of Police, 12*(4), 47–66. Lonsway, K. A. (2003). Tearing down the wall: Problems with consistency, validity, and adverse impact of physical agility testing in police selection. *Police Quarterly, 6*, 237–277.
23. Birzer and Craig, "Gender Differences in Police Physical Ability Test Performance."
24. McElvain, J. P., & Kposowa, A. J. (2008). Police officer characteristics and the likelihood of using deadly force. *Criminal Justice & Behavior, 35*, 505–521. Rabe-Hemp, C. E. (2008). Female officers and the ethic of care: Does officer gender impact police behaviors? *Journal of Criminal Justice, 36*, 426–434.
25. Morash, M., & Greene, J. (1986). Evaluating women on patrol: A critique of contemporary wisdom. *Evaluation Review, 10*, 230–255.
26. Archbold and Schulz, "Making Rank."
27. Dodge, M., Valcore, L., & Klinger, D. (2010). Maintaining separate spheres in policing: Women on SWAT teams. *Women & Criminal Justice, 20*, 218–238.
28. Wertsch, T. L. (1998). Walking the thin blue line. *Women & Criminal Justice, 9*, 23–61. Whetstone, T. S., & Wilson, D. G. (1999). Dilemmas confronting female police officer promotional candidates: Glass ceiling, disenfranchisement or satisfaction? *International Journal of Police Science and Management, 2*(2), 128–143.

29. Schulz, D. M. (2003). Women police chiefs: A statistical profile. *Police Quarterly, 6,* 330–345.

30. Miller, S. L. (1999). *Gender and community policing: Walking the talk.* Boston: Northeastern University Press, p. 68.

31. Tuomey, L. M. (2009). Step up to law enforcement: A successful strategy for recruiting women into the law enforcement profession. *Police Chief, 76*(6). Retrieved from http://www.policechiefmagazine.org/magazine/index.cfm?fuseaction=display_arch&article_id=1820&issue_id=62009.

32. Scarborough, K. E., & Collins, P. A. (2002). *Women in public and private law enforcement.* Woburn, MA: Butterworth-Heinemann.

33. Bureau of Labor Statistics. (n.d.). *Household data, annual averages: Employed persons by detailed occupation, sex, race, and Hispanic or Latino ethnicity.* Retrieved from http://www.bls.gov/cps/cpsaat11.pdf.

34. Martin, S. (1992). The interactive effects of race and sex on women police officers. *Justice Professional, 6,* 383–400. Martin, S. (1979). POLICEwomen and policeWOMEN: Occupational role dilemmas and choices of female officers. *Journal of Police Science and Administration, 2,* 314–323.

35. Dodge, M., & Pogrebin, M. (2001). African-American policewomen: An exploration of professional relationships. *Policing: An International Journal of Police Strategies & Management, 24,* 550–562.

36. Skogan, W. G., & Hartnett, S. M. (1997). *Community policing: Chicago style.* New York: Oxford University Press.

37. Office of Community Oriented Policing Services. (2012). *Community policing defined.* Washington, DC: U.S. Department of Justice. Retrieved from http://www.cops.usdoj.gov/Publications/e051229476_CP-Defined-TEXT_v8_092712.pdf.

38. Cohen, L. E., & Felson, M. (1979). Social change and crime rate trends: A routine activity approach. *American Sociological Review, 44,* 588–605.

39. Kelling, G. L., & Wilson, J. Q. (1982, March). Broken windows: The police and neighborhood safety. *The Atlantic.* Retrieved from http://www.theatlantic.com/magazine/archive/1982/03/broken-windows/304465.

40. National Justice Institute. (2009). *Why crimes occur in hot spots.* Retrieved from http://www.nij.gov/nij/topics/law-enforcement/strategies/hot-spot-policing/why-hot-spots-occur.htm.

41. Sherman, L. W., & Weisburd, D. (1995). General deterrent effects of police patrol in crime hot spots: A randomized, controlled trial. *Justice Quarterly, 12,* 635–648.

42. Sherman, L. W., Gartin, P. R., & Buerger, M. E. (1989). Hot spots of predatory crime: Routine activities and the criminology of place. *Criminology, 27,* 27–55.

43. Hesseling, R. (1994). Displacement: A review of the empirical literature. *Crime Prevention Studies, 3,* 197–230. Eck, J. (1993). The threat of crime displacement. *Criminal Justice Abstracts, 25,* 527–546.

44. Weisburd, D., & Mazerolle, L. G. (2000). Crime and disorder in drug hot spots: Implications for theory and practice in policing. *Police Quarterly, 3,* 331–349.

45. Green, J. A. (1999). Zero tolerance: A case study of police policies and practices in New York City. *Crime & Delinquency, 45,* 171–187.

46. Walker, S., & Katz, C. M. (2002). *The police in America: An introduction.* New York: McGraw-Hill.

47. Katz, C. M., Webb, V. J., & Schaefer, D. R. (2001). An assessment of the impact of quality-of-life policing on crime and disorder. *Justice Quarterly, 18,* 825–877.

48. Ratcliffe, J. H. (2008). *Intelligence-led policing.* New York: Routledge.

49. Ibid.

50. Silverman, E. B. (1999). *NYPD battles crime: Innovative strategies in policing.* Boston: Northeastern University Press.

51. Fisher, C. (Ed.). (2014, March). *Legitimacy and procedural justice: A report by the Police Executive Research Forum (PERF).* Retrieved from http://www.policeforum.org/assets/docs/Free_Online_Documents/Leadership/legitimacy%20and%20procedural%20justice%20-%20a%20new%20element%200f%20police%201eadership.pdf.

52. Fridell, L. A. (2016). *The science of implicit bias and implications for policing.* Switzerland: Springer International Publishing.

53. President's Task Force on 21st Century Policing. (2015, May). *Final repot of the President's Task Force on 21st Century Policing.* Retrieved from http://www.cops.usdoj.gov/pdf/taskforce/taskforce_finalreport.pdf.

54. Terrill, W., Alpert, G., Dunham, R. G., & Smith, M. R. (2003). A management tool for evaluating police use of force: An application of the force factor. *Police Quarterly, 6*(2), 150–171.

55. Bayley, D. H. (1986). The tactical choices of police patrol officers. *Journal of Criminal Justice, 14,* 329–348.

56. Ellis, D., Choi, A., & Blaus, C. (1993). Injuries to police officers attending domestic disturbances: An empirical study. *Canadian Journal of Criminology, 1,* 149–168. Garner, J., & Clemmer, E. (1986). *Danger to police in domestic disturbances: A new look.* Washington, DC: National Institute of Justice.

57. Adams, K., et al. (1999). What we know about police use of force. In *Use of force by police: Overview of national and local data* (pp. 1–14). Washington, DC: U.S. Department of Justice. MacDonald, J. M., Manz, P. W., Alpert, G., & Dunham, R. G. (2002). Police use of force: Examining the relationship between calls for service and the balance of police force and suspect resistance. *Journal of Criminal Justice, 31,* 119–127.

58. U.S. Department of Justice. (2015, March 4). *Department of Justice report regarding the criminal investigation into the shooting death of Michael Brown by Ferguson, Missouri police officer Darren Wilson.* Retrieved from https://www.justice.gov/sites/default/files/opa/press-releases/attachments/2015/03/04/doj_report_on_shooting_of_michael_brown_1.pdf.

59. Fyfe, J. (1995). Training to reduce police-citizen violence. In W. Geller & H. Toch (Eds.), *And justice for all: Understanding and controlling police abuse of force.* Washington, DC: Police Executive Research Forum. Garafolo, J., & Bayley, D. H. (1989). The management of violence by police patrol officers. *Criminology, 27,* 1–27.

60. Adams et al., "What We Know About Police Use of Force." Garner, J. H., & Maxwell, C. D. (1999). Measuring the amount of force used by and against the police in six jurisdictions. In *Use of force by police: Overview of national and local data* (pp. 25–44). Washington, DC: U.S. Department of Justice.

61. Alpert, G. P., & Dunham, R. G. (1999). The force factor: Measuring and assessing police use of force and suspect resistance. In *Use of force by police: Overview of national and local data* (pp. 45–60). Washington, DC: U.S. Department of Justice.

62. *Floyd v. The City of New York,* 959 F. Supp. 2d 540 (S.D.N.Y. 2013). See also *Ligon v. The City of New York,* 925 F. Supp. 2d 478 (S.D.N.Y. 2013).

63. American Civil Liberties Union. (n.d.). *Racial profiling.* Retrieved from https://www.aclu.org/racial-justice/racial-profiling.

64. Carter, D. L., & Katz-Bannister, A. J. (2003). *Racial profiling: Issues and implications for police policy.* Los Angeles: Roxbury.

65. Zagier, A. S. (2014, September 9). Ferguson plans reforms after fatal police shooting. Retrieved from http://www.thehour.com/nation/article/Ferguson-plans-reforms-after-fatal-police-shooting-8070460.php.

66. New York City Bar Association. (2013, May). *Report on the NYPD's stop-and-frisk policy.* Retrieved from http://www2.nycbar.org/pdf/report/uploads/20072495-StopFriskReport.pdf.

67. Ross, J. I. (2012). *Policing issues: Challenges and controversies.* Sudbury, MA: Jones & Bartlett Learning.

68. Ibid.

69. Lieberman, J. D., Koetzle, D., & Sakiyama, M. (2013). Police departments' use of Facebook: Patterns and policy issues. *Police Quarterly, 16*(4), 438–462. Procter, R., Crump, J., Karstedt, S., Voss, A., & Cantijoch, M. (2013). Reading the riots: What were the police doing on Twitter? *Policing and Society: An International Journal of Research and Policy, 23*(4), 413–436.

70. Twitter. (2016). *What's happening.* Retrieved from https://about.twitter.com/company.

71. Procter et al., "Reading the Riots."

72. Swann, P. (2013, June). To serve and protect: How the Boston police used Twitter after marathon attacks. *Public Relations Tactics, 12,* p. 13.

73. Lieberman et al., "Police Departments' Use of Facebook."

74. Stroshine, M. S. (2012). Technological innovations in policing at the dawn of the twenty-first century. In R. G. Dunham & G. P. Alpert (Eds.), *Critical issues in policing* (pp. 168–180). Long Grove, IL: Waveland.

75. *State v. Brossart,* 858 N.W. 2d 275 (N. Dak. 2015).

76. Elinson, Z. (2014, August 15). More officers wearing body cameras. *The Wall Street Journal.* Retrieved from http://online.wsj.com/articles/body-cameras-on-police-can-reduce-use-of-force-citizen-complaints-1408134549.

77. Kraska, P. B. (2001). *Militarizing the American criminal justice system.* Boston: Northeastern University Press.

78. Balko, R. (2013, August 7). Rise of the warrior cop. *The Wall Street Journal.* Retrieved from http://online.wsj.com/news/articles/SB100014241278873233848804578608040780519904.

CHAPTER 6

1. Chambliss, W. J. (2001). *Power, politics, and crime.* Boulder, CO: Westview Press. Quinney, R. (2008). *The social reality of crime* (4th ed.). New Brunswick, NJ: Transaction. Seung-Whan, C. (2010). Fighting terrorism through the rule of law? *Journal of Conflict Resolution, 54,* 940–966. Skaaning, S. (2010). Measuring the rule of law. *Political Research Quarterly, 63,* 449–460.

2. Handler, J. G. (1994). *Ballentine's law dictionary* (legal assistant ed.). Albany, NY: Delmar, p. 431.

3. *Illinois v. Gates,* 462 U.S. 213 (1983).

4. Ibid.

5. *Missouri v. McNeely,* ___ U.S. ___, 133 S. Ct. 1552 (2013).

6. Ross, D. L. (2012). *Messerschmidt v. Millender:* Expanding probable cause and restricting liability. *Criminal Justice Review, 37,* 416–427.

7. *Floyd v. The City of New York; Ligon v. The City of New York.*

8. *Nix v. Williams,* 467 U.S. 431 (1984). *United States v. Leon,* 468 U.S. 897 (1984). See also Jackson, D. W. (1986). Whatever happened to the exclusionary rule? The Burger Court and the Fourth Amendment. *Criminal Justice Policy Review, 1*(2), 156–168. Kaci, J. H. (1987). The exclusionary rule in the year 2000: Due process reborn? *Journal of Contemporary Criminal Justice, 3*(3), 30–42. Ma, Y. (2012). The American exclusionary rule: Is there a lesson to learn from others? *International Criminal Justice Review, 22,* 309–325.

9. *United States v. Leon,* 468 U.S. 897 (1984).

10. *Silverthorne Lumber Co., Inc. v. United States,* 251 U.S. 385 (1920).

11. *California v. Greenwood,* 486 U.S. 35 (1988).

12. Ibid.

13. Marx, G., & Byrne, J. (2011). Technological innovations in crime prevention and policing: A review of the research on implementation and impact. *Cahiers Politiestudies, 3*(20), 17–40.

14. *United States v. Warshak,* 631 F. 3d 266 (2010).

15. Sengupta, S. (2012, November 25). Courts divided over searches of cellphones. *The New York Times.* Retrieved from http://www.nytimes.com/2012/11/26/technology/legality-of-warrantless-cellphone-searches-goes-to-courts-and-legislatures.html.

16. *Florida v. Jardines,* 569 U.S. ___ (2013).

17. *Katz v. United States,* 389 U.S. 347 (1967).

18. Logan, W. A. (2011). Police mistakes of law. *Emory Law Journal, 61*(1), 69–110. Balko, R. (2006). *No SWAT.* Retrieved from http://www.cato.org/publications/commentary/no-swat.

19. Jonsson, R. (2006, November 29). After Atlanta raid tragedy, new scrutiny of police tactics. *Christian Science Monitor.* Retrieved from http://www.csmonitor.com/2006/1129/p03s03-ussc.html.

20. See Vaughn, M. S., & del Carmen, R. V. (1997). The Fourth Amendment as a tool of actuarial justice: The "special needs" exception to the warrant and probable cause requirements. *Crime & Delinquency, 43*(1), 78–103.

21. *Black's law dictionary* (8th ed.). (2004). St. Paul, MN: West.

22. *Miranda v. Arizona,* 384 U.S. 436 (1966).

23. *Harris v. New York,* 401 U.S. 222 (1971).

24. *Berghuis v. Thompkins,* 560 U.S. 370 (2010).

25. Gudjonsson, G. H., & Pearse, J. (2011). Suspect interviews and false confessions. *Current Directions in Psychological Science, 20*(1), 33–37. Kassin, S. M. (2008). False confessions: Causes, consequences, and implications for reform. *Current Directions in Psychological Science, 17,* 249–253.

26. Jenkins, P. (1998). *Moral panic: Changing concepts of the child molester in modern America.* New Haven, CT: Yale University Press. Staller, K. M., & Faller, K. C. (2010). *Seeking justice in child sexual abuse: Shifting burdens and sharing responsibilities.* New York: Columbia University Press.

27. Sutherland, E. H. (1945). Is "white-collar crime" crime? *American Sociological Review, 10,* 132–139. Tappan, P. W. (1947). Who is the criminal? *American Sociological Review, 12,* 96–102.

CHAPTER 7

1. *The Law Dictionary,* www.thelawdictionary.org.

2. *Roe v. Wade,* 410 U.S. 113 (1973).

3. *Obergefell v. Hodges,* ___ U.S. ___, 135 S. Ct. 2071 (2015). See also http://www.supremecourt.gov/opinions/14pdf/14–556_3204.pdf.

4. Supreme Court of the United States. (2014). *The justices' caseload.* Retrieved from http://www.supremecourt.gov/about/justicecaseload.aspx.

5. Gaines, L., & Miller, L. (2006). *Criminal justice in action: The core*. Belmont, CA: Thomson/Wadsworth.

6. National Institute of Justice. (2012). *Drug courts*. Retrieved from http://www.nij.gov/topics/courts/drug-courts/Pages/welcome.aspx.

7. Ibid.

8. Monchick, R., Scheyett, A., & Pfeifer, J. (2006). *Drug court case management: Role, function, and utility* (National Drug Court Institute Monograph Series 7). Washington, DC: Bureau of Justice Assistance. Retrieved from https://www.bja.gov/Publications/Drug_Court_Case_Management.pdf.

9. National Association of Drug Court Professionals. (n.d.). *What are drug courts?* Retrieved from http://www.nadcp.org/learn/what-are-drug-courts.

10. Drug Policy Alliance. (2011). *Drug courts are not the answer: Toward a health-centered approach to drug use*. Retrieved from http://www.drugpolicy.org/drugcourts.

11. National Institute of Justice. (2011). *Domestic violence courts*. Retrieved from http://www.nij.gov/topics/courts/domestic-violence-courts.

12. Labriola, M., Bradley, S., O'Sullivan, C. S., Repel, M., & Moore, S. (2009). *A national portrait of domestic violence courts*. New York: Center for Court Innovation.

13. National Center for State Courts. (n.d.). *Veterans courts: Resource guide*. Retrieved from http://www.ncsc.org/Topics/Problem-Solving-Courts/Veterans-Court/Resource-Guide.aspx.

14. Justice for Vets. (2016). *What is a veterans treatment court?* Retrieved from http://justiceforvets.org/what-is-a-veterans-treatment-court.

15. *Bradwell v. State of Illinois*, 83 U.S. 130, 141–142 (1873).

16. Millhiser, I. (2014, March 19). Only 16 percent of attorneys arguing before the Supreme Court this term were women. *Think Progress*. Retrieved from http://thinkprogress.org/justice/2014/03/19/3416246/only-16-percent-of-attorneys-arguing-before-the-supreme-court-this-term-were-women.

17. National Women's Law Center. (2014, July 31). *Women in the federal judiciary: Still a long way to go*. Retrieved from http://www.nwlc.org/resource/women-federal-judiciary-still-long-way-go-1.

18. Just the Beginning Foundation. (2014). *Irvin C. Mollison*. Retrieved from http://www.jtbf.org/index.&category=United%20States%20Court%200f%20International%20Trade%20Judges.

19. Olivas, M. A. (2011, March 31). *The first Latina and Latino lawyers to argue before the Supreme Court*. Retrieved from http://www.newstaco.com/2011/03/31/the-first-latina-latino-lawyers-to-argue-before-supreme-court.

20. *Examining Board v. Flores de Otero*, 426 U.S. 572 (1976).

CHAPTER 8

1. Birckhead, T. R. (2010). Culture clash: The challenge of lawyering across difference in juvenile court. *Rutgers Law Review, 62*, 959–991. Retrieved from http://pegasus.rutgers.edu/~review/v0162n4/Birckhead.pdf.

2. American Bar Association. (n.d.). *Model rules of professional conduct: Preamble and scope*. Retrieved from http://www.americanbar.org/groups/professional_responsibility/publications/model_rules_of_professional_conduct/model_rules_of_professional_conduct_preamble_scope.html.

3. Innocence Project. (n.d.). *How many innocent people are there in prison?* Retrieved from http://www.innocenceproject.org/Content/How_many_innocent_people_are_there_in_prison.php.

4. U.S. Department of Justice. (n.d.). *About the office*. Retrieved from http://www.justice.gov/ag/about-oag.html.

5. Offices of the United States Attorneys. (n.d.). *Mission*. Retrieved from http://www.justice.gov/usao/about/mission.html.

6. Ibid.

7. U.S. Department of Justice. (2012). *United States attorneys' annual statistical report: fiscal year 2012*. Retrieved from http://www.justice.gov/usao/reading_room/reports/asr2012/12statrpt.pdf.

8. Denver District Attorney's Office. (n.d.). *Mission of the Office of the Denver District Attorney*. Retrieved from http://www.denverda.org.

9. *Brady v. Maryland*, 373 U.S. 83 (1963).

10. Ridolfi, K. M., & Possley, M. (2010). *Preventable error: A report on prosecutorial misconduct in California 1997–2009*. Santa Clara: Santa Clara University School of Law, Northern California Innocence Project. Petro, J., & Petro, N. (2013). The prosecutor and wrongful convictions: Misplaced priorities, misconduct, immunity, and remedies. In C. R. Huff & M. Killias (Eds.), *Wrongful convictions* (pp. 91–110). New York: Routledge.

11. University of Dayton, School of Law. (1997–2003). *Why don't we hear more about grand juries?* Retrieved from http://campus.udayton.edu/~grandjur/faq/faq7.htm. Halsted, J. (1987). The American grand jury: Due process or rights regress? *Criminal Justice Policy Review, 2*, 103–117.

12. Bureau of Justice Statistics. (2014). *Criminal cases*. Retrieved from http://www.bjs.gov/index.cfm?ty=tp&tid=23.

13. See literature review: *The effect of gender on the judicial pretrial decision of bail amount set*. Retrieved from http://www.uscourts.gov/uscourts/federalcourts/pps/fedprob/2006–06/references.html#gender.

14. Goldkamp, J. S., & Gottfredson, M. (1979). Bail decision making and pretrial detention: Surfacing judicial policy. *Law and Human Behavior, 3*, 227–249. Nagel, I. H. (1983). The legal/extra-legal controversy: Judicial decisions in pretrial release. *Law and Society Review, 17*, 481–515.

15. Katz, C. M., & Spohn, C. (1995). The effect of race and gender on bail outcomes: Test of an interactive model. *American Journal of Criminal Justice, 19*, 161–184.

16. Albonetti, C. (1991). An integration of theories to explain judicial discretion. *Social Problems, 38*, 247–266.

17. Figueira-McDonough, J. (1985). Gender differences in informal processing: A look at charge bargaining and sentence reduction in Washington, D.C. *Journal of Research in Crime and Delinquency, 22*, 101–133.

18. Piehl, A., & Bushway, S. (2007). Measuring and explaining charge bargaining. *Journal of Quantitative Criminology, 23*, 105–125.

19. Farnworth, M., & Teske, R. (1995). Gender differences in felony court processing: Three hypotheses of disparity. *Women and Criminal Justice, 6*, 23–44. Johnson, B. (2003). Racial and ethnic disparities in sentencing departures across modes of conviction. *Criminology, 41*, 449–490. Ulmer, J., & Bradley, M. (2006). Variation in trial penalties among serious violent offenses. *Criminology, 44*, 631–670.

20. Albonetti, C. A. (1997). Sentencing under the federal sentencing guidelines: Effects of defendant characteristics, guilty pleas, and departures on sentence outcomes for drug offenses, 1991–1992. *Law & Society Review, 31*, 789–822.

21. Devers, L. (2011, January 24). *Bail decisionmaking: Research summary*. Retrieved from https://www.bja.gov/Publications/BailDecisionmakingResearchSummary.pdf.

22. Waite, J. B. (1923). Challenges to the array. *Michigan Law Review, 21*, 578–581.

23. Daniels, J. P., & Knafo, A. L. (2005). Prospective juror questionnaires made easy. *FDCC Quarterly, 61*,

218–230. Retrieved from http://www.thefederation.org/documents/V61N2_Daniels.pdf.

24. *Batson v. Kentucky,* 476 U.S. 79 (1986).

25. *Hoyt v. Florida,* 368 U.S. 57 (1961).

26. *Taylor v. Louisiana,* 419 U.S. 522 (1975).

27. *J. E. B. v. Alabama ex rel. T. B.,* 511 U.S. 127 (1994).

28. Grossman, J. L. (1994). Women's jury service: Right of citizenship or privilege of difference? *Stanford Law Review, 46,* 1115–1160.

29. *Strauder v. West Virginia,* 100 U.S. 303 (1880).

30. Alschuler, A., & Deiss, A. G. (1994). *A brief history of the criminal jury in the United States.* Retrieved from http://chicagounbound.uchicago.edu/cgi/viewcontent.cgi?article=2010&context=journal_articles.

31. *Elk v. Wilkins,* 112 U.S. 94, 109 (1884).

32. American Bar Association. (2014). *About the American Bar Association.* Retrieved from http://www.americanbar.org/about_the_aba.html.

CHAPTER 9

1. *Federal Rules of Criminal Procedure.* Rule 23(a). Retrieved from http://www.law.cornell.edu/rules/frcrmp/rule_23.

2. See, e.g., Federal Rules of Evidence. (2012). Retrieved from http://www.gpo.gov/fdsys/pkg/USCODE-2011-title28/pdf/USCODE-2011-title28-app-federalru-dup2.pdf.

3. *Federal Rules of Evidence: Rule 102. Purpose.* (n.d.). Retrieved from http://www.law.cornell.edu/rules/fre/rule_102.

4. FindLaw. (n.d.). *"Hearsay" evidence.* Retrieved from http://criminal.findlaw.com/criminal-procedure/hearsay-evidence.html.

5. See, e.g., final charging instructions for New York Criminal Courts: http://www.nycourts.gov/judges/cji/5-SampleCharges/CJI2d.Final_Instructions.pdf.

6. Saks, M. J. (1993). Judicial nullification. *Indiana Law Journal, 68,* 1281–1295.

7. Rottman, D. B., & Strickland, S. M. (2006). *State court organization, 2004.* Washington, DC: U.S. Government Printing Office. Retrieved from http://www.bjs.gov/content/pub/pdf/sc004.pdf; see Table 42.

8. American Judicature Society. (2013). *Jury decision making: Size and unanimity requirements.* Retrieved from https://www.ajs.org/judicial-administration/jury-center/jury-system-overview/jury-decision-making.

9. Mott, N. L., Kauder, N. B., Ostrom, B. J., & Hannaford-Agor, B. L. (2003). A profile of hung juries. *Caseload Highlights, 9*(1). Retrieved from http://www.ncsc-jurystudies.org/~/media/Microsites/Files/CJS/What%20We%20Do/caseload%20highlights%20hung%20juries.ashx.

10. Mistrial. (2014). *Free dictionary.* Retrieved from http://legal-dictionary.thefreedictionary.com/mistrials.

11. Jonakait, R. N. (2003). *The American jury system.* New Haven, CT: Yale University Press, p. 245.

12. To read more about these two cases, the reader is encouraged to consult Stern, S. (2002). Between local knowledge and national politics: Debating rationales for jury nullification after Bushell's case. *Yale Law Journal, 111,* 1815–1859. Retrieved from http://www.law.utoronto.ca/documents/stern/BushellsCase.pdf.

13. The trial of Mr. John Peter Zenger, 17 Howell's St. Tr. 675 (K.B. 1735).

14. Massachusetts Court System. (2009). *Taking the verdict and discharging the jury.* Retrieved from http://www.mass.gov/courts/docs/courts-and-judges/courts/district-court/jury-instructions-criminal/2500-taking-the-verdict-and-discharging-the-jury.pdf.

15. Tonry, M. (1999, September). Reconsidering indeterminate and structured sentencing. *Sentencing & Corrections: Issues for the 21st Century, 2.* Retrieved from https://www.ncjrs.gov/pdffiles1/nij/175722.pdf.

16. Spohn, C. C. (2000). Thirty years of sentencing reform: The quest for a racially neutral sentencing process. In *Policies, processes, and decisions of the criminal justice system.* Retrieved from http://www.justicestudies.com/pubs/livelink3–1.pdf.

17. Irwin, J. (1980). *Prisons in turmoil.* Boston: Little, Brown.

18. Tonry, "Reconsidering Indeterminate and Structured Sentencing."

19. While parole boards were dismantled in many states, prisoners may still be subject to parole supervision following release from prison.

20. Bureau of Justice Assistance. (n.d.). *National assessment of structured sentencing.* Retrieved from https://www.ncjrs.gov/pdffiles/strsent.pdf.

21. Lowenthal, G. T. (1993). Mandatory sentencing laws: Undermining the effectiveness of determinate sentencing reform. *California Law Review, 81*(1), 61–123. Retrieved from http://scholarship.law.berkeley.edu/cgi/viewcontent.cgi?article=1755&context=californialawreview.

22. Ibid.

23. Spohn, "Thirty Years of Sentencing Reform."

24. Table 5.27.2010: Offenders sentenced in U.S. District Courts under the U.S. Sentencing Commission guidelines, by primary offense and age, fiscal year 2010. (n.d.). In *Sourcebook of criminal justice statistics.* Retrieved from http://www.albany.edu/sourcebook/pdf/t5272010.pdf.

25. Table 5.26.2010: Offenders sentenced in U.S. district courts under the U.S. Sentencing Commission guidelines, by primary offense, sex, race, and ethnicity, fiscal year 2010. (n.d.). In *Sourcebook of criminal justice statistics.* Retrieved from http://www.albany.edu/sourcebook/pdf/t5262010.pdf.

26. Table 5.28.2010: Offenders sentenced in U.S. district courts under the U.S. Sentencing Commission guidelines, by primary offense and education level, fiscal year 2010. (n.d.). In *Sourcebook of criminal justice statistics.* Retrieved from http://www.albany.edu/sourcebook/pdf/t5282010.pdf.

27. Blumstein, A., Cohen, J., Martin, S. E., & Tonry, M. (Eds.). (1983). *Research on sentencing: The search for reform.* Washington, DC: National Academy Press.

28. An example of a document declaring the intent to seek the death penalty, from Louisiana: http://www.fjc.gov/public/pdf.nsf/lookup/dpen0005.pdf/$file/dpen0005.pdf.

29. Only Arkansas and South Carolina do not include mandatory appeals. Mandatory appeals, where used, cannot be waived by the defendant.

30. Snell, T. L. (2014, December). *Capital punishment, 2013—Statistical tables.* Retrieved from http://www.bjs.gov/content/pub/pdf/cp13st.pdf.

31. Ibid.

32. Ibid.

33. Phillips, S. (2008). Racial disparities in the capital of capital punishment. *Houston Law Review, 45,* 807–840.

34. Beckett, K., & Evans, H. (2014). *The role of race in Washington State capital sentencing, 1981–2012.* Retrieved from http://www.deathpenaltyinfo.org/documents/WashRaceStudy2014.pdf.

35. Vollum, S. (2012). The death penalty: Ultimate punishment or failed public policy. In F. P. Reddington & G. Bonham Jr. (Eds.), *Flawed criminal justice policies: At the intersection of media, public fear and legislative response* (pp. 121–146). Durham, NC: Carolina Academic Press.

36. Gallup. (2015). *Death penalty.* Retrieved from http://www.gallup.com/poll/1606/death-penalty.aspx.

37. Vollum, "The Death Penalty."

38. Radalet, M., & Bedeau, H. (1987). Miscarriages of justice in potentially capital cases. *Standard Law Review, 40,* 121–181.

39. Snell, T. L. (2014, November). *Capital punishment, 2012—Statistical tables.*

Retrieved from http://www.bjs.gov/content/pub/pdf/cp12st.pdf.

40. Baldus, D. C., & Woodworth, G. (2003). Race discrimination and the death penalty. In J. R. Acker et al. (Eds.), *America's experiment with capital punishment* (2nd ed., pp. 501–551). Durham, NC: Carolina Academic Press.

41. Alarcon, A., & Mitchell, P. (2010). *Executing the will of the voters? A roadmap to mend or end the California legislature's multi-billion dollar death penalty debacle*. Retrieved from http://www.deathpenaltyinfo.org/california-cost-study-2011.

42. Roman, J., Chaflin, A., Sundquist, A., Knight, C., & Darmenov, A. (2008). *The cost of the death penalty in Maryland*. Retrieved from http://www.urban.org/UploadedPDF/411625_md_death_penalty.pdf.

43. Amnesty International. (2013). *Death penalty cost*. Retrieved from http://www.amnestyusa.org/our-work/issues/death-penalty/us-death-penalty-facts/death-penalty-cost.

44. Dieter, R. C. (2009). *Smart on crime: Reconsidering the death penalty in a time of economic crisis*. Washington, DC: Death Penalty Information Center.

45. Hart, T. C., & Rennison, C. (2003). *Reporting crime to the police, 1992–2000*. Retrieved from http://www.bjs.gov/content/pub/pdf/rcp00.pdf.

46. Cassell, P. G., & Joffee, S. (2011). The crime victim's expanding role in a system of public prosecution: A response to the critics of the Crime Victims' Rights Act. *Northwestern University Law Review*. Retrieved from http://www.law.northwestern.edu/depts/legalpub/lawreview/colloquy/2011/1.

47. Office for Victims of Crime. (n.d.). *About OVC*. Retrieved from http://www.ovc.gov/about/index.html.

48. Offices of the United States Attorneys. (n.d.). *Crime victims' rights ombudsman: Crime Victims' Rights Act*. Retrieved from http://www.justice.gov/usao/eousa/vr/crime_victims.html.

49. See, e.g., Massachusetts Victim Bill of Rights: http://www.mass.gov/eopss/law-enforce-and-cj/prisons/dom-violence/massachusetts-victim-bill-of-rights.html.

CHAPTER 10

1. Gudrais, E. (2013, March–April). The prison problem. *Harvard Magazine*. Retrieved from http://harvardmagazine.com/2013/03/the-prison-problem.

2. Kaeble, D., Glaze, L., Tsoutis, A., & Minton, T. (2015, December). *Correctional populations in the United States, 2014*. Retrieved from http://www.bjs.gov/content/pub/pdf/cpus14.pdf.

3. Smith, A., & Berlin, L. (1981). *Treating the criminal offender*. Englewood Cliffs, NJ: Prentice Hall.

4. Petersilia, J. (1998). *Community corrections: Probation, parole, and intermediate sanctions*. New York: Oxford University Press.

5. O'Connor, T. (2011). Intermediate sanctions. *MegaLinks in Criminal Justice*. Retrieved from http://www.drtomoconnor.com/1050/10501ect03a.htm.

6. Kaeble et al., *Correctional Populations in the United States, 2014*.

7. Ibid.

8. Kaeble, D., Maruschak, L. M., & Bonczar, T. P. (2015, November). *Probation and parole in the United States, 2014*. Retrieved from http://www.bjs.gov/content/pub/pdf/ppus14.pdf.

9. Zaitow, B. H., & Thomas, J. (2003). *Women in prison: Gender and social control*. Boulder, CO: Lynne Rienner, p. vii.

10. Kaeble et al., *Probation and Parole in the United States, 2014*.

11. Chiricos, T., Barrick, K., Bales, W., & Bontrager, S. (2007). The labeling of convicted felons and its consequences for recidivism. *Criminology, 45*, 547–581.

12. Kurki, L. (1999). *Incorporating restorative and community justice into American sentencing and corrections: Sentencing and corrections: Issues for the 21st century*. Paper presented at the National Institute of Justice executive sessions on sentencing and corrections.

13. Rogers, B. (2006, September 24). Hit with a DWI, many pick jail over probation. *Houston Chronicle*. Retrieved from http://www.chron.com/news/houston-texas/article/Hit-with-a-DWI-many-pick-jail-over-probation-1856857.php.

14. Readers interested in learning more about ISP programs and their effectiveness are encouraged to read this review: http://cjonline.uc.edu/resources/criminal-justice-research/the-state-of-isp-research-and-policy-implications/.

15. This figure was calculated using data found in Table 3 in Kaeble et al., *Probation and Parole in the United States, 2014*.

16. Kaeble et al., *Probation and Parole in the United States, 2014*, Table 3.

17. See Latessa, E. J., & Smith, P. (2011). *Corrections in the community* (5th ed.). Boston: Anderson.

18. Latessa and Smith, *Corrections in the Community*. Petersilia, J. (1997). Probation in the United States. In M. Tonry (Ed.), *Crime and justice: A review of research* (Vol. 22, pp. 149–200). Chicago: University of Chicago Press.

19. Latessa and Smith, *Corrections in the Community*.

20. Gendreau, P., & Paparozzi, M. (1995, February). Examining what works in community corrections. *Corrections Today*, pp. 28–30.

21. Latessa and Smith, *Corrections in the Community*, pp. 14–15.

22. Petersilia, J., & Turner, S. (1993). *Evaluating intensive supervision probation and parole: Results of a nationwide experiment*. Washington, DC: National Institute of Justice.

23. Cohen, S. (1985). *Visions of social control*. Cambridge, UK: Polity.

24. National Institute of Justice. (2011, September). *Electronic monitoring reduces recidivism*. Retrieved from https://www.ncjrs.gov/pdffiles1/nij/234460.pdf.

25. To read more about the history of federal probation and probation officers, see http://www.history.njd.uscourts.gov/history/us_probation_office.

26. Latessa and Smith, *Corrections in the Community*.

27. Andrews, D., & Bonta, J. (2010). *LSI-R: The Level of Service Inventory–Revised*. Toronto, Canada: Multi-Health System.

28. Walsh, M. K., & Stohr, A. (2011). *Corrections: The essentials*. Thousand Oaks, CA: Sage.

29. Wells, T., Colbert, S., & Slate, R. N. (2006). Gender matters: Differences in state probation officer stress. *Journal of Contemporary Criminal Justice, 22*(1), 63–79.

CHAPTER 11

1. *Furman v. Georgia*, 408 U.S. 238 (1972).

2. Blackmon, D. A. (2008). *Slavery by another name: The re-enslavement of black Americans from the Civil War to World War II*. New York: Knopf Doubleday.

3. Shelden, R. G. (2001). *Controlling the dangerous classes: A critical introduction to the history of criminal justice*. Boston: Allyn & Bacon.

4. Shelden, R. G. (2002). Slavery in the third millennium Part II: Prisons and convict leasing help perpetuate slavery. *The Black Commentator*. Retrieved from http://blackcommentator.com/142/142_slavery_2.html.

5. Hallett, M. A. (2006). *Private prisons in America*. Urbana: University of Illinois Press.

6. Osborne, T. M. (1924). *Prisons and common sense*. Philadelphia: J. P. Lippincott.

7. Bureau of Labor Statistics. (2016, March 30). *Occupational employment and wages, May 2015: 33–3012 correctional officers and jailers*. Retrieved from http://www.bls.gov/oes/current/oes333012.htm.

8. Ibid.

9. Rafter, N. (1985). Gender, prisons and prison history. *Social Science History, 9*, 233–247.

10. Naday, A., Freilich, J., & Mellow, J. (2008). The elusive data on supermax confinement. *Prison Journal, 88*(1), 69–93.

11. Minton, T. D., & Zeng, Z. (2015, June). *Jail inmates at midyear 2014*. Retrieved from http://www.bjs.gov/content/pub/pdf/jim14.pdf.

12. Ibid.

13. Ibid.

14. Ibid.

15. Ibid.

16. Ibid.

17. Ibid.

18. Ibid.

19. Ibid.

20. Ibid.

21. Ibid.

22. Ibid.

23. Ibid.

24. Ibid.

25. Ibid.

26. Ibid.

27. Wegman, J. (2013, July 20). Climbing out of the hole. *The New York Times*. Retrieved from http://www.nytimes.com/2013/07/21/opinion/sunday/climbing-out-of-the-hole.html?_r=0.

28. Cohen, A. (2012, June 18). An American gulag: Descending into madness at supermax. *The Atlantic*. Retrieved from http://www.theatlantic.com/national/archive/2012/06/an-american-gulag-descending-into-madness-at-supermax/258323/.

29. Marcum, C. D., Higgins, G. E., & Tewksbury, R. (2011). Doing time for cyber crime: An examination of the correlates of sentence length in the United States. *International Journal of Cyber Criminology, 5*, 824–835.

30. Ibid.

31. Ibid.

32. Kaeble, D., Glaze, L., Tsoutis, A., & Minton, T. (2016, January 21). *Correctional populations in the United States, 2014*. Retrieved from http://www.bjs.gov/content/pub/pdf/cpus14.pdf. Carson, E. A. (2015, September). *Prisoners in 2014*.

Retrieved from http://www.bjs.gov/content/pub/pdf/p14.pdf.

33. Kaeble et al., *Correctional Populations in the United States, 2014*.

34. Carson, *Prisoners in 2014*.

35. Consult Carson, *Prisoners in 2014*, for a full accounting of states that both grew and shrunk their prison populations from 2013 to 2014.

36. Carson, *Prisoners in 2014*.

37. Public Opinion Strategies & Mellman Group. (2012). *Public opinion on sentencing and corrections in America*. Retrieved from http://www.prisonpolicy.org/scans/PEW_NationalSurveyResearchPaper_FINAL.pdf.

38. 18 U.S.C. § 3582(a).

39. Kaeble et al., *Correctional Populations in the United States, 2014*.

40. Selman-Killingbeck, D. (2010). Prison construction. In M. Shally-Jensen (Ed.), *Encyclopedia of contemporary American social issues* (p. 605). Santa Barbara, CA: ABC-CLIO.

41. U.S. Department of Justice. (1998). *Report to the attorney general: Inspection and review of the Northeast Ohio Correctional Center*. Retrieved from http://www.justice.gov/ag/youngstown/youngstown.htm. Selman-Killingbeck, "Prison Construction."

42. Selman-Killingbeck, "Prison Construction."

43. Cornelius, G. (2007). *The American jail: Cornerstone of modern corrections*. Upper Saddle River, NJ: Prentice Hall.

44. James, D. E., & Glaze, L. E. (2006). *Mental health problems of prison and jail inmates*. Retrieved from http://www.bjs.gov/content/pub/pdf/mhppji.pdf.

45. Mumola, C. J., & Karberg, J. C. (2007). *Drug use and dependence, state and federal prisoners, 2004*. Retrieved from http://www.bjs.gov/content/pub/pdf/dudsfp04.pdf.

46. Powers, J. J. (2013, November 28). *Finally out and among the living*. Retrieved from http://www.coloradoindependent.com/145073/finally-out-and-among-the-living.

47. James and Glaze, *Mental Health Problems*.

48. Carson, *Prisoners in 2014*.

49. Ibid.

50. Ibid.

51. Beck, A. J., Berzofsky, M., Caspar, R., & Krebs, C. (2013, May). *Sexual victimization in prisons and jails reported by inmates, 2011–12*. Retrieved from http://www.bjs.gov/content/pub/pdf/svpjri1112.pdf.

52. Ibid., p. 7.

53. U.S. Department of Justice. (2012, May 16). *National standards to*

prevent, detect, and respond to prison rape. Retrieved from http://ojp.gov/programs/pdfs/prea_final_rule.pdf.

54. Ibid., p. 9.

55. Prison security goes high-tech. (n.d.). *South Source*. Retrieved from http://source.southuniversity.edu/prison-security-goes-hightech-24647.aspx#sthash.Qzy7pHww.dpuf.

56. Ibid.

CHAPTER 12

1. Osterstuck, G. (2012). *What is ethics and how does it affect officers?* Retrieved from http://www.corrections.com/news/article/30421-what-is-ethics-and-how-does-it-affect-officers.

2. Clemmer, D. (1940). *The prison community*. Boston: Christopher, p. 299.

3. Wheeler, S. (1961). Socialization in correctional communities. *American Sociological Review, 26*, 697–712.

4. Fine, G. A., & Manning, P. (2003). Erving Goffman. In G. Ritzer (Ed.), *The Blackwell companion to major contemporary social theorists* (pp. 34–62). Malden, MA: Blackwell.

5. Jiang, S., & Fisher-Giorlando, M. (2002). Inmate misconduct: A test of the deprivation, importation, and situational models. *Prison Journal, 82*, 335–358.

6. Sykes, G. (1958). *The society of captives*. Princeton, NJ: Princeton University Press.

7. Farrington, K. (1992). The modern prison as total institution? Public perception versus objective reality. *Crime & Delinquency, 38*, 6–26. Irwin, J. K. (1981). Sociological studies of the impact of long-term confinement. In D. A. Ward & K. F. Schoen (Eds.), *Confinement in maximum custody* (pp. 49–60). Lexington, MA: D. C. Heath. Irwin, J. K., & Cressey, D. (1962). Thieves, convicts, and the inmate culture. *Social Problems, 10*, 142–155. Jacobs, J. B. (1976). Stratification and conflict among prison inmates. *Journal of Criminal Law and Criminology, 66*, 476–482.

8. Irwin, J. (2002). My life in "crim." In G. Geis & M. Dodge (Eds.), *Lessons of criminology* (pp. 149–164). Cincinnati, OH: Anderson.

9. Irwin, J. K., & Cressey, D. (1962). Thieves, convicts, and the inmate culture. *Social Problems, 10*, 142–155.

10. Flanagan, T. J. (1983). Correlates of institutional misconduct among state prisoners. *Criminology, 21*, 29–39. Steinke, P. (1991). Using

situational factors to predict types of prison violence. *Journal of Offender Rehabilitation, 17,* 119–132.

11. Carson, E. A., & Sabol, W. J. (2012). *Prisoners in 2011* (NCJ 239808). Washington, DC: Bureau of Justice Statistics.

12. Ibid. West, H., Sabol, W. J., & Greenman, S. J. (2010). *Prisoners in 2009* (NCJ 231675). Washington, DC: Bureau of Justice Statistics.

13. McDonald, D. (2009). Empowering female inmates: An exploratory study of a therapeutic community and its impact on the coping skills of substance abusing female inmates. *International Journal of Therapeutic Communities, 30,* 71–88.

14. Greenfeld, L., & Snell, T. L. (1999). *Women offenders* (NCJ 175688). Washington, DC: Bureau of Justice Statistics.

15. Ward, D. A., & Kassebaum, G. G. (1966). *Women's prison: Sex and social structure.* New Brunswick, NJ: Transaction. Giallombardo, R. (1966). *Society of women: A study of women's prison.* New York: John Wiley.

16. Ward and Kassebaum, *Women's Prison.*

17. Bloom, B., & Chesney-Lind, M. (2000). Women in prison: Vengeful equity. In R. Muraskin (Ed.), *It's a crime: Women and justice* (pp. 183–204). Upper Saddle River, NJ: Prentice Hall. Owen, B. A. (1998). *In the mix: Struggle and survival in a women's prison.* Albany: State University of New York Press.

18. Owen, *In the mix.*

19. Edwards, S. M. (1986). Neither bad nor mad: The female violent offender reassessed. *Women's Studies International, 9*(1), 79–87.

20. Liebling, A. (1999). Prison suicide and prisoner coping. In M. Tonry & J. Petersilia (Eds.), *Prison, crime and justice: An annual review of research* (pp. 283–360). Chicago: University of Chicago Press.

21. James, D. E., & Glaze, L. E. (2006). *Mental health problems of prison and jail inmates.* Retrieved from http://www.bjs.gov/content/pub/pdf/mhppji.pdf.

22. Gilligan, C. (1982). *In a different voice.* Cambridge, MA: Harvard University Press.

23. Stadler, W. A., Benson, M. L., & Cullen, F. T. (2013). Revisiting the special sensitivity hypothesis: The prison experience of white-collar inmates. *Justice Quarterly, 30,* 1090–1114.

24. American Psychiatric Association. (2012). *Position statement on segregation of prisoners with mental illness.* Retrieved from http://www.psychiatry.org/File%20Library/Learn/Archives/ps2012_PrisonerSegregation.pdf.

25. American Civil Liberties Union. (2014, February 25). *Written statement of the American Civil Liberties Union before the United States Senate Judiciary Subcommittee on the Constitution, Civil Rights, and Human Rights: Hearing on Reassessing Solitary Confinement II: The Human rights, fiscal, and public safety consequences.* Retrieved from http://solitarywatch.com/wp-content/uploads/2014/02/ACLU-Testimony-for-Solitary-II-Hearing-Final.pdf.

26. United Nations. (2011). *Torture and other cruel, inhuman or degrading treatment or punishment.* Retrieved from http://solitaryconfinement.org/uploads/SpecRapTortureAug2011.pdf.

27. Carroll, L. (1998). *Hacks, blacks, and cons: Race relations in a maximum-security prison.* Lexington, MA: Lexington Books.

28. Florida Department of Corrections. (n.d.). *Major prison gangs.* Retrieved from http://www.dc.state.fl.us/pub/gangs/prison.html.

29. U.S. Department of Justice. (n.d.). *Prison gangs.* Retrieved from http://www.justice.gov/criminal/ocgs/gangs/prison.html.

30. Florida Department of Corrections, *Major Prison Gangs.*

31. Ibid.

32. Kelley, M. B. (2014, February 1). America's 11 most powerful prison gangs. *Business Insider.* Retrieved from http://www.businessinsider.com/most-dangerous-prison-gangs-in-the-us-2014–2?op=1.

33. Associated Press. (2010, July). Vt. commissioner satisfied with inmate assault investigation. Retrieved from http://www.corrections.com/news/article/2311-four-4-types-of-correctional-violence.

34. Davis, A. J. (1982). Sexual assaults in the Philadelphia prison system and sheriff's vans. In A. Scacco (Ed.), *Male rape: A casebook of sexual aggressions* (pp. 107–120). New York: AMS Press.

35. Donaldson, S. (1995). *Rape of incarcerated Americans: A preliminary statistical look.* Fort Bragg, CA: Stop Prisoner Rape. Retrieved from https://www.aclu.org/technology-and-liberty/stephen-donaldson-executive-director-stop-prisoner-rape.

36. Dumond, R. W. (2000). Inmate sexual assault: The plague that persists. *Prison Journal, 80,* 407–414.

37. Lockwood, D. (1980). *Prison sexual violence.* New York: Elsevier.

38. Moster, A. N., & Jeglic, E. L. (2009). Prison warden attitudes toward prison rape and sexual assault findings since the Prison Rape Elimination Act. *Prison Journal, 89,* 65–78.

39. Ibid.

40. Cotton, D. J., & Groth, A. N. (1982). Inmate rape: Prevention and intervention. *Journal of Prison and Jail Health, 2*(1), 47–57. Nacci, P. L., & Kane, T. (1983). The incidence of sex and sexual aggression in federal prisons. *Federal Probation, 47*(4), 31–36. Nacci, P. L., & Kante, T. (1984). Inmate sexual aggression: Some evolving propositions and empirical findings, and mitigating counter-forces. *Journal of Offender Counseling, Services, and Rehabilitation, 9*(1/2), 1–20.

41. Struckman-Johnson, C., & Struckman-Johnson, D. (2010). Stopping prison rape: The evolution of standards recommended by PREA's National Prison Rape Elimination Commission. *Prison Journal, 93,* 335–354.

42. Arkin, D. (2013, June 30). Exploding number of elderly prisoners strains system, taxpayers. NBC News.

43. Human Rights Watch. (2012). *Old behind bars.* Retrieved from http://www.hrw.org/reports/2012/01/27/old-behind-bars-0.

44. American Civil Liberties Union. (2012). *At America's expense: The mass incarceration of the elderly.* Retrieved from https://www.aclu.org/criminal-law-reform/americas-expense-mass-incarceration-elderly.

45. Centers for Disease Control and Prevention. (2006). HIV transmission among male inmates in a state prison system—Georgia, 1992–2005. *Morbidity and Mortality Weekly Report, 55,* 421–426. Retrieved from http://www.cdc.gov/mmwr/preview/mmwrhtml/mm5515a1.htm.

46. Kantor, E. (2006). *HIV transmission and prevention in prisons.* Retrieved from http://hivinsite.ucsf.edu/insite?page=kb-07-04–13.

47. Substance Abuse and Mental Health Services Administration. (1998). *Continuity of offender treatment for substance use disorders from institution to community.* Retrieved from http://www.ncbi.nlm.nih.gov/books/NBK64384.

48. Cote, G., & Hodgins, S. (1990). Co-occurring mental disorders among criminal offenders. *Bulletin of the American Academy of Psychiatry Law, 18,* 271–281. Peters, R. H., & Hills, H. A. (1993). Inmates with co-occurring substance abuse and mental health disorders. In H. J. Steadman & J. J. Cocozza (Eds.), *Providing services for offenders with mental illness and related disorders in prison.* Washington, DC: National

Coalition for the Mentally Ill in the Criminal Justice System.

49. *Cooper v. Pate,* 378 U.S. 546 (1964).

50. *Wolf v. McDonnell,* 418 U.S. 539 (1974).

51. *Sandin v. Conner,* 515 U.S. 472 (1995).

52. *Wilson v. Schoming,* 863 F. Supp 789 (ND IL) (1994).

53. FindLaw. (2014). *Rights of inmates.* Retrieved from http://civilrights.findlaw.com/other-constitutional-rights/rights-of-inmates.html.

54. National Association of Criminal Defense Lawyers. (2013). *Road map to restoration.* Retrieved from http://www.nacdl.org/restoration/roadmapreport.

55. U.S. Census Bureau. (2014). *U.S. world and population clock.* Retrieved from http://www.census.gov/popclock.

56. National Association of Criminal Defense Lawyers, *Road map to restoration.*

57. U.S. Department of Justice. (2015, September 11). *Parole hearings.* Retrieved from https://www.justice.gov/uspc/parole-hearings.

58. Langan, P. A., & Levin, D. J. (2002). Recidivism of prisoners released in 1994. *Federal Sentencing Reporter, 15*(1), 58–65.

59. National Institute of Justice. (2013). *Offender reentry.* Retrieved from http://www.nij.gov/topics/corrections/reentry/pages/welcome.aspx.

60. Petersilia, J. (2003). *When prisoners come home: Parole and prisoner reentry.* New York: Oxford University Press.

61. City of Houston. (2014). *Re-entry programs.* Retrieved from http://www.houstontx.gov/education/prisonerreentry.html.

62. Peeples, C., & Donner, C. (2012). *Getting on after getting out: A reentry guide for Colorado.* Denver: Colorado Criminal Justice Reform Coalition.

63. California Reentry Program. (2014). *About.* Retrieved from http://ca-reentry.org/about.

64. McDonald, D., & Arlinghaus, S. L. (2014). The role of intensive case management services in reentry: The Northern Kentucky Female Offender Reentry Project. *Women & Criminal Justice, 24,* 229–251.

65. Rodriguez, M. N., & Avery, B. (2016, September 1). *Ban the box: U.S. cities, counties, and states adopt fair hiring policies.* Retrieved from http://www.nelp.org/publication/ban-the-box-fair-chance-hiring-state-and-local-guide/.

66. Haney, C. (2003). The psychological impact of incarceration: Implications for postprison adjustment. In J. Travis & M. Waul (Eds.), *Prisoners once removed: The impact of incarceration and reentry on children, families, and communities* (pp. 33–65). Washington, DC: Urban Institute Press.

67. Urban Institute. (2014). *Employment and reentry.* Retrieved from http://www.urban.org/projects/reentry-portfolio/employment.cfm.

68. Mumola, C. J. (2006, November). *Parents under correctional supervision: Past estimates, new measures.* Paper presented at the NIDA Research Meeting, Children of Parents in the Criminal Justice System: Children at Risk, Bethesda, MD.

69. Laub, J. H., & Sampson, R. J. (2003). *Shared beginnings, divergent lives: Delinquent boys to age 70.* Cambridge, MA: Harvard University Press.

70. La Vigne, N. G., Visher C., & Castro, J. (2004). *Chicago prisoners' experiences returning home.* Washington, DC: Urban Institute. Nelson, M., Deess, P., & Allen, C. (1999). *The first month out: Post incarceration experiences in New York City.* New York: Vera Institute of Justice. Shapiro, C., & Schwartz, M. (2001). Coming home: Building on family connections. *Corrections Management Quarterly, 5,* 52–61.

71. Naser, R. L., & Visher, C. A. (2006). Family members' experiences with incarceration and reentry. *Western Criminology Review, 7*(2), 20–31.

72. Tewksbury, R., Jennings, W. G., & Zgoba, K. M. (2012). A longitudinal examination of sex offender recidivism prior to and following the implementation of SORN. *Behavioral Sciences & the Law, 30,* 308–328.

73. Bonnar-Kidd, K. K. (2010). Sexual offender laws and prevention of sexual violence or recidivism. *American Journal of Public Health, 100,* 412–418.

74. Bureau of Labor Statistics. (2015, December 17). Probation officers and correctional treatment specialists. In *Occupational outlook handbook.* Retrieved from http://www.bls.gov/ooh/community-and-social-service/probation-officers-and-correctional-treatment-specialists.htm.

CHAPTER 13

1. Magarey, S. (1978). The invention of juvenile delinquency in early nineteenth-century England. *Labour History, 34,* 11–27.

2. Lawrence, R., & Hemmens, C. (2008). *Juvenile justice: A text/reader.* Thousand Oaks, CA: Sage.

3. Ibid.

4. Ibid.

5. *Ex parte Crouse.* (2008). Retrieved from http://www.faqs.org/childhood/Co-Fa/Ex-Parte-Crouse.html.

6. Grossberg, M. (1985). *Governing the hearth: Law and family in nineteenth-century America.* Chapel Hill: University of North Carolina Press.

7. *Kent v. United States,* 383 U.S. 541 (1966).

8. American Bar Association. (n.d.). *The history of juvenile justice.* Retrieved from http://www.americanbar.org/content/dam/aba/migrated/publiced/features/DYJpart1.authcheckdam.pdf.

9. *In re Gault,* 387 U.S. 1 (1967).

10. *Roper v. Simmons,* 543 U.S. 551 (2005); 112 S. W. 3d 397.

11. Ibid.

12. Office of Juvenile Justice and Delinquency Prevention. (2013). *Statistical briefing book: Jurisdictional boundaries.* Retrieved from http://www.ojjdp.gov/ojstatbb/structure_process/qa04106.asp?qaDate=2012.

13. Congress enacted the Juvenile Justice and Delinquency Prevention Act (Pub. L. No. 93–415, 42 U.S.C. § 5601 et seq.) in 1974. See U.S. Department of Justice, Office of Justice Programs, Office of Juvenile Justice and Delinquency Prevention. (n.d.). Legislation/JJDP Act. Retrieved from http://www.ojjdp.gov/about/legislation.html.

14. Office of Juvenile Justice and Delinquency Prevention. (n.d.). *Programs.* Retrieved from http:www.ojjdp.gov/programs/index.html.

15. Denver's 1993 "summer of violence." (2012, June 28). *Denver Post.* Retrieved from http://blogs.denverpost.com/library/2012/06/28/denvers-1993-summer-violence/2074.

16. Dilulio, J. (1995). The coming of the super-predators. *Weekly Standard, 27,* 23–28.

17. Ibid.

18. Zimring, F. E. (1998). Youth violence epidemic: Myth or reality? *Wake Forest Law Review, 33,* 727.

19. Federal Bureau of Investigation. (2015). Table 38: Arrests by age, 2014. In *Crime in the United States 2014.* Retrieved from https://ucr.fbi.gov/crime-in-the-u.s/2014/crime-in-the-u.s.-2014/tables/table-38. Snyder, H. N. (2003, December). Juvenile arrests 2001. *Juvenile Justice Bulletin.* Retrieved from https://www.ncjrs.gov/pdffiles1/ojjdp/201370.pdf.

20. Snyder, H. N. (2012, October). *Arrests in the United States, 1990–2010.* Retrieved from http://www.bjs.gov/content/pub/pdf/aus9010.pdf.

21. Federal Bureau of Investigation. (2015). Table 37: Current year over previous year arrest trends by sex, 2013–2014. In *Crime in the*

United States 2014. Retrieved from https://www.fbi.gov/about-us/cjis/ucr/crime-in-the-u.s/2014/crime-in-the-u.s.-2014/tables/table-37.

22. Ibid.

23. Chesney-Lind, M., & Shelden, R. B. (2004). *Girls, delinquency, and juvenile justice* (3rd ed.). Belmont, CA: Thomson Wadsworth.

24. Rennison, C. M. (2009). A new look at the gender gap in offending. *Women & Criminal Justice, 19*(3), 171–190.

25. Federal Bureau of Investigation. (2015). Table 43: Arrests by race, 2014. In *Crime in the United States 2014*. Retrieved from https://ucr.fbi.gov/crime-in-the-u.s/2014/crime-in-the-u.s.-2014/tables/table-43.

26. Ibid.

27. Free Dictionary. (2014). *Loco parentis*. Retrieved from http://legal-dictionary.thefreedictionary.com/loco+parentis.

28. Rosenbaum, D. P. (2007). Just say no to DARE. *Criminology & Public Policy, 6*, 815–824. Rosenbaum, D. P., & Hanson, G. S. (1998). Assessing the effects of school-based drug education: A six-year multilevel analysis of Project DARE. *Journal of Research in Crime and Delinquency, 35*, 381–412.

29. Petteruti, A. (2011). *Education under arrest: The case against police in schools*. Washington, DC: Justice Policy Institute.

30. Office of Juvenile Justice and Delinquency Prevention. (n.d.). *Statistical briefing book: Case flow diagram*. Retrieved from http://www.ojjdp.gov/ojstatbb/structure_process/case.html.

31. MacKenzie, D. L., Brame, R., McDowell, D., & Souryal, C. (1995). Boot camp prisons and recidivism in eight states. *Criminology, 33*, 327–357.

32. Letourneau, E. J., & Borduin, C. M. (2008). The effective treatment of juveniles who sexually offend: An ethical imperative. *Ethics Behavior, 18*, 286–306.

33. National Center on Sexual Behavior of Youth. (2003). *NCSBY fact sheet: What research shows about adolescent sex offenders*. Retrieved from http://www.dshs.wa.gov/pdf/ca/NCSBYfactsheet.pdf.

34. Sanborn, J. (2004). The "adultification" of youth. In P. J. Benekos & A. V. Merlo (Eds.), *Controversies in juvenile justice and delinquency* (pp. 143–164). Newark, NJ: LexisNexis.

35. Juvenile Law Center. (2015, February 10). *Reducing transfers to the adult system*. Retrieved from http://www.jlc.org/current-initiatives/youth-criminal-justice-system/reducing-transfers-adult-system.

36. Beck, A., & Harrison, P. M. (2008). *Sexual victimization in state and federal prisons reported by inmates, 2007*. Washington, DC: U.S. Department of Justice, Office of Justice Programs, Bureau of Justice Statistics. Beck, A., Harrison, P. M., & Guerino, P. (2010). *Sexual victimization in juvenile facilities reported by youth, 2008–09*. Washington, DC: U.S. Department of Justice, Office of Justice Programs, Bureau of Justice Statistics.

37. Bishop, D. M., Frazier, C. E., Lanz-Kaduce, L., & Winner, L. (1996). The transfer of juveniles to criminal court: Does it make a difference? *Crime & Delinquency, 42*, 171–191.

38. Campaign for Youth Justice. (2009). *The international consensus against trying youth as adults*. Retrieved from http://www.campaignforyouthjustice.org/documents/InternationalConsensusAgainstTryingYouthAsAdults.pdf. Frost, M., Fagan, J., & Vivona, T. S. (1998). Youth in prisons and training schools: Perceptions and consequences of the treatment-custody dichotomy. *Juvenile and Family Court Journal, 40*, 1–14.

CHAPTER 14

1. 18 U.S.C. § 2331 defines international terrorism and domestic terrorism. Other statutes focus on terrorism. The one cited here captures the essence of these crimes. Please also keep in mind that the United States, while having been the victim of both international and domestic terrorism, has been accused of perpetrating acts of terrorism against other nations.

2. 18 U.S.C. § 2331.

3. Ibid.

4. U.S. Department of Homeland Security. (2012). *Creation of the Department of Homeland Security*. Retrieved from http://www.dhs.gov/creation-department-homeland-security.

5. Peter Andreas, a professor at Brown University's Watson Institute for International Studies, quoted in Koenig, S. (2011, September 8). U.S. Department of Homeland Security: Keeping America safe or costing America too much? *Bangor Daily News*. Retrieved from http://bangordailynews.com/2011/09/08/politics/u-s-department-of-homeland-security-keeping-america-safe-or-costing-america-too-much.

6. U.S. Department of Homeland Security. (2014). *Budget-in-brief: Fiscal year 2014*. Retrieved from http://www.dhs.gov/dhs-budget.

7. U.S. Department of Homeland Security. (2016). *Budget-in-brief: Fiscal year 2016*. Retrieved from https://www.dhs.gov/sites/default/files/publications/FY_2016_DHS_Budget_in_Brief.pdf.

8. See, e.g., Rittgers, D. (2011). *Abolish the Department of Homeland Security*. Washington, DC: Cato Institute. Retrieved from http://object.cato.org/sites/cato.org/files/pubs/pdf/PA683.pdf.

9. White House. (2001, November 13). *President issues military order: Detention, treatment, and trial of certain non-citizens in the war against terrorism*. Retrieved from http://www.mc.mil/Portals/0/Military%20Order%200f%20Nov%2013,%202001.pdf.

10. See http://www.mc.mil.

11. Office of Military Commissions. (n.d.). *Military commissions history*. Retrieved from http://www.mc.mil/ABOUTUS/MilitaryCommissionsHistory.aspx.

12. *Hamdan v. Rumsfeld*, 548 U.S. 557 (2006). Retrieved from http://www.mc.mil/Portals/0/Hamdan%20v%20%20Rumsfeld%20548%20US%20557%20%282006%29%20v2.pdf.

13. H.R. 2467, Military Commissions Act of 2009. Retrieved from http://www.mc.mil/Portals/0/2009%20MCA%20Pub%20%20Law%20111–84.pdf.

14. *Manual for military commissions*. (2010). Retrieved from http://www.mc.mil/Portals/0/2010_Manual_for_Military_Commissions.pdf.

15. United Nations Office on Drugs and Crime. (2014). *Human trafficking*. Retrieved from http://www.unodc.org/unodc/en/human-trafficking/what-is-human-trafficking.html?ref=menuside.

16. Polaris. (2014). *Labor trafficking in the US*. Retrieved from http://www.polarisproject.org/human-trafficking/labor-trafficking-in-the-us.

17. Banks, D., & Kyckelhahn, T. (2011). *Characteristics of suspected human trafficking incidents, 2008–2010* (NCJ 233732). Washington, DC: U.S. Government Printing Office.

18. Clayton, E. W., Krugman, R. D., & Simon, P. (Eds.). (2013). *Confronting commercial sexual exploitation and sex trafficking of minors in the United States*. Washington, DC: National Academies Press. Retrieved from http://www.iom.edu/Reports/2013/Confronting-Commercial-Sexual-Exploitation-and-Sex-Trafficking-of-Minors-in-the-United-States.aspx.

19. Even in death, Byrd has not escaped the wrath of stupidity. In 2004, two men (one 18 and one 19 years old) desecrated his grave with racial slurs and profanities. They were arrested and charged with this crime. See http://www.chron.com/news/houston-texas/article/State-briefs-White-teens-charged-in-grave-1977172.php.

20. Sandholtz, N., Langton, L., & Planty, M. (2013). *Hate crime victimization, 2003–2011* (NCJ 241291). Washington, DC: U.S. Government Printing Office.

21. Ibid.

22. Krebs, C., & Lindquist, C. (2014, December 15). Setting the record straight on "1 in 5." *Time.* Retrieved from http://time.com/3633903/campus-rape-1-in-5-sexual-assault-setting-record-straight/. Krebs, C. P., Lindquist, C. H., Warner, T. D., Fisher, B. S., & Martin, S. L. (2007). *The Campus Sexual Assault (CSA) study.* Washington, DC: US Government Printing Office.

23. Cantor, D., Fisher, B. S., Chibnall, S., Townsend, R., Lee, H., Bruce, C., & Thomas, G. (2015). *Report on the AAU Campus Climate Survey on sexual assault and sexual misconduct.* Rockville, MD: Westat.

24. Cantor et al., *Report on the AAU Campus Climate Survey.* Fernandez, A., & Lizotte A. J. (1995). An analysis of the relationship between campus crime and community crime: Reciprocal effects? In B. S. Fisher & J. J. Sloan III (Eds.), *Campus crime: Legal, social and policy perspectives* (2nd ed., pp. 79–102). Springfield, IL: Charles C Thomas. Fisher, B. S., Daigle, L. E., & Cullen, F. T. (2010). *Unsafe in the ivory tower: The sexual victimization of college women.* Thousand Oaks, CA: Sage. Fisher, B. S., Sloan, J. J., III, Cullen, F. T., & Lu, C. (1998). Crime in the ivory tower: The level and sources of student victimization. *Criminology, 36*(3), 671–710. Fox J. A., & Hellman, D. A. (1985). Location and other correlates of campus crime. *Journal of Criminal Justice, 13,* 429–444. Gardella, J. H., Nichols-Hadeed, C. A., Mastrocinque, J. M., Stone, J. T., Coates, C. A., Sly, C. J., & Cerulli, C. (2014) Beyond Clery Act statistics: A closer look at college victimization based on self-report data. *Journal of Interpersonal Violence, 30*(4), 640–658. Henson, V. A., & Stone, W. E. (1999). Campus crime—An analysis of reported crimes on college and university campuses. *Journal of Criminal Justice, 27*(4), 295–307. Krebs and Lindquist, "Setting the

Record Straight." Krebs et al., *The Campus Sexual Assault (CSA) Study.* McPheters, L. R. (1978). Econometric analysis of factors influencing crime on the campus. *Journal of Criminal Justice, 6,* 47–52. Moriarty, L. J., & Pelfrey, W. V. (1996). Exploring explanations for campus crime: Examining internal and external factors. *Journal of Contemporary Criminal Justice, 12*(1), 108–120. Morriss, S. B. (1993, May). *The influences of campus characteristics on college crime rates.* Paper presented at the 33rd annual forum of the Association for Institutions Research, Chicago. Nobles, M. R., Fox, K. A., Khey, D. N., & Lizotte, A. J. (2012). Community and campus crime: A geospatial examination of the Clery Act. *Crime & Delinquency, 59*(8), 1131–1156. Rennison, C. M. (2015, November). *Violence against females on college campuses—1995–2013.* Paper presented at the 71st meeting of the American Society of Criminology, Washington, DC. Sinozich, S., & Langton, L. (2014). *Rape and sexual assault victimization among college-age females, 1995–2013.* Washington, DC: U.S. Government Printing Office. Sloan, J. J., III. (1992). Campus crime and campus communities: An analysis of crimes known to campus police and security. *Journal of Security Administration, 15,* 31–47. Sloan, J. J., III. (1994). The correlates of campus crime: An analysis of reported crimes on college and university campuses. *Journal of Criminal Justice, 22,* 51–61. Volkwein, J. F., Szelest, B. P., & Lizotte, A. J. (1995). The relationship of campus crime to campus and student characteristics. *Research in Higher Education, 36*(6), 647–670. Wooldredge, J., Cullen, F. T., & Latessa, E. (1995). Predicting the likelihood of faculty victimization: Individual demographics and routine activities. In B. S. Fisher & J. J. Sloan III (Eds.), *Campus crime: Legal, social, and policy perspectives* (2nd ed., pp. 133–122). Springfield, IL: Charles C Thomas.

25. Fisher et al., *Unsafe in the Ivory Tower.* Fisher et al., "Crime in the Ivory Tower."

26. Cantor et al., *Report on the AAU Campus Climate Survey.* Fisher et al., *Unsafe in the Ivory Tower.* Fisher et al., "Crime in the Ivory Tower." Krebs et al., *The Campus Sexual Assault (CSA) Study.* Rennison, *Violence Against Females on College Campuses.* Rennison, C. M., & Addington, L. (2014). Violence against college women: A review to identify

limitations in defining the problem and inform future research. *Trauma, Violence and Abuse, 15*(3), 159–169. Sinozich and Langton, *Rape and Sexual Assault Victimization.*

27. Fox and Hellman, "Location and Other Correlates of Campus Crime." Gardella et al., "Beyond Clery Act Statistics." Henson and Stone, "Campus Crime." McPheters, "Econometric Analysis." Moriarty and Pelfrey, "Exploring Explanations for Campus Crime." Morriss, *The Influences of Campus Characteristics.* Nobles et al., "Community and Campus Crime." Sloan, "The Correlates of Campus Crime." Volkwein et al., "The Relationship of Campus Crime." Wooldredge et al., "Predicting the Likelihood of Faculty Victimization."

28. Voronin, Y. A. (1990). *Measures to control transnational organized crime, summary* (NCJ 184773). Washington DC: U.S. Government Printing Office.

29. United Nations Office on Drugs and Crime. (2014). *Organized crime.* Retrieved from http://www.unodc.org/unodc/en/organized-crime/index.html.

30. United Nations Office on Drugs and Crime. (2014). *United Nations Convention Against Transnational Organized Crime.* Retrieved from http://www.unodc.org/unodc/en/treaties/CTOC/index.html.

31. Ibid.

32. United Nations Office on Drugs and Crime. (2012, October 15). *Transnational crime proceeds in billions, victims in millions, says UNODC chief.* Retrieved from http://www.unodc.org/unodc/en/press/releases/2012/October/transnational-crime-proceeds-in-billions-victims-in-millions-says-unodc-chief.html.

33. Picarelli, J. T. (2013). Responding to transnational organized crime: Supporting research, improving practice. *NIJ Journal, 268,* 4–9.

34. National Human Genome Research Institute. (2014). *Deoxyribonucleic acid (DNA).* Retrieved from http://www.genome.gov/25520880.

35. Zagorski, N. (2006). Profile of Alec J. Jeffreys. *Proceedings of the National Academy of Sciences of the United States of America, 103,* 8918–8920.

36. Ibid.

37. Ibid.

38. Lawson, T. F. (2009). Before the verdict and beyond the verdict: The CSI infection within modern criminal jury trials. *Loyola University Chicago Law Journal, 41,* 119–173.

39. Cole, S., & Dioso, R. (2005, May 13). Law and the lab. *The Wall Street Journal.*